The NIV® STANDARD LESSON COMMENTARY 1999-2000

International Sunday School Lessons

edited by

DOUGLAS REDFORD AND JONATHAN UNDERWOOD

published by
Standard Publishing
Eugene H. Wigginton, President
Mark A. Taylor, Publisher
Richard C. McKinley, Director of Curriculum Development
Carla Crane, Assistant Director of Curriculum Development
Jonathan Underwood, Senior Editor
Hela M. Campbell, Office Editor

Sixth Annual Volume

FREE CD-ROM INCLUDED

The electronic version of *The NIV® Standard Lesson Commentary* and the *QuickVerse®* STEP Book Reader are contained on the CD-ROM so you can:
- Instantly search the complete text of the Commentary for any word, phrase, or Bible reference. Search options include full-text, title-only, case-sensitive, and support of Boolean operators (AND, OR, NOT, etc.).
- Access related articles or information via hyperlinks within the text of each book. (Double-clicking on a highlighted word will access related articles.)
- Print lessons directly from the *QuickVerse®* or customize in any Windows® word processor
- Access Bible maps from *PC-Atlas®!*

PLUS, you'll find additional reference titles locked on the CD. NOTE: These additional resources are made available for your convenience. Standard Publishing does not necessarily endorse the complete contents of any of them.

The electronic version of this book is fully compatible with the new Bible Software Industry standard for reference titles, STEP (Standard Template for Electronic Publishing).

System Requirements:
An IBM or compatible PC running Windows 95 or Windows NT 4.0 or later; 6MB RAM, and 25 MB hard drive space.

For technical support call Parsons Technology at (319) 395-7314.

© 1999
The STANDARD PUBLISHING Company
division of STANDEX INTERNATIONAL Corporation
8121 Hamilton Avenue, Cincinnati, Ohio 45231
Printed in U.S.A.

In This Volume

Special Features

Fall Quarter, 1999
From Slavery to Conquest

Writers

Lesson Development ....*Orrin Root*
Verbal Illustrations ....*Charles R. Boatman*
What Do You Think? ....*Kenton K. Smith*

Discovery Learning ....*Thomas Hutchison (1-4),*
Richard A. Lint (5-9), Steve Simpson (10-13)
Reproducible Activities ....*Thomas Hutchison (1-4),*
Richard A. Lint (5-9), Steve Simpson (10-13)

Winter Quarter, 1999-2000
Immanuel: God With Us

Writers

Lesson Development ....*Johnny Pressley*
Verbal Illustrations ....*L. D. Campbell (1-4),*
David Roadcup (5-9), Richard W. Baynes (10-13)
What Do You Think? ....*Larry Jones (1-4)*
Tom Claibourne (5-9), Charles E. Cook (10-13)

Discovery Learning ....*Ronald G. Davis (1-4),*
Rick Shonkwiler (5-9), Everett Brewer (10-13)
Reproducible Activities........*Ronald G. Davis (1-4),*
Rick Shonkwiler (5-9), Everett Brewer (10-13)

Spring Quarter, 2000
Helping a Church Confront Crisis

Writers

Lesson Development ....*Robert C. Shannon (1-4),*
John W. Wade (5-13)
Verbal Illustrations ....*Charles R. Boatman*
What Do You Think? ....*Kenton K. Smith*

Discovery Learning ....*Virginia Beddow (1-4),*
Richard A. Koffarnus (5-9), Ronald L. Oakes (10-13)
Reproducible Activities........*Virginia Beddow (1-4),*
Richard A. Koffarnus (5-9), Ronald L. Oakes (10-13)

Summer Quarter, 2000
New Life in Christ

Writers

Lesson Development ....*Edwin V. Hayden (1-4),*
J. Michael Shannon (5-13)
Verbal Illustrations...................*Robert C. Shannon*

What Do You Think? ....*Ronald G. Davis*
Discovery Learning.............................*Alan Weber*
Reproducible Activities ....*Alan Weber*

Index of Printed Texts, 1999-2000

The printed texts for 1999-2000 are arranged here in the order in which they appear in the Bible. Opposite each reference is the page number on which the lesson that treats the passage begins in this volume.

Cumulative Index of Printed Texts

A cumulative index for the Scripture passages used in *The NIV Standard Lesson Commentary* for September, 1998—August, 2000 is presented here for your convenience.

Introducing *The NIV®* *Standard Lesson Commentary*

This is the sixth year teachers following the Uniform Lesson Plan have had available this popular commentary based on the *New International Version* of the Scriptures. Teachers familiar with *The NIV® Standard Lesson Commentary* will find in this volume all the features they have come to expect; new users of the *Commentary* will find a wealth of resources never before so close to their fingertips! For the third year a free CD-ROM is included for the convenience of computer users. New last year—and repeated in this year's volume—are some maps and chronological charts included with each quarter. By the end of the current six-year series (see page 12), you can compile quite a handy Bible atlas!

Whether you have used *The NIV® Standard Lesson Commentary* before or not, however, you will quickly find this volume a helpful companion in preparing your Sunday school lessons.

LESSON DEVELOPMENT

The first page of each lesson clearly identifies the title, Scripture, current unit, and lesson aims for the session. A thumb tab identifies the date the lesson will be taught so that it can be found quickly. The date is repeated on each page at the top outside corner.

The first item in the lesson development is a brief rationale for the lesson: **"Why Teach This Lesson?"** Tying the lesson theme to contemporary life, this section puts application at the forefront of your preparation. Then comes the lesson treatment itself, following a three-point structure: introduction, exposition, and conclusion. The **introduction** provides background and other useful information to set the stage, tie the current lessons with earlier ones, and generally give you a handle on the context for the current lesson.

Application from the start!

What follows is a **verse-by-verse Scripture exposition.** The text is printed in the *New International Version*, usually one verse at a time. Bold type sets the text off from commentary so you can read it easily, even if you just want to read through the passage without comment at first. The commentary is interspersed so you can relate the comments to the specific Scripture passage they illuminate.

Verse-by-verse exposition.

The **conclusion** leans heavily toward **application**, giving specific examples of how the principles of the lesson Scripture can be put to practice in real life.

Verbal illustrations, usually two to a lesson, help to illuminate the concepts of the lesson. These are found in the exposition section, providing yet another tool for you to illustrate the Scripture. These are set off in block quotes so they can be easily found or easily jumped over if you choose not to use them.

Verbal illustrations.

MARGINAL NOTES

Many of the most helpful features of this lesson commentary are found in the margins. Occasionally the text suggests some interesting point for discussion. These issues are raised under the heading of **"What Do You Think?"** The question is raised, sometimes from more than one perspective. The Scripture in the main section is relevant, and other Scriptures may also be suggested. No answers are given, however, because these are questions without pat answers. These will encourage your students to wrestle with the big issues without being trite.

Discussion starters.

"**Visuals**" are pictured in the margins, also. These are reproductions of the classroom visuals available from Standard Publishing each quarter to help your

Visual illustrations.

students visualize the points being made. Again, these appear in the margin alongside the Scripture or other part of the lesson where they are most appropriate. NOTE: These are mere **reproductions** of large, colorful classroom visuals available to enhance your lesson presentation. Contact your curriculum supplier to order yours each quarter.

Daily Bible readings.

Daily Bible readings, points to remember, and even prayer ideas are included in the margin near the end of each lesson.

DISCOVERY LEARNING

Student involvement!

For teachers who like to involve their students in the learning process, a page of **Discovery Learning** is included in each lesson. These alternate lesson plans are designed to get the students busy in Bible study and application to discover for themselves the timeless truths of the Scriptures. Each discovery learning plan includes an activity to begin the lesson, a Bible study activity, and an application activity.

Reproducible pages!

The last page of each lesson is a **reproducible page**. These, too, are designed to involve the students in discovery learning. Sometimes they are an integral part of the discovery learning plan. At other times, they provide optional activities that may be introduced at various points in the lesson. Marginal "Option" notes frequently call your attention to an activity on this page. Or you can start with the whole page and build your lesson plan around it, using the other resources in this book.

OPTIONS

This is a lesson planner with lots of options! No matter what style you prefer—lecture, discussion, activities—you'll find resources to plan a great lesson. If you like variety, this will help you design an easy-to-teach lesson unique to your personality and that of your class. Or, if you like a ready-made plan you can teach with minimal preparation time, you'll find that, too. It's all here.

Make it personal.

PLANNING SHEET

Map out your game plan.

Use the lesson planning sheet on page 10 to plan each of your lessons. The page is reproducible, so you can use it to fill in the blanks and plan out your complete lesson each week. List the options and features you have chosen for each lesson, and use it to guide you quickly and easily from one activity to the next.

NIV® BIBLE TEACHER

EASY-TO-READ QUARTERLY FORMAT

Some users of *The NIV® Standard Lesson Commentary* have wished for a quarterly format to use in teaching. Others have wished the type were a little larger and easier to read. Both those desires have been answered with the *NIV® Bible Teacher,* available from your Christian bookstore or from Standard Publishing. It contains the same content as this volume but is published in four quarterly issues and in a larger typeface. Order number 184 for fall, 284 for winter, 384 for spring, and 484 for summer.

Ready . . . AIM . . . Teach!

The Importance of "Lesson Aims" in Teaching

Do you ever wonder whether you are doing any good as the teacher of your class? Does it ever seem you are just passing time in class instead of accomplishing anything meaningful? If so, perhaps you need to take a second look at the "Lesson Aims" (also called "Learning Goals") included in each lesson.

Where Are You Going?

Someone has said, "If you don't know where you are going, then any road will take you there." To know which is the right road, or the right way, one must know where it is he or she wants to be. The same is true in your teaching. Unless you have a clear idea of what you want to accomplish by the end of the class session—where you want your students to be, if you please—then there is no way to know just what you ought to spend your time doing in the class session.

What is your goal in teaching? Surely it is more than providing sixty minutes worth of diversion—you're not just "filling time." And you're not just trying to "cover" a particular portion of Scripture. No, you want more. You want your students to *know* something they may not have known before they came into your classroom. More than that, you want them to *understand* the truths and principles of Scripture that the lesson text presents. Finally, you want the students to *apply* to their lives those things they have come to know and understand.

That is the reason the editors of the *Standard Lesson Commentary* and *The NIV® Standard Lesson Commentary* have been spending so much time in formulating the lesson aims that appear in each lesson in the *Commentaries*. Usually there are three aims for a lesson. The first is a *content* aim. This aim addresses the issue of what facts the student should know as a result of having participated in the study of the assigned lesson text. Verbs like *recall, summarize,* and *tell* will frequently introduce such aims.

Content Aim
What does the text say?

The second aim might be called a *concept* aim. This goal probes beneath the surface of the material to find the timeless principles underlying the facts reported in the Scripture text. This aim takes the learner beyond the knowledge of facts to understanding. This is a necessary link to bring the events of centuries gone by to relevance in our own day. Verbs like *relate, compare,* and *explain* will be more common in introducing these aims.

Concept Aim
What does the text mean?

The third aim is what we might call a *conduct* aim. This is the goal that addresses the issue of application: how will the student's conduct change as a result of participating in this study? These aims may challenge the learner to *make a commitment* or to *suggest a specific action* that he or she can take in the coming week.

Conduct Aim
What does the text demand of me?

The concept aims are especially important in studying the historical narratives in Scripture. It is not enough to know the *facts* about the story of David's killing the giant Goliath. We must also understand the *principles* of faith and courage that moved David to action. Only then can we move on from the content aim— knowing the facts—to the conduct aim—applying this lesson to how we face the giants in our own lives. In some passages, especially in the epistles, the content may be more exposition than narration, more conceptual than historical. In these cases we may find that to know the content of the passage is to know the concept—so separate aims may not be needed. In these cases there may be only two aims instead of three.

No matter how many aims in a lesson, or whether you follow the ones here or develop your own, be sure to start your lesson preparation with a clear understanding of where you want to go. Only then will you be sure to get there!

Lesson Planning Page

List the aims here, either directly from the lesson or revised to suit your individual needs.

LESSON AIMS

Begin with an opening activity like the illustration from the beginning of the lesson, "Into the Lesson" from the Discovery Learning page, a discussion question, or some other appropriate opener.

GETTING STARTED

List in order the activities you will use. These include discussion questions, activities from the discovery learning page and the reproducible page—as well as key points from the commentary section.

LESSON DEVELOPMENT

    I.

    II.

    III.

How will you bring the lesson to a climax, stressing the key point and desired action steps?

CONCLUSION & APPLICATION

Dismiss the class with an activity that reinforces the Bible lesson.

CLOSING ACTIVITY

Fall Quarter, 1999

From Slavery to Conquest
(Exodus, Leviticus, Numbers,
Deuteronomy, Joshua)

Special Features

Lessons

Unit 1: Exodus and Covenant

Unit 2: Wandering in the Wilderness

Unit 3: Entering the Promised Land

About These Lessons

The lessons in this quarter trace the history of Israel from the exodus to the conquest of the promised land. They highlight God's deliverance of his people from bondage in Egypt, the establishment of his covenant with them, the initial failure of the people to enter the land, and their eventual success in doing so under Joshua.

Sep 5
Sep 12
Sep 19
Sep 26
Oct 3
Oct 10
Oct 17
Oct 24
Oct 31
Nov 7
Nov 14
Nov 21
Nov 28

Lessons Learned on the Move

by Orrin Root

Can you imagine an entire nation of people tramping for forty years through rugged country without even wearing out their shoes? It happened (read Deuteronomy 29:5). The account of that migration is as fascinating as Homer's mythic Odyssey, and centuries older. Most important, it is true. It is actual history—and it is the subject of our Sunday school lessons for September, October, and November.

Throughout the Bible, God frequently taught his servants many important lessons while they were "on the move." Hebrews 11:9, 10 says of Abraham, "By faith he made his home in the promised land like a stranger in a foreign country; he lived in tents, as did Isaac and Jacob, who were heirs with him of the same promise. For he was looking forward to the city with foundations, whose architect and builder is God."

Moses, who is a central figure in this quarter's lessons, fled from Egypt to Midian as a fugitive, then returned to Egypt when God called him to lead the

International Sunday School Lesson Cycle
September, 1998—August, 2004

YEAR	FALL QUARTER (Sept., Oct., Nov.)	WINTER QUARTER (Dec., Jan., Feb.)	SPRING QUARTER (Mar., Apr., May)	SUMMER QUARTER (June, July, Aug.)
1998-1999	God Calls a People to Faithful Living (Old Testament Survey)	God Calls Anew in Jesus Christ (New Testament Survey)	That You May Believe (John)	Genesis: Beginnings (Genesis)
1999-2000	From Slavery to Conquest (Exodus, Leviticus, Numbers, Deuteronomy, Joshua)	Immanuel: God With Us (Matthew)	Helping a Church Confront Crisis (1 and 2 Corinthians)	New Life in Christ (Ephesians, Philippians, Colossians, Philemon)
2000-2001	The Emerging Nation (Judges, 1 and 2 Samuel, 1 Kings 1-11, 1 Chronicles, 2 Chronicles 1-9)	Good News of Jesus (Luke)	Continuing Jesus' Work (Acts)	Division and Decline (1 Kings 12-22, 2 Kings 1-17, 2 Chronicles 10-28, Isaiah 1-39, Amos, Hosea, Micah)
2001-2002	Jesus' Ministry (Parables, Miracles, Sermon on the Mount)	Light for All People (Isaiah 9:1-7; 11:1-9; 40-66; Ruth, Jonah, Nahum)	The Power of the Gospel (Romans, Galatians)	Worship and Wisdom for Living (Psalms, Proverbs)
2002-2003	Judgment and Exile (2 Kings 18-25, 2 Chronicles 29-36, Jeremiah, Lamentations, Ezekiel, Habakkuk, Zephaniah)	Portraits of Faith (Personalities in the New Testament)	Jesus: God's Power in Action (Mark)	God Restores a Remnant (Ezra, Nehemiah, Daniel, Joel, Obadiah, Haggai, Zechariah, Malachi)
2003-2004	Faith Faces the World (James, 1 and 2 Peter, 1, 2, 3 John, Jude)	A Child Is Given (Samuel, John the Baptist, Jesus) Lessons From Life (Esther, Job, Ecclesiastes, Song of Solomon)	Jesus Fulfills His Mission (Death, Burial, and Resurrection Texts) Living Expectantly (1, 2 Thessalonians, Revelation)	Hold Fast to the Faith (Hebrews) Guidelines for the Church's Ministry (1, 2 Timothy, Titus)

Israelites out of bondage in that land. Moses' experiences in the desert prepared him for the long, hard years of wandering that the Israelites would have to endure.

David also learned much while "on the go" as a fugitive from the angry, jealous King Saul. A number of David's Psalms were written during this period of his life. They express his love for and trust in God, in spite of the disheartening circumstances he was facing. For example, read Psalm 57, noting what the heading says about the time when it was written.

In the thirteen lessons of this quarter, we shall trace the Israelites' forty-year journey in the wilderness. Obviously we can touch on only the highest of the high points and the lowest of the low. As we observe the Israelites, we shall see the depth of fear and the height of faith, the depth of man's need and the height of God's care. We shall see the wisdom of trusting God and obeying him, and if we are wise we shall determine to trust and obey him too.

What follows is a preview of the thirteen lessons for September, October, and November. They are divided into three units, one unit for each month.

UNIT 1: EXODUS AND COVENANT

September

Lesson 1: God Calls Moses. Most people recall the story of Moses, who was born a Hebrew slave but reared a prince of Egypt. For killing an Egyptian whom he saw mistreating one of the Hebrews, Moses became a fugitive from Egypt and lived as a shepherd in Midian for forty years. Then God sent him back to Egypt to lead the Hebrew slaves to freedom. At first Moses was reluctant to answer God's call; however, assured of God's presence and power, he undertook the task vigorously.

Lesson 2: Crossing the Red Sea. Ten plagues compelled the Pharaoh of Egypt to release the Hebrew slaves. Starting their journey to the land God promised them, they camped beside the Red Sea. Then Pharaoh changed his mind about his decision to release the Hebrews and sent his army after them. But the Lord continued to protect his people. He opened a way through the sea, and the Hebrews passed between walls of water. When the Egyptian soldiers forged ahead into the same path, the liquid walls collapsed and drowned them all.

Lesson 3: The Covenant. The Israelites camped by Mount Sinai, where the Lord demonstrated his presence through impressive sights and sounds. There the Lord gave his people the laws that would govern their life as a nation.

Lesson 4: The Tabernacle and Obedience. While they were encamped at Sinai for approximately a year, the Israelites built a beautiful tabernacle to serve as God's tent among the tents of his people. God promised to bless the people with prosperity and peace if they would obey his law.

UNIT 2: WANDERING IN THE WILDERNESS

October

Lesson 5: The Cloud and the Fire. In the wilderness, God showed the way for his people by going before them in a cloud by day and a fire by night. The cloud served as a signal to indicate when the people should break camp and resume their travels and when they should stop and rest.

Lesson 6: The People's Rebellion. This is perhaps the most tragic incident to be considered in this quarter's lessons. As the Israelites neared the promised land, Moses sent twelve men (one from each of the twelve tribes) to explore the land and to bring back a report. Although the spies gave an encouraging description of the fruit of the land (complete with a visual aid), they also described the residents of the land as giants and themselves as "grasshoppers" in comparison.

Disheartened by the negative elements in the spies' report, the people refused to enter the land. Instead of trusting God to overcome whatever obstacles existed, they became intimidated by those obstacles. They determined to walk by sight, not by faith. As a result, faith was smothered by fear.

Lesson 7: The Desert Years. God ordered the frightened people to turn back to the desert and spend the rest of their lives there. At this they rebelled yet again, and tried to take control of the promised land. But God was not with them in their act of defiance, and they were soundly defeated. Some thirty-eight years would pass before they had another opportunity to enter the land of promise. How foolish it is not to do something when God says, "Do it!" and to do something when God says, "Don't do it!"

Lesson 8: The Great Commandment. While the two previous lessons focused on the Israelites' rebellion against God, this lesson calls attention to the importance of loving and obeying the Lord. It also stresses how vital it is to teach future generations to love and obey him, and to use every available opportunity to do so.

Lesson 9: A Warning. Here God renewed his promise of a good and fruitful land for his people, but warned that they would be destroyed if they forgot his blessings and turned away from him. How necessary is this reminder in our time!

November

UNIT 3: ENTERING THE PROMISED LAND

Lesson 10: Joshua Succeeds Moses. Moses died at the border of the promised land, without ever entering it. He had, however, provided for a successor so that the task of bringing God's people into the land could be completed. Joshua, who had faithfully served as a kind of "apprentice" to Moses, was appointed to provide the necessary leadership.

Lesson 11: Israel Crosses the Jordan River. At the time of year when the Israelites approached the Jordan River, the river was overflowing its banks. However, in a miracle reminiscent of the parting of the Red Sea, God made the water stand up in a heap, leaving an empty riverbed for Israel to cross.

Lesson 12: God Destroys Jericho. Jericho was a well-fortified city, but at Israel's shout the wall collapsed (Joshua 6:20). Charging in from every side, the Israelites took the city. All of its people and its contents were set apart to the Lord to be destroyed. Any items of value were placed in the treasury of the Lord. Only Rahab and her family were spared from the destruction.

Lesson 13: Israel Chooses to Serve the Lord. Israel conquered the rest of the promised land in about seven years of warfare, then settled down to peaceful and prosperous living. In a farewell address, aged Joshua challenged the people: "Choose for yourselves this day whom you will serve" (Joshua 24:15). Together the people promised to sever any ties with idols and to serve the Lord who had given them the good land they possessed.

The challenge of this final lesson is an appropriate one with which to end the quarter. Will we choose to serve the Lord—this day and every day? Are we willing to declare unashamedly, "As for me and my household, we will serve the Lord"? Only by exhibiting such faith can we enter the "promised land" prepared for us—Heaven!

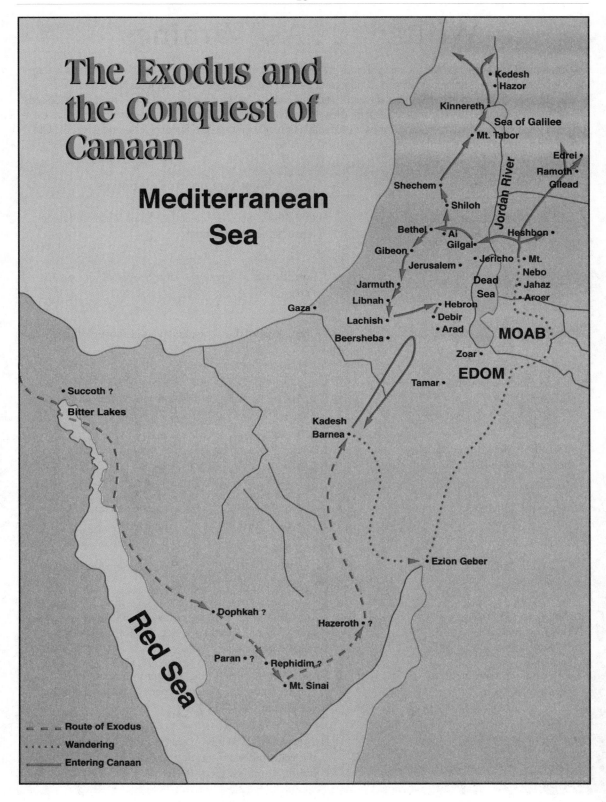

The Exodus and the Conquest of Canaan

Mediterranean Sea

Red Sea

Jordan River

- Kedesh
- Hazor
- Kinnereth
- Sea of Galilee
- Mt. Tabor
- Edrei
- Ramoth Gilead
- Shechem
- Shiloh
- Bethel
- Ai
- Gilgal
- Heshbon
- Gibeon
- Jericho
- Mt. Nebo
- Jerusalem
- Jahaz
- Dead Sea
- Jarmuth
- Hebron
- Aroer
- Libnah
- Debir
- Gaza
- Lachish
- Arad
- Beersheba
- **MOAB**
- Zoar
- **EDOM**
- Tamar
- Kadesh Barnea
- Succoth ?
- Bitter Lakes
- Ezion Geber
- Dophkah ?
- Hazeroth • ?
- Paran • ?
- Rephidim ?
- Mt. Sinai

– – – Route of Exodus

.... Wandering

―――― Entering Canaan

"Written . . . As Warnings"

Sometimes Christians question the value of studying the Old Testament. "We belong to the 'New Covenant,'" they say. "Why study all this stuff about law and sacrifices and the like? We want to know about Jesus and grace!"

But the New Testament frequently cites the Old Testament. In fact—as the chart below shows—many of the lessons of our present quarter's study find reference in the New Testament. Paul said, "These things happened to them as examples and were written down as warnings for us" (1 Corinthians 10:11). If we would know of Jesus and grace, the Old Testament is a good place to start!

Old Testament Event	New Testament References
God Calls Moses (Lesson 1)	**Acts 7:30-34.** Stephen cites the call of Moses in his defense before the Council.
The Passover (Lesson 2)	**1 Corinthians 5:7.** Jesus is "our Passover." (See also 1 Peter 1:19.)
Crossing the Red Sea (Lesson 2)	**1 Corinthians 10:1, 2.** Israel "passed through the sea."
The Law Given Through Moses (Lesson 3)	**Mark 7:9, 10.** Jesus quotes one of the Ten Commandments as a "command of God" and as the words of Moses. (See also John 1:17; 7:19.)
Israel to be a "kingdom of priests," "a holy nation" (Lesson 3).	**1 Peter 2:9** paraphrases Exodus 19:5 in reference to Christians.
Building the Tabernacle (Lesson 4)	**Hebrews 9** describes the tabernacle as a copy of heavenly things (v. 23).
Israel Led by Pillar of Cloud/Fire (Lesson 5)	**1 Corinthians 10:1, 2.** Israel was "under the cloud."
Rebellion in the Desert (Lessons 6, 7, 9)	**1 Corinthians 10:5-13** describes Israel's repeated rebellion. (See also John 3:14; Acts 7:39-43; Hebrews 3:15–4:6.)
The Great Commandment (Lesson 8)	**Mark 12:28-34.** Jesus cites Deuteronomy 6:4, 5 as the "most important commandment." (See also Matthew 4:10; Luke 10:25-27.)
The Fall of Jericho (Lesson 12)	**Hebrews 11:30, 31** says it was faith that brought down the walls of Jericho, noting also the faith of Rahab in hiding the spies. (See also James 2:25.)

From Slavery to Conquest

Unit 1: Exodus and Covenant
(Lessons 1-4)

GOD CALLS MOSES

LESSON 1

WHY TEACH THIS LESSON?

Are you familiar with the "eighty-twenty rule"? Simply put, it says that eighty percent of the work in most churches is done by twenty percent of the members. It's not really a rule, however. In other words, it doesn't have to be that way. It is, instead, a description of the way things are. One of the main reasons the rule holds true is that eighty percent of the people are adept at making excuses. Today's lesson will challenge the excuse-makers in your class. Maybe it will even challenge you!

INTRODUCTION

A. GOD AND MANKIND

Opposition to God always ends in failure or even disaster. We saw that in our lessons from Genesis last summer. Adam and Eve chose to go their own way, and they lost their home in Eden. Mankind after them opposed God till "every inclination of the thoughts of his heart was only evil all the time" (Genesis 6:5), and only eight people survived the flood that followed.

When descendants of those eight grew godless, God chose Abraham (then called Abram) to be the father of a nation that God could call his own. The Lord took Abraham from idolatrous Ur and led him to the land that would belong one day to that nation—the land of Canaan.

Approximately two hundred years later, when there were some seventy people in Abraham's family, the family was welcomed as honored guests in Egypt. But when the family of seventy became a throng of millions, the king of Egypt grew wary of their numbers. Hoping to retard their growth, he made them slaves instead of guests. Yet God remained in control. He had told Abraham that his descendants would dwell in a "country not their own" for four hundred years (Genesis 15:13). Now it was time for them to go back to the land that was theirs, which God had chosen for their home.

B. LESSON BACKGROUND

Nearly every Sunday school student remembers the story of baby Moses. Pharaoh had decreed that any newborn Hebrew boy should be thrown into the river. Moses' mother, however, placed him in a basket and sent the basket floating down the river. Eventually Moses was found by Pharaoh's daughter, who immediately "felt sorry for him" (Exodus 2:6). She brought him up as her own son and gave him the best education that Egypt had to offer (Acts 7:22). Romantic readers like to think he might have been the next king of Egypt if he had been more cautious. One day, however, Moses saw an Egyptian beating a Hebrew, and his anger flared. He killed the oppressor and buried his body in the sand. Moses, a man of great promise and potential, found himself a fugitive, fleeing for his life across the eastern desert.

In the land of Midian, Moses joined the household of a priest named Jethro. He stayed there for forty years, married a daughter of the priest, and started to rear a family. Our text takes up the story at that point.

DEVOTIONAL READING:
EXODUS 6:2-8

BACKGROUND SCRIPTURE:
EXODUS 3

PRINTED TEXT:
EXODUS 3:1-14

LESSON AIMS

After this lesson a student should be able to:

1. Tell the story of God's call to Moses.

2. Compare the call and task God gave Moses with the call and tasks God gives to Christians today.

3. State what he or she believes God has called him or her specifically to do, and suggest one step that can be taken in the coming week to obey that call.

KEY VERSE

God said to Moses, "I AM WHO I AM. This is what you are to say to the Israelites: 'I AM has sent me to you.'" —Exodus 3:14

I. GOD IN THE FIRE (EXODUS 3:1-6)

Moses' father-in-law was a sheep owner as well as a priest. Moses' first contact with the family was at a watering place where Jethro's daughters brought their father's sheep (Exodus 2:15-17). Forty years later, Moses was taking care of the family sheep.

A. SHEPHERD IN THE DESERT (v. 1)

1. Now Moses was tending the flock of Jethro his father-in-law, the priest of Midian, and he led the flock to the far side of the desert and came to Horeb, the mountain of God.

The land of *Midian* was a vast desert area. Pasture is scarce in such country; sheep had to keep moving to find enough to eat. Eventually Moses and his *flock came to Horeb*, also called Sinai. The phrase *the far side of the desert* suggests that Moses had traveled a long way from home at this point. Perhaps Horeb is called *the mountain of God* because God spoke to Moses and later gave the law there; or possibly the Midianites themselves had given the mountain that name for reasons unknown to us.

B. GOD AND HIS ANGEL (vv. 2-4)

2. There the angel of the LORD appeared to him in flames of fire from within a bush. Moses saw that though the bush was on fire it did not burn up.

Students are puzzled because at many points in the Old Testament there seems to be no clear distinction between *the Lord* and his *angel*. Some scholars explain in various ways that the angel either provided the *fire* or was the fire, but God spoke from it. Others believe that the angel was God himself "in one particular phase of his self-revelation." Verse 2 says plainly that *the angel of the Lord appeared . . . in flames of fire from within a bush*; and verse 4 says that *God called . . . from within the bush*. We can accept the facts without understanding all about them.

What Moses saw is quite clear: *the bush was on fire*. That in itself was startling when there was neither a man nor a flash of lightning to start the fire. But what was even more startling was the fact that the bush *did not burn up*. Moses was close enough to see that the small leaves of the desert plant were not withered in the heat, and that the twigs and stems were not being reduced to smoke and ashes.

3. So Moses thought, "I will go over and see this strange sight—why the bush does not burn up."

Moses had never seen such a *sight* before. He went closer to try to determine *why the bush* did *not burn up*.

4. When the LORD saw that he had gone over to look, God called to him from within the bush, "Moses! "Moses!"

And Moses said, "Here I am."

Seeing that the fire had Moses' full attention, God spoke Moses' name clearly and repeated it. If Moses was startled before, now he must have been shocked, if not terrified. But he stood his ground and answered, *Here I am*.

C. HOLY GROUND AND HOLY GOD (vv. 5, 6)

5. "Do not come any closer," God said. "Take off your sandals, for the place where you are standing is holy ground."

Holy ground! If Moses was still moving toward the bush, surely this brought him to a sudden stop. If he was frightened before, now his trembling fingers must have found it hard to untie the thongs of his *sandals*.

WHAT DO YOU THINK?

God got Moses' attention in dramatic fashion when he called Moses. How can we recognize God's call today? How do we know when God wants us to leave the familiar and ordinary—as he called Moses to do—and when he wants us to stay and do his work from within our present situation?

6. *Then he said, "I am the God of your father, the God of Abraham, the God of Isaac, and the God of Jacob." At this, Moses hid his face, because he was afraid to look at God.*

Now the Lord identified himself plainly. He was the God of Heaven and earth who had called the descendants of *Abraham* to be his own. Upon hearing these words, Moses could no longer stare at that fascinating fire. He *hid his face, because he was afraid to look at God*. Later God said to Moses, "You cannot see my face, for no one may see me and live" (Exodus 33:20); but already Moses understood that the sight of Almighty God is not for human eyes.

A MOUNTAINTOP EXPERIENCE

At 29,028 feet, Mount Everest stands as the highest mountain in the world. Not until 1953 did its peak feel the pressure of human footsteps, when Sir Edmund Hillary and Tensing Norgay became the first climbers to see the spectacular view from the "top of the world." Thousands have sought glory in that experience, but through the end of 1996, only 846 people had reached the summit. Only one man, Reinhold Messner, has climbed the mountain alone.

Moses thought that he was alone on "the mountain of God." He had gone there, not in a quest for glory or a spectacular view, but in search of food for his sheep. Instead, what Moses found was a bush that burned with the presence of God and yet was not consumed. As a result, Moses' trip to the mountain was not the culmination of a lifelong quest, but the beginning of a life of service.

Whether our search for meaning in life is as mundane as obtaining our daily bread or as challenging as climbing a breathtaking mountain peak, we should not be surprised to be confronted by God.

He still speaks to those willing to be awed by his presence.   —C. R. B.

II. GOD'S MESSAGE (EXODUS 3:7-12)

Eyes tightly closed and hands covering his face, Moses was humbled, frightened, and trembling with reverent awe. Now he was ready to hear God's message to him. When we approach God's Word with an attitude like that, perhaps we shall understand it better, remember it better, and obey it better. Moses' eyes were closed, but his ears and his mind were opened wide as God continued to speak.

A. A CRY AND A REPLY (vv. 7, 8)

7. *The LORD said, "I have indeed seen the misery of my people in Egypt, I have heard them crying out because of their slave drivers, and I am concerned about their suffering.*

Moses was now eighty years old, and the *misery* of his people had begun long before he was born. Both he and his *suffering* people must have wondered at times if God really knew or cared about their misery, or if he really *heard them crying*. But he did hear; he did know; he did care. That was cheering news to Moses, and it is cheering news to us when we cry in times of suffering.

8. *"So I have come down to rescue them from the hand of the Egyptians and to bring them up out of that land into a good and spacious land, a land flowing with milk and honey—to the home of the Canaanites, Hittites, Amorites, Perizzites, Hivites and Jebusites.*

If news of God's knowledge of his people's misery was encouraging, how Moses' heart must have leaped at this additional news! God had *come down*. He was on the scene, ready for action. The end of bondage was at hand—the liberation of God's people. God himself would *rescue them from the hand of the*

WHAT DO YOU THINK?

Surely Moses' heart often must have yearned for the deliverance of his people whom he had left in bondage when he fled Egypt forty years before. How reassuring it must have been to hear God say he had seen their misery and heard their cry! How can we assure suffering people today that God sees and hears them?

[Perhaps class members can cite examples of how God has demonstrated his care for them or how they have been used by God to minister to some other hurting person.]

WHAT DO YOU THINK?

The lesson writer says, "When a hard job needs to be done, aren't we all more eager to pray for God to do it than we are to dig into it ourselves?" How can we avoid this mistake of trying to substitute prayer for an obedient response to God's call for service?

Egyptians. He would lead them to *a good and spacious land*, a land with plenty of room and resources.

Perhaps Moses' enthusiasm waned a bit upon hearing the list of people already living in that land. It would take courage to invade a country so filled with hostile warriors. But *God* was taking his people there. If he could burn a bush without harming it, couldn't he bring his people unscathed through the fire of battle?

Today we see no bush burning with strange and miraculous fire; we hear God's message from the printed page instead of a living voice. Yet we know all Moses did, and more, about God's mighty power and his unfailing goodness. How can we shrink from any great undertaking when we are sure it is his will?

B. A JOB FOR MOSES (vv. 9, 10)

9. "And now the cry of the Israelites has reached me, and I have seen the way the Egyptians are oppressing them.

The Lord repeated the assurance he had already given Moses.

10. "So now, go. I am sending you to Pharaoh to bring my people the Israelites out of Egypt."

On hearing these words, Moses' soaring heart must have dropped with a thud. That he should go to *Egypt* and rescue his enslaved *people* was not what he had been praying for. When a hard job needs to be done, aren't we all more eager to pray for God to do it than we are to dig into it ourselves? God does many mighty works with no help from us, from the creation of the world to the sunshine that warms us today; but there are also some mighty works that he will do through us or not at all!

DELAYED RESPONSE

Anne-Merete Christensen was a Swedish teenager when she put a letter in a bottle and threw it into the Baltic Sea. After years with no response, she gave up hope of hearing from a pen pal.

However, thirty years later, eight-year-old Otto Fransson found the bottle bobbing near Sweden's eastern shore and retrieved it. He wrote a long-delayed response to Christensen, who by then was a forty-three-year-old married woman with two children of her own.

When God spoke to Moses on the mountain, he was responding to a cry that Israel had been voicing for some four centuries. Moses may well have wondered why it had taken so long for God to respond. But from God's vantage point, that time was well spent in preparing Moses to be his instrument of deliverance.

Who among us has not questioned why God's response to our prayers is so often delayed? Moses' experience teaches us that God always hears us; however, his response often comes through people who, according to his timetable, have finally been prepared to act on his behalf.

Is God preparing you to be an answer to someone's prayer today?   —C. R. B.

C. OBJECTION OVERRULED (vv. 11, 12)

11. Moses said to God, "Who am I, that I should go to Pharaoh and bring the Israelites out of Egypt?"

Who am I? This was a reasonable question. Moses was a fugitive from *Egypt*. There was another *Pharaoh* now, though not the one from whom Moses had fled (Exodus 2:15); but would he be any kinder to a runaway killer? Would even the enslaved *Israelites* pay any attention to a fugitive who had resurfaced after forty years in hiding?

12. And God said, "I will be with you. And this will be the sign to you that it is I who have sent you: When you have brought the people out of Egypt, you will worship God on this mountain."

I will be with you. This was the encouraging promise that put a different face on the job to be done. What appeared too much for Moses was not too much for Moses and God. And how was Moses to know that God would be with him in fulfilling this assignment? When the job was done, Moses and his *people* would worship God on this very *mountain* where God was speaking. In the meantime Moses was to walk by faith. He was to trust and obey.

III. GOD'S NAME (EXODUS 3:13, 14)

After asking, "Who am I?" Moses next asked, "Who is God?" While it may seem odd to us today, this too was a reasonable question. The people of Israel had been in Egypt for approximately four hundred years. During the early stages of that time, they had been treated as honored guests, favored by the government, and allowed to live in Goshen, among the most fertile parts of all the land of Egypt.

Probably the knowledge of God became less rather than greater during those prosperous years in Egypt. Then came a change in the government and the beginning of what became many years of oppression and slavery. Perhaps the people thought of God and cried to him for relief; but the cruel burden of bondage made it hard, if not impossible, to do much effective teaching. Imitating their parents, the children learned to cry plaintively to God, but with little concept of who he was.

A. NEED FOR A NAME (v. 13)

13. Moses said to God, "Suppose I go to the Israelites and say to them, 'The God of your fathers has sent me to you,' and they ask me, 'What is his name?' Then what shall I tell them?"

If Moses would come announcing that the slaves' deliverance was near and claiming to speak on behalf of the *God* of their *fathers*, they would want to know more about that God. It did not seem to them that he had done much for them recently, so why should they expect his help now? *What is his name?* they would ask, hoping his name would give them some insight into his character, his nature, or his power.

B. I AM (v. 14)

14. God said to Moses, "I AM WHO I AM. This is what you are to say to the Israelites: 'I AM has sent me to you.'"

The name *I AM*, spoken by *God*, declares that God is always living and always the same. Coupled with the words of verse 6, this name told the slaves in Egypt that the God calling them to freedom was the same God of majesty and power who had called Abraham from Ur and had brought him to Canaan with wealth and power and honor. That same God could break the shackles of their slavery and bring them to that same land with similar wealth and power and honor.

To all of us, these two verses carry several great thoughts: First, the God who sent Moses is the only God who really is, the only one who actually exists. Other so-called gods are figments of human imagination. They are without life and without power.

Second, the God who sent Moses is eternal. Forever he is, and forever he is the same—past, present, and future. His people can depend on him, not only for all the years of this life on earth, but also throughout the eternity beyond this life.

Third, in a special sense the God who sent Moses is the God of the Hebrews. He is the one who called, blessed, and helped Abraham, Isaac, and Jacob. He is

This visual reminds us of the nature of the God we serve, the great and eternal "I AM," who called to Moses from out of the burning bush.

WHAT DO YOU THINK?

This is an era of compromise and of tolerance gone awry. Many who regard themselves as Christians actually see Christianity as no more authentic than Islam, Buddhism, Hinduism, and other pagan religions. They would regard it as a serious breach of political correctness to speak of the Christian faith as the only way to salvation and eternal life. Yet by revealing himself as I AM, God has demonstrated that he is the only God. How can we emphasize the exclusive nature of worshiping the true God in this age of pluralism?

the one who gave special promises about their descendants as well as about them. In a similar special sense he is the God of Christians, for they are "the Israel of God" (Galatians 6:16). By faith they are "children of Abraham," and thus "are blessed along with Abraham" (Galatians 3:6-9).

CONCLUSION

Moses doubted his ability to do the job, but he could not doubt that God was calling him to do it. Without a clear voice from a flame, how can I recognize God's call? When I see an opportunity, how do I know whether it is God's call to a great work or the devil's invitation to disaster? When I need a leader to follow, how do I know whom to choose?

A. QUALIFICATION

God calls people to do what he qualifies them to do. Several factors combine to qualify a person for a job.

1. *Training.* During the first forty years of his life, Moses became "educated in all the wisdom of the Egyptians and was powerful in speech and action" (Acts 7:22). Who could be better qualified to confront the rulers of Egypt?

2. *Experience.* Many employers are looking for people with experience. During the second forty years of his life, Moses was a shepherd in Midian. He became well acquainted with the desert country and with the needs of livestock as well as people. Who could be better prepared to lead his people and their flocks through such rugged terrain over the next forty years?

3. *Natural talent.* A singer needs a voice. A scholar needs high intelligence. A mechanic needs mechanical aptitude. An evangelist needs to be a "people person." A fine teacher may fail as a farmer, and a fine farmer may fail as a teacher. Moses had talent as well as training and experience. He was the man for the job!

Haven't we all seen a well-schooled preacher who couldn't preach well, or a good preacher who was not good at personal evangelism, or a fine evangelist who was too aggressive in visiting the sick? A big church may have a team of specialists; but a church with only one minister looks for a man of many talents, or one who is strong in the ability most needed in that church.

B. HELP

The new president of a corporation noted, "The secret of success will be to surround myself with people smarter than I am." One who would lead must ask, "Is competent help available?" Anyone looking for a leader must ask, "Is he able to make use of competent help?" Moses needed a talker to help him, and his brother Aaron was just what he needed (Exodus 4:10-16).

A preacher who can't sing looks for a church that has a good song leader, and a church without such a leader may look for a minister skilled in music. A beginning preacher looks for a place with experienced elders, but a new church may need a minister with experience. A preacher unskilled in business looks for a church with a competent treasurer, but a church unskilled in business may look for a minister with knowledge and experience in the business world.

C. THE LORD'S APPROVAL

In choosing a career or a hobby, a task or a game, an employer or an employee, a leader or a follower, a Christian asks, "Will God be pleased with this choice?" If you see anyone or anything that would turn you away from the Lord, turn away from that person or thing. Make a choice that will make you a better Christian.

Discovery Learning

This page contains an alternate lesson plan emphasizing learning activities. Classes desiring such student involvement will find these suggestions helpful. The next page is a reproducible activity page to further enhance discovery learning.

LEARNING GOALS

After this lesson, each student will be able to:

1. Tell the story of God's call to Moses.

2. Compare the call and task God gave Moses with the call and tasks God gives to Christians today.

3. State what he or she believes God has called him or her specifically to do, and suggest one step that can be taken in the coming week to obey that call.

INTO THE LESSON

Bring with you the classified section from a local newspaper. Read several of the "Help Wanted" ads that are very different from each other. Next, ask class members to work in small groups to suggest various tasks God uses people to do today. Provide each group with "Post-it Notes," and ask the students to write their ideas on these notes and then post them on the board to be shared with the rest of the class.

Discuss the following questions. What are some specific situations where God might use a person to speak for him? (*Sharing the gospel, serving in community organizations, etc.*) How can people with particular training, experience, or talent be used by God? (*Teaching ability for preaching and teaching Sunday school classes, musical ability for leading worship, business ability to help administer the church, etc.*)

INTO THE WORD

Once Moses heard that he was the one God would use to deliver his people, he responded with objections and questions (Exodus 3:11; 4:1, 10). Write on the board the following three column headings: "Task Assigned," "Questions and Objections," and "God's Answers." Write, "Go to Egypt and deliver the Israelites (Exodus 3:10)" under "Task Assigned." Review Moses' responses to God by listing them under the next heading. (Who am I? Who is God? What is his name? They will not believe me. I am not qualified. Send someone else. See Exodus 3:11, 13; 4:1, 10, 13.) Under the final heading summarize the response of God to each of these questions or objections. (See Exodus 3:12, 14-22; 4:2-9, 11, 12, 14-17.) In the next section, you will work to identify specific tasks God has for your class members. At that time come back to this chart, and see what questions or objections people might present to God today in light of those special assignments.

INTO LIFE

God met Moses in the ordinary routine of his daily work, and challenged him to a specific task that God had prepared him to accomplish (Exodus 3:1-7). Ask class members, "If God appeared to you and said: 'I have a job for you to do,' what do you think that job might be?"

While God doesn't communicate with us that way today, he still guides us into tasks that are specifically suited for each of us. To help your class members identify specific tasks God may be directing them to accomplish, help them put together a resume to consider ways in which God has prepared them to serve him.

Training: What skills and abilities have you developed through formal or informal classes, job training, seminars, personal study, etc.?

Experience: Have you gone through certain experiences that might equip you to minister more effectively to particular people or in particular situations?

Talents: Has God given you specific abilities that could be used to promote spiritual growth in the lives of others?

Passions or burdens: Do you have a burden for a particular person or a certain group of people? When you think of serving God, is there a particular area of ministry that really excites you?

Opportunities: Are you aware of a particular need that you believe you could meet? Are you in a situation at home, work, the church, or the community that gives you unique opportunities to serve God?

Have class members look over what they have written and then write job descriptions for the ministries they believe God has called them to perform. As a few volunteers name their tasks, write them on the board under the column marked "Task Assigned." Next, ask the entire class to suggest objections or questions that some might offer in resistance to accepting each task. Write these under the "Questions and Objections" heading. Then discuss what God's answer might be to those responses.

Option: Use the reproducible page that follows to help your students compare the tasks God has given them—and the excuses they sometimes use to refuse—with those of Moses' experience.

Close the class time in prayer, thanking God for his direction in our lives. Leave time for class members to commit themselves silently to the task God has for them.

God Calls Moses

When Moses was called by God for a specific job, he responded with a series of questions and objections. After looking at each objection, summarize God's answers to Moses.

TASK ASSIGNED	QUESTIONS AND OBJECTIONS	GOD'S ANSWERS
Go to Egypt and Deliver my people	Who am I? (Exodus 3:10)	Exodus 3:12
	Who is God? What is his name? (Exodus 3:13)	Exodus 3:14-22
	They will not believe me (Exodus 4:1)	Exodus 4:2-9
	I am not qualified (Exodus 4:10)	Exodus 4:11, 12
	Send someone else (Exodus 4:13)	Exodus 4:14-17

Now write down some tasks that God assigns for us to do as Christians today.
Then suggest common questions or objections Christians have about these assignments.
Finally, summarize what you think God's answer would be to those responses.

TASK ASSIGNED	QUESTIONS AND OBJECTIONS	GOD'S ANSWERS

Now complete the next section by describing your personal situation.
What has God assigned you to do?
What questions or objections do you have?
What is God's answer to your response?

TASK ASSIGNED	QUESTIONS AND OBJECTIONS	GOD'S ANSWERS

CROSSING THE RED SEA

LESSON 2

Sep
12

WHY TEACH THIS LESSON?

Israel's crossing of the Red Sea is one of the most famous events in Israelite history. The Canaanites were aware of it in Joshua's day (Joshua 2:10), and it was recited repeatedly in Israelite families down through the centuries. Paul alluded to it in his letter to the Corinthians (1 Corinthians 10:1, 2). It is one of the Bible stories that virtually every child who regularly attends Sunday school can retell.

No doubt the reason for the story's popularity is that so many lessons can be drawn from it. Need to illustrate that the ways of God are greater than the ways of man? This is it. Do you want to teach that God can lead his people to overcome any obstacle? Again, this is a good choice. Perhaps the greatest lesson you can teach from this text is to fear the Lord and and to put one's trust in him (v. 31). You and your students will be wise if that lesson is learned!

INTRODUCTION

A. TEACHING A KING TO OBEY

Last week's lesson focused on Moses, the Hebrew who became first a prince of Egypt, then a fugitive running for his life. After living forty years in Egypt, Moses became a shepherd in Midian for forty years. It seems he was content with that life, and not pleased when the Lord sent him back to Egypt to lead his people to freedom. But the Lord insisted, and Moses went (Exodus 3, 4).

The king of Egypt was not pleased either when Moses came asking him to release God's people so they could observe a religious festival in the desert. Instead of granting the slaves a holiday, he increased their work load. But the Lord had ways of disciplining a disobedient king and his cruel slave drivers: the ten plagues broke their stubborn wills. When the final plague brought death to the firstborn in every Egyptian family, king and people not only agreed to let God's people go, but begged them to go quickly and take whatever items of value they wanted. All of this is recorded in Exodus 5–12.

B. LESSON BACKGROUND

Swiftly a huge caravan was assembled. It included about six hundred thousand men, besides women and children, and countless sheep and cattle (Exodus 12:37, 38). In the Israelites' haste to obtain all they could from the Egyptians (12:35, 36), they must have loaded wagons or oxcarts with lumber, leather, jewelry, and fabrics. We know this because they later used those items to build the tabernacle in the desert (35:4-9). We can imagine that there was more confusion than order in organizing the departure from Egypt, but soon the huge throng was ready to move forward (12:37).

I. STARTING OUT (EXODUS 13:17-22)

The last part of chapter 12 and the first part of chapter 13 are filled with instructions to be followed by God's people throughout the coming centuries. However, for today's lesson we bypass these commands and go on to the record of the actual exodus from Egypt.

DEVOTIONAL READING:
PSALM 106:1-12

BACKGROUND SCRIPTURE:
EXODUS 13:17—14:31

PRINTED TEXT:
EXODUS 13:17-22; 14:21, 22, 26-31

LESSON AIMS

After this lesson a student should be able to:

1. Tell how God led Israel out of Egypt and through the Red Sea.

2. Tell how God has delivered him or her from a specific sin or difficult circumstance.

3. Praise God for his deliverance and seek to go forward in faith.

KEY VERSE

Do not be afraid. Stand firm and you will see the deliverance the LORD will bring you today.
—Exodus 14:13

LESSON 2 NOTES

A. THE LONG WAY (vv. 17, 18)

17. When Pharaoh let the people go, God did not lead them on the road through the Philistine country, though that was shorter. For God said, "If they face war, they might change their minds and return to Egypt."

The people of Israel had lived in Goshen, located in the fertile delta of the Nile River. The direct route to the promised land would have taken them northeast along the Mediterranean seacoast. However, *Philistine country* lay along that route. The Philistines were a tough and hostile people. The Israelites knew nothing about waging *war*; they had been submissive slaves all their lives. Confronted by such a possibility, *they might change their minds and return to Egypt* since they were not far from there at this point. So God led them to Canaan by a much longer route.

18. So God led the people around by the desert road toward the Red Sea. The Israelites went up out of Egypt armed for battle.

Instead of leading his people northeast toward the promised land, *God led* them southeast toward the *desert* country near the *Red Sea*. Thus they bypassed the hostile Philistines.

The word rendered *armed for battle* in the *New International Version* is difficult to translate. The only other time the term is used in the Old Testament it is translated "armed" (Joshua 1:14), so it seems good to some to translate it here consistently with the other use.

Some have noted that since Israel was taking a long way around the Philistines in order to avoid battle, the Hebrew word translated *armed for battle* should not be given a specific military connotation. They propose that the term is better rendered by a more general word such as "equipped," which could have reference to military preparedness, but not necessarily. Thus the Israelites *went up out of Egypt* "equipped" for travel, with wagons and provisions for their journey (but not ready for battle). Whatever this word means, these travelers were expecting a long trip and were prepared for it.

The exact location of where the Israelites crossed the Red Sea has been a matter of much discussion among Bible students. Much of the uncertainty lies in the Hebrew term rendered "Red Sea," which actually means "Sea of Reeds." In addition, this term is used in a variety of ways in the Old Testament. Sometimes it designates the western "arm" of the Red Sea, or the Gulf of Suez (Numbers 33:10, 11); elsewhere, the eastern "arm," or the Gulf of Aqaba, is being described (1 Kings 9:26). Some liberal Bible scholars, attempting to deny the miraculous nature of the crossing, have suggested that this "Sea of Reeds" was merely a marshy area in which the Egyptian chariots got bogged down, allowing Israel to escape. This denies too much of what the Bible says, however, and certainly does not account for the great impression the event made on both the Israelites and the Canaanites (Joshua 2:9, 10).

Some Bible students believe that the crossing occurred at the northern end of the Gulf of Suez. Others point to Exodus 15:22, which says that when the Israelites crossed the sea, they entered the "Desert of Shur." Most scholars locate this desert in the northern part of the Sinai Peninsula, so some suggest that the crossing occurred at an area known as the Bitter Lakes (see the map on page 15), which may have been at that time an extension of the Gulf of Suez.

B. KEEPING A PROMISE (v. 19)

19. Moses took the bones of Joseph with him because Joseph had made the sons of Israel swear an oath. He had said, "God will surely come to your aid, and then you must carry my bones up with you from this place."

WHAT DO YOU THINK?

The Lord led the Israelites away from the warlike Philistines, but then he led them to the Red Sea, with the Egyptian army in hot pursuit. Why do you think he did not let them face the Philistines and deliver them with a miracle as he eventually delivered them from the Egyptians anyway? How do we know when to avoid a confrontation (as with the Philistines) and when to face the problem head on with the power of the Lord (as with crossing the Red Sea)?

The visual for lesson 2 shows a suggested route of the exodus from Egypt. You may want to keep it on display for reference through most of the quarter.

The Exodus and
the Conquest of
Canaan

Mediterranean
Sea

Red Sea

Joseph was a son of *Israel* (Jacob), who had gone to Egypt before his family had. He had become a ruler there and had welcomed his family when a famine drove them to Egypt. Jacob, the head of the family, had died in Egypt, but his body had been taken back to Canaan for burial (Genesis 50:12-14). Confident that God would someday lead all of his people back to the promised land, Joseph had made his fellow Israelites *swear* to take his remains there instead of burying them in Egypt (Genesis 50:24-26). That *oath* had been made long before Moses was born, but it had been handed down from generation to generation. Now Moses was in a position to honor it. Since Joseph's body had been embalmed, the remains were what we would call a mummy rather than merely Joseph's *bones*.

C. GUIDANCE FOR THE JOURNEY (vv. 20-22)

20. After leaving Succoth they camped at Etham on the edge of the desert.

In many Bible atlases, as on the visual for today's lesson and the map on page 15, these place names are printed with question marks because no one knows exactly where they were; but it is clear that the travelers were going southeast toward the Red Sea, and that *Etham was on the edge of the desert*.

21. By day the LORD went ahead of them in a pillar of cloud to guide them on their way and by night in a pillar of fire to give them light, so that they could travel by day or night.

The travelers needed no map or native guide. *The Lord* himself led them with visible signs to show the way. *A pillar of cloud* moved ahead of them every day. By night *a pillar of fire gave light* as well as guidance. Thus they could travel *by day or night*. When the pillar moved, they moved; when the pillar stopped, they stopped.

22. Neither the pillar of cloud by day nor the pillar of fire by night left its place in front of the people.

A *pillar* was always there, *day* or *night*, when *the people* traveled and when they rested. It served, not only as a guide, but also as a constant reminder that God was there and was taking care of them.

A DIVINE PILOT

Bob Frayser was piloting his own plane eastward over Kansas at an altitude of fifty-five hundred feet. A leaking exhaust system allowed carbon monoxide fumes into the cabin, and Frayser lost consciousness. But he didn't die in a fiery crash! He had put his plane on autopilot; and when he passed out, the autopilot kept the plane on a level, straight course.

After some 250 miles, the plane finally ran out of fuel; however, the autopilot kept the plane level as it glided to a landing in a snowy field in Missouri. The plane skidded five hundred feet and stopped in a row of trees. Frayser awakened in a confused state and found his way to a farmhouse a quarter of a mile away. Speaking of his survival with only minor injuries, he said, "Most of the credit I give to the Lord."

The Israelites could see the pillars of cloud and fire that were directing them to their unknown destination. But the real power leading them was God himself—a far surer guide than Frayser's autopilot. And unlike a malfunctioning airplane that caused Frayser to black out, God sustained and protected Israel during their journey from Egypt through the wilderness to the promised land. He fed, healed, and protected them as he led them to freedom.

Today, while God may use less spectacular means, he still protects and guides his children. In all our ways, let us acknowledge him (Proverbs 3:6). —C. R. B.

II. RESCUE (EXODUS 14:21, 22, 26-28)

From Etham the pillar led the travelers on to the shore of the sea (14:1, 2). Meanwhile, however, Pharaoh was having second thoughts about releasing the

---

WHAT DO YOU THINK?

Suppose a member of your class said, "I wish I had a pillar of fire or a cloud to direct me! It seems so hard to determine what God's will is sometimes." How would you respond?

HOW TO SAY IT
Aqaba. OCK-uh-buh.
Canaan. KAY-nun.
Etham. EE-thum.
Goshen. GO-shun.
Midian. MID-ee-un.
Succoth. SOO-kawth.
Suez. SOO-ez.

Hebrews. He had brought on the plagues, including the death of the firstborn, by refusing to let the Hebrews go. Then he had relented and let them go; so his people had lost both their firstborn and their slaves. Many of those grieving over their losses would be blaming Pharaoh personally. Would some of them be thinking of replacing him? If they were, would the army be on their side? What could the king do to regain the respect and support of his people? He knew he could not bring back the dead children, but perhaps he could bring back the slaves. Quickly he marshaled his army—infantry and cavalry and chariots—and raced after the Hebrews. He caught up with them as they were camped by the sea (Exodus 14:5-9).

At first the Israelites panicked. They cried out to Moses, asking why he had led them into that barren wilderness to die. Moses assured them that the Lord would fight in their behalf and that "the Egyptians you see today you will never see again" (v. 13).

Then the guiding cloud became the people's defense. Leaving its place in front of the Israelites, it moved behind them and blocked the pass between them and the Egyptians, keeping the pursuers at bay all night long (vv. 19, 20).

A. DELIVERANCE OF ISRAEL (vv. 21, 22)

21. Then Moses stretched out his hand over the sea, and all that night the LORD drove the sea back with a strong east wind and turned it into dry land. The waters were divided.

Moses did exactly what God told him to do (v. 16), and God did the rest. He made *a strong east wind* do what no wind could do without his express order. It pushed the water to the left and right, exposing the bed of the sea and swiftly turning it *into dry land* over which the people could cross.

22. And the Israelites went through the sea on dry ground, with a wall of water on their right and on their left.

It seems that the guiding cloud now returned to its usual place in front of the Israelites, and they followed it *through the sea.* It must have been quite frightening at first to walk between walls of water, but they bravely followed their guide and were safe.

Once the pillar of cloud was removed and no longer blocked the way before them, the army of Egypt went into action, swift and terrible. Probably the chariots were in the lead, rolling like a wave of death after the fleeing people (v. 23); but then they met the Lord and disaster. Suddenly the chariots lost their wheels. The onslaught of death slowed as horses plunged and swayed, struggling to drag those chariots without wheels. Then panic caught the drivers. The Lord was fighting against them, they realized—the same Lord who had overwhelmed Egypt with those terrible plagues! Desperately they tried to swing the chariots around and race back over the way they had come, but they soon met the oncoming cavalry. Men, horses, and wheeless chariots mingled in wild confusion.

B. DESTRUCTION OF EGYPT (vv. 26-28)

26. Then the LORD said to Moses, "Stretch out your hand over the sea so that the waters may flow back over the Egyptians and their chariots and horsemen."

By this time, all the children of Israel had reached the other side of *the sea.* That dry passageway through the water had served its purpose; now it was time to close it. At Moses' outstretched *hand* the *waters* had been driven back (v. 21); now it summoned them to return.

27. Moses stretched out his hand over the sea, and at daybreak the sea went back to its place. The Egyptians were fleeing toward it, and the LORD swept them into the sea.

WHAT DO YOU THINK?

The Israelites' path to deliverance from the Egyptians took them between towering walls of water. That must have been an awesome—perhaps even frightening—experience. From what frightening situations has God delivered you or someone you know?

Now the towering walls of water came crashing together. Weighed down with battle garb, the men could not swim in that tempestuous sea. Still hitched to the heavy chariots, the horses were helpless too.

28. The water flowed back and covered the chariots and horsemen—the entire army of Pharaoh that had followed the Israelites into the sea. Not one of them survived.

Thus *the army of Pharaoh* was destroyed. *Not one of them survived.* Sooner or later, such is the fate of all those who persist in fighting against God.

III. SAFE AT LAST (EXODUS 14:29-31)

These verses provide a summary of what happened and its impact on those who witnessed it.

A. THE SAVED (v. 29)

29. But the Israelites went through the sea on dry ground, with a wall of water on their right and on their left.

The Israelites had been in deadly peril from the pursuing army and the towering walls of *water*; but they *went through the sea on dry ground*, safe from both dangers.

B. THE SAVIOR (v. 30)

30. That day the LORD saved Israel from the hands of the Egyptians, and Israel saw the Egyptians lying dead on the shore.

The *Egyptians* could have crushed the Israelites, and the sea could have drowned them; but *the Lord* overpowers the armies of nations and controls the movements of the waters of the earth. He made the waters a source of life for his people, and a source of death for their enemies.

C. THE RESULT (v. 31)

31. And when the Israelites saw the great power the LORD displayed against the Egyptians, the people feared the LORD and put their trust in him and in Moses his servant.

The *Israelites* were alive and safe from the *Egyptians*, but this verse mentions other results no less important: they *feared the Lord*, and they *put their trust* not only *in him*, but also *in Moses his servant* whom he appointed and inspired.

We know of this miracle, and Scripture tells us of many others that Moses and his people never saw. Shouldn't we also fear the Lord, believe him, and obey him?

SPLENDID ISOLATION

Juneau, the capital of Alaska, sits in splendid isolation in the southeastern corner of the state. The city backs up to the spectacular glacier-riven, eight-thousand-foot peaks of the Coast Range. On the opposite side is water—what is called the "inside passage" that stretches a thousand miles along the Pacific coast of North America.

Juneau is four and one-half hours by ship from the nearest Alaskan city that has a road system connecting it to the rest of the state. This isolation is both bane and blessing. It is also the subject of continuing debate as to whether the state capital should be moved to Anchorage and whether a road should be built to connect Juneau with the "outside."

The blessing of Juneau's isolation is that it has enabled the city to maintain a pristine beauty, undefiled by the hordes of motor vehicles that crowd most other state capitals. The bane is that the city is inaccessible except by plane or ship.

The Red Sea was first bane, then blessing, to Israel. As Pharaoh's army bore down on the Israelites (standing on the western shore), the sea appeared to be their barrier to salvation. But when they stood on the opposite shore watching the destruction of

DAILY BIBLE READINGS

Monday, Sept. 6—The Feast of Unleavened Bread (Exodus 13:3-10)

Tuesday, Sept. 7—Led by Pillars of Cloud and Fire (Exodus 13:17-22)

Wednesday, Sept. 8—Caught Between Pharaoh and the Sea (Exodus 14:1-9)

Thursday, Sept. 9—Going Forward at God's Command (Exodus 14:10-18)

Friday, Sept. 10—Israel Crosses the Red Sea (Exodus 14:19-25)

Saturday, Sept. 11—God Saves Israel From the Egyptians (Exodus 14:26-31)

Sunday, Sept. 12—Israel Sings of God's Victory (Exodus 15:1-13)

WHAT DO YOU THINK?

"And when the Israelites saw the great power the Lord displayed against the Egyptians, the people feared the Lord and put their trust in him and in Moses his servant" (Exodus 14:31). That's fine for the Israelites, but how about our unbelieving neighbors? How can we lead them to believe in the Lord, or in us as faithful witnesses to him? We can't part the water in the neighborhood pool—can we?

Egypt's army, the Red Sea became a blessing. Now Israel stood in splendid isolation, separated by those same waters from the world that had enslaved it.

   In such circumstances as these, the difference in perspective depends on where one stands with God.

                 —C. R. B.

CONCLUSION

   Why did the Lord take such care to keep the Israelites alive and make them a free people? He had a specific purpose for them. Why has he preserved the church through the centuries, in spite of attacks from without and frequent faithlessness within? He has a purpose for his church. Why has God called you, forgiven you, and made you his own? He has a purpose for you, too.

A. GOD'S PURPOSE FOR ISRAEL

   God stated his purpose for Israel when he called Abraham to be the father of that nation: "All peoples on earth will be blessed through you" (Genesis 12:3). In spite of their many faults and failures, God preserved Abraham's people until they brought into the world the Savior who offers to all the gift of eternal life.

B. GOD'S PURPOSE FOR THE CHURCH

   Today we who follow the Savior are God's chosen people—chosen for the purpose of bringing to all families of the earth the blessing promised through Abraham and given through Christ. How are we doing? Is your church keeping the whole community aware of Christ's offer of life? Is it also supporting missionaries who hold forth the Word of life in distant lands?

C. GOD'S PURPOSE FOR YOU

   I like to think God has called me to prepare Sunday school lessons like this one. I know a young lady who is such a fine teacher that I think God has called her to that work; and she does her best teaching in Sunday school. I once knew an auto mechanic so skilled and so benevolent that I felt sure God had given him a special talent and calling. His chief joy was to take care of the cars that Bible college students drove to their weekend preaching appointments. He did that at reduced rates, and often for no payment at all.

   Whatever God has equipped you to do for a living, are you also finding a way to take part in his great purpose of bringing to all the hope of eternal life?

   Whom do you know who is not a Christian? Have you ever made an opportunity to tell him or her about the way of salvation and the joy of Christian living? Are you ready to begin the great adventure of such telling?

   You don't know how? Then whom do you know who does know how? Maybe you can go with him a few times and see how he does it. Or maybe you can find some other Christians who don't know how. Maybe they would like to meet once a week for a month and get an expert to teach them how to start talking about the most important matters in the world. Between meetings you can practice what he tells you, and then come back for more coaching.

   Involvement in this kind of personal evangelism program is not easy, but what joys it can bring! However, if you keep trying for a year and then are convinced that God did not design you for that service, increase your missionary offering and turn to some ministry better suited to your talent. You can still share your faith informally in personal settings even if evangelism is not your ministry strength.

   If you start out with courage and vigor to do what God wants you to do, he will be with you all the way. Prayer will help; however, a time does come when God tells us to "move on" (Exodus 14:15).

Discovery Learning

This page contains an alternate lesson plan emphasizing learning activities. Classes desiring such student involvement will find these suggestions helpful. The next page is a reproducible activity page to further enhance discovery learning.

LEARNING GOALS

After this lesson a student should be able to:

1. Tell how God led Israel out of Egypt and through the Red Sea.

2. Tell how God has delivered him or her from a specific sin or difficult circumstance.

3. Praise God for his deliverance and seek to go forward in faith.

INTO THE LESSON

Use a bold black marker to write the letters of the word PROBLEM on seven sheets of paper (one letter per sheet). On the backs of the sheets spell RED SEA (the back of the B is blank) with a bold red marker. Display the word PROBLEM at the front of the room before students arrive.

When it is time to begin, ask, "What are some very difficult (or even seemingly impossible) situations you have faced—times when you knew you would make it through only with God's help?" Prompt the discussion with questions like, "How did you react?" "Did you learn any new lessons about God through those experiences?" "Did you wonder why God allowed them to happen, or how he could possibly use the circumstances for any good purpose?"

Observe that in today's lesson we will examine a time when the Israelites faced a similar situation. Begin turning over the letters to reveal the words RED SEA as you tell the class, "Just as God delivered the Israelites through the Red Sea, he will deliver us through our problems and difficult circumstances, too."

INTO THE WORD

Ask a volunteer to read Exodus 13:17-22. Ask the class to listen for the answers to the following questions as the text is read. After the reading, discuss the questions.

• Why did God lead the Israelites through the longer route, avoiding the Philistines? (*So they wouldn't face war and turn back; see Exodus 13:17.*)

• What is the significance of carrying Joseph's bones with them on their journey? (*It was a visual memorial of God's faithfulness, the fulfillment of a promise made over 400 years earlier; see Genesis 50:24, 25.*)

Point out that God led the Israelites to an impassable route and brought the Egyptian army from behind to trap them completely. God allowed the Israelites to face such difficult circumstances to bring glory to himself and to make himself known as the only true God (Exodus 14:1-4). Note the irony that God avoided war between the Israelites and the Philistines but then put the Israelites in an apparently inescapable position with the Egyptian army (Exodus 14:5-9).

Discuss what lessons this should teach us about difficult (or seemingly impossible) situations and about God's providence. (*God protects us from what we cannot handle [1 Corinthians 10:13], but he may also allow us to experience situations where he receives the glory by demonstrating his power [2 Corinthians 12:7-10; Ephesians 3:20, 21; 1 Peter 1:5].*)

Have a volunteer read Exodus 14:21, 22, 26-31. Then divide the class into groups of four to six members each. Ask the groups to work together to summarize how God delivered Israel from an impossible situation and what effect the rescue had on the Israelites. Ask each person in the group to tell how God has delivered him or her from a specific sin or difficult circumstance. Have the groups list as many parallels between God's deliverance of the Israelites from Egypt and his deliverance of his people today from problems or difficult situations as they can. Discuss what these experiences did for the faith of those who went through them.

Allow about ten minutes for the groups to discuss these issues. Then call for reports. List on the chalkboard or a large poster the cumulative list of parallels between Israel's rescue and the rescue of God's people today.

INTO LIFE

Perhaps there are "Red Seas" facing some of your students even now. Ask, "What is one battle you are facing in which you know you need God's help?" Allow volunteers to tell of their situations, but don't pressure anyone to participate. Those who do tell their stories will become models for others, even those unwilling to open up about their situations.

Ask, "What is one risky step of faith that you know you need to take to move forward?" Discuss what is "risky" about such a step, why it is necessary, and what results might be expected.

Option: Use the reproducible page that follows as the basis for your application activity.

Close with prayer for courage as you and your students seek to "move forward" with God in faith.

Crossing the Red Sea

TO CONSIDER:
A PATTERN FOR EXPERIENCING GOD'S POWER

Trust God that he is in control. He will allow you to face only circumstances you can handle (compare Exodus 13:17, 18 with 14:1-4).

Recognize God's purposes. He can use you through this difficult time to demonstrate his power and make his name known (Exodus 14:4).

Call out to God for help. Confess that you cannot take care of this by yourself and you need his help (Exodus 14:13-15).

Move forward by faith. Take the steps you know you should to obediently follow his direction in your life (Exodus 14:15, 16).

Watch God work. He is always at work, but sometimes we are so consumed by our circumstances that we fail to see his hand. Watch him resolve situations that are out of your control. Watch him move people to respond in ways that surprise us (Exodus 14:19-29).

Give God the credit. Verbalize to yourself and others that it is only God who got you through (Exodus 14:30—15:21).

Learn from these experiences. Allow the school of experience to teach you to trust God more.

Remember these things as you face the future. It would even be a good idea to create a "memorial" to God's provision, so that you can see it and be encouraged when you face the difficult times again.

TO DO: CREATE AN ACTION PLAN FOR EXPERIENCING GOD'S POWER

• **Identify a specific battle** you are facing in which you know you need God's help.

How could these lessons help you follow God's direction and move forward?

Write an action plan for steps you could take to follow the pattern above in that situation.

• **Read Exodus 15:1-21** aloud as a song of testimony and praise for God's deliverance of the Israelites.

• **Identify some type of "memorial"** to God's special provision in your life (a diploma, a job offer letter, a personal note from a friend, a medical report, a personal journal recording how God worked in your life at those times, or a song that ministered in a special way to you).

Place it in a spot where you will see it periodically to be reminded of these lessons.

THE COVENANT

WHY TEACH THIS LESSON?

You can focus on the Ten Commandments in this lesson. Indeed, you must to some extent. But even more significant than the Commandments themselves is what they represent—God's covenant. Your students will do well to learn the Ten Commandments. They will do better to appreciate that God is a maker of covenants—and a keeper of his covenants. As he made a covenant with Israel on Sinai, he has made a covenant with us at Calvary!

INTRODUCTION

"1–2–3 TOURIST HOME." So read the sign by the roadside; for this was seventy-five years ago, and the name *motel* had not yet been invented. Behind the sign was a row of tiny cabins, spaced to leave room for cars to park between them. The numbers on the sign were significant. For one dollar you rented a cabin with a table, two chairs, and a bed; but you had to bring your own bedding. For two dollars you got a similar cabin with bedding. For three dollars you got all that and a kitchenette too. There was no running water in the cabins. Bathroom facilities were shared with guests in other cabins. A shower was twenty-five cents extra if you brought your own soap and towel. In each cabin a placard on the wall displayed the following rules:

No drunkenness.
No noise to disturb neighbors.
Keep this home as clean as your own.
Put refuse in the container provided.
Vacate cabin before noon or pay for another day.

A. PRIMITIVE TRAVEL

Traveling from Egypt to the promised land, the people of Israel found no such tourist home. Indeed, modern New York or London could hardly provide hotel accommodations for such a throng. There were perhaps as many as three million men, women, and children, plus uncounted cattle, sheep, and donkeys. The barren desert they traveled had no inns of any kind, no shelter where the weary could stop and rest. They had to bring their own tents as well as everything else they needed.

Still, these travelers needed rules, as people always do when they live close together; and they did not bring their rules from Egypt. There the only rule had been to obey the slave driver or take a beating. So God provided laws for his people. For this lesson we consider the most famous group of those rules—the Ten Commandments, which were carved in stone and "inscribed by the finger of God" (Exodus 31:18).

B. LESSON BACKGROUND

After crossing the Red Sea, the people of Israel continued to move southeast instead of toward the promised land. God continued to lead the way with a pillar of cloud and a pillar of fire. When food supplies were gone, he provided daily

DEVOTIONAL READING:
DEUTERONOMY 4:32-40
BACKGROUND SCRIPTURE:
EXODUS 19:1—20:26
PRINTED TEXT:
EXODUS 19:3-6; 20:2-4, 7, 8, 12-17

Sep
19

LESSON AIMS

After this lesson students should be able to:

1. Tell what God intended Israel to be and how he intended them to live, according to the covenant given at Sinai.

2. Explain how God's intentions for Israel apply to the church.

3. Determine to be a "kingdom of priests" and "a holy nation" by practicing what Jesus called the "greatest" commandments (Matthew 22:38-40).

KEY VERSE

If you obey me fully and keep my covenant, then out of all nations you will be my treasured possession.   —Exodus 19:5

manna from Heaven (Exodus 16). When no water was found, he produced an ample supply from a rock (Exodus 17:1-7).

In the third month of their journey, the travelers came to Mount Sinai—the mountain from which the Lord had sent Moses to Egypt. It was also the place where God had told Moses that the liberated slaves would worship him (Exodus 3:11, 12). The Israelites made their camp on the broad plain beside the towering mountain (Exodus 19:1, 2).

I. GOD'S COVENANT (EXODUS 19:3-6)

Here we see the basic terms of the covenant (agreement or contract) that God was making with his people as they began their life as an independent nation.

A. WHAT GOD HAS DONE (vv. 3, 4)
3. Then Moses went up to God, and the LORD called to him from the mountain and said, "This is what you are to say to the house of Jacob and what you are to tell the people of Israel:

Moses left the camp of the Israelites and *went up* the steep slope of Sinai (we are not told how far) to meet *God. The Lord called to him from the mountain,* speaking in an audible voice, just as he had called to Moses before from a burning bush (Exodus 3:4-10). This time the Lord's message was not for Moses alone. Moses was to relay it to *the house,* or descendants, *of Jacob.* The expressions *people of Israel* and *house of Jacob* are parallel terms and refer to the nation of Israel or, specifically, to the Israelites.
4. "'You yourselves have seen what I did to Egypt, and how I carried you on eagles' wings and brought you to myself.

First, Moses was to remind the people of what they knew very well. *On eagles' wings* is a graceful metaphor for the divine power that had *carried* Israel over all obstacles—the stubborn opposition of *Egypt,* the deep water of the sea, the weary and waterless miles of desert, and the assault of a hostile tribe—and had brought them to God himself at Sinai, his holy mountain. After all this evidence of God's power and favor, his people should have been eager to do things his way.

B. WHAT ISRAEL MUST DO (v. 5a)
5a. "'Now if you obey me fully and keep my covenant. . . .

This describes the part assigned to Israel in the *covenant* that God was making. Israel had no right to claim any of the blessings of that covenant unless the people would *obey* the commandments that God gave them.

C. WHAT ISRAEL MUST BE (vv. 5b, 6)
5b. "'Then out of all nations you will be my treasured possession. Although the whole earth is mine. . . .

The whole earth belongs to God because he made it all. *All nations* are under his sovereignty. However, if the people of Israel faithfully served him, they would be his *treasured possession*—bound to him in a different way, in a higher sense, in a closer relationship.
6. "'You will be for me a kingdom of priests and a holy nation.' These are the words you are to speak to the Israelites."

This verse explains the unique role that would distinguish Israel from all other peoples. God is King; the people of Israel were to be his subjects, obedient to him. One function of *priests* is to teach God's will and way. The people of Israel were to do that for other peoples, not by words only, but by lives lived in obedience to him and blessed by his favor. If the Israelites would do their part, they

WHAT DO YOU THINK?

God reminded Moses that he had carried the Israelites "on eagles' wings," enabling them to soar past all their problems. How has God enabled you to "soar"? Over what problems has he carried you "on eagles' wings"?

WHAT DO YOU THINK?

Israel was to be "a kingdom of priests." We Christians are likewise to be "a royal priesthood" (1 Peter 2:9). What is significant about the role of the priest that you find helpful in following the Lord today?

would also be so prosperous and so happy that all the world would see that it is best to obey the Lord. *A holy nation* is a nation set apart, dedicated to God, and therefore just and righteous and good. Note that Christians are called to fulfill these same responsibilities today (1 Peter 2:9).

This brief message ended as it had begun. God said that his *words* were not for Moses only; he was to deliver them to the multitude camped beside the mountain.

II. DUTIES TO GOD (EXODUS 20:2-4, 7, 8)

Moses delivered the message, and the people promised to be obedient to all God said (19:7, 8). On the third day God came to the mountain amidst awesome sights and sounds (v. 16). At Moses' summons the people gathered on the plain near the mountain. "Mount Sinai was covered with smoke, because the Lord descended on it in fire. The smoke billowed up from it like smoke from a furnace, the whole mountain trembled violently" (v. 18). We can imagine that the people "trembled" as much as the mountain! The long blast of a trumpet grew louder and louder, and the voice of God answered the voice of Moses (v. 19). In the midst of such awe-inspiring surroundings, God spoke the Ten Commandments (20:1).

The visual for today para-phrases the Ten Commandments in a rhyme, which may help your students to memorize the Commandments.

A. EXCLUSIVE WORSHIP (vv. 2-4)

2. *"I am the LORD your God, who brought you out of Egypt, out of the land of slavery.*
With these opening words God announced who he was and reminded the people of what he had done for them.
3. *"You shall have no other gods before me.*
As we noted in our lesson two weeks ago, the Lord is the only God who really exists; there are *no other gods*. Of course, man has been inventing pretend gods for many years, but the Lord's people must not insult him and disgrace themselves by offering any part of their worship to anyone or anything else.
4. *"You shall not make for yourself an idol in the form of anything in heaven above or on the earth beneath or in the waters below."*
This verse is often cited by itself for the sake of brevity, but it really needs to be read with verse 5: "You shall not bow down to them or worship them." God's people are forbidden to make images and worship them. They are not forbidden to make sculptures or paintings or photographs to remember attractive objects or to admire their beauty. We know this because not long afterward, God ordered his people to adorn the tabernacle with representations of various items: cherubim (25:18), flowers (25:33, 34), and pomegranates and bells (28:33, 34). Each of these was a likeness of something, but none was to become an object of worship.

B. REVERENCE (v. 7)

7. *"You shall not misuse the name of the LORD your God, for the LORD will not hold anyone guiltless who misuses his name.*
The word *misuse* translates the Hebrew phrase that is rendered by the familiar "take . . . in vain" of the *King James Version*. According to one lexicon, the Hebrew word meaning "in vain" can have three meanings: (1) evil or wickedness; (2) falsehood; (3) emptiness, nothingness. So it seems that this Commandment is broken when God's *name* is used (1) in connection with any wrong purpose; (2) in swearing to a lie; (3) lightly, frivolously, and without respect for its real meaning.

C. SABBATH OBSERVANCE (v. 8)

8. *"Remember the Sabbath day by keeping it holy."*
Verses 9-11 explain how the *Sabbath day* was to be kept *holy*, or set apart: no work was to be done on that day, the seventh day of the week. It should be noted,

WHAT DO YOU THINK?

As noted in the lesson, views on the Christian's responsibility concerning "the Sabbath" range from a belief that we are bound to all the Sabbath regulations (usually applied to Sunday) to the view that we need not recognize a distinction (short of attending a worship service) at all. What do you think is the proper way for Christians to apply the fourth Commandment? Why?
[See Romans 14:5, 6.]

WHAT DO YOU THINK?

What do you think it means to "honor" one's parents? If it's a matter of obedience (see Ephesians 6:1-3), does it apply to adults as well as children? Why or why not? If there is more to it than obedience, then what does it mean?

however, that the people of Israel understood that some exceptions were allowable. Jesus defended his work of healing on the Sabbath, and even meticulous Pharisees did a certain amount of necessary work on that day (Matthew 12:9-13).

Concerning Sabbath observance by Christians, there are three views that are commonly held:

1. Some say that the Sabbath is based on the pattern of creation (Genesis 2:1-3), and therefore it ought to be observed by all creation until this creation is no more (2 Peter 3:10). Opponents reply that there is neither command nor example of Sabbath observance before the Jewish nation began, that the law was given to Israel only, and that there is neither command nor example of Sabbath observance by the church.

2. Others believe the Sabbath restrictions have been transferred from the seventh day of the week to the first, which is sometimes referred to as the "Christian Sabbath." Opponents reply that the Bible does not say this; it is only a man-made interpretation. Besides, they say, the word *Sabbath* means "seventh," so its restrictions cannot be made to apply to the first day of the week.

3. Still others claim that Christians are not under the law (Romans 6:14; Galatians 5:18). They are guided by Christian teaching recorded in the New Testament. Many things commanded in the law are also taught in the New Testament, but Sabbath observance is not.

It may be noted that a number of both Christians and non-Christians agree that it is good for workers to have a weekly day off, with or without a law. In fact, many workers have two days off each week.

IN MEMORY OF . . .

How should we remember a significant person in our lives? The friends of "Wild Bill" Cottom found a way that they thought was perfectly appropriate. Wild Bill was an inveterate motorcyclist; he started riding when he was twelve years old. At various times in his life he was a racer, mechanic, and dealer, but almost always a friend to anyone on two wheels.

A stroke at age seventy ended Wild Bill's riding days. He spent the next sixteen years working in his shop, where he bought and sold used motorcycles, specializing in antique and British machines.

When Wild Bill died at the age of eighty-six, his body was cremated, and his ashes were placed in the gas tank of an antique Vincent motorcycle. On the day this unusual urn was placed on the wall of Cottom's shop, some fifteen hundred motorcyclists whom he had befriended at one time or another came to pay their respects.

When God asked Israel to honor him and respect the memory of how he had befriended them, he gave more specific instructions: they were to serve him only, refrain from worshiping representations of any creatures he had made, use his name reverently, and reserve one day a week for rest as a symbol of their identification with their Creator. Not too much to ask of Israel if they really loved God, was it?

We who are God's new creation in Christ can show our respect for God in much the same way. Not too much to ask of us either, is it?   —C. R. B.

III. DUTIES TO ONE ANOTHER (EXODUS 20:12-17)

The first four of the Ten Commandments speak of those duties to God that have been discussed above. The final six Commandments instruct us in how we are to relate to our fellow human beings.

A. HONORING PARENTS (v. 12)

12. *"Honor your father and your mother, so that you may live long in the land the* LORD *your God is giving you.*

HOW TO SAY IT

Sinai. SIGH-nye
    or SIGH-nay-eye.

Children must *honor* their parents with respect and obedience. Parents must diligently teach God's law to their children (Deuteronomy 6:6, 7). When this was done, children who honored and obeyed their parents would also honor and obey God. God would then bless them with peace and prosperity in the *land* of promise (Deuteronomy 11:8, 9).

B. FORBIDDEN ACTS (vv. 13-16)

13. "You shall not murder.

We know that with this command God did not mean to forbid all killing, for his law also provided the death penalty for a number of crimes ranging from murder to cursing a parent (Exodus 21:12, 17). God also told his people to "destroy" entire groups of depraved heathen (Deuteronomy 7:1, 2).

14. "You shall not commit adultery.

Pagans of many eras, including those of our own time, have looked on *adultery* as "good clean fun"; but God's law made it one of the transgressions to be punished with death (Deuteronomy 22:22-24).

15. "You shall not steal.

A person has a right to whatever he earns honestly, or buys honestly, or receives as a gift. It is wrong to take it from him without his consent, whether by force, by stealth, or by deceit. Hardly anyone will deny this principle; but so many violate it that we are forced to spend millions for locks and security systems, not to speak of theft insurance for many possessions. Other millions of dollars provide for police and courts and jails. Think what a difference it would make if everyone would put what is right above what is profitable!

16. "You shall not give false testimony against your neighbor.

Of course it is wrong to commit perjury in court; we punish it with fines and imprisonment if it is detected. But what about out-of-court slander, such as the spiteful remark we make about someone we don't like? What about the derogatory gossip we repeat without checking or thinking? If we repeat a false report, do we really escape guilt by saying, "I heard . . ."? My grandmother's rule was: "Don't say anything bad about anyone, even if it's true." She said that made it unnecessary to find out whether any gossip was true or not.

C. FORBIDDEN THOUGHTS (v. 17)

17. "You shall not covet your neighbor's house. You shall not covet your neighbor's wife, or his manservant or maidservant, his ox or donkey, or anything that belongs to your neighbor."

At times this Commandment is abbreviated to *you shall not covet*. In that form it misses the point. To covet is to desire, to want. There's nothing wrong with wanting a good reputation, or new shoes, or even a wife. What's wrong is wanting *anything that belongs to your neighbor*. If your neighbor has something good, you should be happy about it. You wouldn't take it from him if you could. You may feel a longing for many good things, but not that thing.

"GUILTY" OF THE CHRISTMAS SPIRIT

In Pennsylvania a few years ago, the Mercer County Common Pleas Court closed down for two weeks during the Christmas holidays. Prosecutors didn't like to hold trials at that time of year because, as one said, "The holiday spirit lends itself more to not-guilty verdicts." On the other hand, defense lawyers love to have their cases come up at Christmastime!

Perhaps it isn't all to the good that the Christmas spirit interferes with the workings of the justice system, especially if the defendant is guilty! However, it is refreshing

DAILY BIBLE READINGS

Monday, Sept. 13—Israel Camps at Mount Sinai (*Exodus 19:1-9*)

Tuesday, Sept. 14—Israel Meets God at Mount Sinai (*Exodus 19:16-25*)

Wednesday, Sept. 15— Honor God, and Keep the Sabbath (*Exodus 20:1-11*)

Thursday, Sept. 16— Commandments for Life in Community (*Exodus 20:12-21*)

Friday, Sept. 17—Observe God's Statutes and Ordinances (*Deuteronomy 4:1-8*)

Saturday, Sept. 18—Teach Obedience to Generations That Follow (*Deuteronomy 4:9-14*)

Sunday, Sept. 19— Commandments, a Gift of God's Love (*Deuteronomy 4:32-40*)

PRAYER

We love you, Father, because you first loved us. For us you delivered your only begotten Son to death. For you we would give up every selfish thought and wish. Help us, Father; please help us to purify our hearts, and guide our lives by your love. Amen.

WHAT DO YOU THINK?

What can we do to develop a wholehearted love for God as commanded in Matthew 22:37?

THOUGHT TO REMEMBER

God is first; my neighbor is second; I am third.

to hear of some tangible evidence that people actually do think more of the welfare of others at least for a few weeks a year.

The point of the last six Commandments is exactly this: to encourage us to think of the well-being of others rather than of ourselves. In a fashion typical of Old Testament culture, the Commandments are expressed as negatives. However, the New Testament—time and again—turns these same principles into positives. Thus, Christians not only abstain from doing harm to their neighbors; they actively seek their good.

—C. R. B.

CONCLUSION

The last Commandment of the ten turns our thinking in a new direction. Let's go on in that direction for a while. God wants to control our thinking as well as our doing. And really, doesn't our thinking control our doing?

Coveting a neighbor's good looks or popularity or influence can be a potential cause of bearing false witness against him, can't it? Coveting his wife can lead to adultery, coveting his wealth can lead to stealing, and all these covetings can lead to murder. Let's turn to the New Testament for more about this. One who hates his brother is a murderer at heart (1 John 3:15). One who lusts is an adulterer at heart (Matthew 5:27, 28). So let's turn our hearts away from ourselves. Let's love ourselves less, love our neighbors more, and love God most of all.

A. LOVING GOD

The law said to love God with all your being (Deuteronomy 6:5). Jesus said that this was the greatest commandment (Matthew 22:37, 38). If you obey it, you will have no other gods. You will give no shred of worship to anyone or anything else—not the ancient idols of wood and stone, not the modern idols of materialism and pleasure, not even yourself.

If you love God completely, you will never think of misusing his name. You will hold it in reverence and awe.

If you love God with all that is in you, you may conclude that his Sabbath law was for Israel only (Exodus 31:16, 17); but in any case you will hold every day holy to the Lord, and yourself holy every day. "Whatever you do, whether in word or deed, do it all in the name of the Lord Jesus" (Colossians 3:17).

B. LOVING YOUR NEIGHBOR

When we read God's commandments about love, instantly we know that they are not about the kind of love in which young people are said to "fall" every spring without trying. They are about the kind of love that God's people climb into by earnest effort. This love is a heartfelt concern for the welfare of someone else—a concern that moves us to help, even if helping is costly to us.

The law said to love your neighbor as yourself (Leviticus 19:18). Jesus said this too (Matthew 22:39). Your neighbor's place in your heart is below God's, but on a level with your own.

If you love your neighbor as you love yourself, you certainly will not murder him, nor steal from him, nor bear false witness against him, nor commit adultery with his mate. You will not even covet anything he has. Paul summed it up thus: "Love does no harm to its neighbor. Therefore love is the fulfillment of the law" (Romans 13:10). And Jesus said, "All the Law and the Prophets hang on these two commandments" (Matthew 22:40).

God himself inscribed the Ten Commandments on stone, but the two commandments of love are greater than them all. He wrote the love commandments on your heart (Jeremiah 31:33). Let them rule your life.

Discovery Learning

This page contains an alternate lesson plan emphasizing learning activities. Classes desiring such student involvement will find these suggestions helpful. The next page is a reproducible activity page to further enhance discovery learning.

LEARNING GOALS

After this lesson students should be able to:

1. Tell what God intended Israel to be and how he intended them to live, according to the covenant given at Sinai.

2. Explain how God's intentions for Israel apply to the church.

3. Determine to be a "kingdom of priests" and "a holy nation" by practicing what Jesus called the "greatest" commandments (Matthew 22:38-40).

INTO THE LESSON

While we often speak of the Ten Commandments, you may be surprised how few of your class members can actually repeat all of them from memory. To review them together, divide the class into groups of four to six, giving each group a stack of ten large index cards. Give them a few minutes to work together with instructions to write one Commandment on each card.

To review the correct answers, first read the Commandments out loud in incorrect order, and have the groups revise any they wrote incorrectly and/or write ones they missed. When all the groups have complete and accurate sets, ask each one to place the cards in the order the Commandments were given in Exodus 20.

INTO THE WORD

To review the results and to move into the Bible study, have someone read Exodus 19:3-6; 20:2-4, 7, 8, 12-17 aloud. As each Commandment is read, post a card with that Commandment on a wall in the classroom at about head height. Keep them spaced fairly evenly around the room. (These ten cards will be useful later.)

Note that God describes his people as a kingdom of priests and a holy nation (Exodus 19:6). Challenge the class to consider ways that faithfully obeying these ten Commands will distinguish a person or a group of people from the culture around them that does not. To do this, bring several copies of the Sunday newspaper with you to class. Distribute them to the small groups formed earlier, and ask each group to find examples of ways our world is living in violation of the Ten Commandments (stories, articles, advertisements, etc.). As the groups find examples in the newspaper, have them clip the stories and place them on the wall under the card with the corresponding Commandment. Highlight several of the examples found to share discoveries between the groups. Then ask, "How would life be different in specific areas if everyone were obeying that Commandment? How is being radically different from the surrounding culture related to your ability to serve as a 'kingdom of priests' and a 'holy nation'? How would faithful obedience to these Commands encourage others to turn from sin and toward God?"

Observe that people often think of the Ten Commandments as being only negative in orientation—simply prohibitions against things we should not do. Jesus, however, said that the entire law could be summarized by two clear, positively stated guidelines. Ask a volunteer to look up and read Matthew 22:37-40.

It is important to realize that fulfilling the Commandments is more than avoiding certain activities. It includes a positive pursuit of attitudes and actions that demonstrate the spirit and intent of the Commandments. As a class, discuss how these Ten Commandments could be stated in positive terms. (The following are provided as possible suggestions: 1. Trust in God alone. 2. Worship God wholeheartedly and exclusively. 3. Live in a way that honors God's character and reputation. 4. Take time to rest and focus on God. 5. Respect and honor your parents. 6. Value and protect human life. 7. Be faithful to your spouse. 8. Respect the property of others. 9. Live a life of honesty and integrity. 10. Be content with what is your own and pleased for the success of others.)

INTO LIFE

As a class, identify practical things that could be done in each of the above areas to fulfill the true spirit of God's law. Look at the positive statement of individual Commands, and ask, "What should we be doing to show our love for God or our fellow man in this area?" (You can use the next page to facilitate this activity.)

Which of the Commandments do the students think are the most difficult to obey? Are certain Commands harder to obey today than they would have been twenty years ago? a hundred years ago? during the time they were given to the Israelites?

Challenge students to evaluate their lives to identify areas that need attention. They should look for ways their obedience will enhance their testimony to the culture by demonstrating love for God and other people.

The Covenant

People often think of the Ten Commandments as being only negative in orientation, simply prohibitions against things we should not do. Jesus, however, said that the entire law (and prophets) could be summarized by two clear, positively stated guidelines.

Read his message about those summary statements in Matthew 22:37-40.

Now try to restate each of the Ten Commandments in positive terms. A couple of them have been completed to help give you some ideas.

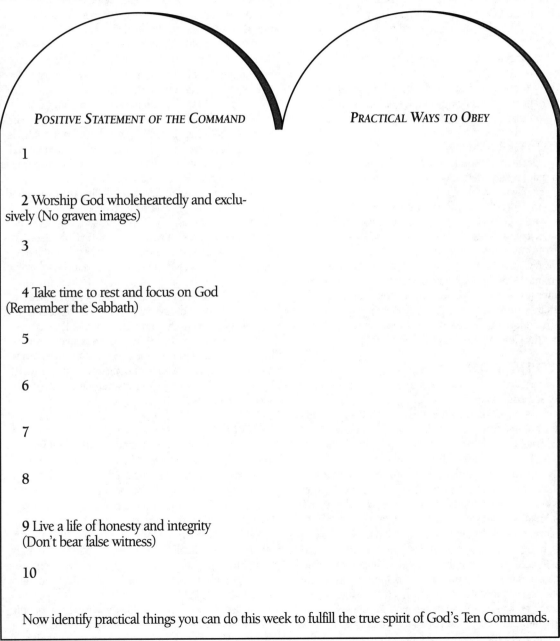

POSITIVE STATEMENT OF THE COMMAND   *PRACTICAL WAYS TO OBEY*

1

2 Worship God wholeheartedly and exclusively (No graven images)

3

4 Take time to rest and focus on God (Remember the Sabbath)

5

6

7

8

9 Live a life of honesty and integrity (Don't bear false witness)

10

Now identify practical things you can do this week to fulfill the true spirit of God's Ten Commands.

THE TABERNACLE AND OBEDIENCE

LESSON 4

WHY TEACH THIS LESSON?

The tabernacle must have been an impressive structure! Covered in exotic skins and furnished with articles of gold, it struck quite a contrast in the barren wilderness through which the Israelites carried it. As the tabernacle typifies the dwelling of God within his people, perhaps the contrast is also typical. Ought not there to be a great contrast between those in whom the Spirit of the Lord dwells and those whose spiritual lives are barren as the desert? Use this lesson to challenge your students to demonstrate with lives of obedience the difference it makes to have the Spirit of God living within them.

INTRODUCTION

In the third month of their journey out of Egypt, the people of Israel set up camp at the foot of Mount Sinai (Exodus 19:1, 2), where they stayed for nearly a year. At Sinai God gave the laws that were to govern his people for centuries; and at Sinai the people constructed an elegant tabernacle according to God's detailed instructions.

A. LAWS FOR A NATION

Last week we considered the Ten Commandments, which God himself inscribed on tablets of stone (Exodus 31:18). We considered also the two great commandments of love, on which "all the Law and the Prophets hang" (Matthew 22:40). Besides these, God also gave a multitude of other commandments, which Moses later wrote in a book (Deuteronomy 31:24-26). We find them, along with much historical material, in the books of Exodus, Leviticus, Numbers, and Deuteronomy.

B. TABERNACLE FOR A NATION

Our English word *tabernacle* is used to translate two Hebrew words that are used quite frequently in the Old Testament. One of the words means "tent." The tabernacle was thus called because it was a temporary structure, made mostly of fabrics and leathers that could be folded or rolled and taken to another campsite. The other word means "dwelling place." The tabernacle was given that name because it was the special place signifying God's presence in the midst of his people.

At Sinai the people were asked to donate materials for the tabernacle, including lumber, fabrics, animal skins, gold, silver, and brass (Exodus 25:1-9; 35:4-9). They responded so generously that Moses had to tell them to stop giving (Exodus 35:20-29; 36:2-7).

God appointed two skilled artisans, Bezalel and Oholiab, to supervise the project. Other skilled men went to work under their direction (Exodus 35:30—36:1). Many women also assisted in this effort. Using raw materials brought from

DEVOTIONAL READING:
PSALM 84

BACKGROUND SCRIPTURE:
EXODUS 40:1-33; LEVITICUS 26

PRINTED TEXT:
EXODUS 40:1-9; LEVITICUS 26:2-6a, 11-13

Sep 26

LESSON AIMS

After this lesson each students should be able to:

1. Describe the tabernacle that Israel was commanded to construct in the wilderness.

2. Tell what the establishment of the tabernacle teaches Christians about how obedience to God is important to the one who would dwell in God's presence.

3. Praise God for making his dwelling among his people.

KEY VERSE

Observe my Sabbaths and have reverence for my sanctuary. I am the LORD. —Leviticus 26:2

This visual shows the tabernacle set up amidst the camps of the tribes of Israel. The inset shows the floor plan and furnishings of the tabernacle.

Egypt, they spun the yarn and wove it into fabrics (Exodus 35:25, 26), which were then used to make the curtains of the tabernacle (36:8). Various parts of the tent and its furnishings are described in Exodus 36:8—38:31.

C. LESSON BACKGROUND

After months of work the various sections of the tabernacle were completed, along with the specific items to be placed within it. Probably these were stacked near the place where the tabernacle was to stand. Moses inspected the work, declared it well done, and blessed those who had contributed to the task (Exodus 39:32-43). Now it was time to assemble the parts so that the tabernacle could be used.

I. SETTING UP THE TABERNACLE (EXODUS 40:1-9)

The roofed tent or tabernacle is described in Exodus 26. It was about forty-five feet long and fifteen feet wide. The sides were fifteen feet high, made of "ten curtains of finely twisted linen" (Exodus 26:1) and supported by a wooden framework. The ceiling was made of "curtains of goat hair" (v. 7), with a leather covering to keep it dry in the infrequent rain. Some students think that there must have been a ridgepole to support a sloping roof so the rain would run off, but there is no mention of this in the Bible. The Bible's silence is no proof that there was none, but there is no compelling reason to believe there was such a pole, either. The roof may well have been flat.

Inside this tabernacle were two rooms. At the west end was the Most Holy Place, also called the Holy of Holies. It was in the shape of a cube, fifteen feet long and wide and high. This was the inner shrine, the very place of God's presence. Here the high priest entered once a year, on the Day of Atonement, to make atonement for the sins of the people (Leviticus 16:11-14, 34). The other room measured fifteen by thirty feet. This was the Holy Place, entered only by priests.

Around this structure was a courtyard approximately 150 feet long and 75 feet wide. It was surrounded by curtains made of additional "finely twisted linen." The entrance at the east end was covered with curtains when not in use.

In today's text we read of the various objects that were placed in the tabernacle.

A. THE TIME (vv. 1, 2)
1. Then the LORD said to Moses:

Thus we are reminded that *the Lord* was directing the construction of this tabernacle. He had given specific instructions for each part of it (chapters 25–27), and now he was directing the assembling of those parts.

2. "Set up the tabernacle, the Tent of Meeting, on the first day of the first month.

The Israelites had begun to measure time by the date of the exodus, which marked God's deliverance of his people. That was considered *the first day of the first month* (Exodus 12:2). Now, one year later, they were celebrating the beginning of the system of worship that God had outlined for them. The first occasion of erecting the tabernacle was to occur on what we might call "New Year's Day." Israel had come to this camping place by Sinai in the third month of the previous year (Exodus 19:1, 2), so they had been there between nine and ten months at this point.

B. THE MOST HOLY PLACE (v. 3)
3. "Place the ark of the Testimony in it and shield the ark with the curtain.

The one piece of furniture to be placed within the Most Holy Place was *the ark of the Testimony*, more often called the ark of the covenant. It was a wooden chest

WHAT DO YOU THINK?

One of the common misconceptions about religion—and Christianity in particular—is that it represents man's search for God. The Bible repeatedly affirms that in the Old Testament and the New, God was revealing himself to mankind. The lesson writer points out that the instructions regarding the tabernacle came from the Lord.

How do you think that applies to Christians or to the church today? How do you reply to people who believe religion to be a human invention instead of a God-given gift?

covered inside and outside with gold. This chest received its name because it held the Ten Commandments—the first and foundational part of God's *Testimony* or covenant with his people. The rest of the covenant, written in a book, was to be kept beside the ark (Deuteronomy 31:24-26). Placed on top of the ark were two golden cherubim, and between them was the exact spot from which God promised to speak to Moses. For a fuller description of the ark, see Exodus 25:10-22.

The curtain separated the Most Holy Place from the Holy Place. Moses was to *shield the ark with the curtain*, not by laying the curtain upon the ark, but by hanging the curtain in its place so that the ark was not visible from the Holy Place.

C. THE HOLY PLACE (vv. 4, 5)
4. "Bring in the table and set out what belongs on it. Then bring in the lampstand and set up its lamps.

Within the Holy Place were three articles of furniture. *The table* of showbread (see Exodus 25:23-30) stood in the north part of the room. As the Lord provided daily manna for his people, it was fitting that their offerings provided bread continually for his tent among them. Twelve loaves, one for each of Israel's twelve tribes, were displayed continually on the table. Each Sabbath Day they were replaced by new loaves. The old ones then became food for the priests, as did some of the other offerings of the people.

The lampstand stood in the south part of the Holy Place. Its seven *lamps* in a straight row provided light for the room even in daytime. The tent had no windows, and the doorway was closed by a hanging curtain that shut out the daylight. See Exodus 25:31-40 for a description of the lampstand.

5. "Place the gold altar of incense in front of the ark of the Testimony and put the curtain at the entrance to the tabernacle.

The third piece of furniture in the Holy Place was *the gold altar*, a small altar on which *incense* was burned. *The ark of the Testimony*, the symbol of God's presence, remained out of sight in the Most Holy Place; the golden altar was placed in front of it with only the veil between. The fragrant smoke rising from the incense was a symbol of the people's prayers rising to God. This golden altar was made of wood covered with gold. Thus it was lighter than a solid gold altar would be, and easier to carry when the people moved to a new campsite. See the precise description of this altar in Exodus 30:1-10.

It should be noted that Hebrews 9:4 describes the golden altar as part of the items in the Most Holy Place, not the Holy Place. This may be due to its close association with the ministry that took place in the Most Holy Place on the Day of Atonement (Leviticus 16:12, 13, 18-20).

The entrance to the tabernacle was located in the east end. It was closed with a curtain. When Moses put these in place, the structure was complete. Now our attention is turned to the enclosed court surrounding the tabernacle, and to the two articles placed in this court.

D. THE COURT (vv. 6-8)
6. "Place the altar of burnt offering in front of the entrance to the tabernacle, the Tent of Meeting.

Outside the doorway of *the tabernacle* was *the altar of burnt offering*, where the bodies of animals were burned in sacrifice to the Lord. This altar had to be strong enough to support a load of firewood and animal flesh, yet light enough to be easily moved. God prescribed a wooden frame seven and a half

HOW TO SAY IT

Oholiab. Uh-HO-lih-ab.

Bezalel. BEE-zah-lel.

Deuteronomy. Due-ter-AHN-uh-me.

Leviticus. Leh-VIT-ih-kuss.

WHAT DO YOU THINK?

The smoke of the incense burned on the tabernacle's altar of incense was to rise continually toward Heaven. The early church was noted for prayer (Acts 2:42), and the church today needs to restore prayer to its primary role. What can we do to make certain our church's prayers are rising continually toward Heaven?

feet square, covered with brass to protect it from the fire. Inside the frame was suspended a brass grate that would support the fire. Read more about it in Exodus 27:1-8.

7. "Place the basin between the Tent of Meeting and the altar and put water in it.

The basin was a brass basin at which the priests were to wash their hands and feet before they entered the Holy Place (Exodus 30:17-21). Its size is not mentioned.

8. "Set up the courtyard around it and put the curtain at the entrance to the courtyard.

Here *the courtyard* designates the curtains set up to enclose the outer court. They were five cubits (about seven and a half feet) high, made of linen, and supported by posts five cubits apart. Exodus 38:17 describes the "bases" or sockets into which the posts were placed as bronze. Perhaps the posts were made of wood, and each one was inserted in a heavy bronze socket that held it upright. The posts were fitted with silver hooks by which to attach them to the linen curtains.

At the east end of the court the *entrance* was thirty feet wide. The *curtain* that enclosed it was richly embroidered. See the description of the courtyard in Exodus 27:9-19 and 38:9-20.

E. THE DEDICATION (v. 9)

9. "Take the anointing oil and anoint the tabernacle and everything in it; consecrate it and all its furnishings, and it will be holy."

Anointing with *oil* was a feature of ancient ceremonies of dedication, whether of people or of objects. Thus Moses was to *consecrate* the *tabernacle* and *all its furnishings*, making the entire structure *holy*.

II. OBEDIENCE AND ITS REWARDS (LEVITICUS 26:2-6a, 11-13)

Now the tabernacle was complete—dedicated, holy, and ready for use. The priests likewise were dedicated and ready for their service. But what about the people? Were they also dedicated? Were they ready to do God's will? In a few verses taken from Leviticus, we see God's call to obedience and his promise of rich rewards.

A. CALL TO OBEDIENCE (vv. 2, 3)

2. "Observe my Sabbaths and have reverence for my sanctuary. I am the LORD.

Verse 1 forbids God's people to make and worship idols, thus repeating the second of the Ten Commandments. Now verse 2 turns to the positive side, mentioning what God's people ought to do in obedience to him. *Observe my Sabbaths* repeats the fourth of the Ten Commandments. God's people must also *reverence* his *sanctuary*. This phrase ties the latter part of our printed text to the first part. God's sanctuary is his holy tabernacle that we have been considering. God's obedient people should approach it with reverence and awe because it is the special place of his residence among them.

3. "If you follow my decrees and are careful to obey my commands,

Here is the call for God's people to obey his *commands*: the Ten studied in last week's lesson and all the rest that are recorded in Exodus, Leviticus, Numbers, and Deuteronomy.

B. REWARDS OF OBEDIENCE (vv. 4-6a)

4. "I will send you rain in its season, and the ground will yield its crops and the trees of the field their fruit.

An abundance of produce is the first reward promised for obedience. If God's people were faithful to him, he would give them *rain* when it was needed—and enough of it to produce good *crops* both in the grainfields and in the *fruit* orchards. In contrast, disobedience would result in drought and crop failure (vv. 18-20).

5. "Your threshing will continue until grape harvest and the grape harvest will continue until planting, and you will eat all the food you want and live in safety in your land.

In that part of the world, reaping normally began in May; but if God's people were obedient to him, the *harvest* would be so abundant that they would hardly be able to finish the *threshing* of their grain in time to begin picking grapes in August. Then the grapes would be so abundant that the people would hardly finish making and storing the wine in time to start planting grain around the end of October for the following year's crop. The people of Israel would have *all the food* they could eat.

The end of verse 5 introduces to us the second reward of obedience: the people would enjoy peace in their *land*. They would be kept safe from invasion and war.

6a. "I will grant peace in the land, and you will lie down and no one will make you afraid."

The promise of *peace* continued. If God's people obeyed him, they would be able to *lie down* and sleep with no fear of an attack from enemies during the night.

NO ACCIDENTAL FIXES

We expect natural disasters to destroy property and injure people, and this is what normally happens. We expect machines and other objects that aren't functioning to require the help of technicians or handymen to make them work properly again. Usually this is so.

However, consider what happened early one morning in January of 1994, when an earthquake measuring 6.6 on the Richter scale struck Los Angeles, California. In the darkness, many people stumbled out of bed fearing for their lives. Then, as a result of this tremor, some strange things happened. A woman whose home was severely damaged owned a pendulum clock that hadn't run for months. It worked after the earthquake. Another woman's refrigerator had sounded "like a diesel truck" before the quake, but afterward it "purred like a kitten." In one place of business, a repairman had tried on numerous occasions to fix the photocopier, but without success. After the earthquake, it worked perfectly!

On the human side of things, a man who had awakened every morning for the past ten years with an aching back found that, after the earthquake, he no longer had any pain.

All of these blessings are simply quirks of circumstance, nothing more than accidental fixes. However, God offered Israel a more certain way to a life of blessedness. If they would follow in his way and keep his commandments, he would bless their land. They could lie down in peace and not be afraid.   —C. R. B.

C. THE CROWNING REWARD (vv. 11-13)

11. "I will put my dwelling place among you, and I will not abhor you.

Here was the crowning promise: God himself would *put* his *dwelling place* among his obedient people. His people would have prosperity and peace (vv. 4-6), but above all they would have God's presence. If they faithfully obeyed him, they would be pleasing to him, and so he would *not abhor* them.

12. "I will walk among you and be your God, and you will be my people.

WHAT DO YOU THINK?

According to Leviticus 26:6, one of the rewards of obedience to God is worry-free sleep. If an Old Testament believer could claim such a promise, how much more should Christians be able to do so! Jesus pointed out that we have no cause for anxiety (Matthew 6:25-34). Paul spoke of the peace that we can experience when we subject our worries to prayer (Philippians 4:6, 7). Peter urged us to cast on God our anxiety (1 Peter 5:7).

What, then, of occasions when we await a report from an oncologist or an ER doctor? What of times when our children get into trouble with the law? Is it wrong for Christians in these and similar situations to have trouble sleeping? Why or why not?

WHAT DO YOU THINK?

God promised to walk among his obedient people. What

encouragement do you find in this promise for today?

[Compare Revelation 1:12, 13, 20; 2:1.]

[Compare Revelation 1:12, 13, 20; 2:1.]

DAILY BIBLE READINGS

Monday, Sept. 20—*God's Command Regarding Tabernacle and Priests (Exodus 40:1-15)*

Tuesday, Sept. 21—*Building the Tabernacle (Exodus 40:16-20)*

Wednesday, Sept. 22—*Equipping the Tabernacle (Exodus 40:21-33)*

Thursday, Sept. 23—*Rewards for Obedience (Leviticus 26:1-13)*

Friday, Sept. 24—*Consequences of Disobedience (Leviticus 26:14-26)*

Saturday, Sept. 25—*Further Punishments (Leviticus 26:27-39)*

Sunday, Sept. 26—*Confession Will Bring Renewal (Leviticus 26:40-46)*

PRAYER

Our Father in Heaven, it is awesome to think that you are also here on earth, that we ourselves are your tabernacle, your dwelling place. Accept the homage of our hearts, we pray, shape us according to your will, and show us how to serve you better. Amen.

THOUGHT TO REMEMBER

As a living stone in God's spiritual house, I must be shaped by his Word and active in his service.

God's residence among his people was symbolized by the elegant tabernacle, but he would not be confined to it. He would *walk among* them: he would be active outside the tabernacle. He would be their *God*, providing for their every need. The people of Israel would be God's *people*—obeying him, trusting him, and depending upon him.

13. "I am the LORD your God, who brought you out of Egypt so that you would no longer be slaves to the Egyptians; I broke the bars of your yoke and enabled you to walk with heads held high."

Who was asking Israel to obey? He was *the Lord*—the only God who actually exists, the Almighty Creator and Keeper of Heaven and earth. To the people of Israel he had demonstrated his power and goodness by rescuing them from slavery in *Egypt*. Now, looking to the future, he offered them rich rewards for obeying him. Knowing his power and goodness, how could they fail to obey?

CONCLUSION

For a long time the tabernacle was God's tent among the tents of his people. Later they replaced God's tent with a temple of stone. When that temple was destroyed, they replaced it with one that stood until it was improved and enlarged by King Herod toward the beginning of the Christian era. But not long after Herod's work was done, that temple was destroyed by the Romans in A.D. 70.

By that time God was building his own replacement for the ancient tent. He was building a "greater and more perfect tabernacle that is not man-made" (Hebrews 9:11). The law provided only "a shadow of the good things that are coming" (Hebrews 10:1). The old tent was only an "illustration" (Hebrews 9:8, 9) of that "greater and more perfect tabernacle." Let's see how the prophetic figure compares with the reality.

A. THE HOLY PLACE

The Holy Place pictures the church. Only priests are allowed to enter there, and Christians constitute a "holy priesthood" (1 Peter 2:5). One task of priests is to teach God's will and way, and that is what we are to do for the world.

In the Holy Place is the table of showbread. Naturally we think of Jesus, "the bread of life" (John 6:35). The ancient priests ate the showbread, and as priests all of us Christians take of the bread that is the Lord's body (Luke 22:19).

In the Holy Place is also the lampstand. We think of Jesus, "the light of the world" (John 8:12); and we think of the Bible, through which the light of Jesus comes to us. This is the light that the church must shine in the midst of a dark world.

The third piece of furniture in the Holy Place is the altar of incense, which stands close to the Most Holy Place, the place of God's presence. The smoke of incense symbolizes the prayers of God's people. From the church such prayers rise continually to the very presence of God.

B. THE MOST HOLY PLACE

The Most Holy Place is the earthly symbol of Heaven. It housed the ark of the Testimony, which was the visible symbol of the presence of the invisible God. Once every year the high priest went into the Most Holy Place, carrying the blood of a sacrifice that was made to atone for the sins of Israel. Once for all Jesus carried into the real Heaven his own blood, offered to atone for our sins. There he appears before God for us (Hebrews 9:24-26) and continues to make intercession for us (Hebrews 7:25).

Discovery Learning

This page contains an alternate lesson plan emphasizing learning activities. Classes desiring such student involvement will find these suggestions helpful. The next page is a reproducible activity page to further enhance discovery learning.

LEARNING GOALS

After participating in this lesson, students should be able to:

1. Describe the tabernacle that Israel was commanded to construct in the wilderness.

2. Tell what the establishment of the tabernacle teaches Christians about how obedience to God is important to the one who would dwell in God's presence.

3. Praise God for making his dwelling among his people.

INTO THE LESSON

Bring to class pictures of several different homes from some home decorating magazines. Include several different types of architecture and styles of decorating. Ask the class to try to describe the owners of the homes by what they observe. What do the furniture, decorating, and landscaping tell you about the owners? Is there a statement they might be trying to make about themselves? About their families? About the importance of having guests? Is there anything else the decor and structure may suggest about the owners and their values?

INTO THE WORD

Today we will examine the tabernacle, described as God's dwelling place among the Israelites. It will help us learn something about God, ourselves, and our worship.

Divide the class into three groups and give the following instructions: "Today you will be preparing copy for a special issue of an architectural or decorating magazine dedicated to the tabernacle described in the Old Testament. Work with the others in your group to prepare a brief diagram and description of the area you have been assigned. [See below.] Describe and explain the purpose for each of the furnishings in that area."

Option: Have students complete the reproducible activity on the next page instead of writing "magazine articles."

Group 1. The Most Holy Place (Exodus 40:3), including the ark of the Testimony (Exodus 25:10-22; Deuteronomy 31:24-26).

Group 2. The Holy Place (Exodus 40:4-5), including the table of showbread (Exodus 25:23-30), the lampstand (Exodus 25:31-40), and the altar of incense (Exodus 30:1-10).

Group 3. The court (Exodus 40:6-8), including the altar of burnt offering (Exodus 27:1-8) and the bronze basin (Exodus 30:17-21).

Allow time for the groups to work; then ask for reports. Draw a composite diagram of the tabernacle and its furnishings on a large poster or on the chalkboard as the groups provide information. Fill in details and explanations from the commentary section as needed.

Have a volunteer read Leviticus 26:2-6a, 11-13. Note that in verses 2 and 3 God commanded the Israelites to "observe my Sabbaths and have reverence for my sanctuary." Clearly worship must be approached with a sense of great respect and awe. Discuss how the design of the tabernacle, as well as the furnishings, communicated this truth. How do we apply this truth in our own church and our own worship services?

Note that the demand for holiness was not just for worship. It applied to all of life and was linked with obedience to God's statutes (v. 3). Review the rewards promised for obedience to God (vv. 4-6). What rewards can Christians expect for such holiness and commitment to obeying God's commands?

INTO LIFE

Read several New Testament passages that describe the dwelling place of God as within Christians individually (e.g., Acts 2:38; Romans 8:10-12; 1 Corinthians 6:19; 2 Timothy 1:14) or in the church as a whole (1 Corinthians 3:16).

Reflect on the lessons learned concerning the respect and care given to the tabernacle as the dwelling place of God, and discuss what those same principles suggest about the need for personal holiness by God's people. If God's tabernacle (later, temple) was to be kept holy, and if we are God's temple today, what kind of demand for holiness does that place on us?

Review the demand for obedience in all areas of life, and discuss the importance of such obedience to Christians. Some believers feel that grace releases us from the demands of obedience. What is wrong with that assumption? How are holiness and obedience related for the Christian?

Have someone read Hebrews 9:1-10 to identify how the work of Christ fulfilled the picture presented of the tabernacle. Then read together as a class the remainder of the chapter (Hebrews 9:11-28). This could be used as a closing prayer, a collective statement of praise for the work of Jesus Christ in providing salvation fully and completely.

The Tabernacle and Obedience

This week's lesson examines the tabernacle, described as God's dwelling place among the Israelites. It will help us understand something about God and our relationship with him. This is true because God is described as the architect, as well as the one who provided building materials (Exodus 12:35, 36; 35:4-9, 21-29; 36:5-7), selected the contractor (Moses), gifted the builders with specific skills (Exodus 35:30–36:1), identified the staff to serve when the tabernacle was completed (the priesthood), and then gave specific instructions for its use.

Read the descriptions of the design as well as the furnishings for each area of the tabernacle. Then summarize lessons we learn from them.

AREA AND FURNISHINGS	WHAT WE LEARN ABOUT GOD	WHAT WE LEARN ABOUT OUR RELATIONSHIP WITH GOD
THE MOST HOLY PLACE (EXODUS 40:3) The ark (Exodus 25:10-22; Deuteronomy 31:24-26)		
THE HOLY PLACE (EXODUS 40:4, 5) Table of showbread (Exodus 25:23-30) The lampstand (Exodus 25:31-40) The altar of gold (Exodus 30:1-10)		
THE COURT (EXODUS 40:6-8) The altar of burnt offering (Exodus 27:1-8) The laver (Exodus 30:17-21)		

The New Testament describes the dwelling place of God as people—specifically those people who know Jesus Christ as their personal Savior (Romans 8:10-12; 1 Corinthians 3:16; 2 Corinthians 6:16; 2 Timothy 1:14).

What lesson should this teach us about God?

What lesson should this teach us about our relationship with God?

THE CLOUD AND THE FIRE

LESSON 5

WHY TEACH THIS LESSON?

Leadership. It is a perennial issue. Each generation seems to decry the lack of leadership in the church, in politics, or in business. Maybe the real issue is followership. If we are not good followers, no leader can be successful. If we do not know whom to follow, we cannot choose a leader.

This lesson addresses the issue of followership. The Israelites followed the cloud and the fire. In truth, they followed God. This lesson will have been a success only if it renews your students' commitment to following God.

INTRODUCTION

A. LIFE AT SINAI

The Israelites began an entirely new way of life when they left Egypt as a free people. Part of that newness was reflected in the way the Israelites started to measure time. The date of the exodus was considered the first day of the first month (Exodus 12:2). They encamped at Sinai "in the third month" (Exodus 19:1) and stayed there the rest of that year. On the first day of the next year they set up the tabernacle, as we saw in last week's lesson (Exodus 40:2). It appears that they then had a month during which to relax after all the work of making the tabernacle, and to observe the week-long feast of Passover in the middle of the month. That was the first anniversary of the Passover in Egypt (Numbers 9:1-14).

B. LESSON BACKGROUND

The next month was busy with several matters of organization. The men available for military service (age twenty or older) were counted, totaling 603,550 (Numbers 1:44-46). The Levites, who were to take care of the tabernacle, were counted, organized, and ceremonially cleansed and dedicated (Numbers 1:47; 3:1-39; 4:1-49; 8:5-26). Each tribe was assigned a certain place in camp for its tents, and a certain position in the order of travel (Numbers 2). Thus prepared, the people were ready to leave Sinai on the twentieth day of the second month of the second year of their journey (Numbers 10:11, 12).

From the beginning of Israel's journey out of Egypt, "By day the Lord went ahead of them in a pillar of cloud to guide them on their way and by night in a pillar of fire" (Exodus 13:21). This week we will read more about those visible signs by which the invisible God guided his people.

I. FACTS FROM EXODUS (EXODUS 40:34-38)

Our text presents facts from Exodus and then facts from Numbers. These facts are so much alike that we may wonder why Moses recorded them twice. Two considerations should lessen our surprise. First, every teacher knows how important it is to repeat facts so that students will remember them. Moses is to be credited with repetition for memory retention. Second, the same facts may be used with different purposes and in different settings. Here again we see Moses' purpose in repeating the information. In Numbers he uses these details as the prelude to the story of the continuing journey from Sinai (Numbers 10:11, 12). In Exodus he

DEVOTIONAL READING:
PSALM 107:1-9

BACKGROUND SCRIPTURE:
EXODUS 40:34-38; NUMBERS 9:15-23

PRINTED TEXT:
EXODUS 40:34-38; NUMBERS 9:15-23

Oct
3

LESSON AIMS

As a result of this lesson, your students should be able to:

1. Tell how God led the Israelites by a pillar of cloud by day and of fire at night.

2. Recall significant moments in their lives when God's guidance sustained them.

3. Stay alert to indications of God's guidance through people and circumstances, and thank him for his guidance.

KEY VERSE

So the cloud of the LORD was over the tabernacle by day, and fire was in the cloud by night, in the sight of all the house of Israel during all their travels.
—Exodus 40:38

LESSON 5 NOTES

uses them as the conclusion to the record of constructing and setting up the tabernacle. We'll consider them in that context first.

A. PRESENCE OF THE CLOUD (vv. 34, 35)

34. Then the cloud covered the Tent of Meeting, and the glory of the LORD filled the tabernacle.

Notice that there is no gap between this passage and the text from Exodus in last week's lesson. There we read that "Moses finished the work" of erecting the tabernacle (Exodus 40:33). For months the people of Israel had worked on this project—shaping the wooden pieces, weaving the fabrics, making the articles of gold and silver and brass—all to provide a *Tent of Meeting* for the Lord in the midst of the tents of his people. Now that tent was completed. From Egypt to Sinai the Lord had gone before them in a *cloud* (Exodus 13:21). Now that cloud settled on the tent constructed for the Lord, and *the glory of the Lord* showed that he was in his tent. We have never seen that glory, but most suppose that it resembled a brilliant light. The Bible tells of one night when it "shone" around some shepherds near Bethlehem (Luke 2:9).

35. Moses could not enter the Tent of Meeting because the cloud had settled upon it, and the glory of the LORD filled the tabernacle.

The *Tent of Meeting* was so designated because this was the place where God promised to meet with Moses and give him the commands that the Israelites were to obey (Exodus 25:22). Earlier, Moses had hidden his face because he was afraid to look at the burning bush from which God spoke to him (Exodus 3:6). Now he found himself in awe before the radiant *glory* that *filled* the new *tabernacle*.

B. MOVEMENT OF THE CLOUD (vv. 36-38)

36. In all the travels of the Israelites, whenever the cloud lifted from above the tabernacle, they would set out.

Whenever the cloud lifted from above the tabernacle, that was the signal for departure. The Levites took the *tabernacle* apart, rolled or folded its fabric and leather, and prepared everything for travel. The people took down their tents, packed their goods, and prepared to move on. If flocks were out grazing, they were brought in quickly. Probably the cloud hovered nearby until the packing was finished. Then it moved away across the desert. The Lord's people followed, each tribe taking its assigned place in the huge caravan.

37. But if the cloud did not lift, they did not set out—until the day it lifted.

The resting *cloud* was the signal for the people to rest. No doubt it remained still every Sabbath day. We are not told if any other special days were considered as occasions when the people did not travel.

38. So the cloud of the LORD was over the tabernacle by day, and fire was in the cloud by night, in the sight of all the house of Israel during all their travels.

All their travels would last forty years, nearly thirty-nine of those after they left Sinai. Never would they have to ask when to break camp or which way to go; never would they have to ask when to stop or how long to stay. The guiding *cloud* was with them all the way, day after day and year after year. When darkness fell the cloud turned to *fire*, providing light for the entire camp.

A PROTECTING PRESENCE

If you live in a large city (and perhaps even if you don't), you have become used to hearing the sound of car alarms going off. The first alarms were simple affairs, flashing the car's headlights and honking its horn. However, false alarms caused people to ignore these warnings.

WHAT DO YOU THINK?

Moses was not able to enter the tabernacle when the "glory of the Lord" filled it. Similarly Isaiah (Isaiah 6) and Peter (Luke 5:8) were overwhelmed by divine glory and felt unworthy of being in the Lord's presence. What occasions or events make you particularly aware of God's glory and make you most appreciative of his grace, without which we could not stand in his presence?

WHAT DO YOU THINK?

The cloud or pillar of fire remained above the tabernacle "in the sight of all the house of Israel during all their travels" to assure the Israelites of God's presence. What assures you of God's presence today? How can you reassure a fellow believer who may doubt the Lord's presence?

So the technology battle between thieves and car owners escalated. Next came alarms with sirens, then alarms with two different sirens. Then came "proximity alarms" that sensed a possible felon approaching the car and uttered a verbal command not to come any closer. Failure to stop would result in all manner of noise to call attention to the disregard for such authority.

One of the more whimsical alarm systems was the Security Bear—a teddy bear to be placed in a spot such as the car's back window. When it sensed changes in the car's internal air pressure (as would be the case if a window were broken or the door opened), it would trigger an alarm "comparable to having a fire engine in your car," according to its manufacturer.

Israel needed no electronic alarm for protection while on its way to the promised land. The sign of Israel's security was more spectacular than any that humans have ever dreamed up. The pillars of cloud and fire comprised the certain symbol of God's presence wherever the Israelites were. In fact, it really didn't matter where the people were; *God* was there with them.   —C. R. B.

II. FACTS FROM NUMBERS (NUMBERS 9:15-23)

In our text from Numbers we see the same facts that were found in our text from Exodus. As noted earlier, the details are set in different surroundings: in Exodus they provide the grand finale for the lengthy story of constructing the tabernacle; in Numbers they are the prelude to the story of the continuing journey from Sinai, which would be announced by the sounding of silver trumpets (Numbers 10:1-10) as well as by the sight of the rising cloud.

A. THE TABERNACLE AND THE CLOUD (vv. 15, 16)

15. On the day the tabernacle, the Tent of the Testimony, was set up, the cloud covered it. From evening till morning the cloud above the tabernacle looked like fire.

The day on which *the tabernacle . . . was set up* was the first day of the new year (Exodus 40:1, 2). The first eight and a half chapters of Numbers tell of other events that followed, including the week-long Passover celebration that began on the fifteenth day of the month. Now comes a flashback to the first day of the month. On that day, *the cloud covered* the tabernacle, as we have seen from Exodus. However, note that here the tent is called by another name: *the Tent of the Testimony*, because it held the foundation of God's testimony, or covenant, with Israel—the Ten Commandments (Hebrews 9:4).

16. That is how it continued to be; the cloud covered it, and at night it looked like fire.

Either the *cloud* or the *fire* was always present, as we saw in Exodus. But here Moses says that the cloud *looked like fire* rather than saying that "fire was in the cloud by night" (Exodus 40:38). This was no ordinary fire! Perhaps it was similar to that fire in a bush from which God had spoken to Moses when he first called him to go to Egypt. That fire had not burned the bush; this fire on the tabernacle did not burn the tabernacle. But each apparent fire indicated the presence of God.

B. THE CLOUD AND THE JOURNEY (vv. 17-23)

17. Whenever the cloud lifted from above the Tent, the Israelites set out; wherever the cloud settled, the Israelites encamped.

This is very clear, both here and in the text from Exodus.

18. At the LORD's command the Israelites set out, and at his command they encamped. As long as the cloud stayed over the tabernacle, they remained in camp.

The Israelites were not merely following a cloud and a fire; they were obeying *the Lord's command.* Obviously the Lord had told Moses at some point that he himself would direct the movement of the cloud and the fire and that the Israelites

WHAT DO YOU THINK?

The lesson writer points out, "The children of Israel were not merely following a cloud and a fire; they were obeying the Lord's command." How would you support that position if an unbeliever challenged the notion that God had led the Israelites?

were to follow when the cloud moved and remain when it was stationary. Thus, every occasion of the cloud's moving or stopping became a commandment of the Lord. The Israelites obeyed.

Moses emphasizes that fact twice in this one verse. Then in the rest of our text he emphasizes it repeatedly. It is as if Moses knew that unbelievers in future times (such as ours) would scoff at the idea that God was really leading those people. Of course, even if Moses did not know that such scoffers would come, God knew and he inspired what Moses wrote. Says a scoffer, "Those people followed wind-driven clouds. It's no wonder a short trip took them forty years!" But that cloud was not driven by the wind, and that fire was not the glow of the moon on the roof of the tent. God moved both cloud and fire according to his will, and God's people obeyed accordingly.

19. When the cloud remained over the tabernacle a long time, the Israelites obeyed the LORD's order and did not set out.

The emphasis of verse 18 is repeated. *The Israelites obeyed the Lord's order.* That charge was to hold *when the cloud remained*, and to move when it moved. Perhaps they were impatient when the cloud *remained* and hung motionless for *a long time*. However, if the cloud remained still, the people *did not set out*.

20. Sometimes the cloud was over the tabernacle only a few days; at the LORD's command they would encamp, and then at his command they would set out.

We understood this well enough from the verses before this. Why does Moses emphasize it again? Perhaps he wanted to impress on our minds the weary monotony of those days in the desert. Travelers eager to be on their way to reach the promised land may have groaned when the cloud did not move in the morning. At other times, footsore travelers may have moaned when it did rise and lead them onward. Still, all of them waited or moved *at the Lord's command*. By doing so they were wise as well as obedient. Without the Lord and his cloud they would have been lost in a trackless desert—and most of them had never been in such country before.

21. Sometimes the cloud stayed only from evening till morning, and when it lifted in the morning, they set out. Whether by day or by night, whenever the cloud lifted, they set out.

Sometimes the *cloud* let the people sleep through the night, then led them on their way *in the morning*. That seems sensible; it's what we do when we're driving thousands of miles across country. But sometimes the cloud took off in the *night*, and we wonder why. Consider how, before cars were air-conditioned, motorists in desert country sometimes drove at night, because it was cooler, and then slept by day in air-conditioned motels. But Israel's tents were not air-conditioned. (Have you ever tried to sleep by day in a tent heated by a broiling sun?) Still, resting would expend less energy than traveling; so even if it was not very comfortable, it may have been wiser to rest in the day and to travel in the cool of the night. Whether the people of Israel could understand or not, they obeyed God.

22. Whether the cloud stayed over the tabernacle for two days or a month or a year, the Israelites would remain in camp and not set out; but when it lifted, they would set out.

Now comes a hint that some of the stops must have seemed unreasonably long to impatient travelers. The people had stayed nearly a year at Sinai, where many of them had been busy preparing different sections of the tabernacle; but now, without such a project to occupy their time, even a month would seem tedious. People who led sheep or goats to pasture would have that leisurely occupation to pass the time, but what would the others do with their time? They had no spare time in Egypt. Could they have known anything about games or other forms

WHAT DO YOU THINK?

The lesson writer points out that the Israelites must have found long delays and nighttime travel hard to understand. Still they obeyed. When do you find God's leading or his commands confusing or troubling? What helps you to obey even when you do not fully understand where God is leading?

WHAT DO YOU THINK?

The movement of the pillar of cloud forced the Israelites to depend on God's timing. What do you find difficult about waiting on God's timing? How do you attempt to meet this challenge?

of recreation? No doubt they eventually invented some activities to pass the time. Yet whether a stop lasted a night, a *month*, or a *year*, the people obeyed the Lord. **23. At the LORD's command they encamped, and at the LORD's command they set out. They obeyed the LORD's order, in accordance with his command through Moses.**

Thus, again, Moses repeats what he has been emphasizing in verse after verse.

KNOWING WHEN IT IS TIME

The *Old Farmer's Almanac* has been published for more than two hundred years, having had only four owners in all that time. Its cover hasn't been changed since 1851. This implies a respect for the old ways of doing things. No doubt, this is one of the reasons for its popularity. The *Almanac* has long been treasured by its readers as a repository of arcane information: for example, how to build a bat house (to attract these efficient mosquito eaters), and the three best ways to hypnotize your chickens!

We may be amused or amazed by such stuff, but the information for which the *Almanac* is most famous is contained in its weather predictions and its tables of tides and astronomical phenomena. Among those who value these data are sailors, fishermen, and people who plant their gardens by the phase of the moon.

When Israel was encamped in the wilderness, they did not need an almanac to tell them when to move on. God's pillar of cloud and pillar of fire were the sign to them of the divine timing for either continuing or stopping their travels.

Unlike Israel, we are not able to tell with such absolute assurance what God's timing is; however, he has given us his Word so that we can know what he wants us to do. Wisdom suggests that Christians give the same careful scrutiny (and more!) to Scripture as some people do to the *Old Farmer's Almanac*.   —C. R. B.

CONCLUSION

Do you sometimes envy the people of Israel? Beset by a problem without an answer, or needing a decision and feeling indecisive, do you long for a cloud to guide you by day, or a fire to give light in the darkness?

A. YOUR FAULTLESS GUIDE

You do have a faultless guide. Dressed modestly in black leather, or perhaps more brightly in cloth, it lies on the coffee table in your home or stands quietly on the bookshelf. What it is you will find written on the outside: *Holy Bible*.

"I know, I know. The Bible is God's Word. It's always right. I believe it. But the Bible doesn't give specific answers to specific questions."

Sometimes it does. Many of our problems involve choices between truth and falsehood, honesty and deception, generosity and greed, kindness and malice, or helpfulness and selfishness. In such cases you know the Bible's answer without even opening its covers. Yet so often the Bible stands quietly on the shelf, while selfish human nature shouts. Seduced by your own lust or desire (James 1:14), you turn away from the guiding cloud. When you find yourself lost in the desert, you say the Bible has failed you. No, you failed the Bible.

"But I'm trying to decide whether to marry this person or not. The Bible doesn't tell me that."

Maybe it does. Perhaps it doesn't use the exact words of the ceremony, but the Bible does picture marriage as a commitment to love, honor, and cherish a person in sickness and in health, in wealth or in poverty, for better or for worse, as long as you both shall live. If you are not ready to make such a commitment to a certain person wholeheartedly and joyfully, the answer is no. If you see that the other person is not ready to match your commitment, the answer again is no.

DAILY BIBLE READINGS

Monday, Sept. 27—God's Glory Fills the Tabernacle (Exodus 40:34-38)

Tuesday, Sept. 28—Led by God's Cloud and Fire (Numbers 9:15-23)

Wednesday, Sept. 29— Journeying Away From Mount Sinai (Numbers 10:29-36)

Thursday, Sept. 30—God Keeps His Covenant Forever (Psalm 105:1-15)

Friday, Oct. 1—God Provided for Israel in Egypt (Psalm 105:16-25)

Saturday, Oct. 2—God Sent Plagues Upon Egypt (Psalm 105:26-36)

Sunday, Oct. 3—God Delivered Israel From Egypt (Psalm 105:37-45)

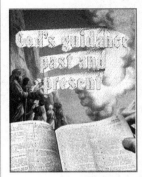

Today's visual demonstrates that we do not need a pillar of cloud or of fire for God to lead us today. He gives us guidance through his Word, the Bible.

PRAYER

How good it is to know you are with us, Father! Though you are "the high and lofty One" who lives in a "high and holy place" (Isaiah 57:15), our joys are more delightful and our sorrows are less oppressive because you are here with us. Thank you, Father. In Jesus' name. Amen.

"I've been thinking about a job that pays a lot more. The Bible doesn't say yes or no to that."

Maybe it does. If the new job would involve you in anything illegal, anything deceptive, any cheating, or any greedy cruelty to customers or competitors, the answer is no. If the new job would open the way to more unselfish service to God and mankind, the answer may be yes. But even then you have other things to consider. If this attractive job would be so all-engrossing that you would have no time for church, your spouse, or your family, the answer is no.

"Why is it so hard to follow the leading of God's Word?" Two reasons are easily seen.

First, the Bible does not lead unless you listen. You need to spend long hours with the Bible, to make it your friend. You need to read it until the reading is a joy and not a duty, until you pick it up with eagerness and lay it down with regret.

Second, the Bible will not lead unless you follow. It only leads; it does not carry you against your will. It says, "Anyone who hates his brother is a murderer" (1 John 3:15); but you yourself must pry the hatred from your heart and fill its place with love, love even for an enemy (Matthew 5:44). Clearly the Bible calls you to forgive (Matthew 6:14, 15), but the devil clamors, "Get even! Get even!" You have to choose.

B. BLESSED ASSURANCE

"Where was God when my loved one died?"

"Where was God when my mate left me?"

"Where was God when I lost my job?"

Every disaster gives rise to questions like these. When agony at midnight will not let you sleep, wouldn't you love to lift the flap of your tent and see the glow of God's fire telling you he is there?

He is there, if you are trusting him. His Word tells you that, too, and his Word is as trustworthy as his fire. "God has said, 'Never will I leave you; never will I forsake you.'" (Hebrews 13:5; also Deuteronomy 31:6, 8). Jesus said, "If anyone loves me, he will obey my teaching. My Father will love him, and we will come to him and make our home with him" (John 14:23).

In our grief, our weakness, our fear, God not only is there; he understands. He knows how we feel. "Where was God when my son died?" So wailed a grieving mother, and a wise counselor replied, "He was right where he was when his own Son died." None of our distress is hidden from him. He knows and he cares.

"Then why doesn't God do something? Why does he allow terrible things to happen to good people?" His Word reminds us, "We know that in all things God works for the good of those who love him" (Romans 8:28). Like Joseph in the Old Testament, we may not be able to realize how he has worked until some time has passed (Genesis 45:4-8; 50:20). But let's think about our own attitude. Do we have to know all God's reasons? Shall we demand an explanation of everything he does or doesn't do? Or shall we trust him? If so, we can join in David's confident song to the Lord:

> If I go up to the heavens, you are there;
> if I make my bed in the depths, you are there.
> If I rise on the wings of the dawn,
> if I settle on the far side of the sea,
> even there your hand will guide me,
> your right hand will hold me fast.
> —Psalm 139:8-10

THOUGHT TO REMEMBER

God is here with us.

Discovery Learning

This page contains an alternate lesson plan emphasizing learning activities. Classes desiring such student involvement will find these suggestions helpful. The next page is a reproducible activity page to further enhance discovery learning.

LEARNING GOALS

After this lesson your students should be able to:

1. Tell how God led the Israelites by a pillar of cloud by day and of fire at night.

2. Recall significant moments in their lives when God's guidance sustained them.

3. Stay alert to indications of God's guidance through people and circumstances, and thank him for his guidance.

INTO THE LESSON

Begin by writing "GOD LEADS US" on the board. That will be the focal point for the lesson.

Probably most of your students will agree that God leads us. However, they may not all agree on the ways that God provides that leadership. Some may say that often it is difficult to tell whether we are following God's leading or our own ideas.

Introduce this lesson on God's leadership by asking each student to select the statement below that most nearly matches how he or she feels about God's leadership in his or her life.

• "I sense God's leadership every day in every phase of my life."

• "I go to God for guidance and leadership whenever I must make a big decision."

• "Most of the time I have a hard time knowing what God wants me to do."

• "I don't need God; I make out okay on my own."

• "I feel a real lack of God's leadership."

Some students may want to talk about God's leadership, but don't push. This lesson will help those who have trouble following God's leadership to move toward a more positive view.

INTO THE WORD

Give half the class a handout that contains the text of Exodus 40:34-38 and the other half one that contains Numbers 9:15-23. Students are to read their texts and underline every phrase that gives information about God's leadership and direction. Suggested responses follow:

• Exodus 40:36—underline the entire verse. God told the Israelites when to go.

• Verse 37—underline the entire verse. God told the Israelites when to stop and how long to stay.

• Verse 38—underline "during all their travels." God's direction continued as long as the Israelites needed it.

• Numbers 9:17—underline the entire verse. God told the people when and where to stop.

• Verse 18—underline the entire verse. God told the people how long to stay where they were.

• Verse 19—underline "when the cloud remained." God demonstrated his continual presence and leadership. The people did not have to wonder if God was still with them and leading them.

• Verse 20—nothing to underline. This verse emphasizes the people's obedience.

• Verse 21—nothing to underline. This verse also emphasizes obedience to God's leadership, with the added idea that the Israelites followed that leadership whether it was by day or by night.

• Verse 22—underline "Whether the cloud stayed over the tabernacle for two days or a month or a year." The Israelites had to wait for God's direction, and waiting can be difficult.

• Verse 23—underline "At the Lord's command . . . through Moses." This verse reemphasizes the people's obedience to God's leadership, with the added idea that Moses was involved in communicating God's direction to the people.

INTO LIFE

Distribute copies of the reproducible page that follows. Allow a few minutes for the students to complete the activities; then lead a discussion of God's guidance based on the handout.

We don't have a cloud or a pillar of fire. So how does God guide us? Below is a list of suggested ways that God uses to communicate his guidance and direction to us. Ask the students to talk about a time when God used each method in their lives.

• The Word of God—the Bible.

• A particularly timely sermon.

• The advice of a trusted Christian friend.

• An open door or a closed door.

• A personal disaster or tragedy.

• A hymn or gospel song.

• A Sunday school lesson.

• A book or an article in a Christian magazine.

In closing, challenge your students to thank God for the guidance and direction that he gives.

Waiting . . . and Waiting . . . and Waiting

Sometimes the Israelites had to wait a month or even a year for God's direction to come (Numbers 9:22). That must have been really hard!

Imagine that you are one of those ancient Israelites—newly released from slavery and now on your own.

- How do you feel about being led about the desert by a cloud and a pillar of fire?

- How do you feel about waiting when you want to go and going when you want to settle down in one place and stay for a while?

- What comfort and assurance do you receive from being able to see the cloud during the day and the fire at night?

Waiting When We Want to Go

As difficult as waiting was for the ancient Israelites, it seems to be even harder for us. We are used to getting what we want instantly. Complete the open-ended sentence below.

"When I have to wait for God's guidance and direction, I usually feel. . . ."

Describe a time when you got impatient and didn't wait for God's direction. What happened?

Describe a time when you felt strongly that you were following God's direction. What gave you that confidence? What was the result?

THE PEOPLE'S REBELLION

WHY TEACH THIS LESSON?

Today's lesson has a frightening relevance. The story of Israel's failure to enter the promised land after the mission of the twelve spies sounds like ancient history until we look just a little closer. What the people did was to decide that they knew better than God. God said go; but they said no. And don't so many people—even Christians—so often say things like, "I know the Bible says this, but I just wouldn't be happy if I did that. And I **know** God wants me to be happy!" When we study the Bible, we do so to find out what God's will is. But are we committed to obedience no matter what? Or do we reserve for ourselves the privilege of deciding whether or not we will obey once we discover God's will? If your students would be like Joshua and Caleb, they will choose obedience—no matter what!

INTRODUCTION

A. TEDIOUS TASKS

Are you old enough to remember what a great day it was when the circus came to town? It arrived in its own private train, and everyone who could leave his work went to watch the unloading. That free show was almost as good as the costly one later in the big top.

Wide-eyed we gazed at sleek lions and tigers resting or pacing in huge crates, monkeys leaping and climbing in smaller ones, great plodding elephants supplying power for the derricks that lifted tall poles into place and spread acres of canvas for the low walls and high roof of a tent bigger than Grandpa's barn.

What an equally busy scene there must have been when Israel's caravan came to a camping place! Can you imagine tents being set up all at once to shelter three million people, including shepherds and herdsmen trying to keep their sheep and cattle out of the way, and Levites carefully assembling the tabernacle in the middle of the camp?

You and I might have found it exciting to watch that busy scene a few times; but those doing the work must have found it monotonous and tiresome, particularly when they had to do it on several consecutive days. But if the cloud guiding them moved, that was their signal to move. No doubt they were grateful for some mornings when the guiding cloud did not stir from the Lord's tent, and the people did not have to stir from theirs.

B. LESSON BACKGROUND

The people of Israel had been at Sinai for nearly a year. Probably there was joy in the camp when the cloud rose in the air, indicating that it was time to move on. Better still, the cloud led them north, toward the promised land! They left Sinai on the twentieth day of the second month (Numbers 10:11); and when they came to Kadesh at the other side of the desert, the grapes were beginning to get ripe (Numbers 13:20). That may have been somewhere in the fifth month, thus making a three-month trip for the Israelites.

From the camp in Kadesh the people could look northward into Canaan. This was the promised land, the land flowing with milk and honey. This was the

DEVOTIONAL READING:
NUMBERS 14:5-19

BACKGROUND SCRIPTURE:
NUMBERS 12:1—14:25

PRINTED TEXT:
NUMBERS 13:1-3, 32—14:4, 20-24

LESSON AIMS

After this lesson a student should be able to:

1. Describe Israel's failure at the border of the promised land, and the tragic result of their failure.

2. Cite examples, from Scripture and their own experience, of both the triumph of living by faith and the tragedy of living in unbelief.

3. Maintain a firm faith in God that is not affected by difficult or challenging circumstances.

Oct
10

KEY VERSE

If the LORD is pleased with us, he will lead us into that land, a land flowing with milk and honey, and will give it to us. Only do not rebel against the LORD.
—Numbers 14:8, 9

LESSON 6 NOTES

home for which they had endured months of grueling travel in the desert. But now, with the promised land closer than ever, the people hesitated.

I. FINDING THE FACTS (NUMBERS 13:1-3, 32, 33)

At this point, the adventurers grew cautious. They came to Moses with a request that spies be sent to study the land so that the people could be better prepared for the task ahead of them (Deuteronomy 1:19-23).

A. CHOSEN SCOUTS (vv. 1-3)

1. The LORD said to Moses. . . .

The idea of studying the land and planning how to take it sounded good to *Moses* (Deuteronomy 1:23), but apparently he did not want to give his approval without asking *the Lord*. Now we will read the Lord's answer.

2. "Send some men to explore the land of Canaan, which I am giving to the Israelites. From each ancestral tribe send one of its leaders."

The Lord told Moses to do what the people asked—to *send* a team of *men* to *explore the land* that they hoped to call their home. Usually these men are referred to as "spies," since their primary purpose was "to spy out the land" (Deuteronomy 1:22). Capturing that land was a project for the entire nation, so every *tribe* was to appoint a representative to be part of the team of spies. Each representative was to be a recognized leader (literally, the Hebrew word translated *leaders* means "one lifted up"; thus, each man selected was to be prominent in his tribe).

3. So at the LORD's command Moses sent them out from the Desert of Paran. All of them were leaders of the Israelites.

Having received divine approval for this plan, Moses, *at the Lord's command*, now dispatched the men who had been selected as spies. Verses 4-31, omitted from our printed text, tell about their expedition. The spies' names are given in verses 4-16. They were to see if the defenders of Canaan were strong or weak and few or many, if the land was productive or barren, if the people lived in tents or in fortified cities, and if there were trees to be found in the land (vv. 17-20). In forty days they traveled approximately two hundred miles northward and searched the land thoroughly (vv. 21, 22).

When the men returned from their expedition, they brought good news and bad news. First, the land was indeed rich and fruitful. They brought samples of its produce to prove so (vv. 23-27). That was encouraging. Second, the defenders of the land were many and strong, and their cities were fortified. That was frightening (vv. 28, 29). One of the spies (Caleb) was bold and confident: "We should go up and take possession of the land, for we can certainly do it" (v. 30). But most of the group had a different opinion: "We can't attack those people; they are stronger than we are" (v. 31).

B. FEARFUL REPORT (vv. 32, 33)

32. And they spread among the Israelites a bad report about the land they had explored. They said, "The land we explored devours those living in it. All the people we saw there are of great size.

True, the land was fertile and productive (v. 27), but the majority of the spies reported that other factors made it undesirable. They claimed that *the land . . . devours those living in it*. Most likely they were referring to the gigantic men living there, who were accustomed to overpowering and destroying weaker peoples who lived near them.

Such a negative report as this came from a frightened, faithless imagination. In addition, the spies' claim that *all the people* were *of great size* was wildly exaggerated,

WHAT DO YOU THINK?

It is easy to look at circumstances that are favorable to our own chosen course of action and decide that God is opening a door for us. But circumstances are not a clear indicator of God's leading. God consented to the people's wishes to investigate the land of Canaan before invading it—even though, by divine foreknowledge, he surely knew what would result. What does that suggest to you about the way God allows us to choose our own course—even when we are wrong? How do we know when God is opening a door and when he is allowing a wrong course of action?

WHAT DO YOU THINK?

In their unbelief the ten spies seemed to exaggerate the size and strength of Canaan's inhabitants. How are we similarly tempted to exaggerate the magnitude of our problems? How can we keep things in perspective?

if not utterly false. The spies had gone through the territory of several peoples. It is hard to believe that *all the people* they saw were giants.

33. "We saw the Nephilim there (the descendants of Anak come from the Nephilim). We seemed like grasshoppers in our own eyes, and we looked the same to them."

The term *Nephilim* is a transliteration of a Hebrew word that seems to mean "fallen ones" or "falling ones." *Today's English Version* uses the translation "giants." Obviously these were men of unusual stature, given the way the Israelites saw themselves in comparison to them. However, the wild exaggeration of scared men is clear once again in the words, *We seemed like grasshoppers in our own eyes.*

TOYING WITH THE TRUTH

Marxist Communism gained a reputation for rewriting history to suit its political or social agenda. For example, when Nikita Khruschev was ousted from power in a bloodless coup in 1964, his name was quickly removed from history books and his face was even removed from official photographs. Then in the middle 1980s, when *perestroika* ("openness") became the new program in Russia, Khruschev's name and face were restored to history because his existence now served official government policy. Other Soviet notables experienced the same fate.

Perhaps it should not surprise us that ten of Israel's spies, for reasons rooted in lack of trust in God, gave a false report about the promised land. They probably could rationalize their falsifications to their own satisfaction, but a good cause is never served by this kind of behavior. In Western society today, government officials, political action groups, advertisers, and even Christian ministries have been known to "massage" the truth. More than anyone else, *Christians* should be known for their careful, truthful handling of the facts. —C. R. B.

II. FAILURE OF FAITH (NUMBERS 14:1-4)

At this point Caleb seemed to stand alone against all the other spies (Numbers 13:30, 31), but later we are told that Joshua was as firm and fearless as Caleb (14:6-9). Thus ten frightened men stood against two confident ones. It is not surprising to see that the people agreed with the frightened majority.

A. MOURNING (v. 1)

1. That night all the people of the community raised their voices and wept aloud.

What a disappointment! These people had traveled many weary miles to find a land flowing with milk and honey. But now it appeared that they could not enter it after all.

Such grief as this could not be kept silent. The Israelites *raised their voices and wept aloud.* Darkness fell, but no one slept in Israel's camp. *That night all the people of the community* continued to weep in bitter disappointment.

B. MURMURING (vv. 2, 3)

2. All the Israelites grumbled against Moses and Aaron, and the whole assembly said to them, "If only we had died in Egypt! Or in this desert!

Soon the people's mourning was mixed with anger. Who was to blame? Why, *Moses and Aaron*, of course! They had enticed the people out of Egypt with promises of bliss, only to have their hopes dashed. They would have been better off if they had *died in Egypt* or somewhere along that tiresome *desert* route than to be slaughtered by giants in Canaan!

Note that these words would later come back to haunt the people, for they indeed *died . . . in this desert* because of their unbelief (vv. 28, 29).

HOW TO SAY IT

Anak. AY-nack.
Canaan. KAY-nun.
Kadesh. KAY-desh.
Khruschev. KROOSH-eff.
Levites. LEE-vites.
Nephilim. Neff-ih-LEEM.
Paran. PAIR-un.
perestroika. pair-ih-STROY-kuh.

DAILY BIBLE READINGS

Monday, Oct. 4—*Aaron and Miriam Jealous of Moses* (Numbers 12:1-9)

Tuesday, Oct. 5—*Miriam Punished With Leprosy* (Numbers 12:10-15)

Wednesday, Oct. 6—*Twelve Sent to Spy Out Canaan* (Numbers 13:1-16)

Thursday, Oct. 7—*The Spies Carry Out Moses' Orders* (Numbers 13:17-24)

Friday, Oct. 8—*Fearful Spies and a Negative Report* (Numbers 13:25-33)

Saturday, Oct. 9—*Israel Rebels Against Moses and Aaron* (Numbers 14:1-12)

Sunday, Oct. 10—*Moses Intercedes for Israel* (Numbers 14:13-25)

3. *"Why is the LORD bringing us to this land only to let us fall by the sword? Our wives and children will be taken as plunder. Wouldn't it be better for us to go back to Egypt?"*

On second thought, the angry people could see that there was too much blame to be borne by Moses and Aaron alone. *The Lord* had enticed them out of Egypt. His cloud and fire had drawn them over those weary miles to this terrible end. Now the men of Israel would be butchered by the swords of giants, and their *wives* and *children* would be forced into abject slavery. Ironically, however, God later declared that those children, whom they thought faced certain doom, would enter the land (v. 31).

Negative thinking seldom stops with one discouraging thought. Especially within a group, it is easy for such thoughts to "snowball" and become worse. Here, as the people's thinking became more and more dismal, they began to entertain another thought: *wouldn't it be better for us to go back to Egypt?*

C. REBELLION (v. 4)
4. *And they said to each other, "We should choose a leader and go back to Egypt."*

Driven by fear, the people's thinking rushed on into even greater folly. "Wouldn't it be better?" became "Let's do it!" A plot was hatched to replace Moses with another *leader* and to *go back* over all those weary miles to the slavery from which they had fled.

According to verses 11-19 (not in our printed text), the Lord suggested a simple way of dealing with the rebels. He could destroy them all, and make Moses the father of a new nation that would carry out his plan.

Immediately Moses protested. That plan would severely damage the Lord's own reputation. All the world knew that he had brought the people of Israel out of Egypt to lead them to Canaan. If he destroyed them now, all the world would think that he was unable to do what he had planned. Moses pleaded for pardon for the rebels.

III. PARDON AND PUNISHMENT (NUMBERS 14:20-24)
A. GOD'S ASSURANCE (v. 20)
20. *The LORD replied, "I have forgiven them, as you asked.*

The Lord declared that he had *forgiven* the rebels: that is, he did not execute them for their treason. That did not mean that their faithlessness and disobedience would make no difference.

B. GOD'S GLORY (v. 21)
21. *"Nevertheless, as surely as I live and as surely as the glory of the LORD fills the whole earth.*

This means that God's declaration in verses 22 and 23 is as certain as are his existence and the presence of his *glory* in the *earth*.

C. FAILURE FOR THE FAITHLESS (vv. 22, 23)
22. *"Not one of the men who saw my glory and the miraculous signs I performed in Egypt and in the desert but who disobeyed me and tested me ten times.*

The *men* of Israel had shown caution when they asked Moses to send spies to explore the promised land, but their caution had turned to cowardice when they refused to advance into the land and take possession of it. Their cowardice was inexcusable because they *saw* God's *glory* in the cloud that led them (Exodus 16:10), on Mount Sinai (Exodus 24:16), and in the tabernacle in the midst of their camp (Exodus 40:34). In addition, the people *saw* God's *miraculous signs*,

---

WHAT DO YOU THINK?

The Israelites were ready to replace Moses with another leader and return to their slavery in Egypt. That seems ridiculous to us today, but many believers do essentially the same thing. Some may forget that they are saved by grace and stray back into the attitude of trying to earn their place in Heaven. (See Galatians 2:16-21; 5:1-6.) Some succumb to the temptation to return to a sinful habit that they had forsaken for Christ. Some believers give up their freedom in Christ when they allow themselves to be dominated by a cult leader's personality and align with his cult. What can we do to maintain our freedom and to resist the lure of these and other rivals?

which had demonstrated both his unconquerable power and his favor toward his people. Still, they did not have faith enough to move into the land God had given them, trusting him for safety and victory.

Each time the people had *tested* the Lord, they had shown their lack of faith. Sometimes the phrase *ten times* is used to mean many times (repeatedly) rather than an exact number. Whether the number is literal or figurative here, it illustrates the repeated faithlessness of Israel. The incidents of the Israelites' testing God are recorded in Exodus 15:22—17:7. They are mentioned in Psalms 78:40, 41; 95:8-11; 106:13-33; 1 Corinthians 10:1-11; Hebrews 3:8, 9.

23. *"Not one of them will ever see the land I promised on oath to their forefathers. No one who has treated me with contempt will ever see it.*

The men of Israel had tested God often. Now, all those twenty years or older, who were earlier counted in the census, would never be allowed to live in the *land* that God had *promised* (vv. 29, 30).

TEN + FEAR = FAILURE
TWO + FAITH = VICTORY

Today's visual demonstrates that "majority rule" is not always right; faith alters the equation. Discuss how we can stand up for our faith even when a vocal majority opposes us.

THE COST OF FAILING THE TEST

There seems to be no end to the schemes people come up with to make money at the expense of others. A business known as Test-A-Mate is a good example. If you think your husband or wife could be tempted into being unfaithful to you, for $250 you can hire Test-A-Mate to "test your mate."

Here's how it works: the suspicious mate looks at a photo album of attractive models for the person to whom he (or she) thinks his mate might be attracted. This person is then sent to the mate's favorite restaurant, health club, or other place where he or she socializes. The decoy does not initiate any conversation; but if the mate does, Test-A-Mate will report on whatever degree of unfaithfulness develops.

Suppose a husband or wife succumbs to the temptation, but later is sorry for having done so. The seeds of doubt have already been sown and may flower into a divorce. Or suppose the mate does not succumb, but finds out about the other's lack of confidence in him or her. What then? The result may still be a broken marriage, even though the suspicious mate may regret having ever initiated such foolishness.

We often forget that sorrow for sin or stupidity may be genuinely felt and expressed, but there are always consequences to our attitudes and actions. Israel discovered this fact of life to its deep regret. The people's lack of faith cost a whole generation the opportunity to enjoy the land that God had promised them.

—C. R. B.

D. SUCCESS FOR THE FAITHFUL (v. 24)

24. *"But because my servant Caleb has a different spirit and follows me wholeheartedly, I will bring him into the land he went to, and his descendants will inherit it."*

Caleb had not doubted, feared, or rebelled. Trusting the Lord, he had strongly urged the people to go on into the *land* without delay (Numbers 13:30). Therefore, he would be allowed to enter that land, to possess a share of it, and to pass it on to *his descendants*. Joshua had been as faithful and obedient as Caleb had (Numbers 14:6-9), and he, too, would find a home there (v. 30).

But all of that was yet to occur. For now, rebellious Israel must turn back into the wilderness, and wander there until all the adults twenty years and older were dead. Of that faithless generation, only faithful Caleb and Joshua would survive to see the land conquered. The next generation, matured and toughened in the arid desert, would finally receive the promised land. With God's help they would make it their own.

WHAT DO YOU THINK?

Caleb and Joshua are famous for their unpopular minority report. When have you had to make such an unpopular stand for God and his Word? How can we prepare ourselves to make such a stand?

[Allow your students to describe how they have taken a stand at their places of work, in political discussions, at school, or even at home. Encourage those who may be making such a stand on a regular basis.]

CONCLUSION

A. OUR OWN MIGRATION

Chapter 10 of 1 Corinthians (verses 1-11) points out that Israel's migration is a picture of our own. God has liberated us from the bondage of sin to lead us home to everlasting joy. Our journey leads through this world's wilderness. It, too, is a land of many hardships, but God is leading all the way. He will not fail us nor forsake us. Will we fail him?

Some Christians lose their nerve when hardships come. They test God with reckless and repeated disobedience, and they die in the wilderness. Others find God's power for overcoming hardship, and they become stronger (James 1:2-4).

B. STORIES OF TRAGEDY AND TRIUMPH

Sam manages a supermarket in our town. He does it well, and his salary provides a good living for him and his family. But Sam is not happy. Ten years ago he owned a bigger store in a bigger town, but that store burned down. Too late, Sam realized that he had let the insurance lapse. He was penniless until he found a job in our town.

Sam was a deacon in the church in that other town, but now he is furious whenever the minister goes to visit him. "Don't talk to me about church!" he storms. "I'm through with God! What did he ever do for me?"

Sam is prosperous now, but how will his story end? Will his final tragedy be worse than the loss of his store?

Holding a "middle management job" with a big firm, Mark was comfortable and happy. He was popular at work, at church, and at the tennis club. Then the firm "downsized," and Mark found himself unemployed. Jobs were available, but they were minimum-wage jobs. Mark scorned them. He had no one but himself to support; he figured he could live on unemployment compensation and his savings. When those resources were exhausted, Mark still scorned minimum-wage work. He took his gun to the next town and robbed a bank; but he was careless about it, and soon he was caught with the loot.

In prison, Mark feels abused. "I didn't do anything wrong," he says. "Not till I had to. Why is the Lord doing this to me?"

What kind of an ending do you foresee for Mark's story? Is there anything he can do to provide a happier one?

Martha is fifty-five years old. Her thirty-year-old son is seriously ill with tuberculosis. The doctor told her that a dry climate might help him, so the two of them drove to Arizona. They were nearly out of gas and money when they came to a little town at the edge of the desert. Martha left her sick son sleeping at the motel while she went to church. Then wonderful things began to happen. Friendly Christians helped Martha find a job. The only vacant house in the little town was too decrepit to be lived in, but men of the church gave it a new roof while women cleaned the inside. With a laugh, the owner said that their work had paid the rent for a year. He himself contributed an old refrigerator, and the women stocked it with food. The newcomers moved in, and neighbors heard Martha singing, "Praise God from whom all blessings flow," as she prepared breakfast.

That's a happy story, yet Martha's son remains very ill. Trouble and grief surely lie ahead—but don't you predict a glorious ending?

You write your own story by what you do while traveling through the deserts of life. Do you want a happy ending?

Discovery Learning

This page contains an alternate lesson plan emphasizing learning activities. Classes desiring such student involvement will find these suggestions helpful. The next page is a reproducible activity page to further enhance discovery learning.

LEARNING GOALS

After this lesson a student should be able to:

1. Describe Israel's failure at the border of the promised land, and the tragic result of their failure.

2. Cite examples, from Scripture and their own experience, of both the triumph of living by faith and the tragedy of living in unbelief.

3. Maintain a firm faith in God that is not affected by difficult or challenging circumstances.

INTO THE LESSON

Begin by telling the adults in your class to imagine they are on a safari. Late one afternoon their vehicle has engine trouble and stops. Since it is too dangerous to camp out in the wild, the guide wants to push ahead on foot to the next station. Even though the road ahead passes through rough and hazardous terrain, he is confident that the entire group can make it. The others in the group want to go back. They would like to go forward, but they are afraid.

If your students were in that safari group, what would they do? At Kadesh, God challenged the Israelites to go forward in faith and enter the promised land. He set before them a choice: overcome obstacles by faith, or shrink back in unbelief.

INTO THE WORD

Divide the class into three-person groups. Tell each group to compare and contrast the two accounts of the sending out of the spies in Numbers 13:1-3 and Deuteronomy 1:19-24. How are the two accounts alike? How are they different? *(They are alike in that both accounts report there were twelve spies, one from each tribe, and that the spies were sent to check out Canaan. The biggest difference is that the Numbers account reports that God told Moses to send the spies, but in Deuteronomy the plan originated with the people.)* Observe that the accounts in Numbers and Deuteronomy have a different perspective, but they are not contradictory. The people could have suggested the plan, and God commanded Moses to go along with them.

Option: Use the reproducible activity on the page that follows. It will connect the following activity with the previous one.

Divide the class into three groups, and assign each group one of these passages: Numbers 14:1-4; 14:20-23; 14:24. The members of each group should look for the "key idea" in their passage.

• Verses 1-4: Faithlessness is contagious and infectious. Faithlessness opens the door to discontent and despair. We often want to blame someone else for the results of our own choices.

• Verses 20-23: Wrong choices bring negative consequences.

• Verse 24: Right choices bring rewards.

Note that there is a significant difference in perspective between the two groups of spies. The ten faithless spies were looking at the conquest of Canaan from a human perspective—they knew they could not defeat the Canaanites in their own strength. Caleb and Joshua were looking at the conquest from God's perspective.

INTO LIFE

Many adults are influenced by the opinions of others and are reluctant to go against the crowd. It is not necessarily wrong to do something simply because everyone else is doing it, but rebelling against God and shrinking back from the challenges he places before us is always wrong no matter who else is doing it.

Discuss the following situations. Ask the students how they would classify the person's actions in each situation: rebellion against God's will, going along with the crowd, accommodation for the sake of convenience, compromise, or some other.

• A. Charlie is invited out to lunch with some guys at work. When he learns they are going to a place that has exotic dancers, he wants to say no, but he's afraid of what the guys will think of him. He keeps quiet and goes along.

• B. Some ladies from church get together every Tuesday for a Bible study. Grace used to enjoy the fellowship, but for the past few weeks one of the ladies has been making hateful comments about a family who just moved into the neighborhood. Grace wants to say something, but she's reluctant to confront the other woman. So she says nothing.

• C. The man with whom Ed carpools to work has no use for God or religion. Knowing Ed is a believer, he said early on he would tolerate no talk of religion. Ed still feels he should talk to this man about Christ, but he doesn't want to risk losing his ride to work, so he says nothing.

In closing, challenge the adults to have the courage to trust God and do the right thing in difficult situations.

Filling in the Gaps

Today's Scripture passage skips over the account of the spies' reconnaissance patrol and their reports. Fill in those gaps by doing some personal investigation and study on the following.

- The path that the spies took (Numbers 13:17-25). List the places explored.

- The reports that the spies gave (Numbers 13:26-31). There was both a majority report and a minority report. Analyze the two reports by answering these questions:

  - Who brought back each report?

  - What did both reports agree on?

  - Where did the two reports disagree?

  - Why was there a difference between the two reports?

  What, if anything, does this suggest to you about situations in your own church where there is a difference of opinion regarding the best course of action to follow? How do you determine the right choice? Majority rule? How?

THE DESERT YEARS

LESSON 7

WHY TEACH THIS LESSON?

Forty years is a long time! Surely the Israelites must have thought so. Forty years had passed since they left Egypt. Now they were finally ready to enter the promised land. They had learned a lot in their wanderings. They had learned that disobedience and faithlessness exact a heavy price. They had learned dependence on God. Most of all, they had learned, "These forty years the Lord your God has been with you, and you have not lacked anything" (Deuteronomy 2:7).

Perhaps you and your class have been waiting a long time for an answer to prayer. An infertile couple is praying for a child. Your church is anxious to build a much needed addition to the facility. The local zoning board has been blocking a national ministry organization from moving into your neighborhood. Whatever "desert" you or your students may be in, this lesson will remind you that the Lord your God has been with you, and he can lead you to the place he wants you to be.

INTRODUCTION

A. NO IRRIGATION NEEDED

"The desert and the parched land will be glad; the wilderness will rejoice and blossom" (Isaiah 35:1). Proudly the guide leading our tour of the Holy Land quoted this prophecy, pointing to wide green fields of wheat where only desert had been not long before. When the nation of Israel was reborn in the twentieth century, soon its people were pumping water from the Sea of Galilee in the north and transporting it through miles of canals to irrigate the desert of the Negev in the south.

As the Israelites stood on the brink of entering the promised land, Moses told them that this land was very different from Egypt, where they had lived so long in bondage. Whereas in Egypt the land was watered "by foot" (probably a reference to irrigation channels that were dug by foot), the promised land required no irrigation whatsoever (Deuteronomy 11:10, 11). The people would have so much land that they would not need to cultivate the desert of the Negev. Their country would be a place of abundance, "a land flowing with milk and honey" (Exodus 3:8).

B. LESSON BACKGROUND

Near the end of their wandering in the desert, the people of Israel came again to the border of the promised land. This time they camped east of the Jordan River. There Moses made a lengthy speech to the nation (Deuteronomy 1:3). He reviewed their forty years in the desert; he repeated the laws God had given; he urged the people to be obedient to God. We take a portion of that speech for today's printed text. We begin with Moses' review of what happened following the events that were the subject of our lesson last week.

I. THE WANDERING BEGINS (DEUTERONOMY 1:41—2:1)

The Israelites had expressed fear, not faith, after they heard the spies' report concerning the land of promise. Because of their unbelief, all the adults twenty years and older (except for faithful Caleb and Joshua) were sentenced to death in

DEVOTIONAL READING:
ISAIAH 35
BACKGROUND SCRIPTURE:
DEUTERONOMY 1:26—2:25
PRINTED TEXT:
DEUTERONOMY 1:41—2:8

LESSON AIMS

After this lesson students should be able to:

1. Tell why the children of Israel were punished with wandering in the wilderness, and summarize their experience there.

2. Relate an example (from Scripture or from personal experience) that illustrates the tragic consequences of disobeying God.

3. Commit themselves to more consistent involvement in the work of the church so that God's kingdom can go forward.

Oct
17

KEY VERSE

The LORD your God has blessed you in all the work of your hands. He has watched over your journey through this vast desert. These forty years the LORD your God has been with you, and you have not lacked anything.
—Deuteronomy 2:7

the wilderness. Only their children (who they had claimed would perish) would be allowed to enter the land. Deuteronomy 1:40 records these tragic words of the Lord following the people's rebellion against him: "But as for you, turn around and set out toward the desert along the route to the Red Sea."

A. WARNING GIVEN (vv. 41, 42)

41. Then you replied, "We have sinned against the LORD. We will go up and fight, as the LORD our God commanded us." So every one of you put on his weapons, thinking it easy to go up into the hill country.

At first the rebels admitted their wrongdoing. They had *sinned* in refusing to advance at the Lord's command, they said. However, they then proceeded to disobey God yet again by refusing to follow his command to turn back into the wilderness. Instead, they determined to *go up and fight*, as they should have done earlier. Apparently they thought the prospect of dying in the desert was worse than the prospect of being killed by the giants in the promised land. So they *put on* their *weapons* and prepared to *go up into the hill country* (or, the higher country).

42. But the LORD said to me, "Tell them, 'Do not go up and fight, because I will not be with you. You will be defeated by your enemies.'"

God gave his answer through Moses. This latter disobedience was no better than the former one. The rebels should obey God's latest command and turn back into the wilderness. It was too late to obey the earlier order that they had refused to obey—the command to go forward and *fight* for the promised land. God would no longer be *with* them in such an effort, so they would be *defeated by* their *enemies*.

B. WARNING IGNORED (v. 43)

43. So I told you, but you would not listen. You rebelled against the LORD's command and in your arrogance you marched up into the hill country.

Moses delivered God's message; however, as one might expect by now, the rebels paid no attention. They ignored God's latest directive, and instead obeyed the earlier one that he had now countermanded. *In* their *arrogance*—choosing their own way in defiance of God's clear command—they *marched up into the hill country* to battle the residents of the promised land.

C. TRAGIC CONSEQUENCES (vv. 44-46)

44. The Amorites who lived in those hills came out against you; they chased you like a swarm of bees and beat you down from Seir all the way to Hormah.

The men of Israel proceeded to enter the territory north of their camp. *The Amorites who lived* there were one of the peoples whom God had commanded the Israelites to destroy once they entered the promised land (Deuteronomy 7:1, 2). But here the Amorites *came out* and *chased* the Israelites *like a swarm of bees*. This presents a vivid picture to anyone who has seen a panic-stricken man running madly, hands flailing wildly at a swarm of hostile bees buzzing around his head. It suggests that the men of Israel panicked and took to their heels, hotly pursued by a swarm of Amorites who struck down as many as they could.

We do not know exactly where *Hormah* was. It appears to have been northeast of Kadesh, within approximately ten miles of Beersheba. Most significant to note here is that rebellious Israel suffered a quick and disastrous defeat.

45. You came back and wept before the LORD, but he paid no attention to your weeping and turned a deaf ear to you.

When the Amorites stopped chasing the Israelites, the survivors *came back* to their camp and *wept before the Lord*. We are not told just what feelings made

WHAT DO YOU THINK?

Having been rebuked for not going up into the land of Canaan, the Israelites attempted too late to obey the Lord and to take the land. They were soundly defeated. What are some modern examples when delayed obedience may fail? If we have been slow to obey, is it better not to? Why or why not?

them weep. Were they merely grieving for their comrades killed by the Amorites? Were they angry with themselves, weeping with shame and sorrow because they had run away rather than fight? Were they angry with the Lord because he had not helped them, even though he had told them plainly that he would not (v. 42)? Were they weeping tears of repentance and promising not to disobey again? Or were several or all of these feelings mingled in their grief? Whatever their feelings were, the facts are plain. They had turned their backs on God, and now his back was turned on them.

We must remember that Moses was telling of this tragedy approximately thirty-eight years after it happened. He said *you*, meaning the men of Israel; but the men actually involved in that tragedy were no longer living. They had died in the desert. Some of Moses' hearers had been children when that attack had failed; some had been born since that time. Now they were coming to the border of the promised land. From the disaster of their fathers, they could learn that it is better to obey God: to advance when he commands, and not to advance when he forbids. This is why Moses' review of the people's history at this time was so important.

46. And so you stayed in Kadesh many days—all the time you spent there.

Perhaps those *many days* were days of mourning for the men who had been killed. Perhaps they were days of indecision. It is not likely that anyone wanted to try another attack, but perhaps some wanted to return to Egypt. Perhaps the Lord's guiding cloud hung motionless, because the Lord wanted his people to have time to think. In that campsite the people had twice disobeyed him. Perhaps those many days of thinking produced a resolution not to disobey God again.

FAILING TO REACH THE GOAL

"You can live to be one hundred!" Promises of long life are the standard pitch for many fad diets. Dr. Stuart Berger was a nutritionist who developed the "Immune Power Diet" and wrote a book titled *Forever Young*. He claimed he could treat cancer and other serious ailments with proper diet and vitamins. But just a few years ago, Dr. Berger died in his sleep at age forty. It seems he could not follow his own dietary advice: he weighed 365 pounds when he died.

J. I. Rodale, a publisher of magazines devoted to health, claimed that he would live to be a hundred; but he died of a heart attack at age seventy-two. Many others, both legitimate doctors and "quacks," have promised that their diet, vitamin combination, exercise regimen, or brand of secret-formula elixir would help one to live longer and better than would normally be expected.

Living to be one hundred is a "promised land" of sorts. Yet most people will not reach it, in part because they don't live up to what they know about good nutrition and a healthy lifestyle.

In that respect, most of us are like the Israelites: they knew what it would take to reach the promised land, but lacked the self-discipline to make it happen. The promised land was a reachable goal, and God would have helped them attain it; but they were disappointed because they failed to accept the challenge. —C. R. B.

D. FURTHER TRAVELS (2:1)

2:1. Then we turned back and set out toward the desert along the route to the Red Sea, as the LORD had directed me. For a long time we made our way around the hill country of Seir.

As we look at the *Red Sea* on the map (page 15), we see that the north end of it is divided into two narrow arms. The west arm is called the Gulf of Suez. That is the part of the Red Sea that the people of Israel crossed as they were leaving Egypt (see lesson 2, page 26). In the first part of this week's text, Israel had

---

WHAT DO YOU THINK?

The Israelites wept before the Lord after their defeat at the hands of the Amorites, but he did not respond to their tears. Suppose a young Christian read this and said, "I am afraid that is how God will respond to my prayers—that he will not listen. How can I be sure he will listen to my prayers?" How would you answer?

WHAT DO YOU THINK?

The Israelites experienced years of wandering as a result of their disobedience. If a person or church seems to be "wandering"—just maintaining, showing no obvious signs of growth—is that evidence of disobedience? Why or why not? What should a "wandering" person or church do to make progress?

Amorites. AM-uh-rites.

Aqaba. OCK-uh-buh.

Arabah. AIR-uh-buh.

Beersheba. Beer-SHE-buh.

Deuteronomy. Due-ter-AHN-uh-me.

Edom. EE-dum.

Edomites. EE-duh-mites.

Elath. EE-lath.

Ezion Geber. EE-zee-on GAY-ber.

Hormah. HOR-muh.

Kadesh. KAY-desh.

Moab. MO-ab.

Negev. NEG-ev.

Seir. SEE-ir.

WHAT DO YOU THINK?

After years of "going nowhere," the Israelites were told, "Turn north." Of course, there is nothing special or spiritual about the direction north, but for Israel it meant going in the right direction to reach their goal. In what way do you need to "turn north"? How can you do that?

camped at Kadesh, near the southern boundary of the promised land. Now, in the latter part of our text, we read that the people *turned* and went back toward the south, but not to Sinai. They went *along the route to the Red Sea*—that is, toward that small east arm of the Red Sea, the Gulf of Aqaba. We know this is the direction they traveled, because *Seir* is the country between that gulf and the Dead Sea. It is about a hundred miles long from south to north.

For the people to have traveled *around the hill country of Seir* means that they lived as nomads, moving about to find pasture for their livestock in a region where pasture was scanty. That continued for *a long time*, thus completing the Israelites' time of wandering in the desert after leaving Kadesh.

CONDEMNED TO WANDER

Fourteen-year-old Jeff Thornton loved to ride his snowboard in the ski areas of the mountains above Los Angeles. As he started his snowboard run on the afternoon of February 7, 1998, fog was beginning to settle in. He became disoriented, lost sight of the signs marking the snowboarding trail, and was soon wandering in the uninhabited mountain wilderness. For six days Jeff stumbled aimlessly in seventy-mile-an-hour winds, subfreezing cold, and snowfall so heavy that rescuers had to call off their search because of "whiteout" conditions.

Then (ironically on Friday the 13th) Jeff was found alive, but with lowered body temperature and severe frostbite. Family and friends rejoiced at the "miracle" and prayed for Jeff's recovery. But as often happens in such cases, his frozen body tissue caused an infection that spread throughout his body. One week after he was found, Jeff died of respiratory problems and heart failure. The wilderness had claimed its victim after all.

The Israelites' lack of faith in God caused them to lose their way spiritually, and they were condemned to wander in another kind of wilderness—the desert of Sinai. Many of them never got out of that wilderness alive. Their wanderings were the direct result of their failure to see the signs that would have kept them "on the trail" to the promised land.

—C. R. B.

II. THE WANDERING ENDS (DEUTERONOMY 2:2-8)

A. GOD'S INSTRUCTIONS (vv. 2-6)

2, 3. *Then the LORD said to me, "You have made your way around this hill country long enough; now turn north.*

The Lord had declared that Israel must live in the desert forty years, because the people had refused to take the promised land when he first had led them to it (Numbers 14:33, 34). That time was now drawing to a close. It was time to move *north* toward the promised land.

4. *"Give the people these orders: 'You are about to pass through the territory of your brothers the descendants of Esau, who live in Seir. They will be afraid of you, but be very careful.*

The Israelites were to *pass through the territory of* their *brothers the descendants of Esau*, who now lived in *Seir* (Genesis 36:8, 9). Esau was nicknamed Edom, which means "red," because he was fond of "red stew" (Genesis 25:29, 30). The nation descended from him is usually called Edom, and his descendants are called Edomites (Genesis 36:9). At this time the heathen tribes living in the promised land had become intolerably wicked. The Lord ordered Israel to "utterly destroy" them (Deuteronomy 7:1, 2; 20:16, 17). But the Edomites were not included in that sentence of destruction. Israel must continue to regard them as *brothers* and show no hostility toward them.

5. *"'Do not provoke them to war, for I will not give you any of their land, not even enough to put your foot on. I have given Esau the hill country of Seir as his own.*

The land promised to Israel did not include a single foot of the *land* of the Edomites. Israel must pass through that territory, but they must take care not to disturb its people.

6. "'You are to pay them in silver for the food you eat and the water you drink.'"

The people of Israel had been living on manna for nearly forty years; likely they would be happy to eat something else for a change. They could buy *food* from the Edomites for a fair price, but they must not take it by force or by threat of force. They must *pay* even for the *water* they would *drink*, for water was scarce in that country. The people of Israel could afford to pay for these items, for they had taken large amounts of *silver* from the Egyptians as they were leaving that country (Exodus 12:35, 36).

B. GOD'S GUIDANCE (v. 7)

7. The LORD your God has blessed you in all the work of your hands. He has watched over your journey through this vast desert. These forty years the LORD your God has been with you, and you have not lacked anything.

The Lord had *blessed* his people during all those years in the *desert*. They had *not lacked anything*, because he had provided manna every day and had brought water from a rock when it was needed. Their clothes had not worn out in *forty years* (Deuteronomy 8:4). Surely they could trust the Lord to provide for them in the present and the future.

C. ON TO CANAAN (v. 8)

8. So we went on past our brothers the descendants of Esau, who live in Seir. We turned from the Arabah road, which comes up from Elath and Ezion Geber, and traveled along the desert road of Moab.

This verse indicates that the Israelites obeyed the Lord's instructions: they *went on past . . . the descendants of Esau* without disturbing them. They *turned from the Arabah road*, which ran northward from *Elath* and *Ezion Geber*, located at the northern edge of the Gulf of Aqaba. They then approached *Moab*, which lay east of the Dead Sea. There again they avoided conflict; instead of entering Moab, they *traveled along the desert road of Moab*, which followed Moab's eastern border. In this way they reached the Jordan River north of the Dead Sea, where they prepared to cross into their new home.

CONCLUSION

> There is a tide in the affairs of men,
> Which, taken at the flood, leads on to fortune;
> Omitted, all the voyage of their life
> Is bound in shallows and in miseries.

In Shakespeare's imagination, those words expressed Brutus's thinking as he planned a crucial battle; and those same words express a truth that is seen in many other enterprises:

There is an opportune time!

A. GOD'S TIME IS BEST

It appeared that the turning point of Israel's migration toward Canaan came at Kadesh. The desert was behind them; the promised land was before them; the Lord was with them. This was the time God had chosen for them to sweep onward like a flood, to overwhelm their enemies, and to take possession of the land he had given them. But in their timid minds the fear of giants conquered their

---

WHAT DO YOU THINK?

In spite of Israel's disobedience God provided for their physical needs throughout the years of wandering. How can we use the fact of God's continual provision for the physical needs of our unsaved friends to lead them to Christ?

The visual for today's lesson recalls several events from Israel's experience. Discuss what the people ought to have learned from each event.

PRAYER

Teach us to put away our selfishness, Father. As you continually give to us, help us to give more of our time, more of our energy, more of our money, and more of ourselves in doing what you want us to do, and in doing it now. In our Master's name. Amen.

THOUGHT TO REMEMBER

You can do more than you think you can.

faith in God. The men of Israel let a golden opportunity slip away, and lived the rest of their lives in the desert.

God's time is always best, but it is not always so easy to see. Do we need more room in our auditorium, our Sunday school classrooms, or our parking lot? Do we need a youth minister, an assistant minister, or a special minister to senior members? How do we know when God would have us supply any or all of these needs?

If more room would enable us to win more people to Christ and to salvation, isn't that a clear indication that now is the time to provide more room? If a youth minister can turn more young people from darkness to light and from the power of Satan to God, doesn't God want that to happen now? If a minister of education can devise a program that will speed Christian growth in all of us, what are we waiting for? If we see a capable person available for any needed ministry, that is an added indication that God's time is now.

B. COUNTING THE COST

Most of us are practical people and cautious about undertaking any big enterprise. We recall that Jesus spoke of counting the cost. If we begin a great work and can't finish it, we invite the contempt of our neighbors instead of their respect. That is clear in Luke 14:25-33.

What does it cost to follow Jesus? It costs all you have. Some of the multitude heard that and said it was too much, but others decided to pay it. Countless others have been willing to do so since then, and that is why the Christian enterprise is still growing. It is still worth the price one pays.

The men of Israel pretended to count the cost of invading the promised land. They claimed that such a venture would cost the lives of all of them, plus the freedom of their wives and children (Numbers 14:3). But that was not really a count; it was a wild exaggeration born of terror. We need an honest count.

C. COUNTING THE RESOURCES

The frightened men of Israel exaggerated the cost and underestimated their resources. They seemed to think that they had nothing but their own strength. God was with them, but they ignored him. They appeared to forget that he still had the power that had overcome Egypt, the Red Sea, and all the dangers of the desert. God continues to do marvelous things through those people who are fully committed to him.

Members of one church extended themselves to enlarge their meeting place, only to find that the added space was useless because there was no room in the parking lot. Some of them were in despair; but after much thought and prayer, the elders proposed the following:

"We're giving all we can to keep up the payments on our bigger place of worship. Now we have to have a bigger parking lot. Obviously we have to give more than we can. Let's think—every person, every family—think of some sacrifice, something we can do without."

One family decided their old station wagon could last another year, and then they found that it lasted *two* years. Another gave up a long-planned trip to Washington, DC. A single man took a part-time job in addition to his regular work. Youngsters gave up movies and candy and snacks, and found lawn-mowing and baby-sitting jobs.

As a result, the parking lot was doubled, and the church grew so rapidly that the loans were paid off in half the expected time. A little later the church employed its very own missionary in a distant land. The pain of sacrifice was forgotten in the joy of accomplishment.

Discovery Learning

This page contains an alternate lesson plan emphasizing learning activities. Classes desiring such student involvement will find these suggestions helpful. The next page is a reproducible activity page to further enhance discovery learning.

LEARNING GOALS

After this lesson students should be able to:

1. Tell why the children of Israel were punished with wandering in the wilderness, and summarize their experience there.

2. Relate an example (from Scripture or from personal experience) that illustrates the tragic consequences of disobeying God.

3. Commit themselves to more consistent involvement in the work of the church so that God's kingdom can go forward.

INTO THE LESSON

Ask your students to review their lives over the past year. Then ask, "What is one thing you did in the past twelve months that you would like to be able to go back and do differently?" Discuss things they did that they would like not to have done, or that they did not but wished they had. What choices or decisions would they make differently?

Remind your students of the choices that the Israelites made at Kadesh. (We learned about those choices in last week's lesson.) They decided to rebel against and disobey God. No doubt during the thirty-eight years they spent in the desert they wished many times for an opportunity to go back and relive those decisions.

INTO THE WORD

In today's lesson the Israelites were again at the threshold of the promised land. Moses reviewed past failures and challenged his people to go forward in faith this time.

Ask a student to read Deuteronomy 1:41—2:8 while the rest of the class listens for things the Israelites did wrong the first time at Kadesh. After the reading, ask, "What mistakes did the Israelites make?"

• They disobeyed and rebelled against God (v. 26).

• They spoke evil against the Lord (v. 27).

• They failed to listen to God, again rebelled, and acted presumptuously (v. 43).

• Because of their disobedience, they were defeated in battle (v. 44).

Now tell the students to suppose that the Israelites could have gone back and relived what they did at Kadesh. What do your students think they would have done differently? How would Israel's history have been changed?

Write the following clichés on the chalkboard. Ask your students to describe incidents in today's Bible passages that illustrate each cliché.

• "We reap what we sow." (*When the Israelites sowed rebellion at Kadesh, they reaped thirty-eight years of wandering in the desert.*)

• "We don't want something until we are told we cannot have it." (*When God told the Israelites to turn back into the desert, they suddenly wanted to invade Canaan.*)

• "Doing the right thing at the wrong time is the same as doing the wrong thing." (*When God said "Go," the people said "No." When God said "No," the people said "Let's go."*)

INTO LIFE

Distribute copies of the reproducible page that follows. After students complete the exercise, say, "At one time or another, we all go through desert experiences. Describe some of your desert experiences and what you have learned from them."

After some discussion, point out that we all suffer for our mistakes. Some of those mistakes are honest errors of judgment, but many of our mistakes are sparked by a rebellious and selfish attitude. For example, an unfaithful husband may come to regret the affair that broke up his marriage; a dishonest worker will likely regret the petty thievery that cost him his job; a tongue-wagging neighbor soon regrets the gossip that ruined a friendship; and a self-absorbed son will eventually regret the vicious and hateful words that drove a spike into his relationship with his father.

As the Israelites looked back on the thirty-eight years they had spent in the desert, they realized that God had been with them and taken care of them. Even though the sin of rebellion had sent them into the desert, God had not abandoned them.

In closing, ask your students where they are in relation to the desert. Are they bitter at God and blaming him for their desert experience? Are they suffering from the heat and sandstorms, but learning and growing? Or are they at the edge of the desert, praising God for his care and deliverance in bringing them through?

Challenge your students to thank God during the coming week for his presence, even when circumstances are difficult and they must spend time in the desert.

Spending Time in the Desert

Some of the Bible's most prominent personalities spent time in the desert. A desert—or wilderness, as it was sometimes called—was a barren, uninhabited ("deserted") place. Often it was an arid or semiarid region, making it uninhabitable since water is so important to the survival of people and animals. The desert was a challenging place in which to make one's living!

See if you can match up the experience with the person who had that experience. Some names may be used more than once.

___ 1. After his conversion, he spent time in the desert of Arabia sorting out what had happened to him (Galatians 1:17).

___ 2. He tended his father-in-law's sheep in the desert of Sinai (Exodus 3:1).

___ 3. He spent forty days in the Desert of Judea, fasting and being tempted by Satan (Luke 4:1, 2).

___ 4. He wasted his inheritance on riotous living, creating for himself a metaphorical desert wasteland (Luke 15:13, 14).

___ 5. He announced the coming of the Messiah by preaching repentance in the Desert of Judea (Matthew 3:1, 2).

___ 6. God sent him into the desert to preach the gospel to a man from Ethiopia (Acts 8:26).

___ 7. They were miraculously sustained in the desert with manna and water from a rock (Deuteronomy 8:15, 16).

___ 8. His own son mounted an insurrection against him, chasing him into the desert (2 Samuel 15:23).

___ 9. He frequently retreated to the desert to get away from the crowds (Mark 6:31, 32).

___ 10. He created a spiritual desert for himself by rebelling against God and committing adultery (Psalm 51:11, 12).

Choose from these names to identify the individuals indicated at the left:

a. King David

b. Moses

c. The Prodigal Son

d. Jesus

e. John the Baptist

f. Saul/Paul

g. Philip

h. The Israelites

KEY

1. f; 2. b; 3. d; 4. c; 5. e; 6. g; 7. h; 8. a; 9. d; 10. a

THE GREAT COMMANDMENT

LESSON 8

WHY TEACH THIS LESSON?

Some Christians bristle at the mention of a "commandment." They believe the New Covenant eliminates the need for obeying commandments because it is a covenant of grace, not law. But it was Jesus who said, "If you love me, you will obey what I command" (John 14:15). The "great commandment," as our lesson title calls it, is also echoed by our Lord. When asked about the greatest commandment, he gave two: "Love the Lord your God with all your heart and with all your soul and with all your mind" and "Love your neighbor as yourself" (Matthew 22:37, 39). The first is clearly from our lesson text, Deuteronomy 6:4, 5. While it is true that the New Covenant is about salvation by grace, it is not true that it has eliminated the need for obedience. As you emphasize loving the Lord in this lesson, you will do well to point out the importance of obedience in that pursuit.

INTRODUCTION

For years the western world has attempted to live by the system of government known as democracy (rule of the people) rather than monarchy (one-man rule). One-man rule is deemed unsatisfactory because the person in power too often becomes greedy and corrupt. In 1215 the English barons forced King John to approve the Magna Carta, which limited the king's power and protected the rights of the barons. Later developments limited the power of the monarch even more, and protected the rights of common people as well as barons.

When the United States came into being near the end of the eighteenth century, its people were determined to be their own rulers. They devised a Constitution for that purpose, and then added ten amendments to protect the rights of the people even more from despotic government. In this new country every man had a part in ruling; it was the very opposite of one-man rule. Through more than two hundred years that nation has been, for the most part, successful; but we all know that its success has been marred many times because ruling commoners can become as corrupt and greedy as ruling kings.

A. ISRAEL'S GOVERNMENT

When Israel came out of Egypt to begin its life as a nation, its government was neither one-man rule nor government by the people. It was one-God rule. The Lord gave the laws; the duty of the people was to obey. History shows both the strength and the weakness of such a nation. Its strength lay in God. His wisdom was flawless. The nation prospered whenever the people obeyed the laws he made. Its weakness lay in the people. Often they did not obey, and poverty and disaster were the result.

It seems that no form of government can work very well without good people.

B. LESSON BACKGROUND

After living for forty years in the desert, the people of Israel came toward the border of the promised land. This was the second time they had approached this good land, for they had failed in their first opportunity to take possession of it.

DEVOTIONAL READING:
DEUTERONOMY 30:11-20

BACKGROUND SCRIPTURE:
DEUTERONOMY 6

PRINTED TEXT:
DEUTERONOMY 6:1-9, 20-25

LESSON AIMS

After completing this lesson students should be able to:

1. Memorize the "great commandment" as found in Deuteronomy 6:4, 5.

2. Tell how the principles for teaching God's Word that are found in today's text apply to modern life.

3. Suggest a plan by which God's will can be communicated more effectively within their homes and to other family members.

Oct 24

KEY VERSE

Hear, O Israel: The LORD our God, the LORD is one. Love the LORD your God with all your heart and with all your soul and with all your strength.
—Deuteronomy 6:4, 5

LESSON 8 NOTES

They camped east of the Jordan River, where Moses talked with them for a lengthy period of time. Last week we considered his brief review of their life in the desert and of God's instructions to them when it was time for them to resume their journey toward Canaan. Today we come to a bit of what he said about the law and about the people's responsibility to keep it and to pass it on to their children. Such teaching was essential if the promised land was to remain their home.

I. ISRAEL AND GOD'S LAW (DEUTERONOMY 6:1-9)

The book of the Bible from which we are reading is called Deuteronomy. That title means "second law" or "repeated law." Chapter 5 tells us that Moses repeated the Ten Commandments, which we studied last month from Exodus 20. Deuteronomy 5 also records that Moses urged the people to obey God's commandments. Chapter 6 continues that exhortation and also encourages the people to think about the obedience of the next generation as well as the present one.

A. RESULTS OF OBEDIENCE (vv. 1-3)

1. These are the commands, decrees and laws the LORD your God directed me to teach you to observe in the land that you are crossing the Jordan to possess.

At Mount Sinai the people had been terrified by the awesome signs of God's presence on the mountain. They had begged that God would not speak to them directly, but would let Moses relay his *commands*. So the Lord had given the rest of his *laws* through Moses (Deuteronomy 5:22-31). Now, some forty years later, Moses was repeating those laws. Some of his hearers had been children when the laws first were given; others had been born later.

2. So that you, your children and their children after them may fear the LORD your God as long as you live by keeping all his decrees and commands that I give you, and so that you may enjoy long life.

Why did God order Moses to give those laws to the people? Three reasons are given: first, so they would *fear the Lord*; second, so they would *keep* (obey) the laws, not only in that generation, but in all generations to come; and third, so their lives would be *long*. God's laws prescribed a healthful and righteous way of living, and that would result in longer life. Long life is specifically tied to the command to honor one's father and mother (Deuteronomy 5:16).

3. Hear, O Israel, and be careful to obey so that it may go well with you and that you may increase greatly in a land flowing with milk and honey, just as the LORD, the God of your fathers, promised you.

Fervently Moses urged his people to obey God's laws, and he continued to relate the beneficial results of obedience. It would *go well* with obedient people: they would have peace, prosperity, good health, and long life. They would *increase greatly* in numbers, in wealth, and in power. The promised land was before the Israelites—*a land flowing with milk and honey*; but it would withhold its plenty if the people were disobedient.

B. LOVING GOD AND HIS LAWS (vv. 4-6)

4. Hear, O Israel: The LORD our God, the LORD is one.

The word *is* in this verse is not found in the original Hebrew; it is inserted by the translators. Hebrew writers often left out the linking verb *is* or *are*. In most cases the meaning is easily understood without it. For example, when a child just learning to talk says, "Milk good," we know he means, "Milk *is* good." But sometimes a different meaning is found by inserting *is* in a different place. In addition to the reading found in the text, the *NIV* lists three other possible translations of the second part of verse 4:

HOW TO SAY IT

Deuteronomy. Due-ter-AHN-uh-me.

Egyptians. Ee-JIP-shuns.

phylacteries. fih-LACK-ter-eez.

The Lord our God is one Lord.
The Lord is our God, the Lord is one.
The Lord is our God, the Lord alone.

Each of these statements is true, and each is appropriate in this context; so which one did Moses have in mind? Perhaps all of them! Remember, the linking verb was not left out accidentally, as if by a child. Moses wrote with full understanding of the dynamics of the Hebrew language. The omission of the linking verb allows a fuller meaning than if we try to insert the verb and limit the meaning to that conveyed by one English construction. Surely all believers will agree with the truths expressed in all of these statements: the Lord is Israel's God, he is one God, and he is the only God.

5. Love the LORD your God with all your heart and with all your soul and with all your strength.

Since there is only one God, his people should give him their total devotion. They should *love* him, and love him with all that is in them. It is not that *heart* and *soul* and *strength* describe separate parts of an individual; rather, all of them together designate the whole person, and *all* of all of them are devoted to the Lord. When this is true, serving the Lord is a joy rather than a burden; obeying his commands is a happy choice rather than a dismal duty.

6. These commandments that I give you today are to be upon your hearts.

Moses' voice was speaking *these commandments*, but they were the Lord's commandments (v. 1). When the Lord occupies one's whole heart, the Lord's words are there with him. One wholly devoted to the Lord finds delight in hearing them, learning them, and obeying them.

C. TEACHING GOD'S LAWS (vv. 7-9)

7. Impress them on your children. Talk about them when you sit at home and when you walk along the road, when you lie down and when you get up.

Everyone who has *children* should give careful attention to this verse. It says much about how to teach God's Word. Such teaching cannot be limited to a few minutes of family devotion, or to a daily half hour of Bible study. It cannot be left to the Sunday school. Even a Christian day school cannot take the place of the parents' teaching. Consider the various "classrooms" described in this verse:

The first is *when you sit at home.* How many of the children's quarrels can be resolved by a careful application of "You shall not covet" (Exodus 20:17) or "Love your neighbor as yourself" (Leviticus 19:18)?

The second is *when you walk along the road.* A roadside tavern may provide an opportunity to teach what God says about the evils of drunkenness. Or if the child recognizes a friend's bicycle parked several houses away from where it belongs, that is a good time to teach a child that God does not endorse the "finders keepers" philosophy, but says we must return the lost property to its owner (cf. Exodus 23:4).

When you lie down at night is a good time to recall any laws that have been broken by children or parents, and to ask forgiveness.

When you get up is a good time to sing, "This is the day the Lord has made; let us rejoice and be glad in it" (Psalm 118:24). That was first sung long after Moses' time, but it has been adapted to a happy chorus in our time and our language. Do you ever sing it in the morning before going to work?

THE TRAGEDY OF NEGLECT

Tragic stories began to come out of Eastern Europe soon after the breakup of the Soviet Union. Tales of government abuse, corruption, and malfeasance in office

WHAT DO YOU THINK?

Like the Jews, we Christians stand firmly for the doctrine of one God. We, too, seek to love him with all our heart, soul, and strength. (See also Matthew 22:34-38.) How would you respond if a visitor to your home challenged your worship of Jesus as a violation of this command in Deuteronomy 6?

These commandments that I give you today are to be upon your hearts. Impress them on your children. Talk about them when you sit at home and when you walk along the road, when you lie down and when you get up.

Deuteronomy 6:6,7,a

Today's visual illustrates the important practice of teaching God's Word to our children. Discuss creative ways parents can do this.

told us how hypocritical were the claims that Marxist Communism was the means to creating a "workers' paradise."

There were perhaps no more heart-rending stories than those that told of children in the state-run nurseries of Communist Romania. Children in these nurseries showed abnormally high levels of stress hormones and demonstrated terrible physical and mental retardation.

Such a scenario is not surprising. Even laboratory experiments with animals have shown us that separation of babies from their mothers and neglect by their caregivers causes an abnormal number of their brain cells to "commit suicide," in the chilling words of one science commentator. The lifelong effect is seen in serious behavior problems, apathetic spirits, learning difficulties, and patterns of chronic illness.

God, of course, knew the effects of parental neglect when he told the Israelites to give special attention to their children, especially when it came to teaching them the laws of God. Parental failure to attend to a child in his or her spiritual development can have even more tragic effects than physical deprivation.   —C. R. B.

8. Tie them as symbols on your hands and bind them on your foreheads.

Pious Jews of later times took this literally, putting short passages of Scripture in small leather cases tied to their *hands* and *foreheads*. These "phylacteries" (cf. Matthew 23:5) may have been better reminders than strings tied on fingers, but surely the Lord's real intent is that his laws should guide all the doing of the hands and all the thinking of the head.

9. Write them on the doorframes of your houses and on your gates.

This too was taken literally in later times. Even today some homes have on the doorposts small leather or metal cases with Scripture verses inside. These too may be useful reminders, but again the figurative meaning is greater: in the morning go out your door to be honest and generous in all your dealings, as God's law demands; in the evening come in to kind and loving family relationships.

II. FOR ALL GENERATIONS (DEUTERONOMY 6:20-25)

The laws that Moses was repeating were not only for the people who heard him; they were for all the coming generations of Israelites.

A. FUTURE QUESTION (v. 20)

20. In the future, when your son asks you, "What is the meaning of the stipulations, decrees and laws the LORD our God has commanded you?"

In the future looks to the time when Israel would be settled in its new home. It speaks of the continual need for faithful parental training. The fact that the child is the one who initiates this conversation about spiritual matters implies that the parents have been diligent in making such matters a priority. They have created a desire in their children to know more.

B. GOD'S MIGHTY ACTS (vv. 21-23)

21. Tell him: "We were slaves of Pharaoh in Egypt, but the LORD brought us out of Egypt with a mighty hand.

The parent's answer should begin with a lesson in history. *The Lord* had rescued the people of Israel from slavery *in Egypt* and had led them to freedom. *A mighty hand* describes his tremendous power in action—power enough to overwhelm great Egypt, and power enough to open a path through the sea. Parents could fill in those details and more for inquiring children.

22. "Before our eyes the LORD sent miraculous signs and wonders—great and terrible—upon Egypt and Pharaoh and his whole household.

WHAT DO YOU THINK?

We do not literally write Bible verses on our hands and foreheads. But what are some practical ways in which we can keep portions of God's Word with us? Why is this important?

WHAT DO YOU THINK?

We do not write Bible verses on the doors or walls of our homes, but what are some practical ways in which we can keep God's Word before us in our homes?

WHAT DO YOU THINK?

Lessons from Israel's history were to be an important aspect of teaching in Jewish homes. How important do you think it is to teach biblical and secular history in Christian homes?

Again the parents could supply details, describing the ten plagues that had driven *Egypt and Pharaoh* to surrender. Only God could do such *miraculous signs and wonders.*

23. "But he brought us out from there to bring us in and give us the land that he promised on oath to our forefathers.

The Lord not only brought Israel *out from* slavery to freedom; he also brought them *in* to a marvelously fruitful *land* that could supply all their needs. From all these facts it was evident that Israel was greatly indebted to the Lord.

C. GOD'S RIGHTEOUS LAWS (vv. 24, 25)

24. "The LORD commanded us to obey all these decrees and to fear the LORD our God, so that we might always prosper and be kept alive, as is the case today.

These decrees came from *the Lord*—the One to whom Israel was deeply indebted. Simple gratitude should motivate every Israelite to *obey*. If that were not enough, God's people ought to *fear* him and be afraid to disobey. They knew about the plagues that had afflicted the disobedient Egyptians (Exodus 7:14—11:10). Surely they did not want to experience such affliction.

Another truth that should never be forgotten is expressed here: fearing and obeying God is *always* for our benefit. God's obedient people are the ones he keeps *alive*. That had been vividly illustrated in the sight of those who were listening to Moses. More than six hundred thousand men of Israel had been disobedient thirty-eight years earlier, refusing to enter the promised land (Deuteronomy 1:19-40), and all those disobedient men had died. Their sons and daughters stood at the border of the promised land. Couldn't they see how important it was to obey God and to teach all future generations to obey him?

KEEPING A MEMORY ALIVE

During the 1950s James Dean was a popular film star. He was also a rebellious idol of many teenagers. Dean was only twenty-four years old when he died tragically in 1955. He was driving his Porsche sports car north from Los Angeles to Salinas, California, when, at about the halfway point of his trip, another car turned left into his path. Dean died instantly in the collision.

Three days after Dean's death, Warner Brothers released "Rebel Without a Cause"—a film in which he had starred—and a rather peculiar fascination with James Dean resulted. Even today, more than four decades later, Dean's memory is renewed annually when his fans trace the route Dean took the day he died. On the anniversary of his death, participants in the "Rebel Run" drive old cars from the 1950s and stop for a few moments at the places where Dean stopped on that fateful day: a gas station, a snack bar, and a country store. Their drive ends at the corner where Dean's life ended.

Much less bizarre (and far more useful) is the tradition initiated by the words of our text today. When children of the Israelites would ask why they kept the words of God, they would be told, not of a drive to death, but of an escape to life. God had set their ancestors free from slavery in Egypt, and the laws and customs of their nation were a timeless reminder of God's goodness. The people were to focus on the victorious beginning of their nation, not on the end of a short but rebellious life. —C. R. B.

25. "And if we are careful to obey all this law before the LORD our God, as he has commanded us, that will be our righteousness."

That will be our righteousness. To right-thinking people, this is very persuasive. Obeying God is right, and that is reason enough to do it. It does please God, yes; and it will cause us to "prosper and be kept alive" (v. 24). But even if doing right brings loss or injury, God's people must still do it.

PRAYER

Please help us, Father. There are so many things we have to do! We do love you. We do want the children to know you and to be glad in Your daily presence. We're trying, Father. Please help us. In Jesus' name. Amen.

THOUGHT TO REMEMBER

You cannot teach another about God and his Word until you know God and his Word.

What Do You Think?

Too many people view the Bible as a rule book, full of dos and don'ts designed to restrict their activities and limit their fun. We need to cultivate an appreciation for the Bible as a love letter from God, a communication from the Originator of life and Source of every good and perfect gift.

How can we promote the love of God's Word in the home and the church?

CONCLUSION

Clearly our text presents three great themes: loving God and his Word, obeying God's Word, and teaching God's Word. Adapted to the New Covenant, these are as important to Christians today as they were to the Israelites in Moses' day.

A. Loving God and His Word

This lesson is titled "The Great Commandment." That title focuses our attention on verse 5 of our text: "Love the Lord your God with all your heart and with all your soul and with all your strength." Jesus said, "This is the first and greatest commandment" (Matthew 22:38). To it verse 6 of our text adds, "These commands that I give you today are to be upon your hearts." God's people not only love God; they also love the words he speaks. Through what he does we know of his power, his greatness, and his majesty; through what he says we learn of his will.

When two people fall in love, all of us notice how they like to be together. They make appointments to meet; they part reluctantly. So when we love God and his words, we spend much time with them, and we do it gladly. If your Bible reading is no more than five minutes before breakfast, you reveal that his words have not taken possession of your heart.

B. Obeying God's Word

When people are in love, selfishness fades. Each one wants to please the other. When we love God, we do what he wants us to do. Serving him is not a burden, but a joy (1 John 5:3). If we find obedience distasteful, we need to examine our love.

We build on a solid foundation when we listen to Jesus and do what he says to do (Matthew 7:24-27). James urges, "Do not merely listen to the word, and so deceive yourselves. Do what it says" (James 1:22). When Jesus said that the first and great command is the command to love God, he added that a second and similar command is this: "Love your neighbor as yourself" (Matthew 22:39; Leviticus 19:18). "Whoever loves God must also love his brother" (1 John 4:21). Such love is expressed in helpfulness, and loving helpfulness is part of the path to a blessed eternity (Matthew 25:31-40). This does not mean that we earn Heaven by doing good on earth; but God prepares Heaven for those who love him, and he gives Heaven to those who show their love by their obedience.

C. Teaching God's Word

If you don't teach God's Word to your children, who will? The public school will not, and that means that for the children who go there a large part of the day is closed to Christian teaching. The public school supervisor of the playground may teach something about fair play and sharing, but she is not likely to mention God. Other children on the street will not help your children learn God's Word. Most TV programs will not help. Who will be talking about God's Word "when you sit at home and when you walk along the road, when you lie down and when you get up"?

Most children will never get such constant teaching except from parents and others whom parents thoughtfully provide. If you employ sitters, do you choose those capable of Christian teaching? If your children are in day care, is Christian teaching done there?

Do you search your Christian bookstore for books that will help your children know God? Or what workable plan can you yourself devise to teach God's commands and "impress them on your children"?

Discovery Learning

This page contains an alternate lesson plan emphasizing learning activities. Classes desiring such student involvement will find these suggestions helpful. The next page is a reproducible activity page to further enhance discovery learning.

LEARNING GOALS

As a result of this lesson, your students should be able to:

1. Memorize the "great commandment" as found in Deuteronomy 6:4, 5.

2. Tell how the principles for teaching God's Word that are found in today's text apply to modern life.

3. Suggest a plan by which God's will can be communicated more effectively within their homes and to other family members.

INTO THE LESSON

If there are parents in your class, introduce this lesson on teaching spiritual truths to children by asking, "What do you say when one of your children asks you, 'Mom/Dad, why do we do it this way?'" In the question, "it" could refer to any custom, tradition, or practice.

How many students are willing to admit that they have given one of the following "explanations"?

"Because that's the way we do it."

"Because I say so."

"Don't ask so many questions."

"Because that's the way my parents did it."

"Because this is what our church teaches."

"Just because."

(This activity is in the student book.)

We teach our children by what we do. But it's essential that we explain the reasons behind the things we do and the way we do them. Today's lesson highlights both teaching religious traditions to children and explaining those traditions.

(If there are no parents in your class, ask your students to talk about times when they questioned *their* parents' customs, traditions, and practices.)

INTO THE WORD

Deuteronomy 6:1-3 says that God gave his people a set of laws. Discuss this question: "Why did God give the laws?" (*For the people's good; so they would know what he expected of them, etc.*)

Tell your students to read Deuteronomy 6:1-9, 20-25 and mark each verse with one or more of the following symbols, as explained below:

+ Every verse that talks about teaching God's commandments (vv. 1, 7, 21-25).

= Every verse that talks about obeying God's commandments (vv. 1, 2, 3, 6, 24, 25).

✔ Every verse that talks about fearing God (vv. 2, 24).

♥ Every verse that talks about loving God as the basis for obedience to his commandments (v. 5).

▲ Every verse that talks about parents teaching their children about God's laws (v. 7).

♦ Every verse that talks about parents teaching their children about the meaning of their religious heritage (vv. 20-25).

After the students have done their individual Bible study, read every verse aloud and discuss which category or categories best describe each one.

Option: Explore the promise of "long life" (Deuteronomy 6:2, 3) more closely by using the reproducible activity on the following page.

INTO LIFE

Deuteronomy 6:6-9 focuses on handling the Word of God. Which descriptive phrase below would your students use to describe how they handle the Word?

- Coffee table decoration.
- Paper weight.
- Dust gatherer.
- Trusted friend.
- Well-worn weapon.
- Sunday-morning special.
- Family heirloom.

Divide the class into three-person groups. Tell your students to translate the contexts for teaching God's Word to children in Deuteronomy 6:7 into contemporary settings:

- "When you sit at home."
  (*Example: at the dinner table.*)
- "When you walk along the road."
  (*Example: driving in the car.*)
- "When you lie down."
  (*Example: at bedtime prayers.*)
- "When you get up."
  (*Example: during family devotions.*)

In closing, hand out index cards and ask each student to write out a Bible verse that he or she would like to keep with him or her. Urge your students to post their cards where they will see them frequently until they are able to keep the verses in their minds without the visual reminders.

A Good Life Guarantees a Long Life— or Does It?

According to Deuteronomy 6:2 and 3, keeping God's laws and commandments results in a long and prosperous life. Since many godly people die young, and many other godly people experience financial adversity, this would be a good debating topic. Conduct your own personal debate by choosing one side of this proposition: "Those who live by God's laws live longer and are more successful than those who don't live by God's laws." (The purpose of this "debate" is not to challenge God's Word but to get at the real meaning of the passage.)

A. Write out five facts that support the side of the proposition that you have chosen.

1. _____

2. _____

3. _____

4. _____

5. _____

B. Now take the other side of the proposition, and see if you can come up with five facts that support that side.

1. _____

2. _____

3. _____

4. _____

5. _____

C. After looking at both sides of the issue, what are your conclusions?

_____

_____

_____

_____

A WARNING

LESSON 9

WHY TEACH THIS LESSON?

The Israelites had been through a lot. Chased by the most powerful army on earth, they had been rescued when God parted the Red Sea. Faced with starvation in the wilderness, they were again rescued by the miraculous provision of manna. Confronted with a critical lack of water, they found God faithful to satisfy their needs once more. In desperate times, God had always provided just what they needed. But once they were in the promised land and had rest from their enemies and an abundance of food and water, would they forget about God?

Your students may have experienced some tough times, but nothing like the forty years Israel spent in the wilderness. Their experience is more like that of Israel in the promised land. In fact, the promised land had nothing to compare with the convenience and ease of modern living. Will your students, like Israel on so many occasions, forget that they depend on God? This lesson is a warning to them as much as it is a report on God's warning to Israel.

INTRODUCTION

"The Lord our God, the Lord is one." So we read last week, and we believe it as firmly as the ancient Israelites did. One evidence of God's unity is the universe he created. It, too, is a unit. Its parts fit together marvelously. For example, gravity and centrifugal force are neatly balanced so that the earth circles around the sun. It does not fall into the sun to be burned, nor does it sail away in space to be frozen. Another example is provided by plants and animals. The animals need oxygen. They take it from the air, and give it back laden with carbon—a waste material. The trees take the carbon and use it to build their trunks and branches. They give back the oxygen for reuse by animals.

Though the problem is often overstated, we humans do sometimes disturb the wonderful balance God built into the world. With automobiles and industries we pollute the air with wastes no living thing can use. With other wastes we pollute the river so that it is not fit for drinking or bathing. Worse still, and this problem is usually understated, we pollute human relationships with enmity and strife.

The Bible is the Manufacturer's manual for all our relationships. It tells us to love God with a passion above all passions and to love our neighbors as ourselves. If all of us would follow its instructions, our relationships would be ideal. But we produce pollutants—and our relationships are poisoned. Thus by our own thinking and acting we rob ourselves of the good things God has provided.

A. PROMISES AND WARNINGS

How we love the promises of God! Truly they are "very great and precious" (2 Peter 1:4). Yet all through the Bible God's promises are balanced by his warnings. Thus far, in our lessons for September and October, we have seen a bright promise held before Israel, the promise of a land "flowing with milk and honey." Along with this promise we have seen the frequent warning that this land is for obedient people, not for those who disobey, and there are many more warnings than we have seen in these lessons. For a notable example, read Deuteronomy

DEVOTIONAL READING:
PSALM 85

BACKGROUND SCRIPTURE:
DEUTERONOMY 8

PRINTED TEXT:
DEUTERONOMY 8:6-20

LESSON AIMS

After participating in this lesson, students should be able to:

1. Summarize the warning given to Israel in today's text.

2. List ways in which it is possible for someone to "forget the Lord your God."

3. Begin a practice or routine that will keep them mindful of God's daily blessings and less inclined to forget his goodness.

Oct
31

KEY VERSE

Be careful that you do not forget the LORD your God, failing to observe his commands, his laws and his decrees that I am giving you this day.

—*Deuteronomy 8:11*

28. Verses 1-14 of that chapter detail precious promises for God's obedient people; verses 15-68 give nearly four times as much space to warnings of terrible disaster for those who disobey. This week our text brings us a shorter example of both promise and warning.

B. LESSON BACKGROUND

Deuteronomy 8 begins with a call to obedience—the same call that we have seen again and again in recent lessons. The frequent repetition emphasizes its importance, and we see the call repeated again in the very first verse of our text.

I. PRECIOUS PROMISES (DEUTERONOMY 8:6-10)

A. CALL TO OBEDIENCE (v. 6)

6. Observe the commands of the LORD your God, walking in his ways and revering him.

Obedience to God involves our actions: we must seek to live each day *walking in his ways*. It involves also our attitude, which is described as *revering him*.

B. PROMISES TO THE OBEDIENT (vv. 7-9)

7. For the LORD your God is bringing you into a good land—a land with streams and pools of water, with springs flowing in the valleys and hills.

Some of those listening to Moses had been teenagers when they left Egypt. They remembered a flat country where the Nile River was the primary water source. They also remembered the vast and desolate wilderness where they had wandered for forty difficult years. Now God was leading them to a very different country, a land of *valleys and hills*. They would find many *pools of water* fed by *springs*.

8. . . . a land with wheat and barley, vines and fig trees, pomegranates, olive oil and honey. . . .

Egypt was a fruitful land where it was irrigated. The promised land was no less fruitful, yet it needed no irrigation. *Wheat and barley* would provide bread, and Israel would move into the land just in time to harvest the grain planted by the former inhabitants. Grapes (the produce from *vines*), figs, *pomegranates*, and olives would ripen after the grain harvest. Bees were busy laying up stores of *honey* from the flowers of spring and summer.

9. . . . a land where bread will not be scarce and you will lack nothing; a land where the rocks are iron and you can dig copper out of the hills.

Food supplies would be abundant in the promised land; there would always be enough to eat. The region of Palestine has never been noted for mining, but it did have deposits of *iron* and *copper* in the northern part and in some of the more mountainous terrain east of the Jordan River.

C. CALL TO GRATITUDE (v. 10)

10. When you have eaten and are satisfied, praise the LORD your God for the good land he has given you.

Praise the Lord and thank him, as all people ought to do for the food they eat. Even now some people see no reason to thank God for food grown and processed by human labor. Skeptics like to tell of the preacher who complimented a farmer by saying, "You and the Lord produced a fine crop on that field."

"Yes," the farmer replied, "but you should see that field when the Lord had it all to himself. It was nothing but a weed patch."

The skeptics, however, forget what the field would be like if the farmer had it all to himself. All his work would be useless if the Lord did not provide sunshine, rain, and air. Not even weeds would grow without the Lord.

WHAT DO YOU THINK?

The lesson writer says that obedience to God involves both our actions and our attitudes. In the New Covenant, which do you think is more important—or are they equally important? Explain why you think the way you do.

[cf. Matthew 7:21; Ephesians 2:8-10; James 2:8.]

WHAT DO YOU THINK?

The promises cited in verses 8 and 9 of our text are extremely appealing to those in an agrarian economy. How do you think God might express his love to us in our technological age?

II. SOLEMN WARNINGS (DEUTERONOMY 8:11-20)

Close on the heels of the promises come the warnings. That arrangement is seen often, for that is where the warnings are most needed. Doesn't it seem absurd that the abundance of God's gifts makes people forget the Giver? Yet the history of Israel seems to show exactly that. People in desperate need cried in their misery to the Lord; and when he gave them all they needed and more, they forgot where their relief came from.

A. BEWARE! (v. 11)

11. Be careful that you do not forget the LORD your God, failing to observe his commands, his laws and his decrees that I am giving you this day.

Be careful is a necessary warning in the midst of a description of a bountiful land. When we have all we need and are "satisfied" (v. 10), we are comfortable, relaxed, and at ease. We have time on our hands. If we think of some activity that would be pleasant, we might not stop to think whether it would be right or not. Not maliciously, but carelessly, we ignore the *commands* that God has given.

B. PERIL OF PROSPERITY (vv. 12-17)

12, 13. Otherwise, when you eat and are satisfied, when you build fine houses and settle down, and when your herds and flocks grow large and your silver and gold increase and all you have is multiplied. . . .

These verses picture the prosperity that would be the norm in the promised land. The people would have all the food they could eat and would live in *fine houses*. Their *herds* of cattle and *flocks* of sheep would be constantly increasing. They would have an abundance of *silver* and *gold*. Nothing would be exempt from God's blessing: *all* they had would be *multiplied*.

14. Then your heart will become proud and you will forget the LORD your God, who brought you out of Egypt, out of the land of slavery.

This verse pictures the peril of prosperity. People who have everything are apt to forget how much help they had in getting it and become *proud*. Moses was speaking these words near the end of the forty years Israel had spent in the wilderness. Those who were under forty years of age had never been slaves in *Egypt*. They knew the oppression of that *slavery* only by hearsay. It would be easy to *forget* how deeply they were indebted to the Lord because he had rescued them.

15. He led you through the vast and dreadful desert, that thirsty and waterless land, with its venomous snakes and scorpions. He brought you water out of hard rock.

Rescue from Egypt was only the beginning of God's benefits to this emerging nation. He had also sustained his people for forty years in the *desert*, a desert that is described as *vast and dreadful*. He protected them from poisonous *snakes and scorpions* in the desert. He brought *water out of hard rock* when people and livestock would have died without it.

16. He gave you manna to eat in the desert, something your fathers had never known, to humble and to test you so that in the end it might go well with you.

The *desert* soil provided no food for human travelers, but God provided *manna*. That and all the other helps mentioned in verse 15 kept the people alive. They also yielded a spiritual benefit by serving to *humble* the people. They could see that they were helpless and had to depend on God. Those years of God's provision also served to *test* the people and show whether they would obey God or not.

HOW TO SAY IT

Babylon. BAB-uh-lun.

Deuteronomy. Due-ter-AHN-uh-me.

WHAT DO YOU THINK?

The lesson writer uses the phrase, "the peril of prosperity." How should Christians deal with material prosperity so as to avoid the peril?

[See also Matthew 6:19-21, 33; 19:23-26; Proverbs 30:8, 9.]

WHAT DO YOU THINK?

Moses said that prosperity might cause the Israelites to forget the great things God had done for them. How can we avoid forgetting God and his blessings?

The result of all these blessings was that at *the end* of their journey God would bless them and give them the promised land. There such want as they had known in the desert would never be known again—if they would obey God.

17. You may say to yourself, "My power and the strength of my hands have produced this wealth for me."

The years in the desert had made the people humble, showing them that they needed to depend on God for daily bread to eat, water to drink, and guidance through an unknown land. Now they were about to move into a land where they would have plenty. The scarcity had made them humble; abundance had the potential to produce the opposite effect.

The people themselves would plow the fields, plant the seed, and harvest the grain. And it was they themselves who would lead their sheep to green pastures and refreshing waters. Then they themselves would sell bread and meat to passing caravans and store up the silver and gold from their sales. Thus they might forget that they were still depending on the Lord just as much as they had depended on him for manna in the desert. They could no more produce rain than they could make a spring flow from desert rock. They could no more produce sunshine than they could produce manna from the sky. But in a land of plenty it would be easy to forget that God's hand was responsible for all that they enjoyed, and instead attribute their success to their own *power*.

REWRITING HISTORY

One of the great controversies to come out of World War II was whether the Japanese nation should acknowledge its guilt in starting the war. For understandable reasons, the post-war government of Japan has been reluctant to acknowledge the unpleasant facts of the nation's wartime past.

None of us likes to admit the wrong we have done. But even more is at stake in this case. Japanese culture places great value in "saving face," and to admit to wartime wrongdoing would violate that principle. So, for more than fifty years, the Japanese government censored school textbooks, deleting accurate descriptions of Japan's unprovoked attack on Pearl Harbor and wartime atrocities such as the Nanking massacre during the invasion of China and medical experiments on human guinea pigs. Finally, in 1997, the Japanese Supreme Court settled the issue by ruling that history should not be rewritten. Truth should be known, no matter how embarrassing it might be.

In later years, Israel would be tempted to say, "All the blessings of the promised land have come because of our own strength." In so doing, they would be "rewriting history," and fooling only themselves. The goodness of their land and their right to it came from the gracious hand of the God whom they all too often forgot.

—C. R. B.

C. CALL TO REMEMBRANCE (v. 18)

18. But remember the LORD your God, for it is he who gives you the ability to produce wealth, and so confirms his covenant, which he swore to your forefathers, as it is today.

God was calling his people to be thoughtful, not careless. He was urging them to *remember* him and all the things that he was doing and how much they depended on him. He would do more than they would to produce their success in the promised land. If their efforts resulted in a bountiful harvest, then it would come about because he gave them the *ability* to do what they were doing. How foolish it would be for the people of Israel to forget him and give themselves all the credit for their success! How foolish it is for people today to do the same!

This chart cites some of the things God had done for Israel. Perhaps your class can list some of the things God has done for us.

Visual for lesson 9

WHAT DO YOU THINK?

According to Deuteronomy 8:18, God "gives you the ability to produce wealth." How important do you think it is for people to know that today? How can we keep that truth known?

D. PENALTY TO THE DISOBEDIENT (vv. 19, 20)

19. If you ever forget the LORD your God and follow other gods and worship and bow down to them, I testify against you today that you will surely be destroyed.

Forgetting God was a serious matter—it was a matter of life and death. In the promised land the people of Israel would depend on God for their living just as surely as they had been depending on him in the wilderness. However, in the promised land they would not see his cloud every day and his fire every night. They would not see his manna lying fresh on the ground every morning.

In half a century there would be a new generation of Israelites, who had never seen these more obvious signs of God's presence. People of that new generation would be able to see and hear the loud religious celebrations of the pagan peoples around them. There would be plenty of food, plenty of wine, and plenty of music and dancing. Eager young people of Israel would begin to ask, "Why not join the fun?"

So as they stood at the border of the promised land, God had Moses tell them why not—bluntly and honestly: if you join that kind of "fun," *you will surely be destroyed*!

A "FREEZE-DRIED" GOD

Your faithful dog Rover is a wonderful companion. He greets you happily when you come home after a hard day's work, he barks to warn of strangers approaching the house, and he is a suitable repository for an abundance of "leftovers" and morsels slipped quietly from the family table by his younger "masters" while Mom and Dad aren't looking.

However, as the saying goes, "Every dog has his day"; and when Rover's days are over, then what? A new way has been found to deal with Rover's remains when he can no longer bring happiness to his human "family." A Florida entrepreneur has developed a technique for freeze-drying family pets so that their owners can have a tangible, physical reminder of the joy-filled days and years their pets once brought them. The cost for this service varies from several hundred dollars to a few thousand.

A freeze-dried pet allows you to keep your pet with you without having to feed it, let it outside, bathe it, or otherwise care for it. Of course, the disadvantage is that you don't really have your pet after all.

God warned Israel that they dare not forget him. If they maintained only some distant memories of him, then the land of plenty that he had given them would be lacking in its most important quality: the presence of the true God in their midst. God will not be a "freeze-dried" memory. —C. R. B.

20. Like the nations the LORD destroyed before you, so you will be destroyed for not obeying the LORD your God.

The Lord had judged the pagan *nations* then living in the promised land and determined they were too wicked to live. He was sending the men of Israel to execute his judgment and destroy them (Deuteronomy 7:1, 2).

If the men of Israel did not follow these orders, those pagans remaining would entice them to serve other gods (Deuteronomy 7:4). If Israel gave in to this temptation, it too would be judged and would *be destroyed* (Numbers 33:55, 56).

CONCLUSION

Our upcoming lessons for November will deal with the conquest of the promised land under Joshua. We will see that God's people fought valiantly, and God gave them victory. Israel possessed the land and remained true to the Lord, as long as faithful Joshua was at the helm.

DAILY BIBLE READINGS

Monday, Oct. 25—*Don't Let Prosperity Spoil You (Deuteronomy 8:1-10)*

Tuesday, Oct. 26—*You Are Not Self-made People (Deuteronomy 8:11-20)*

Wednesday, Oct. 27—*You Were a Rebellious People (Deuteronomy 9:6-14)*

Thursday, Oct. 28—*God Listens to Moses on Your Behalf (Deuteronomy 9:15-21)*

Friday, Oct. 29—*Moses Intercedes for Israel Again (Deuteronomy 9:25-29)*

Saturday, Oct. 30—*Beware of False Prophets (Deuteronomy 13:1-5)*

Sunday, Oct. 31—*Purge Those Who Worship False Gods (Deuteronomy 13:6-11)*

A. ISRAEL'S FAILURE

Sadly, Israel failed to destroy all the pagans as God commanded, and the remnant of them did indeed entice the people of Israel (Judges 2:1-3). After Joshua died, many Israelites took up pagan practices, and Israel suffered (Judges 2:11-15). Later the nation was divided, and idol worship became the state religion of the northern part (1 Kings 12:26-30). In due time the north was destroyed (2 Kings 17:5, 6). Paganism influenced the southern kingdom as well, and it grew until Jerusalem was destroyed and its survivors became captives in Babylon for a time (2 Kings 25:8-11).

B. OUR COMMISSION

As Christians we have a commission different from that of Israel in the promised land. They were sent to destroy the pagans; we are sent to convert them. Our task is to make them disciples of Jesus and teach them to obey him (Matthew 28:18-20).

We undertake our commission with the solemn warning of Jesus ringing in our ears. "You are the salt of the earth. But if the salt loses its saltiness, how can it be made salty again? It is no longer good for anything, except to be thrown out and trampled by men" (Matthew 5:13). If we do not keep the true character of Christianity, we can be destroyed as though we were pagans.

We must see our mission as twofold. First, we are to keep ourselves "salty" (pure and holy). Second, we are to make disciples of all nations.

C. SAMPLES OF SALT

Stephen spoke up for Jesus so clearly that Jesus' enemies stoned him to death (Acts 7:54-60). How many of us have been silenced by a snicker?

Christians in Jerusalem were so enthusiastic in praise of Jesus that non-Christian officials drove them out of town. Then they went everywhere preaching the word (Acts 8:1-4). How long has it been since you spoke up for the Lord in the workplace or at a party or at school?

Sitting on padded pews, some of us find it hard to endure a service an hour long. Meanwhile we read of Christians in Asia who walk ten hours and then sit joyfully on the floor for a four-hour meeting. Early Christians met in the temple every day (Acts 2:46), and they didn't have padded pews, either. Is it possible that our grandchildren will see missionaries come from Thailand to our country and find themselves as unwelcome as western missionaries now are in Moslem countries?

Saul combed Jerusalem to find Christians and put them in jail (Acts 8:3). If you were arrested for being a Christian, could the prosecutor find enough evidence to convict you?

The first Christians sold "their possessions and goods" and "gave to anyone as he had need" (Acts 2:45). This year a statistician reported that the average church member contributes two-and-a-half percent of his income to the church and to Christian causes.

The Israelites were warned not to forget God, but to remember all the good things he had done for them. But what about we who know that Jesus died and rose again for us? It seems that though we have so much more for which to praise God, we too have forgotten him and have become less dependent on him. If this were not the case, wouldn't our world be more Christlike? Wouldn't the average church member be giving much more than two-and-a-half percent of his income to Christian work?

What do you think? Is the salt keeping its savor in our country, in our church—in you? What can you personally do to make it saltier?

Discovery Learning

This page contains an alternate lesson plan emphasizing learning activities. Classes desiring such student involvement will find these suggestions helpful. The next page is a reproducible activity page to further enhance discovery learning.

LEARNING GOALS

After this lesson students should be able to:

1. Summarize the warning given to Israel in today's text.

2. List ways in which it is possible for someone to "forget the Lord your God."

3. Begin a practice or routine that will keep them mindful of God's daily blessings and less inclined to forget his goodness.

INTO THE LESSON

Begin by writing PARADISE on the board. Ask the students to say what they think of when they see that word. What images does it call to their minds? What kind of place is a *paradise?*

Observe that the Israelites had been living in a barren and arid region for forty years. Now they were about to enter a land of abundance—"a land flowing with milk and honey" (Exodus 3:8). In comparison to what they had been experiencing for the past forty years, it would seem like a paradise! But the very bounty and prosperity of the land could be hazardous to the Israelites.

INTO THE WORD

Deuteronomy 8:6-20 is filled with warnings. Moses gave these warnings to his people at the threshold of the promised land. They were to remember the warnings when they had conquered and settled in the land.

Divide the class into four groups, and give each group a different Bible-study assignment based on Deuteronomy 8:6-20. Allow about ten minutes; then call for reports from each group.

Group 1: look for descriptions of the promised land. (See verses 7-9.)

Group 2: look for predictions of the Israelites' success and prosperity in the promised land. (See verses 9, 10, 12, 13, and 17.)

Group 3: look for examples of God's goodness to the Israelites. (See verses 14-16.)

Group 4: look for warnings. (See verses 11, 14, 17-20.)

Deuteronomy 8:6-20 presents challenges. Ask the students to identify at least five challenges cited in the passage. Here are some suggestions.

• Verse 6: A challenge to keep the Lord's commandments and to fear him.

• Verse 10: A challenge to thank God for his goodness.

• Verses 11, 14: A challenge to remember the Lord. ("Do not forget" is an intensive way to say, "Remember.")

• Verses 17 and 18: A challenge to give God the credit when things go right.

• Verses 19 and 20: A challenge to learn from the failures of others.

Option: Use the puzzle on the next page to explore additional warnings in the Bible.

INTO LIFE

Write the following open-ended statements on the chalkboard, and ask the students to provide completions:

"When things go wrong, I usually. . . ."

"When things go right, I usually. . . ."

Students probably will complete the first statement with something similar to ". . . ask God for help" and the second statement with something like ". . . take the credit myself." Expand on that point by asking, "When something good happens in your lives, are you more likely to say, 'Look what I did,' or, 'Look what God did'?" Discuss ways to keep the role of God in mind and to be more ready to give him the credit.

Moses warned the Israelites about the hazards of prosperity. Use the following situations to lead a discussion of the danger of prosperity:

• When Jim first became a Christian, he felt totally dependent on the Lord. He spent a lot of time reading the Bible, praying, and asking for help and direction. Now that he is a "mature" believer, Jim doesn't feel the need for an intensive devotional life. What happened?

• Ten years ago George started his own business. In spite of his best efforts, the business failed. Blaming God for letting him down, George became bitter. He finally was able to start another business. This one is a big success, and George is taking all the credit. What happened?

If your students could spend one minute with each person described above, what would they say? What do they think Jesus would say?

In closing, challenge your students to think of ways they can be more mindful of God's blessings and not forget his goodness. Do they need to set aside a special time of Bible reading and meditating on what God has done? Can some of them start a small group that will encourage them in this direction? Encourage them to think of a specific manner in which they can frequently be reminded of God's goodness.

Heeding the Warnings in the Word

The warnings of the Bible are like the old-time signs at unguarded railroad crossings: "STOP, LOOK, AND LISTEN." Whenever we see a warning in the Bible, we need to STOP anything else that we are doing, LOOK carefully at what it says and means, and LISTEN for instruction from the Holy Spirit.

This crossword puzzle is made up of key words from some of the Bible's warnings.

DOWN

1. "Do not _____ up for yourselves treasures on earth" (Matthew 6:19).

3. "Watch out for false _____" (Matthew 7:15).

4. "_____ foolish controversies" (Titus 3:9).

5. "Avoid every _____ of evil" (1 Thessalonians 5:22).

7. "_____ the devil, and he will flee from you" (James 4:7).

8. "Do not _____ the Lord" (Deuteronomy 8:11).

10. "_____ the Lord your God" (Deuteronomy 6:13).

ACROSS

2. "Keep _____, because you do not know on what day your Lord will come" (Matthew 24:42).

4. "Put on the full _____ of God so that you can take your stand against the devil's schemes" (Ephesians 6:11).

6. "Husbands, _____ your wives" (Ephesians 5:25).

7. "_____, for the kingdom of heaven is near" (Matthew 4:17).

8. "Do not put out the Spirit's _____" (1 Thessalonians 5:19).

9. "You shall not misuse the name of the Lord your _____" (Exodus 20:7).

11. "Do not _____, or you too will be judged" (Matthew 7:1).

12. "You shall not _____" (Exodus 20:15).

13. "Do not _____" (Matthew 6:25).

JOSHUA SUCCEEDS MOSES

WHY TEACH THIS LESSON?

This is a lesson on leadership. No one could miss the critical importance of godly leadership in this account of Joshua's succeeding Moses. One of your lesson aims is that your students will be able to "tell why godly leadership is essential to the accomplishment of God's work." But there is a danger in such a lesson that "non-leaders" will dismiss it as not applicable to them. Worse, it may encourage them to become critics, evaluating leaders by their own understanding of what a leader should be and do without doing anything to help.

You will be remiss if you do not point out the similarity in the instructions to Joshua, the new leader, and the people of Israel, the followers. Even "non-leaders" have a responsibility to act with faith and courage. Challenge all your students, leaders and non-leaders alike, to that high standard!

INTRODUCTION

Older Americans can never forget "the Roosevelt Years"—those twelve years when President Franklin Delano Roosevelt was in the news so constantly that headline writers shortened his name to FDR.

Those years began in the midst of the Great Depression and ended during the turmoil of World War II. Opposition to the President was always strong, but his own attitude was always confident. Cartoonists illustrated it by the jaunty upward tilt of his long cigarette holder.

Then FDR died, and America wondered: could anyone take his place? But a "little man from Missouri" stepped in with courage and determination. Harry Truman was not FDR. He was opposed and belittled, but the country still moved forward. The war ended in triumph; the postwar problems were managed with vigor.

It is traumatic to lose a great leader in troubled times. The years that follow test the mettle, not only of the new leader, but also of those who follow. So it was in Israel.

A. THREE LEADERS

The First Leader. The Moses years were difficult years for Israel. They began in the bitter bondage of Egypt and continued in the years of wandering in the wilderness. The people were frequently critical and disobedient, and sometimes openly rebellious; but for forty years the towering figure of Moses dominated the scene. Then Moses died.

The New Leader. Joshua had been Moses' helper during Moses' forty years of leadership and had proved himself quite capable. Moses had designated him as the next leader. Best of all, the Lord had chosen him for this responsibility. So Joshua assumed this role and did so at a critical time. The people stood at the border of the promised land. It was time to invade—the very point at which Israel had failed before. Would they repeat the mistakes of the past?

The Real Leader. The answer to this question depended on whether Israel would acknowledge its real leader. This, of course, was the Lord. Moses had led well because the Lord had been with him. Now the Lord would be with Joshua.

DEVOTIONAL READING:
NUMBERS 27:12-23
BACKGROUND SCRIPTURE:
DEUTERONOMY 31:1-8; 34
PRINTED TEXT:
DEUTERONOMY 31:1-8; 34:5-9

LESSON AIMS

After this lesson, students should be able to:

1. Describe the transfer of leadership in Israel from Moses to Joshua, according to today's text.

2. Tell why godly leadership is essential to the accomplishment of God's work.

3. Express their appreciation for Jesus' leadership in their lives, and for the leadership of someone in their church.

NOV
7

KEY VERSE

The LORD himself goes before you and will be with you; he will never leave you nor forsake you. Do not be afraid; do not be discouraged. —Deuteronomy 31:8

LESSON 10 NOTES

The Lord would open a way through a flooded Jordan, reduce the walls of Jericho to rubble, and give victory in battle after battle. So Moses encouraged both the people and Joshua to trust the Lord and be strong.

B. LESSON BACKGROUND

This is the fourth lesson that we have taken from Moses' lengthy talk to his people as they stood for the second time at the border of the promised land. He has reviewed the law that God gave the people, their failure to take possession of the promised land at the first opportunity, and their years of wandering in the desert. All of this serves as background for today's lesson. At this point, we are nearing the end of Moses' dramatic speech and nearing the end of his life. What will he say now?

I. ENCOURAGEMENT FOR ISRAEL (DEUTERONOMY 31:1-6)

A. MOSES' LEADERSHIP ENDS (vv. 1, 2)

1. Then Moses went out and spoke these words to all Israel.

All Israel had failed before; *all Israel* must now succeed. So *Moses* gave his word of encouragement to all the people.

2. "I am now a hundred and twenty years old and I am no longer able to lead you. The LORD has said to me, 'You shall not cross the Jordan.'

Moses' life can be divided into three forty-year segments. The first forty years were spent in Egypt. Then he killed an Egyptian and was forced to flee Egypt to save his life. For the next forty years Moses worked as a shepherd in Midian. That period of Moses' life ended abruptly when God called him from out of the burning bush. Over the final forty years Moses led the Israelites out of Egypt's bondage and during their wandering in the desert.

Now he would *lead* no more. The Lord had told him his task was done. Israel must now *cross the Jordan*, but Moses was not to go. This part of the message was not encouraging at all; it was frightening. Israel was losing its leader. Could anyone take his place?

B. GOD'S LEADERSHIP CONTINUES (v. 3a)

3a. "The LORD your God himself will cross over ahead of you. He will destroy these nations before you, and you will take possession of their land.

Who had been Israel's real leader for the past forty years? Not Moses, but *the Lord*. In forty years he had never failed his followers, and he would continue to guide them. How could courage falter under such leadership?

C. JOSHUA'S LEADERSHIP BEGINS (v. 3b)

3b. "Joshua also will cross over ahead of you, as the LORD said.

Often repeated is the story of a small boy who was afraid of the dark at bedtime. He wanted Dad to stay with him.

"Oh, you don't need me," Dad assured him. "God is right here with you."

"I know," the trembling lad replied, "but I need somebody with skin on."

Even with God leading them through the perils beyond the Jordan, the people of Israel needed someone with skin on—a human leader like Moses and like themselves, who would set before them a visible example of fearless faith in action. *Joshua* was to be that leader. *The Lord* had chosen him for that responsibility.

D. PROMISE OF VICTORY (vv. 4, 5)

4. "And the LORD will do to them what he did to Sihon and Og, the kings of the Amorites, whom he destroyed along with their land.

WHAT DO YOU THINK?

Moses knew when to step down as Israel's leader because the Lord told him. In addition, Moses cited his age as a reason for "retiring" from leadership. How can we today know when we ought to give up a position of leadership and let another take up the reins? How much, if any, is age a factor? Why?

The map on the visual for lesson 2 includes the entrance into Canaan (the conquest) as well as the exodus. Refer to that visual as you discuss the great task that lay ahead of Joshua and the Israelites.

Sihon and *Og* were *kings of the Amorites* who had lived in the territory east of the Jordan, the very country where Israel now was camping. Those kings had refused to let Israel pass through their country in peace. But God had *destroyed* these two kings and their armies. He had done that by means of the hands and swords of Israel, but the victories had been so decisive that Israel knew they were from God (Deuteronomy 2:26—3:11). That *land* east of the Jordan was now safely in the possession of Israel. Moses promised that in the same way, God would destroy the hostile peoples west of the Jordan and give their land to Israel.

5. "The LORD will *deliver them to you, and you must do to them all that I have commanded you.*

The Lord will deliver them to you. This repeats the assurance of verse 4. The Lord would hand the enemy peoples over to Israel, who was to "destroy them totally" (Deuteronomy 7:1, 2). God was determined to wipe out the peoples in Canaan because of their wickedness, and Israel was the instrument in his hand to do it.

E. CALL TO COURAGE (v. 6)

6. "Be strong and courageous. Do not be afraid or terrified because of them, for the LORD your God goes with you; he will never leave you nor forsake you."

The encouragement to Israel ended with yet another assurance: the Lord would go *with* his people. Therefore, victory was sure if the men of Israel would do their part. Their part was to *be strong and courageous.* They must approach the task at hand vigorously and fearlessly, confident of victory. If they would do that, they would not fail. The Lord promised it.

II. ENCOURAGEMENT FOR JOSHUA (DEUTERONOMY 31:7, 8)

As the newly appointed leader of the people, Joshua's weight of responsibility exceeded all others'. Moses had a special word of encouragement for him, and of course that word came from the Lord.

A. MOSES' CHALLENGE (v. 7a)

7a. Then Moses summoned Joshua and said to him in the presence of all Israel, "Be strong and courageous.*

The challenge to *Joshua* was similar to that given to the people: *Be strong and courageous.* Later God himself would repeat this command to Joshua (Joshua 1:6, 7, 9). Joshua carried a load vastly greater than anyone else, and he was to carry it no less bravely and vigorously. Moses did not take Joshua aside for private instruction; he sounded this call *in the presence of all Israel.* Thus all the people would see that their commander was one of them, even as he was set apart from them.

B. WORDS OF ASSURANCE (v. 7b)

7b. "For you must go with this people into the land that the LORD swore to their forefathers to give them, and you must divide it among them as their inheritance.*

You must divide it among them as their inheritance. Joshua's responsibility was great, and his task was difficult; but his effort would be crowned with success. Such assurance must have lifted his spirits. And before giving that assurance, Moses stated the basis of it: *the Lord* long before *swore* to give the promised *land* to Israel. Having received an assurance so soundly based, how could Joshua fail to be fearless?

C. GOD'S PROMISE (v. 8)

8. "The LORD himself goes before you and will be with you; he will never leave you nor forsake you. Do not be afraid; do not be discouraged."

WHAT DO YOU THINK?

Many believers are easily discouraged by current events. Declining morality, public scandals, and unjust court decisions, as well as specific cases of rejection or ridicule, are just a few of the problems that we face. How important do you think it is to exhort believers to "be strong and courageous"? Why?

[Perhaps you'll want the class to look up such New Testament promises as those found in Matthew 18:20; 28:18-20; Ephesians 3:14-21; Philippians 2:12, 13; Colossians 1:27; Hebrews 13:5, 6; 1 John 4:4.]

WHAT DO YOU THINK?

Joshua, as the new leader, was especially challenged to "be strong and courageous." What are some ways we can encourage Christian leaders today?

What Do You Think?

Moses knew he would not reach the goal of the Israelites' forty-year trek in the wilderness—even as a whole generation of his followers had not. He might well have been discouraged, but still he was the one who encouraged the others. How might you use Moses' example to encourage a leader who is discouraged about the lack of results he sees in his work?

At the climax of this word of assurance came the comforting promise of God's presence. He is *the Lord*—the invincible, the unconquerable, the Almighty—and he *will be with you!* Not only that, but also he *goes before you.* He leads the way; he bears the brunt of the battle. So *do not be afraid; do not be discouraged!*

Encouragement Needed

An "ultra-race" is what people call the annual 135-mile run/walk from Death Valley, California, to Mount Whitney. It starts at "Badwater," 282 feet below sea level—the lowest spot in North America. The race ends at Whitney Portals, 8,300 feet up the side of the mountain. In between are several mountain ranges that must be crossed. The race must be run in less than sixty hours of physical and emotional torture in temperatures as high as 118 degrees.

Family and friends drive alongside the runners to shout encouragement and to provide support for their physical and emotional needs. Runners have to deal with heat exhaustion, chills, dehydration, muscle cramps, abdominal distress, and hallucinations—and all for a first prize of five hundred dollars!

What did Joshua feel as he faced the battle for the promised land? He did not know the details of what lay ahead, but certainly Moses knew something of the rigorous self-control and the leadership abilities that the task ahead required. So Moses stood beside Joshua in the sight of the entire nation and offered him encouragement, assured him of God's presence, and challenged him to faithfulness. Apparently Moses' actions and words had an impact: Joshua successfully led the people into the promised land.

The question each of us should ask himself is: "Whom do I know who could use my support and encouragement today?"   —C. R. B.

III. CHANGE OF LEADERS (DEUTERONOMY 34:5-9)

For some time we have been reading parts of Moses' speech to the people of Israel as they were camping on the east side of the Jordan River. He finished that message with a poetic blessing on the twelve tribes of Israel (Deuteronomy 33). Then he took leave of his people for the last time and climbed alone to a high peak (Mount Nebo) in the land of Moab. From there he could see a wide sweep of the promised land that he was not to enter (Deuteronomy 34:1-4).

A. Death of Moses (vv. 5-7)

5. And Moses the servant of the Lord died there in Moab, as the Lord had said.

Through forty troubled years, Moses had been a faithful *servant of the Lord.* Almost all the men of Israel had rebelled against God, and had been condemned to die in the desert instead of living in the promised land (Deuteronomy 1:19-40). Moses had not shared in that rebellion; however, even his service had not been perfect. Once when thirsty Israel was clamoring for water, the Lord said to Moses, "Speak to that rock before their eyes and it will pour out its water" (Numbers 20:8). Instead of speaking to the rock, Moses struck it with his rod. Instead of saying, "God will give you water," he said, "Listen, you rebels, must we bring you water out of this rock?" (Numbers 20:10, 11).

Because he did not give God the glory, Moses too was sentenced to die in the desert instead of living in the promised land (Numbers 20:12; Deuteronomy 32:48-52). Thus we read in the verse before us that *Moses . . . died . . . as the Lord had said.* Aaron shared in Moses' guilt, and he died before Moses did (Numbers 20:22-29).

6. He buried him in Moab, in the valley opposite Beth Peor, but to this day no one knows where his grave is.

How to Say It

Amorites. AM-uh-rites.
Beth Peor. Beth PEA-or.
Canaan. KAY-nun.
Deuteronomy. Due-ter-AHN-uh-me.
Jericho. JAIR-ih-ko.
Midian. MID-ee-un.
Moab. MO-ab.
Nebo. NEE-bo.
Sihon. SIGH-hun.

The Lord *buried* Moses *in Moab, in the valley opposite Beth Peor.* Since we do not know the location of Beth Peor with certainty, even now it is true that *to this day no one knows where his grave is.* The Lord himself officiated at Moses' funeral. What an honor!

7. *Moses was a hundred and twenty years old when he died, yet his eyes were not weak nor his strength gone.*

Moses was strong enough to climb the mountain, perhaps the highest one in the vicinity. His *eyes* were good enough to look far across the Jordan, over the length and breadth of the promised land (vv. 1-3). He was not worn out at the age of *a hundred and twenty*; he was strong and active. He died because he had taken to himself and Aaron the credit that belonged to God. Therefore he was not allowed to enjoy the land toward which he had led his people so long and so well.

Although Moses' body lay in an unmarked grave, we can be certain that Moses himself soared from the mountains of Moab to the heights of Heaven, not to be seen again on earth until he would appear to talk about the death of a greater One, the Lord Jesus (Luke 9:28-31). That greater One also came on a mission that would not be completed until after his death.

B. MONTH OF MOURNING (v. 8)

8. *The Israelites grieved for Moses in the plains of Moab thirty days, until the time of weeping and mourning was over.*

Amid the hurried pace of our modern world, we do not take this much time for *mourning,* not even for a popular national hero. Most likely *the Israelites* continued such daily activities as gathering manna and leading their flocks to pasture, but they did delay their advance into the promised land *until the time of weeping and mourning was over.*

HONORING A "LIVING MEMORY"

Jeanne Calment died at 122 years of age on August 5, 1997. She survived all her relatives, including her only grandson. The oldest person in the world at the time of her death, she was an unusually robust individual in spite of her age. At 85 she began taking fencing lessons. At 120 she gave up sweets "for her health." At 121 she released a compact disc with her reminiscences accompanied by music.

Jeanne Calment's passing was mourned by the entire city of Arles, France, where she had lived. The deputy mayor of Arles said, "She was the living memory of our city. Her birthdays were a sort of family holiday."

Moses' death was followed by thirty days of mourning in Israel. Strong and vigorous to the end, Moses had been Israel's personal contact with their amazing past—the "living memory" of the nation. Joshua gave the best testimony to Moses' outstanding leadership by following his faithful example.

How do we best honor the "living memory" of God's dedicated servants? By imitating their faithfulness.   —C. R. B.

C. NEW LEADER (v. 9)

9. *Now Joshua son of Nun was filled with the spirit of wisdom because Moses had laid his hands on him. So the Israelites listened to him and did what the LORD had commanded Moses.*

Joshua was fully prepared and duly commissioned to take the place of leadership that had belonged to Moses. *Moses had laid his hands on him,* indicating that he was passing on the *spirit of wisdom* that God had given to him. Since the Hebrew language has no system of capitalization, we cannot know if the word *spirit* should be capitalized. Whether it is or not, the verse makes clear that Joshua's wisdom came from the Lord. *The Israelites* understood this, so they *listened* to Joshua and obeyed

WHAT DO YOU THINK?

Suppose one of the Israelites had complained that Joshua just wasn't the leader Moses had been. If you had been there, how would you have responded? What if one of them had said, "Joshua is pushing ninety himself—we need a younger leader for this young nation"?

Discuss how you can give new leaders a fair chance in their new roles.

PRAYER

O Father, how poorly we have been following you! How we need your mercy and grace! Forgive us, we pray. We do want to do better this week. In our Master's name. Amen.

THOUGHT TO REMEMBER

Follow the Leader.

DAILY BIBLE READINGS

Monday, Nov. 1—God Will Lead Israel Across Jordan (Deuteronomy 31:1-6)

Tuesday, Nov. 2—Read and Obey the Law (Deuteronomy 31:7-13)

Wednesday, Nov. 3—Joshua Is Commissioned to Succeed Moses (Deuteronomy 31:14-23)

Thursday, Nov. 4—Death of Moses in Moab (Deuteronomy 34:1-7)

Friday, Nov. 5—Moses Is Mourned and Remembered (Deuteronomy 34:8-12)

Saturday, Nov. 6—God's Promise and Command to Joshua (Joshua 1:1-9)

Sunday, Nov. 7—Israel Prepares to Cross the Jordan (Joshua 1:10-16)

him. However, Joshua was only giving the instructions that God had given to Moses long before. The people actually obeyed *the Lord*. In the next two lessons, we will see examples of the wonderful way in which the Lord led them.

CONCLUSION

A. THE REAL LEADER

In previous lessons we have seen Moses leading a nation so disobedient, so rebellious, and so stubborn that it took forty years to make a trip from Egypt to the promised land that should have taken closer to a year and a half. Though it took forty years, Moses did at last bring to the edge of the promised land a nation disciplined, toughened, and courageous enough to take the land. Why was Moses successful? Because, with rare exceptions, he himself was obedient to the real leader—the Lord.

This week we see Joshua stepping into Moses' place of leadership. In the weeks ahead, we shall see Joshua leading his people across the Jordan, capturing Jericho, and sweeping on in victory to make the promised land the Israelites' own. Why were they successful? Because both Joshua and the people were following the real leader—the Lord.

In the promised land the people were secure and prosperous as long as Joshua lived to lead them, and longer. But when the leaders of the invasion died, the next generation of Israelites began to disobey their real leader. Without his protection, the people soon fell prey to their enemies (Judges 2:6-15).

Centuries later, God's people were so disobedient that God delivered them over to the power of Babylon for seventy years. And centuries after that, in a horrible climax of disobedience, the rulers of Israel crucified the Son of God. In so doing, the chief priests declared, "We have no king but Caesar" (John 19:15). They had rejected outright their real leader.

B. FOLLOW THE LEADER

"I will build my church," said Jesus (Matthew 16:18). And he continues to build it. It rests on the foundation of the apostles and prophets who told us of God's will, but Jesus himself is the "chief cornerstone" (Ephesians 2:19, 20).

Today are we following our real leader? How can we follow him better? Two thoughts should be evident.

First, we must listen. Jesus speaks to us through the pages of the New Testament. Some editions print the quoted words of Jesus in red ink so we can identify them at a glance, but we must not think that no other words tell us of Jesus' will. He speaks to us also through the writing of his inspired apostles and prophets: Matthew, Mark, Luke, John, Paul, Peter, James, and Jude. Do you know all these too well to be misled by someone who misrepresents them?

Second, we must "not merely listen to the word," but "do what it says" (James 1:22). Does the word of Christ "dwell in you richly" so that you obey it automatically (Colossians 3:16)? Do you do whatever you do "in the name of the Lord Jesus" (Colossians 3:17)?

Honestly, do you love God with all that is in you (Matthew 22:37, 38)? How have you shown it in the past week?

Do you really love your neighbor as yourself (Matthew 22:39)? How have you shown it?

More than this, do you "love your enemies and pray for those who persecute you" (Matthew 5:44)? Can you think of any recent examples where you have shown that kind of love?

This week, do you want to do more in obedience to our real leader—Jesus?

Discovery Learning

This page contains an alternate lesson plan emphasizing learning activities. Classes desiring such student involvement will find these suggestions helpful. The next page is a reproducible activity page to further enhance discovery learning.

LEARNING GOALS

After this lesson students should be able to:

1. Describe the transfer of leadership in Israel from Moses to Joshua, according to today's text.

2. Tell why godly leadership is essential to the accomplishment of God's work.

3. Express appreciation for Jesus' leadership in their lives, and for the leadership of someone in their church.

INTO THE LESSON

Divide your class into three or four smaller groups. Give each group a newspaper and ask the members to scan the paper for articles featuring dynamic leaders or changes in leadership. (Obviously you will need to have collected newspapers during the days before this class session. The longer you have spent collecting them, the greater will be the variety of story lines.) If you don't have newspapers, ask each group to select a historical leader about whom they are knowledgeable (e.g., George Washington, Alexander the Great, Winston Churchill, a famous sports coach). Ask the groups to discuss among themselves what made these leaders so important.

Allow your students five minutes to work. Then ask a representative from each group to explain either why the featured leader is/was dynamic or what difficulties (if any) the change in leadership caused. What leadership qualities does/did the leader in question possess? What distinguishes this leader from others?

Stress to the class the importance of a good leader. Israel had one: Moses. In today's text we see the mantle of leadership passed to Joshua.

INTO THE WORD

Begin by reading the printed text (Deuteronomy 31:1-8; 34:5-9). Ask your class, "Why was Moses not permitted to enter the promised land?" and "How do you think Moses felt about not completing the task after dedicating forty years of his life to it?" (*For the first question, refer to Numbers 20:8-12; Deuteronomy 32:48-52. The second question is more subjective and should evoke a variety of answers.*)

Ask, "How do you feel when a new leader assumes authority over our country?" (*The answer to this question probably depends on the new leader's "politics," the popularity of the previous leader, the kinds of turmoil the former*

leader caused or calmed, and similar issues.) Ask, "How do you think you would have felt about having someone replace Moses?" After a brief discussion you can probably conclude that most people would feel a bit uneasy. Ask the class to look in the text to find as many promises as they can that God gave Israel to reassure them at this critical time. (*God would go before them; God would destroy the enemy nations; Israel would possess the land; the Lord would not fail them; the Lord would not forsake them.*)

Ask, "How do you suppose Joshua felt? What reasons can you think of that might have left him apprehensive about his new role?" (*Following a popular leader is difficult, even in the best of circumstances. Joshua had not only Moses' "shadow" to think of, but he faced opposition from hostile forces and was leading a group with a history of mutiny.*) Ask the class to list God's promises to Joshua to reassure him. (*Moses reminded him that God had sworn to give Israel the land; Joshua would "divide it among them as their inheritance"; the Lord would go before Joshua; he would be with Joshua, and he would not fail or forsake Joshua.*)

Option: Use the reproducible page that follows to explore Joshua's qualifications for leadership and then to apply those qualifications to leaders today.

INTO LIFE

Give a three-inch-by-five-inch index card to each member of your class. Say, "This lesson reminds us of leaders in our own lives. Often we understand how much responsibility such people carry, but we fail to show them the appreciation they deserve."

Remind your students that Jesus is the foremost authority in their lives, and a model leader at that. Discuss how they could better appreciate Jesus' authority in their own lives (prayer, devotion time, ministry, service).

Second, ask each student to think of a leader he or she respects in the church and write the leader's name on the note card. (No names should be spoken aloud.) Give these instructions: "Think of three ways you can express appreciation this week to the person whose name you have written. Such appreciation can range from verbal acknowledgments to services rendered. Write down the ideas you think of."

Challenge your students to follow through in the tasks they have written. Then close with a prayer of appreciation for the leaders in your church.

Resume of a Godly Leader

In today's text, God reveals to Moses that his plan for him is complete, and that someone else is to lead the Israelites into the promised land. Moses was a trusted leader, and his absence would leave huge sandals to fill. God chose Joshua as Moses' replacement. Why was Joshua such a good choice? Complete Joshua's resume below. Use biblical references and any biblical helps necessary to complete the task.

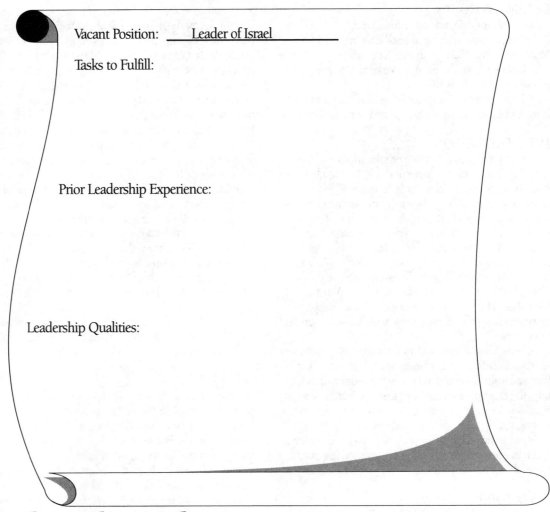

Vacant Position: _____Leader of Israel_____

Tasks to Fulfill:

Prior Leadership Experience:

Leadership Qualities:

Modern-day Joshuas:

Think of a leader in your own church who has helped you in your walk with Christ. Identify three ways in which you can show your appreciation to this leader throughout the week and beyond.

ISRAEL CROSSES THE JORDAN RIVER

LESSON 11

WHY TEACH THIS LESSON?

We can imagine the awe felt by the Israelites as the waters of the Jordan stopped and the riverbed dried up before them. They knew it was God's handiwork, so they felt confidence in his leading. We wonder what the residents of Canaan thought. No doubt there were scouts from Jericho keeping an eye on the vast people camped just across the Jordan from their walled city. They must have seen the Israelites cross the Jordan and reported it hastily to their incredulous superiors. What utter dread must have filled their hearts as they contemplated facing in battle these people who could stop flooded rivers!

But it wasn't the people who could control the river; it was their God—our God. As you teach this lesson, urge your students to worship the great and awesome God who led Israel across the Jordan and who leads us even today!

INTRODUCTION

A. REFLECTIONS ON RAIN

"It never rains in summertime." So says an advertising sign in Tel Aviv, and nearly always it is true in Israel. Once, in the time of Samuel, there was a heavy rain during harvesttime, but everyone knew that it was a miracle (1 Samuel 12:16-18).

Do you remember learning about why such dry summers occur in that part of the world? When warm weather comes, the dry land is warmed much faster than the waters of the Mediterranean Sea. When moisture-laden sea air moves inland, it is warmed and dried by the warm earth, so there is no rain. In winter the same principle works the other way. The land cools faster than the sea. When sea air moves inland, it is cooled by the cool earth. Its moisture condenses into rain or, on some occasions, snow.

B. LESSON BACKGROUND

It appears that the rainy season had ended while the people of Israel were mourning the death of Moses (Deuteronomy 34:8). For weeks after that, the runoff from the tributaries to the north (which included the melting from the snows on higher elevations such as Mount Hermon) continued to pour into the Jordan. Soon the river flowed out of its banks, spreading over the valley floor that is sometimes called the plain of Jordan.

As we have observed in our previous studies from Deuteronomy, the people of Israel were camped on the east side of the Jordan. There appeared to be no way for them to get their families and goods and livestock across the river. They would have to wait for the high waters to recede. But God had other plans, and he revealed them to Joshua, who had taken Moses' place as the leader of Israel. The camp of Israel had been some miles from the river; now it was moved closer (Joshua 3:1). Then came the day when Joshua told the people to prepare

DEVOTIONAL READING:
JOSHUA 4:15-24
BACKGROUND SCRIPTURE:
JOSHUA 3
PRINTED TEXT:
JOSHUA 3:7-17

LESSON AIMS

After this lesson, students should be able to:

1. Summarize the plan by which God led the children of Israel across the Jordan River.

2. Recall times in their lives when God's guidance saw them through difficult circumstances.

3. Suggest a way to "memorialize" these and future occasions so that they will not be forgotten

Nov
14

KEY VERSE

Be strong and courageous. Do not be terrified; do not be discouraged, for the LORD your God will be with you wherever you go.
—Joshua 1:9

for another move. "Tomorrow," he said, "the Lord will do amazing things among you" (Joshua 3:5).

I. GOD'S WORDS (JOSHUA 3:7-13)

Like Moses before him, Joshua was the second in command in Israel. The first in command was the Lord. Joshua gave no order to Israel until he had received an order from God.

A. FOR JOSHUA (v. 7)

7. And the LORD said to Joshua, "Today I will begin to exalt you in the eyes of all Israel, so they may know that I am with you as I was with Moses.

Ultimately the people of Israel owed their allegiance to *the Lord*, not to *Joshua* alone. They would accept Joshua as their leader if they knew the Lord was *with* him. All through the past forty years the Lord had been *with Moses* and had demonstrated that fact in unmistakable ways. For example, at one time there had been a rebellion against Moses. To show that the Lord was on Moses' side, the earth had swallowed the rebels (Numbers 16:1-33).

Now Joshua was beginning his leadership of Israel, and the Lord was about to show how he would be with Joshua just as he had been with Moses. He would do this, not by having rebels destroyed, but by enabling Joshua to foretell a great miracle (v. 13). This miracle would indicate that God was with all the people and would do great things for them (v. 10); Joshua's prediction would demonstrate that God was with Joshua. Thus God would *exalt* Joshua and make him great *in the eyes of all Israel*.

B. FOR THE PRIESTS (v. 8)

8. "Tell the priests who carry the ark of the covenant: 'When you reach the edge of the Jordan's waters, go and stand in the river.'"

The priests who carry the ark of the covenant were to lead the march straight into the flooded river. As they waded into the shallow water at the edge, they were to *stand in the river*. The water would then vanish before them (v. 13). Verse 17 adds that the priests carrying the ark would then go on to the middle of the river and remain standing there until all the people crossed over.

C. FOR THE PEOPLE (vv. 9-13)

9. Joshua said to the Israelites, "Come here and listen to the words of the LORD your God.

Joshua wanted *the Israelites* to *come* as close as they could so that all of them could hear him. He began by declaring that they would *listen to the words of the Lord*, not merely the words of Joshua.

10. "This is how you will know that the living God is among you and that he will certainly drive out before you the Canaanites, Hittites, Hivites, Perizzites, Girgashites, Amorites and Jebusites.

Seven warlike peoples lived in the country west of the Jordan—the land that the Lord had promised to Israel. It would take courage to march into that country—more courage than the fathers of those Israelites had exhibited thirty-eight years earlier. Intimidated by giants and high city walls, that previous generation had balked at the border of the promised land, refusing to capture the land God had given them.

Now, as the new generation of Israelites was gathered before the Jordan, the giants and the high city walls were still present. The seven peoples listed by Joshua were the same ones mentioned by Moses in Deuteronomy 7:1. The coming battle

WHAT DO YOU THINK?

One reason for the miraculous crossing of the Jordan was to give Joshua credibility as the new leader of Israel (to "exalt [him] in the eyes of all Israel"). How does a Christian leader gain credibility today? What do you look for in a leader? Why?

WHAT DO YOU THINK?

It was an encouragement to the nation of Israel to see the ark of the covenant—the symbol of God's presence—going before them. What encourages you in following the Lord? What reassures you that God himself goes before you and with you?

was not one for Israel to undertake alone. They would need *the living God* to be *among* them. Joshua proceeded to give the people a sign to prove that this was so.

11. "See, the ark of the covenant of the Lord of all the earth will go into the Jordan ahead of you.

The *ark of the covenant* was a symbol of God's presence and favor. It held the Ten Commandments engraved on enduring stone—the symbol of God's enduring and unchanging authority. He was leading the way into the flooded *Jordan* and into the battles beyond it. Israel could confidently follow without fear.

12. Now then, choose twelve men from the tribes of Israel, one from each tribe.

What these *twelve men* were to do is not described at this point, but it will be a part of the miracle that is soon to take place. We shall come back to them later in the lesson.

13. "And as soon as the priests who carry the ark of the LORD—the Lord of all the earth—set foot in the Jordan, its waters flowing downstream will be cut off and stand up in a heap."

Now Joshua described the convincing sign promised in verse 10. Soon the *priests* would wade into the *Jordan*, carrying *the ark of the Lord*. At the touch of their feet, the water in front of them would flow on down toward the Dead Sea; but the *waters* upstream would *be cut off and stand up in a heap*, forming a growing mountain of water somewhere to the north. In front of Israel would be a dry riverbed. The people would walk across it without getting their feet wet.

Can you imagine a more convincing proof of the presence and power of the Lord? The similarity of this miracle to the crossing of the Red Sea would assure the people that the Lord who had brought the previous generation safely out of Egypt would bring them safely into the promised land and allow them to possess it.

AGAINST THE "LAWS OF NATURE"

Ann Landers is a famous purveyor of advice on many issues. Occasionally she prints items purportedly taken from the tests and papers of grade-school children. A recent list included the following from some fifth and sixth graders:

- "The law of gravity says no fair jumping up without coming back down."
- "You can listen to thunder and tell how close you came to getting hit. If you don't hear it, you got hit, so never mind."
- "A vibration is a motion that cannot make up its mind which way it wants to go."

These childlike perceptions of how things work in the world are unsophisticated; but like adult hypotheses, they are attempts to apply some sense of regularity to what happens in God's creation. We trust this regularity and call exceptions to it "miracles."

When Joshua prophesied what would happen when the priests stepped into the Jordan River, he was saying, in effect, "You should follow my leading, for God has told me that a miracle will take place. He will make things happen that could not happen except by the power of God. The God who led Moses and your parents across the Red Sea is leading us now." That same God will lead us here and now and into eternity!

—C. R. B.

II. GOD'S ACTIONS (JOSHUA 3:14-17)

A. THE TRUSTING START (vv. 14, 15)

14. So when the people broke camp to cross the Jordan, the priests carrying the ark of the covenant went ahead of them.

Slowly the huge caravan was formed. The *priests carrying the ark of the covenant* led the way. The *people* left their campsite and followed at a respectful distance

HOW TO SAY IT

Adam. Uh-DAHM.

Amorites. AM-uh-rites.

Arabah. AIR-uh-bah.

Canaanites. KAY-nuh-nites.

Cincinnatus. Sin-sih-NAT-us.

Deuteronomy. Due-ter-AHN-uh-me.

Girgashites. GUR-guh-shites.

Hittites. HIT-tites.

Hivites. HI-vites.

Jebusites. JEB-you-sites.

Jericho. JAIR-ih-ko.

Mediterranean. MED-uh-tuh-RAY-nee-un.

Perizzites. PAIR-ih-zites.

Sinai. SIGH-nye or SIGH-nay-eye.

Zarethan. ZAIR-uh-than.

WHAT DO YOU THINK?

When the Israelites obeyed, the Lord made a way for them to cross the flooded Jordan. How can that fact strengthen our faith in the Lord's power to make a way for us through difficult circumstances?

(Joshua 3:4). All Israel *broke camp* and prepared to approach the flooded *Jordan*, though not one of them could possibly wade across it.

15. Now the Jordan is at flood stage all during harvest. Yet as soon as the priests who carried the ark reached the Jordan and their feet touched the water's edge. . . .

This was the crucial moment in the promised sign of God's presence and power. Once the priests' *feet touched the water's edge*, it was time for the miracle to begin (v. 13). The fact that the *Jordan is at flood stage all during harvest* is mentioned to underscore the magnificence of the sign.

B. THE OPENED WAY (v. 16)

16. The water from upstream stopped flowing. It piled up in a heap a great distance away, at a town called Adam in the vicinity of Zarethan, while the water flowing down to the Sea of the Arabah (the Salt Sea) was completely cut off. So the people crossed over opposite Jericho.

What happened was so unusual and marvelous that it was hard to find words to describe it. Some details of the record are not clear, but the main facts are indisputable. The water *from upstream* simply *piled up in a heap*. That heap was upstream from Israel, of course, but it is hard to tell just where. The text describes the place as being *a great distance away, at a town called Adam in the vicinity of Zarethan*.

All of this would be somewhat less confusing if we knew where Adam and Zarethan were, but their exact locations are uncertain. The scene becomes more dramatic if we suppose that the people could see the waters rising swiftly into a mountain north of them, but the record does not make it clear whether the mound was in sight. At the same time, the waters right in front of Israel were *cut off*, or separated, and kept on flowing down toward *the Sea of the Arabah (the Salt Sea)*. (These are two ways of describing the body of water we usually call the Dead Sea. The term *Arabah* describes that part of the Jordan Valley that included the region around the Dead Sea.)

As a result of all of this, in front of the people of Israel was no water at all—only the empty bed of a river! Very easily the people *crossed over* that waterless ground, going straight toward the city of *Jericho*, which was just a few miles west of the river.

C. THE SAFE ARRIVAL (v. 17)

17. The priests who carried the ark of the covenant of the LORD stood firm on dry ground in the middle of the Jordan, while all Israel passed by until the whole nation had completed the crossing on dry ground.

Carrying *the ark of the covenant of the Lord*, the priests proceeded forward until they came to the middle of the dry riverbed. There the priests *stood firm* while *all Israel passed by* and went on to the west bank of the river. The ark was the symbol of God's presence and authority. Positioned there in the middle of the *dry ground*, it pictured God holding back the flooded Jordan while his people crossed to the other side.

When all the Israelites were gathered safely on the high ground west of the river, Joshua called to the priests; and they too walked the rest of the way across. Then the mountain of water came down with a rush, filling the wide channel, covering the banks, and spreading over the plain; but it did not reach the spot that Israel had chosen for a new campground. Read about all of this in Joshua 4:15-18.

What happened to those twelve men mentioned in verse 12 of our text? One of them was from each of the twelve tribes of Israel, remember? Thus they

WHAT DO YOU THINK?

Of course, it was the priests, not the people in general, who had their faith most sorely tested in the crossing of the Jordan. They were the ones who stepped into water—the others saw the waters cut off before they entered the riverbed. And the priests had to stand in the middle of the riverbed while the rest of the people hurried on by. What does this suggest to you about leadership?

formed a committee representing the entire nation, and they had a special job to do. They were to get twelve stones from the middle of the river and carry them to the west bank. There Joshua would build the stones into a monument in memory of the miraculous crossing (Joshua 4:1-7).

Over the course of many generations, that monument would be seen by travelers, including family groups who would eventually go to Jerusalem for the annual feasts. Parents would tell their children of the miraculous crossing, and those children would repeat the story years later to their children. That story would lead to others: the crossing of the Red Sea, the providing of manna in the desert, the miraculous supplying of water from dry rock, and the giving of the Ten Commandments from Sinai. Thus through many centuries this simple monument would help to perpetuate the knowledge of God's power and God's care for his people.

HISTORY REPEATS ITSELF

Some people believe that a spacecraft from outer space crashed near Roswell, New Mexico, in 1947, killing the extraterrestrial aliens aboard. "UFOlogists" refuse to accept the U.S. government's denial that an alien crash took place. In 1997, fifty years later, true believers placed a plaque on a ranch near the supposed site of the crash. It said, "We don't know who they were; we don't know why they came; we only know they changed our view of the universe."

The plaque was put in place as part of a weekend celebration. The owner of the land at the "crash site" charged fifteen dollars per person for a tour of the area. Campsites for the weekend cost ninety dollars. Hundreds of people attended the six-day festival. A comic later remarked, "As in the past, nothing happened, but this time there were more witnesses." In other words, history repeated itself when an alien spaceship didn't crash there this time either!

There was no doubt about what happened when the priests carrying the ark of the covenant stepped into the Jordan River. At the defining moment when Israel became a free people, leaving Egypt behind, the Red Sea had parted and they had walked across on dry land. Now, as God led them to the land they would call their own, history indeed repeated itself and they crossed the Jordan on dry ground.

When God is at work, history is under his control.   —C. R. B.

CONCLUSION

Once they reached the west side of the Jordan, the people of Israel could never forget how they got there. For them the Lord had overcome the flooded river, and for them he could overcome the flood of pagan warriors that awaited them. Buoyed by that faith, the Israelites plunged into that pagan flood and moved on from victory to victory. And through the years that followed, a simple monument of uncut stones by the river told each new generation about God's power and care, and called each new generation to trust and obey him.

A. MEMORIAL MONUMENTS

Since I live in Cincinnati, I have seen beside the Ohio River a statue of Cincinnatus and his plow. It calls to mind that ancient hero who turned his back on fame and fortune and went home to cultivate his farm. To every thoughtful passerby it says that growing food for the hungry can be as noble as leading an army; and to me personally it says that writing Sunday school lessons can be noble too, if I do it well.

In downtown Cincinnati I see another memorial monument. It is a statue of James A. Garfield, a minister of the gospel who became President of the United States. In the course of that service he was assassinated. As I pause to meditate, that silent statue tells me that faithful service to God and man is dearer than life

WHAT DO YOU THINK?

Joshua 4:1-8 tells how the twelve men selected in verse 12 of the text collected stones from the riverbed for a monument to commemorate the crossing of the Jordan. What can we do to fix firmly in our memories those occasions when God's guidance and help have been especially evident?

Today's visual applies our Key Verse (Joshua 1:9) to trials we may face today. Discuss what trials confront your class today. How can you find courage to face them?

PRAYER

How great thou art, our Father and our God! From the day when you created the heavens and the earth to this present day, your power and your goodness have been evident in every generation. Thank you for such a clear testimony, Father, and thank you for our memories. In Jesus' name. Amen.

THOUGHT TO REMEMBER

Lord God of Hosts, be with us yet,
Lest we forget—lest we forget!

itself. That agrees with the words of Jesus: "If anyone would come after me, he must deny himself and take up his cross and follow me" (Matthew 16:24).

Probably your town has a memorial monument, too. When you stop to think, what do you hear it saying?

B. PERSONAL MEMORIES

When I was a child I nearly drowned. I was unconscious under the water when a man rescued me. He laid me on the ground, limp and pale and apparently lifeless. Mouth-to-mouth resuscitation was unknown then, but the Lord restored my breathing.

As a teenager I had typhoid fever and nearly died. But one day the Lord took away the fever, and I am alive today.

When I was middle-aged, I was involved in a terrible crash on the highway. Seeing the mangled remains of my car afterward, people said, "Nobody came out of that one alive!" As a matter of fact, my whole family came out alive. How can that be explained unless the Lord had a hand in it?

Think of your own life. Haven't you seen some wonderful works of God? Don't they compel you to trust God and obey him today, tomorrow, and forever?

C. NATIONAL MEMORIES

The nation of Israel remembered the crossing of the Jordan and other wonderful works that showed God's power and his favor to Israel. With rare exceptions, that memory kept Israel faithful to God through their years of fighting for the promised land, and for years after the fighting was over and the land was won. However, within the next generation the memory grew dim, and national faithfulness began to wane (Judges 2:7-15). In that bit of history lies a warning for every nation.

People in the United States of America pause each year on the fourth day of July to remember how their forefathers declared their independence from Great Britain and then procured it "with a firm reliance on the protection of divine Providence." While they continue to exercise their independence, do U.S. citizens still continue that "firm reliance"?

On the same continent the citizens of Mexico observe a similar day of independence on the sixteenth day of September. But do they remember that "the Most High is sovereign over the kingdoms of men and gives them to anyone he wishes" (Daniel 4:17)?

On the first of July the citizens of the largest country in North America observe Canada Day. They pause to remember and celebrate the consolidation of four separate provinces into one nation. But do the people and the government remember to trust and obey the Lord who "is sovereign over the kingdoms of men"?

During the latter half of the nineteenth century, Great Britain's influence in the world reached its peak. On Queen Victoria's Diamond Jubilee in 1897, Britain's navies gathered to the homeland for a happy celebration. Then, as the great ships steamed away on their worldwide missions, a thoughtful poet, Rudyard Kipling, penned a prayer that is most relevant to our times:

> If, drunk with sight of power, we loose
> Wild tongues that have not Thee in awe—
> Such boasting as the Gentiles use
> Or lesser breeds without the Law—
> Lord God of Hosts, be with us yet,
> Lest we forget—lest we forget!

Discovery Learning

This page contains an alternate lesson plan emphasizing learning activities. Classes desiring such student involvement will find these suggestions helpful. The next page is a reproducible activity page to further enhance discovery learning.

LEARNING GOALS

After this lesson students should be able to:

1. Summarize the plan by which God led the children of Israel across the Jordan River.

2. Recall times in their lives when God's guidance saw them through difficult circumstances.

3. Suggest a way to "memorialize" these and future occasions so they will not be forgotten.

INTO THE LESSON

If you are able to do so in your classroom, arrange the chairs in a "maze" before the students arrive. Ask for a volunteer at the beginning of class. Blindfold the volunteer and stand him at the start of the maze. Direct him through the maze with vocal commands only (e.g., "turn right," or "turn left, take two steps, and turn right"). If you have a small classroom, secure a larger room for this activity. One can also arrange the students in a maze and navigate the blindfolded student through a maze of his own classmates. The point is to show how leadership is needed in a time of difficulty. We need to follow God's guidance in life.

If the maze idea won't work, ask the students to think of a time when God's guidance led them through a difficult time in their lives. It need not be too personal. Ask your students to share some of their experiences. Prepare to share an experience or two of your own.

Observe that in our lesson today we'll see Israel at an extremely vulnerable time in its history. Not only did the people have to ford a swollen river, but they needed to conquer seven hostile peoples before finding rest in the promised land. Israel needed God's guidance now more than ever.

INTO THE WORD

Ask a volunteer to read today's Scripture aloud (Joshua 3:7-17). Use the contents of the lesson commentary to give a brief lecture on this passage. If possible, provide a map of the area so students can visualize the Bible passage. (See the visual for lesson 2.)

Ask your students to construct a chronological occurrence of events. Ask the students to call out randomly some of the events mentioned in the text while you write them on the chalkboard or on a large poster. Then work together to determine the chronological order of the events. Write numbers (1, 2, 3, etc.) next to the

events to show which happened first, second, third, etc. A summary of the significant events follows:

God speaks to Joshua; Joshua tells the people what God said to do; the priests carry the ark into the river; the flow of water stops; Israel crosses on dry ground; twelve men collect stones for a memorial; the priests come out of the riverbed; the river resumes its normal flow.

Discuss the significance of the priests' carrying the ark into the waters first. (*It demonstrated that God was leading them into the new territory. How can we be sure God is leading today?*)

Ask a student to read the account of the Red Sea crossing (Exodus 14:15-31). What similarities exist between these two miracles? (*Both were signs from God to his people. Both involved a halt in natural occurrences. Each event signaled a dramatic change in the national situation of Israel. You may note other similarities.*)

Ask, "What was the first thing the Israelites did after each crossing?" (*They memorialized the event—with a song, Exodus 15, and a monument, Joshua 4.*) Discuss the importance of taking note of God's guidance in our lives.

INTO LIFE

Distribute copies of the reproducible page that follows. Ask your students to use this page to recall times when God helped them through difficult circumstances. Urge them to find ways to memorialize these events. Perhaps they can write songs or poems or stories of their events. Others might record the instances in prayer logs, or set aside specific times to pray and thank God for his guidance.

As a class, find some way of memorializing God's guidance in general. Perhaps you could write a skit about God's guidance and perform it for the rest of the church. If your class does not wish to perform the skit for the entire church, at least record the skit on video. If your class is more "hands-on," make a trophy or a plaque to display in the classroom. During the week prior to class, collect any craft items you feel might aid this exercise (e.g., construction paper, glue, shoe boxes, paint, balsa wood, Styrofoam, etc.). The final product may not be the most attractive specimen, but it will remind the students of today's lesson each time they see it.

To close, gather in a prayer circle and thank God for his guidance in the past and for his continued guidance throughout the coming week.

A Monumental Experience

Read the account in Joshua 4. What was the purpose of the monument constructed by the Israelites? Have you ever "built a monument" to commemorate a time when God led you through a difficult impasse? Below are twelve "stones," symbolizing the twelve stones the Israelites used in Joshua 4. In each stone, write one word that sufficiently reminds you of an instance of God's guidance in your life. Try to fill all twelve stones. Afterward, say a prayer of thanks for each stone.

GOD DESTROYS JERICHO

LESSON 12

WHY TEACH THIS LESSON?

"Old habits die hard," according to an old saying—and which of us has not found it to be painfully true? New converts are frustrated that temptations from their former way of life continue to plague them, and longtime saints wonder why certain vices still seem attractive. For new Christian or old, some temptations loom like mighty strongholds, strong and seemingly impregnable.

This lesson will help your students know that even the toughest foe will fall when we put ourselves in God's hands. As Israel trusted him and saw the mighty walls of Jericho fall, so we can trust him to tear down Satan's fortresses in our own lives.

INTRODUCTION

A. AN END, YET A BEGINNING

Driving westward across the great plains of middle America, we come in sight of the Rocky Mountains. At first they are only a silhouette on the horizon, as if cut from cardboard and pasted on the distant sky. Then, as we drive on, we come to a breathtaking but bewildering arrangement of mountains. We find a pass and leave a summit behind, only to see another summit looming ahead.

Geographically, the Jordan River is situated in a valley. Yet in importance, the crossing of that river was a high peak in the migration of Israel. Dangerous peaks of battle still loomed ahead, but in a sense that crossing brought the Israelites to the end of their journey. They were in the promised land! They pitched their camp in Gilgal, between the river and the city of Jericho.

B. LESSON BACKGROUND

During their years in the desert the Israelites had been guilty of frequent criticism of Moses, and in some cases open rebellion. But the Lord had intervened decisively in favor of Moses. (See, for example, the account of Miriam and Aaron's criticism of Moses in Numbers 12.) At this point it seems that the new generation of Israelites had learned their lesson. They clearly understood that the Lord was in charge and that he was giving orders through Joshua, who had taken the place of Moses. Commands were obeyed without question or protest, even when it was hard to see the importance or usefulness of them.

In Gilgal the Israelites observed the Passover forty years after the first Passover—the one they had observed in Egypt. They used the produce of the promised land for their food, and never again did they find manna lying around their camp in the morning (Joshua 5:10-12). For a time they lay quietly in camp, awaiting further instructions.

I. BATTLE PLAN (JOSHUA 6:1-5)

In God's own time he gave the order for Israel to advance to battle. With the command he provided a battle plan. Joshua passed it on to the Israelites, and they obeyed—even though they must have been quite mystified. This was a strange plan for conquering a city.

DEVOTIONAL READING:
PSALM 47

BACKGROUND SCRIPTURE:
JOSHUA 6

PRINTED TEXT:
JOSHUA 6:1-5, 15-20

LESSON AIMS

After this lesson, each student will be able to:

1. Summarize how God delivered the city of Jericho into the hands of the Israelites.

2. Tell how Christians today are to face the wicked "Jerichos" around them.

3. Express the need for personal holiness in today's world, and tell how he or she will cultivate it through time with God each day.

KEY VERSE

The seventh time around, when the priests sounded the trumpet blast, Joshua commanded the people, "Shout! For the LORD has given you the city!"   —Joshua 6:16

Nov
21

LESSON 12 NOTES

A. FRIGHTENED CITY (v. 1)

1. Now Jericho was tightly shut up because of the Israelites. No one went out and no one came in.

Before the Israelites crossed the Jordan, their spies learned that the people on the west bank were terrified of them. People of that region had heard how Israel had crossed the Red Sea forty years earlier, and how they had recently destroyed two nations east of the Jordan (Joshua 2:9-11). The residents of *Jericho* must have panicked when another miracle brought the invaders across the Jordan, for it looked as if Jericho would be next.

The frightened inhabitants of Jericho took refuge in the city and kept the gates locked day and night. *No one went out and no one came in.* They could only hope that the city walls would keep them safe.

THE CHILL OF GOD'S DISPLEASURE

The winter of 1988-89 covered much of North America with record-breaking cold. The cold wave came out of the Arctic, swept through Alaska and across Canada, and proceeded into the midwestern states of the U.S. Temperatures stayed bitterly cold for several days in a row.

In the Alaskan town of Coldfoot—an aptly named community fifty miles north of the Arctic Circle—the temperature was reported to have dropped to -82°, which was colder than the official North American record set in the Canadian Yukon some forty years earlier.

All across Alaska (and elsewhere throughout Canada and the United States), schools and businesses closed, and people stayed inside their homes to survive. Food supplies were disrupted, and in some cases heating fuel wouldn't burn!

When the threat of external danger is so great, the only wise action is to stay inside until the peril is past. So it was in Jericho when Israel began its ominous march around the city wall. The air temperature may have been warm, but an emotional chill of terrible proportions must have settled over the doomed city.

Israel's solemn march around Jericho indicated the awful chill of God's displeasure with the city's wickedness. Unlike a weather front moving across a region, this bitter "season" of judgment would not go away.   —C. R. B.

B. PROMISE OF VICTORY (v. 2)

2. Then the LORD said to Joshua, "See, I have delivered Jericho into your hands, along with its king and its fighting men.

Already *the Lord* had determined the outcome of the battle of *Jericho*. Both *its king and its fighting men* would be helpless before the onslaught of Israel. God had *delivered* them into Joshua's *hands*.

C. INSTRUCTIONS (vv. 3-5)

3. "March around the city once with all the armed men. Do this for six days.

Having assured the Israelites of victory, the Lord proceeded to outline how that victory was to be achieved. For six days no blow was to be struck, either against the walls of stone or against a human enemy. The *armed men* (the fighting men of Israel) were simply to *march around the city once*.

This reference to a specific group of Israelites (the *armed men*) makes it doubtful that all the Israelites marched around the city (which would have involved around two to three million people). Verses 9 and 13 tell us that the armed men along with a "rear guard" marched around Jericho. According to one estimate, ancient Jericho would have covered no more than four or five acres.

4. "Have seven priests carry trumpets of rams' horns in front of the ark. On the seventh day, march around the city seven times, with the priests blowing the trumpets.

HOW TO SAY IT

Achan. AY-can.
Gideon. GID-ee-un.
Gilgal. GIL-gal.
Jericho. JAIR-ih-ko.
Miriam. MEER-ee-um.
Rahab. RAY-hab.

WHAT DO YOU THINK?

For six days the Israelites were just "going in circles," but then they saw God's promise fulfilled. Sometimes in our service for the Lord, it may seem as if we're just "spinning our wheels" or "going in circles." How might the event in today's text encourage us in such times?

The *ark* of the covenant was to be carried in the great procession. To call attention to the ark, *seven priests* were to march in front of it, *blowing the trumpets* as they went. Perhaps the people of Jericho knew that it was the symbol of Israel's God—the God who had made the water of the Red Sea stand up like walls, and made the water of the Jordan pile up in a heap—or perhaps their pagan minds supposed that the ark actually was that God.

On the *seventh day*, that great procession would *march around the city seven times.* The frequency of the number *seven* in these instructions highlighted their sacred significance (*seven* often symbolizes completeness in the Bible).

What was the point of all this marching? God did not explain, but we may suppose that these actions served to create a sense of panic and foreboding within the residents of Jericho. Probably they would not sleep well at night, as they wondered about that army marching outside their walls each day. On the seventh day they would grow more apprehensive as the marching went on and on and on. By the time the walls came down, they would have been weakened by a week of fitful sleep and daily anxiety; so their defense was not what it might have been when the Israelite soldiers stormed the city.

Perhaps, too, it was a lesson to Israel. What good is marching around a walled city? None, if that is all there is. But when their marching was an act of obedience to God, it was extremely valuable. This method may have been chosen for the same reason God later chose to deliver Israel through Gideon and only three hundred men: "in order that Israel may not boast against me that her own strength has saved her" (Judges 7:2).

5. "When you hear them sound a long blast on the trumpets, have all the people give a loud shout; then the wall of the city will collapse and the people will go up, every man straight in."

We are not told what sound the trumpeters were making prior to the seventh circuit; but when that final round of the city was completed, they would *sound a long blast.* The marchers were to remain silent through the week (v. 10), but that long blast would be the signal for *all the people* to *give a loud shout.* Such a deafening roar would alarm the frightened defenders even more. Then *the city wall* would *collapse,* and panic would seize all in Jericho as *every man* among Israel's fighting men would charge over the fallen stones *straight in* to the city. Probably those men were numerous enough to reach all the way around small Jericho, so they could enter the city from all directions.

II. CARRYING OUT THE PLAN (JOSHUA 6:15-20)

Verses 6-14 tell how God's battle plan was carried out for six days. The armed men led the way in marching around Jericho. Then came seven priests blowing their trumpets, followed by other priests carrying the ark of the covenant in the middle of the marching column. The rest of the armed men (or "rear guard") followed at the end. Our printed text leaps over those six days and brings us to the events of the critical seventh day.

A. THE LONG MARCH (v. 15)
15. On the seventh day, they got up at daybreak and marched around the city seven times in the same manner, except that on that day they circled the city seven times.

We know the people of Jericho were afraid of the Israelites (Joshua 2:11). Their fears and anxiety must have escalated when the marchers did not stop after one circuit as they always had done before, but *marched around the city seven times.*

WHAT DO YOU THINK?

Some scoffers have suggested that the vibration created by the loud shout of all those Israelites is what caused the wall of Jericho to fall. How would you respond to such a claim?

Today's visual pictures the collapse of the walls of Jericho, in fulfillment of God's promise in verse 16.

B. THE SIGNAL (v. 16)

16. The seventh time around, when the priests sounded the trumpet blast, Joshua commanded the people, "Shout! For the LORD has given you the city!

Following the loud *trumpet blast* of the *priests*, *Joshua* repeated the command to *shout*. That shout was the Israelites' battle cry. When it was given, the wall would collapse and they would rush into the city (v. 5). Joshua assured the people, *The Lord has given you the city*. Victory would be quick and complete.

C. FURTHER INSTRUCTIONS (vv. 17-19)

17. "The city and all that is in it are to be devoted to the LORD. Only Rahab the prostitute and all who are with her in her house shall be spared, because she hid the spies we sent.

Now came additional instructions concerning the treatment of *the city* once it was captured. Jericho and all the people, animals, and objects in it were to be *devoted to the Lord* and designated as his property. Just as the firstfruits of every harvest belonged to the Lord (Deuteronomy 26:1-4), so this first city taken from the pagans on the west bank was to be the Lord's.

In the case of Jericho, the setting apart was not so that these people and items could be used in God's service; it was so that they could be objects of his righteous judgment. The peoples living in the promised land were ripe for such judgment because of their idolatry and utter wickedness. Israel, in contrast, was to be "holy," or set apart, as God's obedient people. The difference between these two kinds of setting apart is clear from a study of Deuteronomy 7:1-6.

Verses 18 and 19 tell more about these instructions concerning Jericho, but the last part of verse 17 tells of an exception to the destruction. *Rahab* and her family were to be spared because she had saved the lives of Israel's *spies* when they came to Jericho (Joshua 2).

CERTAIN DISASTER

"Asteroid May Hit Earth in 2028!" read the newspaper headlines on March 12, 1998. The International Astronomical Union had announced that a mile-wide asteroid was expected to get as close as thirty thousand miles from earth in the year 2028. The television news that evening featured computer-generated pictures of the devastation that would be caused worldwide if the asteroid were to hit the earth. Hope was expressed that within the thirty years before the event was to happen, science would figure out a way to save the human race.

However, even before the grocery store tabloids were able to rush into print with the news, on the following day other astronomers claimed that the asteroid would miss the earth by six hundred thousand miles. They had discovered more data that put the celestial event at a much more comfortable distance.

The citizens of Jericho had only seven days in which to await their destruction. There would be no escape from the judgment of God. When Israel's trumpets blew on the seventh day, Jericho's walls would come crashing down; and only one woman and her family would be saved. Her prior service to the Lord and his people resulted in her deliverance from divine judgment.

The testimony of Scripture is that God's judgment is certain. Only those whose righteousness is found in him shall escape. —C. R. B.

18. "But keep away from the devoted things, so that you will not bring about your own destruction by taking any of them. Otherwise you will make the camp of Israel liable to destruction and bring trouble on it.

No one in Israel was to be enriched by any of the wealth of Jericho; all of it was the Lord's. Anyone who violated this order would be doomed to *destruction* along with the city. In addition, he would *bring trouble* upon the entire *camp of Israel*. Read Joshua 7 to see how this tragically came to pass when one man (Achan) ventured to steal some of the spoil of the city.

19. *"All the silver and gold and the articles of bronze and iron are sacred to the* Lord *and must go into his treasury."*

Every living thing in Jericho, human or animal, was to be killed (v. 21). The city was to be burned (v. 24), including the houses and their contents, in a huge sacrifice to the Lord. The metals that could not be destroyed by fire were to be put *into* the Lord's *treasury.*

Eventually other cities in the promised land would be conquered. Then the children of Israel would be permitted to live in the houses, eat the wheat and barley, use the animals, and pocket the treasure. This first captured city, however, belonged to the Lord.

D. Victory (v. 20)

20. *When the trumpets sounded, the people shouted, and at the sound of the trumpet, when the people gave a loud shout, the wall collapsed; so every man charged straight in, and they took the city.*

The plan of battle was carried out exactly as God had given it. *The trumpets sounded* a long blast, *the people shouted* at the top of their voices, the city *wall collapsed*, the men of Israel swarmed into Jericho from every side, *and they took the city*.

The citizens of Jericho had been demoralized already by a week of fear. The collapse of the wall must have brought them to utter despair. Women and children were killed along with the men. So were oxen, sheep, and donkeys (v. 21).

We may shrink in horror from such genocide, the devastation of an entire city. Can there be any justice in the killing of an innocent baby in his mother's arms? Can it be possible that God ordered such destruction?

Yes, he could and he did. What conclusion can we draw from a lesson like this?

CONCLUSION

God's justice is as real as his mercy. His punishment is as real as his love. In bringing Israel to the promised land, God had two purposes. One was to provide a homeland for the people he had chosen to bring a blessing to all families of the earth. The other was to wipe out several peoples that were not fit to live.

But the children—even babies not yet old enough to talk—what justice could there be in their deaths?

Let's think about that for a minute. Was their death justice, or was it mercy? Was it cruelty, or was it an act of kindness? Which would be better for those children: to die in their innocence and live forever in Heaven, or to live and grow up in sinful Jericho and suffer the "second death" of Hell?

A. God's Judgment

In another age "The Lord saw how great man's wickedness on the earth had become, and that every inclination of the thoughts of his heart was only evil all the time" (Genesis 6:5). People like that were not fit to live, and God destroyed them with a great flood—innocent babies along with wicked parents (Genesis 6–8).

In a later time, God chose one man (Abraham) to be the father of a nation that he designated as his chosen people. He destroyed the people of Jericho and other evil people and gave his own people a land flowing with milk and honey. But

What Do You Think?

The Israelites faced godless Jericho and destroyed everyone and everything in it—except faithful Rahab and her family (v. 17, cf. Hebrews 11:31). Today we face a godless society, and what shall we do? We can't "wipe them out"! What lessons are here for us?

Daily Bible Readings

Monday, Nov. 15—*The Passover Celebrated at Gilgal (Joshua 5:10-15)*

Tuesday, Nov. 16—*Israel Begins Conquest of Jericho (Joshua 6:1-7)*

Wednesday, Nov. 17—*Six-Day March Around Jericho's Walls (Joshua 6:8-14)*

Thursday, Nov. 18—*Destruction of Jericho by Israel (Joshua 6:15-20)*

Friday, Nov. 19—*Rahab and Her Family Are Spared (Joshua 6:22-25, 27)*

Saturday, Nov. 20—*Joshua Renews the Covenant (Joshua 8:30-35)*

Sunday, Nov. 21—*A Sacred Song of Remembrance (Psalm 44:1-8)*

PRAYER

*Lord, lay some soul upon my
   heart,
And love that soul through me;
And may I nobly do my part
To win that soul for Thee.*

            —Dr. Leon Tucker

THOUGHT TO REMEMBER

We are to influence our Jerichos for good; we are not to be influenced by them for evil.

WHAT DO YOU THINK?

Many critics today accuse Christians of being judgmental, intolerant, and hypocritical. Unfortunately there are believers who elicit such charges by behavior that is out of harmony with the teaching and example of Christ. But often these charges are leveled at Christians who are merely taking a firm stand on the side of Biblical morality. How do we respond to such charges?

God's chosen people became so ungodly that God sent pagan armies to destroy Jerusalem and drag his people to captivity in Babylon.

"The Lord is compassionate and gracious, slow to anger, abounding in love" (Psalm 103:8). But to those who spurn his mercy and persist in doing wrong, "God is a consuming fire" (Hebrews 12:29). The meek and lowly Jesus, the loving Savior of mankind, will someday say to some, "Depart from me, you who are cursed, into the eternal fire prepared for the devil and his angels" (Matthew 25:41). He will also say, "Come, you who are blessed by my Father; take your inheritance, the kingdom prepared for you since the creation of the world" (Matthew 25:34). Because of his love and grace, we can choose which of these statements we will hear.

B. OUR JUDGMENT

"Do not judge." We can hardly say a word against obvious evil without hearing those words of Jesus quoted. But Jesus also said, "Make a right judgment." The first of these sayings is a warning that we can expect to be judged by the same kind of judgment we use (Matthew 7:1-5). The second is a call to make our judgment agree with God's (John 7:24).

Very clearly God's Word describes some things as bad. If we accept them as good, we contradict God's judgment. That puts us on the way to being like the people of Jericho, who were not fit to live.

Some popular television programs seem to have been made in Jericho! Perhaps you have seen on TV a story in which illicit sex seems to be the normal conclusion of a date, or a story that glorifies homosexuals proudly coming "out of the closet." God says that fornicators and homosexuals "will not inherit the kingdom of God." They belong in Jericho, along with idolaters, adulterers, thieves, the greedy, drunkards, slanderers, and swindlers (1 Corinthians 6:9, 10). It is not we who judge the wrongdoers; it is God. Wrong is condemned in his Word as plainly as it is glorified in some TV programs, movies, magazines, and newspapers.

Yet God also has a word of hope for the evildoers. They do not have to stay as they are. They can be washed and sanctified and justified "in the name of the Lord Jesus Christ and by the Spirit of our God" (1 Corinthians 6:11).

C. OUR DUTY

If we are to live as God's people today, we have a threefold duty.

First, we are to keep ourselves pure (1 John 3:2, 3). We are not to be contaminated by the sins of ancient Jericho that run rampant in the modern towns where we live. We must recognize evil, no matter how adroitly it is camouflaged, and resolutely turn away from it.

Second, we are not to destroy but to restore a brother who has drifted or has been enticed into the sins of Jericho. Gently, not angrily, we are to lead him back home. We are to watch ourselves lest we be tempted, too (Galatians 6:1).

Third, we are to take the good news of life to every Jericho in the world today (Mark 16:15, 16). The wages of sin is death; but we are commissioned to let every sinner know that he does not have to die—every sinner in Jericho, every sinner in our national capital, every sinner in our hometown. But we cannot and must not conceal the promise that he will die unless he trusts and obeys the Savior.

We are not called to take a sword, a rifle, or a bomb and kill all the sinners in any Jericho. We are called instead to be winsome, to carry good news, and to plead, "Be reconciled to God" (2 Corinthians 5:20).

What shall we do this week to fulfill our duty?

Discovery Learning

This page contains an alternate lesson plan emphasizing learning activities. Classes desiring such student involvement will find these suggestions helpful. The next page is a reproducible activity page to further enhance discovery learning.

LEARNING GOALS

After participating in this lesson, each student will be able to:

1. Summarize how God delivered the city of Jericho into the hands of the Israelites.

2. Tell how Christians today are to face the wicked "Jerichos" around them.

3. Express the need for personal holiness in today's world, and tell how he or she will cultivate it through time with God each day.

INTO THE LESSON

Ask a dramatically inclined person, preferably not one of your students, to dress as a person of Joshua's day and to come and relate the story of the fallen city of Jericho through the eyes of an average Israelite. His soliloquy should summarize the story and offer down-to-earth commentary (e.g., "It seemed a silly thing to do, but we'd seen God do some pretty amazing stuff!"). The soliloquy can be humorous or serious and should last two to three minutes.

INTO THE WORD

Divide your class into two groups. Supply each group with paper, pencils, and any Bible helps you can. Assign Group 1 to read Joshua 6:1-16 and Group 2 to read Joshua 6:17-27. Each group should answer its assigned questions below. (Do not give the answers, which follow in italic type in parenthesis.) After a time of discussion, ask each group to summarize its passage and offer answers to the rest of the class.

GROUP 1:

1. How was Israel's method of the siege of Jericho different from those normally used? (*Most sieges of the day spanned a great length of time. Armies would attempt to destroy or scale city walls, or they would merely cut off the city from outside help, including food supplies, and starve the inhabitants. Needless to say, armies never toppled walls by yelling.*)

2. What were the advantages of this unusual siege method? (*Many cities were prepared for an ordinary siege and would have fought well against it. In the meantime, the Israelites might have lost patience in a siege that went on for weeks or even months. God's method gave a decisive victory in just a week.*)

3. Joshua 5:15 names the commander of the Lord's army. Who was this commander, and how was he glorified? (*God, of course, was the commander, and he was glorified by the miraculous defeat of Jericho.*)

GROUP 2:

1. What was to be saved and what was to be destroyed? (*Everything was to be destroyed except silver, gold, iron, and brass vessels, which were added to the treasury of the Lord.*)

2. How was this a just punishment, since it meant the deaths of innocent children? (*See the comments under "Conclusion," pages 109, 110.*)

3. What is the significance of Rahab's being saved from destruction? (*There is still redemption for those who turn from sin and embrace God's will.*)

INTO LIFE

On a chalkboard write "Modern-Day Jericho." Ask your students to list ways in which our society resembles Jericho (metaphorically). Examples include pornography, adultery, fornication, greed, abortion, idolatry, etc. What potential do these evils have to corrupt a Christian's life?

Ask your students how they feel they should respond to the following situations:

— Coarse talk in the workplace.

— A pornography shop in town.

— A Christian friend who is unfaithful to his or her spouse.

— A friend or a relative who is an alcoholic.

God does not command us to destroy all evil. There is redemption. Rahab's deliverance in today's text is an example of this. Because of her obedience to God's will, she did not suffer the punishment that the rest of Jericho did. Though we are called to flee from sinful acts, we are also called to share the gospel with the people who do them.

Give each student a copy of "A Seven-Day Siege" from page 112. Every day, starting today, each student should set aside five minutes to write a journal entry about an aspect of modern Jericho that troubles him or her and pray for God's guidance. (Keep this exercise confidential and encourage the students to choose items that especially tempt them.) Use the remaining class time to complete the first day of this exercise.

A Seven-Day Siege

There are many aspects of the post-modern world that resemble Jericho of old, and these aspects tempt all of us. The purpose of this exercise is to indicate privately one of these and launch a seven-day siege in the spirit of the Israelites' march on Jericho. Start by identifying one aspect of modern-day Jericho that tempts you the most (the answers need not be shared with anyone). Starting with Sunday and ending with Saturday, set aside five minutes a day to record how you have overcome or have been overcome by this problem area. Complement your journal time with Bible reading (for each day there is listed a passage about a well-known Bible character who overcame a weakness or adversity). Finish each session with a prayer for guidance and assistance.

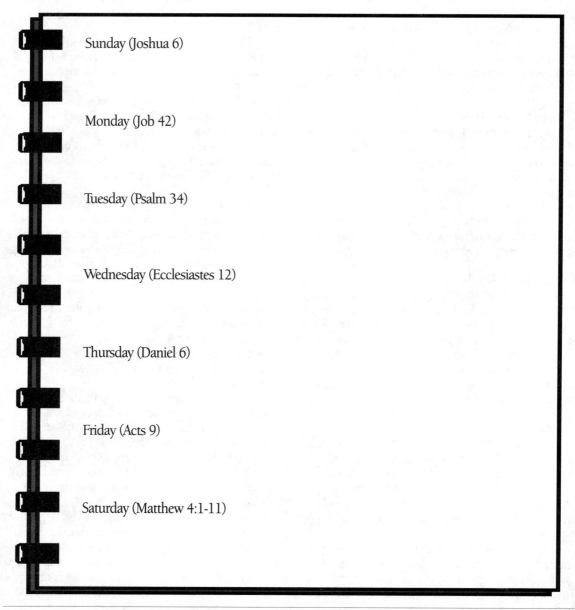

Sunday (Joshua 6)

Monday (Job 42)

Tuesday (Psalm 34)

Wednesday (Ecclesiastes 12)

Thursday (Daniel 6)

Friday (Acts 9)

Saturday (Matthew 4:1-11)

ISRAEL CHOOSES TO SERVE THE LORD

LESSON 13

WHY TEACH THIS LESSON?

This lesson will challenge everyone in your class. For those who have not yet accepted Jesus Christ as their Savior, the challenge is that famous call in Joshua 24:15: "Choose for yourselves this day whom you will serve." Remind them that "now is the day of salvation" (2 Corinthians 6:2).

But there is a challenge also for the believers—who are, no doubt, in the majority—in your class. It is the same one with which Joshua challenged the Israelites when they glibly promised to obey the Lord: "You are not able to serve the Lord" (Joshua 24:19). Use this lesson to remind your students that having accepted the Lord was just the beginning. It is to the one who is "faithful to the point of death" that Jesus promised the crown of life (Revelation 2:10).

INTRODUCTION

On May 14, 1948, the Jews in Palestine boldly proclaimed that the nation of Israel was again established in its ancient homeland, where no nation of Israel had been for 1878 years (since the destruction of Jerusalem by the Romans). Other nations in the vicinity objected violently. Fierce fighting continued for about a year, and was ended only by armistice rather than real peace. Today, fifty-one years later, the objectors are still objecting, sometimes with violence.

This was not the first time that the people of Israel had won or lost that land. They lost the northern part of it to Assyria in 722 B.C., and the southern part to Babylon in 586 B.C. By permission of the Persians, who later conquered Babylon, the Jews recovered part of it without war, though not without objection from nearby residents. In a violent and bloody war they lost it to the Romans in A.D. 70, not to reclaim it until this century.

A. THE FIRST TIME

It was Joshua and his troops who established the nation of Israel in the promised land for the first time. God had first promised the land of Canaan to Abraham, but he and his family never possessed the land; instead "he made his home in the promised land like a stranger in a foreign country" (Hebrews 11:8, 9). Abraham's grandson Jacob moved the family to Egypt to escape famine, but there the family remained for more than four hundred years, until Moses led them out. Forty years after they had left Egypt, Joshua led the Israelites across the Jordan River. There they destroyed Jericho and then fought for some seven years to establish themselves in the land, dividing it up among their tribes. With the firm hand of Joshua at the helm, the nation stayed faithful to God, and prosperous.

B. LESSON BACKGROUND

Like his predecessor Moses, Joshua could not be expected to lead the people forever. He grew old (Joshua 23:1), more than a century old (Joshua 24:29). He

DEVOTIONAL READING:
JOSHUA 24:14-24
BACKGROUND SCRIPTURE:
JOSHUA 24
PRINTED TEXT:
JOSHUA 24:1, 2a, 14-25

LESSON AIMS

After this lesson students should be able to:

1. Summarize Joshua's challenge to the children of Israel that is found in today's text.

2. List some of the "gods" in today's world that clamor for us to choose them, thus turning our focus away from serving God.

3. Make every day a day in which they will choose to serve God above anything else.

KEY VERSE

And the people said to Joshua, "We will serve the LORD our God and obey him."—Joshua 24:24

NOV
28

called together the leaders of all Israel for the assembly that is recorded in chapter 23. For today's lesson we bypass that gathering and go on to chapter 24, which records Joshua's farewell address to the entire nation.

I. A CALL TO CHOOSE (JOSHUA 24:1, 2a, 14, 15)

Shechem was an appropriate place for a national meeting. It was located near the center of Israel's territory, making it easier for people throughout the land to attend. In addition, Shechem had already played a significant part in Israel's history (Genesis 12:6, 7).

Shechem was situated in a narrow valley between Mount Gerizim and Mount Ebal, where Moses had commanded the people to gather and renew their commitment to obey God (Deuteronomy 27:9-13). Israel gathered there earlier under Joshua's leadership to do this (Joshua 8:30-35). The rising terrain on either side of the valley provided a natural amphitheater.

A. FOR ALL THE PEOPLE (vv. 1, 2a)

1. Then Joshua assembled all the tribes of Israel at Shechem. He summoned the elders, leaders, judges and officials of Israel, and they presented themselves before God.

All the tribes of Israel, a huge throng, met *at Shechem*. An appeal was given to the prominent men of every tribe, clan, and family. Perhaps they came forward and stood with *Joshua* as he spoke. Thus they would show that they agreed with what he was saying. Previously he had consulted them and enlisted their support (Joshua 23:2). Together *they presented themselves before God*. They knew that God was present with them, seeing what they did and hearing what they said.

2a. Joshua said to all the people. . . .

This part of a verse is included in our text to make it plain that Joshua spoke the words that we read in the rest of the printed text (vv. 14-25). Before giving that challenge, however, Joshua repeated a message that God had given him for the people. It is recorded in verses 2-13, where God reviewed the history of Israel from the time Abraham left Ur of the Chaldees to the time in which Joshua was speaking.

B. THE RIGHT CHOICE (v. 14).

14. "Now fear the LORD and serve him with all faithfulness. Throw away the gods your forefathers worshiped beyond the River and in Egypt, and serve the LORD.

Verses 2-13 reminded the people that God had faithfully helped Abraham and his descendants and had brought them to this moment of triumph. Therefore these people ought to *fear* and *serve* him, not in mere form and ritual, but *with all faithfulness*. To do that they must *throw away* idols of all kinds. The real God must be the only God in their minds and hearts.

The *River* in this verse is the Euphrates. Abraham had come from Ur, *beyond* (east of) the Euphrates. In that land Abraham's *forefathers* had worshiped idols (v. 2). More recently the forefathers of the Israelites had lived in *Egypt*, a land of many false *gods*. Joshua urged that no worship or service should be given to any god but *the Lord*, the true God—the One who had blessed and helped Israel abundantly.

C. WRONG CHOICES (v. 15a)

15a. "But if serving the LORD seems undesirable to you, then choose for yourselves this day whom you will serve, whether the gods your forefathers served beyond the River, or the gods of the Amorites, in whose land you are living.

Joshua realized that he could not compel his fellow Israelites to do what he was urging. To serve the Lord was costly. But they ought to remember that the

WHAT DO YOU THINK?

The leaders of Israel "presented themselves before God." They recognized him as their Sovereign Lord and made themselves accountable to him. How might leaders today "present themselves before God"? What advantage do you think there would be to such a practice?

WHAT DO YOU THINK?

Someone might say that Joshua had a very tolerant attitude: he offered the Israelites their choice of gods. They might paraphrase Joshua: "If you don't want to serve Yahweh, that's okay. Choose some of the Mesopotamian, Egyptian, or Amorite (i.e., Canaanite) gods!" How would you respond to such a suggestion?

Lord was the One who had helped and blessed them continually ever since the time of Abraham.

Here the word *Amorites* is a general name for all the hostile people who had lived in the promised land before the Israelites came. Not all of these peoples had been "totally destroyed" at this point, as God had commanded (Deuteronomy 7:1, 2). There was still the possibility that their *gods* could seduce the Lord's people.

D. JOSHUA'S CHOICE (v. 15b)

15b. "But as for me and my household, we will serve the LORD."

Joshua's choice was made, and he would never waver. Only Yahweh is worthy of worship. Joyfully Joshua announced that he and his family would *serve* him.

IMPORTANT CHOICES

Martha Van Sloten thought she had recovered from cancer surgery—but two years later she was dying. Lisa, her nineteen-year-old daughter, dropped out of college to help care for her sisters, who were only eight and four years old.

Shortly before Martha died, her husband, Richard, began to have seizures. He was found to have a very aggressive brain tumor. Knowing what the future held, the couple began to plan for their children's future. Their medical bills were increasing, they had only limited life insurance, and they wanted to find a way to keep the family intact. Few choices are more momentous than that last one. One other extremely significant choice was this one: how would they respond to God in such a crisis?

Richard's response was this: "I thank God for his blessings. I get to make arrangements for my wife and for me. I get to remind my little girls that I love them . . . I've tried to conduct myself in a way that will make my daughters proud of me."

Joshua held out to Israel a life-and-death choice: spiritual life or spiritual death. It is the same choice that all of us get; the circumstances of our lives are all that differ. Do we choose to face life's challenges in a way that makes others proud of us? Do we choose to respond to God in a way that brings glory to him?   —C. R. B.

II. A REASONABLE CHOICE (JOSHUA 24:16-18)

A. ISRAEL'S RESPONSE (v. 16)

16. Then the people answered, "Far be it from us to forsake the LORD to serve other gods!

Four options had been presented: serve the Lord, worship the idols of Mesopotamia that Abraham had long ago rejected, worship the gods of Egypt that the Lord had soundly defeated not fifty years earlier, or worship the Canaanite idols as the defeated peoples around them were doing. Vigorously *the people* declared their choice: they agreed with Joshua. They too would serve *the Lord*.

B. BASIS FOR ISRAEL'S CHOICE (vv. 17, 18)

17. "It was the LORD our God himself who brought us and our fathers up out of Egypt, from that land of slavery, and performed those great signs before our eyes. He protected us on our entire journey and among all the nations through which we traveled.

The people of Israel were indebted to *the Lord* for many things. They acknowledged all his deeds that had been mentioned earlier (vv. 5-11). Simple gratitude ought to lead them to give all their worship to the One who had done so much for them.

18. "And the LORD drove out before us all the nations, including the Amorites, who lived in the land. We too will serve the LORD, because he is our God."

As noted under verse 15, *Amorites* is a general name for all the hostile peoples who had *lived in the land* before the Israelites came. Joshua 9:1 names six groups

This visual is an attractive reminder of Joshua's pledge. It's one that more of us might hang on our walls to express our own commitment to the Lord.

WHAT DO YOU THINK?

The people pledged to serve the Lord, rehearsing many of the things God had done for them. What things has God done for you, for which you feel indebted to him and are compelled to serve him?

DAILY BIBLE READINGS

Monday, Nov. 22—*Joshua Summons Israel to Remember God (Joshua 23:1-5)*

Tuesday, Nov. 23—*Israel Exhorted to Love and Obey God (Joshua 23:6-10)*

Wednesday, Nov. 24—*Joshua Warns Against Unfaithfulness to God (Joshua 23:11-16)*

Thursday, Nov. 25—*Joshua Rehearses Israel's History (Joshua 24:1-13)*

Friday, Nov. 26—*Israel Promises to Be Faithful (Joshua 24:14-18)*

Saturday, Nov. 27—*Israel Renews the Covenant (Joshua 24:19-24)*

Sunday, Nov. 28—*Death of Joshua and Eleazar (Joshua 24:29-33)*

who lived west of the Jordan; Deuteronomy 3:1, 2 names two kings who ruled east of the river. The Lord had given Israel victory over all of these. That was one more good reason for Israel to *serve the Lord*. It seems that there was no dissenting voice as the people expressed their desire to make the same choice that Joshua had made.

III. A CONCLUDING CHALLENGE (JOSHUA 24:19, 20)

The people made the right choice. But no doubt wise old Joshua could see that they had made it too lightly, not realizing all it implied. Instead of praising their choice, he issued a strong challenge.

A. A DEMANDING CHOICE (v. 19)

19a. Joshua said to the people, "You are not able to serve the Lord.

Can you imagine how this statement shook the complacent *people?* They had made the same choice *Joshua* had made, the one he obviously wanted them to make. Then Joshua said, "You can't do it!" What in the world could he mean? *19b. "He is a holy God; he is a jealous God. He will not forgive your rebellion and your sins.*

God is *holy.* He is altogether good, separated from anything that is bad or even questionable. His word to the people was, "Be holy because I, the Lord your God, am holy" (Leviticus 19:2). Were the people of Israel ready for that? Are we?

God is *jealous.* He will not tolerate a rival in the minds and hearts of his people (Exodus 20:3). He wants their total devotion. Were the people of Israel ready for that? Are we?

God *will not forgive your rebellion and your sins.* That jolts us, and it must have jolted those who heard Joshua say it. The law describes several offerings to atone for sin and bring forgiveness (Leviticus 4:1—6:7). What could Joshua mean?

Perhaps he meant that God will not forgive a person's sins if that one treats lightly the issue of sin in his or her life. God will not forgive one's transgressions while that one keeps on transgressing, thus showing that he prefers to do wrong rather than right. Were the people of Israel ready to serve so demanding a God? Are we?

B. A CLEAR WARNING (v. 20)

20. "If you forsake the LORD and serve foreign gods, he will turn and bring disaster on you and make an end of you, after he has been good to you."

For three months our lessons have dwelt on the *good* that God did for his people. But he would not always do them good, regardless of what they would do. They were promising to serve him. If they broke that promise, then he would do them harm instead of good—and it would be no trivial harm. God would *bring disaster on* them *and make an end of* them.

Were the people ready to pledge themselves to God under these conditions? Are we?

IV. A SOLEMN PLEDGE (JOSHUA 24:21-25)

Too lightly, too easily the people of Israel had pledged to serve God (vv. 16-18). Joshua had made them stop and think. It was a demanding commitment, and failure to meet its demands would be tragic (vv. 19, 20). Were the people still ready to make that pledge?

A. PLEDGE OF SERVICE (v. 21)

21. But the people said to Joshua, "No! We will serve the LORD."

Joshua had said, "You are not able to serve the Lord" (v. 19). To that the people responded, *No:* it is not so. They said, *We will serve the Lord.* They were pledging to meet all the demands of such service, to be holy and obedient to God.

B. WITNESSES OF THE PLEDGE (v. 22)
22. Then Joshua said, "You are witnesses against yourselves that you have chosen to serve the LORD."

"Yes, we are witnesses," they replied.

There were no disinterested parties present to witness the promise that was made, so Joshua said that the very people who made the promise would be *witnesses.* If they later failed to *serve the Lord,* they would have to testify against themselves. They would have to admit that they had made a promise and broken it.

The people agreed: *we are witnesses.* They were affirming that they had made a solemn pledge to serve the Lord.

C. KEEPING THE PLEDGE (v. 23)
23. "Now then," said Joshua, "throw away the foreign gods that are among you and yield your hearts to the LORD, the God of Israel."

Twice the people had promised to serve the Lord, to worship and obey him (vv. 18, 21). Now they had to demonstrate, immediately and completely, their sincerity about this promise. Joshua challenged them to get rid of any pagan *gods,* or idols, that they still had.

During their recent years of war, the Israelites had destroyed several towns in the promised land and taken the possessions of those towns as booty. No doubt the spoils included some pagan idols. Also, the Israelites who had lived in Egypt had brought many things of value from that land (Exodus 12:35, 36). Perhaps some of the Egyptian idols were included. Every idol of any kind had to go, for the Lord said, "You shall have no other gods before me" (Exodus 20:3).

REMINDERS OF AN UNGODLY PAST
Forty or fifty years ago, one of the finest gifts a college-bound high-school graduate could receive was a portable manual typewriter. But, as the saying goes, "That was then; this is now." Next came electric typewriters and then computers. Today, many college students take their class notes on "laptops." Colleges are wiring their dormitories for the Internet and local networks so that students can do research right in their rooms.

Typewriters are becoming outmoded reminders of a pre-electronic past. Many children have grown up on computers, not knowing what a typewriter is. A recent cartoon showed a child watching her mother using a typewriter. The child was saying, "Wow! Cool! A keyboard with a built-in printer!" Today, a typewriter may best be kept around as an ornament to embellish a home or office decorated with antiques!

Israel had some "decorations" on hand also: the idols that their ancestors had brought with them out of Egypt, as well as those that the people had collected as spoils from their conquest of Canaan. Joshua told the people to destroy them all. These were not mere "antiques" or harmless household decor; they were physical reminders of Israel's idolatrous past. Joshua wanted to make sure that even the slightest temptation to return to that past was eliminated.

Is there anything from our past that keeps us from making and living out a sincere commitment to God?   —C. R. B.

D. THE PLEDGE REPEATED (v. 24)
24. And the people said to Joshua, "We will serve the LORD our God and obey him."

WHAT DO YOU THINK?
Joshua was careful to point out to the Israelites that serving the Lord would cost them something in terms of holy, godly living. How much do you think Christians need to be reminded of the cost of following Jesus Christ? What has it cost you?

HOW TO SAY IT
Amorites. AM-uh-rites.
Assyria. Uh-SEAR-ee-uh.
Babylon. BAB-uh-lun.
Canaan. KAY-nun.
Chaldees. Kal-DEEZ.
Ebal. EE-bul.
Euphrates. You-FRAY-teez.
Gerizim. GAIR-ih-zim or
   Guh-RYE-zim.
Jericho. JAIR-ih-ko.
Shechem. SHEK-em or
   SHEE-kem.

The *people* had made this pledge twice before (vv. 18, 21). Each time Joshua had responded by helping them understand what they were promising. Now, with a fuller understanding, they voiced their pledge the third time.

E. THE PLEDGE RECORDED (v. 25)

25. On that day Joshua made a covenant for the people, and there at Shechem he drew up for them decrees and laws.

The text of this lesson clearly shows the nature of the *covenant* (the agreement or contract) that was made *that day*. It was a reaffirmation of the covenant made at Sinai about half a century earlier, and it included those *decrees* and *laws* that would guide the conduct of *the people* in the promised land.

Verses 26 and 27 add that Joshua recorded the words of this covenant "in the Book of the Law of God." He also set up a stone as a monument—a perpetual reminder of the covenant reaffirmed at *Shechem*.

CONCLUSION

A. TO BE CONTINUED

Next September we shall return to this story at the point where we are leaving it now. We shall see the people of Israel failing to keep the covenant they made. We shall see their obedience turning to disobedience, and their peace and prosperity turning to constant harassment and impoverishment at the hands of their enemies. See Judges 2:11-15 for a preview of that dismal time. The covenant made at Sinai and reaffirmed at Shechem failed, not because there was anything wrong with it, but because the people failed to worship and obey God as they had promised to do.

B. THE NEW COVENANT

It is good, then, that in December we will turn our thoughts to Jesus, the mediator of a New Covenant. For three months our study will center on him, focusing on Matthew's Gospel. Then for six months we will be looking at various New Testament epistles. We will be reminded of the marvelous blessings of the New Covenant, foretold in Jeremiah 31:31-34. It provides the only sufficient atonement for sins; thus it is able to offer the forgiveness of those sins.

As Christians we rejoice in what the New Covenant supplies. But still the call of Joshua comes to us today, and tomorrow, and every day of our lives: "Choose for yourselves this day whom you will serve."

Almost everyone agrees that earning a living is important. In doing so we can serve God, for he encourages us to earn our living (2 Thessalonians 3:12), support our families (1 Timothy 5:8), and give to the needy (Ephesians 4:28). However, if our eagerness to make money compels us to give up worship at church, or Bible study at home, or time with our families, are we not serving money rather than God (Matthew 6:24)?

Most of us spend some of our money and more of our time on recreation, fun, or simply relaxing. That is not necessarily disobedient to God. Paul says, "Physical training is of some value" (1 Timothy 4:8). God's ancient Sabbath law offers clear evidence that every worker needs some time off, even if he prefers relaxation to exercise. But if our time off is filled with actions displeasing to God (Galatians 5:19-21), or if we become "couch potatoes" who do nothing but view salacious shows or magazines, or if "fun" crowds out worship and church work, are we not among those whose "god is their stomach" (Philippians 3:19)?

Can you think of other choices that can be made instead of serving the Lord? Whatever they are, and whatever they offer, will you still serve the Lord?

Discovery Learning

*This page contains an alternate lesson plan emphasizing learning activities. Classes
desiring such student involvement will find these suggestions helpful. The next page
is a reproducible activity page to further enhance discovery learning.*

LEARNING GOALS

After this lesson students should be able to:

1. Summarize Joshua's challenge to the children of Israel that is found in today's text.

2. List some of the "gods" in today's world that clamor for us to choose them, thus turning our focus away from serving God.

3. Make every day a day in which they will choose to serve God above anything else.

INTO THE LESSON

Before the students arrive, write the words, "Choose for yourselves this day," on the chalkboard. As the students arrive, engage them in conversation about choices. What choices did they have to make this morning? (What outfits to wear, what to have for breakfast—or whether to have breakfast! Did some have to decide whether to come to class?)

Observe that we make choices every day. Some are routine, and we scarcely even notice we have made a choice. Others are more significant, and we are sometimes hard-pressed to make "the right choice." In our lesson today, Israel was faced with a choice—a choice that would determine much about what kind of future they would have in the promised land!

INTO THE WORD

To read today's text, prepare a handout with Joshua 24:1, 2a, 14-25 printed on it, with verses 16-18, 21, 22b, and 24 in bold type. Distribute the handout and announce that you will read the type that is not bold, and the class is to read together what is in bold.

After the text is read, divide the class into three groups. Give the first group a sheet of poster board and some markers. Ask the group to read verses 14-18 and make a poster that describes the choice Israel had to make. They may use words or simple pictures to illustrate Israel's choice to serve God instead of Mesopotamian, Egyptian, or Amorite (i.e., Canaanite) gods.

The second group should examine verses 19-22 and write a poem that describes the warning Joshua gave and the Israelites' response. Provide pens or pencils as needed and some paper.

Provide the third group with a variety of craft supplies and ask them to make a visual reminder of Israel's promise based on verses 23-25. They might make a poster or plaque with the words of verse 24, or perhaps they will make a "yield" sign with the words of verse 23. Let them be creative!

Allow the groups time to work; then take a few minutes to display the results of each group's efforts.

INTO LIFE

In life we are constantly bombarded by other gods and other lifestyles. It is crucial that we decide in whom to put our faith. Many choose God without giving it any thought and, in turn, are unprepared for when another choice is offered.

Ask your students to name some of the "gods" that clamor for our attention. "Gods" can refer to anything from other religions (Islam, Judaism, Buddhism, New Age) to postmodern philosophies (humanism, pluralism) to possessions (cite specific objects) to activities (such as one's occupation, sports, or watching TV). Write these on the chalkboard as the class names them.

Explain to your students that we live in a world that seeks to fill a spiritual void. Some seek fulfillment in God, others seek it elsewhere—in one or more of the "gods" you have already listed. Even those who believe in the Lord are frequently challenged to give one of these "gods" first place in their lives.

Distribute pencils or pens and copies of the reproducible activity "Choose for Yourselves . . ." on page 120 to the class. Ask each student to write in the left column the names of some of the other "gods" that clamor for attention in his or her life. (These will be kept private.) In the center column the student should write some of the ways this temptation appears. (For example, one of the rivals might be "materialism." This rival may vie for attention through slick advertisements on TV or in print, through a co-worker who frequently brags about new purchases he or she has made, or through a spouse who complains that the family doesn't have enough nice things because they give too much to the church.) Then have the student write in the right column an answer to each temptation showing why serving the Lord is superior to the respective rival.

Finally, ask the students to write the words of Joshua 24:23 across the bottom of the page. Encourage the students to keep these papers as reminders to put the Lord first. Close the session with a prayer of commitment.

Choose for Yourselves....

In this week's passage, Joshua challenges the Israelites to choose whom to serve: God, or the gods their ancestors chose; God, or the many gods of the land in which they dwell.

As Christians, we find ourselves in the same position as the Israelites. There are numerous "gods" who clamor for our attention today. In the left column on the chart below list as many of these "gods" as you can. In the center column write how each of these rivals tempts you and lures you to follow it. Finally, write in the right column one or two reasons that following the true God is the preferred choice over each rival.

RIVAL "GODS"	WAYS THEY TEMPT ME	WHY GOD IS SUPERIOR

Write the words of Joshua 24:23 below. Use large letters. Keep this page as a reminder not to fall for the puny rival gods that seek to replace the true God in your life.

Winter Quarter, 1999-2000

Immanuel: God With Us (Matthew)

Special Features

Lessons

Unit 1: Beginnings: Birth and Ministry

Unit 2: Ministry: Wonderful Words and Works

Unit 3: Fulfillment: Atonement and Final Commission

About These Lessons

These lessons, all taken from the Gospel of Matthew, lead the reader to one inescapable conclusion: Jesus was indeed Immanuel ("God With Us"), and he demonstrated this through his matchless words and mighty works. Although Matthew's Gospel was written primarily for a Jewish readership, the good news of which he writes is meant to be told to "all nations."

Dec 5
Dec 12
Dec 19
Dec 26
Jan 2
Jan 9
Jan 16
Jan 23
Jan 30
Feb 6
Feb 13
Feb 20
Feb 27

Sweetest Story Ever Heard

by Johnny Pressley

> Tell me the story of Jesus,
> Write on my heart every word;
> Tell me the story most precious,
> Sweetest that ever was heard.
> —Fanny J. Crosby

Are there things in your life that you especially enjoy because you have become accustomed to them? Your own bed and pillow? A comfortable pair of shoes? Your family's favorite home-cooked meals? Old, familiar songs? The company of family and friends?

Most of us like to try new products, sample new foods, and buy brand-new items. But have you noticed how we all have some old familiar favorites that we keep going back to because we enjoy them so?

The gospel story of Jesus is one of those "old familiar favorites" that we love to keep going back to again and again. At the same time, some may think that a lesson series on the life of Jesus could be nothing more than a repetition of what we have heard many times already. How quickly this attitude can change when we dig into the Scriptures and witness again the richness of the Gospel texts, and the deeper insights waiting to be discovered! With each reading of familiar texts of Scripture, we see truths that we had not observed before; and our understanding and comprehension are enhanced. Old lessons yield new applications to our ever-changing lives.

Perhaps more wonderful than all of this is simply the opportunity to hear again the beloved stories we have cherished from our youth and to let them touch and bless our hearts once more. They never fail to fill us with peace and joy, kindling anew a burning passion to know Christ even more.

As Fanny J. Crosby declared, the story of Jesus is a story "most precious," the "sweetest that ever was heard." When that is our attitude toward the Gospel story of our Lord, we will long to hear it told again and again.

BEGINNINGS

The lessons for this quarter are all taken from Matthew's account of the life of Jesus. They cover the full range of Jesus' days on this earth, from his birth in Bethlehem to his ascension back to Heaven. Some of the lesson texts focus upon what Jesus did while others call attention to what he taught. Together they present a well-rounded portrait of his life and ministry.

The first unit of lessons is entitled "Beginnings: Birth and Ministry." **Lesson 1,** "King's Herald and Baptism," tells the story of John the Baptist and his role as the forerunner of the promised Messiah. With his austere manner and rough attire, John "prepared the way of the Lord" by creating within the hearts of the Jewish people an expectation that the Messiah's long-awaited arrival was near.

Lesson 2, "Temptations and Ministry," picks up Matthew's account immediately after the baptism of Jesus. Before his messianic ministry began, Jesus was first tested by the subtle craftiness of the devil; and, like gold in a refiner's fire, his faith proved to be genuine. Each of the well-known temptations in the wilderness was cleverly designed to undermine Jesus' plans for ministry. By focusing upon God's will and relying upon his Word, Jesus won a crucial victory. Our study of

Matthew 4 will remind us how we too can counter the deceptions of the devil.

Lesson 3, "Birth of Jesus," takes us back to the announcement of Jesus' birth to his earthly father Joseph. Matthew 1 presents a portrait of Joseph as a quiet man of faith, who, though rarely mentioned in Scripture, played a significant role in God's scheme of redemption.

Lesson 4, "Coming of the Wise Men," is taken from the account in Matthew 2 of the search for the Christ child by the wise men from the East. The familiar story of their homage to the child and the precious gifts they presented to him will challenge us to keep an attitude of worship and adoration in all our Christmas activities.

MINISTRY

The second unit of lessons, entitled "Ministry: Wonderful Words and Works," presents five examples of the teaching and healing ministry of Jesus. It also affords us a glimpse of the twelve closest disciples of Jesus as well as a look at some of his bitterest enemies.

Lesson 5, "The Twelve Disciples," uses select verses from three different chapters in Matthew to show how Jesus selected, groomed, and then sent forth into service the group of twelve men we now know as his apostles. The challenge of discipleship and service that he presented to them will serve as a reminder of his calling to us.

Lesson 6, "Teachings on Prayer," gives us the opportunity to look again at what may be the most famous and beloved prayer in Scripture—Jesus' "model prayer" in Matthew 6. Jesus gave this prayer to his disciples as an example to guide them in their own prayer lives. And though many of us have already memorized this prayer and often repeat it in our Lord's day worship, we will seek some practical lessons from this prayer that will guide us as we construct our own personal expressions of prayer to God.

Lesson 7, "Miracles of Compassion," uses some of the incidents recorded in Matthew 9 to present a "typical day" in the healing ministry of Jesus. A woman who for twelve years had suffered from severe bleeding, a young girl who had died, two blind men, and an entire crowd of afflicted people all benefited from Jesus' compassion. Though his powers were beyond our abilities, his manner of compassion and concern will challenge us as we try to respond with mercy to the needs of people around us.

Lesson 8, "Opposition to Jesus," looks at the unpleasant side of Jesus' ministry. While great multitudes often flocked around Jesus, listening to his words with wonder and amazement, always lurking in their midst were groups such as the scribes and Pharisees. Matthew 12 illustrates the kind of critical barrage Jesus regularly faced from his enemies and the incisive response he was capable of giving.

Lesson 9, "Laborers in the Vineyard," presents one of the many memorable parables of Jesus. The concept of the grace of God in this parable was difficult for Jesus' audience to grasp; but then, it is a concept with which many today still struggle.

FULFILLMENT

The last unit of lessons, "Fulfillment: Atonement and Final Commission," focuses upon the climax of Jesus' life and ministry: his death and resurrection and his final words to the church.

Lesson 10, "Entry Into Jerusalem," celebrates Jesus' triumphal entry into Jerusalem. On that "Palm Sunday" beginning the week that was climaxed by his

JANUARY

FEBRUARY

crucifixion, Jesus received some of the kind of praise and exaltation that he truly deserves. Our goal in studying Matthew 21 will be to seek ways to enrich our own expressions of worship to our triumphant Lord and Savior.

Lesson 11, "Anticipation of Christ's Return," reminds us that someday Jesus will return to earth to gather up his people and take them home to Heaven. Selected passages from Matthew 24 and 25 will emphasize Jesus' clarion call for readiness. While many today study second coming texts for clues and signs of the end, this lesson will demonstrate the real purpose of such texts: to challenge us to pursue godly living daily and actively so that we will be found ready on the day Jesus returns.

Lesson 12, "Death of Jesus," is perhaps the most moving lesson in this series, for it focuses on the description in Matthew 27 of the terrible suffering of Jesus on the cross. We sing of how we "love that old cross" as we reflect upon the salvation that Jesus' death brought about; but then we draw back in horror as we realize the depth of the pain that Jesus endured because of our sins. Calvary is the heart of the gospel and the key to our redemption from sin.

Lesson 13, "Resurrection and Commission," brings the story of Jesus to a fitting conclusion. The final chapter of Matthew's Gospel tells of the women's discovery that the tomb of their Master was empty. Through this lesson we will relive the excitement and joy of the good news that our Savior has conquered death. And we will be reminded of that to which the church must give top priority—Jesus' Great Commission to take the gospel to "all nations."

Without question, the story of Jesus bears repeating time and time again, for it is indeed the "sweetest that ever was heard."

Palestine

in the Time of Christ

Caesarea Philippi ★

Suggested site of the Sermon on the Mount

Mediterranean Sea

GALILEE

★ Korazin
Capernaum ★

Sea of Galilee

★ Nazareth   Gadara ★

SAMARIA

Samaria ★

★ **Sychar**

Jordan River

PEREA

Mount of Temptation

Emmaus ★

Site of Baptism

Jerusalem Bethany

Bethlehem ★

Dead Sea

JUDEA

Jerusalem (from the east)

Hinnom Valley

■ **Place of the Last Supper?**
□ **Herod's Palace**
● **Tomb of Jesus?**

■ **House of Caiaphas?**
Tower of Mariamne
● **Golgotha?**

■ **Palace of Herod Antipas**

Praetorium (Antonia Fortress)

Tyropoeon Valley

Kidron Valley

Garden of Gethsemane ● **Mount of Olives**

CHRONOLOGICAL OUTLINE OF SELECTED EVENTS IN MATTHEW

Early Period

Lesson 3	Genealogy (1:1-17)	
Lessons 3, 4	Birth of Jesus (1:18—2:12)	4 B.C.
	Flight to Egypt and Return to Nazareth (2:13-23)	

Beginning of Jesus' Ministry

A.D. 26

Lesson 1	John's Ministry (3:1-12)
Lesson 1	Baptism of Jesus (3:13-17)
Lesson 2	Temptation (4:1-11)

The Galilean Ministry

A.D. 27

Lesson 5	Calling of Four Fishermen (4:18-22)	
	Teaching and Miracles in Capernaum (8:14-17)	
Lesson 5	Call of Matthew (9:9-13)	
	Teaching and Healing the Multitudes (12:15-21)	A.D. 28
Lesson 6	The Sermon on the Mount (5:1—8:1)	
Lesson 8	Opposition to Jesus (12:22-45)	
	The Great Sermon in Parables (13:1-35)	
Lesson 7	Miracles of Compassion (9:18-38)	A.D. 29
Lesson 5	Twelve Apostles Named (10:1-4)	
	Feeding of Five Thousand (14:13-21)	
	Peter's Great Confession (16:13-20)	
	The Transfiguration (17:1-8)	

Journey to Judea

A.D. 30

	Jesus in Perea (19:1-12)
	The Rich Young Ruler (19:16-22)
Lesson 9	Parable of Laborers in the Vineyard (20:1-16)
	The Blind Men at Jericho (20:29-34)

The Final Days

Lesson 10	The Triumphal Entry (21:1-17)
	Day of Questions (22:1-46)
Lesson 11	Prediction of the Second Coming (24:45-51)
Lesson 11	Parable of Ten Virgins (25:1-13)
	The Passover Meal and the Lord's Supper (26:17-29)
	Agony in the Garden (26:36-46)
	Arrest and Trials of Jesus (26:47—27:26)
Lesson 12	Death of Jesus (27:27-66)
Lesson 13	Resurrection (28:1-15)
Lesson 13	The Great Commission (28:16-20)

KING'S HERALD AND BAPTISM

LESSON 1

WHY TEACH THIS LESSON?

"Do not conform any longer to the pattern of this world," Paul wrote (Romans 12:2). Today's lesson will provide you and your students a good role model for applying Paul's command to real life. John the Baptist was a nonconformist of the first order. His clothing was functional but not stylish. His diet was—to modern palates—bizzare! But more important than such externals as food and dress was his uncommon devotion to truth. The trappings of wealth and power meant nothing to John, so those who displayed them could not intimidate John. He would tell the truth; he would speak God's message. Are your students as bold?

INTRODUCTION

A. TALKIN' ABOUT HEAVEN

One of the old spirituals has the line: "Everybody talkin' about Heaven ain't goin' there." Jesus confirmed that it is true that many who think they are "on good terms" with God will be surprised to learn otherwise at the Judgment. Some who claimed to be Christians during their lives will be turned away. They will say, "Lord, Lord, did we not prophesy in your name, and in your name drive out demons and perform many miracles?" (Matthew 7:22). But they will be rejected because, "Not everyone who says to me, 'Lord, Lord,' will enter the kingdom of heaven, but only he who does the will of my Father who is in heaven" (v. 21).

Most of us have heard that Christians ought to "practice what we preach." A more contemporary version of this principle is that we must "walk the talk." But no matter how one says it, the simple truth is that it is not enough just to talk about being a Christian—we need to live as though we mean it. After all, the old spiritual is right: not everyone talking about Heaven is going to be there.

B. LESSON BACKGROUND

The Gospel of Matthew tells the story of the ministry of Jesus, from his baptism to his death and resurrection. However, as Matthew indicates, the ministry of Jesus actually began with the ministry of John the Baptist. John had been commissioned by God to announce the imminent arrival of the Jewish people's long-awaited Messiah and to issue a call for all those who were ready to join the Messiah in establishing the kingdom of God. John was not one to mince words; he made it very clear that the joys of the messianic kingdom are for only those who are willing to humble themselves before God and repent of their sins.

I. HEED GOD'S CALL (MATTHEW 3:1-6)

A. A RUGGED PREACHER (vv. 1-4)

1. In those days John the Baptist came, preaching in the Desert of Judea.

John the Baptist conducted a ministry unlike that of anyone else in his day. The contents of his *preaching* were not of his own devising, but were given to him by

DEVOTIONAL READING:
MATTHEW 21:23-27
BACKGROUND SCRIPTURE:
MATTHEW 3
PRINTED TEXT:
MATTHEW 3:1-17

LESSON AIMS

After this lesson students will be able to:

1. Summarize the message of John the Baptist and how he fulfilled his role as the herald of Jesus.

2. Compare and contrast the reason Jesus was baptized with the reasons believers are baptized today.

3. Examine their lives and state changes they will make in order to "fulfill . . . righteousness."

KEY VERSE

I baptize you with water for repentance. But after me will come one who is more powerful than I, whose sandals I am not fit to carry. He will baptize you with the Holy Spirit and with fire.

—Matthew 3:11

This visual shows some of the sites where the events studied this quarter took place. Keep it on display throughout the quarter.

WHAT DO YOU THINK?

The people went to the wilderness in droves to hear a word from the Lord in the preaching of John the Baptist. People in our society have not lost their spiritual appetite, but they do not always know where to find the truth. Where do spiritually hungry people go for food in our modern world? How can we convince them that only in Jesus is there spiritual food to satisfy their need?

God. John was not welcomed or accepted by the religious leaders of his day, and thus he withdrew from their jurisdiction to the *Desert*, or less populated areas, of the province *of Judea*.

2. . . . and saying, "Repent, for the kingdom of heaven is near."

We can be certain that John's sermons were considerably longer than this one sentence. What Matthew has done is to record for us the essence of John's preaching. For centuries the Jews had waited for the fulfillment of the messianic prophecies. John declared that the time of fulfillment was *near*.

What is referred to in Matthew as the *kingdom of heaven* is described in the Gospel of Mark as "the kingdom of God." These are parallel phrases, as can be seen by comparing Matthew 13 and Mark 4. In neither case is the focus upon a place (a kingdom located in Heaven, or a territory on earth), but upon a relationship. We are in a *"kingdom* relationship" with *heaven* when God is our King and we are his servants. It is in this sense that John could say that the *kingdom of heaven* would appear on earth shortly. The anointed King had already been born and was about to begin his ministry. Then, after his resurrection, when "all power" would be given to him (Matthew 28:18), Jesus would begin to summon all people through the gospel to enter into a kingdom relationship with him by accepting him as their Lord and King.

3. This is he who was spoken of through the prophet Isaiah: "A voice of one calling in the desert, 'Prepare the way for the Lord, make straight paths for him.'"

This quotation is taken from Isaiah 40:3, one of Isaiah's several prophecies of the coming Messiah. The imagery here is that of an "advance team" preparing for a visit from a royal dignitary. Roads are smoothed out (potholes are filled in), and people are made ready to greet their visiting king. John was the "advance team" for Jesus—the road builder who made *straight paths for him*, and the *voice* (herald) who trumpeted the King's arrival.

4. John's clothes were made of camel's hair, and he had a leather belt around his waist. His food was locusts and wild honey.

John the Baptist is noted for his austere manner of living. He lived out in the wilderness areas away from the cities of Judea. His *camel's hair* clothing was rougher than other fabric, but also more durable and thus better suited for his outdoor lifestyle. The *leather belt* held his robe together and also allowed him to gather up the bottom of his robe so he could move freely when he traveled through rocky terrain or waded into the Jordan River.

John's *food* consisted of *locusts and wild honey* (and probably anything else edible that he could take from the land). His choices were small and simple, but healthful. We should not imagine John to have been a sickly, malnourished man, but a healthy, vigorous outdoorsman who made quite an impression upon all who ventured out to see this prophet of God.

B. A RECEPTIVE PUBLIC (vv. 5, 6)

5. People went out to him from Jerusalem and all Judea and the whole region of the Jordan.

The ministry of John was extremely well received. Though the religious leaders despised him, the multitudes loved him. So great was their regard for John that the Pharisees hesitated to make public statements critical of John, for fear of agitating the crowds (Matthew 21:26).

6. Confessing their sins, they were baptized by him in the Jordan River.

As his nickname implies, John "the Baptist" (or "the Baptizer") was known for performing baptisms. Such a practice must have been rare or even non-existent in John's day for the title to have much meaning. First-century Judaism did devise a "proselyte baptism" to initiate Gentile converts into the Jewish faith, and the Jewish sect known as the Essenes used baptism to symbolize spiritual cleansing. But there is no clear evidence that these pre-dated John's baptism. John's baptism was unique, both in its form and its purpose, and was intended to prepare the people spiritually for the arrival of the Messiah and the kingdom of God.

The baptism of John was like Christian baptism in its outward form, but not in its meaning. John's baptism was not linked to "the gift of the Holy Spirit" (Acts 2:38). His audience was not told that they would be "buried with Christ" (Romans 6:3-6) or experience a "putting on" of Christ (Galatians 3:27). John offered a "baptism of repentance" that anticipated the coming of the Messiah and his salvation (Acts 19:4). This is how the link between John's baptism and remission of sins (Mark 1:4; Luke 3:3) should be understood. His baptism looked forward to the time when remission of sins could be offered as a result of Jesus' death and resurrection, just as the sacrifices under the law of Moses had looked forward to Christ's perfect sacrifice. Note that believers in Jesus who had been baptized with John's baptism were later challenged with the gospel to finish what they had started and to be "baptized into the name of the Lord Jesus" (Acts 19:1-5).

II. PREPARE FOR JUDGMENT (MATTHEW 3:7-12)
A. FRUITS OF REPENTANCE (vv. 7-10)
7. But when he saw many of the Pharisees and Sadducees coming to where he was baptizing, he said to them: "You brood of vipers! Who warned you to flee from the coming wrath?

John's strange behavior and enticing message drew a diverse crowd. Along with the listeners who were genuinely interested, there were the curiosity seekers and the scoffers. The latter category included the *Pharisees and Sadducees*, the leaders of the Jewish community. They opposed John's ministry because he operated outside their oversight and disrupted the religious *status quo*. They came, not to grow in spirit, but to gather evidence that could be used to silence John.

Like one of the ancient prophets, John courageously challenged the malicious hypocrisy of the Pharisees and Sadducees when they attended his preaching. He called them a *brood of vipers*, using snakes as a symbol of evil and deception—an image that recalled the activity of the serpent in the garden of Eden.

8. "Produce fruit in keeping with repentance.

Just as "faith without deeds is dead" (James 2:26), so likewise *repentance* that does not bear *fruit* is nothing more than empty words. Biblical repentance is more than remorse at getting caught or regret at how badly a situation turned out. It is an honest acknowledgment of having done wrong and a genuine desire to set things right as best we can.

One obvious fruit of repentance would be a verbal apology to someone we have wronged. Usually what we would rather do is to ignore a problem and hope it goes away; however, what we need to do is to muster the courage to face our friends and say, "I was wrong and I am sorry for what I did." Sometimes the obvious fruit of repentance is to offer to make restitution for the harm we have done, and perhaps, like Zacchaeus, even add a bonus to underscore our sincerity (Luke 19:8). And, of course, nothing says "repentance" better than to change our behavior for the good and cease to do the sin in question.

In the case of deeply ingrained habits that do not easily go away, repentance may not be able to produce an immediate end to the sin. But a genuine desire to quit will seek out aggressive measures for effecting change, such as agreeing to work with counseling, setting up an accountability relationship, or staying away from people and places that tempt us to renew our sin.

WHAT DO YOU THINK?

Just as in John's day, people in our generation may not immediately embrace the good news of Jesus Christ. Negative experiences with Christianity and society's perception of the church have left a number of people very resistant to the gospel. How can Christians open the hearts of others to receive the gospel?

WHAT DO YOU THINK?

How important do you think it was for John to emphasize repentance in preparation for Jesus' ministry? Why?

How much is John's emphasis on repentance a model for us? Why? How well do you think our church is doing in following John's example? How might we improve?

A changed heart should result in a changed life. Neither standing in a crowd by the river Jordan nor sitting in a church pew will make us right with God unless our lives exhibit genuine fruits of repentance.

ONLY HUMAN

Dr. Laura Schlessinger is the host of a popular talk radio program. She says the question she most often receives from her radio audience is this: "Now that I've done all these things I shouldn't have done, how can I avoid the consequences I knew about, but denied and just hoped wouldn't happen?"

Dr. Schlessinger confesses that her pet peeve is the frequent protest that one is "only human."

"*Only* human?" she asks. "As if one's humanness were a blueprint for instinctive, reflective reactions to situations, like the rest of the animal kingdom. I see being 'human' as the unique opportunity to use our minds and wills to act in ways that elevate us above the animal kingdom."

Schlessinger then underscores her point with an illustration from the classic film, "The African Queen." Charlie, who is played by Humphrey Bogart, invokes the "only human" excuse to explain his drunkenness the evening before. Rosie, the missionary who is played by Katherine Hepburn, looks up from her Bible and sharply replies, "We were put on earth to rise above our nature."

Nothing says repentance better than change. When we truly repent, we "rise above our nature" and begin to live as our Creator meant for us to live. —L. D. C.

WHAT DO YOU THINK?

The self-righteousness of the Sadducees and Pharisees was rooted in genealogical pride—they were children of Abraham—and the accuracy with which they, by their own accounting, had kept God's commandments. How do religious people today develop a self-righteous attitude? How can we prevent having such an attitude?

9. *"And do not think you can say to yourselves, 'We have Abraham as our father.' I tell you that out of these stones God can raise up children for Abraham.*

A genuine faith and repentance are required of all who would approach God, including his "chosen people." Though the Jewish people may be the natural heirs of the messianic promises to *Abraham* their *father*, the blessings are actually bestowed upon those who imitate the faith of Abraham, and that regardless of ancestry (Galatians 3:26-29). There is no privileged status when it comes to the grace of God—or the judgment of God.

10. *"The ax is already at the root of the trees, and every tree that does not produce good fruit will be cut down and thrown into the fire.*

As the woodsman holds the *ax* blade next to the *root* of a *tree* in order to prepare to strike it, so also the judgment of God is already being planned for those who fail to produce the *good fruit* of faith and repentance.

B. WHEAT AND CHAFF (vv. 11, 12)

11. *"I baptize you with water for repentance. But after me will come one who is more powerful than I, whose sandals I am not fit to carry. He will baptize you with the Holy Spirit and with fire.*

WHAT DO YOU THINK?

John used a vivid illustration to demonstrate his view of his ministry. Jesus' role was so superior to his, he said, that he was not worthy even to carry Jesus' sandals. In an age that seems to worship "self-esteem," this kind of self-effacement sounds strange. How do you think one should balance self-esteem and humility?

John operated with a clear understanding of his relationship to Jesus. Desiring no glory for himself, all that he did was for the advancement of the Messiah's ministry. He knew that his was a temporary role that must soon "become less," even as Jesus' role "must become greater" (John 3:30). His humility was such that he did not consider himself worthy of even carrying the Messiah's *sandals*. In the other Gospels John says he is not worthy to "untie" the Messiah's shoes (Mark 1:7; Luke 3:16; John 1:27). No doubt these references to handling shoes were occasioned by the ancient practice of washing one's feet upon entering a home. This was a task for the lowliest household servant. John said he was unworthy to perform even this lowly task for the Messiah.

Some believe that the fulfillment of John's words about the Messiah's baptizing *with the Holy Spirit and with fire* came through what the apostles experienced on the Day of Pentecost (Acts 2:1-4). Others, noting that John's words were addressed to the multitudes, think it is more inclusive. Jesus seems to have referred to John's words here in Acts 1:5, when he told the apostles they would shortly "be baptized with the Holy Spirit," clearly a reference to Pentecost. In that instance, he did not mention baptism with fire, which this context explains is a reference to judgment. All who resist the Spirit-led ministry of Jesus and his apostles after him will experience this baptism of fire.

12. *"His winnowing fork is in his hand, and he will clear his threshing floor, gathering his wheat into the barn and burning up the chaff with unquenchable fire."*

After *wheat* was cut at the harvest, it was taken to the *threshing floor*, where the grain was separated from the straw, usually by having oxen trample it or drag a sled over it to break the grain out of the husks that surrounded it. The straw could then easily be removed, but the grain was still mixed with *chaff* (the husks and small, broken pieces of straw). So the grain, including the chaff, was then scooped up with a *winnowing fork* and tossed into the air. The wind separated the light chaff from the heavier grain. The grain was then stored for later use, and the chaff was scooped up and burned.

John's picture of wheat and chaff clearly portrays the idea of a day of judgment when the saints will be separated from the sinners. Just as God's "ax" is already being lined up against the unfruitful tree (v. 10), so also His *fork is in his hand*, ready to separate the useless chaff from the grain, and to burn up the chaff in the *unquenchable fire* of Hell.

III. DO WHAT IS RIGHT (MATTHEW 3:13-17)

A. JESUS' OBEDIENCE (vv. 13-15)

13. *Then Jesus came from Galilee to the Jordan to be baptized by John.*

Jesus was born in the southern province of Judea, in the town of Bethlehem, but he was raised at Nazareth in the northern province of *Galilee*. When he was thirty years old (Luke 3:23) and ready to begin his ministry, he traveled to the *Jordan* River to the location where *John* was baptizing.

14. *But John tried to deter him, saying, "I need to be baptized by you, and do you come to me?"*

At this point, John had not yet received the divinely appointed sign that Jesus was indeed the Messiah. That would accompany Jesus' baptism (John 1:32-34). However, John may have known something about Jesus' miraculous birth and his exemplary character, which made him hesitant to baptize Jesus. The mothers of John and Jesus were related (Luke 1:36), and thus information about one may have become known by the other.

15. *Jesus replied, "Let it be so now; it is proper for us to do this to fulfill all righteousness." Then John consented.*

Jesus instructed John to permit him to be baptized because doing so would *fulfill all righteousness*; that is, it would be the "right thing" before God. Jesus understood that John's baptism expressed more than just repentance from sin, but also a readiness for the kingdom of God. Thus Jesus thought it "right" that he submit to baptism in order to express before God his own readiness for the kingdom of God and his willingness to assume God's appointed role for him in that kingdom as the Messiah who must suffer and die for the sins of the world (John 1:29).

THE CRITIC

When John F. Kennedy was President of the United States, newspaper columnists frequently wrote advising Kennedy how he could do a better job. In response

HOW TO SAY IT

Essenes. Eh-SEENZ.
Isaiah. Eye-ZAY-uh.
Pharisees. FAIR-ih-seez.
Sadducees. SAD-you-seez.
Zacchaeus. Zack-KEE-us.

PRAYER

Father, accept our humble admission of sin. Help us to change and grow in holiness through Jesus Christ, in whose name we pray. Amen.

THOUGHT TO REMEMBER

"Do not merely listen to the word, and so deceive yourselves. Do what it says" (James 1:22).

to these critics, Kennedy told a story of a legendary baseball player. "He never failed to hit when at bat and never dropped a ball," Kennedy said. "Grounders never dribbled between his legs. He threw with unerring accuracy. In the field and on the bases he had the speed and grace of a leopard. He never tired or missed a signal. In fact, he would have been one of the all-time greats except for one thing—no one was ever able to get him to put down his soft drink and hot dog and come out of the press box to play."

Jesus did not simply command us to be baptized; Jesus himself was baptized. Jesus was not a critic; he was a doer. What he instructed others to do he did. He set the ultimate example through a lifestyle that modeled the teachings that he gave. Though Jesus had no reason to repent (because he was without sin), he showed us what we are to do by being baptized. He not only taught us the right thing to do; he did what was right. —L. D. C.

B. GOD'S APPROVAL (vv. 16, 17)

16. As soon as Jesus was baptized, he went up out of the water. At that moment heaven was opened, and he saw the Spirit of God descending like a dove and lighting on him.

The Gospel of John explains this descent of *the Spirit of God* on Jesus when he *was baptized* as a sign to mark Jesus as the Messiah (John 1:32, 33). He did not receive the Spirit at this point, as if he had not possessed the Spirit before. As God's Son, Jesus was one with the Father and the Spirit. The descent of the Spirit marked the beginning of Jesus' Spirit-empowered ministry. Immediately after that Jesus, "led by the Spirit," defeated the devil in the wilderness (Matthew 4:1ff.). From that time on, he worked miracles by the power of the Spirit (Matthew 12:28).

17. And a voice from heaven said, "This is my Son, whom I love; with him I am well pleased."

God's *voice from heaven* confirmed that what Jesus had said to John was true. Baptism was the right thing for him to do to start his messianic ministry. The words *this is my Son* were derived from the Old Testament prophecies that identified the Messiah as that person designated by God as "my Son" (Psalm 2:7). God was *well pleased* with what Jesus had done on this day.

Though our experience in Christian baptism is not identical to that of Jesus, our attitude should be the same as his. He knew what God wanted him to do, and he took action to "fulfill all righteousness"—to do the right thing before God. Many today question whether or not they need to be baptized as long as they have a genuine faith in Christ. But since baptism is part of our Great Commission for evangelism (Matthew 28:18-20; Mark 16:15, 16), is stated in Scripture as a command (Acts 2:38; 22:16), and is the consistent practice of converted believers in the book of Acts, then there should be no debate. Faith does whatever God says to do because it is the right thing to do.

CONCLUSION

How do you know when it is time to change the oil in your car? Many auto mechanics leave a sticker on the windshield to remind you when your next oil change should take place. Some may send a postcard notice as that time approaches. Some newer cars even have a red warning light to let you know it is time for a change.

Over and over through his messengers and in his Word God has issued a call for repentance from sin. As we reflect on the ministry of John the Baptist, let us allow this story to serve as a spiritual "warning light," telling us that it is time for a change.

Discovery Learning

This page contains an alternate lesson plan emphasizing learning activities. Classes desiring such student involvement will find these suggestions helpful. The next page is a reproducible activity page to further enhance discovery learning.

LEARNING GOALS

After this lesson students should be able to:

1. Summarize the message of John the Baptist and how he fulfilled his role as the herald of Jesus.

2. Compare and contrast the reason Jesus was baptized with the reasons believers are baptized today.

3. Examine their lives and state changes they will make in order to "fulfill . . . righteousness."

INTO THE LESSON

Purchase ten bananas. Write one letter of the word *repentance* on each. (Any felt-tip marker should work.) Hand a banana to each of the first ten students who arrive for your study. As class begins, ask those holding bananas to read their letters aloud, one at a time, at random. Direct the group to listen carefully and to guess what word the letters, if arranged properly, could spell. If they need help, have the letters read a second time or have the students with bananas to stand and show the letters.

Once the word *repentance* is seen, emphasize this as the theme of John's preaching and of today's lesson. Ask the banana holders to keep their fruit handy for later use.

INTO THE WORD

As the class follows in their own Bibles (or in the student books), have a volunteer read Matthew 3:1-17. Divide the class into three groups. Ask one group to discuss John's relationship with the people, a second group to discuss his relationship with the religious authorities, and a third to discuss his relationship to Jesus.

If you or someone in your class has a talent for drama, plan an "interview of John the Baptizer." Give your John role player all the following references to read prior to today's class: Matthew 3:1-17; 14:3-12; Mark 1:1-11; 6:17-29; Luke 1:5-80; 3:1-22; 7:16-35; John 1:15-37; 3:23—4:1; 10:41. Prepare some interview questions on cards or slips of paper to be distributed randomly to class members. (Give the person playing John a copy of these questions.) Here are some samples that can highlight John's life and ministry. Allow the class members to ask additional questions based on their small group studies.

• How did your parents communicate to you regarding your God-given purpose?

• Describe your life in the Judean wilderness.

• Where did you get the idea of baptizing people as a symbol of cleansing?

• Matthew tells us only that you preached, "Repent, for the kingdom of heaven is near!" Please elaborate on the content of your sermons.

• How was the baptism you performed different from the baptism later demanded by the Christian evangelists?

• Why did you call the Pharisees and Sadducees "vipers"? Isn't that harsh and judgmental?

• You didn't feel worthy to baptize Jesus. Why didn't you simply refuse?

• You offended many important people in your preaching ministry. Wasn't some of your preaching foolishly risky?

• What did you mean by "fruit in keeping with repentance"?

At the end, you will want to discuss the accuracy and reasonable nature of "John's" answers, especially to those questions that call for answers not specifically found in the Scriptures.

INTO LIFE

Have the class return to its small groups to discuss these questions. (You may give each group all the questions or divide the questions among the groups.)

1. Jesus' coming to John to be baptized is an example of a variety of righteous traits in the person of Jesus. What are some of those traits?

2. The imagery of baptism is a perfect symbol of its essence and meaning. How so?

3. John the Baptizer, as a servant of God, demonstrates some characteristics that are universal to God's servants and some that are peculiar to his specific ministry. Which are which?

After a brief statement by each of your discussion groups, return to the class members who held the bananas. Ask, "How is the banana a worthy symbol of the key word of today's text: *repentance?*" Accept various responses; anticipate someone noting that the banana is not useful . . . until it "makes a drastic change," until it "takes on a new appearance"; it must be peeled! If your personal budget permits, give each of the other members of your class a banana to carry home as a symbol and a reminder of today's key truth—and possibly a conversation starter.

What's In a Nickname?

John "the Baptist" carries a "nickname" befitting part of his important ministry. How might each of the following be appropriate nicknames for John?

JOHN THE ROAD BUILDER—

JOHN THE VOICE—

JOHN THE RUGGED OUTDOORSMAN—

JOHN THE VIPER SPOTTER—

JOHN THE HUMBLE—

JOHN THE OBEDIENT—

JOHN THE LESSER—

JOHN THE POPULAR—

JOHN THE AX WIELDER—

JOHN THE COUNTRY PREACHER—

If you were to be given a nickname for your character and your service on behalf of God, what might it be? Fill in your name and appropriate appellations here:

_____ the _____

_____ the _____

Repentance Fruit

John demanded that his audience repent, but he also expected them to "produce fruit in keeping with repentance." On the bowl of fruit pictured here, write in what you believe to be "fruit in keeping with repentance." (Hint: it might include some of the internal and external traits highlighted in Galatians 5:22, 23 and some of the "opposites" of Galatians 5:19-21.)

TEMPTATIONS AND MINISTRY

LESSON 2

WHY TEACH THIS LESSON?

Familiar stories from the Bible offer a special challenge: "How can this material be presented in a fresh and inspiring manner?" The account of Jesus' temptations in the desert is one such story. The three recorded temptations have been compared with 1 John 2:16 and applied to the kinds of temptations we all face. Note has been taken of Hebrews 4:15 as well, observing that Jesus has been "tempted in every way, just as we are." So what will you do with this text today?

Much of the same, of course. These are important facts to know. The application of Jesus' experience to our own can help us in our daily walk with the Lord. What will make this lesson fresh could well be the candor with which you, the teacher, share from your own experience how the same methods Jesus used to deal with temptation still work today. Can you do that?

INTRODUCTION

A. SHAMEFUL PRACTICES

What kind of parents would kill their own children? The idea is almost unthinkable to most of us, for we like to think that all parents cherish their children as much as we do. And yet we know from news reports that this kind of shocking incident happens with increasing frequency.

How strange it is, then, to read in the Old Testament that sometimes parents would offer their children as burnt sacrifices to the pagan god Molech. How awful that some of the Hebrew parents began to join the pagans in this horrific practice! The prophet Ezekiel describes the wrath of God against those from among his people who "sacrificed their children" on the pagan altars (Ezekiel 23:37). And then, as if their sin were not great enough already, with utter hypocrisy they would enter the sanctuary of God with an offering "on the very day" they had killed their own children (Ezekiel 23:38, 39).

However, inconsistent behavior toward God is not confined to the Old Testament age! Jesus rebuked the Pharisees of his day for their hypocrisy. They took great pains with small details such as setting aside a tithe of all their income, including the vegetables out of their gardens (Matthew 23:23). Yet they blatantly violated some of the greater demands of God's moral standard by such actions as defrauding widows and orphans out of the few possessions they had (Matthew 23:14).

We do well to heed the Bible's warning that God is not pleased with a partial obedience that obeys only those portions of his Word that are agreeable to us. We must learn to put the will of God above our own desires in *all* areas of our lives.

B. LESSON BACKGROUND

Though the baptism of Jesus marked the official beginning of his ministry, he did not come before the public until weeks later. The first item on God's agenda was a private time of testing. Jesus was "led by the Spirit" (Matthew 4:1) into a

DEVOTIONAL READING:
LUKE 4:14-21
BACKGROUND SCRIPTURE:
MATTHEW 4:1-17
PRINTED TEXT:
MATTHEW 4:1-16

LESSON AIMS

After this lesson each student will be able to:

1. Tell how Satan tempted Jesus and how Jesus resisted Satan in the wilderness.

2. Tell what principles for dealing with temptation can be drawn from Jesus' experience.

3. Devise a plan to overcome a personally troubling temptation by using Jesus' experience in the wilderness as a model.

KEY VERSE

Jesus said to him, "Away from me, Satan! For it is written: 'Worship the Lord your God, and serve him only.'"—Matthew 4:10

LESSON 2 NOTES

Then, Jesus was led by the Spirit into the desert to be tempted by the devil.
Matthew 4:1, NIV

The visual for today's lesson shows the traditional site for the temptations of Jesus. Display it as you begin your study of the lesson text.

WHAT DO YOU THINK?

The Bible does not tell us what Jesus did during his forty-day fast, but we know that a Jewish fast usually involved intense prayer and meditation. What do you think Jesus prayed about? What can we learn from this experience?

WHAT DO YOU THINK?

Satan chose food for his first temptation. He knew Jesus had no moral weakness, but even the Son of God in human form had a need and a craving for food. What can we learn about temptation from this?

desert area. There Satan took the opportunity to try to distract Jesus from his divine calling, but Jesus firmly resisted all of Satan's temptations. In doing so he demonstrated the genuineness of the faith commitment that he had earlier declared through his baptism.

I. TRUSTING GOD'S WORD (MATTHEW 4:1-4)

A. NOT MOTIVATED BY FEELINGS (vv. 1-3)

1. Then Jesus was led by the Spirit into the desert to be tempted by the devil.

The precise location of Jesus' confrontation with the devil is not disclosed in any of the Gospels. However, the term *desert* conveys the idea of an area isolated from cities and villages. There were several such locations on both sides of the Jordan River, where Jesus could have gone following his baptism. The Gospel of Mark notes that Jesus was "sent" by the Holy Spirit into the desert (Mark 1:12). Jesus' time of testing was no coincidence; it was by God's design. (The visual for today's lesson—shown at left—pictures the site traditionally held to be the location of this testing.)

2. After fasting forty days and forty nights, he was hungry.

The fact that Jesus spent his *forty days and forty nights* in the desert *fasting* likely indicates that he was spending a significant amount of time each day in prayer and meditation. The issue for Jesus that would have been serious enough to warrant such intense prayer and fasting was the messianic ministry that now lay before him. Fasting was typically done for short periods of time, from one day up to a week. Thus Jesus' *forty days* of fasting was quite exceptional and somewhat risky. The human body can easily adapt to a few days without food. But with extended fasting there comes a point at which physical strength and health begin to decline. To say that Jesus *was hungry* at that point is quite an understatement.

Forty days of fasting is not humanly impossible, as some have contended. Modern-day protesters have often conducted "hunger strikes" for forty days and longer. But the result is always a physically weakened condition.

3. The tempter came to him and said, "If you are the Son of God, tell these stones to become bread."

In the three desert temptations, Satan demonstrates why he is to be acknowledged as a master of his craft, deserving of the title *the tempter*. Each temptation Jesus faced was carefully aimed at his present situation, striking where he was most vulnerable and in a manner that could actually have seemed reasonable and thus all the more tempting.

Satan's first temptation focused on Jesus' physical weakness and hunger. The devil knew that after forty days of fasting, Jesus would have a strong desire for food as well as a genuine need for nourishment. He also knew that when an enticing opportunity (temptation) matches a person's inner desires, the conditions are right for sin to occur (James 1:14, 15). Our own experience with sin bears out this truth, for we can recall occasions when our moral judgment and good intentions were set aside because we felt overwhelmed by the desires of our flesh.

Satan also took care to package his temptation in the most appealing manner. *If you are the Son of God*, he said, reflecting back on Jesus' baptism. Jesus had heard the voice from Heaven say, "This is my Son" (Matthew 3:17), and he knew that he was "led by the Spirit" (4:1); but he had yet to do anything truly messianic or supernatural. So far he had simply been alone for forty days in a wilderness. Perhaps the devil was suggesting that Jesus attempt a miracle with the *stones* just to take advantage of his special status as the Son of God. Or he may have proposed that Jesus use his powers to preserve his life so that he would be able to carry out his messianic calling.

Whatever the intent of Satan's words, they constituted a subtle attempt to get Jesus to give up trusting in God for his needs and to take some initiative on his own. But since the Holy Spirit had directed him into the desert, the Holy Spirit was the one who should tell him what to do next. To move ahead of the Spirit would have been a sin.

The Snake

The story is told of a man who was walking through the woods on a cold winter day. As he was walking, he came upon a poisonous snake. Startled, he took a step back and noticed that the snake was freezing cold. The snake looked up at the man and said, "Please, sir, pick me up and warm me in your arms."

The man refused, saying, "No, if I pick you up, you will only bite me and I will surely die."

The snake replied, "But you would be helping me—why would I bite you?"

The man thought for a moment, while the viper continued to plead for the man to help him. Finally the man picked up the snake and put him inside his coat. As soon as the snake warmed up, he bit the man. As the man was dying, he asked the snake why he had bitten him. The snake responded, "You knew who I was before you picked me up; you just chose to see me in a different light."

This is how Satan wants us to treat sin. He wants us to see it in a different light, so that he can steer us into excuses and rationalizations. Satan glamorizes sin and makes it look delightful, when it is actually destructive. We must see sin as it really is, and we must see the one who tries to make us sin for who he really is—the deadliest of serpents.   —L. D. C.

B. Relying on God (v. 4)

4. Jesus answered, "It is written: 'Man does not live on bread alone, but on every word that comes from the mouth of God.'"

Jesus responded to the devil's clever temptation with a resounding "no," quoting from Deuteronomy 8:3. Jesus could identify with the full context of this passage, which describes how the children of Israel wandered for forty years in another wilderness, living each day by the manna that fell from Heaven. Though their bodies longed for this miraculous bread, Moses cautioned them that their greater desire should always be for the Word of God.

II. SERVING GOD'S WILL (MATTHEW 4:5-7)

A. Not Acting With Presumption (vv. 5, 6)

5. Then the devil took him to the holy city and had him stand on the highest point of the temple.

The order of the second and third temptations in Matthew's account are the reverse of Luke 4:5-12. We assume that one of the Gospel writers was following a chronological order, while the other may have been telling the events according to the emphasis he wanted to make (perhaps desiring to end with what he considered the most pivotal of the three temptations).

The second temptation in Matthew's account of the testing of Jesus took place in *the holy city* of Jerusalem, at the top of one of the several towers built onto the roof of the temple complex to give it a look of grandeur. The text does not indicate how the devil took Jesus from the wilderness near the Jordan to this new location. He may have challenged Jesus to travel to Jerusalem and meet him at *the highest point of the temple*, but it is more likely that he used supernatural powers and transported Jesus there immediately.

What Do You Think?

Jesus used Scripture to defend himself against Satan. How is that significant to you? What does it suggest to you about how to deal with your own temptations? How can you prepare yourself to be able to do that?

WHAT DO YOU THINK?

In his second temptation Satan challenged Jesus to test God to see whether he would keep his promises. How are Christians sometimes tempted to test God? How can we resist these temptations?

6. *"If you are the Son of God," he said, "throw yourself down. For it is written: 'He will command his angels concerning you, and they will lift you up in their hands, so that you will not strike your foot against a stone.'"*

Showing his versatility in crafting temptations, Satan "fought fire with fire." Jesus had rebuffed the first temptation with a Scripture quotation; the tempter responded with his own text of Scripture. His quotation of Psalm 91:11, 12 was accurate, but, as we would expect, his application of it was misleading.

Psalm 91 is not really a messianic prophecy. It is the testimony of a man who remained faithful to God under difficult circumstances and thus received God's protection because of his unfailing trust. Satan was suggesting that the promise of divine protection should apply to the Messiah most of all. After all, the Messiah is the faithful servant par excellence, and thus should be entitled to the help of *angels* if ever needed.

Once again, Satan was encouraging Jesus to exploit his relationship as the *Son of God* and obligate the Father to intervene and rescue his Son. Perhaps the temptation here was to follow a different course of ministry from the one laid out for him, which included service and the submission to death. Instead, Satan suggested that Jesus make a grandstand show to attract the crowds. Then Jesus could begin his messianic ministry with a great following.

B. HUMBLE BEFORE GOD (v. 7)

7. *Jesus answered him, "It is also written: 'Do not put the Lord your God to the test.'"*

Jesus was not one to be outdone in a contest involving Scripture. Returning once again to the book of Deuteronomy, Jesus quoted a verse that effectively called the devil's bluff: *Do not put the Lord your God to the test* (cf. Deuteronomy 6:16). No one, including the Messiah, should presume to tell God what to do. God was under no obligation to send angels to rescue Jesus, had he thrown himself off the temple tower. Jesus' duty was to wait until God chose to act by his own initiative in his own time.

III. SEEKING GOD'S GLORY (MATTHEW 4:8-10)

A. NOT THINKING OF SELF (vv. 8, 9)

8. *Again, the devil took him to a very high mountain and showed him all the kingdoms of the world and their splendor.*

For the third temptation the location shifted to an unnamed *mountain* peak. Of course, there is no mountain in the world from which one could actually see *all the kingdoms of the world.* Some suggest that Jesus may have been on a mountain from which he could see two or three large cities, which would have represented all civilizations. However, it is more likely that the devil used his supernatural powers and presented a vision of each of the major cities and kingdoms of the world. Luke's account speaks of Jesus' seeing the kingdoms "in an instant" (Luke 4:5). This brings to mind a rapidly moving vision with pictures in quick succession, or perhaps in some kind of montage with images overlapping one another. In any event, it would have been an impressive sight to behold.

9. *"All this I will give you," he said, "if you will bow down and worship me."*

It might seem that Satan was losing his touch if he imagined for a moment that Jesus would *bow down and worship* him. However, when this temptation is understood properly, one is led to conclude that this may have been the most crucial test of the three. For what the devil appears to be offering Jesus is actually an attractive concession to his messiahship.

The Old Testament prophecies often foretold that the Messiah would eventually obtain the right to rule all nations in behalf of God. The devil was offering to

WHAT DO YOU THINK?

Satan offered Jesus an easier path to glory. What kind of shortcuts does Satan offer us? How can we guard against his trickery?

step aside and let Jesus lay claim to the world right now, without any struggle or conflict. The one concession: allow the devil a moment to enjoy having his "sworn enemy," the Son of God, bow before him in submission. To put it another way, Satan was telling Jesus, "Let me win this one time, and then you can have it all."

Oh, the subtle strength of this temptation! Here was a shortcut to Jesus' messianic destiny—a chance to bypass the horrible suffering of Calvary. The agony that awaited him was so great that it "troubled" his spirit to even speak about it (John 12:27; 13:21). In Jesus' final moments before his arrest and crucifixion he prayed, "If it is possible, may this cup be taken from me" (Matthew 26:39). He wanted to serve God faithfully in his role as Messiah, but he dreaded the price he had to pay. It had seemed as though there was no other way for him to reign as Lord of creation except through his death—that is, no other way until now.

THE HIGH COST OF SHORTCUTS

There was once an extremely wealthy man who employed a very devoted and responsible contractor. One day the wealthy man asked the contractor to build him a home. He gave the contractor the specific instructions that he wanted him to follow, and he told him to use only the finest materials. The man also gave the contractor all the money that building the house would require. Then the man left on a business trip, with the instructions that he wanted the house done by the time he returned.

The contractor had begun building the home, when he thought to himself, "I have worked for this man for many years. I have been dedicated and hard-working, yet I live in a small home and am barely able to put food on my plate—while this man lives in luxury and pays me next to nothing." So the contractor decided that he would make some money from his employer by taking certain shortcuts in his work. When he ordered the materials for the house, he bought cheaper items than the plan called for, especially in materials that would be covered up so checking on them would be difficult or impossible. Then he pocketed the rest of the money.

When the wealthy man returned from his trip, he came out to see the house. Then he said to the contractor, "You have been a hard-working, dedicated employee all these years, and I want to reward you." Then he handed the house key to the contractor and said, "Here, this is your house."

Satan tried to get Jesus to take a shortcut that would have bypassed the cross. Jesus, Satan claimed, would be able to rule over all the nations immediately, without having to suffer a horrible death. But Jesus refused to take any shortcuts. He stood his ground and remained obedient to the will of his Father.   —L. D. C.

B. FOCUSED ON GOD (v. 10)

10. Jesus said to him, "Away from me, Satan! For it is written: 'Worship the Lord your God, and serve him only.'"

Drawing for a third time from Deuteronomy, Jesus reminded the devil what our "jealous" God requires: *Worship the Lord your God, and serve him only* (cf. Deuteronomy 6:13). Jesus could not give to Satan that which is reserved exclusively for God, even though it would have benefited him greatly. For Jesus there was no room for compromise with the plan laid out for him by his Father.

IV. FULFILLING GOD'S PLAN (MATTHEW 4:11-16)

A. APPROVED BY GOD (v. 11)

11. Then the devil left him, and angels came and attended him.

After his third defeat, Satan retreated to rethink his strategy and to watch for another opportune moment to tempt Jesus (Luke 4:13). He left behind a fragile

HOW TO SAY IT

Antipas. AN-tih-pus.
Capernaum. Kuh-PER-nay-um.
Deuteronomy. Due-ter-AHN-uh-me.
Ezekiel. Ee-ZEEK-yul or Ee-ZEEK-ee-ul.
Isaiah. Eye-ZAY-uh.
messianic. mess-ee-AN-ik.
Molech. MO-lek.
Naphtali. NAF-tuh-lye.
Perea. Peh-REE-uh.
Zebulun. ZEB-you-lun.

PRAYER

Heavenly Father, when we are weak you are strong. So when we are tempted to sin, help us to "hope in the Lord," knowing that you will renew our strength. In Jesus' name. Amen.

THOUGHT TO REMEMBER

"For I have come down from heaven not to do my will but to do the will of him who sent me" (John 6:38).

form—one who had been weakened physically from the forty days of fasting, and was now also drained emotionally and spiritually as a result of his intense conflict with the devil. But now that he had proven himself entirely faithful, God was pleased to fulfill the promise of Psalm 91:11, 12 and send *angels* to assist Jesus in the recovery of his strength.

B. READY FOR SERVICE (vv. 12-16)

12. When Jesus heard that John had been put in prison, he returned to Galilee.

Soon after the time of tempting was completed, John the Baptist was arrested by Herod Antipas, who ruled as king of *Galilee* and Perea (Matthew 14:3). Perhaps because this arrest implied danger for Jesus as well, he departed from the southern territory of the Jews where John had been ministering. The northern district of Galilee became the focal point of his ministry. From Matthew's Gospel we might think this move happened immediately after the wilderness temptations. John, however, records several events in an early Judean ministry (chapters 1–3), which must have lasted for a few months before Jesus departed for Galilee.

13, 14. Leaving Nazareth, he went and lived in Capernaum, which was by the lake in the area of Zebulun and Naphtali—to fulfill what was said through the prophet Isaiah:

The headquarters for Jesus' Galilean ministry was the city of *Capernaum*, located on the northwest shore of the Sea of Galilee. When Joshua allotted the promised land to the twelve tribes of Israel, this territory was given to the tribes of *Zebulun and Naphtali*. Though these tribal divisions no longer existed by Jesus' day, Matthew noted the old territorial names in order to show the fulfillment of an Old Testament prophecy from *Isaiah* (9:1, 2), which he proceeded to quote.

15, 16. "Land of Zebulun and land of Naphtali, the way to the sea, along the Jordan, Galilee of the Gentiles—the people living in darkness have seen a great light; on those living in the land of the shadow of death a light has dawned."

The *land of Zebulun and . . . of Naphtali* was never of any great significance in Old Testament history. Its location made it especially more vulnerable to the influence of the pagan peoples who lived to the north of Israel. Yet in spite of the presence of such spiritual *darkness*, this territory saw *a great light*. Its *people* were blessed by the ministry of the one whom Isaiah proceeded to describe in chapter 9 as "Wonderful Counselor, Mighty God, Everlasting Father, Prince of Peace" (Isaiah 9:6).

CONCLUSION

In *Mere Christianity*, C. S. Lewis writes that it is those who refuse to give in to temptations who face the greatest spiritual challenges. Those who give up, Lewis says, never know just how tough temptation can get. It is only those who fight to the end who know the full strength of the devil's craft. And as for Jesus Christ, "because he was the only man who never yielded to temptation, [he] is also the only man who knows to the full what temptation means."

Because of his strong dedication to the will of God, Jesus attracted the most powerful temptations Satan had to offer; and yet he was always "without sin" (Hebrews 4:15). It is to our benefit to study the Gospel accounts of the wilderness temptations so that we might learn from Jesus' success. We watch him ignore the desires of the flesh that so readily lead us into sin (James 1:14, 15). We observe the way he used Scripture as a spiritual sword against the devil (Ephesians 6:17). We see how he set aside his own personal interests as he focused on God's will for his life (Philippians 2:3-8). Our fervent desire should be to imitate Jesus' faithfulness and thereby join him in victory over the devil.

Discovery Learning

This page contains an alternate lesson plan emphasizing learning activities. Classes desiring such student involvement will find these suggestions helpful. The next page is a reproducible activity page to further enhance discovery learning.

LEARNING GOALS

After this lesson students should be able to:

1. Tell how Satan tempted Jesus and how Jesus resisted Satan in the desert.

2. Tell what principles for dealing with temptation can be drawn from Jesus' experience.

3. Devise a plan to overcome a personally troubling temptation by using Jesus' experience in the desert as a model.

INTO THE LESSON

As class begins, display the following list with the heading, "TODAY'S TOUGHEST TEMPTATIONS." Ask your class to take a few minutes and jot them down in order of "most common" to "least common" in contemporary society: tell a lie, commit fornication, practice gluttony, envy another's position, want to be rich and powerful, break governmental law, leave something important (and good) undone, elevate self above others, use foul or profane language, grumble about circumstances, gossip about another person.

After a few minutes, ask several to tell what they put at the top and the bottom of their lists. Sample the class for uniformity and differences. Ask the class to suggest other temptations they could add to the list. Make the transition to Bible study by pointing out that in today's text, the Master Teacher teaches us all how to deal with "Today's Toughest Temptations."

INTO THE WORD

Have Matthew 4:1-16 read aloud by three readers: one for Jesus' words, one for Satan's words, and one for the connecting narrative words.

Read the following generalizations about temptations and have the students agree or disagree with each, using elements of today's narrative and text to support their positions. Pause after each statement for learner response.

1. Temptations are always "reasonable."

2. Temptations always attack human weaknesses, that is, lusts.

3. Temptations are all "fathered" by the devil.

4. Temptations are persistent.

5. Temptations may be either blatant or subtle.

6. Temptations lose their strength in the presence of Scripture.

7. Temptations always carry with them a doubt of God's power and care.

8. Temptations thrive in the company of stress.

9. Temptations are allowed by God, but never come from God.

10. Temptations do not have to "succeed."

As the class reacts and questions, introduce the following Scriptures at appropriate times: James 1:14, 15; Hebrews 4:15; Matthew 6:13; Luke 8:6, 13; 1 Corinthians 10:13; Galatians 4:13, 14; Revelation 3:10; James 1:2-4; 2 Peter 2:9; 1 Thessalonians 3:5. You may want to assign these texts to be found, held, and introduced appropriately, before beginning this activity.

INTO LIFE

Introduce this activity by stating the key principle of dealing with temptations, as seen in today's text: *confront temptation with the power of God's truth!* Give each person in half of your class a blue index card with a text from the following list written on it. These students should find and read these texts.

Give each person in the other half of the class a red index card with one of the "temptations" from the list written on it. (There are two references for each temptation, so prepare two cards for each temptation.)

Ask your class to stand and circulate, exchanging cards without speaking until they come to a person who holds a "matching" card, that is, until a temptation is matched with a verse that could well be used to overcome it. When matches are made, those holding the two cards should be seated. The one who has read the verse should recognize the match; the one who held the temptation card should now keep the verse card, look up the Scripture, and read it. When all matches have been made, ask the group to report on their matches.

Matthew 6:12 and Matthew 18:21, 22: **spirit of vengeance**; Proverbs 8:7 and Ephesians 4:15: **lying**; Leviticus 19:13 and Romans 12:17: **cheating**; 1 Corinthians 6:18 and 1 Peter 2:11: **sensual pleasure**; 2 Corinthians 9:7 and Acts 20:35: **greed, stinginess**; Hebrews 10:25 and 1 John 2:17: **indifference to godliness**; 1 Thessalonians 5:14 and Psalm 37:7, 8: **impatience**; Philippians 4:11 and 1 Corinthians 10:10: **grumbling**. (A similar activity can be found in the student book.)

Close with a prayer for strength to handle temptations.

Meet the Enemy . . . Know the Enemy

Jesus was led of the Spirit into the isolation of the desert to meet and "be tempted by the devil." He had to meet the enemy . . . and demonstrate his utter superiority over him. Meet the enemy of God's children in the following passages. What is his dominant characteristic(s) in each? Put the letter of your choices in front of each.

_____ 1. Job 1:6-12; 2:1-8	A. brazen
_____ 2. Acts 26:18	B. cruel
_____ 3. 1 Peter 5:8	C. deceitful
_____ 4. Revelation 20:10	D. doomed
_____ 5. 2 Corinthians 11:13, 14	E. lying
_____ 6. John 8:44	F. accusing
_____ 7. Zechariah 3:1-4	G. powerful
_____ 8. Revelation 2:9, 13, 24	H. ravenous

Are there other adjectives you would use of the enemy? Write them here:

Know Yourself . . . Beat the Enemy

To the left here, identify a few temptations most common in your daily Christian walk. To the right—using a concordance or a Christian friend!—find a Scripture you should memorize and use against the temptation—just as the Lord confronted temptations in the desert.

TEMPTATION	SCRIPTURAL "ANTIDOTE"
_____	_____
_____	_____
_____	_____
_____	_____
_____	_____
_____	_____

BIRTH OF JESUS

LESSON 3

DEVOTIONAL READING:
JOHN 1:1-14
BACKGROUND SCRIPTURE:
MATTHEW 1
PRINTED TEXT:
MATTHEW 1:1-6, 18-25

Dec
19

WHY TEACH THIS LESSON?

If last week's lesson text provided a familiar Bible story, then this week's text provides one even more so. Even non-Christians know the basic facts of the nativity story—even if they do not believe them to be "facts." What may be unfamiliar is the portion of the genealogy with which the lesson opens.

The contrast between the familiar and unfamiliar may give you an opportunity to challenge your students in a way the "Christmas story" has not challenged them before. In the familiar we see some of the major characters in the drama of human redemption—names known to virtually everyone: Mary and Joseph. In the unfamiliar we see names like Perez and Hezron and Salmon—names unknown to us but important enough in God's estimation to be included in the inspired record.

Not many of us will make such an impression on our society that our names will appear in the history books of future generations. That fact may make some of us uncomfortable. Like George Bailey, we may wonder if our lives make any difference at all. But just as Perez and Hezron and Salmon were important to the working of God's redemption plan, so are we. Our names might not be written in history books, but God has a book, too. If our names are written there, that is what counts!

INTRODUCTION

A. SMALL PARTS

"There are no small parts, just small actors." Such is the bold front often put up by actors and actresses who are assigned roles that they think are less than what their talents deserve. The words may appear to reflect a humble acceptance of one's circumstances, but in reality they may be nothing more than "sour grapes."

In the record of sacred Scripture, there are hundreds of "small parts," played by godly characters for whom we are given little information regarding their lives and service for God. Joseph, the earthly father of Jesus, is one such minor character, receiving far less attention in Scripture than his wife Mary, John the Baptist's parents, or even the shepherds who traveled from their fields to Bethlehem. And yet, though Joseph's role in God's grand "drama of salvation" may seem small, he was faithful to his divine calling. He left behind an example worthy of our study and our imitation.

B. LESSON BACKGROUND

The ministry of Jesus began with his baptism in the Jordan River and his testing in the wilderness. But the character and direction of his ministry was set some thirty years earlier at his birth. At that time several people received messages from God telling them what they could expect from this special child: his mother Mary (Luke 1:26-38), his earthly father Joseph (Matthew 1:20, 21), a group of shepherds (Luke 2:8-14), an old man named Simeon (Luke 2:25-35), and an aged widow and prophetess named Anna (Luke 2:36-38). The revelation

LESSON AIMS

After this lesson each student will be able to:

1. Tell how God's providence was active in preparing Joseph to be the Messiah's earthly father.

2. Tell why a "behind-the-scenes" obedience, such as that of Joseph, is essential to the achievement of God's purposes.

3. Plan one or more acts of kindness during this Christmas season, which, though they may be done privately, will show Christ's love to others.

KEY VERSE

She will give birth to a son, and you are to give him the name Jesus, because he will save his people from their sins.

—Matthew 1:21

LESSON 3 NOTES

each received was brief, but it included crucial information about the person and work of Jesus. Our lesson today will focus on that prophecy given to Joseph.

I. ROYAL LINEAGE (MATTHEW 1:1-6)

A. SON OF ABRAHAM (vv. 1, 2)

1. A record of the genealogy of Jesus Christ the son of David, the son of Abraham.

Matthew's Gospel, directed primarily to a Jewish readership, begins with a tracing of Jesus' roots back to two of the most prominent individuals in Jewish history. *Abraham* was the father of the Jewish nation, and *David* was her greatest king.

There are some peculiarities to note regarding Matthew's *genealogy*. First, it is not intended to be a comprehensive listing of all Jesus' paternal ancestors. Matthew has selected certain names to mention and has elected to skip others. He later notes (v. 17) that he has provided fourteen names from the patriarchal period (Abraham to David), fourteen from the monarchy (David to the Babylonian captivity), and fourteen from the post-exilic period (the captivity to the birth of Christ). One should keep in mind that it was not an uncommon practice among the Jews to selectively design a genealogy to accomplish a specific objective. Perhaps, in Matthew's case, this objective was to facilitate memorization of Jesus' ancestry.

In Jewish genealogies such as Matthew's, the term *father* does not necessarily imply a direct father-son relationship, because a man was considered the "father" of all of his descendants. Thus Jesus is identified as *the son of David* and *the son of Abraham*, though in fact he was many generations removed from both men.

Another significant point regarding Matthew's genealogy of Christ is that it does not match the genealogy provided in Luke's Gospel (Luke 3:23-38). The traditional explanation is still the most acceptable: Matthew is tracing Jesus' ancestry through Joseph, while Luke is tracing his lineage through Mary.

2. Abraham was the father of Isaac, Isaac the father of Jacob, Jacob the father of Judah and his brothers.

Matthew's genealogy of Christ begins with *Abraham*—the first and greatest of the patriarchs ("father rulers"). During the days prior to the establishment of formal government structures among the Jews, the patriarchs exercised authority over their family clans and all who lived within their boundaries. Abraham's position was handed down to his son *Isaac*, whose birth was a special gift from God to Abraham when he was old, and to his wife Sarah, who—until then—had been barren.

Isaac fathered twin sons, Esau and *Jacob*—the latter and younger of the two having been chosen by God before his birth to assume the patriarchal role of his grandfather and father. Jacob fathered twelve sons, from whom the twelve tribes of Israel were descended.

Passing over his first three sons because of offenses they committed against him, Jacob chose *Judah* to carry on the patriarchal tradition. And as Jacob on his deathbed made clear to Judah, this special blessing also included the privilege of being the "father" of the future kings of Israel as well as of the ultimate King, the Messiah (Genesis 49:10).

THE TRUTH OF THE BIBLE

Myron Augsburger tells of a young man from India who left his Hindu religion to become a Christian after reading the first chapter of Matthew. When he was asked what there was about the genealogy that led to his conversion, the man replied that for the first time in his life he had found a religion that is rooted in history.

HOW TO SAY IT

Ahaz. AY-haz.
Amminadab. Uh-MIN-uh-dab.
Bathsheba. Bath-SHE-buh.
Boaz. BO-az.
Emmanuel. Ih-MAN-you-el.
Esau. EE-saw.
Gabriel. GAY-bree-ul.
Herod. HAIR-ud.
Hezron. HEZZ-ron.
Hittite. HIT-ite.
Immanuel. Ih-MAN-you-el.
Isaiah. Eye-ZAY-uh.
Jericho. JAIR-ih-co.
Nahshon. NAH-shahn.
Obed. OH-bed.
Perez. PAIR-ezz.
Rahab. RAY-hab.
Salmon. SAL-mun.
Sheol. SHE-ol.
Simeon. SIM-ee-un.
Tamar. TAY-mer.
Uriah. Yu-RYE-uh.
Zerah. ZAIR-uh.

Hinduism and Buddhism are based on mythology, and the young man found Christianity's historicity a refreshing contrast.

Many people today try to disregard the Bible as a myth. They suggest that the authors of the books of the Bible simply made up the stories they record. In fact, however, the Bible is historically accurate. Matthew makes this point evident by accurately tracing the lineage of Jesus back to Abraham.

It is clearly demonstrated throughout the Bible that its authors were divinely inspired to be completely accurate. "All Scripture," Paul tells us, "is God-breathed and is useful for teaching, rebuking, correcting and training in righteousness, so that the man of God may be thoroughly equipped for every good work" (2 Timothy 3:16, 17). From its history to its moral teaching to its claim to tell of the only way of salvation, the Bible is completely reliable and trustworthy. —L. D. C.

B. SON OF DAVID (vv. 3-6)

3. Judah the father of Perez and Zerah, whose mother was Tamar, Perez the father of Hezron, Hezron the father of Ram.

Most of the names that follow *Judah* identify obscure individuals for whom Scripture gives little if any biographical information. Judah once had an adulterous encounter with his daughter-in-law *Tamar*, resulting in the birth of twin boys (Genesis 38:27-30). The younger of the two was named *Zerah*. The firstborn, *Perez*, is known for slipping ahead of his brother during the time of birth, after his brother had thrust one hand out ahead of him then withdrew it. Perez thus inherited the special royal lineage, which he passed along to his son *Hezron*, who did the same with his son *Ram*.

4. Ram the father of Amminadab, Amminadab the father of Nahshon, Nahshon the father of Salmon.

The royal lineage continued through *Amminadab*, the father-in-law of Moses' brother Aaron (Exodus 6:23). Amminadab's son *Nahshon* became the leader of the tribe of Judah during the forty-year march through the wilderness (Numbers 2:3; 10:14). The royal heritage was then passed on to his son *Salmon*.

5. Salmon the father of Boaz, whose mother was Rahab, Boaz the father of Obed, whose mother was Ruth, Obed the father of Jesse.

It is with *Salmon* that the first gap appears in Matthew's genealogy. The Old Testament provides no information regarding Salmon, making it difficult to know where to place him in Jesus' ancestry. It is only in Matthew that we learn that Salmon was married to Rahab, the prostitute of Jericho who hid the Hebrew spies (Joshua 2). That information would place Salmon in the time of Joshua's conquest of Canaan. However, *Boaz*, who was David's great-grandfather, should be placed in the latter half of the period of the Judges, who ruled for some three hundred years (Judges 11:26). Salmon was thus a few generations removed from Boaz's actual father. In this case, Salmon was *the father of* Boaz in the sense that he "was the ancestor of" Boaz.

Boaz was a wealthy farmer who married *Ruth*, whose story of exceptional faith is told in the Old Testament book that bears her name. The lineage passed from Boaz to his son *Obed*, and then to his son *Jesse*, the father of King David. Boaz lived in Bethlehem (Ruth 2:1-4), which became known as the "town of David" and where centuries later Jesus was born (Luke 2:4, 11).

6. And Jesse the father of King David. David was the father of Solomon, whose mother had been Uriah's wife.

King *Solomon* was gifted by God with exceptional wisdom and was blessed with Israel's largest and wealthiest kingdom (2 Chronicles 1:7-12). His *mother*, Bathsheba, had been *Uriah's wife*. (Uriah, a Hittite, was one of King David's

DAILY BIBLE READINGS

Monday, Dec. 13—The Genealogy of Jesus the Messiah (Matthew 1:1-11)

Tuesday, Dec. 14—Jesus' Genealogy Completed (Matthew 1:12-17)

Wednesday, Dec. 15—The Birth of Jesus the Messiah (Matthew 1:18-25)

Thursday, Dec. 16—Jesus Christ, God's Eternal Word (John 1:1-14)

Friday, Dec. 17—The Angel Gabriel Visits Mary (Luke 1:26-38)

Saturday, Dec. 18—Mary Visits Her Cousin Elizabeth (Luke 1:39-45)

Sunday, Dec. 19—Mary's Song of Praise (Luke 1:46-56)

WHAT DO YOU THINK?

Four women are mentioned in the portion of Jesus' genealogy chosen for our printed text. Two were prostitutes (Tamar, Genesis 38:24, and Rahab—i.e., Rahab, Joshua 2:1), and one had an adulterous affair with King David (the wife of Uriah—i.e., Bathsheba). Ruth had a pagan past. What, if anything, does the presence of such characters in Jesus' ancestry suggest to you?

military officers.) Bathsheba's adulterous affair with David led to a royal plot to have Uriah die in battle so that David could marry the widow and cover up her unexpected pregnancy. However, Nathan the prophet exposed the sin and told David that his and Bathsheba's child would die. Solomon, then, was the second child born to David and Bathsheba (2 Samuel 11:1—12:25).

David was the greatest king to rule Israel. Though his life and reign were not perfect, his heart was fully committed to God; and he became the standard by which future kings were measured (1 Kings 15:3, 11; 2 Kings 16:2; 18:1-3). David also became the symbol of the coming Messiah-King, who was acknowledged as the "Son of David" (Matthew 21:9; 22:41, 42).

II. GODLY MAN (MATTHEW 1:18-21)

A. DIFFICULT SITUATION (vv. 18, 19)

18. This is how the birth of Jesus Christ came about: His mother Mary was pledged to be married to Joseph, but before they came together, she was found to be with child through the Holy Spirit.

The Gospel of Luke records the announcement to *Mary* by the angel Gabriel that she had been chosen by God to give birth to the promised Messiah (Luke 1:26-38). The *Holy Spirit* would use his supernatural power to cause Mary to become pregnant. With our modern, scientific understanding of reproduction and conception, we are often curious to know exactly what the Holy Spirit did. But all we know for certain is that the *birth of Jesus Christ* involved no intimacy with a man. The Holy Spirit truly performed a miracle.

Mary's pregnancy became known while she was still engaged (*pledged to be married*) to her fiancé *Joseph*. This could have been a scandalous discovery for Joseph and his family. The couple had at no time come *together* in sexual intimacy—in fact, Mary had been separated from Joseph for three months in Judea (Luke 1:39, 56). Thus Joseph would have to assume that the child had been conceived as a result of intimacy with some other man. And since Mary had apparently not yet informed Joseph of Gabriel's message, he had no reason to believe anything other than that she had been unfaithful to her betrothal pledge.

19. Because Joseph her husband was a righteous man and did not want to expose her to public disgrace, he had in mind to divorce her quietly.

Joseph is here called Mary's *husband*, a term that emphasizes the serious nature of the betrothal. A couple who was betrothed were not to live together or sleep together, but they had entered a relationship as binding and as exclusive as marriage. Violations of this pledge were treated as violations of the marriage covenant, for which the law of Moses required the death penalty (Leviticus 20:10).

First-century Judaism did not have the legal authorization from Rome to carry out executions, and thus other measures were typically used to punish sexual infidelity. Anyone violating the betrothal pledge could be publicly denounced and humiliated, effectively shutting him or her out from any future marriage prospects (at least from any good ones). Furthermore, the violator's family could be assessed damages for bringing shame to the innocent party.

Regarding Mary, Joseph decided not *to expose her to public disgrace* by seeking punitive measures, but *divorce her quietly*. Herein lies a testimony to the gracious character of Joseph. Even when he believed he had been wronged and shamed, there was a gentle and compassionate spirit in his response. As a *righteous man* he was prepared to seek justice, and yet his was a justice tempered by mercy. It is not difficult to understand why God selected Joseph to serve as one of the parents who would nurture and guide the young Messiah in his development.

WHAT DO YOU THINK?

People in Joseph's day, even as today, would have believed Joseph quite justified in making a public example of Mary. But Joseph rose above that and acted honorably. Have you ever been in a situation in which you could have exacted revenge on a person—and most people would have believed you were entitled to it? How does one choose the "righteous" option of tempering justice with mercy?

B. BLESSED PROMISE (vv. 20, 21)

20. But after he had considered this, an angel of the Lord appeared to him in a dream and said, "Joseph son of David, do not be afraid to take Mary home as your wife, because what is conceived in her is from the Holy Spirit.

Matthew's nativity account does not name the angel who appeared to Joseph at this time, then later following the visit by the wise men (Matthew 2:13), and again after the death of Herod (v. 19). The designation *angel of the Lord* could apply to any angel, but its parallel use for Gabriel in Luke's account (Luke 1:11) supports the idea that he was also Joseph's messenger from God.

Joseph was instructed not to break off the betrothal as he had intended to do, but to *take Mary home as* his *wife*. He was then informed of the miraculous nature of Mary's pregnancy. This information would dispel any thought of infidelity by Mary, as well as indicate to Joseph the exceptional calling to which he and Mary were being summoned by God.

21. She will give birth to a son, and you are to give him the name Jesus, because he will save his people from their sins."

The *name Jesus* is the Greek form of the Hebrew word meaning "Jehovah is salvation" (from the Hebrew spelling comes the familiar name *Joshua*). The angel emphasized the spiritual nature of the messianic mission when he declared that *he will save his people from their sins*. First-century Judaism did anticipate some spiritual blessings from the Messiah, but it focused more on the idea of a political ruler who would deliver the Jewish people from the domination of the Romans.

Jesus, however, understood his spiritual priority and never wavered from it. His friend and forerunner John the Baptist spoke of "the Lamb of God, who takes away the sin of the world" (John 1:29). Jesus himself passed over any talk of earthly kingdoms and simply declared that the Son of Man had come "to give his life as a ransom for many" (Mark 10:45).

III. OBEDIENT SERVANT (MATTHEW 1:22-25)

A. DIVINE PLAN (vv. 22, 23)

22. All this took place to fulfill what the Lord had said through the prophet.

The appearance of an angel to the earthly father of the Messiah is not the prophecy fulfilled in this instance. There was no such prophecy. The fulfilled prophecy was the child's miraculous conception by the Holy Spirit.

23. "The virgin will be with child and will give birth to a son, and they will call him Immanuel"—which means, "God with us."

Matthew quotes one of the most famous messianic prophecies of the Old Testament, found in Isaiah 7:14. This is a text cherished by Christians, especially during the Christmas season. Old Testament scholars often debate the meaning of this sentence in its original context, arguing over whether or not Isaiah meant to point to the pregnancy of a "young woman" in the days when the prophecy was spoken to King Ahaz of Judah, with Matthew then adding a messianic implication to the passage centuries later.

While the issues involved can be quite complex, there are some simple observations that are worth noting. First, the "sign" Isaiah intended to give King Ahaz was to be "as deep as Sheol or high as heaven" (Isaiah 7:11, *New American Standard Bible*). This implies that Isaiah had in mind a supernatural event, such as would be the case with the miraculous conception of the Messiah. Also note that Matthew's interpretation of Isaiah 7:14 was given under the inspiration of the Holy Spirit. Whatever other applications to his own time Isaiah may or may not have had in mind when he spoke these words, Matthew assures us that the miraculous birth of Jesus was the fulfillment of Isaiah's prophecy.

Today's visual pictures Joseph as the angel speaks to him in a dream, telling him that the Son to be born to Mary is the Savior: Jesus!

WHAT DO YOU THINK?

Both Mary and Joseph knew Jesus had come to bring salvation. They probably did not know, however, that he would die a sacrificial death to make salvation possible. Most people in Mary and Joseph's generation looked for a political hero. How can one participate in God's plan if he or she does not understand God's plan?

WHAT DO YOU THINK?

Many people have no concept of a personal relationship with God. God is too "other-worldly" in their thinking. Even if they acknowledge Jesus as the Son of God, his physical presence was experienced for a short time some two thousand years ago, and they are unable to appreciate any benefit for today. What do you find most significant to your own life about Jesus as "God with us"?

The name *Immanuel* (also spelled "Emmanuel") literally means "with us is God," as Matthew tells his readers. This was sometimes used as a kind of "battle cry" by the Jews in times of trouble, expressing confidence that God was present with and fighting for the cause of his people. However, with the Son of God's incarnation on earth, *God with us* achieves its ultimate fulfillment.

B. WILLING OBEDIENCE (vv. 24, 25)

24. When Joseph woke up, he did what the angel of the Lord had commanded him and took Mary home as his wife.

True to the character we have earlier observed regarding *Joseph*, he obeyed the message from God. By doing so, he would have taken the shame of Mary unto himself. Observers would now wonder if he was in fact the man who had taken sexual liberties with this young lady, and, if not, why he would go through with the marriage plans. And certainly no one could be expected to believe a story about a supernatural conception. Joseph knew that his personal reputation might suffer from this decision, but he was fully committed to the will of God.

ACCEPTING YOUR ROLE

Cheryl had been practicing for days—looking over her script, reading it out loud, and perfecting her delivery in front of a mirror. She was trying out for the high school play, and was hoping to be given the part of Dorothy in the school's presentation of *The Wizard of Oz*. Cheryl especially wanted to play the lead since this was her senior year. But Cheryl did not get the part; in fact, a freshman was assigned the role of Dorothy. Cheryl was understandably disappointed.

Later the director of the play approached Cheryl and told her that there were still a lot of minor roles to be filled, but not enough people to fill them. Would she accept one of these? Cheryl could have said, "You didn't need me when I wanted to play Dorothy, the main character; now you want me for a less important part." But she didn't. Instead, Cheryl accepted her new role and worked hard at the practices. The play would not have been the success that it was, if people such as Cheryl had not been available and willing to play the minor roles.

Joseph also had to accept a role that was far different from what he might have chosen for himself. Perhaps he looked forward to a happy, peaceful life in Nazareth with his new bride Mary. But God had another role for Joseph—as the earthly father of the Messiah. Joseph humbly accepted his role and faithfully carried out all the responsibilities that went with it.

When we are doing God's will, no role is minor or insignificant.   —L. D. C.

25. But he had no union with her until she gave birth to a son. And he gave him the name Jesus.

For Matthew to say that Joseph *had no union with* Mary (in an intimate way) until after Jesus' *birth* implies that Joseph and Mary did eventually establish a normal marriage relationship. Later references to Jesus' brothers and sisters confirm this (e.g., Matthew 13:55, 56).

CONCLUSION

How many others in Jesus' ancestry could also give evidence, like Joseph, of faithful service to God, if only they had the opportunity to have their story told? How many servants of Christ over the course of church history have labored in obscurity—their devotion to duty known only to God? And how many of us are quietly doing our best to serve the Lord with the gifts and opportunities he provides, giving no thought to receiving recognition and applause?

Discovery Learning

This page contains an alternate lesson plan emphasizing learning activities. Classes desiring such student involvement will find these suggestions helpful. The next page is a reproducible activity page to further enhance discovery learning.

LEARNING GOALS

After this lesson each student will be able to:

1. Tell how God's providence was active in preparing Joseph to be the Messiah's earthly father.

2. Tell why a "behind-the-scenes" obedience, such as that of Joseph, is essential to the achievement of God's purposes.

3. Plan one or more acts of kindness during this Christmas season, which, though they may be done privately, will show Christ's love to others.

INTO THE LESSON

Cut from poster board twenty-eight strips two inches by ten inches. Punch holes in the ends of all the strips. Pair the strips and then write on each pair the names of a father and son from Matthew 1:2-6: Abraham and Isaac, Isaac and Jacob, and so on until David and Solomon.

Connect the father-son pairs with string or yarn, about twelve to fifteen inches long. Position one name "upside down" to the other so you can hand each connected pair of strips to a class member to wear over his/her neck, one name (the father) showing to the front, the other name (the son) showing to the back.

Once the class assembles, ask the students to stand. Direct each student with father-son labels to find the person who carries a "son's" name that matches his or her "father's" name. (Students without labels may assist those who do.) As the students identify the proper matches, have the group line up in correct genealogical order.

Once finished, stress to your class the value that the Jews placed on such genealogical carefulness. Note also that many roles that seem unimportant or behind the scenes are actually of great value to God and his kingdom.

INTO THE WORD

Read Matthew 1:1-6, 18-25. Give paper and pens to your class and ask them to write numbers 1 to 10 for the following true-false quiz about Joseph, based on the second half of today's text. Allow students to respond not only with T and F, but with D for "don't know" or P for "probably."

Read each statement carefully and slowly, repeating some as necessary. (1) Just as he had to Mary, the angel appeared to Joseph to reveal God's plan. (2) Joseph knew about Mary's pregnancy from the very beginning; she told him immediately. (3) Justice, in the Jewish

scheme, would have allowed Joseph to call disgrace upon his wife-to-be. (4) Joseph, whom the text calls "righteous," could also be called Joseph the "kind." (5) Divorce was appropriate in the circumstances in which Joseph and Mary found themselves. (6) Joseph found out from the angel of the Lord that Mary was pregnant. (7) Joseph believed in the Holy Spirit of God. (8) Joseph called the Son given to Mary and him Jesus, because that was his father's name. (9) Joseph was familiar with the prophecy of Isaiah about a virgin giving birth to a son. (10) Joseph was a carpenter.

As you review the questions for answers and comment, consider the following. (1) False. Mary met the angel face to face; Joseph's encounter was in a dream. (2) False. Apparently Mary went to visit Elizabeth immediately after the angel spoke with her; see Luke 1:39. Joseph probably learned of her pregnancy after she returned. (3) True (Matthew 1:19). (4) True. Verse 19 labels Joseph "righteous," but also suggests his kindness in the matter. (5) True; betrothal was considered as binding as marriage. (6) False; Joseph already knew when the angel spoke to him (verses 18-20). (7) Probably; the Spirit is part of Old Testament revelation, not novel to the New. (8) False. Joseph named the child Jesus because the angel told him to; see verses 21, 25. (9) Probably; Joseph certainly had opportunity to know Old Testament Scripture, and there was a scroll of Isaiah in Nazareth; see Luke 4:16-20. (10) True. Not so identified in this text, but see Matthew 13:55.

INTO LIFE

Some today are touting "Random Acts of Kindness"; encourage your class to perform "Private Acts of Kindness" after the order of Joseph's kindness. Give each member a small envelope and an index card. Ask each to write on that card a kindness he/she knows is needed by someone outside the class group. Have all the cards put into the envelopes; then collect the envelopes and drop them in a large grocery bag. Ask each member to draw a card from the bag on the way out of the class and to do the suggested kindness anonymously during this holiday season. Suggest a few possibilities: a family that needs food, a child who will be unlikely to receive gifts, a homebound person who needs a "shower" of cards. Tell the class to give clear, complete information on the cards they put into the bag.

Joseph, Father

Joseph "stands in the shadows," as far as the events of the Christmas story are concerned. One writer calls him "a minor character," filling one of the "hundreds of 'small parts'" in the stories of Scripture. Yet his is a critical role in the incarnation of God's Son: He will be Jesus' father! To the left and right of the poem that follows, cite relevant Bible verses from today's text—and others, perhaps—that tell the same information as that contained in the poem. Draw lines from your references to the relevant information in the poem. (One example is done for you to illustrate the idea.)

Joseph, Father

Joseph, standing in the shadows,
Father, holy in God's scheme,
Wondering how his God will finish,
Story started in a dream.

Joseph, dreaming in the clamor,
Father to whom angel came:
"Do not set your spouse aside now;
"Give her Child my special name."

"Jesus, born of Holy Spirit;   ——— Matthew 1:18
"Mary's pregnant by His plan:
"Child will need an earthly father;
"He must learn to be a Man."

Joseph, standing in the shadows,
Father, ready for his Son,
Now he waits for God to finish,
Story only now begun.

Playing the Joseph Role

Are you small enough to play the big role of Joseph? Are you big enough to play the small role of Joseph? What are the attributes of Joseph that you find most commendable—attributes that God also must have seen and liked?

COMING OF THE WISE MEN

LESSON 4

WHY TEACH THIS LESSON?

Some people might say the wise men demonstrated their wisdom by stopping to ask directions! Some men do seem to believe it to be a symbol of manhood to be able to find a location—or to do anything, for that matter—without assistance. Admitting that they need help is an embarrassment they just can't face!

But the whole story of the incarnation is one of help. Man could not help himself out of the predicament of sin, so God sent the Savior. The wise men recognized their need. Wise men and women today also recognize their need for the Savior. This lesson will be a helpful reminder of that fact.

INTRODUCTION

A. "ANYONE CAN PLAY THE PART"

"Anyone can play the part of a shepherd or a wise man." Such is the rule generally observed by all who direct boys and girls in church Christmas pageants, simply because (as is the case with many Bible stories) there are not a lot of female characters. Consider, for example, a dramatization of David and the Israelites against Goliath and the Philistines, Paul and Silas in prison, or Jesus and the apostles at the last supper in the upper room. Even in the nativity story the only female part is that of Mary. In order for many girls to have parts in these presentations, we usually hand a bathrobe to anyone who is interested in acting and adopt the policy that "anyone can play the part of a shepherd or a wise man."

This practical rule conveys an important spiritual truth. The nativity accounts of Matthew and Luke portray the wise men and shepherds as noble individuals who, when confronted with Jesus Christ, humbled themselves before him and gave him their worship. Their example can be, and should be, imitated by all of us, no matter who we are. "Anyone can play the part of a shepherd or a wise man," especially the part of giving one's all to Jesus our Lord and King.

B. LESSON BACKGROUND

The account of the birth of Christ in the Gospel of Matthew focuses on two events. As we noted last week, chapter 1 records an angel's message to Joseph that Mary was pregnant through the work of the Holy Spirit and that she would give birth to a Son who should be named Jesus. This week we will see that chapter 2 describes the visit of wise men from the East and King Herod's attempt to kill the Christ child. Located chronologically between the events of Matthew 1 and 2 is the familiar story of Luke 2.

During the final stage of Mary's pregnancy, Joseph and his fiancée traveled south from their hometown of Nazareth to Bethlehem, their ancestral home. The birth of Jesus occurred after the couple found temporary shelter, since there was "no room for them in the inn" (Luke 2:7). On the same day as the birth, angels appeared in the night sky to shepherds tending their flocks in a field. The angels directed the shepherds into town to locate the newly arrived Messiah.

For the next several weeks, Joseph and his new family apparently settled in Bethlehem. Whether this was a temporary arrangement to allow mother and

DEVOTIONAL READING:
PSALM 98
BACKGROUND SCRIPTURE:
MATTHEW 2
PRINTED TEXT:
MATTHEW 2:1-12

Dec
26

LESSON AIMS

This lesson is intended to help each student:

1. Retell the story of the visit of the wise men to see the child Jesus.

2. Tell what qualities shown by the wise men are worthy of imitation by Christians today.

3. Suggest a specific way to give oneself more fully to the Lord and his work in the coming year.

KEY VERSE

"Where is the one who has been born king of the Jews? We saw his star in the east and have come to worship him."
—Matthew 2:2

WHAT DO YOU THINK?

It seems reasonable to believe that the king of the Jews would be found in the capital city of the Jews; so the wise men looked for him in Jerusalem. Where do people look for Jesus today? How can we help them to find him when they look in our church or in our homes?

WHAT DO YOU THINK?

Many honest seekers for God enter church buildings every Sunday, hoping to find Jesus. They expect to find him in the words and actions of his people. They assume his people will reach out to them with sincere hearts. What can we do to make his presence felt more?

Where is he that is born King of the Jews? for we have seen his star in the east, and are come to worship him.

Matthew 2:2

This visual pictures the wise men in Jerusalem looking for the king of the Jews. Discuss how we can direct people today to the Savior, even when they are looking in the wrong places.

child time to prepare for the long trip home to Nazareth or Joseph had decided to remain in Bethlehem is not clear. In any event, it was during this period that the wise men came to honor the one "born king of the Jews" (Matthew 2:2).

I. A NOBLE QUEST (MATTHEW 2:1-6)

A. STARTING IN THE EAST (vv. 1, 2)

1. After Jesus was born in Bethlehem in Judea, during the time of King Herod, Magi from the east came to Jerusalem.

The word *Magi* resembles the Greek word used to describe the individuals whom we generally call "wise men." It was a title used by religious wise men in several countries of the Middle East, notably Persia and Arabia. The wise men who searched for the Christ child were renowned as "stargazers" who studied the night sky looking for divine clues to the future. Some believe they were proselyte converts to Judaism; others, that they were simply scholars interested in knowing more about the Jewish messianic hope, a subject that people in all of the regions surrounding Jerusalem would have known something about. After all, many Jews had been dispersed throughout the known world centuries earlier by the Assyrians and Babylonians. Also, Jerusalem was located on a major trade route in the Middle Eastern world. Foreign travelers passing through could easily pick up bits and pieces of Jewish thought.

The wise men had more than a passing interest in the Messiah, however. They came to "worship" him (v. 2), not just to greet him. And they appear to have been more than mere astrologers, too, receiving direct communication from God (v. 12).

2. . . . and asked, "Where is the one who has been born king of the Jews? We saw his star in the east and have come to worship him."

Matthew does not explain the nature of the *star in the east*. Some propose that the star was a bright meteor; others suggest a close alignment of two or more planets, at least one of which the wise men believed was linked to the fortune of Israel, or to the Messiah in particular. This appearance or alignment suggested to the wise men that something pivotal was about to happen. Some students think it very important that no movement is actually attributed to the star until after the visit of the wise men to Jerusalem (v. 9). To them, the fact that the wise men journeyed to Jerusalem rather than to Bethlehem suggests that the star was not yet guiding them to the birthplace; they were simply assuming that the *king of the Jews* would be born in the capital city of the Jews.

Other students are quick to point out that while no earlier movement is mentioned, it remains quite possible that the star had been leading the wise men. If so, it probably would have led them along the normal trade route from the East, which would have taken them through Jerusalem. These students suggest that clouds may have obscured the star for a time, which would account for the wise men's premature assumption that they had arrived at the proper location when they reached Jerusalem and for their joy at seeing the star as they left the city (v. 10).

Whatever the precise nature of the star, it is clear that it was more than a natural phenomenon. God may have used a meteor or an alignment of planets to get the wise men's attention, or he may have created a special sign in the sky. But then he caused that heavenly light to move and to indicate the exact location where the wise men would find Jesus (v. 9). That is not natural. There is no reason to believe that the wise men's quest was guided by mere assumptions based on astrology. The fact that God later spoke to the wise men (v. 12) suggests to some that he may well have spoken to them earlier, explaining the light in the sky. In any event, the star was a divine sign guiding the wise men on a divine mission.

B. STOPPING AT JERUSALEM (vv. 3, 4)

3. When King Herod heard this he was disturbed, and all Jerusalem with him.

The *Herod* of the nativity story was the first and most notable of the Herodian line of rulers. Known as Herod the Great, he ruled from approximately 37 B.C. to 4 B.C. over Galilee, Judea, and portions of the surrounding territory. (This is not the same Herod who would later be an antagonist of Jesus during his ministry. That was his son Herod Antipas, who ruled Galilee and Perea from 4 B.C. to A.D. 39.)

Our knowledge of Herod the Great through sources outside the Bible enables us to approximate the date of Jesus' birth. Herod died in the latter half of March in the year 4 B.C., at which time Joseph and Mary returned home from Egypt, where they had gone to protect the baby Jesus (Matthew 2:15). Counting backward from this date, and allowing three to four months for the events noted in the Gospels—the forty-day wait until Jesus could be "presented" in the temple (Luke 2:22), the visit of the wise men, the journey to Egypt, and a short stay there—the birth of Jesus could have occurred anywhere between November of 5 B.C. and January of 4 B.C.

It should be evident from all of this that our modern Western calendar is three to four years in error. The "Gregorian Calendar," devised in 1582, was calculated to center on the birth of Christ. Thus, many Christians today assume that A.D. 1, for example, corresponds to Christ's first year on earth, and that his death at age 33 took place in A.D. 33. However, we now know from other research that these calculations were slightly off. Jesus' birth likely occurred in the winter of 5–4 B.C., and his death was in A.D. 30.

None of this should be of great concern to us because calendars are a human contrivance that have been modified frequently throughout the ages. What matters most to us is the historical reality that the Son of God "became flesh" (John 1:14) and was born upon this earth.

4. When he had called together all the people's chief priests and teachers of the law, he asked them where the Christ was to be born.

Herod the Great was noted for his political cunning, but not for his Old Testament scholarship. Thus he had to ask the *chief priests*, who administered the Jewish religious system, and the *teachers of the law*, who were the leading Bible scholars, where the *Christ* was prophesied *to be born*.

C. PROCEEDING TO BETHLEHEM (vv. 5, 6)

5. "In Bethlehem in Judea," they replied, "for this is what the prophet has written:

The town of *Bethlehem* was located approximately five miles southwest of Jerusalem. It was a small town in the hill country of *Judea*, and was generally considered to be of little importance except for two matters of note. Bethlehem could lay claim to being "the town of David," because it was the hometown of the shepherd boy who became king (1 Samuel 16:1). And it was, according to Old Testament prophecy, the future birthplace of the Messiah and thus destined one day for prominence.

6. "'But you, Bethlehem, in the land of Judah, are by no means least among the rulers of Judah; for out of you will come a ruler who will be the shepherd of my people Israel.'"

Micah 5:2 is the Old Testament prophecy that identified *Bethlehem* as the Messiah's birthplace. As noted last week regarding Isaiah 7:14 (quoted in Matthew 1:23), modern Old Testament scholarship often debates whether or not Micah was actually speaking of someone from his own day, with Matthew later reading into the text a messianic meaning. However, the response of the chief priests and scribes

WHAT DO YOU THINK?

Herod was "disturbed." And when Herod was disturbed, someone has said, *everyone* was disturbed! What "disturbs" government officials today about the church or religion? How should Christians respond when government officials are disturbed in this way—or when they disturb us?

WHAT DO YOU THINK?

Bethlehem in the first century was considered to be of little importance. How has God used little-known people, places, and events to bless your life? What lessons, if any, do you see in that for us today?

to Herod indicates that even Jewish thinking already understood what Matthew recorded by inspiration of the Holy Spirit—that Micah predicted the birth of the Messiah in Bethlehem of *Judah* (called in verse 4 by the Greek name of *Judea*).

Here we see a reason why the church has often used fulfilled prophecies as an important element of "apologetics," or the defense of the Christian faith. Jesus fulfilled all messianic prophecies, even those that spoke of precise details outside of his control, such as the condition of his mother (a virgin) and the place of his birth (Bethlehem).

II. A DEVIOUS KING (MATTHEW 2:7, 8)

A. PLOTTING HIS EVIL (v. 7)

7. Then Herod called the Magi secretly and found out from them the exact time the star had appeared.

The initial inquiries of the *Magi* may have been in public areas such as the temple, where crowds of people could hear their story and be "disturbed" (v. 3). But shortly thereafter they were summoned to a private meeting with *Herod*. The king wanted to know *the exact time the star had appeared*; apparently he pressed the unsuspecting wise men for a precise date when they first noticed the heavenly sign.

Herod's subsequent actions reveal the motive behind his interest in the star. Assuming that the star first appeared on the day the new King was born, he calculated the age of the child in order to know the age of the person he should look for as he tried to have the new King killed. His order to kill all male children two years old and younger (v. 16) may indicate that the star had first appeared two years earlier, and thus much earlier than the actual birth of Christ. More likely, Herod was giving his soldiers a "margin for error" to make sure they did not miss the one boy he was after.

Matthew's description of King Herod's deceitful ploy with the wise men is consistent with other historical records. Throughout his reign Herod "distinguished" himself with his cunning and cruelty, but in the final year prior to his death his mental state was so greatly diminished that he experienced delusions of persecution accompanied by violent outbursts. His paranoia became so great that he killed anyone he suspected of plotting against him, including members of his immediate family. It was in this state of mind that he interrogated the wise men for information that would help him locate and destroy this child whom he suspected of being a new rival in Bethlehem.

B. PREPARING TO KILL (v. 8)

8. He sent them to Bethlehem and said, "Go and make a careful search for the child. As soon as you find him, report to me, so that I too may go and worship him."

Herod's subterfuge was set in motion. If the *child* was being hidden by his family for protection, the location was more likely to be revealed to foreign dignitaries seeking to honor the future King than to armed soldiers scouring the town. Herod would await the *report* of the wise men and then launch his deadly assault.

FUNNY, ISN'T IT?

I recently received an e-mail that had a very thought-provoking message. It said, "Funny how ten dollars looks so big when we take it to church and so small when we take it to the store. Funny how big an hour serving God looks and how small it seems when spent playing golf, fishing, or playing bridge. Funny how laborious it is to read a chapter in the Bible and how easy it is to read a hundred pages of a best-selling novel. Funny how we believe what a person or newspapers say, but question what the Bible says. Funny how we can't think of anything to say when we pray, but don't have any difficulty thinking of things to talk about with a friend. Funny how we need two or three weeks to fit a church event into our schedule, but can adjust it at the last minute for a social event. Funny, isn't it?"

Well, obviously it isn't funny, and neither was the hypocritical attitude that King Herod displayed. He lied to the wise men and told them that he wanted to know the location of the Christ child in order to worship him; but in reality he wanted to kill him. Some Christians, though their attitude toward Jesus is not malicious as Herod's was, still demonstrate a disparity between their lives and their words. Jesus deserves more than our words. He gave up everything to save us. He humbled himself and was "made in human likeness" (Philippians 2:7) so that we could be saved from the eternal punishment that we deserve for our sins.

Yet, like Herod, we want to be king—king of our own lives—and we do not want anyone else to have control over us. First Corinthians 6:19, 20 says that we are not our own, but "were bought at a price. Therefore honor God with your body." Jesus is worthy of our total devotion.   —L. D. C.

III. A ROYAL CHILD (MATTHEW 2:9-12)

A. REVEALED BY GOD (vv. 9, 10)

9. After they had heard the king, they went on their way, and the star they had seen in the east went ahead of them until it stopped over the place where the child was.

The wise men now had the information they needed to locate the town where the new King was born, but they still did not know where in that town they would find the right child. However, in Bethlehem God provided another sign to assist the wise men. The *star they had seen in the east went ahead of them until it stopped over the place where the child* Jesus and his family were staying. Such movement by the star clearly suggests God's guidance and not merely a natural phenomenon.

10. When they saw the star, they were overjoyed.

It has already been suggested that the *star* may have disappeared at some point when the wise men arrived in Judea, later to return after they departed from Jerusalem for Bethlehem. Another way to understand Matthew's statement is to read it in light of the previous verse: the wise men *were overjoyed* upon seeing the star point to the location of the Messiah. They were pleased to have divine assistance hasten their search, and thrilled to reach at long last the goal of their long journey.

B. DESERVING OF WORSHIP (v. 11)

11. On coming to the house, they saw the child with his mother Mary, and they bowed down and worshiped him. Then they opened their treasures and presented him with gifts of gold and of incense and of myrrh.

Many modern portrayals of the visit of the wise men stray from the actual biblical description. For example, the wise men did not kneel before a manger in a stable along with the shepherds; instead, they found the family settled in a *house.*

All of this makes sense when we examine the biblical data. The wise men did not arrive with their expensive gifts until after Jesus' birth; otherwise at the forty-day presentation of their *child* in the temple, Joseph and Mary would have offered the required lamb sacrifice rather than the poor person's alternative of two turtledoves or pigeons (Luke 2:22-24). Also note that the biblical text at no point indicates the number of wise men or that they held positions as "kings." It is the number of gifts and their royal flavor that suggest the popular idea of "we three kings."

WHAT DO YOU THINK?

The wise men were men of high reputation. While they may not have been worshiped by others, they were looked on with great favor. How strange to think of these travelers going to such expense and trouble to find the king of the Jews! It is stranger still to find them worshiping a child. Their attitude was clearly one of wonder and praise. What significance do you see in their humble attitude toward Jesus? What can we do to follow their example?

PRAYER

Father, help us to be eager students of your Word, who are devoted fully to your Son and committed to living a life of service and praise. In Jesus' name we pray. Amen.

THOUGHT TO REMEMBER

Consider the difference between King Herod and King Jesus: Herod killed others so he could live; Jesus died so that others could live.

DAILY BIBLE READINGS

Monday, Dec. 20—The Birth of Jesus (Luke 2:1-7)

Tuesday, Dec. 21—Jesus' Birth Announced to Shepherds (Luke 2:8-20)

Wednesday, Dec. 22—Jesus Is Presented in the Temple (Luke 2:21-27)

Thursday, Dec. 23—Simeon and Anna Praise God (Luke 2:28-38)

Friday, Dec. 24—Wise Men Inquire About Jesus' Birth (Matthew 2:1-6)

Saturday, Dec. 25—Wise Men Visit and Honor Jesus (Matthew 2:7-12)

Sunday Dec. 26—Herod's Wrath Is Unleashed (Matthew 2:13-18)

The wise men treated Jesus in a royal manner, bowing before him in worship and presenting to him costly *gifts* suitable for a king. We recognize *gold* for the beautiful and expensive treasure that it is. The *incense* and *myrrh* were very expensive tree resins—the former derived from a type of balsam tree, the latter from something akin to a sturdy shrub. Incense was burned in a dish in order to release into the air a sweet-smelling smoke; it was also used in perfumes and medicines. Likewise myrrh was an ingredient in fragrances and medicines, and in addition was often used as an embalming agent (John 19:39).

All three of these gifts were befitting of royalty and served as genuine expressions of adoration and praise. While Herod deceitfully spoke of worship, the wise men truly offered it.

C. SUBJECT TO DANGER (v. 12)

12. And having been warned in a dream not to go back to Herod, they returned to their country by another route.

This time God spoke directly to the wise men *in a dream*. Herod's evil scheme was exposed, and the wise men discreetly returned to *their country*, carrying with them the secret of their discovery. Matthew goes on to report that Herod became enraged when he realized his plans had been thwarted and ordered the execution of all male children two years of age and under (v. 16).

Like the wise men, Joseph was also warned in a dream of the imminent danger from Herod and was ordered to flee the king's jurisdiction and hide his family in Egypt (vv. 13, 14). There they remained for a short while until after the death of Herod the Great, at which time an angel instructed Joseph to return to his homeland (vv. 19-23) and nurture the child who would one day become Messiah and King.

HONORING THE REAL KING

Henry Ward Beecher was one of the most respected preachers in the United States during the latter part of the nineteenth century. He was so popular that people would travel from all over the country to listen to him preach. It was not uncommon for him to have more than three thousand people gather to hear him on a Sunday morning!

One Sunday, during the peak of his popularity, Beecher was away, so he asked his brother Thomas to preach for him. When Thomas Beecher got up to preach that morning, many in the congregation got up and headed for the door. Quickly he called out: "May I have your attention, please? All who came here this morning to worship Henry Ward Beecher may now leave. All who came to worship God may stay."

The wise men's purpose in traveling from the East was clear: they had come to worship King Jesus. They had not come to please King Herod. When God told them that Herod was being deceitful and intended to kill Jesus, the wise men followed God's instructions and traveled homeward by another route. They knew who the real King was.

—L. D. C.

CONCLUSION

It is a popular refrain, often found on holiday cards: "Wise men still seek him." It reminds us of the diligence of the wise men in seeking the one "born king of the Jews" until they found him. And it challenges us to follow their example: to seek after the One whom God sent to earth as Lord and King, to bow before him in worship and homage, and to give him the best gifts we have—our hearts committed to his will and our lives devoted to his service. The lessons learned from the story of the wise men are very much applicable in our modern times: wise men still seek him.

Discovery Learning

This page contains an alternate lesson plan emphasizing learning activities. Classes desiring such student involvement will find these suggestions helpful. The next page is a reproducible activity page to further enhance discovery learning.

LEARNING GOALS

After this lesson each student will be able to:

1. Retell the story of the visit of the wise men to see the child Jesus.

2. Tell what qualities shown by the wise men are worthy of imitation by Christians today.

3. Suggest a specific way to give of oneself more fully to the Lord and his work in the coming year.

INTO THE LESSON

As learners arrive, hand each one a card or note bearing one of the following letters: **M, A, G,** or **I.** Ask the learners to assemble in four groups by matching letters with others: **M**'s together, **A**'s together, etc.

Direct each group to devise an alliterative title for these visitors to the child Jesus, using the key letter assigned to the group. Give this example: "If we were using the word *wise,* and you were in the **W** group, you might come up with something like 'Wise Wanderers Wanting to Worship the Worthy.'" Challenge them to get as many alliterative words into their titles as possible.

Here are some samples: **M:** Matthew's Mysterious Male, Meandering Messiah-seekers. **A:** Aggressive, Adoring Astronomers Asking Assistance Arrive for Adulation of the Anointed. **G:** Generous and Glad Givers of Gracious Gifts to God. **I:** Intelligent Inquirers Interested in the Immortal "I Am."

INTO THE WORD

Use the activity "Magi Knowledge—Or Lack of It!" from the next page to explore what we really know about the Magi (wise men). Then present the following statements, one at a time, to your class. Ask the students to find support in Matthew 2 that indicates that each statement is true. (1) Wise men come prepared to worship. (2) Wise men tolerate difficulties in order to get to worship. (3) Wise men seek and value the company of other wise men. (4) Wise men give significant and costly gifts. (5) Wise men listen to all of God's directions. (6) Wise men do not hesitate to ask for help. (7) Wise men avoid trouble if they know about it and can. (8) Wise men know good, better, and best; they choose the best. (9) Wise men value inquiry and wonder. (10) Wise men do not hesitate to humble themselves in the presence of a greater One.

(Number 1 refers to the gifts the Magi carefully carried —and at great risk along the way—in order to present them to the new "king of the Jews." Number 2 relates to the long miles—perhaps hundreds of desert miles—that they traveled. Number 3 shows their studied consensus and mutual plan in coming. Number 4 is quite obvious. Number 5 pertains both to their following the star and to the dream given to save their lives. Numbers 6 and 7 are obvious. Number 8 relates to these wise men who were well studied and obviously prosperous, the good and the better, but they still chose to pursue the Messiah, the Best. Wise men [number 9] were the scientists and scholars of their day; they were joyous in knowledge, intrigued by possibility. Number 10 is the surest evidence of their wisdom; though no doubt honored in their homelands, they recognized their inferiority to Jesus.)

INTO LIFE

Refer to the Introduction section of the commentary, where the writer says, "Anyone can play the part of . . . a wise man." Summarize the writer's description of the common practice of recruiting anyone for the role in a Christmas drama or pageant.

Then display several wardrobe items that a wise man might have worn. (You might borrow such items from the church's drama ministry—or, if your class has a good imagination, "fake" them by holding each up "invisibly," in the manner of "The Emperor's New Clothes"!)

As you hold up each item, ask your class members to suggest what attributes of the wise man's wardrobe it might represent. For example, hold up a tunic (sleeveless knee-length undergarment): "The wise person needs to hold certain things close to his heart, hidden from men, known only to God: his faith in God's directions for life and worship." Hold up a scarf that might have covered the wise man's face and neck: "The wise person always needs to know when to open his mouth and when to close it; this scarf can cover his mouth at all the right times—to avoid the harm that can come from having it open!" Let the class "imagine" and freely conjecture.

If it is possible—and affordable—present each class member with a clothes hanger to take home. Direct the students to attach little tags bearing the words, "What the Fashionable Wise Man/Woman is Wearing," and keep the hangers in their closets or dressing rooms as daily reminders of today's study.

Magi Knowledge—Or Lack of It!

What do we know about the Magi (wise men) who came to honor the newborn king of the Jews? Answer *yes* or *no* to each of the following issues.

YES NO

____ ____ 1. What country(ies) they came from

____ ____ 2. Exactly what they saw in the east

____ ____ 3. Exactly when the star appeared, in relation to Jesus' birth

____ ____ 4. How many were in the company

____ ____ 5. How they knew about the coming "King of the Jews"

____ ____ 6. What religion they held

____ ____ 7. When they arrived in Bethlehem, in relation to Jesus' birth

____ ____ 8. Why they chose the gifts they offered

____ ____ 9. Why Matthew, of the four Gospel writers, tells their story

____ ____ 10. How they escaped Herod's plot and anger

By the Spirit's wisdom, all we know is essentially this: God allowed these men to know of his Son's birth, and they wanted to—had to!—come and worship him. What else is essential—for any person?

Life With a "PG" Rating

Wise men make Planned Gifts. Wise men Praise God. Make a plan for your giving to God in the coming year. Call it your "PG Plan." How will your giving praise God? How will it not?

THE TWELVE DISCIPLES

LESSON 5

WHY TEACH THIS LESSON?

When I was a boy, I learned a song that named the twelve disciples. We did a lot of that kind of thing in our Sunday school. Learning Bible facts was important to the leaders of the Sunday school, but they knew learning could also be fun. So we sang the song and learned the names of the disciples along the way. I still sing that song to myself when I need to recall the names of all the disciples!

The song did not let us off easy, however. After we named the disciples, we had to sing, "He has called us, too; He has called us, too. . . . We are his disciples, We his work must do!"

You must not let your students off easy, either! This lesson is intended for more than the students' learning the names of twelve men and how Jesus called them. It is intended to be a call to discipleship.

Do you have non-Christians attending your class? Good for you! Use this lesson as a gentle nudge toward their making a commitment. And for the rest of the students, it is a reminder that discipleship is about more than attending Sunday school sessions and worship services. It's about following Jesus.

INTRODUCTION

A. READY AND WILLING

When Pearl Harbor was bombed on December 7, 1941, that day became for Americans "a day that will live in infamy." But the following day, December 8, was a day of patriotic pride, which ushered in a period of vigorous American response to the bombing. For weeks after the bombing of Pearl Harbor, Americans volunteered in droves for military duty, ready and willing to stop the threat of world domination and to defend American honor.

Another recruitment call has been issued. It started on the shores of the Sea of Galilee with four fishermen, and continues today. Our Lord and Savior is looking for disciples to spread his gospel message to the uttermost parts of the earth, and then to teach and nurture those who respond. Our challenge as Christians is simply this: are we ready and willing to serve?

B. LESSON BACKGROUND

Having taken a brief interlude to look at the birth of Christ, our study returns to the ministry of Jesus as recorded in the Gospel of Matthew. Following Jesus' baptism in the Jordan River and his testing in the desert (lessons 1 and 2), he was ready to begin three and a half years of teaching and preaching to the people of Israel.

One of Jesus' first tasks was to seek out some men who would assist him in his ministry. Those who agreed to work with him he called "disciples," from the Greek word referring to a student who followed his teacher around so that he could learn from him. (In ancient times a teacher would often leave the classroom setting and simply walk about, teaching as he walked.) Anyone who accepted the call to be a disciple of Jesus had to spend significant time with him and had to be prepared to follow him wherever and whenever he traveled.

DEVOTIONAL READING:
MATTHEW 10:5-16
BACKGROUND SCRIPTURE:
MATTHEW 4:18-22; 9:9-13; 10:1-4
PRINTED TEXT:
MATTHEW 4:18-22; 9:9-13; 10:1-4

Jan
2

LESSON AIMS

After this lesson a student should be able to:

1. Name the twelve apostles and tell a little of the background of some of them.

2. Tell how the calling of Jesus' first disciples instructs us today about responding to Jesus' call.

3. Express a commitment to being a disciple of Jesus.

KEY VERSE

"Come, follow me," Jesus said, "and I will make you fishers of men." —Matthew 4:19

At one point Jesus selected twelve from this group of disciples to serve in a more demanding role as "apostles." Our lesson today focuses on the calling of those men.

I. FOUR FISHERMEN (MATTHEW 4:18-22)

A. FISHERS OF MEN (vv. 18-20)

18. As Jesus was walking beside the Sea of Galilee, he saw two brothers, Simon called Peter and his brother Andrew. They were casting a net into the lake, for they were fishermen.

The bulk of Jesus' ministry took place in the towns on the west side of the Sea of Galilee, a large freshwater lake in the northern province of Galilee, about sixty miles north of Jerusalem. It was referred to as an inland "sea" because of its large size (thirteen miles long by eight miles wide), and because it exhibited wave movements and storm activity comparable to those of a typical coastal sea.

Jesus' ministry was headquartered on the west side of the Sea of Galilee in the city of Capernaum (Matthew 4:13). Not far from Capernaum was the smaller town of Bethsaida, identified in Scripture as the hometown of Peter, Andrew, and Philip (John 1:44). (Note that this is a different Bethsaida from the location on the northeast side of the Sea of Galilee, where, according to Luke 9:10-17, Jesus fed the five thousand.)

The most prominent of all the men Jesus summoned to follow him as disciples or apostles was *Simon called Peter.* While *Simon* was his birth name, Jesus gave him the new name "Cephas" (Aramaic) or *Peter* (Greek), both of which mean "small stone" (John 1:42). Peter's brother *Andrew* was apparently the more reserved of the two men; but it is to his credit that Andrew introduced Peter to Jesus (John 1:40, 41), and later informed Jesus about some Greeks who wanted to see him (John 12:20-22). It was also Andrew, who, in a crowd of five thousand men, discovered the little boy with five loaves of bread and two pieces of fish (John 6:8, 9).

19. "Come, follow me," Jesus said, "and I will make you fishers of men."

Luke (5:1-11) tells more details of this event, which likely culminated in Jesus' invitation: *Come, follow me . . . and I will make you fishers of men.*

20. At once they left their nets and followed him.

One should not assume from Matthew's brief account that all Jesus had to do was to introduce himself to men like Peter and Andrew, say "Follow me," and *at once* they would quit their fishing business to become full-time disciples. The men Jesus called into service were already well acquainted with him.

Andrew first became acquainted with Jesus when he was a disciple of John the Baptist. When Jesus returned from the desert temptations, Andrew and an unnamed disciple began following Jesus, encouraged by John's testimony (John 1:35-40). Shortly thereafter, Andrew introduced his brother Simon to Jesus (vv. 41, 42). The two brothers lived and fished in Bethsaida near Capernaum (v. 44), which became the headquarters for Jesus' ministry. They would have had weeks, perhaps even months, to hear Jesus teach before he called them to travel with him in full-time ministry. By the time he asked, they were ready to say yes.

B. FOLLOWERS OF CHRIST (vv. 21, 22)

21. Going on from there, he saw two other brothers, James the son of Zebedee and his brother John. They were in a boat with their father Zebedee, preparing their nets. Jesus called them.

WHAT DO YOU THINK?

At least three factors were involved in Jesus' process of calling his "apostles": seeking men who would be willing to assist him; giving limited exposure to the type of work they would do; and challenging them to follow him. Do you think these same steps might be used to motivate people to discipleship today? If so, how?

This chart from the visuals packet will help your students to sort out the chronology of the events you will study this quarter. Display it throughout the remainder of the quarter.

Peter and Andrew were partners in the fishing business with another pair of brothers, *James* and *John*, and their father *Zebedee* (Luke 5:10). Jesus likewise summoned these brothers to give up their fishing career and follow him. Once again the groundwork for this call had likely been laid by Jesus' preaching and teaching during his early Judean ministry.

22. And immediately they left the boat and their father and followed him.

We should not imagine that the two sets of brothers left the family business in a predicament by their departure. We know that Zebedee had hired servants to assist him (Mark 1:20). We can assume that the parents were pleased with their sons' decision to follow Jesus, for Zebedee's wife was one of several women from Galilee who supported Jesus' ministry (most likely in a financial way) and stood near the cross as he died (Matthew 27:55, 56).

OBEDIENCE WITHOUT QUESTION

First Samuel 15 tells how God instructed King Saul of Israel to go to war against the Amalekites. Saul was instructed to "totally destroy" them because of their past mistreatment of the Israelites (vv. 2, 3). Saul proceeded to defeat the Amalekites in battle; but instead of completely destroying the enemy, he kept their king and some of their livestock alive. The Lord told his prophet Samuel to confront Saul about his blatant disobedience. Seeking to justify his behavior, Saul claimed that he kept the livestock alive to sacrifice them to the Lord. But Samuel replied, "To obey is better than sacrifice" (v. 22).

The four fishermen whom Jesus called to be apostles had this factor in common: they were obedient. When Jesus invited them to come and follow him, they followed. Their obedience is a great example to us today.

Mother Theresa once said, "There is no demand so unreasonable that God cannot make it of my life." This thought should be planted deeply in the thinking of each of us. Jesus said, "If you love me, you will obey what I command" (John 14:15). The acid test of the love that we sing about or talk about on Sunday morning is our daily obedience Sunday afternoon through Saturday night. —D. R.

II. ONE TAX COLLECTOR (MATTHEW 9:9-13)

A. RECEPTIVE FOLLOWER (vv. 9, 10)

9. As Jesus went on from there, he saw a man named Matthew sitting at the tax collector's booth. "Follow me," he told him, and Matthew got up and followed him.

Some weeks or perhaps months after the calling of the four fishermen, Jesus enlisted *Matthew* into his service as a full-time disciple. Once again, the readiness with which he responded indicates that he had already met Jesus, listened to his message, and given serious thought to this decision. His *tax collector's booth* was located near the shore of the Sea of Galilee (Mark 2:13, 14). Thus he, like the four fishermen, was residing in the area where Jesus concentrated his preaching and teaching.

Matthew was also known as Levi (Mark 2:14; Luke 5:27), which was most likely his original name. Luke, who wrote not only the third Gospel but also the book of Acts, refers to him by the name Matthew, which means "gift of God," in Acts 1:13. Matthew's writing and recording skills, possibly developed in his position as a tax collector, later served him well; he wrote the longest of the four Gospels, and the one distinguished for its fuller summaries of the teachings of Jesus.

10. While Jesus was having dinner at Matthew's house, many tax collectors and "sinners" came and ate with him and his disciples.

Matthew's account says, literally, that Jesus came to dinner at "the house." It is Luke who notes that this was *Matthew's house*, and that Jesus was Matthew's

HOW TO SAY IT

Alphaeus. Al-FEE-us.
Amalekites. AM-uh-leh-kites or Uh-MAL-ih-kites.
Aramaic. Air-uh-MAY-ick.
Bartholomew. Bar-THAH-luh-mew.
Bethsaida. Beth-SAY-uh-duh.
Canaanite. KAY-nun-ite.
Capernaum. Kuh-PER-nay-um.
Cephas. SEE-fus.
Didymus. DID-uh-mus.
Iscariot. Iss-CARE-ee-ut.
Joses. JOE-sez.
Nathanael. Nuh-THAN-yull.
Pharisees. FAIR-ih-seez.
Sadducees. SAD-you-seez.
Sanhedrin. San-HEED-run or SAN-huh-drin.
Thaddaeus. THAD-ee-us.
Zacchaeus. Zack-KEE-us.
Zealot. ZEL-ut.
Zebedee. ZEB-uh-dee.

WHAT DO YOU THINK?

Jesus was criticized for associating with "sinners." Though he defended his actions, the Bible does warn us about our associations. (See 2 Corinthians 6:14-18.) At the same time, we are told to be "light" and "salt" in the world (Matthew 5:13-16). Where do we draw the line? How much contact do you think we as Christians should maintain with unbelievers? Why?

guest of honor (Luke 5:29). The place was filled with infamous outcasts of Jewish society—perhaps the only friends a tax collector could claim as his own, being an outcast himself. Matthew had invited other *tax collectors*, all of them despised by the Jews for collaborating with the Roman government. They also had the reputation, usually well-earned, of being dishonest and coercive. (Recall the words of Zacchaeus to Jesus in Luke 19:8.)

There were also other *sinners* present, which in this context usually refers to those who made their living in a disreputable manner, such as prostitutes (Matthew 21:31, 32). Matthew's joy at being accepted by Jesus knew no bounds, and thus he cared not with whom he celebrated. In fact, this banquet may have been intended as his first evangelistic effort.

EVANGELISM—WITH NO STRINGS ATTACHED

Evangelism needs to be a part of every Christian's life and needs to be the heartbeat of every church. Minister Steve Sjorgren (*Sor*-gren) tells the true story of Joe Delaney and his eight-year-old son Jared, who were playing catch in their backyard. Jared asked, "Dad, is there a God?" Joe explained that he wasn't really sure if God existed or not. "I'll be right back," Jared shouted as he ran into the house.

Moments later, he returned with a helium balloon from the circus, a pen, and an index card. "I'm going to send God an airmail message," Jared explained. "Dear God," he wrote, "if you are real and you are there, send people who know you to Dad and me."

"God, I hope you are watching," Joe thought as they watched the balloon and message sail away.

Two days later, Joe and Jared pulled into a car wash sponsored by Sjorgren's church. When Joe asked, "How much?" he was told, "It's free. No strings attached."

"But why are you doing this?" Joe asked.

"We just wanted to show God's love in a practical way," Sjorgren answered.

"Are you guys Christians—the kind of Christians who really believe in God?" Joe asked.

Sjorgren replied, "Yes, we're that kind of Christians." From that encounter, Steve led Joe to accept Christ.

When Matthew chose to follow Jesus, he found something that he wanted to share with his friends. That is the reason he invited them—and Jesus—to his house. Let us follow his example and develop a similar passion for caring about and reaching out to the lost.   —D. R.

B. RESENTFUL PHARISEES (vv. 11-13)

11. When the Pharisees saw this, they asked his disciples, "Why does your teacher eat with tax collectors and 'sinners'?"

The *Pharisees* were one of the two most prominent of the Jewish religious groups. (The Sadducees were the other.) They exercised a powerful influence over the laws and rituals of Judaism. They were the "sworn enemies" of Jesus throughout his years of ministry, ultimately becoming the group with the most influence in the Jewish Sanhedrin—the council that officially sentenced Jesus to death on the false charge of blasphemy. Of course, the other party that was represented on the Sanhedrin, the Sadducees, was equally hostile toward Jesus.

The Pharisees could not understand how any preacher who wanted to be taken seriously could participate in a gathering of people who were at odds with the high moral code of the Mosaic law. Their criticism of Jesus implied that he had compromised his convictions and was condoning the lifestyles of *tax collectors and sinners* by his presence with them.

12. On hearing this, Jesus said, "It is not the healthy who need a doctor, but the sick.

What the Pharisees always failed to take into account was the evangelistic duty that God's people have toward those who are lost. They claimed that associating with sinners would tarnish their godly image and place them too close to dangerous influences.

While this may have been a ruse to justify the Pharisees' prejudices, there is a concern here with which Christians can identify. We enjoy being with people who share our religious convictions, and we are often troubled to be around sinful words and activities. Even so, the *sick* need to be visited by a *doctor* if they are ever to recover their spiritual health and vitality. Thus the New Testament rule for Christians is that we develop relationships with the people of this world by which we can graciously challenge their sinful lives and bring them to salvation. Our role model is Jesus, who could eat with sinners and yet firmly say, "Go now and leave your life of sin" (John 8:11).

13. But go and learn what this means: 'I desire mercy, not sacrifice.' For I have not come to call the righteous, but sinners."

Jesus, the Master Teacher, suggested a homework assignment for these who presumed to know the full will of God: *learn* the meaning of Hosea 6:6. The prophet Hosea criticized Israel for its hypocrisy. The people correctly practiced the religious rituals and sacrifices of Judaism, but they did not apply the meaning of it to their hearts. Theirs was a religious formalism that concentrated on outward appearances but failed to grasp deeper spiritual truths.

A heart truly devoted to God must demonstrate *mercy* to all *sinners*. Even though we may be repulsed by the lifestyles of such individuals, the love of God should draw us near to them. We must recognize that God could have been repulsed by our sins as well and could have left us to perish in them. Jesus' newest disciple was one who had quickly learned the spirit of genuine service to God.

III. TWELVE APOSTLES (MATTHEW 10:1-4)

A. SET APART FOR SERVICE (v. 1)

1. He called his twelve disciples to him and gave them authority to drive out evil spirits and to heal every disease and sickness.

Of the many disciples who followed Jesus during his ministry, he selected twelve, "that they might be with him and that he might send them out to preach" (Mark 3:14). These twelve are known as the *twelve disciples,* reflecting Jesus' desire "that they might be with him." A disciple followed his teacher, learning from him in a variety of settings. They are also known as the twelve "apostles" (see verse 2), which reflects the latter part of the charge: "that he might send them out to preach." The word *apostle* literally means "one sent out."

The apostles eventually served as the human agents who formed part of the foundation of Christ's church (Ephesians 2:20). They were commissioned to be the primary authors of the New Testament Scripture that guides the church (John 14:26; 15:26, 27). They were the first recipients of the Great Commission to evangelize all peoples throughout the world (Matthew 28:18-20).

These twelve had been with Jesus for several months, learning from him and serving with him. Now they were ready for an assignment on their own. They had seen how Jesus taught and acted with authority. Now they would be empowered—at least temporarily—with miraculous gifts that they could use to establish their credentials as God's messengers (Matthew 10:5-15).

WHAT DO YOU THINK?

Jesus' answer to his critics included a clear statement of his purpose: "I have not come to call the righteous, but sinners." What is our purpose—individually as disciples and corporately as a church? How can we keep our purpose clearly in mind at all times?

WHAT DO YOU THINK?

How can we, as Jesus' disciples, avoid the tendency of the Pharisees to focus only on outward appearances? What steps would help us exercise mercy toward others without condoning their sinful actions or lifestyle?

WHAT DO YOU THINK?

When asked to take positions of ministry in the church, some people refuse because they do not know how. In fact, Jesus did spend three years training his disciples. How much training and discipling do you think are necessary before a person can effectively serve in Christ's church? Why?

[See Ephesians 4:11-13; 1 Peter 4:10, 11.]

PRAYER

Father, help us to be ready and willing to serve, whenever and wherever you present the opportunity. In Jesus' name. Amen.

WHAT DO YOU THINK?

What does the wide diversity seen in Jesus' first disciples suggest to you about the makeup of the church? Can a church with similar diversity survive today? Why or why not?

THOUGHT TO REMEMBER

Jesus calls us: by Thy mercies, Savior, may we hear Thy call, Give our hearts to Thy obedience, Serve and love Thee best of all.
       —Cecil F. Alexander

B. SELECTED AS APOSTLES (vv. 2-4)

2. *These are the names of the twelve apostles: first, Simon (who is called Peter) and his brother Andrew; James son of Zebedee, and his brother John. . . .*

All four of the New Testament passages that list the *twelve apostles* (Matthew 10:2-4; Mark 3:16-19; Luke 6:13-16; Acts 1:13) begin with the four fishermen: *Peter, Andrew, James,* and *John.* As previously noted, they were among the earliest disciples called by Jesus. Also, in every list found in the Gospels, Peter appears first and Judas last.

3. *. . . Philip and Bartholomew; Thomas and Matthew the tax collector; James son of Alphaeus, and Thaddaeus. . . .*

For most of the remaining apostles, little information about them (if any) can be found in Scripture. It was noted earlier that *Philip* was a native of Bethsaida (John 1:44). *Bartholomew* is apparently the apostle referred to in the Gospel of John as Nathanael (John 1:45-51; 21:2). Nathanael was introduced to Jesus by his friend Philip (John 1:45), and the two are listed side-by-side (as Philip and Bartholomew) in the listings of apostles found in the Gospels.

Thomas was also known as Didymus (John 11:16), which means "twin." *James son of Alphaeus* may have been the brother of *Matthew the tax collector,* since Matthew's father was also named Alphaeus (Mark 2:14). Perhaps to distinguish him from James the brother of John (Acts 12:2), he is sometimes referred to as "James the younger" (Mark 15:40). James's mother's name was Mary, and he had a brother named Joses (Mark 15:40).

Thaddaeus was also known as "Judas son of James" (Luke 6:16; Acts 1:13); however, the word "son" is not in the Greek text. The translators of the *New International Version* have chosen to use it to describe the relationship between Judas and James, but we cannot say with certainty how they were related.

4. *. . . Simon the Zealot and Judas Iscariot, who betrayed him.*

The description of *Simon* as a *Zealot* calls attention to his membership in a radical liberation party called the Zealots, which was known for the extreme and violent actions it took against Roman officials. Certainly the most interesting matchup among the apostles was this former anti-Roman Zealot (Simon) working with a former Roman tax collector (Matthew).

The name *Iscariot* probably referred to Judas's native town in southern Judea. *Judas* served as the "treasurer" of the apostles (John 12:6; 13:29), and probably started his service to Jesus with good intentions. But as almost everyone realizes, his ending was tragic, and he will always be known as "Judas the traitor."

It was this diverse group of men whom Jesus used to proclaim the message of his kingdom. Several of them were highly unlikely candidates for leadership in such an enterprise, yet all (except for Judas) left behind a legacy of faithful service to Jesus.

CONCLUSION

When we try to recruit helpers for any project in the church, we sometimes use the expression: "The key is not ability, but availability." Christian service is enhanced by our gifts and abilities, education and experience, and personalities and attitudes. Certainly leadership positions must be limited to those who are Biblically qualified. But with God the key to effective ministry is a desire to serve. God seems to enjoy taking unlikely candidates—such as four fishermen, a tax collector, and a political radical—and making them a testimony to his grace and power.

Any of us can engage in some kind of meaningful service for Jesus' kingdom, if only we are willing to answer the call to discipleship.

Discovery Learning

This page contains an alternate lesson plan emphasizing learning activities. Classes desiring such student involvement will find these suggestions helpful. The next page is a reproducible activity page to further enhance discovery learning.

LEARNING GOALS

After participating in this lesson, a student should be able to:

1. Name the twelve apostles and tell a little of the background of some of them.

2. Tell how the calling of Jesus' first disciples instructs us today about responding to Jesus' call.

3. Express a commitment to being a disciple of Jesus.

INTO THE LESSON

As students arrive, put them in groups of three or four members each. (People who arrive a little later can join the existing groups, up to about six in a group.) Give each group a slip of paper on which you have written a task from the list below and this set of instructions: "If you were choosing a team to accomplish this task, what qualities would you look for among the participants? List four to six qualities." Assign these and/or other tasks: plant a garden, build a house, win a basketball game, develop a new ministry in your church.

After a few minutes, ask the groups to reveal their lists. Record the answers on a chalkboard or overhead transparency. Ask, "What common characteristics are listed?" (Integrity, vision, passion, detail-orientation.) "Why are some characteristics different?" (Tasks are different, individuals are different, skill levels are different.)

Next, ask, "How would you recruit people to be a part of your team?" Answers may include telephone calls, letters or notes, e-mail, or face-to-face meetings.

Note that today's study focuses on Jesus' calling of the twelve apostles. We will see how each came when Jesus called, characteristics of some of them, and how we can follow Jesus today.

INTO THE WORD

Encourage members to complete the following activity in groups of three or four. Make sure that each has a copy. (This activity is also in the student book.) Give them ten to twelve minutes to complete the exercise, matching the letter with the correct name.

1. Peter	2. Andrew	3. James
4. John	5. Matthew	6. Philip
7. Bartholomew	8. Thomas	9. James
10. Thaddaeus	11. Simon	12. Judas

a. One of two brothers, known for his temper and martyrdom (Luke 9:54; Acts 12:2).

b. A Galilean who brought a friend to Jesus (John 1:44, 45).

c. Referred to as "Judas son of James" (Luke 6:16; Acts 1:13).

d. The original "doubter," but first to confess Jesus as Lord (John 20:25, 28).

e. The keeper of the money bag, or treasurer, of the Twelve (John 12:6; 13:29).

f. Also known as "the younger" (Mark 15:40).

g. Fisherman who confessed his own sinfulness, yet stood like a rock (Luke 5:5-8; John 1:42).

h. Most beloved by Jesus (John 13:23; 19:26; 21:24).

i. Tax collector (Matthew 9:9; Mark 2:14).

j. A "Zealot," member of an anti-Rome faction (Luke 6:15).

k. Originally a follower of John the Baptist, brought his brother to Jesus (John 1:40-42).

l. Also named Nathanael, a man of honest motives (John 1:45-49).

(*Answers:* 1, g; 2, k; 3, a; 4, h; 5, i; 6, b; 7, l; 8, d; 9, f; 10, c; 11, j; 12, e.)

When most of the students have finished, discuss their answers, explaining background information and details from the lesson commentary. Particularly note that Scripture indicates some prior knowledge of Jesus before this specialized call. Say, "We see that Jesus called a variety of people to be his first disciples. This unique group fulfilled a unique mission."

INTO LIFE

Reflect back to the "Into the Lesson" section where we discussed qualities necessary for different tasks. Remind students that the church's mission is to seek and to save the lost. Distribute three-by-five index cards and instruct each student to list two or three qualities he or she possesses that can be used in this mission. (These could include: gregarious personality, communication skills, persistence, a winsome smile, as well as evangelism training or leadership skills.)

Ask one or two volunteers to read their lists to the class. Then have the class open their Bibles to Matthew 28:19, 20, and have a volunteer read it aloud. Say, "Jesus will use in his mission the qualities you have listed. Write, 'Matthew 28:19, 20' over your list of qualities. Silently pray a prayer of commitment to use your personal qualities in participating in the Great Commission."

Hurdles to Answering God's Call

Read Matthew 4:18-22; 9:9-13; 10:1-4, as well as other Scriptures on the twelve apostles. (You can locate additional Scripture references in the cross references in a reference edition Bible or from a concordance.) List on the hurdles below some of the circumstances that could have stood in their way of answering Jesus' call.

Personal Hurdles

Now list some of the things that keep you from fully answering God's call for your life. Over those concerns write Matthew 28:19, 20 (after you have read it).

TEACHINGS ON PRAYER

LESSON 6

WHY TEACH THIS LESSON?

Curriculum planners struggle with the decisions they have to make about what topics to include in a series of Bible lessons. Of all the themes the Bible addresses, which few will be included in a particular unit, and which will be ignored until some other time? Which topics demand to be taught, and which topics can be left for the Bible reader to discover on his or her own? Which issues are directly relevant to today, and which require an understanding of ancient culture to translate the timeless principles involved?

The Bible offers some help in this, but it rarely gives specific topics. Jesus ordered us to be "teaching [disciples] to obey everything I have commanded"— much too broad a subject for one lesson! Paul said, "The things you have heard me say . . . entrust to reliable men who will also be qualified to teach others" (2 Timothy 2:2). Even if we equate his epistles with the things he had said (since we didn't hear him say anything), we still have more than one unit's worth of lessons!

Today's lesson has clear biblical support—not just in content, but as a theme. "Teach us to pray" the disciples requested (Luke 11:1). If it was good enough for Jesus and the Twelve, it's good enough for you and your class this morning!

INTRODUCTION

A. ALL THE WORLD'S A STAGE

"All the world's a stage, and all the men and women merely players." William Shakespeare penned this famous line (*As You Like It*, Act II, Scene 7) to illustrate the changes that we all experience throughout our lives. We work through different "stages" of life, from childhood to old age, like an actor changing roles from one play to the next until at the end we finally make our grand exit. Today this quotation is often used to make the claim that all of life is mere acting and pretending. We say and do what is required of us, whether we actually mean it or not.

While the latter idea was not Shakespeare's intent, it does describe the way too many people approach life, pretending to be genuine and putting on a show for others to see. And all too easily this can be the way we practice our Christianity—singing, praying, and giving—with more concern for outward form than for the inner attitude of worship and devotion.

B. LESSON BACKGROUND

Most of Matthew's Gospel is concerned with Jesus' ministry in Galilee. This ministry included three major tours of Galilee, in which Jesus visited several cities, preaching and doing miracles (Matthew 4:23; Luke 8:1; Matthew 9:35). It was in connection with the third tour that Jesus called the Twelve together, gave them power to work miracles, and sent them out on a tour of their own, as noted in last week's lesson.

Today's lesson backs up to the time between the first and second tours, during the second year of Jesus' ministry. Jesus spent most of these months on the west side of the Sea of Galilee, in the vicinity of Capernaum and Bethsaida. His teaching and miracles attracted throngs of people (Matthew 12:15; Mark 3:9, 10).

DEVOTIONAL READING:
LUKE 11:1-13
BACKGROUND SCRIPTURE:
MATTHEW 6:1-15
PRINTED TEXT:
MATTHEW 6:1-15

LESSON AIMS

After this lesson students should be able to:

1. Summarize Jesus' teaching about prayer in this portion of the Sermon on the Mount.

2. Explain the difference between "letting your light shine" and "blowing your own horn."

3. Suggest specific steps that they can take to make their prayer lives conform to Jesus' teaching.

Jan
9

KEY VERSE

When you pray, go into your room, close the door and pray to your Father, who is unseen. Then your Father, who sees what is done in secret, will reward you.
—Matthew 6:6

LESSON 6 NOTES

DAILY BIBLE READINGS

Monday, Jan. 3—*A Call to Love Enemies (Matthew 5:43-48)*

Tuesday, Jan. 4—*Instructions About Giving and Prayer (Matthew 6:1-6)*

Wednesday, Jan. 5—*The Lord's Prayer (Matthew 6:7-15)*

Thursday, Jan. 6—*Ask, Seek, Knock: God Will Respond (Matthew 7:7-11)*

Friday, Jan. 7—*Persevere in Prayer (Luke 11:5-13)*

Saturday, Jan. 8—*A Parable on Perseverance in Prayer (Luke 18:1-8)*

Sunday, Jan. 9—*The Pharisee and the Tax Collector (Luke 18:9-14)*

HOW TO SAY IT

Baal. BAY-ul.

Bethsaida. Beth-SAY-uh-duh.

Capernaum. Kuh-PER-nay-um.

hypocrites. HIP-uh-krits.

Isaiah. Eye-ZAY-uh.

Lazarus. LAZ-uh-rus.

Levites. LEE-vites.

Macedonians. Mass-uh-DOE-nee-unz.

synagogues. SIN-uh-gogs.

In order to speak to crowds that must have numbered in the thousands, Jesus had to devise creative ways to be seen and heard. In today's lesson, for example, he took his place on the side of a small mountain in order to project his voice over the crowd (Matthew 5:1). It was from this location that Jesus preached what is known as his "Sermon on the Mount" (Matthew 5–7).

The Sermon on the Mount is the longest recorded sermon of Jesus, containing such familiar teachings as the Beatitudes, the admonition not to worry (because God takes care of the birds of the air and clothes the lilies of the field), and the parable of the wise and the foolish builders. In the middle of this are Jesus' instructions regarding worship and devotion, giving, and prayer. Its importance is suggested by the early placement Matthew gives it in his Gospel, even though several events in the eighth, ninth, and twelfth chapters actually occurred before Jesus preached this sermon.

I. A HUMBLE GIFT (MATTHEW 6:1-4)

A. NOT FOR SHOW (vv. 1, 2)

1. Be careful not to do your 'acts of righteousness' before men, to be seen by them. If you do, you will have no reward from your Father in heaven.

The law of Moses required the Jews to give tithes and offerings regularly to support the ministry of the Levites (Numbers 18:21-24), who in turn gave a tithe of what they received in order to provide for the priests (vv. 25-32). In addition to these offerings, those who had the means to provide for their own families were also expected to make charitable donations to the poor (Deuteronomy 15:11).

Here Jesus was concerned with more than just financial giving, as the term *acts of righteousness* indicates. He is critical of any who do such acts *before men, to be seen by them*. The Greek word translated *to be seen* is the source of our English word "theater." The idea is that of someone putting on a show, as if "on stage," with the desire to be noticed and applauded by observers.

2. So when you give to the needy, do not announce it with trumpets, as the hypocrites do in the synagogues and on the streets, to be honored by men. I tell you the truth, they have received their reward in full.

The imagery of sounding *trumpets* to announce the giving of a charitable donation is probably hyperbole—that is, an exaggeration to emphasize a point. There may not have been actual trumpets blowing near the treasury boxes in the local *synagogues* or in the Jerusalem temple, but hypocrites could always find a way to draw attention to themselves. In first-century Judaism it was not uncommon for the collection receptacles to be placed in prominent locations where individuals would walk in front of the crowd and deposit their gifts. On one occasion Jesus sat with his disciples and watched people come forward and give their money, aware of how much each one was giving (Mark 12:41-44).

The modern church is not exempt from Jesus' warning against doing good deeds in order *to be honored by men*. Some Christians long to receive public acknowledgment and appreciation for their gifts, to be included in a posted list of donors, or to be singled out in some other manner. And they are offended if not given their due. Some like to mention how much they give or do for others—in casual conversation, public testimonies, and even in lessons or sermons. How easy it is for any of us to set aside humility for a moment and to *announce* our good works *with trumpets*, or, as we might say it today, "toot our own horn."

B. GIVEN WITH DISCRETION (vv. 3, 4)

3. But when you give to the needy, do not let your left hand know what your right hand is doing.

Here Jesus used the imagery of the human body to illustrate the concept of giving with discretion. Just as our *left hand* and our *right hand* can at the same time be holding two different objects or performing two different functions, so each of us should be busy serving the Lord as best we can, without a concern for whether others notice how much we are doing.

Let us note that there is a place in Jesus' teaching for a desire that others see our good deeds—not that we might receive the praise of others (v. 2), but to set an example for them to follow. Earlier in this sermon Jesus said, "Let your light shine before men, that they may see your good deeds and praise your Father in heaven" (Matthew 5:16). For those of us who serve as leaders in the church, it is good for others to see that we "practice what we preach" so that they can be encouraged to heed our teaching and imitate our godly example. We should speak of our spiritual activities in very general terms for the purpose of illustration and edification, and always with humility and moderation.

The key difference between "be careful not to do your 'acts of righteousness' before men" (v. 1) and "let your light shine before men" (Matthew 5:16) is the intent of the heart. We can discover a proper balance when we start with a humble spirit.

4. . . . so that your giving may be in secret. Then your Father, who sees what is done in secret, will reward you.

Here Jesus established a principle for all gifts and deeds of service. If we seek the notice and applause of men, then we forfeit a claim to heavenly blessings (v. 1). God gives us our "just deserts" by holding back the bounty he is able to bestow, because our heart is set on being "honored by men" (v. 2).

Still, there is a positive side to this principle. If we are motivated by a devotion to God, with no thought for the praise of men, then our *Father* will *reward* us. His blessings have eternal implications, and they can also result in the praise and appreciation of others—not because we sought it, but because he was pleased to give it.

FLINT, SPONGE, OR HONEYCOMB?

There are three types of givers when it comes to stewardship—the flint, the sponge, and the honeycomb. To get anything out of the flint, you must hammer it. You hit it and hope you are coming from the right angle—and even then you get only chips and sparks. To get water out of a wet sponge, you squeeze it. The more pressure you exert, the more water you will get. But remove the lid from a jar of honey with the comb inside and take out a generous piece of the honeycomb. That piece of honeycomb will overflow with its own sweetness.

Jesus talked about our attitudes and our motives in personal stewardship. He tells us it is not only the gift we give, but also the condition of our hearts when we are giving, that is important to the Lord. Our attitude in giving counts!

Paul mirrors this very thought when he writes in 2 Corinthians 9:7 and tells us, "Each man should give what he has decided in his heart to give, not reluctantly or under compulsion, for God loves a cheerful giver." When we come to the place in our love for the Lord that we are giving from the purest of motives and from a spirit of joy, we are overflowing in a "honeycomb" style of giving.

Each one of us, then, must answer the question, "Am I flint, sponge, or honeycomb?"   —D. R.

II. A GENUINE DEVOTION (MATTHEW 6:5-8)

A. FOCUSED UPON GOD (vv. 5, 6)

5. And when you pray, do not be like the hypocrites, for they love to pray standing in the synagogues and on the street corners to be seen of men. I tell you the truth, they have received their reward in full.

WHAT DO YOU THINK?

In most churches Jesus' words about giving "in secret" are applied very literally to financial contributions. At the same time, when people give volunteer service, we have appreciation dinners, publish their names in the bulletin and newsletter, etc. Why do you think we don't take Jesus as literally about these "acts of righteousness"?

Jesus' description of the *hypocrites* sounds like the teachers of the law, of whom he said on another occasion, "They devour widows' houses and for a show make lengthy prayers. Such men will be punished most severely" (Mark 12:40). To *love to pray* is certainly commendable; however, these teachers loved the opportunity that praying gave them to call attention to their high level of spirituality. Rather than seek out a prayer chamber in the temple or a quiet place of retreat, they preferred to stand and pray in the midst of public activity: in the *synagogues* and even on the *corners* of busy *streets*.

6. But when you pray, go into your room, close the door and pray to your Father, who is unseen. Then your Father, who sees what is done in secret, will reward you.

Instead of a public display of prayer, Jesus counseled that we withdraw from busy places for our personal prayer time. The word *room* describes an inner room of a house, such as a bedroom. Of course, Jesus was not requiring the use of a bedroom for prayer; he was simply illustrating the type of setting that is most appropriate.

Some have erroneously concluded that a public prayer in an assembly contradicts this text. However, Jesus himself prayed aloud on several occasions, such as when he fed the multitude (Matthew 14:19) and when he approached the tomb of Lazarus (John 11:41, 42). Prayer was a regular part of the worship gatherings of the early church (Acts 2:42), and on special occasions was the main reason for a church to assemble (Acts 12:12).

Public prayer is appropriate when done in a manner consistent with Jesus' principle of humility and discretion. The person who prays aloud should speak directly to God, not for the ears of the assembly (though with a clarity that will allow the people to comprehend and then say a genuine "Amen!" or "So be it!"). The wording should reflect an eloquence befitting God, but not with the intent of impressing men.

When the thoughts of all assembled are directed heavenward, then a public prayer has been done well.

B. LED BY FAITH (vv. 7, 8)

7. And when you pray, do not keep on babbling like pagans, for they think they will be heard because of their many words.

The *babbling* of the *pagans* included a chanting of key words and phrases over and over with the hope that such incessant repetition or *many words* would eventually win the favor of a deity. (Recall the cries of the prophets of Baal in 1 Kings 18:26-29.) Such prayer was not so much a conversation with God, or even a well-worded petition to God, as a verbal appeasement of God. The *New American Standard Bible* speaks of "meaningless repetition."

We Christians, however, can also be guilty of repeating traditional prayer phrases without giving them careful thought. Our prayers before meals and at bedtime can easily become routine as we repeat familiar words. In addition, the public prayers in our worship services (especially the invocation, the benediction, and the prayers for the Lord's Supper and the offering) can seem like trite formulas when the same phrases are repeated time after time. Even the name of "God" or "Lord" can fall into the category of vain repetitions when routinely attached to every sentence, as if God's name were a magic formula. It is easy to understand why we repeat that which is familiar, and how difficult it is to be creative all the time. Nevertheless, our goal should be to put serious thought behind each word we use, even the familiar ones.

Some people think that reciting "the Lord's Prayer" (below) or reading aloud a written prayer contradicts Jesus' prohibition against meaningless words. However, the key to Jesus' criticism is not repetition, but meaningless repetition. As long as

---

WHAT DO YOU THINK?

What guidelines would you suggest regarding public prayers?

WHAT DO YOU THINK?

How much thought should we give to our words before leading a public prayer? On the one hand, there is a danger in preparing our words so carefully that we fall into the unhealthy pattern of trying to impress those who hear. Yet, if we give no thought to our choice of words, we run the risk of becoming casual or flippant with the Lord God of the universe. So, what do you think— how can we prepare thoughtful, reverent prayers without becoming stiff or ceremonious?

one's words are spoken with care and not repeated like a magical formula, the repetition itself is not a problem.

8. Do not be like them, for your Father knows what you need before you ask him.

Prayer should not be a religious ritual, but a loving communication between us and our *Father*. We were created by God for fellowship with him, and thus he enjoys hearing us talk to him in the expression of a personal relationship.

Of course, an omniscient God who knows all things does not need to hear our prayers in order to know our needs; he *knows before* we *ask him*. He expects us to speak our petitions in prayer because of the joy he experiences in the fellowship that occurs. Just because a parent understands the needs of his or her children does not mean that there should be no communication regarding these matters.

III. A MODEL PRAYER (MATTHEW 6:9-15)

A. RESPECT FOR GOD (vv. 9, 10)

9. This, then, is how you should pray: "Our Father in heaven, hallowed be your name.

What we refer to as "the Lord's Prayer" is a beloved text often memorized and repeated by Christians, and regarded on a par with the Twenty-third Psalm and John 3:16. On another occasion, Jesus repeated this prayer in response to a request from his disciples that he teach them how to pray properly (Luke 11:1-4).

Prayer should begin with an address to God that expresses our highest respect for him. There is a sense of familiarity in addressing God as *Our Father*, yet there is also a formality in noting that he is our heavenly Father, exalted far above his creation. His *name* is to be *hallowed*, or revered as holy and special. The Ten Commandments declare that God's name is not to be "misused" (Exodus 20:7), but treated with great care and reverence. We would do well in our prayers not to become too casual with God, thinking of him as our "Daddy in the Sky" or the "Big Man Upstairs," but to approach him with all the adoration he so richly deserves.

10. ". . . your kingdom come, your will be done on earth as it is in heaven.

What is this *kingdom* that Jesus told us to pray would *come*? Actually the Greek word for *kingdom* does not refer so much to a place or an organization as to a relationship with God. The "kingdom of God" describes God's authority and rule being exercised over those individuals who express their allegiance to his lordship. To pray *your kingdom come* is to pledge submission to God, or, as the parallel phrase says, to declare that *your will be done* in all that we do. The angels in *heaven* give God their total submission (Hebrews 1:6). May we on *earth* give him the same respect and devotion.

B. REQUEST FOR NEEDS (vv. 11-13)

11. "Give us today our daily bread.

We should not be embarrassed when we use our prayer time to make requests for the items we believe we need. Certainly to focus our prayers exclusively upon our own needs would be out of balance. But if we first approach God with the reverence he deserves, then we can in good conscience proceed to our petitions. To ask for God's assistance is an expression of our dependence on him; thus our requests honor him as our Creator and Provider.

By mentioning something as routine as *our daily bread*, Jesus was indicating that any concern we have is appropriate to bring before God. The fact that God numbers the hairs on our heads (Matthew 10:30) shows that even the minor details of our lives are of interest to him.

12. "Forgive us our debts, as we also have forgiven our debtors.

While it is proper to petition God for our physical needs, we should never forget our spiritual needs. It is especially helpful that Jesus gave us the example of

Our Father which art in heaven,
Hallowed be thy name.
Thy kingdom come.
Thy will be done in earth,
as it is in heaven.
Give us this day our daily bread.
And forgive us our debts,
as we forgive our debtors.
And lead us not into temptation,
but deliver us from evil:
For thine is the kingdom,
and the power, and
the glory, for ever.
Amen.

This display of the Lord's Model Prayer will be useful for your lesson today and on many occasions even after this quarter of study has concluded.

WHAT DO YOU THINK?

The lesson writer says, "To pray 'your kingdom come' is to pledge submission to God." If our prayer is sincere, what kind of actions would you expect to see demonstrating this submission?

praying for forgiveness. We are reminded that we must not take sin for granted; rather, we must honestly acknowledge when we have sinned (1 John 1:8-10) and then must "produce fruit in keeping with repentance" (Matthew 3:8; cf. Acts 26:20). One of those fruits is our willingness to *forgive* others, which reflects our understanding of God's forgiveness toward us. This is brought out most clearly in Jesus' parable of the unforgiving servant (Matthew 18:21-35).

13. *"And lead us not into temptation, but deliver us from the evil one."*

"No temptation has seized you except what is common to man. And God is faithful; he will not let you be tempted beyond what you can bear. But when you are tempted, he will also provide a way out so that you can stand up under it" (1 Corinthians 10:13). Paul's promise provides a helpful commentary on Jesus' prayer. When we express in prayer our complete trust and dependence upon God, we can be assured that he will look out for our spiritual well-being.

Note that the *New International Version* does not include the portion of the prayer that begins with "For thine is the kingdom" in the *King James Version*. These words do not appear in the oldest known manuscripts of Matthew. At the same time, the words offer a fitting conclusion to the model prayer, focusing on the majesty of God just as the prayer's opening words have done.

PLUG IN!

A man popped his morning bagel into the toaster. He waited for the pleasant aroma he usually detected when the bagel was toasting, but even after several minutes there was no aroma. He looked inside the toaster, and the metal strips that were usually bright orange were cold and dark. Pulling the toaster away from the wall, he found that the toaster had not been plugged in after the counter had been cleaned the day before. He plugged the appliance in, and in just a few moments he was enjoying his toasted bagel. His lesson for the day: everything works better when it's plugged in!

At times we are tempted to allow several days to go by without prayer. When we do this, we realize that the power we need to confront temptation, to speak a good word for the Lord, and to carry out other spiritual disciplines is not with us as we would like.

Prayer is the Christian's source of power: no prayer—no power. Plug yourself in daily to the most exciting power source in the universe: our Savior, the Son of God!

—D. R.

C. LIVING BY GRACE (vv. 14, 15)

14. *For if you forgive men when they sin against you, your heavenly Father will also forgive you.*

God's grace is not deserved or earned, and yet there is a "fairness" to grace. That which we ask God to give to us without merit, we must also be willing to give to others on the same terms.

15. *But if you do not forgive men their sins, your Father will not forgive your sins.*

Jesus confirms that what we say is in our hearts must also be translated into real life before God and man, or it is not genuine. Grace must become more than a point of theology; it must govern how we live and how we treat others.

CONCLUSION

Jesus quoted the prophet Isaiah (29:13) in expressing his frustration with some of the people to whom he ministered: "These people honor me with their lips, but their hearts are far from me. They worship me in vain; . . ." (Matthew 15:8, 9). The lesson is clear. We can practice the required rituals and say the proper words, but if it is all outward display rather than conviction of the heart, then it is of no value.

Discovery Learning

This page contains an alternate lesson plan emphasizing learning activities. Classes desiring such student involvement will find these suggestions helpful. The next page is a reproducible activity page to further enhance discovery learning.

LEARNING GOALS

After this lesson students should be able to:

1. Summarize Jesus' teaching about prayer in this portion of the Sermon on the Mount.

2. Explain the difference between "letting your light shine" and "blowing your own horn."

3. Suggest specific steps that they can take to make their prayer lives conform to Jesus' teaching.

INTO THE LESSON

Bring to class a flashlight, a blinking light, a bicycle horn or air horn, and a megaphone. (A megaphone can be made by rolling a sheet of paper into a cone, leaving openings at each end.)

Ask for volunteers each to take one of the objects and operate it in turn. Be sure that the flashlight is not waved around. Ask, "What is the reason for using this object?" Answers may vary: sound a warning, let your presence be known, draw attention to the operator.

Note that the flashlight can quietly point the way for someone who is lost or who is searching. Today's lesson warns us to check our motives in giving and praying. Are we trying to draw attention to ourselves for man's praise or to give glory to God? We will explore this issue in our lesson.

INTO THE WORD

This lesson presents some of Jesus' teaching in a time when crowds followed everywhere to hear what he had to say. (See the "Lesson Background" in the commentary for information concerning the setting of this Scripture.) Emphasize that Jesus was challenging his would-be disciples to live differently from other people, even those who appeared religious.

Ask three volunteers to read the text for today. One reads Matthew 6:1-4; the second reads Matthew 6:5-8; the third reads Matthew 6:9-15. Use these discussion questions with the class. The commentary will help to complete the answers.

Matthew 6:1-4 (Group 1)

1. What is Jesus' concern? (*The showiness of gift-giving for the sake of the giver.*)

2. How does this contrast with genuine, compassionate giving to the poor? (*Genuine giving is the matter of a humble heart. Its intent is to bring glory to God.*)

3. What is the promise to each? What is meant by "reward"? (*Each will receive his reward. For some the craving of men's applause will wind up being empty. For the humble, God will give blessing with eternal implications.*)

Matthew 6:5-8 (Group 2)

1. What does hypocritical prayer look like? (*It is "me-focused," showy; often uses trite formulas.*)

2. What does sincere prayer look like? (*It is "God-focused." It is done out of the limelight. It is from the heart of the believer.*)

3. If God knows what we need, why should we pray? (*Prayer is loving communication with God. We pray because we wish to interact with him and experience mutual joy.*)

Matthew 6:9-15 (Group 3)

1. What concerns for God are expressed in this prayer? (*His name be respected, his authority and rule be exercised, his purpose be accomplished.*)

2. What concerns for personal well-being are expressed? (*Our daily physical needs are met. Our daily spiritual needs are met: for forgiveness, guidance, and deliverance.*)

3. Why are personal forgiveness, forgiving others, and prayer linked? (*We need to recognize that God expects us to live out what we pray and to show grace toward others.*)

INTO LIFE

It is often easy to fall into established patterns of worshiping and serving God—patterns and forms that are comfortable to us. We need to monitor our motives to be sure we are seeking to bring glory to God.

Prepare a poster, overhead transparency, or chalkboard with the following headings. "1. Pray Regularly"; "2. Pray in Secret"; "3. Pray With Your Heart"; and "4. Pray Intentionally." Ask the students to give specific ideas as to how one should accomplish the activity in each heading. Use the printed text and other ideas. Examples may include the following: 1. Mark your calendar for prayer time. 2. Have a special place for prayer. 3. Write out your prayers. 4. Use this model prayer as an example.

Have each student choose the one area of these four in which he or she most needs improvement. Ask each one to discuss with a neighbor one or two ways to improve. Then close the session with prayer, in these groups of two, for strength and resolve to obey Christ.

Prayer in the New Testament

Read each of the following Scriptures and note what is said about the object of the prayer, the focus of the prayer, and the asked-for outcome of the prayer.

TEXT	OBJECT	FOCUS	OUTCOME
Matthew 6:9-15			
Ephesians 1:15-23			
Ephesians 3:14-21			
Philippians 1:3-11			

My Prayer Life

Reading through the prayers listed, we recognize several practical applications. These prayers can easily serve as models for our prayer life.

What would it be like to pray in the above manner?

What are you doing to build your prayer life?

Give examples of answered prayer in your life.

What is the most important lesson to be learned from these Scriptures?

What will you do differently today because of this study on prayer?

MIRACLES OF COMPASSION

LESSON 7

WHY TEACH THIS LESSON?

A dead child. A woman with an incurable bleeding disorder. Two blind men. What do they all have in common? Quite simply, Jesus Christ. In today's lesson you and your class will examine the miraculous encounters each of these people had with Jesus. Beyond that you will note that Jesus healed all kinds of illnesses and diseases. People did not have to "qualify" for Jesus' attention. They did not have to earn a hearing with him. They just had to have a need. Jesus saw them, "harassed and helpless, like sheep without a shepherd" (Matthew 9:36). As the Good Shepherd, of course, he had to act in their behalf.

All around us are people with needs. We can't raise their dead or heal all their diseases, but we can show them compassion. And we can introduce them to Jesus Christ. If your students miss that, they will have missed the whole lesson!

INTRODUCTION

A. BIRDS OF THE AIR

A duck hunter hits his target as it flies overhead, and then sends out his bird dog to retrieve it. A cat crouches under a bush, preparing to make a dash toward the unsuspecting birds in the birdbath. A baby bird ventures out of its nest too soon and falls to the ground below. Numerous times each day the words of Jesus come true: "Are not two sparrows sold for a penny? Yet not one of them will fall to the ground apart from the will of your Father" (Matthew 10:29). The Creator of all life notices everything he has created; nothing that happens escapes his watchful eye.

Jesus exemplified the compassion of God in his ministry as day after day he reached out to those around him who were hurting. And it should come as no surprise that so much of his time was spent helping others. After all, if God notices even a tiny bird that falls, he will certainly take an interest in those created in his own image when they are in need. For as Jesus went on to explain, "So don't be afraid; you are worth more than many sparrows" (v. 31).

B. LESSON BACKGROUND

The Old Testament book of Isaiah is sometimes referred to as "the Fifth Gospel" because it contains so many detailed prophecies regarding the coming Messiah, particularly his birth, his suffering, and his death. The prophet even predicts the impact of the Messiah's daily ministry. In one place he writes: "Then will the eyes of the blind be opened and the ears of the deaf unstopped. Then will the lame leap like a deer, and the mute tongue shout for joy" (Isaiah 35:5, 6).

Jesus invested much of his ministry in performing miracles of healing. And while these miracles fulfilled prophecy and provided supernatural evidence that Jesus was God's appointed Messiah (John 5:36; Acts 2:22), there was much more to his miracles than this. Jesus was motivated by compassion. He truly cared about the people he touched and healed. He sympathized with the families who grieved. He healed, not only because he needed to for the sake of his mission, but because he wanted to for the sake of the people.

DEVOTIONAL READING:
MATTHEW 11:2-6

BACKGROUND SCRIPTURE:
MATTHEW 9:18-38

PRINTED TEXT:
MATTHEW 9:18-31, 35, 36

LESSON AIMS

After this lesson each student will be able to:

1. Retell the miracles performed by Jesus and recounted in today's text.

2. Tell how these miracles show the compassion of Jesus.

3. Demonstrate Jesus' compassion this week to someone in need.

Jan
16

KEY VERSE

When he saw the crowds, he had compassion on them, because they were harassed and helpless, like sheep without a shepherd.   —Matthew 9:36

LESSON 7 NOTES

I. ACT OF DESPERATION (MATTHEW 9:18-22)

A. WHEN ALL ELSE FAILS (vv. 18-21)

18. While he was saying this, a ruler came and knelt before him and said, "My daughter has just died. But come and put your hand on her, and she will live."

Each day crowds of people gathered around Jesus with requests for healing. As soon as one person had been helped, there would be many others waiting their turn. The appearance of a father with a request regarding his *daughter* was not unusual; what was unusual was the position this man held.

The man who approached Jesus on this day was a *ruler* named Jairus (Mark 5:22), a religious official in one of the local Jewish synagogues. Since he knew of Jesus' reputation, he may have been from the Capernaum area, where Jesus focused much of his ministry. His daughter was twelve years old (Luke 8:42), suffering from an unknown ailment. Both Mark and Luke note that the girl was dying (Mark 5:23; Luke 8:42), while Matthew says that she had *just died*. According to Mark's fuller account of the story, the girl was "dying" when Jairus left home to seek out Jesus. Later, while they were walking toward his house, Jairus received word that the girl had since died (Mark 5:35). Apparently Matthew is giving an abbreviated version that emphasizes the condition of the child when Jesus arrived at her home.

The religious leaders in general had not given Jesus' ministry a friendly reception, and most of them remained adversaries until the day they crucified him. We do not know whether Jairus had once been part of this official opposition, but there was no place for animosity now—not with his daughter dying, and with no one else to turn to. He *knelt before* Jesus and expressed great respect for him, proclaiming his faith in Jesus' healing power.

ASK JESUS

Jairus did the one thing he believed necessary to save his daughter: *he asked Jesus for help*. No one else could do for his daughter what Jesus could.

A minister planted a new church, which very quickly experienced a surge of growth. After several months, three couples whose involvement and financial commitment had been especially helpful had to move out of town because of a change in employment or some other cause. While the church maintained its health, it began to struggle financially.

One Sunday during the traditional "summer slump," the offering came to $700, far short of the weekly need. The deficit, combined with other bills that had to be paid, put the church in need of $2,200 by the following Friday to meet expenses.

The minister remembered Jairus and his boldness in approaching Jesus. He got on his knees and laid the needs of the church before the Lord. Literally while he was praying, the phone rang. One of the relatively inactive members of the church asked the minister to come to his house that afternoon, saying that he wanted to make a donation to the church. So the minister drove to the man's house, picked up the envelope he offered, and returned to his office.

On the way, the minister had prayed and asked the Lord to make the gift at least $1,000 to put toward the needed $2,200. When he opened the envelope, he found to his amazement a check for $10,000! Not only did the gift supply the church's immediate need, but it also helped get the church through the rest of the summer.

Ask Jesus. He heard Jairus. He heard the minister of the new church. And he will hear you, if you will ask.

—D. R.

19. Jesus got up and went with him, and so did his disciples.

Jesus did not hesitate to respond to Jairus's desperate need and his humble spirit.

WHAT DO YOU THINK?

The lesson writer notes that most of the religious leaders in Jesus' day were openly hostile toward his ministry. Now here came one of them asking Jesus for help. How should we react today when a person who has been antagonistic toward Christ and the church begins attending church as a result of a crisis that has left him or her desperate?

20. Just then a woman who had been subject to bleeding for twelve years came up behind him and touched the edge of his cloak.

The most we are told about the plight of this *woman*, even by the physician Luke, is that she had some kind of persistent internal *bleeding* that could not be healed (Luke 8:43). She had used all of her resources to pay for various medical treatments, but they had only made her situation worse (Mark 5:26). Note that her *twelve years* of suffering matches the girl's age of twelve years. It seems, perhaps, more than coincidental, but the Scripture makes nothing of the similarity. We, therefore, ought to be cautious about drawing conclusions from it.

21. She said to herself, "If I only touch his cloak, I will be healed."

Here was a daring act of faith. At this point in the ministry of Jesus there is no record of someone's being *healed* by touching Jesus' clothing. How this woman arrived at this idea, we are not told. But "desperate times call for desperate measures." Since her situation seemed hopeless otherwise, she was willing to try.

B. GOD IS ABLE (v. 22)

22. Jesus turned and saw her. "Take heart, daughter," he said, "your faith has healed you." And the woman was healed from that moment.

Not only was the woman *healed from that moment*, but, more precisely, at the very moment she "touched the edge of his cloak" (Luke 8:44). The timing was so exact that there was no mistaking the source of her healing.

Mark notes that Jesus felt healing power leave his body when the woman touched his robe. The disciples were dumbfounded when Jesus asked, "Who touched my clothes?" because there were many people touching him. But Jesus looked directly at those around him until finally the woman confessed that she was the one who had touched him and received healing (Mark 5:30-33). Jesus sought out her confession, not to rebuke her for an unauthorized action, but that he might receive credit for the blessing she had received from God through his messianic ministry. The testimony of this miracle to Jesus' power was not to be lost on this crowd.

Your faith has healed you, Jesus then said to the woman. She had exhausted the healing arts of mankind, but to no avail. Believing that God was her only recourse left and that Jesus was the way to approach God, she touched him and was blessed for her faith.

II. CHALLENGE TO REASON (MATTHEW 9:23-26)

A. WHEN ALL HOPE IS GONE (vv. 23, 24)

23. When Jesus entered the ruler's house and saw the flute players and the noisy crowd.

By the time Jesus arrived at Jairus's house, not only had his daughter died, but the mourners had assembled. As was typical for that culture, neighbors would quickly gather at the home of the deceased and put on a *noisy* display of emotions on behalf of the grieving family (who tended to remain secluded inside the home). *Flute players* would play sad funeral dirges, and people would publicly weep while uttering loud wailing sounds. Mark accurately describes the sound as a "commotion" (Mark 5:38).

24. . . . he said, "Go away. The girl is not dead but asleep." But they laughed at him.

Jesus' statement *the girl is not dead but asleep* was met with derisive laughter, for his words defied all reason and logic. But these scoffers would later remember what Jesus said, and how a dead girl came to life again as if she had only been sleeping.

WHAT DO YOU THINK?

What are some situations that can seem hopeless to people today? What, if anything, does today's text offer to people in hopeless situations?

DAILY BIBLE READINGS

Monday, Jan. 10—Jesus Continues His Healing Work (Matthew 8:1-17)

Tuesday, Jan. 11—Jesus Heals the Gadarene Demoniacs (Matthew 8:28—9:1)

Wednesday, Jan. 12—Jesus Heals a Paralytic (Matthew 9:2-8)

Thursday, Jan. 13—Jesus Gives Life and Healing (Matthew 9:18-26)

Friday, Jan. 14—Jesus Heals the Blind and Mute (Matthew 9:27-38)

Saturday, Jan. 15—Jesus Heals a Man's Withered Hand (Matthew 12:9-14)

Sunday, Jan. 16—The Faith of a Canaanite Woman (Matthew 15:21-31)

HOW TO SAY IT

Capernaum. Kuh-PER-nay-um.
Isaiah. Eye-ZAY-uh.
Jairus. JYE-rus or JAY-ih-rus.
messianic. mess-ee-AN-ick.

B. GOD GIVES LIFE (vv. 25, 26)

25. After the crowd had been put outside, he went in and took the girl by the hand, and she got up.

Jesus cleared the house of all spectators except for the girl's parents and his three closest disciples—Peter, James, and John (Luke 8:51). The crowd was removed because their mocking attitude made them unworthy of taking part in the special event that was soon to occur.

Jesus *took the girl by the hand*, summoned her to arise (Mark 5:41), and she *got up* . Once again, there was no doubt that a miracle had occurred and that Jesus was the source of it.

26. News of this spread through all that region.

As he often did during his Galilean ministry, Jesus gave the parents of the girl strict orders not to broadcast this miracle (Mark 5:43). The persistent problem Jesus faced was that his miracles often drew larger crowds than he could manage. As thousands pressed in upon him, they presented a danger to themselves and to his disciples (Luke 12:1).

In addition the crowds also wanted to manipulate Jesus' ministry by forcing him to keep on healing when he wanted to preach (Mark 1:32-38) or to lead them as an earthly king (John 6:15). In some cases Jesus stayed away from the cities in order to avoid the huge crowds, yet they always seemed to find him anyway (Mark 1:45). Here, in spite of what Jesus said, *news of this spread through all that region*; because the joy of experiencing God's power when all hope is gone is too great to keep locked up inside.

III. CRY FOR MERCY (MATTHEW 9:27-31)

A. WHEN PEOPLE SUFFER (vv. 27, 28)

27. As Jesus went on from there, two blind men followed him, calling out, "Have mercy on us, Son of David!"

Raising the dead is such an extraordinary miracle that it would provide an appropriate occasion to stop and take a break for the remainder of the day. Actually, Jesus had had a full day of healing, including having to travel slowly through a massive crowd over whatever distance it took to reach the home of Jairus. It was apparently time for him to retire for the day. Thus he did not stop to heal the *two blind men* (or apparently anyone else) who called out to him along the way, but kept moving forward.

One of the hard truths for a compassionate heart to accept is that we do not have the time or energy to help everyone who calls out for us. Even as Jesus balanced healing with his preaching and teaching, so we must balance our service for Christ with our other work and family responsibilities. And, like Jesus, we must be disciplined enough to know when to quit and refresh ourselves in order to be prepared adequately for later tasks.

28. When he had gone indoors, the blind men came to him, and he asked them, "Do you believe that I am able to do this?"

"Yes, Lord," they replied.

Matthew notes that Jesus went *indoors*, but he does not tell us where. It is not likely that Jesus went back to the home of Jairus, but to a place where he and his disciples could rest each evening. It may have been the home of a family member or friend of Jesus or of one of the disciples. It was probably the home that served as his "headquarters" whenever he was in Capernaum.

These *blind men* pleaded for a hearing with Jesus, driven as they were by the misery of darkness and alienation that they endured day after day. They cried out for mercy and drew the attention of Jesus by the faith and persistence that they

WHAT DO YOU THINK?

There will always be hurting people and undone work. Yet we must remember Jesus' example. He knew that if he did not regularly withdraw to be with God the Father, he would not be able to minister adequately to the multitudes clamoring for his attention.

As we try to help hurting people, how can we determine when it is time to withdraw for personal refreshment and renewal, and when we should stay and minister to one more person?

demonstrated when they followed him all the way home. This was no easy task for blind men on crowded streets, but they refused to abandon their cause.

B. GOD MAKES A WAY (vv. 29-31)

29. Then he touched their eyes and said, "According to your faith will it be done to you."

Jesus enjoys distributing his blessings *according to* one's *faith*. However, this should not be understood to mean that possessing faith automatically results in a life of blessings. Many faithful saints will suffer much in this lifetime, and only after they have departed this world will they "rest from their labor" (Revelation 14:13). We are to give thanks in every situation (1 Thessalonians 5:18), acknowledging that even in the most trying of circumstances God is working for our good (Romans 8:28)—a perspective that can be grasped only *according to* one's *faith*.

30. And their sight was restored. Jesus warned them sternly, "See that no one knows about this."

Once again Jesus *warned . . . sternly* those whom he healed not to draw more attention to him. The crowd-control problem was sometimes so great that Jesus could not even rest in a house without people seeking to get in.

31. But they went out and spread the news about him all over that region.

The *news* of miraculous healing continued to *spread*, despite Jesus' best efforts to slow it down. If only Christians had the same enthusiasm today for publicizing the greater "healing" that has occurred in our souls—the forgiveness of our sins and life anew in the Spirit!

IV. HEART OF COMPASSION (MATTHEW 9:35, 36)

A. WHEN PEOPLE ARE LOST (v. 35)

35. Jesus went through all the towns and villages, teaching in their synagogues, preaching the good news of the kingdom and healing every disease and sickness.

This verse provides a good summary of the priorities of Jesus' ministry. His first concern was his *teaching* and *preaching*, which he confirmed through his *healing* ministry.

The theme of Jesus' preaching was *the good news of the kingdom*. Jesus taught that his kingdom was not something to be seen and touched, but something "within you" (Luke 17:21). He told Pilate that his kingdom was "not of this world" (John 18:36). For Jesus, the *kingdom* means a relationship with the King, not a geographical region. The kingdom of God exists wherever there is someone in total submission to the will of God, for when there is someone in charge (a king) and someone who serves (the subject), then there is a kingdom.

Thus when Jesus preached about the kingdom of God, he was preparing hearts for the challenge he would later issue through the Great Commission. The church is to go out and "make disciples" (Matthew 28:19)—that is, recruit people who will commit themselves to Jesus as their Master, Lord, and King. While a "heavenly kingdom" awaits the faithful (2 Timothy 4:18), our kingdom relationship begins now when we make a faith commitment to the lordship of Jesus Christ.

Jesus was able to heal *every disease and sickness*. His ministry of healing stands in sharp contrast with the so-called faith healers of today. Whereas Jesus would take on any physical affliction (and even death), modern faith healers are selective. Generally avoiding congenital ailments and incurable diseases, they usually focus on internal conditions that are not easily or immediately substantiated. And, as we have already noted, Jesus' healings were instantaneous, occurring at the moment he acted or spoke, and never produced a failure. What a contrast to the modern healer who makes several attempts to cure, then blames any failure

WHAT DO YOU THINK?

In the case of the infirm woman, Jesus deliberately called attention to her so that, according to our lesson writer, "he might receive credit for the blessing she had received from God." But Jairus was told not to broadcast the miracle of raising his daughter (Mark 5:43) and the blind men were also charged, "See that no one knows about this." Why do you suppose Jesus wanted one miracle known but not the others? What difference does it make today?

on the lack of faith of those who come to him. Whatever is actually going on with contemporary faith healers, it is no match for what Scripture tells us Jesus did.

B. GOD STILL CARES (v. 36)

36. When he saw the crowds, he had compassion on them, because they were harassed and helpless, like sheep without a shepherd.

Both the English word *compassion* and the Greek word behind it literally mean "to feel with" someone else. The spirit of compassion is to feel someone else's hurts and pains, then desire to relieve their misery.

Jesus was motivated by the spirit of compassion. Although there was a "theological necessity" for his healings, supplying divine proof for his messianic claims, his was a heart that could not look upon hurting people without longing to reach out and relieve their misery.

ACTING WITH COMPASSION

Just as Jesus "had compassion" concerning the needs of others, so we as his followers need to cultivate hearts of compassion.

A godly gentleman served as an elder in his church. He was active in many areas of the life of the congregation and was involved in several parachurch organizations as well. His commitment to the kingdom of God made him highly respected in his church and community.

One day, while the elder was doing some finishing touches on a house he was building, a young man from across the street, who was "high" on a heavy amount of illegal drugs, entered the house where the elder was working and took this man's life. He was caught, convicted of the crime, and eventually sent to prison for a lengthy term.

While the young man was awaiting trial, the wife of the elder began coming to the jail where he was kept and spending time with the man who had killed her husband. Displaying a tremendous heart of compassion, she took him cookies and gave him her husband's Bible to read. In time, the minister of the church where the man had been an elder baptized this young man into Jesus Christ.

The actions of this elder's wife truly demonstrated the compassion of Jesus to one of the "sheep without a shepherd." Her courageous witness illustrates an important principle: the world can never know the compassion of Jesus without experiencing it through his people.

—D. R.

CONCLUSION

No one wants to have to make an emergency phone call. But check out the phone(s) in most of our homes and you will see that we are ready to call for help if necessary. Our speed dial buttons are set with the emergency numbers we need to summon the police and rescue squad, as well as to contact close family members. Perhaps there is an emergency sticker on the phone, reminding our children to dial 911. And for those occasions when we leave the children with a baby-sitter, there will be a note with special instructions for the evening. We hope we never need all of these numbers, but we are ready just the same.

Now for a spiritual inventory. Do we have God's "number" ready to call in times of need? Often, when problems come our way, we scramble to deal with them the best that we can, only to realize later that we forgot to support our efforts with prayer. Too often God is an afterthought; we come to him only after we have exhausted our own resources, finally realizing that we need *his* help.

Oh, the unnecessary grief we bring upon ourselves when we do not think to call first upon the wise and understanding compassion of our Father in Heaven!

WHAT DO YOU THINK?

Jesus was moved with compassion for the people, seeing them as "sheep without a shepherd." What do you think would happen if all Christians began to see people with the same compassion Jesus had?

Today's visual challenges us to see the multitudes of today as Jesus saw the crowds in his day: as "sheep without a shepherd."

PRAYER

Father, help us to draw near to you in times of trouble. Then help us to imitate our Lord and Savior by assisting those around us who are in need of acts of compassion. We ask in his name. Amen.

THOUGHT TO REMEMBER

Others will never know of the compassion of Christ unless they see it in his followers.

Discovery Learning

This page contains an alternate lesson plan emphasizing learning activities. Classes desiring such student involvement will find these suggestions helpful. The next page is a reproducible activity page to further enhance discovery learning.

LEARNING GOALS

After this lesson each student will be able to:

1. Retell the miracles performed by Jesus that are recounted in today's text.

2. Tell how these miracles show the compassion of Jesus.

3. Demonstrate Jesus' compassion this week to someone in need.

INTO THE LESSON

Today's lesson deals with Jesus' compassion, his motive for ministry and miracles. Call attention to the fact that one of the characteristics of a Christian is to be compassionate.

Prepare a chart or chalkboard with the acrostic COMPASSION written down the side. Say, "What are some words, beginning with these letters, that describe a person with compassion?" (*Examples include Comforting, Openness, Motivated, Purposeful, Awareness, Sensitivity, Serving, Intense, Observant, Needs-oriented.*) This activity is in the student book.

Many of us in this class today have experienced Christ's compassion in our lives. As we explore today's text, we will determine to show compassion to others.

INTO THE WORD

Prepare a mini-lecture on Jesus' miracles in the New Testament. Use material in the commentary section, noting the purpose being apologetic, the motive being compassion, and the balance needed for ministry.

Option: Use the reproducible activity "Words of Hope" on page 182 to introduce the Bible study.

Distribute the following true/false quiz based on today's text. In groups of two to four, students are to read the Scripture (Matthew 9:18-31, 35, 36) and complete the quiz. Reasons for the answers are printed to help the teacher discuss the material further.

1. The ruler asked Jesus to speak and his daughter would be healed. (*False, v. 18; he asked Jesus to touch her.*)

2. The woman with bleeding had been ill twelve years. (*True, v. 20.*)

3. Jesus touched the woman to heal her. (*False, v. 20; the woman touched Jesus' clothing.*)

4. Jesus told the woman that his faith had made her well. (*False, v. 22; Jesus said her faith had made her whole. See the commentary notes for a treatment of this issue.*)

5. Jesus told the people that the girl was asleep. (*True, v. 23. Of course, they knew that she was dead; the commentary gives additional notes concerning Jesus' challenge to the crowd.*)

6. Jesus asked the blind men if they believed he could heal them. (*True, v. 28; even their behavior speaks of their belief.*)

7. Jesus encouraged the men to speak freely of his miracle. (*False, v. 30; the commentary speaks of the intensity of the crowd.*)

8. Jesus' miracles were instantaneous. (*True; see the comments on v. 35 to expand on this point.*)

9. Jesus' compassion was for those without a shepherd. (*True, v. 36. Be sure to emphasize to your students that Jesus has compassion for them as well.*)

INTO LIFE

Ask, "If you had been in the crowd for any of these miracles, what would you have felt? What would you have thought? How does this help you to understand the goodness of God? If you had been there, could you have kept quiet concerning these miracles?"

During the week, as you prepare for this lesson, collect newspaper and magazine articles showing the compassion of people toward others. Distribute these articles to your groups, asking them to identify the situation, the compassion shown, and the results. For example, you may find stories about a hospitalized child and individuals who raised money to help with the bills, bringing thanks from grateful parents.

We recognize a person's compassion by his or her actions. How did Jesus' actions show his compassion? (*He desired to reach out and relieve misery. He was willing to be "inconvenienced" to help. He met real needs.*)

Have each group make a list of issues people face today and the ways in which compassion can be shown. Give each group a copy of the second activity on page 182, "Hope for the Hopeless," to facilitate this. Be sure to involve each group by using its suggestions.

Have each class member choose a situation familiar to him or her in which compassion is necessary. Encourage each to list the need, the person involved, and the response the student will give. Have each student choose a prayer partner. Share the concern. Pray for strength to act. Establish a time when a checkup will be made on the commitment.

Words of Hope

Read Matthew 9:18-33, 35, 36. Throughout the passage Jesus gives words of hope. Write the biblical reference and the words of hope given in each of the hearts below.

Hope for the Hopeless

Write below various situations that seem to be hopeless. Next to each write how Jesus might answer and show hope to the person(s) involved.

HOPELESS SITUATION   *HOW JESUS MIGHT ANSWER*

OPPOSITION TO JESUS

LESSON 8

WHY TEACH THIS LESSON?

We live in an age of transition. For many, the changes in society are a source of anxiety and frustration. Of special concern to Christians is the drift in morality. Behavior that once was a source of embarrassment is now a source of pride. The respect once given to people of faith has turned to ridicule and disdain.

What is hard for some to believe is that things are more "normal" now than they used to be! Over the centuries and around the world, opposition to Christians and what they believe has been the norm more often than not. Jesus said it would be so. "If the world hates you, keep in mind that it hated me first," he said. "If they persecuted me, they will persecute you also" (John 15:18, 20).

So use this lesson on the opposition that Jesus faced as a wake-up call. Your students, if they have not already, will face the same kind of slander and vicious attacks that Jesus faced. Are they ready?

INTRODUCTION

A. A SIGN OPPOSED

No matter how wrong the world may seem, all is forgotten when we hold a baby in our arms. For those few moments we see innocence, beauty, and hope for a brighter future. And when we return to the cares of this life, we always treasure our memories of that precious, innocent child.

As Mary, the mother of Jesus, held her special child in her arms, there was much that she could have "pondered . . . in her heart" (Luke 2:19). "What a glorious future must lie ahead for my Son!" she may have thought as she reflected on the words that the angel Gabriel had spoken to her months earlier (Luke 1:28-37). Yet how troubled her thoughts must have become when she and Joseph met an old man named Simeon in the temple and heard his prophecy that the child would be "a sign to be opposed" (Luke 2:34, *New American Standard Bible*). Simeon went on to tell Mary, "And a sword will pierce your own soul too" (Luke 2:35). The word *too* indicates that the sword would pierce Jesus as well—a veiled reference to his death.

In last week's lesson we noted how huge crowds often surrounded Jesus during his ministry—seeking his assistance, clinging to his every word. The "flip side" of this popularity is that Jesus' years of ministry were marked by severe opposition from start to finish, culminating in his crucifixion at Calvary.

B. LESSON BACKGROUND

The first instance of opposition to Jesus during his public ministry occurred shortly after he had established his headquarters in Capernaum (Matthew 4:13). He made a brief trip to Jerusalem for the Passover (John 2:13). While he was there, he chased the merchants out of the temple (John 2:14-16). The hostile response from the religious leaders was only a foretaste of what Jesus would experience each time he returned to the city of Jerusalem.

In addition, opposition to Jesus was present even in his hometown of Nazareth. The first time he visited and identified himself as the Messiah of

DEVOTIONAL READING:
MATTHEW 12:1-14

BACKGROUND SCRIPTURE:
MATTHEW 12

PRINTED TEXT:
MATTHEW 12:22-32, 38-41

LESSON AIMS

After participating in this lesson, each student will be able to:

1. Summarize the controversy between Jesus and the Pharisees described in today's text.

2. Tell how Jesus' acts and teachings answer those who oppose Christianity today.

3. Prepare a statement of faith that answers the criticisms he or she most often hears from unbelievers.

Jan
23

KEY VERSE

He who is not with me is against me, and he who does not gather with me scatters.
—*Matthew 12:30*

LESSON 8 NOTES

prophecy, his former neighbors were so offended that they attempted to force him off a cliff (Luke 4:16-29).

The encounter that is the subject of today's lesson was not as dangerous as the one in Nazareth, but it was more vicious. On this occasion the assault did not involve the threat of physical violence; instead, it came in the form of a most slanderous charge: that Jesus was actually an agent of Satan. The battle lines were clearly being drawn.

I. KINGDOM OF GOD (MATTHEW 12:22-30)
A. BOLD CHALLENGE (vv. 22-24)
22. Then they brought him a demon-possessed man who was blind and mute, and Jesus healed him, so that he could both talk and see.

While all supernatural healings are amazing events, releasing a person from the control of a demonic spirit is special in that it involves a face-to-face confrontation with an evil and powerful enemy. When the seventy disciples reported to Jesus about the miraculous signs they had performed, their greatest thrill was in casting out demons (Luke 10:17).

One of the characteristics of demon possession revealed in Scripture is that demons tended to abuse their victims physically. The people Jesus confronted were often afflicted with ailments such as the lack of sight and speech (the man in our text is an example), or with torments such as causing the victim to cut himself with sharp objects (Mark 5:5) or to throw himself into a fire (Matthew 17:15).

23. All the people were astonished and said, "Could this be the Son of David?"

When Jesus challenged the power of Satan and cast out demons, some wondered if he might be *the Son of David*—one of several expressions for the Messiah (Matthew 22:42). This is not to say that any person who cast out demons had to be the Messiah, for Jesus' disciples could also do this. But miraculous signs served to confirm the claims made by the person working the miracles (John 3:2; 5:36; 10:38; 14:11). Thus Jesus' claim to be the Messiah was reinforced by his miraculous power over demons.

24. But when the Pharisees heard this, they said, "It is only by Beelzebub, the prince of demons, that this fellow drives out demons."

Beelzebub is a variant spelling of the ancient name "Baal-Zebub," which was the title of one of the local Canaanite pagan gods in Old Testament times (2 Kings 1:2). Some Bible students believe that *Beelzebub* (meaning "lord of the flies") was a name meant to ridicule the actual name of the supposed deity, which was *Beelzebul* (meaning "lord of the house"). In fact, Beelzebul is the form of the name that appears in the Greek text of this passage. The significance of the name "lord of the house" is especially clear in the context of Jesus' response to the Pharisees' charge (see verse 29).

For now, let us note that by the first century, Beelzebul had become one of the titles that the Jews used for Satan. This means that the charge the Pharisees leveled against Jesus was the lowest form of slander against someone claiming to represent God. They were crediting Jesus' miraculous works to the power of Satan. The implication of such a charge was either that Jesus was himself deceived regarding who was empowering him, or that he was knowingly working in league with the devil and thus operating under false pretenses. Jesus could not allow such an accusation to go unchallenged.

B. FOOLISH IDEA (vv. 25-27)
25. Jesus knew their thoughts and said to them, "Every kingdom divided against itself will be ruined, and every city or household divided against itself will not stand.

WHAT DO YOU THINK?

People in Jesus' day had differing views about his identity. Today, as well, people have many wrong views of Jesus: that he is merely a man who discovered a divine idea, that he is something similar to Michael the archangel (an important being created by God), that he is a "Son" of God, but not "God the Son," or that he was a prophet or even a mere man who was wrongly deified by his followers. How can we help people to know Jesus for who he really is?

These words constitute a principle that has stood the test of time. Any organization that allows internal conflicts to continue unchecked is destined for failure. **26. If Satan drives out Satan, he is divided against himself. How then can his kingdom stand?**

Jesus offered a very rational application of the "house divided" principle to the slanderous charge against him. Suppose it were true that Jesus was operating by the powers of *Satan*. Considering the aggressiveness with which Jesus had attacked demonic spirits during his ministry thus far, did it make sense that Satan would support such a ministry? Only a fool would continue to supply the supernatural power that was being used against him. The logical conclusion is that Satan cannot be the source of Jesus' power, or he would have cut it off long ago. **27. And if I drive out demons by Beelzebub, by whom do your people drive them out? So then, they will be your judges.**

The next argument Jesus used also shows the foolishness (as well as the hypocrisy) of the Pharisees' accusation against him. They taught their own *people* (that is, their disciples) how to *drive out demons*. Thus to argue that it requires a Satanic power to cast out demons would in effect be an indictment against themselves.

Jesus' incidental reference to the Pharisees' casting out demons raises the question of just what exactly these men were capable of doing, and by what means. We would not expect that the Pharisees were empowered by the Holy Spirit, given their opposition to the work of the Holy Spirit in Jesus Christ. Nor is it likely that they were empowered by Satan, using the same logic Jesus used to defend himself. If they were successful in casting out demons, then perhaps they were doing it through the means that Jesus suggested his disciples use: "prayer" (Mark 9:29).

The difference between this approach and a supernatural gift such as the one Jesus and his disciples possessed is that the gift can effect an immediate release from the demon, with all the evidence of a miracle in the eyes of those who observe. Prayer, on the other hand, takes time to accomplish its objective. It may have been this difference that accounted for the crowds' being "astonished" at the manner in which Jesus cast out demons (v. 23). His work was a powerful, instantaneous miracle of God, not simply an eventual response to fervent and persistent prayer.

C. STRONG STAND (vv. 28-30)

28. But if I drive out demons by the Spirit of God, then the kingdom of God has come upon you.

Jesus could not be operating by the power of Satan, since he continually assaulted the kingdom of Satan. He was obviously doing something bigger than what was achieved through prayer and fasting, since he obtained immediate and impressive results. By the process of elimination, Jesus had proven that he was empowered by the *Spirit of God*.

Now came the challenging implication for the Pharisees: the power of God within Jesus confirmed the claims being made by Jesus. He is the Messiah, the Son of David. *The kingdom of God has come upon you*, for the King himself was standing before them.

29. Or again, how can anyone enter a strong man's house and carry off his possessions unless he first ties up the strong man? Then he can rob his house.

Jesus provided a further application of his "house divided" principle. Each time he freed an individual from demonic influence, he took from Satan people whom Satan saw as his own *possessions*. Consider how this language was, in effect, a response to the original charge of the Pharisees. If Satan is, as the Pharisees

WHAT DO YOU THINK?

Some people apply Jesus' statement about a kingdom divided against itself to the church. Do you think this is a valid application? Why or why not? If so, what duties or responsibilities does it lay on us?

WHAT DO YOU THINK?

The biblical evidence is clear as to who Jesus was, what he taught, and what he demands. In what way did Jesus' call to make a decisive choice between his kingdom and the kingdom of this world become clear to you? How can you use your experience to help someone else to come to know the Lord?

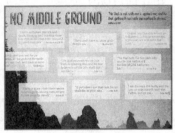

Today's visual is a timely reminder that we must choose to be either with Jesus or against him. There truly is "No Middle Ground."

called him, *Beelzebul* (the "lord of the house"), then Jesus must be very powerful if he is able to enter into such a *strong man's house*, tie him up, and then *rob* him by seizing his *possessions* (those under his influence). There is only one power capable of meeting such a challenge: Jesus must possess the power of God.

30. He who is not with me is against me, and he who does not gather with me scatters.

The battle lines were drawn. The Pharisees knew too much about the power of Jesus to take a neutral position with any kind of intellectual or moral integrity. The choice facing them was clear: either to support Jesus in his messianic ministry, or, by default, to be rejected by Jesus and by God.

II. SIN AGAINST THE SPIRIT (MATTHEW 12:31, 32)

A. UNPARDONABLE SIN (v. 31)

31. And so I tell you, every sin and blasphemy will be forgiven men, but the blasphemy against the Spirit will not be forgiven.

One of the most terrifying warnings in Scripture is this reference to a sin that is "unpardonable." There are many theories regarding the *blasphemy against the Spirit*, but most have little to do with the incident that we have seen developing in this chapter. The key to interpreting this verse (or any verse of Scripture, for that matter) is to look at the context.

Since the Pharisees were being warned about this sin, they had apparently not yet crossed the line. Even so, it was their charge that Jesus was empowered by Satan rather than the Holy Spirit that led to this warning. Starting with this understanding, we can draw some reasonable conclusions from this text.

First, blasphemy against the Holy Spirit has something to do with denying the Spirit's powerful witness to Jesus Christ. Furthermore, it is a slander against the Holy Spirit; for when his divine powers are said to be Satan's powers, he is truly being "blasphemed." Blasphemy against the Holy Spirit also seems to involve a deliberate and willful rejection of the Holy Spirit's evidence on behalf of Jesus. Such an attitude is not an honest doubt that needs more time to reason through the data; it is a recognition of the truth and a refusal to accept it. This is the line the Pharisees were being warned not to cross.

Perhaps this sin can best be likened to the attitude of Satan himself. He knows the truth about Jesus; he and all his cohorts "believe" in Jesus (James 2:19). And yet Satan has willfully chosen to reject the authority of God and to oppose the ministry of Jesus. This is a perversion of the will so deep that one cannot recover from it, and therefore God cannot forgive.

Let us keep in mind that this is not a sin we would expect to see often, if ever. After all, even Jesus' staunchest enemies, the Pharisees, had not yet reached this level of opposition. Thus, we should continue to evangelize all those who reject the gospel of Jesus Christ; because what we will likely confront is not the willful and final rejection of a truth that these individuals know, but the resistance of a truth of which they have not yet been persuaded.

As for the Christian who is worried that he may have committed the unpardonable sin at some point in his past, the fact that he is troubled by this possibility suggests that he has never reached this level of perversion. He is to be encouraged to repent of the sins he has committed and renew his pledge of faith to Christ.

B. ETERNAL CONSEQUENCES (v. 32)

32. Anyone who speaks a word against the Son of Man will be forgiven, but anyone who speaks against the Holy Spirit will not be forgiven, either in this age or in the age to come."

Why is speaking *against the Son of Man* more tolerable than speaking *against the Holy Spirit*? Consider that Jesus made his exceptional claims while he was in his incarnate state, and it is always reasonable to be cautious when a man claims to be God. While preaching in human form, Jesus looked not unlike any other man who might make such an incredible claim—and there were many in his day who claimed to be great leaders (cf. Acts 5:34-39). There was nothing about Jesus' appearance that would have given him an advantage over these other claimants—or over those who Jesus predicted would come after him (Matthew 24:5).

Thus to "speak against Jesus" and doubt his claims would not be unreasonable—that is, until the Holy Spirit provided indisputable, supernatural witness to Christ through the apostles (John 14:26; 16:13, 14; 17:20). A rejection at this point would not be against the Son of Man, but against the Holy Spirit who testifies on his behalf.

The consequences of blaspheming against the Spirit and his witness to Jesus are as severe as one can imagine: it *will not be forgiven, either in this age or in the age to come*. The Spirit's word concerning Jesus is God's last word. One rejects it at his own eternal peril.

III. SIGN OF JONAH (MATTHEW 12:38-41)

A. CLOSED MIND (v. 38)

38. Then some of the Pharisees and teachers of the law said to him, "Teacher, we want to see a miraculous sign from you."

There was something less than honest about the demand of the *Pharisees and teachers of the law* for a *miraculous sign*. This becomes especially apparent when one notes that Jesus had just provided several such signs (vv. 15, 22). Apparently the scribes and Pharisees expected to set the terms for the sign they demanded and to name the type of miracle they wanted to see.

B. SURE SIGN (vv. 39, 40)

39. He answered, "A wicked and adulterous generation asks for a miraculous sign! But none will be given it except the sign of the prophet Jonah.

The Pharisees and their compatriots were *a wicked and adulterous generation*. They had committed spiritual adultery in failing to live as God's covenant people. And, like the adulterous husband who cheats on his wife, they were being malicious and dishonest in their discussion with Jesus. They said that if they were given the proper *sign*, they would believe Jesus' claims. Their opposition to Jesus remained so strong, however, that they would never have changed their minds, no matter how many signs he gave them.

Jesus was willing, however, to grant his critics a special sign—*the sign of the prophet Jonah*. What Jesus offered as the ultimate proof for his claims was a third-day resurrection (Matthew 16:21; John 2:18-22). Certainly a resurrection miracle in and of itself is extraordinary; but naming the day of the resurrection is even more impressive, and thus provides even stronger credentials for Jesus.

The key to this sign of the resurrection is that it would most assuredly be an act of God. Once Jesus was dead, he would be totally dependent upon the actions of God, because dead people do not perform miracles (or do any other works). If Jesus rose from the grave on the third day, there would be no other reasonable explanation except the hand of God. The third-day resurrection promise became the ultimate sign for Jesus and the test by which his word would be proven to be either genuine or false (Romans 1:3, 4). And it is the miracle upon which our faith stands firm today (1 Corinthians 15:12-20).

WHAT DO YOU THINK?

If a Christian friend came to you and said he was afraid that he had committed the "unpardonable sin," what would you say?

[See John 16:8; Romans 5:6-11; 8:1-4; 1 John 1:5–2:2.]

HOW TO SAY IT

Assyria. Uh-SEAR-ee-uh.
Baal-Zebub. BAY-ul-ZEE-bub.
Beelzebub. Bih-EL-zih-bub.
Beelzebul. Bih-EL-zih-bull.
Calvary. CAL-vuh-ree.
Canaanite. KAY-nun-ite.
Capernaum. Kuh-PER-nay-um.
Gabriel. GAY-bree-ul.
messianic. mess-ee-AN-ick.
Nazareth. NAZ-uh-reth.
Nineveh. NIN-uh-vuh.
Pharisees. FAIR-uh-seez.
Simeon. SIM-ee-un.

40. "For as Jonah was three days and three nights in the belly of a huge fish, so the Son of Man will be three days and three nights in the heart of the earth.

Some Christians are bothered by the biblical account of Jesus' death on a Friday afternoon and his resurrection on a Sunday morning, because it does not comprise three days and three nights. The problem is resolved when we understand the Jewish practice of "rounding off" numbers when counting time, in adding, and (as we saw in lesson 3) in recording a genealogy. It is important to observe that the Jewish people who were present when the resurrection happened counted Sunday as the "third day" since the crucifixion of Christ (Luke 24:21; 1 Corinthians 15:4). Jesus fulfilled his third-day resurrection sign.

C. CLEAR WARNING (v. 41)

41. "The men of Nineveh will stand up at the judgment with this generation and condemn it; for they repented at the preaching of Jonah, and now one greater than Jonah is here."

What greater shame could there be for the Jewish leaders than to have an evil, pagan nation like Assyria (whose capital was *Nineveh*) *condemn* them at God's final *judgment*? At least *the men of Nineveh* recognized their need to change their ways. The Pharisees were unwilling to do this, in spite of the fact that *one greater than Jonah is here*.

GET TO THE HEART

A man working in his garden noticed a large, green, healthy-looking squash plant. The stems appeared to be strong, and the leaves were large and full. A few days later, however, he noticed that the plant had wilted terribly. Within a few days it was completely dead. Pulling up the plant and examining its roots, the man discovered a bore worm, which could not be seen from the outside. That worm had eaten the heart out of the stem of the plant.

The religious leaders who confronted Jesus had allowed sin to penetrate their hearts to the place that they were attributing Jesus' miracles to Satan. This should alert us to the need to deal with temptation as soon as it appears. We must attack it early and refuse to allow it to get a foothold. Failing to do this can lead to disaster. In the case of the religious leaders, Jesus pronounced them ripe for God's judgment.

Three disciplines will prevent sin from "eating the heart out" of our relationship with Christ: (1) taking time daily for the Word of God; (2) empowering ourselves with prayer; and (3) seeking serious, significant fellowship with other believers. These disciplines will help us find the power and strength to keep sin from controlling our lives and to keep our walk with Christ alive and meaningful.   —D. R.

CONCLUSION

Imagine that you have committed a crime and that your conscience is racked with guilt. You believe that the only way to get a good night's sleep again is to admit your wrongdoing to someone and get it out of your system. So you confess what you have done to your friendly neighbor. If your neighbor is a professional counselor, he can hold your confession in confidence. But if your neighbor is a policeman, get ready to be arrested. In this case, your neighbor has sworn an oath to uphold the law, and he is honor bound to act on the information you gave him. He knows too much now to ignore your situation. He must do what is right.

The supernatural witness for Jesus Christ is overwhelming. The only honest recourse we have is to accept his claim to be our Savior and Lord. We know too much to ignore him. Now we must do what is right.

PRAYER

Father, we thank you for accrediting Jesus before us by your power, and we readily claim him as our Lord. In his name. Amen.

THOUGHT TO REMEMBER

The evidence for Jesus is too overpowering to overlook.

Discovery Learning

This page contains an alternate lesson plan emphasizing learning activities. Classes desiring such student involvement will find these suggestions helpful. The next page is a reproducible activity page to further enhance discovery learning.

LEARNING GOALS

After this lesson the student will be able to:

1. Summarize the controversy between Jesus and the Pharisees described in today's text.

2. Tell how Jesus' acts and teachings answer those who oppose Christianity today.

3. Prepare a statement of faith that answers the criticisms he or she most often hears from unbelievers.

INTO THE LESSON

A children's rhyme goes, "Sticks and stones may break my bones, but words will never hurt me." In groups of two or three, ask class members to critique that rhyme. Say, "Do you agree or disagree with this rhyme?" Ask each group to write two reasons for its chosen answer. Most will agree that words can, indeed, hurt—even if they do not cause *physical* injury.

Observe that words can also be helpful. While some are "fighting words," others are building words. Ask the class to suggest some building words and some fighting words. (Building words include: "Great job!" "I agree." "Keep it up." Fighting words include: "I disagree." "You are completely wrong!" "No way!") Discuss the difference between the two types of words. Can these words ever be confused? How does one disagree without using "fighting words"?

Make the transition to today's lesson by noting that today we will see how Jesus used some strong words to denounce the vicious attacks of his enemies.

INTO THE WORD

Distribute copies of the reproducible activity "Details, Please" from the next page. Give the students a few minutes to complete the activity; then review. With the basic facts in hand, you are ready to look a little deeper.

Give a brief background lecture on the tension between Jesus and the Pharisees (see page 183) while you write these headings on the chalkboard: "Situation of the Demon-possessed Man"; "Crowd's Reaction"; "Pharisees' Rejection"; and "Jesus' Response." Have students search the text to fill in data under each heading. Be sure to cover the reasons for the Pharisees' challenge to Jesus (public embarrassment and the questioning of his claims to be God). This was a highly charged atmosphere.

Divide the class into three groups. Give each group five to eight minutes for the following Bible study.

Group one is to survey the text and determine the central points of Jesus' answer to the Pharisees. (For example: Standing here, in your midst, is the King himself!)

Group two is to create a list of ways by which Jesus answered his critics. Students could respond: his miracles (casting out the demon[s], healing, resurrection), his words (do not misrepresent the work of the Holy Spirit), and his warning (do not miss what I am doing or you will miss God).

Group three is to prepare a short list of implications from verse 30 for today. Responses could include: reaching out to the lost with the teachings of Jesus, seeking to relieve some of the physical problems people face, or encouraging those with broken hearts.

INTO LIFE

Ask each group to report its findings, leading a group discussion on the points in each report. Emphasize the need to be sure about the teachings of Jesus on the need for strong faith.

Choose one or more of the following options to apply today's text.

1. Keep the students in their small groups, and ask each group to create a list of the most often heard criticisms of Jesus today. This list might include the following: "His miracles are fantasy"; "He did not rise from the dead"; "He has done nothing for me"; "This is nothing but a bunch of moralists taking away my fun!"

Next, answer the objections. Create a brief statement of faith that the student can carry with him or her. Emphasize that we do not substitute a statement of faith for Scripture, but the statement can be helpful for understanding.

2. Prepare several "bumper-sticker" sized strips of colored paper and give one to each student. Be sure to have a marking pen for each person.

Group the students in the same groups of two or three as at the beginning of the session. In these smaller groups encourage the students to create bumper stickers that will give testimony to the truth of Jesus as Lord. Have students display and explain their bumper stickers to the class.

3. Use the lower half of the following reproducible page to discuss breaking down barriers today.

Close the session in prayer for boldness to confront false images of Christ and for strength to face opposition.

Details, Please

Read Matthew 12:22-32, 38-41. Close your Bible and put the following details in the order in which they occurred, using "1" in the blank for the first event, "2" for the second, etc. After you have finished, go back to the text to check your answers.

___ The Pharisees oppose Jesus.

___ The Pharisees and teachers want a sign.

___ Jesus warns about speaking blasphemy against the Holy Spirit.

___ Jesus teaches that he has power by the Spirit of God.

___ Jesus heals the demon-possessed man.

___ A demon-possessed man is brought to Jesus.

___ Jesus rebukes the Pharisees for their unbelief.

___ Jesus said the men of Nineveh would condemn the current generation.

___ People are astounded by Jesus' miracle of healing.

___ Jesus tells of his death, burial, and resurrection.

Barriers to Belief

What barriers to belief do we confront today? Unscramble the words below to see what barriers people have in their lives that seem to prevent them from believing in Jesus as Lord.

gkarnodubc _____

direp _____

imayfl _____

tsauts _____

oerwp _____

Write the name of one person who has had criticisms of Jesus.

Determine two or three things you can say that will defend your faith in Jesus to this person.

LABORERS IN THE VINEYARD

LESSON 9

WHY TEACH THIS LESSON?

"Equal pay for equal work." It has a ring of fairness to it that seems unquestionable. It's the principle on which women and minorities have based their appeals to be treated—and compensated—fairly in the workplace. If two people do the same work, they should receive the same pay. Right?

Actually, this lesson will challenge that principle. It's a bit too simplistic for all the exigencies of real life. It leaves no room for grace. This lesson gives you a chance to help your students balance fairness—the goal of the "equal-pay-for-equal-work principle"—and grace. Of the two, grace is always to be preferred!

INTRODUCTION

A. I WOULD DO IT FOR NOTHING

Is there any kind of activity you enjoy so much that you would pay to do it? Of course there is. We pay admission fees all the time in order to participate in activities that entertain and amuse us. Is there a job you would gladly do because of the satisfaction it gives you, even if it did not offer the pay and benefits of other types of employment? Many of us, in fact, have the privilege of working in occupations we enjoy that much. Are there family and friends whom you would help when they were in need, with no thought of being paid for your services? For Christians the answer should be a definite *yes*. The fact is that for most of us there are many things we will "do for nothing."

At the same time, when we are working for a living, we do expect reasonable pay. We want to be treated fairly, and we may leave a job if we are dissatisfied with our working conditions. This is all well and good where our job is concerned because our family responsibilities require that we give some concern for the income and benefits we can provide. However, these thoughts are out of place when considering our service for the Lord. This work we do because we ought to and because we want to, not because of any reward we hope to attain. The Christian service we do, we do "for nothing," and yet we receive an abundance of spiritual riches from the vast treasures of God's grace.

B. LESSON BACKGROUND

The "Parable of the Laborers in the Vineyard," as recorded in Matthew 20, was spoken by Jesus within three or four months of the end of his ministry. (The reader can sense that the end is near by noting that next week's lesson from Matthew 21 covers Jesus' triumphal entry into Jerusalem a few days before his crucifixion.)

During the closing months of his three-and-a-half-year ministry, Jesus gave several parables and lessons on service and stewardship, perhaps in anticipation of the call for laborers that he would issue following his death and resurrection. The Great Commission would challenge his disciples to take on the task of spreading the gospel message throughout the world. Those who remembered the parable of the laborers in the vineyard and others like it would know the kind of response Jesus expected to see.

DEVOTIONAL READING:
MATTHEW 20:20-28
BACKGROUND SCRIPTURE:
MATTHEW 19:16–20:16
PRINTED TEXT:
MATTHEW 20:1-16

LESSON AIMS

After this lesson a student should be able to:

1. Retell Jesus' parable of the laborers in the vineyard.

2. Explain the principle by which the owner of the vineyard dealt with his workers and how this applies to God's dealings with us.

3. Express gratitude for God's grace in his or her own life as well as for the demonstrations of God's grace in another's life.

Jan
30

KEY VERSE

So the last will be first, and the first will be last.
—Matthew 20:16

I. THE MASTER'S CALL (MATTHEW 20:1-7)

A. WILLING WORKERS (vv. 1, 2)

1. For the kingdom of heaven is like a landowner who went out early in the morning to hire men to work in his vineyard.

This parable about *the kingdom of heaven* is not about the place we call Heaven, but about the principles established by Heaven's King and how they apply to our lives on earth.

The parable revolves around an unidentified *landowner* of a sizable estate. It is the time of year for harvesting his grape *vineyard*, and thus he is seeking *to hire men to work*. Naturally he would have his regular crew of hired hands and servants who assist him all year long; but for a brief period, while the grapes are ripe for picking, he needs all the help he can get.

Already one application of this parable to the work of *the kingdom of heaven* should be apparent. There is always before the church an urgency to take the gospel to the world as quickly as we can. Every day untold numbers of people die without Christ—and without hope. Our urgency is multiplied by the fact that there is so much work to be done and so few willing to serve.

2. He agreed to pay them a denarius for the day and sent them into his vineyard.

The precise value (according to today's currency) of the Roman coin known as a *denarius* is difficult to assess, because such estimates are always subject to change. The easiest way to calculate its worth is to think in terms of one day's wages. This single coin was the typical daily pay for a common laborer with no professional skills, and it possessed a modest spending power adequate to supply a family's basic needs. The landowner in Jesus' parable was offering a fair wage for harvest labor.

B. REINFORCEMENTS (vv. 3-7)

3. About the third hour he went out and saw others standing in the marketplace doing nothing.

Around mid-morning the landowner was still looking for workers. By the Jewish reckoning of time, this was *the third hour* after sunrise, approximately 9:00 A.M.

The men who were *standing in the marketplace doing nothing* were probably not being lazy, but were simply waiting for someone to hire them. These were "day laborers" who gathered in this central location each day at this time of year. Landowners would know to come by in the early morning hours and choose as many workers as needed for that day. Those who worked well and impressed an owner would be asked to come directly to the fields each day until the harvest was completed. Whenever a landowner needed more laborers, he returned to the marketplace.

4. He told them, "You also go and work in my vineyard, and I will pay you whatever is right."

As noted earlier, the standard wage for this type of work was one denarius for a full day's labor. Since this second group of workers would not be working a full day, a typical landowner would calculate the appropriate percentage of a day's wage. It was not necessary that our owner declare the exact amount he would pay at this time; his statement *whatever is right* assured the workers that he would *pay* them a fair amount based on—they would reasonably suppose—the denarius.

5. So they went.

He went out again about the sixth hour and the ninth hour and did the same thing.

It was unusual to be hiring day laborers as late as *the sixth hour* (12:00 noon) and *the ninth hour* (3:00 P.M.), but it could happen if unforeseen events occurred during the day (such as an approaching storm) that necessitated a faster pace than originally planned. This late-hiring scenario is quite appropriate, however, for our kingdom of Heaven lesson; because in our case there are never enough workers to "harvest" the whole world before the approaching "storm" of God's judgment arrives. God will always be seeking new laborers for his fields, even in the "late hours" of history.

6. About the eleventh hour he went out and found still others standing around. He asked them, "Why have you been standing here all day long doing nothing?"

With only one hour left in the working day, the landowner was still eager at *the eleventh hour* (5:00 P.M.) to hire anyone willing to work for him. Is this a realistic scenario from biblical times? Perhaps only when the situation was most desperate. But then, when the analogy is made to a world racing toward an eternity of torment, the situation *is* most desperate.

7. "Because no one has hired us," they answered. He said to them, "You also go and work in my vineyard."

The final crew of workers for the day was sent into the *vineyard*. Their contribution could never be equal to those who had invested more time, but their labors would benefit the landowner just the same. Every person's contribution was appreciated by the landowner, whose greatest concern was harvesting as much as possible while there was still time.

In our spiritual application of this parable, we realize that it is never too late to become actively involved in service for the kingdom of Heaven. Certainly the ideal situation is to "remember your Creator in the days of your youth" (Ecclesiastes 12:1) and give a lifetime of devotion and service to our Lord. A good youth ministry or camp program will issue such challenges to our young people as early as possible. Our Bible colleges typically draw those who are recent high school graduates and are ready to be trained for service. Those who get serious about their faith commitment late in life may wonder sometimes if they have arrived too late to make any significant contribution to the Lord's work. Jesus' parable reminds us that God welcomes even the "eleventh-hour laborer" to serve in his fields. The task at hand is too important to turn away anyone who is willing to help.

GROWING THROUGH INVOLVEMENT

Judy's minister had finished preaching a series of sermons on the topic, "Using Your Spiritual Gifts." After the last sermon, she went to see him. She wanted to serve the Lord, she said, but she had no spiritual gift. The minister told her that he was sure she had been gifted by the Lord in some way. Sensing that Judy was a lady of great compassion (and thus someone with the gift of mercy), he urged her to begin making weekly visits to one of the church's shut-ins, who was living in a nursing home.

After several visits, one of the attendants at the nursing home asked Judy if she had any Bible stories on video tape that she could show to the residents of the home. She replied that she did and would be glad to bring those the following week. Judy was very uncomfortable with the idea of teaching or leading discussions, however, and she told the attendant that she did not want to do that.

The next week she brought the tape and showed it to a few of the residents. After they had seen the video, one of the residents raised her hand and asked a question. There was no one there to give an answer except Judy, so she responded to the resident's question as best she could. Before long, Judy was conducting a weekly Bible study with several people in the nursing home. She then began teaching a women's class at the church, which has grown incredibly over the years. And all this from a woman who had "no spiritual gift!"

WHAT DO YOU THINK?

The lesson writer notes that the landowner's "greatest concern was harvesting as much as possible while there was still time." The workers may or may not have shared this concern. God does not want "anyone to perish, but everyone to come to repentance" (2 Peter 3:9). What do you think distracts Christian workers from this view? How can we bring our view more into line with God's?

WHAT DO YOU THINK?

Where do you see yourself— as an early-morning worker, a third-hour worker, sixth-hour worker, ninth-hour worker, or eleventh-hour worker? Why? How does this view of yourself motivate you in Christian service?

HOW TO SAY IT

denarii. dih-NAIR-ee or dih-NAIR-eye.
denarius. dih-NAIR-ee-us.
Ecclesiastes. Ik-LEEZ-ee-AS-teez.

Whether we begin our labors for Christ early in life or much later, the Lord is always interested in our willingness to serve him. It's never too late to get busy in his vineyard!

—D. R.

II. THE WORKERS' PAY (MATTHEW 20:8-12)

A. SURPRISE (vv. 8-10)

8. When evening came, the owner of the vineyard said to his foreman, "Call the workers and pay them their wages, beginning with the last ones hired and going on to the first."

At the end of the day the landowner explained to his *foreman* how he wanted the wages to be made. There was no standard procedure in biblical times for the order in which to pay workers. For the sake of the lesson of this parable, Jesus had his owner pay *beginning with the last ones hired and going on to the first.*

9. The workers who were hired about the eleventh hour came and each received a denarius.

The first surprise was the generous pay *received* by those who had worked for only one hour. No one, not even the *"eleventh hour* workers" themselves, would have imagined such a thing. Of course, none of the people in this group complained about their pay! All were thrilled to receive more than they had anticipated, and were probably eager to be hired for the next day.

10. So when those came who were hired first, they expected to receive more. But each one of them also received a denarius.

The second surprise was not one of joy, but of shock and disbelief. Those *who were hired first* and had worked the full day *received* the very same pay as those who had worked only one hour! The workers who had previously benefited from the owner's generosity probably assumed that those who had worked the longest would receive more than they did. No one could believe what was happening.

B. COMPLAINT (vv. 11, 12)

11. When they received it, they began to grumble against the landowner.

To say that those who were hired first *began to grumble* would likely be an understatement. This situation would have had all the makings of a riot. Most of us can identify with these workers' complaint. The vineyard owner appeared to treat his best workers unfairly.

12. "These men who were hired last worked only one hour," they said, "and you have made them equal to us who have borne the burden of the work and the heat of the day."

If one knows anything about Jesus' method of teaching, he knows that this story is leading toward an important spiritual lesson. Our thinking about fairness will probably be challenged. However, even before we reach the conclusion to this parable, there is something we should note. Those who grumbled did so only after they compared their situation with that of the other workers. If they had not known what the others had been paid, they would probably have been happy to receive their denarii. Their bitterness surfaced when they observed others being given an advantage they had not received.

Keeping an eye on what others have or receive is a sure road to discontent. A child thinks it is unfair if he or she does not receive the same thing a brother or sister received. The oldest child grumbles when her younger siblings get to do something she was not permitted to do at their age. An employee is upset when he thinks that his salary and benefits are not comparable to those of his fellow workers. The church member is offended when others are publicly thanked for their service and she is not mentioned.

WHAT DO YOU THINK?

What steps can we take to prevent the comparative spirit seen in the parable?

The complaint of the workers who had toiled the longest may seem reasonable at first; but when we realize that theirs was a judgment based on how they thought they should have been treated in comparison with others, we should be cautious about joining their cause.

III. THE LORD'S GRACE (MATTHEW 20:13-16)

A. FAIRNESS (vv. 13, 14)

13. But he answered one of them, "Friend, I am not being unfair to you. Didn't you agree to work for a denarius?

No matter how unfair this situation might seem to us, the first group of laborers had not been cheated. The landowner had, in fact, upheld his original agreement with them. He had given them a *denarius* for their day's labor—just as he had promised.

This story gives us a more biblical view of fairness than what we sometimes assume. Fairness should not be judged on the basis of how we are treated in comparison to others, but on whether or not the terms to which we agreed have been honored. The question should not be, "Did others receive any advantage over me?" but rather, "Has any agreement or promise to me been broken?"

Consider how God deals with us. We are not all given the same spiritual gifts, for the Holy Spirit distributes his gifts with much variety (1 Corinthians 12:4-6). Likewise, God's providence does not produce blessing and suffering among us in equal measure. The fact that we are treated differently by God is no basis for accusing God of being unfair to us, for he has never promised us equality of gifts and experiences. God has promised to love each one of us fully and to value all human life as a special creation made in his image. He has promised eternal blessings to every one who remains faithful to him. But at no time has God ever been unfair to us, for God never violates a promise. Fairness does not require equal or comparable treatment of others, but simply that a person live up to his word.

14. "Take your pay and go. I want to give the man who was hired last the same as I gave you.

In this case, the landowner's decision was final. He had not been unfair to anyone, despite their expectations. Those who have a complaint should *take* what they have received and *go*. They have no basis for a charge against the landowner, except that which derives from their envy of the blessings received by others.

B. GENEROSITY (v. 15)

15. "Don't I have the right to do what I want with my own money? Or are you envious because I am generous?"

Is there something familiar about the idea of giving someone more than what his effort deserves? There should be. After all, this is the meaning of grace.

Grace is a free gift that is given simply because the giver chooses to do so. Grace does not necessarily make sense, especially when we are on the sidelines watching others receive it. But grace is not bound by our sense of what is fair as we compare ourselves with others. Grace cannot be demanded or expected, nor is it regulated by our opinions of it. Grace does not answer to anyone except the heart of the giver himself.

We who are the beneficiaries of the greatest act of grace the world has ever known should not feel cheated when, in the daily circumstances of life, we see others experience a generosity not offered to us. We should be humbled by the vineyard owner's question regarding envy: *Are you envious because I am generous?*

WHAT DO YOU THINK?

Jesus' parable demonstrates the astonishing grace and generosity of God toward the undeserving. How can we become better at showing that same grace in our treatment of others?

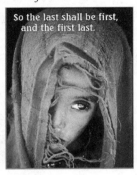

So the last shall be first, and the first last.

A Picture of Grace

You are on your way to church, but running a bit late because of some delays at home. So you apply just a bit more pressure to the accelerator. All of a sudden, a patrolman pulls up behind you. You pull off the road and get your license and registration ready. The officer comes to your window and says you were doing fifty-five in a thirty-five miles-per-hour zone. Then he asks where you are going, and you sheepishly tell him you are on your way to church. He asks for your license and registration and tells you he will be back. Before long the officer comes to your window to give you the "bad news."

At this point, what would grace look like? Would it be the officer's saying to you, "This time I'm going to give you just a warning"? This would certainly look like grace, but it would more accurately be called compassion.

Suppose the officer said, "I'm going to have to give you a ticket because you broke the law; you were exceeding the speed limit. However, I have decided to go to court with you and pay the fine myself." That would be grace. And that is exactly what our heavenly Father did when Jesus went to the cross for our sins. God paid the debt himself.

The vineyard workers who had labored the entire day did not seem to understand that the owner had the right to extend all the compassion and grace that he wanted to extend, since he was the owner. It was his right and privilege to handle the situation as he desired.

May God's "amazing grace" keep us ever dependent on him and genuinely grateful for his blessings—not only in our lives but in the lives of others.   —D. R.

C. Humility (v. 16)
16. So the last will be first, and the first will be last.

The first portion of this expression fits the parable quite well: *the last will be first.* Those hired near the end of the work day were indeed treated as if they had been among those who had been *first* in service. This calls attention to a prominent biblical theme: God takes great pleasure in lifting up the lowly and exalting those who are humble in spirit.

The latter statement is likewise an important lesson: *the first will be last.* Some have misread these words, wondering if they mean that those who have given God their best will actually end up being slighted by God. Not at all. The intent of this latter expression is related to that of the former. Just as God exalts those who are humble, he will eventually humble those who are exalted in their own eyes. Those who compare themselves with others and think that they are more deserving of God's grace must learn that no one actually deserves grace.

God will not disregard those who give him a "full day's labor." He will bless them richly, but only if they maintain a humble spirit in relation to others.

CONCLUSION

Some games are designed to be played in teams, where people work together and use the strengths that each member is able to contribute. Other games are intended to be played "every man for himself." Such games have their place, but in team sports the every-man-for-himself attitude is a ticket to disaster.

The Christian life is meant to be conducted as a team effort rather than every man for himself. It was never God's intent that his people "go it alone," but that they work together for a common goal—the ministry of the gospel to a lost and dying world. We are not to envy one another, but to encourage and support one another in all circumstances, both good and bad. And while it is the bond of love that holds us together, it is the grace of God that humbles us and makes us suitable vessels for his service.

Discovery Learning

This page contains an alternate lesson plan emphasizing learning activities. Classes desiring such student involvement will find these suggestions helpful. The next page is a reproducible activity page to further enhance discovery learning.

LEARNING GOALS

After participating in this lesson, each student will be able to:

1. Retell Jesus' parable of the laborers in the vineyard.

2. Explain the principle by which the owner of the vineyard dealt with his workers and how this applies to God's dealings with us.

3. Express gratitude for God's grace in his or her own life as well as for the demonstrations of God's grace in another's life.

INTO THE LESSON

Ask every other student to turn to the person on his or her right and discuss the following: "What is the best job that you ever had? Why?"

Allow four to five minutes for discussion; then ask the pairs to report. List on a poster or chalk board the jobs cited. Ask, "Is it fair that some jobs pay more than others? Why or why not?"

After four minutes, make the transition to the lesson by saying, "The text we are studying today contains Jesus' parable of the laborers in the vineyard. The actions of the vineyard owner challenge many people's sense of fairness. We will see that the parable is about more than being fair; it's about being more than fair!"

INTO THE WORD

Ask a volunteer to read today's text, Matthew 20:1-16. Then divide your class into three groups. Distribute the following outline to each group. (Allow about a third of a page under each point for students to make notes.)

A. The Call
B. The Complaint
C. The Conclusion

Give the following questions to Group A:

1. To whom is the call given? (*Laborers*)

2. What are the terms of the call? (*Work in my vineyard for a day's pay.*)

3. What is the master's response to the need for more workers? (*Hire more when needed.*)

Assign these questions to Group B:

4. How are the workers compensated? (*Each is paid a day's wage.*)

5. Who is the first compensated? (*The last hired.*)

6. What concerns are raised? (*It's not fair that some are paid the same as we for less work.*)

Give these questions to Group C:

7. What is the master's initial answer? (*I did nothing wrong.*)

8. Why did the master compensate as he did? (*Because that was the agreement made at hiring.*)

9. What principles are stated at the end of this parable? (*The last will be first, and the first will be last.*)

Call the groups together after several minutes and discuss together their answers to the questions, filling in the outline. Use the lesson commentary to answer any questions or expand on any thoughts raised.

Make the transition to the application phase of the session by saying, "It is apparent that the early workers began to compare themselves with and to envy the latter workers. We want to explore how this concept carries over into the church today."

INTO LIFE

Using today's text, have each group (from the three groups formed earlier) write a definition of *fairness* and of *grace*. After allowing the groups a few minutes to work, ask them to compare their definitions of *fairness* with this definition from the lesson commentary: "Fairness should not be judged on the basis of how we are treated in comparison to others, but on whether or not the terms to which we agreed have been honored." Discuss how this is seen in the text. Then discuss the definitions of grace, noting how the landowner was motivated more by grace (giving the workers who worked least what they needed, rather than what they deserved).

Ask the students to think of situations when they thought they were treated unfairly. Ask them to consider whether their standards of fairness were the same as the standards you have discussed today. Perhaps they need to see that grace was at work for another and to rejoice in that rather than feel slighted. And if they truly were treated unfairly, perhaps they need to practice grace toward the offending party.

Conclude this lesson by having five volunteers read the following Scripture passages: Romans 5:8; 1 Corinthians 12:4-6; Ephesians 1:3-14; Matthew 20:13; Matthew 20:15. Note the lesson writer's comments concerning God's generosity and grace (page 195).

Close by asking each person to offer a silent prayer expressing gratitude for God's grace in his or her own life and thanking him for another person's grace gifts.

More Than Fair

We easily succumb to the tendency to say, "That's not fair." That is the particular lament of many Christians. In the Scriptures, note how God treats us more than fair. List what God has given to us. You may want to find other related verses as well.

Romans 5:1, 2, 8

Romans 8:1

Romans 8:37-39

1 Corinthians 12:4-6

Ephesians 1:3-14

Colossians 1:21-23

Workers in His Vineyard

Read Ephesians 2:8-10. These verses teach that because of God's grace we can be effective workers for him. On the grapes in the cluster below are a few services or works to be done for Jesus. Pick one by circling (or write in your own).

ENTRY INTO JERUSALEM

LESSON 10

WHY TEACH THIS LESSON?

It was the beginning of the end. In our lesson text for today we see Jesus on the first day of the final week of his life on earth. It was marked by celebration and re-joicing, but he knew the cheers would not last. By Friday he would be on a cross. If ever there were a time to avoid conflict or soften his rebukes, this was it. But he did not. In fact, some of the most confrontational acts of Jesus' ministry occurred in the final week. One of them, the cleansing of the temple, probably did as much to move the leaders from wishing Jesus dead to actually plotting his demise as any other single act in all of Jesus' ministry.

Some of your students are at crossroads in their lives. They, too, may be at the beginning of the end. They may be tempted to back off from their commitment to the Father's will. Use this lesson to encourage them to follow the Lord's example.

INTRODUCTION

A. IMPROMPTU GREETINGS

Do you remember the old expression, "If I knew that you were coming I would have baked a cake"? The line expresses both surprise and appreciation to unexpected guests. According to the statement our friends deserve special treat-ment; and we would gladly give it to them if we have sufficient notice to prepare that special treatment. Too often, though, we have to do the best we can with the situation we are given.

The Passover crowd gathered in Jerusalem on the first day of Jesus' final week had no idea when the day began that they would witness the arrival of the Mes-siah-King of prophecy. Had they known, surely they would have made grand preparations for his arrival. As it was, they did the best they could under the cir-cumstances, and with palm branches and shouts of adoration they honored the King. So significant was Jesus' "triumphal entry" that it is recorded by all four Gospel writers.

B. LESSON BACKGROUND

The twenty-first chapter of Matthew's Gospel begins his account of Jesus' final week, which culminated in his death at the end of the week and his resurrection on the first day of the following week. The events of this week actually began on Saturday evening with a dinner in Jesus' honor in the town of Bethany, about two miles southeast of Jerusalem. The host for these festivities was a man called "Simon the Leper" (Matthew 26:6), probably so named because he had at some point been healed by Jesus. Also in attendance were Jesus' close friend Lazarus and his sisters Mary and Martha (John 12:1-3). Though this episode occurred before the events recorded in chapter 21 (cf. John 12:1, 2), Matthew saves the telling of it until chapter 26 (vv. 6-13). There he uses this incident in combina-tion with two other events to recount Jesus' betrayal, as a prelude to his record of the death of Christ in chapter 27.

Following the dinner on Saturday evening, Jesus made his "triumphal entry" into Jerusalem on Sunday. The day we now call "Palm Sunday" commemorates

DEVOTIONAL READING:
LUKE 19:29-44
BACKGROUND SCRIPTURE:
MATTHEW 21:1-17
PRINTED TEXT:
MATTHEW 21:1-13

LESSON AIMS

After this lesson students should be able to:

1. Summarize the events sur-rounding Jesus' triumphal entry into Jerusalem.

2. Explain what made Jesus' triumphal entry so significant.

3. Take specific steps to elimi-nate something from their lives that keeps Jesus from ruling as Lord and King.

Feb
6

KEY VERSE

*"Say to the Daughter of Zion,
'See, your king comes to you,
gentle and riding on a donkey, on
a colt, the foal of a donkey.'"*
—Matthew 21:5

LESSON 10 NOTES

HOW TO SAY IT

BETHANY. BETH-uh-nee.
BETHPHAGE. BETH-fuh-gee.
GETHSEMANE. Geth-SEM-uh-nee.
HOSANNA. Ho-SAN-uh.
ISAIAH. Eye-ZAY-uh.
JEREMIAH. Jair-uh-MY-uh.
KIDRON. KID-ron.
LAZARUS. LAZ-uh-rus.
MESSIANIC. mess-ee-AN-ick.
NAZARETH. NAZ-uh-reth.
ZECHARIAH. Zek-uh-RYE-uh.

WHAT DO YOU THINK?

There seems always to be more things to do in the church than there are people to do them. Studies show that 80% of the work done is accomplished by 20% of the people. A few in the church are probably doing too much; many are doing little or nothing! When you are asked to take a responsibility or perform a task in the church, the person asking is basically telling you, "The Lord needs your service." How do you decide what your response will be?

that electrifying day when Jesus was given a royal welcome as he entered the city of Jerusalem in fulfillment of prophecy.

I. OBEY THE MASTER (MATTHEW 21:1-6)

A. FINDING AN ANIMAL (vv. 1-3)

1. As they approached Jerusalem and came to Bethphage on the Mount of Olives, Jesus sent two disciples.

The day after the dinner in Bethany, Jesus and his disciples began to walk the approximately two miles to *Jerusalem*. This road took them over the *Mount of Olives*, down a steep descent, and into Jerusalem from the east side.

The Mount of Olives is a ridge running north-south just across the Kidron Valley from Jerusalem. It is the highest peak on the east side, providing a strategic view of Jerusalem. Historical sources of Jesus' day tell us a person could stand on the top of the mount and see clearly into the temple courts. In ancient times the terrain was thick with olive groves, thus providing the origin of the mount's name.

Somewhere on the lower slopes of the Mount of Olives was a place known as Gethsemane, which means "olive press." We suppose it was one of many olive groves on the mountain. Gethsemane was a favorite place of prayer for Jesus (Luke 22:39; John 18:2). He retreated there each evening of his final week (Luke 21:37), and it was there that his disciples slept as he prayed on the night that he was arrested (Matthew 26:36-46).

Somewhere on the Mount of Olives was the village of *Bethphage*, along—or a short distance from—the main road on which Jesus was walking. It was there that *two disciples* of Jesus obtained the donkey used for the triumphal entry.

2. . . . saying to them, "Go to the village ahead of you, and at once you will find a donkey tied there, with her colt by her. Untie them and bring them to me.

Jesus knew exactly what his two disciples would *find* when they entered the *village* of Bethphage. The focus of their search was the young *colt* of a *donkey*, for that was the animal Jesus actually rode (and the only one mentioned in the accounts of Mark and Luke).

This particular colt was special in that he had not yet been ridden by any person (Mark 11:2). Perhaps the reason his mother was also brought along was to steady this young donkey during his first experience at being ridden. The task on this day was both his first and his most important ever—to transport the promised Messiah-King during his royal procession.

3. "If anyone says anything to you, tell him that the Lord needs them, and he will send them right away."

In a small village such as Bethphage, one might expect that two strangers taking off with someone else's property would be challenged. Mark and Luke tell us that the disciples were, indeed, questioned about taking the animals (Mark 11:5; Luke 19:33). However, when informed that the animals would be used by Jesus, the owners were pleased to oblige.

It is possible that the use of the animals for this occasion had been prearranged. Or it may be that this request was just as impromptu as it appears in the biblical text, and that the owners responded favorably out of respect for Jesus and a desire to assist in his ministry. In either case, their attitude is an example for us. When called upon by Jesus, they were ready to serve, and we should be as well.

B. FULFILLING GOD'S WILL (vv. 4-6)

4. This took place to fulfill what was spoken through the prophet:

According to Matthew, the triumphal entry on the donkey was a fulfillment of the prophecy in Zechariah 9:9. In a chapter that speaks of God's judgment coming on Israel's enemies, Zechariah foretold the coming of the Messiah-King to Jerusalem, at which time he would establish among God's people a "peace" that would never come to an end (Zechariah 9:10).

5. *"Say to the Daughter of Zion, 'See, your king comes to you, gentle and riding on a donkey, on a colt, the foal of a donkey.'"*

The precise details of this prophecy given centuries before the time of Jesus are amazing. The Messiah would publicly reveal himself to the city of Jerusalem, referred to here as the *Daughter of Zion*. The sign of the Messiah would be a grand and royal entrance—not by just any means, but specifically by riding on *a colt, the foal of a donkey*. This prophetic sign was so clear that the crowd who observed Jesus on this occasion immediately began to proclaim the coming of "the Son of David" (v. 9). What appeared to be very humble and unassuming was actually an unmistakable sign heralding the arrival of the long-awaited *king*.

The *gentle* appearance of the Messiah-King was intended to symbolize the peace that he would establish upon the earth. For royalty to parade on a white horse symbolized military might and a readiness to do battle with the enemy—a most appropriate symbol for Jesus' second coming (Revelation 19:11). In contrast, the use of a gentle animal such as the donkey symbolized a reign of peace and security.

There are some today who interpret Zechariah 9 as predicting a political peace for the nation of Israel. The history of Israel since the days of Zechariah has been marked by foreign domination and by frequent conflicts with surrounding peoples. Thus some believe that this prophecy has not yet been fulfilled, and will not be fulfilled until the arrival of a future period of peace on earth for the Jews.

Matthew, however, declares that Zechariah's prophecy was fulfilled at Jesus' triumphal entry into Jerusalem. Indeed, we know that through Jesus' death and resurrection, which occurred a few days later, peace has been established among God's people—a peace between sinners and God, as well as a peace between Jew and Gentile (Ephesians 2:11-22). If Zechariah's promise of peace is thus understood to be a spiritual peace, then we can join Matthew in proclaiming that Jesus has fulfilled this Old Testament messianic prophecy.

"ALL CREATURES GREAT AND SMALL"

Have you ever thought about the prominence of animals in the Bible? Animals play an important role in many Bible stories, and are often used symbolically. Herbert Lockyer has compiled an entire book that lists and comments on *All the Animals in the Bible*—a volume with hundreds of entries!

It is not surprising that Jesus entered Jerusalem riding, rather than on foot. What was unusual was that he, the Messiah-King, sat astride a small and humble beast of burden rather than atop a great white horse. Though many in the crowd would have been familiar with the Zechariah prophecy that Matthew cites, they were likely confused by such a humble image—inappropriate, it seemed, for Israel's King and Deliverer.

Our understanding, however, is aided by the New Testament Scriptures, which elaborate on the humility of Christ and the non-political nature of his kingdom. (See Philippians 2:6-11.) The Suffering Servant reigns as a selfless, modest, and lowly prince. Thus the colt of a donkey was an appropriate animal for Jesus' "triumphal entry" into the holy city. The donkey is a fitting symbol of the condescension that prompted the Son of God to leave a heavenly throne and die on a shameful cross.

Now re-exalted, the Messiah will return one day on a royal white horse, as "King of Kings and Lord of Lords" (Revelation 19:11-16).   —R. W. B.

6. *The disciples went and did as Jesus had instructed them.*

DAILY BIBLE READINGS

Monday, Jan. 31—Jesus Sets His Face Toward Jerusalem (Luke 9:51-56)

Tuesday, Feb. 1—Jesus Enters Jerusalem Amid Hosannas (Matthew 21:1-11)

Wednesday, Feb. 2—Jesus Cleanses the Temple (Matthew 21:12-17)

Thursday, Feb. 3—Chief Priests and Elders Resist Jesus (Matthew 21:23-27)

Friday, Feb. 4—Parable of the Wicked Tenants (Matthew 21:33-46)

Saturday, Feb. 5—A Question About the Resurrection (Matthew 22:23-33)

Sunday, Feb. 6—The Greatest Commandment of All (Matthew 22:34-46)

WHAT DO YOU THINK?

The disciples "did as Jesus had instructed them." Why is it sometimes difficult for us to do what God's Word instructs us to do? How can we make a better effort to do what the Lord commands?

This story teaches a good lesson regarding our duty to the Lord, for it presents the worthy examples of individuals who were willing to be used in the service of Jesus. The two *disciples* were ready to do *as Jesus had instructed them*, and the owners of the donkey were eager to offer what they had for Jesus' sake (even the donkey proved to be useful to our Lord). There is no better way to honor Jesus Christ than to offer him our willing obedience in all things.

II. HONOR THE KING (MATTHEW 21:7-11)

A. BRINGING HIM GLORY (vv. 7, 8)

7. They brought the donkey and the colt, placed their cloaks on them, and Jesus sat on them.

Lacking a saddle, the disciples laid some of their *cloaks* (the outer garments they were wearing) on the backs of the animals. It seems strange that they thus equipped both animals, since Jesus could ride only one. Perhaps they put some cloaks on the larger animal, assuming Jesus could not ride an unbroken colt, but then Jesus insisted they cover the younger one. Or maybe one of the disciples—Peter, perhaps—thought he would ride one of the animals alongside Jesus! That, of course, did not happen.

8. A very large crowd spread their cloaks on the road, while others cut branches from the trees and spread them on the road.

As the crowd along the road saw the "sign of Zechariah" approaching, they quickly caught the spirit of a royal procession. In a special gesture of homage, they placed their *cloaks* on the ground for Jesus to ride upon (see 2 Kings 9:13). Since the road passing over the Mount of Olives went through a heavily wooded area, many in the crowd *cut branches from the trees and spread them* in Jesus' path. The Gospel of John specifically refers to the use of palm branches (John 12:13). This is the source of our modern designation of "Palm Sunday."

While no numerical estimate of the size of the crowd is given in the four Gospels, Matthew does describe it as *very large*. Given that this was the Passover season, Jerusalem would have had well over one hundred thousand guests. There was no shortage of people on hand to produce an immense crowd! As the Pharisees watched the proceedings, they remarked with envy and bitterness that "the whole world has gone after him!" (John 12:19).

WHAT DO YOU THINK?

Many in the crowd that shouted "Hosanna" on one day were, just a few days later, shouting "Crucify!" In what ways are we sometimes just as fickle? How can we resist the temptation to "change our tune" when the crowd shifts?

B. SHOUTING HIS PRAISE (vv. 9-11)

9. The crowds that went ahead of him and those that followed shouted,
> **"Hosanna to the Son of David!"**
> **"Blessed is he who comes in the name of the Lord!"**
> **"Hosanna in the highest!"**

The *crowds* that gathered did not simply observe what transpired but joined in the procession. Many of them marched in front of Jesus and announced his coming. Others stood and watched him pass, then fell in behind the parade. All were shouting messianic tributes of praise. They celebrated the arrival of *the Son of David*, a reference to the Messiah-King who would literally descend from the family of David and establish a kingdom no less glorious than that of his father David. This King would come *in the name of the Lord*—that is, with the authority and power of God.

On this day the multitudes wished for Jesus nothing but God's finest blessings. They shouted *Hosanna*, from a Hebrew word meaning, "Save, we pray." It was their desire that God save and preserve the life of this King and grant him success with his messianic plans. How ironic that only five days later many in this same crowd would be crying, "Crucify! Crucify!" (John 19:6).

WHO DOESN'T LOVE A PARADE?

Most people enjoy a parade—watching it on television or, especially, being along the parade route to see it firsthand. The floats, the bands, the sights, sounds, and crowds—all of it makes for a pretty exciting spectacle!

As Jesus came into Jerusalem, he too generated so much excitement that "a very large crowd" was soon taking part in the celebration. But all too soon the "oohs" and "aahs" turned into shouts of contempt. In just a few days, crowds of worshipers became an angry mob of self-appointed executioners, crying, "Crucify him!"

Some people love a parade only as long as the *crowd* loves a parade. A few disenchanted observers, if they are vocal enough, can quickly turn the mood of the masses toward hatred and violence. It's called "mob psychology"—a dark and scary side of human nature.

It may have appeared to some that Jesus' parade ended at Calvary. But that was only a pause in the action; by God's resurrection power, Jesus' parade became once again a march of triumph.   —R. W. B.

This visual contrasts Jesus' arrival in Jerusalem, "gentle and riding on a donkey," with his awesome second coming in power and in glory.

Coming In Meekness   Coming In Might

10. When Jesus entered Jerusalem, the whole city was stirred and asked "Who is this?"

As *Jesus entered Jerusalem*, it quickly became apparent to those inside the *city* that something unusual was happening. Such a crowd and commotion suggested that an important person was arriving, but apparently they could not tell who it was.

Who is this? they asked. Some of those asking probably were visitors in town who did not know anything about Jesus. Those who did know of him may have joined the crowd as they learned that Jesus was in the middle of it. They would want to see this One who had been at the center of popular admiration and official controversy for the past three years.

11. The crowds answered, "This is Jesus, the prophet from Nazareth in Galilee."

Despite the messianic overtones of the crowd's earlier accolades, they gave a moderate answer to the question of Jesus' identity. To describe him as a *prophet* was far less controversial than to label him the Messiah. Perhaps we are seeing already the fickle nature of the people.

The Gospel of Mark notes that it was near evening when Jesus arrived within the walls of Jerusalem (Mark 11:11). Thus, he did not stay long that day. The events reported later in this text took place on the following day.

Well before the time Jesus arrived in the city, "near the place where the road goes down the Mount of Olives" (Luke 19:37), the Pharisees had urged Jesus to silence the crowd and dismiss them, for their jubilation was getting out of hand. Jesus refused, adding that, "If they keep quiet, the stones will cry out" (Luke 19:39, 40). It was not possible to contain the excitement being felt over the arrival of the long-awaited King of prophecy. One can imagine that this excitement fairly exploded once the crowd had entered the city. It was a day of unbridled celebration and praise, quite fitting for the One who is our Lord and King.

III. RESPECT THE LORD (MATTHEW 21:12, 13)

A. CLEANSING THE TEMPLE (v. 12)

12. Jesus entered the temple area and drove out all who were buying and selling there. He overturned the tables of the money changers and the benches of those selling doves.

As noted above, the "cleansing of the temple" took place on the day following Jesus' triumphal entry (Mark 11:11-17). No doubt Jesus deliberately planned to separate the two events to allow the crowd to settle down. Had he immediately *entered the temple area* and rid it of the abuses taking place there, the frenzied

WHAT DO YOU THINK?

If Jesus were to come into a contemporary church, what might he observe, if anything, that would cause him to respond similarly to the way he reacted to what was going on at the temple?

(Be careful that this question does not open the door for class members to complain about whatever they personally do not like in the worship service. Note that the actions of selling and exchanging money in and of themselves were not wrong, but the abuse and exploitation associated with them were.)

PRAYER

Father, we thank you for sending your Son to save us, and to reign over us as the Prince of Peace. Help us to be his humble and obedient servants. In Jesus' name we pray. Amen.

WHAT DO YOU THINK?

God's house, or temple, is not the church building, but the church—believers collectively (1 Corinthians 3:16, 17) and individually (1 Corinthians 6:19, 20). To what extent, then, do you think Jesus' words about honoring God's house apply to us today?

THOUGHT TO REMEMBER

"Hosanna to the Son of David! Blessed is he who comes in the name of the Lord!" (Matthew 21:9).

crowd might well have broken out in a riot. By waiting until the next day, Jesus was able to cleanse the temple in a manner that demonstrated his high authority as Messiah-King. This was no mob action, but wholly the act of Jesus.

By the time of Jesus, the chief priests and Pharisees had turned the temple into a religious marketplace. Initially their intentions may have been quite commendable. Those traveling to the temple from great distances for the Passover or other occasions would find it more convenient to buy their sacrificial lambs and birds at the temple rather than having to transport them to Jerusalem. Likewise, tithes and offerings had to be converted to acceptable Jewish coins by *the money changers*.

At some point, however, this convenience had turned into a racket. Some sources indicate that perfectly good animals were often rejected as inadequate in order to coerce travelers into purchasing from the temple market. The exchange fees charged by the money changers became exorbitant. The system had become corrupt and was badly in need of reform. The problem was that the spiritual leaders who should have sought reform needed to be reformed themselves.

In his role as Messiah, Jesus *drove out* the merchandisers and *overturned the tables of the money changers*. Furthermore, he would not allow pedestrians to take shortcuts across the temple grounds while they conducted their business (Mark 11:16). There is no indication that Jesus harmed anyone, but there was a clear expression of his anger against the defilement of God's holy temple.

B. TEACHING THE TRUTH (v. 13)
13. *"It is written," he said to them, "'My house will be called a house of prayer,' but you are making it a 'den of robbers.'"*

The phrase *den of robbers* was taken from Jeremiah, who lamented the fact that the people who gathered for worship in his day were so evil to each other throughout the week that the temple became, whenever they were present, a "den of robbers" (Jeremiah 7:11). The situation was even worse in Jesus' day. The thievery that once had been practiced outside the temple was now actually being conducted, under priestly sanction, on temple grounds. Jesus' cleansing of the temple was intended to remove such corruption.

However, there was more to Jesus' actions. Using the language of the prophet Isaiah, Jesus also declared that the temple was meant to be a *house of prayer* (Isaiah 56:7) where people could remove themselves from the cares of this world and focus their attention upon God. The merchants within the temple interfered with the solemn and serene setting intended by God. Thus Jesus was able to "cleanse" the temple of both its corruption and its distractions. And though it is likely that the abuses resumed shortly after his death, he had at least established an ideal that thoughtful worshipers of God must keep in mind.

CONCLUSION
In announcing the coming of the Messiah, the prophet Isaiah used the imagery of a road crew, whose task was to prepare a royal highway for the grand arrival of a visiting dignitary. "A voice of one calling: 'In the desert prepare the way for the Lord; make straight in the wilderness a highway for our God. Every valley shall be raised up, every mountain and hill made low; the rough ground shall become level, the rugged places a plain. And the glory of the Lord will be revealed, and all mankind together will see it'" (Isaiah 40:3-5).

The spirit of honoring the arrival of Jesus as King was present at his triumphal entry. May it ever be present in our hearts each time we gather in worship to celebrate our Lord Jesus Christ. May it be present each day as we seek to honor and serve him before a dying world.

Discovery Learning

This page contains an alternate lesson plan emphasizing learning activities. Classes desiring such student involvement will find these suggestions helpful. The next page is a reproducible activity page to further enhance discovery learning.

LEARNING GOALS

After this lesson students should be able to:

1. Summarize the events surrounding Jesus' triumphal entry into Jerusalem.

2. Explain what made Jesus' triumphal entry so significant.

3. Take specific steps to eliminate something from their lives that keeps Jesus from ruling as Lord and King.

INTO THE LESSON

To open today's class, rent and play a clip from a video that shows a ticker-tape parade. (*The Right Stuff* or *The Spirit of America* with James Stewart would do nicely.) If you have a class member who is interested in videos, this would be a good time to invite this person to help. This person could rent the video and cue it to the appropriate section. He or she could also set up the equipment in the room.

Introduce the clip by saying, "Everyone loves a parade. As you watch this clip, see if you can identify the parade being dramatized." After showing the tape, make the transition to the Bible study by saying, "Our lesson today examines an event that was similar to a ticker-tape parade—Jesus' triumphal entry into Jerusalem. As we study Matthew 21:1-13, look for similarities with the parade we saw on the movie clip."

INTO THE WORD

Have a volunteer read Matthew 21:1-13. Then use one or more of the following activities to lead a study of the text.

Word Search

Distribute copies of the reproducible page that follows and allow time for the students to find the sixteen words from the text. Use the words to discuss the key details of the text.

Parallel Passage Study

The triumphal entry is one of the few events recorded in all four Gospels. Have your class study the parallel accounts by listing similarities and differences in the four accounts: Matthew 21:1-13; Mark 11:1-19; Luke 19:28-43; and John 12:12-19. For example, Matthew alone mentions the foal's mother, while John doesn't mention Jesus' sending two disciples to get the animal. Prepare a chart with four columns (headed with the names Matthew, Mark, Luke, and John). Put items that are the same in more than one Gospel on the same line. Unique items in a column should be on separate lines from anything in any other column.

Choral Reading

Matthew 21:1-17 lends itself well to a choral reading. Assign the parts of narrator, Jesus, the quotes from the Old Testament (Zechariah, Psalms, Isaiah, and Jeremiah), and the crowds. Encourage readers to read dramatically with exaggerated expression.

Invite the students to ask questions about the text, seeking to answer them with the help of the commentary section of this book.

INTO LIFE

Choose one or both of the following activities to apply the message of today's text.

Praise Service

Depending on the time available, you may want to have a praise service to conclude today's class session. Have your class members select songs from church hymnbooks or song sheets. Tell your class to look especially for songs related to today's text, that is, with phrases like "Hosanna" or "Blessed is he who comes in the name of the Lord."

Cleansing Your Temple

Tell the class, "When Jesus visited the temple at the beginning of his final week, he cleansed it from activities and actions that had corrupted it. According to 1 Corinthians 6:19, 20, the believer's body is the temple of God today. Please bow your heads and prayerfully consider each of these questions based on today's Scripture." (Allow fifteen seconds of silence between questions.)

1. Are there any "money changers" that need to be removed from your temple of God today?

2. Are there any areas of greed that are corrupting your temple today?

3. Which description best applies to your temple of God today: a house of prayer or a den of robbers?

4. Are there activities that look religious to others but, in reality, interfere with God's spiritual purposes in your temple?

Word Search

Find sixteen words from the Matthew 21:1-17 account of the triumphal entry that are hidden in this word search. (All words go down or to the right; none go up, backward, or diagonally.)

```
E  V  D  I  E  C  W  F  J  X  G  T  Y  S  K
T  Q  I  B  R  J  J  I  E  C  K  W  L  D  H
I  N  F  A  N  T  S  L  R  B  D  O  V  E  S
C  L  O  A  K  S  Z  M  U  X  O  B  M  N  Z
O  D  A  H  S  J  A  L  S  E  N  N  A  O  P
L  H  L  K  N  T  B  N  A  D  K  I  N  G  X
T  R  I  U  M  P  H  A  L     E  N  T  R  Y
F  G  T  U  H  R  G  W  E  V  Y  E  O  O  B
M  C  R  E  I  A  Q  R  M  F  R  N  W  B  D
U  T  E  L  D  I  S  C  I  P  L  E  S  B  X
F  J  E  S  U  S  V  U  T  C  M  A  P  E  A
C  K  S  S  B  E  T  H  A  N  Y  B  Q  R  S
```

He Is Lord!

Is Jesus Lord of your life? Color each section to show the extent to which Jesus is Lord of each of these areas of your life:

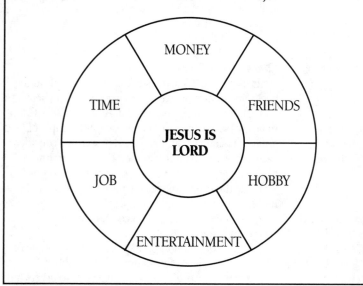

MONEY

TIME

FRIENDS

JESUS IS LORD

JOB

HOBBY

ENTERTAINMENT

KEY TO WORD SEARCH:

Find these words horizontally: infants, doves, cloaks, king, disciples, Jesus, Bethany

Find these words vertically: Jerusalem, two, foal, donkey, colt, praise, robber, trees

Note also the title near the center of the puzzle grid: Triumphal Entry

---

ANTICIPATION OF CHRIST'S RETURN

LESSON 11

WHY TEACH THIS LESSON?

If your class and others in the church know your lesson topics in advance, there could be a better than average attendance for today's lesson. The topic of the second coming of Jesus seems always to draw a crowd. Unfortunately, the crowds are often more interested in speculation than in Scripture, in guesses than in God!

You won't be setting any dates in today's lesson! You won't be making any predictions about the rise and fall of nations. What you will be doing is applying the truth that Jesus is coming back to the simple acts of faithfulness you and your class are already doing. If you do nothing more than help the students appreciate the urgency and significance of everyday faithfulness, your lesson will have been a success.

INTRODUCTION

A. CHARTS FOR SALE

"Bible Prophecy Chart for Sale—Used Only Once." What an amusing sign this would be at a garage sale for some Bible prophecy preachers, who have often attempted to guess the date of Christ's return by searching for clues in the Scripture. Church history records twenty centuries of such theorizing about the date of Christ's return, with none of the efforts having proved successful. Even so, every day new guesses replace the old failed ones, and time eventually takes its toll on additional prophecy speculators.

Today's lesson offers a more solid alternative to the study of the second coming of Christ. Rather than urging us to seek signs pointing to the time this event will take place, Jesus' words encourage us to stay ready at all times, always recognizing that today could be the day that he returns.

B. LESSON BACKGROUND

Today's lesson material is part of the teaching that Jesus probably gave on Tuesday of his final week. Most of this day was spent in the temple, presenting lessons in parables to the Passover crowds, fielding difficult questions from his enemies, and rebuking the hypocrisy of the scribes and Pharisees. The evening was spent in a private setting with his closest disciples. The Gospel of Matthew devotes most of five chapters to this busy day of public and private teaching (Matthew 21:23—25:46).

As Jesus and the disciples were leaving the temple area at the end of the day, some of the disciples commented on the impressive stones of the temple buildings (Mark 13:1). Jesus startled them when he said that a day would come when the temple would be destroyed, with not one stone left upon another (Matthew 24:2).

Once they arrived at the seclusion of the Mount of Olives, the stunned disciples asked Jesus to elaborate on his statement. Their questions were simple

DEVOTIONAL READING:
MATTHEW 24:36-44
BACKGROUND SCRIPTURE:
MATTHEW 24:1—25:13
PRINTED TEXT:
MATTHEW 24:45—25:13

LESSON AIMS

After this lesson students should be able to:

1. Tell what Jesus' teachings concerning the unfaithful servant and the ten virgins say about his second coming.

2. Explain the difference between being wise and foolish regarding Jesus' second coming.

3. List some specific steps they can take to prepare for the return of Jesus and to increase its impact on their daily living.

Feb
13

KEY VERSE

Therefore keep watch, because you do not know the day or the hour. —Matthew 25:13

enough. When will the temple be destroyed, and what will be the sign that the end of the age has arrived (Matthew 24:3)? Jesus' answer, recorded in Matthew 24, remains one of the most controversial passages in the Gospels.

Some Bible students maintain that Matthew 24 predicts the fall of Jerusalem, including the destruction of the temple, at the hands of the Roman army in A.D. 70. Others insist that it is focused exclusively on signs that will foretell the end of time and the second coming of Christ. Most students see both the fall of Jerusalem and the second coming reflected here. Of these, some see Jesus alternating back and forth in his discussion of the two, while others believe that Jesus is linking the two events, with the end of the temple as a foretaste of the end of the world.

Regardless of the approach one takes to this chapter, it seems obvious that by verse 36 Jesus is focusing attention on the day when he will return to earth. He speaks of "that day or hour" as being unknown to all but our heavenly Father (v. 36) and tells us to "keep watch" every day for his coming (v. 42). Thus begins a series of lessons on the theme of staying ready for Christ's return.

I. FAITHFUL SERVICE (MATTHEW 24:45-47)

A. STEWARDS OF GOD (v. 45)

45. Who then is the faithful and wise servant, whom the master has put in charge of the servants in his household to give them their food at the proper time?

The individual *whom the master has put in charge of the servants in his household* describes the person designated as a household "steward." He was the slave who supervised other slaves. His job included overseeing the performance of assigned duties, including the administration of discipline when needed. His job was to make sure everything was done in a manner pleasing to the master. He would also *give* the servants *their food at the proper time*—that is, he would see that all of them were properly fed, housed, and cared for.

We Christians likewise are stewards in the household of God. We have been entrusted with spiritual gifts and service opportunities, and are expected to do the best we can with them to please the Master (1 Peter 4:10, 11). Paul reminds us that "those who have been given a trust must prove faithful" (1 Corinthians 4:2).

B. BLESSED AND EXALTED (vv. 46, 47)

46. It will be good for that servant whose master finds him doing so when he returns.

A wealthy landowner could be away from home for several days or weeks at a time, pursuing business dealings abroad or attending to political affairs. While he was gone he would expect his house to operate as if he were there personally overseeing it. If he returned to find everything in excellent order, the steward could expect to be rewarded by his *master*.

47. I tell you the truth, he will put him in charge of all his possessions.

Any servant in ancient times who did his job well and proved himself to be of special value would naturally be promoted to a position of greater responsibility, where his competence would bear even greater fruit for the master. That is how an ordinary servant could become a household steward, and how the steward in Jesus' illustration could move on to more important leadership duties.

While this parable refers primarily to our readiness for the second coming of Christ, it carries immediate application to our present service in the kingdom of God. Those who minister and serve in the church in a commendable manner are often encouraged to try more challenging areas of service. There is a real satisfaction we receive in being noticed and appreciated for our work and in being desired for other labors.

WHAT DO YOU THINK?

These parables are about being ready to give an accounting of our service when the Lord returns. The "faithful and wise servant" is the one who has nothing for which to be ashamed on that day. Of course, we are asked to account for our actions in a variety of settings in this life as well. What application do you think this concept has for Christians at the workplace?

WHAT DO YOU THINK?

The lesson writer says, "There is a real satisfaction we receive in being noticed and appreciated for our work" in the church. But what if we work hard and are not noticed? What applications do you find in this parable for ministry in the church?

II. FOOLISH ACTIONS (MATTHEW 24:48-51)

A. EVIL STEWARDS (vv. 48, 49)

48. But suppose that servant is wicked and says to himself, "My master is staying away a long time."

In contrast to the "faithful and wise" steward of verse 45, Jesus introduced a *wicked* steward. This *servant* thought he could ignore his duties as long as he did not get "caught." Since he believed his *master* had been delayed and would not catch him in inactivity or abuse, he began to misuse his position of trust.

Many Bible teachers will use the idea that the Lord's return is upon us to motivate good behavior—lest the Lord "catch us" doing wrong when he returns! The fact of the matter is, we ought to do right whether the Lord's return is going to be today or is still far off in the future.

At the same time, if we believe the Lord's return is far off in the future, we may be tempted to treat spiritual matters with little or no urgency. We intend to do the things we ought, but later. We need to keep in mind that the Lord may return very soon; it is urgent that we do all we can as soon as we can—particularly when it comes to winning the lost.

As for the unsaved, they may view Christ's apparent delay in returning as proof that believing in his second coming is futile. By the time Peter wrote his second epistle (approximately thirty years after Jesus' resurrection and ascension) there were already "scoffers" making fun of the Christian hope of a second coming because of the "long" delay (2 Peter 3:3, 4). But Peter understood the concept of a "delay" based on God's timetable rather than our expectations (Acts 1:6, 7). He explains: "With the Lord a day is like a thousand years, and a thousand years are like a day" (2 Peter 3:8). From God's perspective, Jesus has been gone only "a couple of days," and who knows how many more "days" the church is to wait? We would do well to learn patience and practice readiness.

49. . . . and he then begins to beat his fellow servants and to eat and drink with drunkards.

"Dereliction of duty" is the official charge we would declare against this evil steward today. When he dared to *beat his fellow servants*, he was violating the trust that his master had placed in him. Also, when he began to *eat and drink with drunkards*, he was shirking his assigned duty to carefully oversee the master's business at home. He would certainly not be rewarded as the faithful steward was if he were caught participating in such activity.

B. CURSED AND TORMENTED (vv. 50, 51)

50. The master of that servant will come on a day when he does not expect him and at an hour he is not aware of.

The evil steward thought the way many so often think—that they have plenty of time to take care of business. But who among us has not watched family and friends die sooner than expected and, for many, spiritually unprepared?

One day some generation in this planet's history will experience the day of Christ's return. No doubt it will occur when least expected. Many will find themselves unprepared for the judgment to follow, because they assumed that they had plenty of time to get ready. Who knows? We could be that generation of people for whom the Lord comes *at an hour* that we are *not aware of*.

51. He will cut him to pieces and assign him a place with the hypocrites, where there will be weeping and gnashing of teeth.

In biblical times it was considered a serious threat to the social stability for servants not to perform their duties faithfully. Rebellious attitudes could become widespread among the servant population, collapsing the whole societal structure.

Coming In Meekness   Coming In Might

Display the poster from last week's lesson to illustrate the lesson today. Discuss how different Jesus' return will be from his first coming.

WHAT DO YOU THINK?

Patience is a fruit of the Holy Spirit (Galatians 5:22) that we are all expected to possess, yet many of us struggle to manifest it in our endeavors and in our relationships. Someone has said that the longest time known to man is the time it takes for the traffic light to turn green, and the shortest is the time it takes for the guy behind you to honk his horn when it does.

If I asked your spouse or best friend if you are patient, what would he or she say? Why? Why do you think we have so much difficulty being patient, individually and as a society?

Landowners were permitted to take strong punitive measures against servants who needed to be disciplined. Imprisonment and even torture were permitted.

The horror of the imagery of Hell in this verse is designed to teach us a valuable lesson: as we await the return of our Lord for a day of accounting before God, we need to get ready and stay ready.

ARE YOU READY?

The lady picking strawberries in the row next to me—I'll call her Susan—was explaining how difficult it had been to move her father and mother out of their house in Cleveland and into an assisted-living facility in Cincinnati. They were in their nineties and had become unable to care for themselves. Now they were having trouble adjusting to their infirmities and to living in a new environment.

Susan (an only daughter) and her husband had insisted on and assisted with the move. When it was completed, they were exhausted and "stressed out"; so they decided to take a "spring break." But on their way to Hilton Head, South Carolina—without symptoms or warning—Susan's comparatively young husband suddenly dropped dead, the victim of a heart attack.

Susan said she wasn't ready for that. Of course, she wasn't! But a more important question arises: was *he* ready? That is, was he ready to meet his Maker?

Are *you* ready to meet *your* Maker? Christ's return or your physical death is certain; the timing of either event is *uncertain*. Given those truths, "what kind of people ought you to be?" (2 Peter 3:11).   —R. W. B.

III. FULLY PREPARED (MATTHEW 25:1-7)

A. IMPORTANT DUTIES (vv. 1-4)

1. At that time the kingdom of heaven will be like ten virgins who took their lamps and went out to meet the bridegroom.

The *virgins* of this parable were comparable to today's bridesmaids. They themselves were not yet married but were sending off one of their own to be married. They would gather at the site of the wedding festivities, whether in the home of the bride or groom or in another location, and then go out and greet the *bridegroom* and his entourage as they approached, ushering them into the house in a stately manner. Not knowing the precise time of the bridegroom's arrival, the virgins needed to bring their *lamps* in case he did not come until dark.

2. Five of them were foolish and five were wise.

Before Jesus even described the virgins' actions, he gave an assessment of their readiness for duty on behalf of the bride and groom. *Five* of them were called *foolish*, while the other *five* were designated as *wise*.

3. The foolish ones took their lamps but did not take any oil with them.

When Jesus says that the *foolish* virgins *did not take any oil with them*, he means that they did not carry "vessels" of oil for refilling their lamps, as did the wise virgins (v. 4). Their lamps would have been filled and burning as soon as the sun set, but they would not have the means for replenishing their lamps if the bridegroom's coming was delayed.

4. The wise, however, took oil in jars along with their lamps.

In contrast to the foolish virgins, the *wise* virgins did anticipate the possibility of a delay and brought along *jars* with extra *oil*. The foolish virgins may have had good intentions, but they were short-sighted in their planning. Such a special event as a wedding deserved the kind of foresight demonstrated by the wise virgins.

B. READY WHEN CALLED (vv. 5-7)

5. The bridegroom was a long time in coming, and they all became drowsy and fell asleep.

The *bridegroom* could have been delayed by business that needed to be concluded before he could give his attention to the wedding activities. Some suggest that he and his family and friends may have had their own preliminary celebration that had run late. Whatever the cause, such a delay would not have been uncommon where people were not as time conscious as Westerners are today. For an event like this, people would not so much have designated a time for it to begin as they would have appointed a particular day. The virgins would simply have been told that the bridegroom's party would arrive sometime that evening.

Some have concluded that it was wrong for the foolish virgins to have slept. But that was not the problem; after all, even the wise virgins fell asleep. A watchman would awaken the entire household in plenty of time for people to take their positions (vv. 6, 7); thus resting was a reasonable thing to do.

6. At midnight the cry rang out: "Here's the bridegroom! Come out to meet him!"

The *cry* was sounded *at midnight*, approximately six hours after the lamps had been lit at sunset. By this time, probably all of the lamps had gone out or would soon do so.

7. Then all the virgins woke up and trimmed their lamps.

The *virgins* quickly *trimmed their lamps* by removing the burned portion of the wick and pulling out a fresh wick. It quickly became apparent to the foolish virgins that their oil supply was inadequate. The five virgins who had thought to bring extra oil added it to their lamps and were fully prepared for the bridegroom's arrival.

THE BRIDEGROOM IS COMING!

A grandmother recently shared the account of her grandson's wedding reception, which was nearly a disaster. The caterer failed to bring even half enough food to feed the more than two hundred guests. (A "free-will" offering had to be received to order pizza!) The specially ordered cake, to be complete with a fountain in the center, was delivered "downsized" and *incomplete*—with no fountain. The audio tape intended to provide big-band sounds was mistakenly replaced by a recording of the Monkees! The bride was in tears most of the evening, and the groom was fuming.

Even the best-made plans can go awry on the most careful planners. Apparently none of the aforementioned mishaps was due to poor preparation on the part of the bride or the groom. But *someone* dropped the ball—or several someones, perhaps.

Weddings require enormous amounts of time and effort in preparation. The "wedding supper of the Lamb" (Revelation 19:9) also demands diligent planning. To be ready for the coming of our Bridegroom is our most important challenge. To ignore personal preparation for that day is most foolish. Proper attention to details, double-checking instructions, clear and frequent communication, and fulfilling responsibilities "to the letter" will enhance our readiness for the day of Christ's return.   —R. W. B.

IV. FUTILE EFFORTS (MATTHEW 25:8-13)

A. DESPERATE REQUEST (vv. 8, 9)

8. The foolish ones said to the wise, "Give us some of your oil; our lamps are going out."

The *foolish* virgins' request that the *wise* share their *oil* sounds reasonable to Christians who appreciate the biblical idea of sharing what you have with others and helping your friends when they are in need.

9. "No," they replied, "there may not be enough for both us and you. Instead, go to those who sell oil and buy some for yourselves."

The wise virgins realized that if they shared their limited supply of oil, then none of the attendants would have enough in their lamps to be certain that they

---

HOW TO SAY IT

HYPOCRITES. *HIP-uh-krits.*
PHARISEES. *FAIR-ih-seez.*

WHAT DO YOU THINK?

Can you think of an instance in which you were asked to "bail out" someone who had failed to fulfill a responsibility or make adequate preparation? What did you do? How did you arrive at your decision?

PRAYER

*Father, help us to be more dili-
gent in our pursuit of holiness
and service. May we never take
time for granted, knowing that it
is a limited and precious re-
source. In Jesus' name. Amen.*

WHAT DO YOU THINK?

*So often we intend to do bet-
ter than we do! What can be said
for good intentions? How can we
turn good intentions into good
actions?*

THOUGHT TO REMEMBER

*"Look, he is coming with the
clouds, and every eye will see him,
even those who pierced him; and
all the peoples of the earth will
mourn because of him. So shall it
be! Amen"* (Revelation 1:7).

could keep them lighted for the remaining six hours until morning. The wedding celebration would thus be spoiled. The wise virgins must have realized that five lamps capable of remaining lighted through the night were better than ten lamps shining brightly at first but later failing.

Though it is true that sharing with others is usually a good practice, in this case there was a greater principle to be considered. The first loyalty of the wise virgins was to their duty on behalf of the bridegroom. Their refusal to share was not based on a selfish spirit, but on a clear perception of their duty.

B. KEPT FROM ENTERING (vv. 10-13)
10. But while they were on their way to buy the oil, the bridegroom arrived. The virgins who were ready went in with him to the wedding banquet. And the door was shut.

Had this been a real event and not a parable, the foolish virgins probably never would have found a shop owner willing to reopen his store after midnight. Their return was significant to the point Jesus was making, so after some delay, they did return with oil. In the meantime, however, the *wedding* party had entered the *banquet* hall and *the door was shut*. In such cases, a guard was often posted to keep any curious but uninvited neighbors outside.

11. Later the others also came. "Sir! Sir!" they said. "Open the door for us!"

Eventually the foolish virgins returned with fresh oil and trimmed lamps, ready to fulfill their duties. Perhaps it had been their intention to do a good job; they simply had failed to plan adequately. Now they were asking for a second chance.

12. But he replied, "I tell you the truth, I don't know you."

The good intentions of the foolish virgins were worthless once the door was secured. For the bridegroom to say *I don't know you* does not mean that he did not recognize these ladies, but that he had no use for their services now. After all, he had no reason to care for these who had given him so little care earlier.

13. Therefore keep watch, because you do not know the day or the hour.

The lesson from this parable should be obvious to all readers. The second coming of Christ will not be announced in advance so that we can plan on when to get our lives ready for the judgment. "No one knows about that day or hour, not even the angels in heaven, nor the Son, but only the Father," Jesus declared in this same passage (Matthew 24:36). Here is the one clear instruction he has given to all his disciples regarding the second coming: stay ready every moment of every day.

CONCLUSION

Watch children playing a game that requires them to try out new skills, and you will often hear someone ask for a "do over." This means that, even though a child has failed at some part of the game and according to the rules should forfeit a turn to someone else, he is given a second chance. And since the other children would enjoy having that same privilege if they failed, a "do over" is generally granted.

Wouldn't it be great if life gave out a few "do overs" when we messed up? Unfortunately, we adults know from the classroom of experience that such is not often the case. God has given each of us a limited amount of time to accomplish whatever we wish to do with our lives, and he expects us to use our time and resources wisely. Missed opportunities are rarely repeated. Those who delay in addressing spiritual matters are making a mistake they will regret throughout eternity, unless they take steps to set their spiritual houses in order.

There is no better day for doing this than *today*.

Discovery Learning

This page contains an alternate lesson plan emphasizing learning activities. Classes desiring such student involvement will find these suggestions helpful. The next page is a reproducible activity page to further enhance discovery learning.

LEARNING GOALS

After this lesson students should be able to:

1. Tell what Jesus' teachings concerning the unfaithful servant and the ten virgins say about his second coming.

2. Explain the difference between being wise and foolish regarding Jesus' second coming.

3. List some specific steps they can take to prepare for the return of Jesus and to increase its impact on their daily living.

INTO THE LESSON

This lesson looks at character qualities and skills necessary to be a faithful and wise servant. To get into the lesson, ask your class members to write help-wanted ads that might appear if Jesus were advertising for disciples today in the "Help Wanted" section of the newspaper. Warm up for the writing period by identifying some qualities that Jesus expects in his servants. For example, he wants faithfulness, ability to work alone and in groups, perseverance, and the like. Ask for volunteers to read their ads to the class.

Make the transition to the Bible study by saying, "Jesus is actively seeking servants to work in his kingdom today. We've seen the qualities that we think he would want. Today's text tells us what he expects. Some of you may even have thought of the qualities identified in Matthew 24:45—25:13. Let's compare our ideas with what Jesus taught in this passage."

INTO THE WORD

Ask a volunteer to read Matthew 24:45—25:13. Then choose one or more of the following activities to study the text. Or divide the students into three groups and assign one activity to each.

Concordance Study

These parables employ terms that Jesus used regularly. Understanding how Jesus used these terms in other places will broaden our understanding of this passage. Provide copies of the reproducible page that follows for your students to use in class. Have them complete the exercise.

Drama

Drama can be a powerful Bible study tool because it requires us to examine the text carefully to determine the characters, story line, tone of voice, etc. Ask your class members to act out the two parables in today's lesson. In the first parable they will need characters to represent Jesus, the wise servant, the wicked servant, and the other servants. In the second, they will need five foolish virgins, five wise virgins, the crier, the oil merchant, and the doorman.

Cartooning

Every class has members who like to doodle and draw. A cartooning activity will appeal to them and allow them a chance to use their skills. For this activity you will need to assemble pencils, paper, erasers, and a means of displaying the finished work, such as a clothesline and clips or masking tape and a blank wall.

Instruct the class to draw cartoon strips that will tell the two parables in this lesson. They may want to work in pairs or small groups to decide how many frames need to be drawn to tell the story completely. Then one frame could be assigned to each person. Assure them that the quality of the drawing is not the critical point, but a faithful telling of the story.

INTO LIFE

The common thread in both parables is that Jesus' return will be at a time when he is not expected, and some will not be prepared for his return. Give each person an index card and a pen. Ask each person to write down the name of a service or project that is not complete because of procrastination. Then ask him or her to set a date by when it will be completed and to select a partner who will agree to pray and/or help him or her complete the project. Close the class with a prayer time, with each pair praying for one another's project.

Option

Distribute several copies of older hymnbooks to your class members. Make sure the books include songs like, "Toiling On," "Work, for the Night Is Coming," or "There's a Place for Every Worker." Invite your class to do a hymn study. They will compare ideas from today's Bible passage with the ideas from these and other hymns. For example, "toiling on" is the basic message of Matthew 24:45-51. Close the class by singing one or more songs of commitment to be wise and faithful servants until Jesus comes again.

Concordance Study

The stories of the wise and wicked servants and the ten virgins include terms that Jesus used regularly. Understanding how Jesus used these terms in other places will broaden our understanding of this passage. Below are the results of a concordance study. Look up these references to "weeping and gnashing of teeth," "wicked servant," "hypocrites," and "keep watch." In the blank following each reference write a brief description of the significance of the term: to whom it applies, cause, solution, or some other note that summarizes the way the reference helps you understand the term in Jesus' teaching.

Weeping and gnashing of teeth

Matthew 8:12 _____

Matthew 13:42 _____

Matthew 13:50 _____

Matthew 22:13 _____

Matthew 24:51 _____

Matthew 25:30 _____

Luke 13:28 _____

Keep watch

Matthew 24:42 _____

Matthew 25:13 _____

Matthew 26:38 _____

Matthew 26:40 _____

Mark 13:34 _____

Mark 13:35 _____

Mark 14:34 _____

Mark 14:37 _____

Hypocrites

Matthew 6:2 _____

Matthew 6:5 _____

Matthew 6:16 _____

Matthew 15:7 _____

Matthew 22:18 _____

Matthew 23:13 _____

Matthew 23:29 _____

Matthew 24:51 _____

Mark 7:6 _____

Luke 12:56 _____

Luke 13:15 _____

Wicked servant

Matthew 18:32 _____

Matthew 24:48 _____

Matthew 25:26 _____

Luke 19:22 _____

Which verse seems to be addressed most specifically to you? What can you do this week to respond to its message or warning?

Immanuel: God With Us

Unit 3: Fulfillment: Atonement and Final Commission
(Lessons 10-13)

DEATH OF JESUS

LESSON 12

WHY TEACH THIS LESSON?

It's always a tender moment. A hero is reunited with the person whose life the hero saved. You've probably seen some of these reunions on television programs like *Rescue 911!* Occasionally a victim who was rescued, after time to recuperate from injuries sustained, is brought on the program to meet the man or woman who risked life and limb on behalf of the victim. Often there are tears—tears of joy and gratitude. This is not something the victim takes lightly!

Today's lesson should help your students feel somewhat like those victims. It is too easy for Christians to begin to take for granted their privileged status in Christ. You see it in irregular attendance in worship services, in half-hearted service, in lackluster enthusiasm.

But Jesus went to the cross for us! He is a greater Hero than any you will see on *Rescue 911!* If the heroes on that and similar programs deserve the gratitude and admiration of the victims with whom they are occasionally reunited, then what kind of love and gratitude ought we to show toward Jesus? Challenge your students with that thought today.

INTRODUCTION

A. CHERISHED SYMBOLS

We Christians have several religious symbols that speak volumes without ever having to be explained. We see a rainbow and immediately think of Noah and the great flood. We see a manger with straw and fondly recall the birth of Jesus, or the emblem of a dove descending and imagine our Lord's baptism in the Jordan River.

Of all of these symbols, perhaps none is more cherished than the cross. While for the Jew the cross was an offensive "stumbling block" and for the Gentiles it was a "foolishness" that they could not understand, for the Christian the cross speaks of "Christ the power of God and the wisdom of God" (1 Corinthians 1:23, 24). In the cross the Christian sees an object in which he can rightfully "boast," as did Paul (Galatians 6:14).

B. LESSON BACKGROUND

At the heart of the Christian faith is the death of Christ on the cross. "Good Friday," as we call it today, brought the culminating event of Jesus' final week. On Thursday evening Jesus ate his "Last Supper" with the apostles in an upper room, where he instituted the Lord's Supper. Later in the evening he prayed in the garden of Gethsemane while three of his disciples slept. There he was arrested by the temple guards and taken through a series of Jewish and Roman "trials" before finally being condemned to die by the Roman governor, Pontius Pilate.

Early Friday morning Jesus carried his own cross (most likely one of the beams, which weighed thirty to forty pounds) and made the slow march to a site outside Jerusalem known as Golgotha (Aramaic) or Calvary (Latin). It was there that our Lord and Savior was crucified.

DEVOTIONAL READING:
JOHN 19:16-30
BACKGROUND SCRIPTURE:
MATTHEW 27:32-61
PRINTED TEXT:
MATTHEW 27:35-54

LESSON AIMS

After this lesson students should be able to:

1. Relate the important details of Jesus' crucifixion according to today's text.

2. Tell how these details reveal the degree of shame and suffering that Jesus experienced on the cross.

3. Renew their love for and commitment to Jesus, recognizing that he endured the agony of the cross for them.

Feb
20

KEY VERSE

"Surely he was the Son of God!" —*Matthew 27:54*

WHAT DO YOU THINK?

Shame was a major part of the punishment of crucifixion. The victim's clothing was taken, he was verbally assaulted, and he was made a public spectacle. Surely nothing we suffer even comes close, but in what ways do Christians sometimes suffer shame for their faith? How can we maintain our faith in the face of ridicule?

I. PUBLIC SHAME (MATTHEW 27:35-38)

A. CLOTHING REMOVED (vv. 35, 36)

35. When they had crucified him, they divided up his clothes by casting lots.

Part of the "spoils" of guard duty at a crucifixion was the right to confiscate a condemned man's clothing. The usual band of four soldiers would divide the *clothes* four ways, with each soldier getting a fair share. The prize among Jesus' clothing was his soft and seamless undergarment, which was worn beneath his outer robe. This was a valuable item that would be rendered worthless if torn into four pieces. Thus the soldiers participated in *casting lots* (the equivalent of rolling dice) to determine which one of them could claim the entire garment. John notes in his Gospel (John 19:23, 24) that all of this fulfilled the prophecy in Psalm 22:18, which is part of a messianic Psalm that foretells several of the indignities to be experienced by the Messiah at the hands of his enemies.

36. And sitting down, they kept watch over him there.

There was no concern that a crucifixion victim might break free from his cross and escape, for his hands and feet were securely nailed to the cross (in some cases they were tied). The guards were posted in order to prevent anyone from rescuing the victim.

THE SHAME OF IT

There is something hideous and bloodthirsty in the human condition. Consider the popularity of movies with gore, horror, and violence. Consider also the "rubbernecking" of motorists passing a highway accident and slowing to a snail's pace to see the wreckage. A morbid curiosity lurks just beneath the surface of their facade of sophistication. One wonders how many today would turn out to watch a public execution—too many, perhaps, from a supposedly civilized, "polite" society.

The same morbid curiosity likely drew many to the scene at Golgotha where three men were crucified. The crowd looked and leered, they taunted and jeered, as these nearly-naked men suffered unspeakable indignities. Jeremiah certainly was right when he declared, "The heart is deceitful above all things" (Jeremiah 17:9).

The crucifixion of Christ marked a shameful day for the human race. Thankfully, he "endured the cross, scorning its shame, and sat down at the right hand of the throne of God" (Hebrews 12:2).   —R. W. B.

B. TREATED LIKE A CRIMINAL (vv. 37, 38)

37. Above his head they placed the written charge against him: THIS IS JESUS, THE KING OF THE JEWS.

In a typical crucifixion, a placard was posted on the cross to inform observers of the criminal charges *against* the victim. The sign *above* Jesus' *head* gave the identity of the accused, *This is Jesus*, and the *charge* against him, *the King of the Jews*. The accusation against Jesus was treason, for his claim to be a King was twisted to imply that he wanted to usurp the authority of the Roman emperor.

The phrase *King of the Jews* was added by Pilate to poke fun at the Jewish leaders, because he knew that it would offend them to speak of this man they hated as being their king (John 19:21, 22). The sign was written in Hebrew (or Aramaic), Greek, and Latin (John 19:20) so that all passersby (including the many travelers who were present for the Passover) could read it and know why this man was being put to death.

38. Two robbers were crucified with him, one on his right and one on his left.

It was the practice of the Romans to hold condemned criminals in prison until there were several who could be *crucified* at the same time, thereby requiring only one set of guards (rather than a set for each victim). Because the Jewish leaders insisted that Pilate execute Jesus without delay, the soldiers had to work with the number they had available at that time—in this case, only *two robbers*. It would have been bad enough for Jesus to be crucified alone, but for a righteous and innocent man it was an agonizing shame to be associated with common criminals.

II. HATEFUL SCORN (MATTHEW 27:39-44)

A. FROM THE CROWD (vv. 39, 40)

39. *Those who passed by hurled insults at him, shaking their heads.*

The Romans designed crucifixion to be a public spectator event. Crosses were placed next to major highways, often up on a hill, for all to see. The intent was to draw a large crowd who would witness an excruciating and humiliating death for the worst kind of criminals. The crowd itself was encouraged to participate through mocking and derision. All of this was designed, not only to torment the criminal, but also to teach the people a lesson: do not violate the laws of Rome and risk putting yourself in this same situation.

40. . . . *and saying, "You who are going to destroy the temple and build it in three days, save yourself! Come down from the cross, if you are the Son of God!"*

Near the beginning of his ministry, Jesus had spoken the prophetic words, "*Destroy* this *temple*, and I will raise it again *in three days*" (John 2:19). Though he was not understood at the time, even by his own disciples, the apostle John explains that Jesus was referring to the "temple" of his body being destroyed by his enemies and then resurrected by God (vv. 21, 22). These words were perverted by the false witnesses who came forward at Jesus' trial (Mark 14:57, 58).

How Jesus' enemies must have relished this scenario! *Come down from the cross, if you are the Son of God!* they cried. Jesus could only bear these indignities in silence—the cross was the very reason that he, the Son of God, had come to earth.

B. FROM THE LEADERS (vv. 41-43)

41. *In the same way the chief priests, the teachers of the law and the elders mocked him.*

The *chief priests, the teachers of the law, and the elders* had been bitter enemies throughout Jesus' ministry. Jesus had warned his disciples that these three groups of leaders would be instrumental in putting him to death (Matthew 16:21). What pleasure they must now have experienced in being able to deride Jesus without fear of a reprisal! Finally, they thought, they were getting the last word.

42. *"He saved others," they said, "but he can't save himself! He's the King of Israel! Let him come down now from the cross, and we will believe in him.*

Jesus' enemies scorned his ministry of healing and his claim to be the Savior sent from Heaven. The one who promised and provided salvation to *others* was now unable to provide it for *himself*.

More than once the Pharisees had demanded that Jesus give them a sign to validate his message (Matthew 12:38). They had witnessed dozens of miracles by Jesus, but they wanted to name their own "test case"—something they believed to be impossible for anyone but God. Now they saw their opportunity to name the sign. They would *believe* Jesus, they said, if he would *come down now from the cross*. But he had already announced the one sign that he would give: the "sign of . . . Jonah" (Matthew 12:39, 40). He must remain on the cross and die, so that in three days he could provide the true sign that he is the Son of God (Romans 1:3, 4).

43. *He trusts in God. Let God rescue him now if he wants him, for he said, 'I am the Son of God.'"*

Of all the derision that Jesus endured on the cross, these words may have hurt the most. His whole life had been spent devoted to God's will. He had been faithful in all his duties. If anyone deserved to be spared this suffering, he did.

WHAT DO YOU THINK?

Ironically, the chief priests, teachers of the law, and the elders were right when they said, "He saved others, but he can't save himself!" Jesus could have saved himself, but then he would not have been the atoning sacrifice for our sins. If he would save others, he had to refuse to save himself to do it. Under what circumstances would you be willing to sacrifice yourself for the sake of another?

[Consider also that Paul urges us to offer our bodies as "living sacrifices" to God (Romans 12:1). Discuss how this sacrifice imitates the example of Jesus on the cross.]

C. FROM THE THIEVES (v. 44)

44. In the same way the robbers who were crucified with him also heaped insults on him.

As if the insults of his enemies were not enough, Jesus was also verbally attacked by strangers who had no reason to dislike him. There should have been a common bond between Jesus and *the robbers* as they faced this horrible death together; yet they too *heaped insults on him*, mocking Jesus with the same kind of ridicule. (Luke notes, however, that one of the thieves later reconsidered and repented—Luke 23:39-43.)

III. JESUS' DEATH (MATTHEW 27:45-50)

A. CRY OF AGONY (vv. 45, 46)

45. From the sixth hour until the ninth hour darkness came over all the land.

According to Mark's Gospel, the crucifixion of Jesus began, by Jewish reckoning, at "the third hour" (Mark 15:25) after sunrise, which was approximately 9:00 in the morning. This unusual *darkness* set in at *the sixth hour* (12:00 noon) and lasted for three hours.

46. About the ninth hour Jesus cried out in a loud voice, "Eloi, Eloi, lama sabachthani?"—which means, "My God, my God, why have you forsaken me?"

Jesus died at *about the ninth hour* (3:00 P.M.), after six agonizing hours on the cross. In his final moments he *cried out* (in Aramaic) the lament from Psalm 22:1: *My God, my God, why have you forsaken me?* Many Christians have wondered how Jesus could have spoken such words. Surely he knew that God would never abandon him. And yet the prophet Isaiah did speak of a tension between Father and Son at Calvary, as the Messiah "carried our sorrows" and was "stricken by God, smitten by him, and afflicted" in our place (Isaiah 53:4). There was a sense in which Jesus was being *forsaken* and punished by God as the substitutionary atonement for our sins.

Perhaps, however, Jesus was thinking about more than just the opening verse of Psalm 22, and would have quoted the rest of the passage had he had the strength to do so. After David described the misery he was suffering at the hands of men and voiced his despair with God for not responding quickly, he still expressed his belief that God would eventually rescue him (vv. 22-25). In the midst of his agony on the cross, Jesus still knew that God would "rescue" him in due time on the third day.

B. LOSS OF STRENGTH (vv. 47-49)

47. When some of those standing there heard this, they said, "He's calling Elijah."

At this point in the crucifixion, Jesus would have been extremely weak. His tongue was likely swollen and his throat dry. His lungs would have been struggling for air, making it difficult for him to speak. His words *Eloi, Eloi* ("my God, my God") were probably spoken in such whispered tones that they sounded to the crowd like the name *Elijah*. The onlookers assumed that Jesus was *calling* for the prophet Elijah to descend from Heaven and rescue him.

48. Immediately one of them ran and got a sponge. He filled it with wine vinegar, put it on a stick, and offered it to Jesus to drink.

The *drink* offered to Jesus at this time was quite different from that which he had refused earlier that day. As the Roman soldiers prepared to drive the spikes through his hands and feet, they offered him a mixed drink of wine, gall, and myrrh (Matthew 27:34; Mark 15:23). Each of the ingredients acted to numb a person temporarily, much as an anesthesia would do, so that the victim would not die prematurely of shock when his body was pierced and thus avoid the hours of agony on the cross. Since Jesus came to the cross with the intent of suffering as an atoning sacrifice, he refused to drink anything that would diminish what he had agreed to do before God.

The drink offered six hours later was a mild *wine vinegar*. It would not have the numbing effect of the earlier drink, but it would ease the pain of Jesus' throat enough for him to speak clearly his final words before he died.

49. The rest said, "Now leave him alone. Let's see if Elijah comes to save him."

The mistaken idea that Jesus was calling for *Elijah* to come and *save him* merely added to the mocking and derision that Jesus had experienced from his first moments on the cross.

C. MOMENT OF DEATH (v. 50)

50. And when Jesus had cried out again in a loud voice, he gave up his spirit.

Now that his throat was moistened enough for him to speak for a moment, Jesus *cried out again in a loud voice*, "It is finished" (John 19:30), and then, "Father, into your hands I commit my spirit" (Luke 23:46). When these words were spoken, Jesus' *spirit* departed from his body.

TRAVESTY OF JUSTICE—MIRACLE OF MERCY

A young man sits in a Southern prison for signing a check he was not authorized to sign. He didn't forge the check; he didn't steal the money. He simply was not licensed to receive investments on behalf of his brother's firm.

To many, the punishment seems excessive; his accusers seem to carry a vendetta. Lesser charges could have been filed, or a minimal sentence imposed. Thus far the parole board has been inflexible—some would say unreasonable. This prisoner, who has a wife and three children, may be incarcerated for as long as fifteen years! It has been called by many a travesty of justice.

Jesus of Nazareth, at age thirty-three, was arrested late one night in a garden where he went to pray. He was dragged before an illegally convened court, charged with blasphemy for telling the truth, and hauled off to the governor's palace to be tried and sentenced without "due process." Even the governor proclaimed this respected preacher and compassionate healer innocent, then later succumbed to mob pressure and ordered him to be executed. Jesus had committed no crime yet paid the supreme penalty. It was by all standards a travesty of justice!

But God, in his incomprehensible grace, turned the crucifixion of Christ into a miracle of mercy. He "made him who had no sin to be sin for us, so that in him we might become the righteousness of God" (2 Corinthians 5:21).   —R. W. B.

IV. GOD'S RESPONSE (MATTHEW 27:51-54)

A. ATONEMENT ACCOMPLISHED (v. 51)

51. At that moment the curtain of the temple was torn in two from top to bottom. The earth shook and the rocks split.

The main portion of the *temple* consisted of two rooms. The outer chamber (the Holy Place) was serviced by priests each day. The inner chamber (the Holy of Holies) symbolized the presence of God. Only the high priest could enter this room and did so only once a year on the Day of Atonement.

Between these two rooms was a *curtain* that barred admission into the Holy of Holies. Each year the high priest carried the blood of an animal sacrifice into the inner room and presented it to God. The fact that he had to do this year after year indicated that this sacrifice was imperfect (Hebrews 10:1-4). Full atonement for sin was not yet accomplished.

However, at the moment Jesus died this curtain was *torn in two from top to bottom*. That the tearing originated from the top indicated an act of God, announcing

WHAT DO YOU THINK?

There are many reasons that people become convinced that Jesus is "the Son of God." What was the primary reason that brought you to this belief?

Today's visual captures the dramatic moment when the centurion at the cross realized the death of Jesus was unlike any other crucifixion he had ever seen.

Truly this was the Son of God.

PRAYER

Father, help us never to lose our love for the cross of Calvary or for the One who died there so that we might live with you forever. It is in his name that we pray. Amen.

THOUGHT TO REMEMBER

"He was pierced for our transgressions, he was crushed for our iniquities; the punishment that brought us peace was upon him, and by his wounds we are healed" (Isaiah 53:5).

that on the cross an acceptable sacrifice had finally been offered—the sinless Lamb of God. God now declares that anyone may draw near to him and enter the Most Holy Place through the atoning blood of Jesus (Hebrews 9:11, 12; 10:19-22).

B. DEATH DEFEATED (vv. 52, 53)

52. The tombs broke open and the bodies of many holy people who had died were raised to life.

The previous verse mentions a great earthquake that occurred the moment Jesus died. Its primary impact was to crack open some of the *tombs* outside the city of Jerusalem. These graves were not like our Western burial places, six feet underground, but caves sealed with large stones. Many of these stones were cracked by the earthquake, with the pieces falling to the side and creating a means of exit. All of this was a prelude to the resurrections that followed.

53. They came out of the tombs, and after Jesus' resurrection they went into the holy city and appeared to many people.

These resurrections did not occur at the time of the earthquake on Friday; they occurred *after Jesus' resurrection* on Sunday. No details are given regarding who these people were, how long they lived this second time, and what happened when they *appeared to many people* in Jerusalem. We can assume that these were godly people (they are called "holy people" in verse 52) who had anticipated the coming of the Messiah and were now beneficiaries of his power. Whatever the case, their brief reprieve from death was a God-given symbol of an even greater miracle. Death had been defeated through the work of Jesus Christ—not just for a short while, but for eternity.

C. WITNESSES SPEAK (v. 54)

54. When the centurion and those with him who were guarding Jesus saw the earthquake and all that had happened, they were terrified, and exclaimed, "Surely he was the Son of God!"

The *centurion* was the officer in charge of the shifts of soldiers who stood guard duty around the crosses. He and *those with him* (probably some of his men) must have been deeply moved by the manner in which Jesus humbly died in the face of great ridicule and scorn, and by the supernatural phenomena that accompanied his death. Our English translation makes it seem that these witnesses now believed in the deity of Jesus. However, the Greek text is more accurately rendered, "This was a son of God," the equivalent to Luke's expression, "This was a righteous man" (Luke 23:47). The centurion was declaring that Jesus was a godly man, undeserving of the treatment he had received. Perhaps he interpreted the darkness and the earthquake as indicators that some god in Heaven was obviously not pleased with the way Jesus had been treated.

We can hope that this very rudimentary faith eventually matured in this centurion, as well as in the others at the cross that day, leading them to a saving commitment to Jesus as the promised Christ and the true Son of God.

CONCLUSION

What is the best way to conclude this study after reflecting so intensely upon the death of Christ? Perhaps the classic words of George Bennard can provide a fitting closing thought.

> On a hill far away stood an old rugged cross,
>   The emblem of suffering and shame;
> And I love that old cross where the dearest and best
>   For a world of lost sinners was slain.

Discovery Learning

This page contains an alternate lesson plan emphasizing learning activities. Classes desiring such student involvement will find these suggestions helpful. The next page is a reproducible activity page to further enhance discovery learning.

LEARNING GOALS

After this lesson students should be able to:

1. Relate the important details of Jesus' crucifixion according to today's text.

2. Tell how these details reveal the degree of shame and suffering that Jesus experienced on the cross.

3. Renew their love for and commitment to Jesus, recognizing that he endured the agony of the cross for them.

INTO THE LESSON

The account of the last hours of Jesus' life is familiar to most Bible students. Give them the following "true-false-maybe" quiz to reveal how fuzzy they may be on the details, to raise questions, and to motivate them for study. (Answers with references are provided in parentheses to aid you in discussing the quiz after the students complete it.)

1. The final hours of Jesus' life are recorded in all four Gospels. (*True; Matthew 27, Mark 15, Luke 23, John 19*)

2. Jesus said he could have called ten thousand angels to his rescue. (*False; twelve legions—some 72,000 angels, Matthew 26:53*)

3. Jesus refused wine mixed with gall. (*True; Matthew 27:34*)

4. It was dark from noon until three o'clock on the day Jesus died. (*True; Matthew 27:45*)

5. Jesus accepted a sponge soaked in wine vinegar. (*True; Matthew 27:48*)

6. Jesus died at about 6:00 P.M. (*False; 3:00 P.M., Matthew 27:45-50*)

7. The centurion at the crucifixion expressed his faith in Jesus. (*Maybe; Matthew 27:54*)

INTO THE WORD

If you can, rent or borrow a video of the crucifixion, particularly if you can find one based solely on Matthew's account. (*Visual Entertainment* has such a video.) This is a good opportunity to recruit some help from a class member who has video interest and equipment. Have him or her cue the video to the appropriate parts of the text. This person can also be sure the equipment is set up and ready for the class time.

After the viewing, have a volunteer read the text, Matthew 27:35-54. Compare the video with the text for accuracy. Then use one or more of the following options to explore the text.

Interview

The intense drama of the final hours of Jesus' life can best be understood by considering them from the perspective of the participants. Divide your class into groups to prepare interviews with the following characters: the centurion, one of the robbers crucified with Jesus, someone standing nearby who heard what Jesus said, and one of the women who watched (verses 55, 56).

Diary or Journal Entry

Did the comment of the centurion who was in charge of the crucifixion mean he was a convert? Or was he simply observing that Jesus was an innocent man unjustly condemned? We cannot tell for sure, but it is interesting to speculate based on what is recorded. Have your class write a journal or diary entry that the centurion might have written that day.

Group Discussion

Assign a group to discuss various aspects of the suffering of Jesus in his death. Read through the passage looking for indications (stated or implied) of each of these kinds of suffering: physical, emotional, mental, volitional, and spiritual.

INTO LIFE

Choose one of the following activities to make application and to conclude today's session.

Communion Devotion

The events in this lesson often come to mind as we observe the Lord's Supper. Conclude today's lesson by asking your students to write a devotional thought to be used in preparation for the Lord's Supper. Ask if it might be used in your church services today or soon.

Write a Song

Have your class write new words to a familiar melody. Let the first stanza tell about the events, the middle stanzas deal with the emotions of the participants, and the final stanzas call for us to respond to these events in life application. Assign these three sections to three groups from your class. If time is too short for songwriting, write prose paragraphs following the same guidelines.

If the class does write a song, sing it together and close with prayer.

Responding to the Cross of Christ

1 Peter 2:24 says that Jesus "bore our sins in his body on the tree, so that we might die to sins and live for righteousness."

On the cross below, write the names of your sins that Jesus took to the cross. Then write a prayer of thanks and a prayer of commitment in the appropriate boxes below.

My Prayer of Thanks:

My Prayer to Live for Righteousness:

RESURRECTION AND COMMISSION

LESSON 13

WHY TEACH THIS LESSON?

Matthew begins with the birth of "Immanuel . . . 'God with us'" (Matthew 1:23). It closes with the promise of Jesus, "Surely I am with you always, to the very end of the age" (28:20). Our study of Matthew has used the words of the angel in Joseph's dream as its theme. What more fitting way, then, to conclude the study than with the great promise of Jesus' presence with us!

That, then, is one reason to teach this lesson—to bring to a fitting close our study. Another is the reassurance such a promise will give your students. Jesus is with us; he will always be with us! Yet there are more reasons. The title, "Resurrection and Commission," suggest two more. First is the resurrection. The fact that Jesus rose from the dead is vital to our faith. Any chance we have to reinforce students' belief in that fact is a chance not to be squandered!

And then there is commission. Too many Christians want to conclude their study with a reaffirmation of the resurrection and a reassurance of Jesus' presence. If you allow that, without a recommitment to the Great Commission, your lesson will have fallen short of its potential.

INTRODUCTION

A. A FITTING ENDING

What a disappointment it is when an otherwise good movie concludes with a bad ending! Sometimes the ending is anticlimactic and not nearly as exciting as the action that led up to it. At other times a movie critic will express dismay at what is often called a "Hollywood ending," where the hero or heroine experiences a somewhat farfetched turn of events just so the movie can have a happy ending. It leaves us yearning for something more realistic, more fitting with the story line. Or perhaps the story line takes a sudden turn for the worse, and we leave feeling grief for a character we had come to like but who made an unfortunate choice or met an untimely end at the conclusion of the film.

Matthew draws his Gospel to a conclusion with what is indeed a fitting ending to his account of the life of Jesus Christ. Matthew does not leave us with an anticlimactic or grievous finish with Jesus' body lying dead in the grave. Nor does he create some dramatic rescue attempt by the disciples of Jesus. What he records is truly a "grand finale" well suited for the story he has told: the power of Almighty God reaches down to earth to complete the plan he began in his Son Jesus Christ by raising him from the dead. In this case, the truth is better by far than any fiction Matthew might have dreamed up!

B. LESSON BACKGROUND

Shortly after Jesus died on the cross, a secret disciple named Joseph of Arimathea asked the Roman governor Pilate for permission to bury the body (John 19:38). Assisted by Nicodemus, a Pharisee who had visited Jesus by night during

DEVOTIONAL READING:
JOHN 20:19-31
BACKGROUND SCRIPTURE:
MATTHEW 27:62—28:20
PRINTED TEXT:
MATTHEW 28:1-10, 16-20

LESSON AIMS

After this lesson each student will be able to:

1. Summarize Matthew's record of Jesus' resurrection and the commission he gave his disciples.

2. Tell why the Great Commission must remain a priority for today's church, in spite of other concerns that the church is often asked to address.

3. Think of a specific individual who needs to hear the good news about Jesus, and plan to tell that person this week.

KEY VERSE

"Therefore go and make disciples of all nations, baptizing them in the name of the Father and of the Son and of the Holy Spirit, and teaching them to obey everything I have commanded you. And surely I am with you always, to the very end of the age."
—*Matthew 28:19, 20*

Feb
27

the early months of his ministry (John 3:1, 2), Joseph quickly placed Jesus' body in a tomb. (He had less than three hours to move the body and seal the tomb before the Sabbath began at sundown.) Joseph used a "new tomb," one "cut out of the rock" (Matthew 27:60) for his own family, because it was near the vicinity of the crucifixion (John 19:41, 42).

As Joseph closed the tomb with a big stone, some of the women who had supported Jesus throughout his ministry stood nearby and watched. They then returned to their quarters to prepare spices and other materials that they would use to complete the burial process on Sunday, after the Sabbath was over (Luke 23:55, 56). The day after the crucifixion, the chief priests and Pharisees persuaded Pilate to station Roman guards at the tomb, in order to keep Jesus' disciples from stealing the body and then spreading news of an alleged "resurrection" (Matthew 27:62-66). The scene was being set for a most astonishing discovery.

I. GOOD NEWS (MATTHEW 28:1-7)
A. GOD HAS ACTED (vv. 1-4)
1. After the Sabbath, at dawn on the first day of the week, Mary Magdalene and the other Mary went to look at the tomb.

Matthew names two of the women who went to Jesus' *tomb* early on Sunday morning. *Mary Magdalene* was the most prominent of the several women who supported Jesus' ministry, having become a follower after Jesus cast seven demons out of her (Mark 16:9). *The other Mary* was the mother of one of Jesus' disciples, "James the younger," and his brother Joses (Mark 15:40; 16:1).

Mark notes that the two Marys were accompanied by a woman named Salome (Mark 16:1), who may well have been the same woman Matthew identifies as the mother of two other disciples, James and John (Matthew 27:56). Luke adds the name of Joanna (24:10). Having served Jesus faithfully while he was alive and having witnessed his horrible crucifixion and his burial (Matthew 27:55, 56, 61), these women—and perhaps others—were now about to pay due respect to their Master.

The women came to the tomb *at dawn on the first day of the week.* As they neared it, they suddenly realized that they would need help rolling the large stone away from the entrance (Mark 16:3). But God had a means of entry already planned for them.

2. There was a violent earthquake, for an angel of the Lord came down from heaven and, going to the tomb, rolled back the stone and sat on it.

The precise timing of Jesus' resurrection is not indicated in any of the Gospel accounts, but we have traditionally assumed that the *violent earthquake* occurred at the moment he arose and departed the tomb. According to Matthew, the earthquake occurred when *an angel of the Lord came down from heaven* and moved the heavy *stone* to the side. The stone was not moved to let Jesus out; he later demonstrated that he could pass through walls (John 20:19, 26). Instead, it was moved to let the witnesses in so that they could testify that the tomb was empty.

3. His appearance was like lightning, and his clothes were white as snow.

The angel's *appearance* shone with the unearthly brilliance of a blinding, *white* light. It is not likely that the radiant glory was that of the angel himself; rather, it was a reflection of the glory of God. It is common in Scripture for angels sent by God to be characterized by his radiance, just as "the glory of the Lord shone around them" when an angel announced the birth of Jesus to the shepherds (Luke 2:9). The radiant glory displayed at the tomb was intended to declare, along with the earthquake, that God's power had raised Jesus to life.

4. The guards were so afraid of him that they shook and became like dead men.

The sight of the angel terrified the Roman *guards*, who for a moment froze like *dead men*. However, they must have regained their composure quickly and fled; because the other Gospel accounts indicate that the tomb was unguarded when the women arrived. The power of God had provided, not only the removal of the heavy stone, but also unobstructed access to the tomb.

B. CHRIST IS RISEN (vv. 5-7)

5. The angel said to the women, "Do not be afraid, for I know that are looking for Jesus, who was crucified.

By the time *the women* arrived at the tomb, the Gospel accounts indicate that *the angel* was no longer sitting on the stone. Luke simply states that they found the stone removed, entered the tomb, and discovered that the body of Jesus was missing (Luke 24:2, 3). It was then that "two men in clothes that gleamed like lightning" were observed in the darkness of the tomb (Luke 24:4). Matthew and Mark mention only the one who did the speaking and who was "sitting on the right side" (Mark 16:5). This angel told the women that he knew why they had come: to locate the body of *Jesus, who was crucified*. He must have piqued their curiosity when he asked, "Why do you look for the living among the dead?" (Luke 24:5).

6. He is not here; he has risen, just as he said. Come and see the place where he lay.

The message of what is often called "Easter" Sunday is succinctly expressed in these words of the angel: *He is not here; he has risen*. It was time to make known the glorious news, although the full impact of the angel's words was not grasped by the women or the disciples until later that day.

Jesus' resurrection happened just *as he said* it would. The angel reminded the women that Jesus had taught his disciples that "the Son of Man must be delivered into the hands of sinful men, be crucified and on the third day be raised again" (Luke 24:6, 7). The women then "remembered his words" (v. 8).

There was great significance in having an opportunity to *see the place where he lay*. Not only did it confirm that the tomb was empty, but to the observant eye it provided evidence of a miracle. When the apostle John later inspected the tomb, he noticed that the linen strips that had been wrapped around the body of Jesus were still lying in the tomb undisturbed. The cloth that had been tied around Jesus' head was lying separate from the linen cloths, in the place where the head had been. It appeared as if the body of Jesus had not been taken, but had simply vanished, leaving the burial clothing still in place.

When John saw this, he believed in the resurrection of Jesus (John 20:6-8). Perhaps seeing the place where Jesus' body had been laid had a similar effect on the women.

"OUT-OF-TOMB" EXPERIENCE

· In recent years, much has been written by and/or about people who claim to have had "out-of-body" experiences. Many individuals receive such reports with a good bit of skepticism. Most of the accounts include similar elements, such as "hovering above one's body" or "passing through a long tunnel toward a bright light." Could these simply be personalized versions of someone else's experience? Is it possible that impressionable people are pre-programmed to dream or visualize what others have described?

Make no mistake—Jesus had a "*real*-death, out-of-*tomb*" experience. He really died on the cross, and his body lay on a stone shelf in a grave for three days. On the third day, God raised him from the dead and miraculously ushered him out of that tomb.

At first the reports of Jesus' "out-of-tomb" experience were received with skepticism and doubt. But no one has ever invalidated the Gospel accounts of Christ's

WHAT DO YOU THINK?

The lesson writer says, "There was great significance in having an opportunity to see the place where the Lord lay." What else do you find especially significant in the resurrection account— something that demands belief in the resurrection?

HOW TO SAY IT

Arimathea. AIR-uh-muh-THEE-uh (th as in thin).
Joses. JOE-sez.
Magdalene. MAG-duh-leen or Mag-duh-LEE-nee.
Nicodemus. Nick-uh-DEE-mus.
Pharisee. FAIR-ih-see.
Pilate. PIE-lut.
Salome. Suh-LO-me.

resurrection. Jesus' experience will one day be ours, according to his promise: "Because I live, you also will live" (John 14:19).　　　—R. W. B.

7. Then go quickly and tell his disciples: 'He has risen from the dead and is going ahead of you into Galilee. There you will see him.' Now I have told you."

The women were sent by the angel to *tell* Jesus' *disciples* that he had *risen from the dead*. Mark reports that Jesus especially mentioned telling Peter (Mark 16:7). Perhaps Jesus intended to let Peter know that his denials of Jesus could be forgiven. They need not separate him from fellowship with the risen Lord.

The angel's message also included instructions for the disciples to meet Jesus in *Galilee*. During his last supper in the upper room, Jesus had told his disciples to meet him there following his resurrection (Matthew 26:32). But since they had not yet grasped the truth of Jesus' resurrection, they did not sense the urgency of going to Galilee. Now, however, it was time for them to proceed there.

The reason for going to Galilee is not stated. Perhaps it was for safety. (The disciples were certainly in fear of the Jews in Jerusalem, as seen in John 20:19.) Whatever the reason, the angel's command served as a test of the disciples' faith. Would they travel to Galilee simply on the women's claim that they had seen an angel of God, or would their limited faith require a resurrection appearance of Jesus to them? We are told that they did not believe the women, nor the testimony of others that Jesus was alive (Mark 16:11-13). Later Jesus rebuked the disciples for their refusal to accept such testimony (Mark 16:14).

II. GLORIOUS SIGHT (MATTHEW 28:8-10)

A. MIXED EMOTIONS (v. 8)

8. So the women hurried away from the tomb, afraid yet filled with joy, and ran to tell his disciples.

After seeing an angel and hearing his message that Jesus was alive, the *women* were not sure what to think. They experienced great *joy* at such good news, yet they were beset by fear. Nevertheless, the women *hurried away from the tomb* and faithfully reported what they had seen and heard.

B. BLESSED ENCOUNTER (vv. 9, 10)

9. Suddenly Jesus met them. "Greetings," he said. They came to him, clasped his feet and worshiped him.

Although Mary Magdalene came to the tomb with the other women, at some point she apparently became separated from them. John's account indicates that when Mary saw that the stone had been rolled away from the tomb, she immediately ran to tell Peter and John the news (though incorrect) that someone had taken the body of Jesus (John 20:1, 2). Thus Mary did not see the angel at the tomb and was not present at the appearance of Jesus recorded by Matthew.

Having summoned Peter and John, Mary returned alone to the tomb, where Jesus appeared to her (John 20:11-18). Mark 16:9 tells us that Jesus appeared to Mary Magdalene *first*. So Mary had returned to the tomb and had seen Jesus before his appearance to the women reported by Matthew in this account.

Once these women saw the risen Jesus, they fell prostrate before him and *clasped his feet*. This was an act of humility and worship. The touch also served to verify that the women were not hallucinating, but were indeed seeing Jesus alive.

10. Then Jesus said to them, "Do not be afraid. Go and tell my brothers to go to Galilee; there they will see me."

Jesus repeated the instruction for the women to tell the disciples to *go to Galilee* and meet him (v. 7). No doubt the women relayed the command faithfully, but the disciples "did not believe the women, because their words seemed to them like nonsense" (Luke 24:11). Apparently it was not until after Thomas had the opportunity to see the resurrected Jesus and voice his belief (John 20:26-29) that the eleven departed for Galilee as they had been instructed (Matthew 28:16).

Though it would have been commendable for the disciples to believe in the resurrection without hesitation, their reluctance serves to confirm the truth of the resurrection for us. Contrary to the skeptics who suggest that the disciples were so eager to believe in a resurrection that they imagined seeing Jesus alive, the Gospel accounts indicate that their minds were not at all predisposed for such a hallucination. They had to be convinced by solid evidence, thus providing us with a firm basis for believing their witness to the resurrected Christ.

III. GREAT COMMISSION (MATTHEW 28:16-20)

A. LORD'S AUTHORITY (vv. 16-18)

16. Then the eleven disciples went to Galilee, to the mountain where Jesus had told them to go.

The *eleven disciples* (minus Judas) finally gathered in *Galilee* as instructed by Jesus. The designated *mountain* is not identified in the Gospels. It may be that Jesus called his disciples back to a mountain that had played a prominent role during his Galilean ministry.

17. When they saw him, they worshiped him; but some doubted.

The eleven had come to believe in Jesus' resurrection while in Jerusalem, thus they were prepared to worship him when he appeared before them on the mountain. Apparently other disciples from Jesus' Galilean ministry were permitted to join the eleven on the mountain, for Matthew says that there were *some* present who *doubted*. The apostle Paul notes that following his resurrection Jesus once appeared to as many as five hundred believers at one time (1 Corinthians 15:6). Perhaps this gathering was that occasion.

18. Then Jesus came to them and said, "All authority in heaven and on earth has been given to me.

It is significant that Jesus began his words with a declaration of his *authority*, for he was about to issue orders that would establish the first priority for every disciple from then until the end of time. Only on the basis of his authority as the Lord of *heaven* and *earth* could he give such a command!

This is the same authority Jesus demonstrated again and again throughout his ministry. His disciples were amazed when he stilled the storm, marveling, "What kind of man is this? Even the winds and the waves obey him!" (Matthew 8:27). When Jesus healed the paralytic, he demonstrated that he had "*authority* on earth to forgive sins" (Matthew 9:6).

Yet there was something climactic about Jesus' announcement here. He was about to return to the glory that he had with the Father "before the world began" (John 17:5). Jesus' time on earth was a time of submission, of being a "servant" (Philippians 2:6-8). He and his authority were about to be exalted by God the Father (Philippians 2:9-11). When he ascended to Heaven forty days after his resurrection (Acts 1:3, 9), he was seated on the throne of Heaven at the right hand of God (Acts 2:32, 33). Jesus' identity as "Lord and Christ" (Acts 2:36) now takes on an even greater significance than when the disciples called him "Lord" (John 13:13) or when Peter confessed him as the "Christ" (Matthew 16:16).

That Jesus possesses all authority has a practical and daily application to our lives. It challenges us to look within to see if in our hearts we truly honor Jesus as Lord and King. Saving faith is not just believing facts about Jesus, but accepting Jesus as the supreme authority in our lives.

WHAT DO YOU THINK?

The resurrection was, at first, a test of faith for the disciples. Would they believe the women? Would they go to Galilee? Would they recall and believe Jesus' own predictions?

In what ways is the resurrection a test of our own faith today?

WHAT DO YOU THINK?

If it is true that all authority in Heaven and earth has been given to Jesus, how ought this reality to affect the daily conduct of our lives?

WHAT DO YOU THINK?

How can we assure that our focus is clearly on making "disciples of all nations"?

This visual illustrates six actual mission works in different parts of the world. Use it to challenge your students to take Christ's commission seriously.

PRAYER

Father, we thank you for the many lessons we have learned about Jesus through the Gospel of Matthew. May our lives be fully devoted to you and to your Son. In his name. Amen.

THOUGHT TO REMEMBER

The final command of Jesus (the Great Commission) should be the church's first priority.

B. CHURCH'S PRIORITY (vv. 19, 20)

19. Therefore go and make disciples of all nations, baptizing them in the name of the Father and of the Son and of the Holy Spirit.

We call Jesus' instructions for evangelizing the world the "Great Commission," for it represents the "marching orders" for the church. The other three Gospel writers also record the Great Commission, though in different contexts with different wording (Mark 16:15, 16; Luke 24:46-49; John 20:21-23). This repetition implies that evangelizing the world was considered a top priority by Jesus and should be viewed as such by his followers.

We are to *make disciples of all nations*, or followers of Christ of as many people as we can. Those willing to make such a commitment are to be immersed in water, which is the actual meaning of the Greek word rendered *baptizing*. When applied to a believer, it washes away sins (Acts 22:16) and then empowers him for Christian living with the sanctifying "gift of the *Holy Spirit*" (Acts 2:38; Romans 8:11-13).

Though the theological world loves to debate the subject of baptism, for most believers all that needs to be said is that, in his Great Commission, Jesus commanded that it be done. Since he has all authority, our obedience to him in this matter should be unhesitating and without question.

20. . . . and teaching them to obey everything I have commanded you. And surely I am with you always, to the very end of the age."

Our task of evangelism is not complete when a person rises from the waters of baptism. There remains a lifetime of *teaching*, for the Word of God has a depth that is never exhausted; and our lives are always in need of constant challenge and growth. As the church performs its dual task of evangelism and nurturing, Jesus promises to be *with* us and thus to support us, even *to the very end of the age*.

WHO'S YOUR BOSS?

Our four-year-old grandson has been taught by his mother that whenever grandparents are baby-sitting him, they are "in charge." He has never questioned nor challenged our authority. Rarely has he protested our instructions or prohibitions. Never has he said, "You can't tell me what to do; you're not my boss!"

Jesus prefaced his final commission by claiming "all authority in heaven and on earth." Christians may rarely, if ever, openly question Christ's authority, yet many believers have not taken seriously all of his commandments. Isn't ignoring the clear instructions of someone in authority the same as saying, "You're not my boss!"?

The Great Commission is so called because it defines the "supreme task of the church: world evangelization" (Oswald Smith). Though millions of Christians are aware of what it says, dozens of people groups and countries have not yet been told the good news of salvation.

Personal evangelism continues to be one of the "bugaboos" of Christian discipleship. Though Christ has earned the right to send us into our own "spheres of influence" and even unto the ends of the earth with the gospel, many fail to honor his authority and comply with his command. We must recognize his lordship before we will trust and obey him.

Who's *your* boss?

—R. W. B.

CONCLUSION

A study of the life of Christ should be a moving experience. We are moved to admiration as we observe the manner in which Jesus ministered and as we listen to his words of teaching. We are moved to wonder and awe as we watch him die the horrible death of the cross. And now may we be moved to devotion and service as he stands before us as our risen Savior and Lord.

Discovery Learning

*This page contains an alternate lesson plan emphasizing learning activities. Classes
desiring such student involvement will find these suggestions helpful. The next page
is a reproducible activity page to further enhance discovery learning.*

LEARNING GOALS

After this lesson each student will be able to:

1. Summarize Matthew's record of Jesus' resurrection
and the commission he gave his disciples.

2. Tell why the Great Commission must remain a priority for today's church, in spite of other concerns that
the church is often asked to address.

3. Think of a specific individual who needs to hear
the good news about Jesus, and plan to tell that person
this week.

INTO THE LESSON

Use one of the following to introduce today's lesson.

Believe It or Not

Ripley's Believe It or Not is a collection of incredible
facts. Borrow a copy from your library. Select some samples to introduce today's lesson.

Make the transition to the Bible study by saying,
"These are incredible accounts of astonishing events. We
probably would have to see some of them to believe
them. In the disciples' thinking the resurrection of Jesus
was an unbelievable event. In fact, they refused to believe until they examined the evidence firsthand. Let's
look at the evidence for ourselves."

Circle Response

Seat the class or a small group in a circle. Go around
the circle and have each person complete the following
sentence. "I believe the purpose of the church is. . . ."
You may want to list responses on a chalkboard or
poster. Give each person a chance to respond once before anyone gives a second response.

INTO THE WORD

Ask a volunteer to read Matthew 28:1-10, 16-20.
Work together to develop an outline of the text. Ask
class members to call out significant facts from the text.
Then work together to arrange them into an outline.
Group several events together under heads that tie them
together. The lesson outline reflected in the headings of
the commentary section can serve as an example.

Option: Use the reproducible activity "'G' Is for . . ."
on the following page for the basis of a Bible study.

Ask the class, "Can you imagine the drama of seeing
the risen Lord and hearing him give the Great Commis-

sion?" Briefly discuss what that must have been like.
Then ask each class member to write a diary entry that
one of the apostles might have written the night after
Jesus gave the Great Commission.

INTO LIFE

Conducting an interview is a non-threatening way for
your class members to involve others in a discussion
about the basic message of Christ and Christianity. Challenge your class members to interview ten people this
week, asking questions about the resurrection of Jesus.
They should take notes recording people's responses
and bring them to class next week. Here are two questions to get your class started. Add to them as necessary.

1. Do you believe that Jesus rose from the dead? Why
or why not?

2. What difference does it make in your life?

If there is time remaining in the class session, use one
or both of the following additional application exercises.

Write a Letter

Probably several young people from your church are
away from home at college or in military service. These
people need your class members' support to stand firm
and true against attacks on their faith.

Ask each class member to select one of these and
write him or her a letter of encouragement. Some of the
insights from this lesson on the resurrection and Great
Commission should be shared. Be sure to have names
and addresses, zip codes, stationery, envelopes, pens,
and stamps available for your class members.

Evangelism Training

Many Christians know that they should share their
faith and make disciples, but they lack the skills and
experience to be effective. Ask your church leaders to
sponsor a course in witnessing and disciple making. This
class should include classroom instruction, observation
of others, and practical experience. If it is certain that
such a course will be available, conclude today's class by
inviting and urging your class members to enroll!

Ten Most Wanted

Use the reproducible activity "Ten Most Wanted" to
help your students identify individuals with whom they
can share their faith.

"G" Is for . . .

This activity is brought to you by the letter "G." Each of the answers to these questions from Matthew 28:1-20 contains the letter "G."

What Jesus said when he met the women. _____

What Jesus commanded his disciples to do. _____

How long Jesus promised to be with his disciples. _____

A lady who went to the tomb on the first day of the week. _____

Where Jesus told the women he would meet his disciples. _____

Who appeared to the women at the tomb. _____

Who became like dead men. _____

The first thing we are commanded to do in making disciples. _____

The other command we are to obey in making disciples. _____

What we are to teach disciples to obey. _____

Ten Most Wanted

Think of the people you know who are not Christians. Of these, choose ten whom you would most like to see accept the Lord, or the ten on whom you believe you are most likely to be able to have some influence to lead them to the Lord. Write their names below.

_____   _____

_____   _____

_____   _____

_____   _____

_____   _____

Pray daily for these ten people. Pray for opportunities to share your faith with them. Pray that God will put others in their lives who can influence them.

Then choose one of the names. Look for ways to introduce him or her to Christ.

Spring Quarter, 2000

Helping a Church Confront Crisis
(1 & 2 Corinthians)

Special Features

Lessons

Unit 1: Christ, the Basis for Unity

Unit 2: Unity in Human Relationships

Unit 3: Unity Expressed in Ministry

About These Lessons

This quarter finds us in some of the most practical material in the New Testament. Within five years of its establishment, the church at Corinth was having profound problems, which Paul addressed in his letters to the Corinthian believers. His help for that church will bless your class and your church as you study Paul's Corinthian letters this quarter.

Mar 5

Mar 12

Mar 19

Mar 26

Apr 2

Apr 9

Apr 16

Apr 23

Apr 30

May 7

May 14

May 21

May 28

Not Another Crisis!

by John W. Wade

Every time we pick up a newspaper or listen to the TV news, the word *crisis* leaps out at us. From day to day, even hour to hour, it seems that we are confronted with another crisis. Now we have to deal with another one in our Sunday school lessons, for this quarter's lessons are entitled, "Helping a Church Confront Crisis."

The word *crisis* comes from the Greek word *krisis*, which in turn is derived from a verb meaning to "judge," "separate," or "select." A dictionary definition of *crisis* is "a time of great danger or trouble, whose outcome decides whether possible bad consequences will follow." The Chinese symbol for *crisis* consists of a combination of two symbols—one meaning "danger" and the other meaning "opportunity." That seems an appropriate way to describe the lessons in this quarter, which are based on 1 and 2 Corinthians. Each lesson deals with an issue that posed a serious threat to the young church at Corinth. At the same time, each issue also offered the opportunity for growth toward maturity.

Because of the frequency and intensity of the crises around us today, we may be inclined to think that no other period in history has ever encountered the problems we are facing. However, every period has had its share of problems. The church in Corinth was certainly no exception.

We need to remember that the church of Jesus Christ has lived its entire history in a crisis; Christians have always been engaged in a spiritual warfare with Satan and his hosts. We can be sure that this conflict will continue until God finally triumphs over Satan. If this is the case, we must ask how the crises experienced by the Corinthian church are relevant to us today. The lessons of this quarter will provide answers to that question. They will show how the problems that troubled the Corinthian church—including divisiveness, worldliness, abuse of spiritual gifts, personal ambitions, and pettiness—are surprisingly contemporary.

UNIT 1: CHRIST, THE BASIS FOR UNITY

In **lesson 1** Paul, who had learned of divisions that had formed among the Corinthian Christians, makes an earnest plea for unity. This first lesson does not touch on all the causes for the lack of unity; later lessons will examine some of these. Paul's plea for unity is based on the person and work of Christ. "Is Christ divided?" he asks. "Was Paul crucified for you? Were you baptized into the name of Paul?" In the face of all the divisions that exist within the church today, these are still important issues to raise.

Lesson 2 deals with "The Holy Spirit as Teacher." Other activities of the Holy Spirit will be treated in later lessons. The focus in this lesson is his work in revealing truth to Paul and other inspired leaders.

Leadership is the theme of **lesson 3**. Few factors are more important to the growth of the church than dedicated leadership. Paul deals with some aspects of this issue in 1 Corinthians 4. The key qualification of leaders is that they must consider themselves "servants of Christ." They must also be good stewards of the "secret things of God," which have been given to them as a "trust" (1 Corinthians 4:1, 2). Humility and integrity form the foundation upon which any effective leadership in Christ's church must be built.

Lesson 4 deals with a serious moral problem within the Corinthian church. Such a circumstance was perhaps more apt to surface in a city like Corinth, since so many of the Corinthian Christians came to Christ out of a paganism that included frequent sexual promiscuity. How timely this lesson is in our culture, where moral standards once accepted without question have been seriously eroded by the corrosive winds of secularism! Combine this with the rampant "me-ism" of our times, and the result is a situation not greatly different from the one Paul faced in Corinth.

UNIT 2: UNITY IN HUMAN RELATIONSHIPS

APRIL

First Corinthians 7:1-16, which deals with marriage and related matters, is the basis for **lesson 5**. Few today have any doubts that marriage and the home are under siege in our society. Nor does anyone deny that unless we find ways to make our homes more stable, our nation faces a devastating future. The standards that Paul lays down—sexual fidelity in marriage and a serious commitment to the marital vows—are not popular with many today, but they remain God's standards. As a teacher you will need to handle this lesson with sensitivity and compassion.

Our culture puts a great deal of emphasis upon education and knowledge. These certainly are important; however, in **lesson 6** Paul points out that intellectual superiority can create an arrogance that disregards the sensitivities of others. He emphasizes the importance of showing love and concern to weaker brethren, even to the point of limiting some of one's own freedoms for the sake of others.

In **lesson 7** Paul answers some of the questions that had been raised in the Corinthian church about "spiritual gifts." This issue is quite controversial in many churches today. It is important to keep in mind that "to each one the manifestation of the Spirit is given for the common good" (1 Corinthians 12:7). Whatever gifts and abilities an individual has should be put to use for the good of the entire church.

The printed text for **lesson 8**, taken from 1 Corinthians 15, is an appropriate study for Easter Sunday. The resurrection story needs to be retold, not only for those who have never heard it or do not understand it, but also for faithful saints who never tire of it.

"Love's Better Way," the subject of **lesson 9**, leads us through 1 Corinthians 13, the "love chapter" of the Bible. The lessons of this chapter are not difficult to understand, but they can be difficult to implement, even for mature believers. Young Christians must learn these lessons, but mature saints need to relearn them and apply them to new situations. Christians must never take for granted that they already know all there is to know about love.

UNIT 3: UNITY EXPRESSED IN MINISTRY

MAY

Lesson 10 introduces the third unit in this quarter. It is also the first lesson based on a text from 2 Corinthians. We might note here that some students believe this was actually the third or even the fourth letter Paul wrote to the Corinthians, with one or two epistles having been lost. Theories advanced to explain the Corinthian correspondence are varied and complicated; they are best left to more technical studies. Suffice it to say we have the message the Spirit wanted us to have from Paul's Corinthian correspondence.

In this lesson we find a reference to one who had done some earlier wrong but had repented. This is probably the man mentioned in 1 Corinthians 5. This lesson gives us, then, "the rest of the story" begun in lesson 4, and tells us the discipline exercised by the church was successful.

No one ever promised that being a follower of Christ and living the Christian life would be easy, especially the apostle Paul. In **lesson 11** we consider his teaching on the "Trials and Triumphs of Christian Ministry." Paul's experiences as a messenger for Christ made him an "expert" on the pain and agony of ministry. While many in our world today endure physical suffering—beatings, imprisonment, and even death—for their faith, we in the Western world may never experience such opposition. However, in certain situations our faith and how we live it out may produce emotional pain in the form of ridicule and discrimination. When these occasions arise (and they are likely to if we take our faith seriously), we can look to the example of Paul, whose faith empowered him to triumph over anything Satan could throw at him.

One important area of Christian ministry is our use of the material resources that God has entrusted to us. **Lesson 12**, "Collection for Jerusalem Christians," will give you an opportunity to stress several facets of Christian stewardship. Giving should never be approached as a legalistic requirement, so that it is done "reluctantly or under compulsion." Rather, we should rejoice that we have the opportunity to share our blessings with others; for "God loves a cheerful giver" (2 Corinthians 9:7).

Lesson 13 concludes this series of studies from the Corinthian letters. It is also a fitting conclusion for this quarter's final unit, which emphasizes ministry. During his ministry to the Corinthians, Paul had come under sharp criticism from some within the church. Any person who becomes a leader will face some degree of criticism. How one handles it will go a long way in determining how successful he will be as a leader. Paul set the example of dealing both firmly and yet gently with criticism. As an apostle he had the authority to deal firmly with any troublemakers; but he chose to act with humility and gentleness, desiring to work in such a way as to build the Corinthians up, not to tear them down (2 Corinthians 13:10).

May God help us do likewise in addressing similar situations in the body of Christ today.

ANCIENT CORINTH

North market

North stoa

Temple of Apollo

Northwest stoa

Basilica

Lechaeum Road

Peribolos of Apollo

Pirene

Julian basilica

Northwest shops

Captives facade

Propylaea

Temple

A G O R A

West shops

Judgment Seat

Central shops

Central shops

South stoa

South basilica

0   500   1000 yards

0   500   1000 meters

© Carta

Senate house

To Cenchrea

WORLD OF PAUL'S MINISTRY

BLACK SEA

Rome

Philippi

Ephesus

Corinth

Tarsus

MEDITERRANEAN SEA

CORINTH

Long Wall

Long Wall

Asclepium

Roman Amphitheater

Area of large map

Sanctuary of Demeter and Kore

Sanctuary of Aphrodite

ACROCORINTH

Upper Pirene (Spring)

© Carta

Chronology of Paul's Missionary Journeys

(And of Epistles Written at the Same Time)

DATE	
A.D. **47-49**	FIRST MISSIONARY JOURNEY (ACTS 13:1—14:28)
A.D. **52-54**	SECOND MISSIONARY JOURNEY (ACTS 15:40—18:22)
52	Thessalonian epistles written (from Corinth, 1 Thessalonians 3:1-6; Acts 18:5)
A.D. **54–58**	THIRD MISSIONARY JOURNEY (ACTS 18:23—20:38)
54/55-57	Three-year ministry in Ephesus (Acts 20:31)
56	1 Corinthians written (from Ephesus, 1 Corinthians 16:8, 9)
56/57	Possible second trip by Paul to Corinth, since he mentions coming to the Corinthians for the "third time" in 2 Corinthians 13:1
57	Arrival in Macedonia (Acts 20:1-6)
57/58	2 Corinthians written (from Macedonia, 2 Corinthians 2:12, 13; 7:5-7)
58	Galatians written (from Macedonia, or possibly from Corinth)
58	Romans written (from Corinth, Romans 16:23; 1 Corinthians 1:14) in anticipation of Paul's visiting Rome
A.D. **58**	PAUL ARRESTED IN JERUSALEM (ACTS 21:17-33)

Helping a Church Confront Crisis
Unit 1: Christ, the Basis for Unity
(Lessons 1-4)

APPEAL FOR UNITY

WHY TEACH THIS LESSON?

In our study of Matthew in the previous quarter we heard Jesus' rebuke of those who claimed he cast out demons by the power of the devil. "Every kingdom divided against itself will be ruined," he said, "and every city or household divided against itself will not stand" (Matthew 12:25). In that answer are both the need and the urgency for today's lesson.

Jesus' point was that, if Satan's kingdom were divided, it would fall. As is true of Satan's kingdom, so it is true of the Lord's. If that kingdom is divided, it is weak—it cannot stand. We have the power we need in Christ, but that power is diffused in division. Thus, we need this appeal to unity.

Jesus also made it clear that Satan's kingdom was not, and is not, divided. It remains a formidable foe. It is no match for the power of Jesus, and Jesus' casting out of demons proved that. But it is very powerful just the same. Thus there is an urgency in today's appeal for unity. Unity in the body of Christ is more than a preference—it is vital to our mission, to our survival!

And don't allow the class to spend all its time lamenting the denominational divisions in the world today. As distressing as such division is, the situation Paul addressed was on a local level. Breaking down the walls between denominations will happen only as each local congregation banishes the divisions and factions within its own walls. Use this lesson to urge every member to a recommitment to following the Bible as his or her only rule of faith and practice, and to rallying others to unity on that basis.

INTRODUCTION

A. SADDENED, YET ENCOURAGED

In the days when the Soviet Union was a world power, an American minister spent some years visiting and preaching among congregations behind the Iron Curtain. When he went there, he expected to find the churches united. After all, they were facing the common enemies of Communism and militant atheism. He pictured them like the pioneers of the American West, drawing their wagons into a circle to support each other in the face of danger. Instead, he was shocked to find the same kinds of disagreements, divisions, power struggles, and personality conflicts so common within the churches of the free world.

At first the minister was quite depressed by his discovery, but then he came to realize that the devil is not creative. Only God is creative. The devil uses the same tactics all over the world, in every place and in all generations. Sadly, these methods almost always work.

When we become the cause of division in the family of God, we do not advance God's cause but Satan's. When we work for peace and unity in the body of Christ, we help to advance the cause for which he died.

B. LESSON BACKGROUND

The city of Corinth was one of the great commercial centers of the first-century world. It was located on a very narrow strip of land that connected the two

DEVOTIONAL READING:
1 CORINTHIANS 1:18-25
BACKGROUND SCRIPTURE:
1 CORINTHIANS 1:1-17
PRINTED TEXT:
1 CORINTHIANS 1:2-17

LESSON AIMS

After participating in this lesson, each student should be able to:

1. Explain what was causing division within the church at Corinth.

2. Tell why division is so destructive to the church and its message.

3. Tell how a divided church can find oneness in Christ.

KEY VERSE

I appeal to you, brothers, in the name of our Lord Jesus Christ, that all of you agree with one another so that there may be no divisions among you and that you may be perfectly united in mind and thought.
—1 Corinthians 1:10

Today's visual will give your students a better understanding of the location and features of the city of Corinth. Post it before the session begins.

WHAT DO YOU THINK?

According to the New Testament, Christians are saints, disciples, and brothers. How can we use these titles to promote and preserve unity?

land masses of Greece. The city had harbors on two seas, the Aegean to the east and the Adriatic to the west. Rather than go around the great stretch of southern Greece (called the Pelopenessus), ships unloaded in one harbor, carried their goods overland, and reloaded on another ship in the other harbor. This gave Corinth many opportunities for employment and for the accumulation of wealth through the taxation of any items that passed through its harbors.

Like many seaport cities Corinth was also the center of frequent immorality. Two temples in particular dominated the city: that of Apollo (the sun god) and that of Aphrodite (the goddess of love and beauty). The latter housed more than a thousand temple prostitutes. Corinth's reputation for immorality was so widespread that it became a byword for vice: the verb "to Corinthianize" was coined to mean "to engage in sexual immorality." It is easy to see why Corinth was an especially challenging place to start a church, and why it appeared to present more problems for Paul than any other church with which he was associated.

Paul came to Corinth from Athens during his second missionary journey. Acts 18:1-18 records his initial visit there. Aquila and Priscilla were among his first contacts in Corinth (it is not clear from Scripture whether they were led to Christ through Paul's efforts or were already Christians when Paul met them). A close bond developed since, like Paul, Aquila and Priscilla were tentmakers.

Paul stayed in Corinth for about eighteen months (Acts 18:11). Eventually his success became so great that he encountered serious opposition. Jewish leaders brought him before Gallio, an official of the province of Achaia (where Corinth was located), but Gallio refused to hear the case. Paul then traveled to Ephesus, where he made a brief stop, then proceeded on to Jerusalem. He returned to Ephesus on his third missionary journey and stayed there for three years (Acts 20:31). It was from Ephesus that he wrote 1 Corinthians, in approximately A.D. 56.

I. WINSOME GREETING (1 CORINTHIANS 1:2, 3)

A. TWO TERMS TO UNDERSTAND (v. 2)

2. To the church of God in Corinth, to those sanctified in Christ Jesus and called to be holy, together with all those everywhere who call on the name of our Lord Jesus Christ—their Lord and ours.

The word *church* is used to translate the Greek word *ekklesia*, which, in New Testament times, referred to a meeting or assembly. Literally the word means, "called-out ones." It described the gathering of the citizens of Greek cities to discuss affairs of government (something comparable to a town hall meeting). The term became an appropriate one to apply to those "called . . . out of darkness into [God's] wonderful light" (1 Peter 2:9).

The word *sanctified* means set apart for a *holy* purpose. In the Bible the word is used of buildings, objects, and people. It does not imply a higher level of Christian commitment. Similarly, the noun "saints," which comes from the same root as *sanctified* and *holy,* is frequently used in the New Testament as a reference simply to Christians, not to people who are known for their extraordinary commitment to God. All believers are *called to be holy*—or called to be "saints," as some versions translate it. Such devoted followers of *our Lord Jesus Christ* are needed *everywhere* to serve as his ambassadors.

B. TWO GIFTS TO RECEIVE (v. 3)

3. Grace and peace to you from God our Father and the Lord Jesus Christ.

Paul uses this same greeting of *grace* and *peace* in all of his letters, and it is always in the same order: *grace* then *peace*. This is important, for until one has experienced the grace of God, he cannot hope to experience the peace of God. Both are gifts from *God our Father*, not personal achievements. The use of the word *peace* is particularly significant in this letter to a congregation where there was so little peace.

II. WORD OF GRATITUDE (1 CORINTHIANS 1:4-9)

A. PAUL'S PRACTICE (v. 4)

4. I always thank God for you because of his grace given you in Christ Jesus.

While Paul was aware of the many problems troubling the Corinthians, he began his remarks to them with words of commendation, not criticism. With the exception of Galatians, all of Paul's letters in the New Testament begin with words of encouragement similar to *I always thank God for you.*

How often do we thank God for other believers? Do we thank him for believers who are imperfect, immature, and struggling (as Paul did here)? Do we thank him for the believers we have known who have taught us, inspired us, and encouraged us in our walk with Christ?

B. SPIRITUAL RICHES (vv. 5, 6)

5, 6. For in him you have been enriched in every way—in all your speaking and in all your knowledge—because our testimony about Christ was confirmed in you.

Some believe that the words *speaking* and *knowledge* refer to the related gifts of the Spirit—speaking in tongues and the "message of knowledge" (1 Corinthians 12:8, 10). Others think that they refer to spiritual blessings given to all the Corinthians. The significance of Paul's mentioning these blessings lay in the fact that the Greek world placed great emphasis on wisdom and on eloquence in speech—points to which Paul will refer shortly in this letter (1:19-30; 2:1-5). Here he affirms that the Corinthians, through God's grace, had nothing to be ashamed of in these important areas.

TWO KINDS OF RICHES

Lottery fever has taken over America. It is a disease for which there is neither a vaccine to prevent it nor an antibiotic to cure it. In recent years, most states in the nation have legalized gambling in lotteries, casinos, or riverboats.

In May of 1998 an Illinois couple won the Iowa "Power Ball" lottery. It was a record prize at the time. The couple chose to receive the lump sum of more than $104 million, rather than twenty-five annual payments totaling $196 million. They must have thought that 104 million "birds in the hand" were worth 196 million "birds in the bush"!

The odds against winning that lottery were eighty million to one. Think of it this way: suppose you laid a continuous row of quarters, touching each other, from Washington, D.C., to Tulsa, Oklahoma. Picking the right quarter would have won the Iowa "Power Ball" lottery!

After winning such a prize, many individuals say, "It's not going to change the way we live." Later, however, a high percentage of such winners find that their wealth has brought them far more grief than happiness. Not so with the riches of which Paul writes! The gracious gifts of God's Spirit bring us peace and satisfaction. One who has been enriched in this way knows what true wealth is. —C. R. B.

C. SPIRITUAL GIFTS (v. 7)

7. Therefore you do not lack any spiritual gift as you eagerly wait for our Lord Jesus Christ to be revealed.

The term *spiritual gift* includes both the miraculous gifts of the Spirit listed in 1 Corinthians 12:8-10 and also those gifts that are not miraculous (as in Romans

---

WHAT DO YOU THINK?

Paul characteristically thanked God for the believers to whom he wrote. What benefits do you think would result if we all developed the habit of thanking God for all our brothers and sisters in Christ?

HOW TO SAY IT

Achaia. Uh-KAY-uh.
Adriatic. Ay-dree-AT-ik.
Aegean. Ay-JEE-un.
Aphrodite. AF-ruh-DITE-ee.
Apollo. Uh-PAHL-o.
Apollos. Uh-PAHL-us.
Aquila. ACK-wih-luh.
Aramaic. Air-uh-MAY-ik.
Cephas. SEE-fus.
Chloe. KLO-ee.
Corinth. KOR-inth.
Corinthianize. Kor-IN-thee-un-ize.
Corinthians. Kor-IN-thee-unz.
Crispus. KRIS-pus.
ekklesia (Greek). ek-lay-SEE-uh.
Ephesus. EF-uh-sus.
Gaius. GAY-us.
Gallio. GAL-ee-o.
Pelopenessus. PELL-uh-puh-NEE-sus.
Priscilla. Prih-SIL-uh.
Stephanas. STEF-uh-nass.

12:6-8; Ephesians 4:11-13). The possession of such gifts was not to be an occasion of personal pride. When exercised by individuals, gifts are to be used to benefit the entire congregation and to prepare people for the coming *of our Lord Jesus Christ*. Clearly the Corinthians were not deficient in the possession of spiritual gifts; they were deficient in the attitude required to use those gifts as the Giver intended.

D. THE FAITHFUL GOD (vv. 8, 9)

8, 9. He will keep you strong to the end, so that you will be blameless on the day of our Lord Jesus Christ. God, who has called you into fellowship with his Son Jesus Christ our Lord, is faithful.

That you will be blameless is rendered in one translation in these words: "so that nobody can accuse you of anything." While we are called to good works (Ephesians 2:10), it is only God's grace and not our personal goodness that will allow us to plead "not guilty" when we stand in the judgment before God *on the day of our Lord Jesus Christ*. That day will be the time when final judgment is rendered (Matthew 25:31, 32).

III. CALL FOR AGREEMENT (1 CORINTHIANS 1:10-12)

A. PAUL'S PLEA (v. 10)

10. I appeal to you, brothers, in the name of our Lord Jesus Christ, that all of you agree with one another so that there may be no divisions among you and that you may be perfectly united in mind and thought.

Paul urged that the Corinthians *all . . . agree with one another*. This does not mean that he expected individuals to have no differing viewpoints. There was— and is—room for private opinions. However, Paul wanted believers to say that which would work for the common good of all believers (Romans 15:6; Ephesians 4:29). He was urging a unity of purpose in Christ.

Paul's challenge to be *perfectly united in mind and thought* may seem to present an unattainable standard. However, the word *perfectly* means "completely." As Christians we do not have to agree on everything, but our disagreements must not be allowed to divide the church. We should all seek to have the mind of Christ, which means "being like-minded, having the same love, being one in spirit and purpose" (Philippians 2:2).

B. CHLOE'S REPORT (v. 11)

11. My brothers, some from Chloe's household have informed me that there are quarrels among you.

We do not know who *Chloe* was, nor what members of her *household* went to see Paul in Ephesus with the news about the *quarrels* or dissension within the Corinthian church. They were a credible source, however, and Paul took their allegations seriously.

C. DIVIDED LOYALTIES (v. 12)

12. What I mean is this: One of you says, "I follow Paul"; another, "I follow Apollos"; another, "I follow Cephas"; still another, "I follow Christ."

People in the Corinthian church had become closely attached to different leaders. This was the primary cause of the friction that had developed within the church.

Apollos had come to Ephesus, apparently after Paul's first visit (Acts 18:24—19:1), and had then proceeded to Corinth. *Cephas* was the Aramaic name for the apostle Peter. The specific factors leading to the formation of these groups are not

WHAT DO YOU THINK?

Differing opinions and disagreements regarding minor matters are inevitable in any congregation. What principles can we follow to keep such opinions and disagreements from becoming divisive?

WHAT DO YOU THINK?

Word of the contentions in the Corinthian church had reached Paul in Ephesus. It seems that bad news regarding a congregation spreads rapidly. How much does that bother you? What is most troubling to you about that?

mentioned. Perhaps some included Jewish Christians (particularly Peter's group), while the others (such as the followers of Apollos) tended to draw Gentile Christians. Those claiming loyalty to Christ may have claimed to belong to Christ in some exclusive sense, or perhaps took some measure of pride in refusing to be labeled by the names of human leaders.

Jesus prayed that all who believed in him might be one, "that the world may believe that you have sent me" (John 17:21). He knew that the world would believe the message of a united church more readily than that of a divided church. The schisms in Corinth were working against the desires of the Head of the church.

A DIVIDED FAMILY

A couple who had filed for divorce three times went to see a Fresno, California, minister. They supposedly wanted to try once more to patch things up. The counseling session came to an abrupt end, however, when the couple started shooting at each other!

When the woman started to walk out of the counseling session, her husband pulled out a gun and shot her. Not mortally wounded, she reached into her purse, turned, and shot him in the shoulder. The couple went outside, where the wife fell to the ground and the husband fired several more shots at her. Both survived, and both were charged with attempted murder. It would be a gross understatement to say that this was not a happy family.

Just as God intends for marriage and family life to provide contentment and mutual support for all concerned, this is also what he intends for his spiritual family—the church. The church in Corinth, however, was not "one big, happy family." Instead of contentment there was quarreling over personal loyalties—loyalties that were a symptom of some deeper spiritual problems to which Paul would later call their attention.

This is typical of troubled families and troubled churches—usually their problems consist of several overlapping layers of disturbing issues. But God wants *all* families—both ours and his—to live in peace and unity.   —C. R. B.

IV. PERSUASIVE ARGUMENT (1 CORINTHIANS 1:13-17)

A. THREE IMPORTANT QUESTIONS (v. 13)

13. Is Christ divided? Was Paul crucified for you? Were you baptized into the name of Paul?

The sin of division is highlighted in Paul's question, *Is Christ divided?* Just as Christ had only one physical body, so the church is to be his one spiritual body (1 Corinthians 12:12; Ephesians 4:4). The obvious answer to Paul's question is *no*.

Next, Paul asked a question with an equally evident answer: *Was Paul crucified for you?* Clearly not—Christians must hold allegiance to only one Person, and that is the Person who gave his life for them at the cross. No human preacher or teacher, however brilliant or prominent, could ever do for us what Jesus did.

The third question raised by Paul was, *Were you baptized into the name of Paul?* This raises the issue of the One by whose name or authority baptism takes place. Baptism is an act commanded by Christ (Matthew 28:18, 19; Mark 16:16) and brings a person "into Christ" (Romans 6:3; Galatians 3:27). Baptism joins a person only to Christ, not to Peter, Paul, Apollos, or whoever does the baptizing.

These were three powerful arguments intended to persuade the Christians at Corinth to think seriously about the divisions they had created. They had become sidetracked from the doctrines that really mattered.

WHAT DO YOU THINK?

One of the factions in the Corinthian church was centered around Paul's name. But Paul frequently discouraged this in his writings. Christian leaders today must take care to prevent those they influence from forming a divisive faction within a church. How can they do this?

DAILY BIBLE READINGS

Monday, Feb. 28—Paul Greets the Corinthian Christians (1 Corinthians 1:1-9)

Tuesday, Feb. 29—Divisions Among Corinthian Christians (1 Corinthians 1:10-17)

Wednesday, Mar. 1—God's Power and Wisdom in Christ (1 Corinthians 1:18-25)

Thursday, Mar. 2—Christ Jesus, Source of Our Life (1 Corinthians 1:26-31)

Friday, Mar. 3—Paul Encourages Timothy (2 Timothy 1:3-14)

Saturday, Mar. 4—Serve Jesus Christ Faithfully (2 Timothy 2:1-13)

Sunday, Mar. 5—The Ways of God's Servant (2 Timothy 2:14-26)

B. PAUL'S RECOLLECTION (vv. 14-16)

14-16. I am thankful that I did not baptize any of you except Crispus and Gaius, so no one can say that you were baptized into my name. (Yes, I also baptized the household of Stephanas; beyond that, I don't remember if I baptized anyone else.)

The mention of baptism in the previous verse led to Paul's further consideration of this topic. He kept no records of people whom he had *baptized*; he depended on his memory. *Crispus* was the ruler of the synagogue at Corinth (Acts 18:8). *Gaius* may have been the same man mentioned in Romans 16:23 as Paul's host when he wrote the letter to the Romans (since Paul most likely wrote Romans from Corinth). *The household of Stephanas* is described as Paul's "first converts in Achaia" (1 Corinthians 16:15).

Paul was not diminishing the importance of baptism. He was simply expressing his gratitude that others had done most of the baptizing, in view of the divisions that had developed over individuals.

C. PAUL'S COMMISSION (v. 17)

17. For Christ did not send me to baptize, but to preach the gospel—not with words of human wisdom, lest the cross of Christ be emptied of its power.

Again, Paul's intent was not to disparage baptism; if anything, these words and those of verse 16 show how important baptism is. Baptism is meant to be the common experience of all Christians and, thus, a point of unity for them. To focus on who does the baptizing draws attention away from baptism's real significance. When one considers how much Paul had to say about baptism in his letters (Romans 6:3-6; 1 Corinthians 12:13; Galatians 3:27; Ephesians 4:5; Colossians 2:12; Titus 3:5), it is clear that he did not consider it an unimportant topic nor an insignificant act.

In most cases, it seems that Paul's primary concern in his evangelistic efforts was to *preach the gospel*, while others baptized the converts. If we consider Paul's poor health (apparently alluded to in 1 Corinthians 2:3; 2 Corinthians 12:7-10; Galatians 4:13), we can see why others would have done the physical work of baptizing whenever possible. In addition, knowing the way that some people can become attached to certain personalities, we can see the wisdom of someone other than Paul doing the actual baptizing. With the Corinthians, Paul could use the argument that he had baptized very few people to make his case for unity in Christ, not division based on loyalty to human teachers.

CONCLUSION

It is so easy to be sidetracked into issues that are tangents, thus losing sight of the "big picture." The heart of the gospel is that Christ died for us, was buried, and rose again (1 Corinthians 15:3, 4). Keeping focused on those fundamentals will give us a sense of perspective when we evaluate other issues.

However, with the church at Corinth, doctrine was not the primary issue that divided the Christians (it seldom is, even today). Often believers divide over power struggles or personality conflicts. Because we do not want to admit that these quarrels are really the consequence of our sinful attitudes, we sometimes hide behind an alleged controversy over what is a very minor issue. We do not want to admit that *we* are at fault, so we magnify the differences of opinion that exist and present ourselves as "defending the faith."

Yes, we must be true to the fundamental doctrines of our faith. But we must also keep in mind that those fundamentals include keeping "the unity of the Spirit through the bond of peace" (Ephesians 4:3) and practicing the "most excellent way" of love (1 Corinthians 12:31).

Discovery Learning

This page contains an alternate lesson plan emphasizing learning activities. Classes desiring such student involvement will find these suggestions helpful. The next page is a reproducible activity page to further enhance discovery learning.

LEARNING GOALS

After today's lesson, each adult will be able to:

1. Explain what was causing division within the church at Corinth.

2. Tell why division is so destructive to the church and its message.

3. Tell how a divided church can find oneness in Christ.

INTO THE LESSON

Before class, ask two or three pairs of class members, or other adults, to prepare brief (one minute or less) skits that show people being divisive about a church situation. You might suggest that a pair discuss the minister's sermon, a change in the worship service, or the choice of color for the new carpet in the fellowship hall. Tell them to exaggerate and add humor if they like, but to make the spirit of divisiveness obvious. (You may want to caution the pairs about avoiding any "sticky" issue in your church.)

Begin the class by playing a recording of the first verse of "They'll Know We Are Christians by Our Love" and then letting your first pair perform their skit. Without comment, play the chorus again and let the second pair present its skit.

Say, "Did any of these scenes sound or look familiar? Unfortunately, divisiveness does happen sometimes in our churches. This is not a new problem arising in our time. In the first century the apostle Paul learned about problems in the church in Corinth. This quarter we will be studying what he wrote to confront those crises."

INTO THE WORD

Begin with a lecture by yourself or a student on the background information for today's study. (See pages 237 and 238 in the commentary.) Half of your students are probably people who learn best by "seeing" the information, so illustrate the lecture. Use a map showing Corinth and the other cities mentioned in the background material. Display some teaching pictures of Paul preaching in Athens, working with Aquila and Priscilla, and teaching in Ephesus.

Have a volunteer read 1 Corinthians 1:1-9. Use the commentary to explain some of the key terms, such as *church of God, sanctified,* and *grace and peace.*

Read 1 Corinthians 1:10-17. Use the following questions to help students analyze these verses. (They are

also in the student book.) This can be done with the class as a whole, or divide into smaller groups for discussion and have the groups report their results after a short time.

• What is Paul's attitude toward the division and the Christians at Corinth? *It is serious, but the Corinthians are still brethren; he is glad he didn't baptize more people to add to the problem.*

• What seems to be the cause of the division? *People are claiming allegiance with one of the leaders to the point of forming parties/cliques.*

• Why might a Corinthian believer want to be associated with one of the men listed—Paul, Apollos, Cephas, Christ? *Status because of who taught and/or baptized them, devotion to the person.*

• Note the three questions with the obvious answer, "No." Why do you think Paul asks them? *To persuade the believers to think seriously about the things they were doing; to divert attention from human leaders to the Christ.*

INTO LIFE

Distribute copies of the reproducible page that follows. Reproduce the chart also on an overhead transparency or on a large poster.

Have the class work in groups of four or five people each to brainstorm answers for the chart. As a group completes its work, tell members to discuss why division is so destructive to a church and its mission to win people to Christ.

After a few minutes, ask each group to report two ideas for each category. Write their ideas on the chart on the transparency or poster for all to see.

Ask, "What destruction did your group describe as the result of division in a church?" Write down key phrases so that they become part of the total picture in front of the students.

Review the suggestions. Close the class session by asking the students to write specific actions they can take to promote unity within the local church. When most students have stopped writing, play a recording of the entire song, "They'll Know We Are Christians by Our Love." If you cannot find a recording, read the words of the song (all the verses) to the class.

Close the session with a prayer for unity, asking God for help to carry out the specific ideas that were suggested in class.

Saying and Doing

On the chart below cite some phrases and actions that can lead to division or unity in the church.

Phrases That Contribute to Division	Phrases That Encourage Unity
Actions That Lead to Division	**Actions That Encourage Unity**

As I think about my life, I can hear myself saying . . .

or

but I want to hear myself saying. . . .

As I think about my actions in the life of this congregation, I can see and feel myself doing things that could lead to division, like. . . .

I want to encourage unity, so I will. . . .

THE HOLY SPIRIT AS TEACHER

LESSON 2

WHY TEACH THIS LESSON?

Popular personalities are able to attract large followings today. Through their own charisma and persuasive speech, certain preachers, politicians, and others are able to convince many people to accept their ideas. Often the ideas have little merit, and their acceptance wanes as soon as the leader is no longer on the scene.

This is not what God intended for his church. Paul recognized it, and he went out of his way to present the gospel in its own power and not in his own eloquence. That power is the power of the Holy Spirit, who inspired the writing of the Scriptures (2 Timothy 3:16). This lesson should reinforce your students' confidence in the Bible as their infallible guide.

INTRODUCTION

A. PAUL'S ELOQUENCE

One need only read 1 Corinthians 13 to know that the apostle Paul was an eloquent man. It would be hard to find more expressive words in any of the world's literature! However, Paul did not want the Corinthians to be moved simply by eloquence. He wanted them to be moved by his message—"Jesus Christ and him crucified"—and not by the manner of its delivery.

B. LESSON BACKGROUND

As we noted in last week's Lesson Background (page 237), Paul came to Corinth from Athens during his second missionary journey. Some Bible students believe that Paul left Athens with a sense of having failed there. Pointing to 1 Corinthians 2:2—"I resolved to know nothing while I was with you except Jesus Christ and him crucified"—they suggest Paul thought he had tried too hard to appeal to the philosophical thinking of his audience in Athens, at the expense of diminishing the power of the gospel. This verse, they say, signals a change in Paul's method. Other students think such a conclusion reads too much into this verse. They believe Paul's words should be seen in contrast to the Corinthians' own overemphasis on human wisdom rather than in contrast to an earlier method tried by Paul.

Whatever we conclude about Paul's evaluation of his work at Athens, there is no mistaking the determination he expresses in today's lesson text. Every Christian would do well to cultivate this same passion for making Christ known to others.

I. PAUL'S TESTIMONY (1 CORINTHIANS 2:1-5)

A. THE METHOD (v. 1)

1. When I came to you, brothers, I did not come with eloquence or superior wisdom as I proclaimed to you the testimony about God.

Paul was a highly educated man. He could have used this training to draw attention to himself. But people might have gone away saying, "What a great man

DEVOTIONAL READING:

1 CORINTHIANS 3:1-9

BACKGROUND SCRIPTURE:

1 CORINTHIANS 2, 3

PRINTED TEXT:

1 CORINTHIANS 2:1-16

LESSON AIMS

After participating in this lesson, students should be able to:

1. Explain the Holy Spirit's role in revealing the gospel message.

2. Tell why it is important to base one's faith on the Spirit-given message of Christ and not on man-made wisdom.

3. Express faith in Christ, as revealed by the Spirit's wisdom.

KEY VERSE

We have not received the spirit of the world but the Spirit who is from God, that we may understand what God has freely given us. —1 Corinthians 2:12

Paul is!" Paul wanted them to go away saying, "What a great Savior Jesus is!" *Eloquence* and *superior wisdom* are powerful tools for those who seek a following for themselves. Paul, however, was seeking a following for the Lord. Thus he was determined to focus his hearers' attention on the *testimony about God*—that is, what God did, through Jesus, at the cross.

It would be wrong to use this passage to claim that excellence is not important in Christian work. We should never put forth haphazard or shoddy efforts in serving the Lord. However, no one should use his gifts in such a way as to call attention to the gifts and not to the gospel. Paul did not want to come to Corinth with overpowering oratory or impressive demonstrations of wisdom. Such methods may have drawn a crowd, but the results would not last.

B. THE MESSAGE (v. 2)

2. For I resolved to know nothing while I was with you except Jesus Christ and him crucified.

Paul had already emphasized the centrality of *Jesus Christ and him crucified* to the Christian message (1:17-24). He did so knowing that many would be offended by such preaching (1:18, 23). The Greeks at Corinth could not imagine a deity who died for men. They thought that only criminals died on crosses. But Paul refused to tailor his message to suit the sensitivities or prejudices of his audience. Too much was at stake!

C. THE MESSENGER (v. 3)

3. I came to you in weakness and fear, and with much trembling.

Many artists have painted self-portraits, including Michelangelo, van Gogh, and Rembrandt. It is estimated that Rembrandt painted between fifty and sixty self-portraits. Many of these are quite realistic and not very flattering. Paul's verbal self-portrait in today's lesson text is not a flattering one. He describes himself as a man who *came* to the Corinthians *in weakness and fear, and with much trembling*. Sometimes we tend to draw the apostle Paul larger than life. We picture him as a man who was always bold and confident, and never timid, hesitant, or afraid. This verse tells us exactly the opposite. Paul felt quite inadequate to proclaim properly so great a message as the gospel.

All Christians have felt this inadequacy, and it is right that they should. No one is really qualified to handle so sublime a message. All must say with Paul, "Who is equal to such a task?" (2 Corinthians 2:16).

D. THE MOTIVE (vv. 4, 5)

4. My message and my preaching were not with wise and persuasive words, but with a demonstration of the Spirit's power.

We have various words to describe speakers who use *wise and persuasive words* to appeal to people, including demagogue, rabble-rouser, and propagandist. These individuals usually employ deception or distortion rather than truth to get their message across. Paul believed that the truth of the gospel can stand on its own merits without being promoted by such devious means. To use such tactics smothers the *demonstration of the Spirit's power* that is central to the gospel (Romans 1:16; 1 Thessalonians 1:5).

5. . . . so that your faith might not rest on men's wisdom, but on God's power.

Here is the reason Paul refused to use "eloquence or superior wisdom" (v. 1) or "wise and persuasive words" (v. 4) in presenting the gospel to the Corinthians. He did not want their *faith* to *rest* in the method of presentation, which was based on *men's wisdom*, but in the content of the gospel, which magnifies *God's*

WHAT DO YOU THINK?

Contemporary thought puts much value in self-esteem and self-acceptance. In order to draw crowds, then, some churches and evangelists have begun to emphasize positive thinking and "feel-good" messages. This is in contrast to Paul's emphasis on "Jesus Christ and him crucified." What dangers do you see in the contemporary practice?

WHAT DO YOU THINK?

Paul's preaching was accompanied by "a demonstration of the Spirit's power." Of course, Paul spoke by the inspiration of the Spirit, and he worked miracles by the power of the Spirit. How can modern preaching and teaching exhibit "a demonstration of the Spirit's power"?

How do Ephesians 6:19, 20 and 2 Timothy 4:1-5 address this issue?

power to save lost sinners through his Son's death on the cross. This verse is a helpful warning to us to examine whatever methods we use in presenting the gospel, lest those methods draw attention away from the crucified Christ.

II. TRUE WISDOM (1 CORINTHIANS 2:6-13)

A. NOT OF THIS WORLD (v. 6)

6. We do, however, speak a message of wisdom among the mature, but not the wisdom of this age or of the rulers of this age, who are coming to nothing.

Paul had already noted the futility of *the wisdom of this age* in attempting to know God (1 Corinthians 1:18-21). Often the *rulers of this age* are governed by such wisdom, and find themselves frustrated that their policies and laws fail to accomplish their desired ends. Those who are *mature* in Christ should turn away from such false wisdom and embrace the higher, spiritual wisdom that comes from heaven (James 3:17).

THE CURE THAT REALLY WORKS

Emily Rosa was just eleven years old when she became the youngest person ever to author a scientific paper published in the *Journal of the American Medical Association*. Her article was the result of a fourth-grade science project. It was heralded as "brilliant" by a physician whose specialty is bringing medical fraud to light.

"Therapeutic touch healers" practice their "art" by moving their hands above a patient's body in an effort to realign the "energy fields" that illness has disturbed. They have claimed that their method is helpful in treating AIDS, cancer, and other illnesses.

Emily tested twenty-one such therapeutic touch healers and demonstrated that they could *not* reliably sense their patients' energy fields—a claim on which rests their alleged ability to heal.

Human wisdom often uses strange ideas and deceptive techniques to tell us how to cure our souls' diseases, unlike the revelation of God that we have in Scripture. The Bible gives us truth that does not depend on either human wisdom or human folly. It comes from the One who made us and knows us better than anyone. It will always serve as an accurate standard by which to measure any rival claims.   —C. R. B.

B. ORDAINED OF GOD (v. 7)

7. No, we speak of God's secret wisdom, a wisdom that has been hidden and that God destined for our glory before time began.

The Greek word translated here as *secret* is the source of our word *mystery*. Today we use the terms *secret* and *mystery* much differently from how they are used in the New Testament. Usually we are talking about something that is unknown or something deliberately kept hidden. Pagan religions in the Greek world were often referred to as "mystery religions" because they claimed to offer their adherents knowledge and insights available from no other source. New converts were initiated in secret ceremonies.

In the New Testament, however, these terms describe something that once was *hidden* from man's understanding but has now been revealed by God. *God's secret wisdom* (his plan to save the world through the crucified Christ) was something he *destined*, or determined, *before time began*. (See 1 Peter 1:18-20.) But until God chose to reveal it, it remained secret, a mystery. Though parts of this plan were outlined in the Old Testament, the full revelation of his plan did not occur until the New Testament era.

C. UNKNOWN BY RULERS (v. 8)

8. None of the rulers of this age understood it, for if they had, they would not have crucified the Lord of glory.

WHAT DO YOU THINK?

What are some specific contrasts you see between "the wisdom of this age" and the wisdom of God?

[Cite James 3:13-18 for some ideas.]

HOW TO SAY IT

Athens. ATH-unz.
Corinth. KOR-inth.
Corinthians. Kor-IN-thee-unz.
Isaiah. Eye-ZAY-uh.
Michelangelo. My-kull-AN-jell-o.
Rembrandt. REM-brant.
van Gogh. van GO.

Earthly rulers are called, as in verse 6, *rulers of this age*. The reference to those who *crucified the Lord of glory* indicates that they include Pilate, Herod, and the religious leaders in Jerusalem whose efforts resulted in Jesus' death. These men failed to recognize the wisdom that Jesus represented and that guided God's plan concerning him. This did not exonerate them, of course. (See Romans 3:5-8.) They had many opportunities to learn of that wisdom, but they rejected those opportunities.

Here, as elsewhere in the New Testament, the cross is linked with *glory* (John 12:23, 28; Galatians 6:14; Philippians 2:8, 9; Revelation 5:12). It is remarkable that the cross, which was a symbol of shame and humiliation, should in Christian thought be turned into an emblem of glory. Today we do not think it at all strange to sing, "In the Cross of Christ I Glory." However, we should never forget that the way of the cross can still be marked by occasions of humiliation and persecution for the followers of Jesus.

D. BEYOND MAN'S THINKING (v. 9)

9. However, as it is written: "No eye has seen, no ear has heard, no mind has conceived what God has prepared for those who love him"—

Isaiah 64:4, from which this quotation is taken, does not include the line *no mind has conceived*. Apparently Paul was paraphrasing this text, yet providing, under the inspiration of the Holy Spirit, a correct understanding of its meaning.

Given the context, *what God has prepared* comprises the mystery of the gospel. It is not something invented by natural means, something the *eye* could observe or the *ear* could hear. It was not *conceived* in the *mind* of man, but was, instead, revealed by God's Spirit (v. 10).

Christians through the years have also seen this promise as a reference to future blessings and to Heaven in particular. That application is justified—though with some limitation. Just as no one in Isaiah's day could have imagined the grandeur of the Christian religion, so no one in our day can imagine the grandeur of Heaven. God has revealed something of that glory to us, but the images are sketchy and the details few. We know it will be a great and marvelous experience to be with the Lord in Heaven, but we cannot imagine just how awesome it will be.

E. TAUGHT BY GOD'S SPIRIT (vv. 10-13)

10, 11. . . . but God has revealed it to us by his Spirit. The Spirit searches all things, even the deep things of God. For who among men knows the thoughts of a man except the man's spirit within him? In the same way no one knows the thoughts of God except the Spirit of God.

The word *searches* does not mean that the *Spirit* has difficulty finding out *the deep things of God*. It describes his access, as part of what we often call the Trinity (2 Corinthians 13:14), to these deep truths. The Spirit comprehends these truths and is thus able to reveal them to us.

When Paul says that God *has revealed* these matters to us, he is linking the preceding verse about eye and ear and heart to the truths we now know. No man could have discovered these truths by his own effort or through the use of the five senses. The initiative had to come from God. If he had not revealed these truths, they would have remained unknown.

In verse 11 Paul uses the illustration of the human *spirit* to give us insight into the mind of God. No other human can know what a person is thinking; that person must reveal the content of his thoughts. In the same way, only the *Spirit of God* has insight into *the thoughts of God*. They cannot be known by human beings except through revelation. This is the reason the Holy Spirit was given to the apostles (John 14:26; 16:13).

WHAT DO YOU THINK?

The lesson writer says the gospel message could never have been invented by human creativity. How would you answer a skeptic who contended that it was?

12. We have not received the spirit of the world but the Spirit who is from God, that we may understand what God has freely given us.

Paul's use of the word *we* suggests he is talking about the apostles, not about Christians in general. (Earlier he uses "you" and "your" when speaking of all believers; see vv. 1-5.) The apostles certainly received a measure of the Spirit that far exceeds that of any other human being, then or now. Paul observed to the Corinthians that he could speak in tongues "more than all of you" (1 Corinthians 14:18). The apostles' ability to impart gifts by the laying on of hands was so extraordinary that Simon the sorcerer tried in vain to purchase it (Acts 8:14-19).

In the phrase *the spirit of the world*, the *world* may refer to those influences in our surroundings that lure us from God. Perhaps Paul is thinking of one of the "spirits" of whom Christians are warned in 1 John 4:1-3. Whatever the phrase may mean, it is undoubtedly linked to "the wisdom of this age" mentioned in verse 6. The greater emphasis should be on the word *world*. The Spirit who inspired Paul was not of the world, but *from God*.

13. This is what we speak, not in words taught us by human wisdom but in words taught by the Spirit, expressing spiritual truths in spiritual words.

Paul insisted that the content of his message was not to be found in *human wisdom*, just as he contended in the previous verse that the power behind the message was not of this world. Paul's message was not the product of human creativity or skill. It consisted of words from God himself—*taught by the Spirit*.

The only way we humans can understand anything is by means of words, so it was necessary that the divine revelation be given to Paul in words and that those words be taught by the Holy Spirit. This is in keeping with Jesus' promise of what the Spirit would do for the apostles (John 14:26; 16:13). To know this should bolster our confidence in the words of Scripture. While the personalities of the biblical writers and their purposes in writing come through in their choice of words, we can affirm without hesitation that God governed their words so that they were prevented from error.

The verse ends with a difficult phrase to interpret: *expressing spiritual truths in spiritual words*. The Greek text simply reads "comparing spiritual with spiritual," so it is hard to know what nouns should be added to accompany each adjective. In addition, the verb rendered "expressing" can also mean "interpret," "combine," "compare," or "explain." The translation found in our text here goes well with the thought of the previous verse. Others suggest reading the phrase, "interpreting spiritual truths to spiritual men," which would link this verse with the content of the next one.

III. RECEIVING WISDOM (1 CORINTHIANS 2:14-16)

A. THE NATURAL MAN (v. 14)

14. The man without the Spirit does not accept the things that come from the Spirit of God, for they are foolishness to him, and he cannot understand them, because they are spiritually discerned.

Paul said "we" (that is, the inspired apostles) did receive the message *from the Spirit of God*. The *man without the Spirit*, who *does not accept the things that come from the Spirit of God*, must be seen, then, in contrast to the apostles. Such a one is limited to physical means of receiving information, such as the eyes and ears (v. 9). These are inadequate to receive the truths of God, which are *spiritually discerned*.

B. THE SPIRITUAL MAN (vv. 15, 16)

15. The spiritual man makes judgments about all things, but he himself is not subject to any man's judgment.

The visual for today's lesson illustrates the source of Paul's teaching. Post it as you begin to discuss verse 12 of the lesson text.

WHAT DO YOU THINK?

Paul said, "The man without the Spirit does not accept the things that come from the Spirit of God" (1 Corinthians 2:14). Yet Jesus promised that the Holy Spirit would "convict the world of guilt in regard to sin and righteousness and judgment" (John 16:8). How would you resolve this apparent contradiction?

PRAYER

Lord, forgive us when we trust in human personalities and the power of human eloquence, and do not trust wholly in Jesus Christ. We pray in his name. Amen.

THOUGHT TO REMEMBER

Without God's revelation of truth to us in the Scriptures, we are left alone to grope in spiritual darkness.

The spiritual man is one who is inspired by the Spirit. No one can pass judgment on the apostles' message; it comes from the Holy Spirit. The inspired messenger was able to make *judgments* about or discern (it is the same Greek word here as in verse 14) *all things* by the standard of truth taught by the Spirit.

As verse 9 has a dual application, we also see a secondary application in verses 14 and 15. There is a noticeable difference between the Christian, especially a mature Christian, and one who has no interest in spiritual matters. The indwelling Spirit in the Christian's life makes a difference! One who has ordered his or her life according to "the things that come from the Spirit of God" (v. 14) is equipped with the spiritual wisdom needed to be discerning in life. Such wisdom comes from God's Word, which "is useful for teaching, rebuking, correcting and training in righteousness" (2 Timothy 3:16). The natural man, or the unbeliever, considers the things of God "foolishness" (v. 14); he cannot discern or understand the thinking of one who is spiritual. Things that are obvious to believers mystify the unsaved.

TWO KINDS OF PEOPLE

As the saying goes, "There are two kinds of people in the world." In this case, I'm thinking of those who find mathematics fascinating, as opposed to the rest of us who have been out of school for a few years and have forgotten much of what we once knew about math. We may still be able to use $\pi r2$, but quick—do you recall what a prime number is? (Answer: it is a number divisible only by itself and 1.)

A fascination with prime numbers was the driving force guiding Roland Clarkson, a nineteen-year-old college student who, two years ago, found the largest prime number yet discovered. It is 909,526 digits long, would fill a four-hundred-page book, would stretch for more than a mile if written out in one line, and would take 277 hours to say! Roland's "natural curiosity about math," as he describes it, led him to search for the number on a computer. He ran his computer part-time for forty-six days before coming up with the record-setting prime number.

There is another distinction, however, that is far more important than mathematicians and non-mathematicians. That is the distinction between natural and spiritual. The natural person lives life on the surface, content with the material things of this present world. The spiritual person has a deep interest in the real values in life—the things that *really* make a difference.

Which kind of person are you?
—C. R. B.

16. *"For who has known the mind of the Lord that he may instruct him?" But we have the mind of Christ.*

Here Paul takes his thought from Isaiah 40:13. No one can know *the mind of the Lord* unless he chooses to reveal his thinking to us. No one can *instruct* God, but we can (and must) be instructed by him. Because God has revealed the truth to us in Scripture, we are able to know *the mind of Christ* and how he wants us to live.

CONCLUSION

Paul wanted the Corinthian Christians to keep their focus on Jesus—not on him, not on clever words, not on eloquent phrases, but on the Lord Jesus Christ. He knew that only through the crucified Lord could one know "the power of God and the wisdom of God" (1 Corinthians 1:24).

Certainly spreading the good news deserves the use of our best gifts and abilities, but we must never forget that the power is always in the gospel itself. That gospel came from God and not from human wisdom. It carries within it "the power of God for the salvation of everyone who believes" (Romans 1:16). It has changed lives throughout the years, and it will continue to do so until Jesus comes.

Discovery Learning

This page contains an alternate lesson plan emphasizing learning activities. Classes desiring such student involvement will find these suggestions helpful. The next page is a reproducible activity page to further enhance discovery learning.

LEARNING GOALS

After today's lesson each adult will be able to:

1. Explain the Holy Spirit's role in revealing the gospel message.

2. Tell why it is important to base one's faith on the Spirit-given message of Christ and not on man-made wisdom.

3. Express faith in Christ, as revealed by the Spirit's wisdom.

INTO THE LESSON

Before class, prepare a collection of objects that would be recognized by people familiar with their subject or category, but not easily recognized by those who are not. For example, when people are asked what kind of car a person was driving, some people can name the model, make, and year. Another person might say, "Well, it was white." From dealers' showrooms you could collect pictures of cars that are very similar in appearance and blot out the identifying names.

To begin class, show the pictures—perhaps posted on a wall where people can look at them as they arrive. Ask class members to identify the make and model of each car. After they have had some fun with this, say, "Those of you who are familiar with cars probably had no trouble distinguishing one car from another. But some of you did have trouble because you don't know enough about the subject. In today's lesson, we will learn from Paul that we need to be able to distinguish God's wisdom from man-made wisdom."

INTO THE WORD

Today's lesson is vital for Christians. Man's "wisdom" presents a message or value structure quite different from the timeless principles given through the Spirit in God's Word. In fact, it varies from culture to culture and from generation to generation. Such an important lesson can best be learned through a lecture of important content, followed by lots of time to apply it to life.

Read 1 Corinthians 2:1-16 to the class, clarifying the content with the material in the commentary as you read. Make an overhead transparency of the main points of the lesson outline and reveal each point as you go.

When you talk about verse 7, hold up a mystery novel. "When we read a good mystery, we consider many answers to the question, 'Who did it?' But we don't know the *real* answer until the author tells us. In the same way, we can make up all the answers we want to the mysteries of life, but we don't know the real answers until the Author of life tells us. And we find those answers in his Word—the Bible."

INTO LIFE

When talking about basing one's faith on the Spirit-given message rather than man-made wisdom, there are some issues on which many Christians are agreed. For example, man-made wisdom asserts that a person is born with his/her sexual orientation, so practicing one's homosexuality is not sin. The first chapter of Romans makes it clear, however, that God's timeless principle says that such practice is sin. (See vv. 26, 27.)

Distribute copies of the reproducible page that follows and ask your students to form groups of four or five. Have each group focus on one area of life (e.g., the workplace, neighborhood, family, etc.) and contrast what the world's wisdom says with what God's wisdom says. (Some suggested contrasts follow.)

Workplace: *World says, "Get ahead at any cost." "Watch out for number one." "The end justifies the means." God's Word says, "Do to others as you would have them do to you." "You shall not steal." "You shall not give false testimony." "Serve wholeheartedly, as if you were serving the Lord. . . . Masters, treat your slaves in the same way."*

Neighborhood: *World says, "Nice guys finish last." "I have my rights." "You can take only so much." God's Word says, "Do to others as you would have them do unto you." "If someone strikes you on one cheek, turn to him the other also." "Love your neighbor." "Love your enemies." "You shall not covet your neighbor's. . . ." "If you forgive men when they sin against you. . . ."*

Family: *World says, "Quantity of time doesn't matter as long as it is 'quality' time." "One parent is as effective as two." "Who needs marriage? True love is more important than a piece of paper." "You need to meet my needs." God says, "Do not commit adultery." "Do not store up treasures on earth." "Do not worry about your life." "Honor your father and your mother." "Do everything without complaining."*

Remind students that Christians have the help of the Holy Spirit to do what is difficult. Guide them to make specific plans of how to let the Holy Spirit work in their lives and how they can help one another to live such lives. Let students pray in their small groups.

What Kind of Wisdom?

"This is what we speak, not in words taught us by human wisdom but in words taught by the Spirit, expressing spiritual truths in spiritual words" (1 Corinthians 2:13). Man's wisdom presents a value structure and lifestyle that are different from those that follow the timeless principles given through the Spirit in the Bible. Even if a Christian has made a decision to live a lifestyle that follows God's principles, it can be difficult. The Christian must constantly evaluate life's challenges and questions against the Bible or risk following the world's wisdom—perhaps without even realizing it! Use the exercise below to practice that kind of evaluation.

Write in the conversational balloons phrases or sentences that reflect the values and attitudes of worldly people today. Then write in the book outline a paraphrase of some timeless principle from God's Spirit given in his Word. For example, if you were thinking about the workplace, you might write in the conversational balloon, "They won't miss one little box of paper clips." In the Bible you might write, "Thieves . . . will not inherit the kingdom of God."

THE CHURCH AND ITS LEADERS

LESSON 3

WHY TEACH THIS LESSON?

Your classroom is probably full of leaders! Parents are entrusted with leadership of those who will comprise the next generation of adults. Probably there are some teachers in your classroom, school teachers as well as those who teach in a variety of settings in the church. Perhaps there are elders and deacons—perhaps even some ministry staff personnel if your church is a large one. Are there civic leaders in your class? How about scout leaders? Is anyone in a management position at his or her place of work?

Even those students who wear no titles of leadership are probably leaders in some way. So even though this lesson addresses the church's leaders directly, every student should be challenged to use his or her leadership influence for the Lord. Even secular positions can be used to demonstrate godly character and a Christian witness. You will want to remind your students of that fact today.

INTRODUCTION

A. LEADING AND SERVING

A minister once related that he was asked to come to a certain church and speak on leadership. He agreed; however, when he stood to speak, he surprised the congregation by announcing that his topic would be, not leadership, but servanthood.

There are many ways to serve in the Lord's church. Being a leader should be considered one of them. In Romans 12:8 Paul describes leadership as a gift given by God. Just as some have the gift of preaching and some the gift of encouragement, some have the gift of leadership. Those who have been given this gift should not see it as an occasion of pride nor as an opportunity to exercise power, but as a calling to glorify God and minister to others. Every leader is a servant. Leadership is one way of serving the Lord!

It is natural that we are drawn to some personalities more than others. That is unavoidable. We will feel a kinship with some leaders that we will not sense with other leaders. However, we should never permit this to lead to conflict. We should never assume that the person we like is always right nor that the person we don't like is always wrong. The head must rule the heart here.

B. LESSON BACKGROUND

Paul established the church at Corinth in approximately A.D. 52. After he left there, Apollos, who had been preaching in Ephesus, then traveled to Corinth (Acts 18:24—19:1). Apollos was a native of Alexandria (in Egypt), which was one of the most renowned centers of learning in the world at that time. He was undoubtedly highly educated. He possessed a thorough knowledge of the Scriptures and was very effective as an evangelist, being "a learned man" (Acts 18:24-28).

It was only natural that people would be drawn to such a highly educated and articulate speaker as Apollos. In Corinth, as we noted in lesson 1, the church had

DEVOTIONAL READING:

1 PETER 5:1-11

BACKGROUND SCRIPTURE:

1 CORINTHIANS 4:1-13

PRINTED TEXT:

1 CORINTHIANS 4:1-13

LESSON AIMS

After this lesson each student will be able to:

1. Summarize how Paul viewed his apostolic ministry according to this text.

2. Tell why the concept of receiving a "trust" is appropriate for any leader in the church.

3. Speak or write a message of appreciation and encouragement to the leaders of his or her church.

KEY VERSE

So then, men ought to regard us as servants of Christ and as those entrusted with the secret things of God.

—1 Corinthians 4:1

divided into factions, one of which declared its allegiance to Apollos and another to Paul (1 Corinthians 1:12). Perhaps the original converts in Corinth were those who were attached to Paul, while newer converts were drawn to Apollos. (Often people feel a special bond to the person who led them to Christ.)

Of course, Paul and Apollos themselves could not have cared less about who "liked" either of them better than the other. It had become clear, however, that such loyalties were producing conflict that was having a devastating effect on the Corinthian church. Some were taking "pride in one man over against another" (1 Corinthians 4:6). Paul had already told the church that individuals such as he and Apollos were simply "God's fellow workers" (3:9) and that the Corinthians should cease "boasting about men" (v. 21). In today's text Paul elaborates on this point.

I. SERVANTS AND STEWARDS (1 CORINTHIANS 4:1, 2)

A. WE ARE SERVANTS (v. 1a)

1a. So then, men ought to regard us as servants of Christ.

When Paul says *us*, he means to include primarily himself, Peter (Cephas), and Apollos, since they are mentioned at the end of the previous chapter (3:22) and were the leaders around whom the various groups in Corinth had formed (1:12). However, Paul's words convey an important message to all leaders in the church.

The literal meaning of the Greek word translated *servants* is "under-rowers." In New Testament times, this word was used to describe the slaves who pulled the oars and moved a ship forward. These under-rowers were confined to the dark, smelly hold of the ship. Such a picture of humble, unnoticed service provided the image Paul wanted us to have of himself and of all leaders in Christ's church.

B. WE ARE STEWARDS (v. 1b)

1b. . . . and as those entrusted with the secret things of God.

The words *secret things* was discussed in last week's lesson (see the comments under 1 Corinthians 2:7). There it was noted that God has revealed, not hidden, his secrets. Christians have been *entrusted* with, or made stewards of, this revealed truth. As such, we are charged with the proper handling of it.

C. WE MUST BE FAITHFUL (v. 2)

2. Now it is required that those who have been given a trust must prove faithful.

There is a necessary quality *required* of *those who have been given a trust*: they *must prove faithful*. At the bank you will find a person known as a trust officer. That individual is entrusted with the care and investment of other people's money. Thus he must be someone of dependable character, or *trust*worthy.

The same qualification must be found in those who are entrusted with God's eternal truth. They must never forget that they are Christians only because someone else took his or her calling as a steward seriously.

II. HUMAN AND DIVINE JUDGMENT (1 CORINTHIANS 4:3-5)

A. OTHERS' VIEWPOINT (v. 3)

3. I care very little if I am judged by you or by any human court; indeed, I do not even judge myself.

When Paul says *I care very little*, he is referring to the evaluation some in Corinth had of his work. Apparently, they had *judged* Paul and attempted to disparage his work and his ministry. Perhaps they claimed that Apollos was a better preacher than Paul, or that Peter—as one of the original twelve apostles—was more important than Paul. Paul did not want the Corinthians to put any stock in such futile comparisons.

So then, men ought to regard us as servants of Christ and as those entrusted with the secret things of God.

1 Corinthians 4:1 +?

This verse does not suggest that the judgment of others is of no significance. Certainly it is important what others think of us as Christians. We must set a good example. It is no small thing when what we are or what we do causes people to turn a deaf ear to the gospel. It is a small matter if someone thinks another is a more capable worker than we are.

Paul's words *I do not even judge myself* mean that he is not wasting time comparing his effectiveness or his popularity with others. As he earlier stated, "What, after all, is Apollos? And what is Paul? Only servants, through whom you came to believe—as the Lord has assigned to each his task" (3:5).

B. GOD'S PERSPECTIVE (vv. 4, 5)

4. My conscience is clear, but that does not make me innocent. It is the Lord who judges me.

Paul states that his *conscience is clear*, yet he realizes that such self-evaluation *does not make* him *innocent*. In his own mind he believed that he had been a faithful steward at Corinth; however, *the Lord* alone is the One capable of judging such matters.

5. Therefore judge nothing before the appointed time; wait till the Lord comes. He will bring to light what is hidden in darkness and will expose the motives of men's hearts. At that time each will receive his praise from God.

Paul urged the Corinthians not to *judge* anything prematurely—that is, *before the appointed time* of final judgment comes. Apparently some had already made a decision about Paul's faithfulness as a servant of Christ. They had rendered a verdict before the trial was over! Paul told them that they must not do this. All of us must wait for the time appointed for judgment, which will take place when *the Lord* returns.

Paul adds some details regarding the final judgment. On that day the Lord *will bring to light what is hidden in darkness*. Only God knows all the facts. He will bring into the open both our secret sins and our secret virtues. In addition, he knows *the motives of men's hearts*. He will reveal not only what we did, but why we did it. It is his *praise*, or approval, that Paul seeks.

THE POWER OF PERCEPTION

If you were told you had to live on Iceland or Greenland—and you knew nothing about the two islands except their names—which would you choose? In spite of its name, Iceland is famous for its volcanoes, and its winters are no more harsh than those of the New England coast.

Greenland, on the other hand, is covered by a permanent ice cap. In A.D. 984 the Norse explorer, Eric the Red, was trying to entice settlers to leave the relative warmth of Iceland and Scandinavia and move to a land he had discovered, which is the largest island on the planet. Both Scandinavia and Iceland benefit from the warm Gulf Stream current, so Eric had to exercise some creative thinking if his goal of populating his new land was to be realized. He was equal to the task: he called the island "Greenland." (Modern advertising executives should think of Eric as their patron saint!)

We are sometimes greatly misled by our perception of what is valuable, and advertisers play on our weakness. They keep telling us that if we had a better house or a nicer car or finer clothes, others would have a better image of us.

Paul tells us otherwise: the person who truly pleases God is the one who willingly seeks to be a servant—a faithful, trustworthy steward of what his Master has entrusted to him. The world may consider this a waste of time and effort; however, we serve a cause "not of this world."

Which perception are we more concerned about?   —C. R. B.

HOW TO SAY IT

Alexandria. Al-ex-AN-dree-uh.
Apollos. Uh-PAHL-us.
Cephas. SEE-fus.
Corinth. KOR-inth.
Corinthians. Kor-IN-thee-unz.
Ephesus. EF-uh-sus.

III. PAUL AND APOLLOS (1 CORINTHIANS 4:6, 7)

A. CONCRETE EXAMPLES (v. 6)

6. Now, brothers, I have applied these things to myself and Apollos for your benefit, so that you may learn from us the meaning of the saying, "Do not go beyond what is written." Then you will not take pride in one man over against another.

Paul now *applied* the principles he had just stated to himself *and Apollos*. The Corinthians' loyalties were not to be divided, pitting *one man over against another*, but united in following *what is written*—most likely a reference to Scripture. If all submit to the authority of Scripture, then it is far more likely that individuals will *not take pride* in their efforts to set one teacher above another.

B. SOBERING QUESTIONS (v. 7)

7. For who makes you different from anyone else? What do you have that you did not receive? And if you did receive it, why do you boast as though you did not?

The fact that members of God's family are *different from* one another in gifts and abilities should not become a source of contention (as it had in Corinth). Instead, all gifts and abilities should be used to further the work of the kingdom.

One of the most humbling questions we should ask ourselves is, *What do you have that you did not receive?* We are simply stewards—nothing more—and there is no reason for us to *boast* about our achievements.

IV. PRIDE AND HUMILITY (1 CORINTHIANS 4:8-11)

A. FROM SARCASM TO TENDERNESS (v. 8)

8. Already you have all you want! Already you have become rich! You have become kings—and that without us! How I wish that you really had become kings so that we might be kings with you!

Occasionally we find touches of irony and sarcasm in the Bible. It is obvious that the meaning of the speaker's words is just the opposite of what he says. We do the same today, as when we spill something and say, "Oh, that was smart!" Biblical examples can be found in 1 Kings 18:27 and Amos 4:4.

Here, when Paul describes the Corinthians as *rich* and as those who *have become kings*, his language reflects the conceit that had come to characterize the Corinthians' attitude and that had resulted in their divisions. In their own estimation, they had attained spiritual maturity. But in reality, they had a long way to go!

Paul then moved quickly from this strong tone of irony to more tender words that reflected his sincere concern for the Corinthians. He loved them and truly wished that their evaluation of themselves were accurate—that they *really had become kings* as they desired. But did they really understand what it meant to thus reign with Christ? Paul proceeded to elaborate on this point.

B. THE APOSTLES' SHAME (v. 9)

9. For it seems to me that God has put us apostles on display at the end of the procession, like men condemned to die in the arena. We have been made a spectacle to the whole universe, to angels as well as to men.

While we often think of the apostolic office as an exalted one, Paul described it in very different terms. Did the Corinthians want to "reign" as the apostles did? Then here is Paul's personal experience of "reigning": being *condemned to die* and being *made a spectacle*. The Greek word rendered *spectacle* here is the word from which we get our English word "theater." The picture behind this word was a familiar one in Paul's world. At the end of the gladiatorial contests, those gladiators who were doomed to die were stripped of their armor, led before the crowd, and

---

WHAT DO YOU THINK?

Why is it important that we acknowledge frequently that our talents and gifts have been given to us by God?

DAILY BIBLE READINGS

Monday, Mar. 13—Apollos and Paul, Servants of Christ (1 Corinthians 4:1-7)

Tuesday, Mar. 14—The Ministry of the Apostles (1 Corinthians 4:8-13)

Wednesday, Mar. 15—Paul's Fatherly Love for the Corinthians (1 Corinthians 4:14-21)

Thursday, Mar. 16—Clothe Yourselves With Humility (1 Peter 5:1-5)

Friday, Mar. 17—Faithful Leaders Will Encounter Suffering (1 Peter 5:6-11)

Saturday, Mar. 18—Do Not Judge One Another (Romans 14:1-12)

Sunday, Mar. 19—Live in Harmony With One Another (Romans 15:1-6)

then taken to the coliseum to be killed by wild animals. In the same way, the apostles suffered shame, suffering, and even death for Christ (Acts 12:1, 2; 2 Corinthians 1:9; 4:11).

The Corinthians' understanding of serving Christ seems similar to that of James and John. We are told how they approached Jesus about "reigning" with him by being given the chief seats in his kingdom. Jesus responded by challenging them to drink the cup he was going to drink and be baptized with the baptism he would experience (Mark 10:35-40). They would indeed reign with Christ, but only on his terms, not theirs. The Corinthians needed to learn this same lesson.

C. A TOUCHING COMPARISON (v. 10)

10. We are fools for Christ, but you are so wise in Christ! We are weak, but you are strong! You are honored, we are dishonored!

Here Paul continues his ironic tone. People in the world saw individuals such as Paul as *fools* because they chose to forsake all and follow Jesus. In contrast, many at Corinth thought themselves *wise, strong,* and *honored.* But in their perceived wisdom, strength, and honor, had they lost sight of what it meant to follow Jesus? The contrast is both striking and touching. It was meant, not to shame the Corinthians, but to warn them (v. 14). It is easy to see how deeply Paul loved these people and how concerned he was for their spiritual welfare.

D. SUFFERING FOR CHRIST'S SAKE (v. 11)

11. To this very hour we go hungry and thirsty, we are in rags, we are brutally treated, we are homeless.

We do not know of any specific occasions when Paul experienced being *hungry* and *thirsty* or was *in rags.* He later wrote to the Philippians that he had known such need and appreciated their giving to supply that need (Philippians 4:10-13).

Acts 14:19 and 16:22-24 record occasions Paul may have been thinking of when he writes that he had been *brutally treated.* (The instances in Acts 21:30-32 and 23:2 took place after Paul wrote the Corinthians.) A partial summary of Paul's sufferings for Christ is found in 2 Corinthians 11:23-28. Like Abraham, who lived "like a stranger in a foreign country" (Hebrews 11:9), and Jesus, who had no place to lay his head (Matthew 8:20), Paul considered himself *homeless.* His true citizenship was in Heaven (Philippians 3:20).

V. WORKING AND ENDURING (1 CORINTHIANS 4:12, 13)

A. TOILING ON (v. 12a)

12a. We work hard with our own hands.

Paul supported himself throughout most of his ministry (Acts 20:34), though he did on some occasions receive outside support (Philippians 4:14-18). Generally he preferred to be self-supporting as an example of how Christians ought to conduct themselves (1 Corinthians 9:15; 1 Thessalonians 2:9; 2 Thessalonians 3:8, 9). But he vigorously defended his right and the rights of fellow Christian workers to be supported by other believers (1 Corinthians 9:1-14).

B. FACING OPPOSITION (vv. 12b, 13)

12b, 13a. When we are cursed, we bless; when we are persecuted, we endure it; when we are slandered, we answer kindly.

Paul's words about being *cursed* should call our attention to Jesus' teaching in the Sermon on the Mount. He taught his followers to respond to verbal abuse and slander by rejoicing, blessing the persecutors, and praying for them

WHAT DO YOU THINK?

How can we express our appreciation to workers in the church who labor without thought of earthly rewards?

(Matthew 5:10-12, 44; cf. Luke 6:28). Peter reminds us that Jesus himself responded in this way to those who mistreated him (1 Peter 2:23).

To speak of being *persecuted* reminds us of the teaching in 1 Peter 2:19-21 and 4:12-16 that Christians who suffer should bear their suffering patiently. Even when *slandered* they should *answer kindly* and thus follow the example of Jesus.

If the Corinthians really want to "become kings" in Christ (v. 8) and become wise, strong, and honored (v. 10), here is the path they must take. What an example we have both in Jesus and in Paul!

13b. Up to this moment we have become the scum of the earth, the refuse of the world.

We occasionally refer to someone who is particularly despicable as *the scum of the earth*. Paul notes that this is the way some have treated him and his fellow apostles.

A word of similar meaning is the term *refuse*. The Greek word behind this term was used in New Testament times to describe condemned criminals who were viewed by society with particular scorn. In the eyes of the world, this is how Paul and the apostles were viewed. Today, in many parts of the world, Christians are looked at with an equal degree of contempt. However, it is not the world's approval that we seek, for we are "dead to the world" (Galatians 6:14). Only one view matters, and that is Christ's.

TREATED LIKE DIRT

Throughout most of modern history, great art has usually represented the world fairly accurately (that is, as most observers saw it). However, the twentieth century witnessed a revolution in artistic expression. Some very bizarre forms of "art" have become commonplace.

In New York City a few years ago, "conceptual artist" Walter DeMaria created a work that gave new meaning to the term, the "field" of art. DeMaria's work was entitled "Earth Room." That's just what it was: a room containing 3,600 square feet of dirt, two feet deep. Bill Dilworth, curator of the gallery where DeMaria's work was displayed, claimed that the work "has more of an emotional range than the 'Mona Lisa' or the Sistine Chapel." (Dilworth seems to have missed something there.)

It's a strange world where dirt is treated as if it were art, and art is treated as if it were dirt! But that's really not too different from Paul's description of how he and the other apostles were viewed: as "the scum of the earth, the refuse of the world" (1 Corinthians 4:13). For all of the mistreatment that Paul suffered and all of the effort that he expended, for all of the good that he did and the blessings he brought to others, many people still "treated him like dirt." But he had a clearer vision of reality than his enemies did. He wasn't fooled by their idle talk, nor did he try to see value in their delusions. —C. R. B.

CONCLUSION

The verse that follows today's printed text reveals Paul's purpose in writing to the Corinthians as he has. He tells them, "I am not writing this to shame you, but to warn you, as my dear children" (1 Corinthians 4:14). He does not write to get even with those who have mistreated him. He writes to warn them that they must not be too fascinated with receiving earthly glory for their spiritual service.

If we receive praise and appreciation for our service to the Lord, that is fine. We should be grateful for such appreciation, but we should not work for it. Our primary calling is to work for Jesus, serving him in a sinful world. Our chief recognition will be in the world to come. Jesus said that the smallest act of service done in his name will not be overlooked. Even a cup of cold water will be rewarded (Matthew 10:42).

Discovery Learning

This page contains an alternate lesson plan emphasizing learning activities. Classes desiring such student involvement will find these suggestions helpful. The next page is a reproducible activity page to further enhance discovery learning.

LEARNING GOALS

After participating in this lesson, each student will be able to:

1. Summarize how Paul viewed his apostolic ministry according to this text.

2. Tell why the concept of receiving a "trust" is appropriate for any leader in the church.

3. Speak or write a message of appreciation and encouragement to the leaders of his or her church.

INTO THE LESSON

Before class, create two piles on the floor or on a table. In one pile place items that represent riches and honor (such as a crown, a trophy, and a purse); in the other pile place rags and trash.

Begin class by asking, "If you could possess everything in one of these piles, which one would you choose?"

Comment on the fact that it is natural that we would select the riches and symbols of honor. Note the irony, then, in Paul's assessment of himself as "the scum of the earth" and "the refuse of the world" (1 Corinthians 4:13).

INTO THE WORD

Provide some background for today's lesson by noting the cliques that had formed in Corinth when the believers put too much emphasis on human leaders (1 Corinthians 1:12). Note that Paul tells us how we ought to view Christian leaders in 1 Corinthians 4. Say, "Paul uses himself and Apollos to illustrate how the people should view their leaders. Let's analyze the chapter to discover what he says and then pull out principles that apply to all leaders in the church today." If your students completed the exercise in their student books, let them report their findings. If your students use the student books in class, assign them to complete the chart now in small groups or individually.

Read the chapter aloud. (Let your voice reveal the sarcasm of verses 8-10.) Then have the class make two lists: "Paul's View of Himself" and "Principles for Leaders in Any Age." They can do this in small groups or as a class. Have someone write the group's ideas on the chalkboard or a large poster. (A similar activity appears in the student book, *NIV Bible Student.*)

Paul's View of Himself: servant of Christ, entrusted with secret things of God, obligated to prove faithful, has clear conscience, spectacle to whole universe/scum of the earth, father through the gospel, consistent in his teaching of the gospel.

Principles for Leaders in Any Age: God will judge all people's motives, don't take pride over one another, all that we have we received, we may become a spectacle or scum of the earth, we should respond as the apostles did (verses 12, 13).

INTO LIFE

After reading the list of principles for leaders of all ages, ask pairs to describe when they have experienced or observed another church leader or teacher carrying out any of the principles on the list. (Letting people talk in pairs will allow shy people to feel comfortable answering. They often give excellent answers that will now be heard by a partner who can later urge the quiet person to tell a good example to the whole class.)

Ask for two or three volunteers to describe positive examples of leaders who have followed the principles.

Observe that Paul and the apostles lived in the way he described without expecting praise or appreciation, and we know from our study that leaders today should do the same. But it is hard to live that way, so it is always good to encourage leaders and let them know that we recognize their willingness to bear the hardships of leadership.

Distribute envelopes and stationery. (Photocopy the next page on colored paper to make an attractive yet inexpensive "stationery" for this activity.) Tell students to write to any leaders in your church. To avoid having a few people get all the letters, you might post a list of categories of leadership on the wall or chalkboard, or post a list of leaders and teachers. If appropriate, you could let people check off the name of the person to whom they are writing so that each leader will get at least one note.

Some people may not feel comfortable trying to express their thoughts on paper. Let them work with others to write a group letter or prepare a different way to show appreciation. (For example, some might bake a pie for a leadership meeting or volunteer to help carry out a task.)

Close with directed prayer. Name a category of leaders (ministers, elders, deacons, ministry team leaders/committee chairmen, superintendents, teachers, coordinators, music directors, etc.) and allow at least a minute of silence for the students to pray for these leaders. Then name another category and allow a minute of prayer, etc.

NEED FOR CHURCH DISCIPLINE

LESSON 4

WHY TEACH THIS LESSON?

In a permissive society like ours any talk of discipline may seem strange. If your class includes a lot of visitors, this lesson may sort out those who are genuinely interested in discipleship from those who are more curious than committed. Like the crowds who deserted Jesus in John 6, they may find this lesson "a hard teaching" (John 6:60). But for those who will hear it and accept it, this lesson could renew their commitment to following the Lord. Its call to moral purity is a breath of freshness in the stale air of relativism that hovers over our land.

INTRODUCTION

A. ONE TOUGH CHAPTER

There are some chapters in 1 Corinthians that we genuinely enjoy reading. Chapter 13 is pure poetry. Chapter 15 may be the greatest commentary on the resurrection of Jesus ever written.

First Corinthians 5, however, is quite another story. It reflects a sternness about a delicate situation that may make us uncomfortable. But it, too, is a part of God's Word and merits our study and consideration. All of the book was meant to be taken seriously by those to whom it was first sent, and all of it has value for Christians today.

B. LESSON BACKGROUND

As noted in the Lesson Background of the first lesson in this quarter (see pages 237, 238), the church at Corinth was located in a very sinful city. Like many seaport cities, prostitution was rampant there. In Corinth, however, there was a particularly evil side to it; for many prostitutes were affiliated with the pagan temples. Thus one could easily combine vice with "worship."

Such a corrupt atmosphere certainly provided a challenging environment for the Christian message, which emphasized personal purity. The church there was an island of holiness in a sea of evil—at least, it ought to have been.

I. TAKING SIN SERIOUSLY (1 CORINTHIANS 5:1, 2)

A. AN UNUSUAL SIN (v. 1)

1. It is actually reported that there is sexual immorality among you, and of a kind that does not occur even among pagans: A man has his father's wife.

The words *actually reported* suggest that Paul's information was more than mere hearsay. This sin was common knowledge—not just a piece of private gossip. It seems to have been flaunted before both the public and the church.

The Greek word translated *sexual immorality* is *porneia*, from which comes our word "pornography." The immoral act that Paul cited was that *a man* had *his father's wife*. Such language indicates that Paul was most likely describing an incestuous relationship between this man and his stepmother.

DEVOTIONAL READING:
JAMES 3:13-18
BACKGROUND SCRIPTURE:
1 CORINTHIANS 5:1—6:11
PRINTED TEXT:
1 CORINTHIANS 5

Mar
26

LESSON AIMS

After this lesson a student should be able to:

1. Tell why discipline was needed in Corinth and how Paul said it should be administered.

2. Explain the purpose of church discipline, and tell how that purpose would influence the administration of discipline.

3. Cultivate personal holiness with greater dedication, and support his or her church's efforts on the rare occasions when discipline may be necessary.

KEY VERSE

Therefore let us keep the Festival, not with the old yeast, the yeast of malice and wickedness, but with bread without yeast, the bread of sincerity and truth.
—1 Corinthians 5:8

LESSON 4 NOTES

WHAT DO YOU THINK?

The sin Paul dealt with in 1 Corinthians 5 was apparently a matter of public knowledge. Why did this make it particularly serious? What effects would it have on other Christians? What would be the effect on unbelievers?

Various questions may arise regarding the details of this relationship. Was this woman's husband dead? Was she divorced from her husband? Were they merely separated? The same questions could be asked regarding the man involved. However, such details are not provided. The shame of the sin called for the action that Paul later recommended, not for additional, and unnecessary, details.

In any case, this relationship was regarded as incest by Greeks, Romans, and Jews. (See the Old Testament teaching on this subject in Leviticus 18:8.) That a sin so widely condemned by even the *pagans* should be condoned by Christians was unthinkable. Even the excessively pagan environment in Corinth, which was not noted for its sexual purity, frowned on such an act.

B. AN UNUSUAL REACTION (v. 2)
2. And you are proud! Shouldn't you rather have been filled with grief and have put out of your fellowship the man who did this?

In the previous chapter (from which part of last week's text was taken), Paul spoke of the Corinthians' misdirected pride (vv. 6, 18, 19). Here he points out how inappropriate such pride is in dealing with a situation that should have concerned them greatly. Apparently their pride had led them to tolerate this situation instead of take action to correct it. They sound like people in our own day— *proud* that they can tolerate what others condemn!

The Corinthians should have been *filled with grief* over the sin in their presence. Note that the proper response is not anger. We can easily get angry when we are disappointed in someone's behavior, but the proper response is one of sorrow and heartache. Apparently caught up in their pride in their own supposed spiritual attainments, the Corinthians had chosen to ignore a situation that should have troubled them deeply.

When Paul expresses his desire that the man might be *put out of your fellowship*, he clearly means that this individual should be removed from the church. Why does Paul say nothing about the woman involved? Perhaps she was not a member of the church. If so, she was outside the church's jurisdiction—a point with which Paul concludes his discussion of this issue (vv. 12, 13).

HOW MUCH SIN SHOULD WE TOLERATE?

An Ohio man with numerous convictions for drunk driving drove for years without his driver's license. His eighteen convictions had no effect on his behavior.

After conviction number eighteen, a judge handed down a sentence that brought shocked responses. A representative of MADD (Mothers Against Drunk Driving) denounced the sentence as being too lenient. A sheriff called it "very squirrely!"

The judge ordered the man to spend the first week of each of the next five years in jail; when he rides in a car, he must either be handcuffed to the door on the passenger side or have someone sit between him and the driver; and he must move within easy walking distance of a liquor store so he isn't tempted to drive while drunk.

From what Paul says about the immoral member of the Corinthian church, it would appear that his sin involved unrepentant, habitual behavior similar to that of the Ohio drunk driver. The reason for the shocked reactions to the judge's sentence is that people have started to realize the need to get serious about punishing drunk driving. The Corinthian church, however, appears to have had no limit to the amount of sinful behavior they were willing to tolerate!   —C. R. B.

Ruins are all that remain of the pagan temples where many in ancient Corinth were seduced into immoral behavior. Discuss the lures Satan uses in our own culture.

II. MAINTAINING PURITY (1 CORINTHIANS 5:3-8)
A. A VERDICT REACHED (v. 3)
3. Even though I am not physically present, I am with you in spirit. And I have already passed judgment on the one who did this, just as if I were present.

Since Paul was *not physically present* with the Corinthians, how could he be involved in the verdict concerning the guilty man? The answer is that this matter did not involve some unsubstantiated rumor or idle bit of gossip that may or may not have been true. It would have been a great mistake to rush to judgment merely on the basis of idle talk. Situations can be misunderstood and people can be misrepresented. But that was not the case here. There was no question of the truth of the reports that Paul had heard.

The term *judgment* does not mean that Paul was condemning the man for eternity at this point. He was expressing his decision regarding how this critical matter should be handled *as if* he *were present*.

B. AN ACTION JOINTLY TAKEN (v. 4)
4. When you are assembled in the name of our Lord Jesus and I am with you in spirit, and the power of our Lord Jesus is present.

To invoke *the name of our Lord Jesus* is to place in the most solemn of categories the occasion when the church will be *assembled* to address the situation at hand. Not only the name but the *power* of Jesus was to be acknowledged in this assembly. This is not to say that the name and power of Jesus were not present at other assemblies of the church. Paul is simply emphasizing these factors because of the grave situation confronting the Corinthians.

Was this a meeting called for the very purpose of dealing with the immoral man? Or was this part of a regular gathering of the church? It is difficult to tell. If the latter, were any visitors dismissed before discussing a matter such as this? Perhaps they were allowed to remain in the assembly so that they could see a demonstration of the church's commitment to purity.

While Paul would not be at this gathering, he told the Corinthians that his *spirit* would be there. This does not suggest some miraculous presence, but rather the need to recognize Paul's authority as an apostle and his role as a spiritual father to the Corinthians (1 Corinthians 4:14, 15). Paul had founded this church and certainly possessed some influence because of that. But he also recognized that the congregation had some authority, too, as well as a grave responsibility to deal correctly with the matter at hand.

C. AN OBJECTIVE SOUGHT (v 5)
5. . . . hand this man over to Satan, so that the sinful nature may be destroyed and his spirit saved on the day of the Lord.

From a spiritual standpoint, there are two rulers and two kingdoms. Satan is "the prince of this world" (John 12:31; 16:11), and Jesus is the Head of the church (Ephesians 1:22, 23; 4:15, 16). To *hand this man over to Satan* simply means to put him out of the church so that he may return to the world, or Satan's kingdom. It is sometimes called "withdrawing fellowship" from the guilty one.

What is indicated by the phrase *that the sinful nature may be destroyed*? Certainly Paul was not telling the Corinthians to punish this man physically in any way, nor was he allowing Satan to kill him! The term *sinful nature* is actually the Greek word for *flesh* and should be understood as describing the kind of perspective that lives in defiance of God's authority and in pursuit of one's own desires. Such a rebellious attitude must be *destroyed* so that the man in question will no longer be guided by immoral standards.

We should not overlook the objective of putting this man out of the church. It was *so that . . . his spirit* may be *saved*—in other words, that the spirit may be delivered from the control of the flesh and that the willingness of the spirit may triumph over fleshly weakness (to use Jesus' words in Matthew 26:41). The

WHAT DO YOU THINK?

Anyone who has dealt with problems in the church knows it can be difficult to separate facts from rumors, opinions, and speculations. What principles would you suggest that leaders can follow in ascertaining the facts?

WHAT DO YOU THINK?

If a person in our church were being disciplined by the same standard as described in our text, how would you do it?

church's action was meant to be a kind of "shock treatment" to the man. It was not merely a means of punishment; it was intended as a wake-up call. Its goal was that the man would repent and would thus be saved. And, from what we read in 2 Corinthians 2:5-11, it worked! There we find that the man did repent, and Paul ordered him restored to the fellowship of the church. When congregations today exercise church discipline, it must be for this very same purpose.

The day of the Lord refers to the return of Christ and to the judgment that will take place at that time. Paul's desire was that whatever discipline the church administered now would prepare the person being disciplined for that day. Any discipline he undergoes now will be worth it if by so doing he escapes the eternal punishment of Hell.

D. An Old Testament Example (vv. 6, 7)

6. Your boasting is not good. Don't you know that a little yeast works through the whole batch of dough?

Again Paul cites the pride and *boasting* of the Corinthians. In view of the many problems about which Paul writes in this letter, they had very little reason to boast. But this matter was especially troubling. They were taking sin far too lightly. The church itself was being put in danger.

In a day when most families baked their own bread, the image of *yeast* was an appropriate one. As most know, when *a little yeast* is introduced into the *dough*, it soon spreads through *the whole batch*.

7. Get rid of the old yeast that you may be a new batch without yeast—as you really are. For Christ, our Passover lamb, has been sacrificed.

While *yeast* can be used in a positive sense (Matthew 13:33), it usually carries a negative connotation in Scripture (Matthew 16:6, 12; Mark 8:14, 15; Galatians 5:7-9). Here the *Passover* ritual of purging the house of yeast is invoked to illustrate the removal of evil influences—*the old yeast*. At the time of the exodus from Egypt, the Jews were instructed to remove all yeast from their houses (Exodus 12:14-20). This purging became an annual custom in preparation for Passover. The custom was to sweep one's house thoroughly before preparing the Passover meal so that even the crumbs of any bread made with yeast would be discarded. Such a cleansing is used here as an analogy to the spiritual cleansing that the Corinthians needed to undergo.

The presence of the immoral relationship in the church was dangerous. If this sin were tolerated, then other sin would also be tolerated—the yeast would spread. The Corinthians needed to *get rid of* these influences and become *a new batch* of dough, free of any harmful influences. Individually we all need to go through the same process of spiritual renewal from time to time: to examine ourselves, purge whatever sin is present from our lives, and renew our commitment to purity.

Paul's description of *Christ, our Passover lamb* calls to mind another important Old Testament link to the New Testament. Just as a lamb was killed at the time of the first Passover (and annually at the celebration of the feast by the Israelites), so Jesus the Lamb of God was crucified at the time of the Passover. The lamb slain in Egypt died to mark the Israelites' freedom from bondage there; the Lamb of God died for our freedom from sin (John 1:29). With this parallel in mind we should, like the Corinthians, get rid of the old yeast, or evil influences, that have the potential of keeping us in bondage to sin.

E. A Practical Application (v. 8)

8. Therefore let us keep the Festival, not with the old yeast, the yeast of malice and wickedness, but with bread without yeast, the bread of sincerity and truth.

What Do You Think?

If a congregation is lax in disciplining members guilty of sexual sin, what kind of message does that send to members in general?

That Paul is not referring to an obligation to *keep the Festival* literally is clear from his reference to *the bread of sincerity and truth*. Paul is not referring to the Lord's Supper or to any kind of religious observance. He is continuing his challenge to the Corinthians to rid themselves of the *old yeast* mentioned in the previous verse. All *malice and wickedness* must be purged from the thoughts, words, and acts of the people so that they may reflect the holiness God desires in his church (Ephesians 5:27).

III. WATCHING FRIENDSHIPS (1 CORINTHIANS 5:9-11)

A. PROPER CONTACT (vv. 9, 10)

9. I have written you in my letter not to associate with sexually immoral people.

Some students believe that Paul refers here to an earlier *letter* from himself to the Corinthians—one that has not been preserved. Such a conclusion is not necessary, however. The expression can also be understood to refer to the letter Paul was writing at that time. Paul used the same construction with the verb "sent" in Ephesians 6:22; Philippians 2:28; and Colossians 4:8.

Paul had written in verse 2 of the present chapter that the brother guilty of fornication should be "put out of your fellowship." Now, lest some assume he meant Christians were *not to associate with sexually immoral people* in any way, Paul will clarify his instructions.

10. . . . not at all meaning the people of this world who are immoral, or the greedy and swindlers, or idolaters. In that case you would have to leave this world.

If we separated ourselves altogether from *this world* and from worldly people, there would be no evangelism of the lost. We have not been called to *leave this world*; instead, we are to "go into all the world" (Mark 16:15). We dare not shun those who need the witness of Christians the most. We must build a bridge of friendship to win them—always being cautious as to who is influencing whom.

In addition to the *immoral*, Paul speaks of the *greedy*. While this term is usually applied to material greed, it can refer to all forms of desire for self-indulgence. The Greek word translated as *swindlers* conveys the idea of seizing something by force. *Idolaters* were common in Corinth, given its numerous pagan temples.

B. IMPROPER CONTACT (v. 11)

11. But now I am writing you that you must not associate with anyone who calls himself a brother but is sexually immoral or greedy, an idolater or a slanderer, a drunkard or a swindler. With such a man do not even eat.

There is a difference between the kind of association one has with an evil person whom he is trying to win to Christ and the kind of association one has with a *brother* who persists in sin and refuses to repent. The former situation is acceptable, for it is part of the Christian's obedience to Christ. The latter situation is what had developed in Corinth, and it was totally unacceptable.

It is important to distinguish between the circumstance in Corinth and that described by Paul in Galatians 6:1: "Brothers, if someone is caught in a sin, you who are spiritual should restore him gently. But watch yourself, or you also may be tempted." Here Paul is presenting a case involving someone who has yielded to temptation in a particular instance and needs assistance and encouragement. All of us are imperfect in this regard, and when these situations occur, we need to help one another. We must not shoot our own wounded. The problem in Corinth, however, involved a person who wanted to continue in sin (cf. Romans 6:1) and still be considered a brother in Christ.

To *associate* with such an individual would have a devastating effect on the church's influence on its surroundings. If the Corinthians did not address the

---

WHAT DO YOU THINK?

What are some principles we can utilize to guide us in our association with unbelievers?

HOW TO SAY IT

Corinth. KOR-inth.
Corinthians. Kor-IN-thee-unz.
Hymenaeus. High-meh-NEE-us.
porneia (Greek). por-NYE-uh or por-NAY-uh.

PRAYER

O Lord, keep us from the sins of the flesh. Keep us also from the sin of self-righteousness. Give us hearts that care about sinners and grieve over their sin. Give us courage to apply discipline if it is ever needed. In Jesus' name. Amen.

THOUGHT TO REMEMBER

The church is a hospital for those who are sick, not a rest home for those who are well.

DAILY BIBLE READINGS

Monday, Mar. 20—*Sexual Immorality Defiles the Church (1 Corinthians 5:1-8)*

Tuesday, Mar. 21—*Stay Away From Sexual Immorality (1 Corinthians 5:9-13)*

Wednesday, Mar. 22—*Resist Lawsuits Among Believers (1 Corinthians 6:1-11)*

Thursday, Mar. 23—*Watch Your Tongue! (James 3:1-12)*

Friday, Mar. 24—*Choose Wisdom That Is From Above (James 3:13-18)*

Saturday, Mar. 25—*Submit to God's Will and Way (James 4:1-10)*

Sunday, Mar. 26—*Seek Humility and Avoid Judging (James 4:11-17)*

immorality, they would give the impression that the church approved of such behavior. Their laxness would lead others into similar sins. Note that the four sins listed previously by Paul are repeated in this verse, and two more are added. A *slanderer* is one who speaks evil of others. Also added is the *drunkard*.

With *such a man* the Corinthians could *not even eat*. This probably is not a direct reference to the Lord's Supper. Eating together constituted an expression of kinship between those who shared a meal, so Paul told the Corinthians to withhold such expressions from the immoral brother.

IV. JUDGING CORRECTLY (1 CORINTHIANS 5:12, 13)

A. THE CHURCH'S RESPONSIBILITY (v. 12)

12. What business is it of mine to judge those outside the church? Are you not to judge those inside?

Neither Paul nor the church was to apply his counsel to those *outside the church*. The congregation itself should take responsibility for its own—for those *inside* the church.

It is not to be expected that non-Christians will behave like Christians. We should not be surprised that people outside of Christ do not try to live like Christ. But we can expect people who are Christians to live like Christ, and we should be very saddened when they do not.

B. GOD'S RESPONSIBILITY (v. 13)

13. God will judge those outside. "Expel the wicked man from among you."

The church is not to take the kind of actions with *those outside* (those not a part of the church) that it takes in disciplining a member. God has instituted civic authorities to discipline wrongdoers in the world (Romans 13:1-5). The final judgment of the world will, of course, be left to God himself (Romans 2:16).

That Paul's directive *Expel the wicked man from among you* appears in quotation marks calls attention to the fact that it is drawn from the Old Testament. Such words appear among the laws found in Deuteronomy (17:7; 19:19; 21:21; 22:21; 24:7) and are often accompanied by a command to put an offender to death. Paul's previous words make clear, however, that such a command was not a part of his instructions to the Corinthians.

CONCLUSION

We make a great mistake if we isolate this passage in 1 Corinthians from the rest of the book. In the church at Corinth there were many people committing many wrong acts.

There were divisive people.

There were people taking Christian brothers to court.

There were people conducting themselves improperly in worship.

Yet Paul did not say to put any of these out of the church! The incident found in today's text is very unusual. In fact, besides this incident, the only other reference to a similar act of church discipline is found in 1 Timothy 1:19, 20. There Paul writes that he has "handed over to Satan" Hymenaeus and Alexander, "to be taught not to blaspheme."

If this kind of action occurred rarely in the New Testament church, we should not be surprised that it occurs rarely today. It is likely that no more than once in a lifetime would a congregation face a situation that demanded such radical action. It was rare then and it should be rare now. Two factors in particular seem to call for discipline in a given situation: if there is widespread knowledge of the sin and if there is a refusal to repent.

Discovery Learning

This page contains an alternate lesson plan emphasizing learning activities. Classes desiring such student involvement will find these suggestions helpful. The next page is a reproducible activity page to further enhance discovery learning.

LEARNING GOALS

After today's lesson each adult will be able to:

1. Tell why discipline was needed in Corinth and how Paul said it should be administered.

2. Explain the purpose of church discipline, and tell how that purpose would influence the administration of discipline.

3. Cultivate personal holiness with greater dedication, and support his or her church's efforts on the rare occasions when discipline may be necessary.

INTO THE LESSON

Write the following statement on the chalkboard or a large poster: *"Church leaders should not remove fellowship from a member."*

Distribute half-sheets of paper and ask each student to write whether he agrees or disagrees and to write one reason he believes as he does. Then collect the papers and notice how many agree and how many disagree. Read one or two reasons on each side.

Make your transition into the Bible study with a statement like, "Let's find out what Paul said about the goal and process of church discipline."

INTO THE WORD

Use an overhead transparency, a poster, or the chalkboard to display three headings: *A Problem, A Timeless Principle,* and *An Application.* Ask the students to read through the text and suggest what should be cited under each heading. (The student book has an activity to assist in this.)

Problem: *It was commonly known in Corinth (and obviously beyond) that a man within the church was involved immorally with his father's wife. Instead of mourning the behavior, the church was ignoring it!*

Principle: *We always want the sinner to repent and be saved.*

Application: *Ignoring the sin was having two negative consequences: the other members of the church were in danger of becoming dull so that they would be more likely to sin, and the man was not being challenged to repent so that he could be saved. Paul wants the church to withdraw close fellowship from him.*

Read 2 Corinthians 2:6, 7 and 7:9-12 to reinforce the fact that the goal of the church discipline was achieved. The man repented!

INTO LIFE

Distribute copies of the reproducible page that follows. To help your students understand how Paul's principle might be applied today, let small groups analyze the cases on that page. If you have enough students to form three groups, give each group one of the cases. If you have fewer than three groups, have everyone work on all the cases. If you have more than three groups, assign one or more of the cases to more than one group.

Allow time for the groups to develop plans; then ask for reports. Use the following to guide your discussion:

Case 1. This sin is publicly known. Failure to act can cause JKL to think that his sin is "no big deal" and others to assume his behavior is condoned by Christians in this church. He has done it before; he needs to be confronted in order to break the pattern of sin, repent, and be saved. If he repents, the church leadership can work out a program of prayer, support, and study for his spiritual growth. If he fails to repent, they must withdraw fellowship from him. If he repents in the future, they should restore him to fellowship.

Case 2. At this point this sin is not commonly known. This puts the responsibility on those who saw her to follow the Matthew 18 passage: go privately and confront RST with love and prayer. If she repents, pray with her; offer support and accountability for spiritual healing. If she does not repent, go to the elders. If she then repents, everyone should pray and work together to help her restore a strong relationship with God. If she still does not repent, the church will withdraw fellowship with the prayer that she will yet come to repentance.

Case 3. The church leadership must take this sin seriously. Recognize that others who may know about it may decide that such behavior is acceptable; act with the goal to save BCD. Since they no longer have authority over him, they should follow the principles of Matthew 18. They should also involve the elders of the new congregation where BCD is now serving. If he repents, he will need their help to hold him accountable for his spiritual recovery. If he does not repent, the elders need to be on the alert for possible repetition of sin.

Summarize all the discoveries made during the class session so that students can hear one more time the purpose and the process of discipline. Then read 1 Corinthians 5:6-8—Paul's admonition to live a life of personal holiness.

To close the session, lead the class in a time of silent personal introspection and prayer.

Administering Church Discipline

Today's text from 1 Corinthians 5 taken with what Jesus said in Matthew 18:15-17 gives us several practical guidelines to follow in matters of church discipline.

GUIDELINES FROM 1 CORINTHIANS 5
- Take seriously sin by a Christian, especially sin that is publicly known.
- Recognize that failure to take responsibility can lead others to sin.
- Act with the goal of saving the person.
- Withdraw close fellowship so that the church is purified.
- When the person repents, restore the person to fellowship.

GUIDELINES FROM MATTHEW 18:15-17
- Admonish privately the person who sins. If he listens, you have been successful.
- If he does not repent, take one or two others with you.
- If he still refuses to repent, get the church leaders involved.
- If he still refuses to repent, treat him as a pagan.

Consider one or more of the following case studies. Applying the guidelines above, prepare a step-by-step plan for how the leaders of the church should deal with the people involved in each case. Be prepared to explain why each step is appropriate and necessary.

CASE 1: THE EMBEZZLING EMPLOYEE
A story in the local newspaper reports that JKL has been convicted of embezzling funds from a local business. Some investigation reveals that he was fired from his previous job for the same reason. He, his wife, and his children have been active members of your congregation for over ten years.

Applying the principles cited above, what should the church leaders do? Be prepared to explain why you think they should take each step.

CASE 2: THE MOTEL RENDEZVOUS
While you and a friend were delivering publicity posters to local businesses, you saw RST and a man come out of a motel room. They kissed and then got into separate cars to drive off. RST and her husband (not the man at the motel) are in your Sunday school class.

Applying the principles cited above, what steps will you take? Be prepared to explain why you would take each step.

CASE 3: THE DEPARTED MINISTER
BCD, the minister, recently resigned and moved to a position as minister in another church. The elders have met because they have discovered that, before he left, BCD removed all the fixtures from the parsonage and emptied the benevolence account. He is no longer a member of the church under the elders' authority, but they believe they need to do something about his sin. What should they do?

MARRIAGE

WHY TEACH THIS LESSON?

A few years ago a number of so-called experts were predicting an end to the institution of marriage. It was out of date and impractical, they asserted. The modern generation would discard it like out-of-fashion clothing.

While they were not right about marriage being discarded, perhaps they were correct on one level. Though marriage is still popular, it has changed radically. Getting married was once synonymous with "setting up housekeeping"; now most couples enter a marriage already living together. While marriage was once expected to be a lifetime commitment, more and more couples approach it as a convenience. They will drop out as soon as the marriage becomes inconvenient. Even such an axiomatic truth that marriage is for a man and a woman is being challenged in court and legislature as homosexuals argue for the "right" to marry and to enjoy the social and economic privileges accorded to marriage partners. Marriage, as we once knew it, has come to an end for many, many people.

Does the Bible have anything to say to our post-modern society about marriage? This lesson will convince you that it does. The question is, "Will society listen?"

INTRODUCTION

A. A NINETY-TEN MARRIAGE

Many years ago I was visiting an older couple who had experienced more than half a century of happy married life together. "I'm sure the secret to your long marriage is that both of you accepted it as a fifty-fifty partnership."

"No, son," the husband quickly replied. "Our marriage has always been a ninety-ten partnership."

"You mean you got your way ninety percent of the time, and she got her way only ten percent of the time?" I asked in surprise.

"No! What I mean is that each of us was willing to go ninety percent of the way in any matter, and as a result the other never had to go more than ten percent of the way."

Heeding that wise advice from an older generation would go a long way toward solving many marital problems today.

B. LESSON BACKGROUND

Today's lesson introduces the second unit in this quarter's study from Paul's letters to the Corinthians. Unit 1 dealt with Christ as the basis for unity. Unit 2 shows how Christ provides a basis for unity in human relationships.

Our lesson today deals with one of the fundamental institutions in any society—marriage. Marriage provides the cement that holds a society together and helps it function in a healthy, positive way. It is no empty truism that as the homes go, so goes the nation.

We have already noted that Corinth was a city steeped in paganism, making it an especially challenging location to plant a church. Throughout the city were numerous symbols of blatant sexuality, including the temple of Aphrodite, where more than a thousand sacred prostitutes plied their trade. When the Corinthians became

DEVOTIONAL READING:
1 CORINTHIANS 7:25-35
BACKGROUND SCRIPTURE:
1 CORINTHIANS 6:12—7:16
PRINTED TEXT:
1 CORINTHIANS 7:1-16

Apr
2

LESSON AIMS

After completing this lesson, each student should be able to:

1. Recite the standards Paul set for both married and single persons in our text.

2. Tell how today's society illustrates the folly of abandoning God's guidelines for marriage.

3. Take steps to promote and model these guidelines in the family, the church, and the community.

KEY VERSE

Do you not know that your body is a temple of the Holy Spirit, who is in you, whom you have received from God? You are not your own.

—1 Corinthians 6:19

Christians, no doubt it was difficult for many of them to rid themselves of all of their pagan values and beliefs. For example, it appears that some began to question whether or not a married person should share physical intimacy with his or her spouse. Such intimacy had always been linked with pagan deities and practices.

The Corinthians expressed their concerns about these issues in a letter to Paul, as verse 1 of today's text indicates ("Now for the matters you wrote about"). Paul then addressed not only these questions, but several other marriage issues.

I. CONCERNING MARRIAGE (1 CORINTHIANS 7:1-7)

A. NOT REQUIRED OF ALL (vv. 1, 2)

1. Now for the matters you wrote about: It is good for a man not to marry.

In the verses immediately preceding our printed text (6:12-20) Paul had raised the issue of sexual immorality, warning the Corinthians of its disastrous consequences. Now, in chapter 7, he begins to suggest some ways that the people could guard themselves against the polluting forces around them and uphold God's standards in all their relationships.

Some believe that Paul's statement It is good for a man not to marry quotes the letter the Corinthians have written Paul and describes what some in the church were teaching. More likely, Paul was introducing his teaching on the value—at least in certain situations—of celibacy (cf. verses 26, 32-35). Paul himself was unmarried (note verse 7), though it is not clear whether he never married or was a widower. He had chosen to remain unmarried in order to give himself completely to his strenuous and dangerous ministry. Those who make a similar choice have exercised their "own gift from God," as Paul states in verse 7.

2. But since there is so much immorality, each man should have his own wife, and each woman her own husband.

Even though Paul commended celibacy, he recognized that it was not typical and that not everyone would be able to live within such limits. Surrounded as the Corinthians were with sexual symbols, language, and acts, it is not surprising that many would find living the celibate life an unbearable burden. Paul knew it was not reasonable to expect everyone to live as he lived.

Given such conditions, it was appropriate for many of the Corinthians that they enter marriage in order to avoid immorality. We should understand that this seemingly negative view of marriage does not present the total picture of the marital state or the sole reason for marriage. The fact that God instituted marriage in the garden of Eden and gave his highest blessing to it (Genesis 2:24; Matthew 19:4, 5) should make it obvious that marriage is much more than simply a protection against the temptation of immorality.

B. CONJUGAL OBLIGATIONS (vv. 3-5)

3. The husband should fulfill his marital duty to his wife, and likewise the wife to her husband.

The marital duty mentioned here refers to the physical intimacy of marriage. The Greek word literally means "debt." Such an obligation is not one-sided, falling upon either spouse alone, but must be shared equally by both husband and wife.

4. The wife's body does not belong to her alone but also to her husband. In the same way, the husband's body does not belong to him alone but also to his wife.

In marriage a man and a woman become "one flesh" (Genesis 2:24). This expression has a broad application, covering many aspects of the marriage relationship, but it certainly includes conjugal relations. Each member of the marriage partnership must be sensitive to the needs of the other. Difficulties arise when one partner makes selfish demands without considering the other. As our culture

WHAT DO YOU THINK?

Paul noted that sexual temptations in Corinth were strong enough that some should marry to avoid immorality. What similarities to this situation do you see in our society?

WHAT DO YOU THINK?

A husband's and wife's bodies belong to one another. How can the recognition of this truth contribute to a successful marriage?

increasingly encourages persons to be self-centered, it should not surprise us that marriage problems are multiplied.

A Moral Earthquake

In January of 1994, the Northridge earthquake hit Southern California, toppling freeway overpasses, collapsing parking garages, and demolishing many businesses. Thousands of church buildings and homes were severely damaged, and many people died or were injured.

Ironically, California's largest egg farm (producing one million eggs every day) lay just five miles from the epicenter of the quake. The egg farm suffered a broken water line and *one broken egg!* One manager at the farm told his workers, "We had a 6.6 earthquake that broke fewer eggs than you guys do when we're working!"

A far more lethal moral earthquake shook Western civilization in the last half of the twentieth century. The so-called "sexual revolution" caused our society to view marriage as a quaint relic of the past. The idea that some people (for moral reasons) would remain celibate outside of marriage was no longer seen as self-discipline; it was "repression"—something to be mocked by the cultural "movers and shakers." The moral quake of the sexual revolution shattered lives, destroyed families, caused the indiscriminate death of millions of babies, and promoted irresponsible behavior among innumerable teenagers and adults.

The long-term damage from this shaking of the biblical norms for sexual behavior has been far greater than all the damage done by any mere earthquake.   —C. R. B.

5. Do not deprive each other except by mutual consent and for a time, so that you may devote yourselves to prayer. Then come together again so that Satan will not tempt you because of your lack of self-control.

Here Paul stresses just how vital conjugal obligations are: one who is not willing to accept such responsibilities is said to *deprive* his or her spouse. At the same time, Paul recognized that there may be occasions when sexual relations are to be forsaken, but only *by mutual consent* and *for a time* (temporarily). Paul cites a specific situation that may occur when one involves himself or herself in a special period of *prayer*. But this period should be brief, lest *Satan* use this time apart to *tempt* one to sacrifice his or her *self-control* and be unfaithful.

Paul's statement does not address many modern situations that may require the temporary separation of husband and wife. While many of these circumstances may be considered secular rather than spiritual (for examples, military service or employment far from home), they can create similar problems. Most of us know of situations where such separations have opened the door for Satan to gain a foothold and wreak havoc in a marriage.

C. Qualifying Statements (vv. 6, 7)
6. I say this as a concession, not as a command.

Most likely Paul's *concession* refers to what Paul has just stated in the previous verse. He is granting permission for abstinence from sexual relations during times of prayer or certain other activities. But this teaching is not a *command* (it is not found in the teachings of Jesus or elsewhere in Scripture)—only a *concession*.

Since such abstinence is permitted but not commanded, some have questioned whether such a statement carries the kind of divine authority that we associate with the Scriptures. We must understand that the apostle Paul, even in this case, was a divinely inspired messenger of God, and that what he speaks as a *concession* is still communicated under the inspiration of God's Holy Spirit.

7. I wish that all men were as I am. But each man has his own gift from God; one has this gift, another has that.

What Do You Think?

Suppose a friend told you he was considering taking a job in a far-off city, but that his wife could not leave her job until she was vested—eighteen months from now. Considering what Paul says about marriage's being a hedge against immorality, and his warning not to "deprive" one's spouse, how would you advise your friend? Why?

WHAT DO YOU THINK?

Paul's recommendation of the celibate life seems to have hinged on current circumstances (see 1 Corinthians 7:26). Under what conditions today might it be advisable for a Christian to shun marriage?

The Greek word *men* in this verse is generic, including both men and women. Paul's desire was that *all* Christians remain celibate *as* he himself was. The extreme demands of Paul's ministry made celibacy almost an absolute must in his case. However, he readily acknowledged that not every Christian has been given this *gift*.

"IF ONLY . . ."

"If only . . ." is a game played by many of us. Life would be better—maybe even *perfect*—if only this or that were different. The most popular form of the game is probably "If only I were rich. . . ." Numbers two and three on the list may be, "If only I were married . . ." and "If only I hadn't married. . . ."

Gregg Warren claims to have a solution for all these problems. If you are distraught over being single or having married the "wrong person," Warren says, you no longer have to be troubled about it. Write out your problem, burn the paper, and send him the ashes (along with five dollars). He will carry the ashes aloft in his plane—cleverly named "Worry Free"—and dump them out over Carefree, Arizona. Warren is a Buddhist, and his idea is a technological adaptation of an ancient Buddhist practice. In the first six months after he began this service, Warren handled some five thousand requests!

God's way, however, is better than the Buddhist way. Paul wrote that one should consider his or her marital status a "gift from God" (1 Corinthians 7:7). Worrying about such a matter is not productive. Trusting and being faithful to the Lord will have a profoundly positive effect—whatever our status.   —C. R. B.

II. OTHER CIRCUMSTANCES (1 CORINTHIANS 7:8-16)

A. THE UNMARRIED AND WIDOWS (vv. 8, 9)

8, 9. Now to the unmarried and the widows I say: It is good for them to stay unmarried, as I am. But if they cannot control themselves, they should marry, for it is better to marry than to burn with passion.

Paul next considered those who were *unmarried* or were *widows*. While he does not specifically include widowers, it seems reasonable to suppose that they would be covered by his advice. Once again he states his preference that those not presently married should *stay* in that state. At the same time, he recognized that remaining celibate would be extremely difficult for some persons. Many of those in the Corinthian church to whom Paul was writing were recent converts, and they had not yet developed the spiritual strength to resist sexual temptations. Those with stronger sex drives or who were surrounded by especially enticing temptations would likely be overwhelmed. For them, Paul conceded, *it is better to marry than to burn with passion.*

B. SEPARATION (vv. 10, 11)

10. To the married I give this command (not I, but the Lord): A wife must not separate from her husband.

Paul's words *not I, but the Lord* indicate that the teaching in these verses reflected what *the Lord* (Jesus) had taught concerning marriage and divorce. At this point in time, Paul may have had access to some of the Gospel accounts of how Jesus dealt with the matter of divorce. But even without these written records, Paul spoke with the authority of an inspired apostle, echoing Christ's teaching in this matter (Mark 10:2-12). (That the Greek word rendered *separate* refers to divorce, not to mere separation, is indicated by its use in Mark 10:9: "Therefore what God has joined together, let man not separate.")

11. But if she does, she must remain unmarried or else be reconciled to her husband. And a husband must not divorce his wife.

The visual for today's lesson is a reminder that love, purity, and unity are required for the kind of marriage that Paul urges in our text.

In the event that someone should "separate" from his or her spouse, the Christian should *remain unmarried* or else *be reconciled* to the mate. A commitment to stay unmarried would keep open the possibility of eventual reconciliation. Paul did not raise the issue of adultery as an acceptable reason for divorce (see Matthew 5:32), but what he says here does not contradict that teaching.

C. THOSE MARRIED TO UNBELIEVERS (vv. 12-16)

12, 13. To the rest I say this (I, not the Lord): If any brother has a wife who is not a believer and she is willing to live with him, he must not divorce her. And if a woman has a husband who is not a believer and he is willing to live with her, she must not divorce him.

As Christianity reached out into the pagan society of the first century, it would not have been unusual for a person to become a Christian while his or her spouse remained a pagan. We can readily imagine some of the conflicts that must have arisen in some of those households.

In dealing with the issue of divorce in the previous verses, Paul presented the word of the Lord Jesus. However, in dealing with the problem of a Christian married to an unbeliever, he says *to the rest I say this (I, not the Lord)*. This should not be taken to mean that Paul's teaching on this subject did not reflect the will of Christ or that he was not inspired at this point. He was simply saying that Jesus did not address the issue of a Christian married to an unbeliever during his earthly ministry. Now, under the inspiration of the Holy Spirit, Paul provided counsel not previously given on this subject. He did so as a divinely inspired apostle (1 Corinthians 7:40), making his words authoritative.

Paul taught that a Christian is to remain in the "mixed marriage" with an unbeliever, no matter how inconvenient it might be, as long as the unbeliever is *willing* to abide in it. The pagan culture of Paul's day typically had different standards for men and women, but Paul said the same standard applies here for both.

Perhaps a more common situation today occurs when a Christian marries an unbeliever. We need to teach our young people to seek their marriage partners among Christians (2 Corinthians 6:14-18). Yet, in spite of our best efforts, some will marry outside the faith. When this occurs, we need to encourage them to build solid marriages without compromising their commitment to the Lord.

14. For the unbelieving husband has been sanctified through his wife, and the unbelieving wife has been sanctified through her believing husband. Otherwise your children would be unclean, but as it is, they are holy.

Paul now explained why a Christian should remain in a marriage with an unbeliever as long as possible: *the unbelieving husband has been sanctified through his wife*, while *the unbelieving wife has been sanctified through her believing husband*. Bible students have held various views about what this statement means. It certainly does not mean that an unbeliever will come to enjoy the blessings of salvation simply because he or she happens to be married to a Christian. Salvation always requires the sinner to make a personal commitment to the Lord and cannot be gained by mere contact with a Christian.

Paul probably means that a Christian marriage partner has a unique opportunity to present the claims of the gospel to his or her mate by word and, even more important, by deed. Most of us can think of persons who patiently and graciously witnessed to their mate and after many years finally led him or her to the Lord. In this sense the unbeliever who has become a Christian is thus *sanctified*, or set apart to the Lord.

Not only does a Christian marriage partner have an opportunity to witness to his or her mate, but also to rear the *children* to become Christians. The children of

WHAT DO YOU THINK?

How can Christian parents prepare their children for successful marriage?

HOW TO SAY IT

Aphrodite. Af-ruh-DITE-ee.
Corinth. KOR-inth.
Corinthians. Kor-IN-thee-unz.

THOUGHT TO REMEMBER

"Therefore what God has joined together, let man not separate" (Mark 10:9).

such a marriage are *unclean* in the sense that they are not Christians and will not become Christians unless they are properly taught. The home, even when one partner is not a Christian, is still the best place for a child to learn about the Lord.

15. But if the unbeliever leaves, let him do so. A believing man or woman is not bound in such circumstances; God has called us to live in peace.

If the unbeliever leaves—if he or she chooses not to live with the Christian spouse—the *believing man or woman is not bound* and is released from all attempts to keep the marriage together. Some believe that, since the marriage bonds are thus broken, the Christian is free to remarry. According to this interpretation, Paul has added abandonment to adultery (Matthew 5:32) as a biblical basis for divorce and remarriage.

Other Bible students oppose this view, insisting that Paul's teaching on not being *bound* only frees the Christian from the obligation of trying to maintain a marriage with an unwilling partner. Since remarriage is not mentioned here, they believe we have no right to infer that it is included as a part of Paul's teaching.

One thing is certain: *God has called us to live in peace.* God wants us to have harmony, not discord, in our marriages. No Christian should intentionally foster strife in a marriage and thereby pressure the unbelieving spouse to seek to end the marriage.

16. How do you know, wife, whether you will save your husband? Or, how do you know, husband, whether you will save your wife?

A Christian married to an unbeliever may think that the chances of converting his or her unbelieving spouse are remote indeed. But even in situations that seem hopeless, we must never underestimate the power of a believer's consistent, compassionate witness. Christians who are married to non-Christians should find strength and hope in this verse. And certainly they need the prayers and support of other Christians.

CONCLUSION

The teachings of Christ and the apostle Paul concerning marriage and divorce are not easy to accept in our modern culture. Keep in mind, however, that down through history those who have tried to follow the teachings of the Bible have often found themselves at odds with their culture. All too often Christians, when faced with such confrontations, have compromised their convictions and surrendered to the culture.

Divorce is one of the major problems facing our homes today; and because the home is the foundation of the nation, it is therefore a major problem facing our nation. Within two generations we have moved from a situation in which divorces were rather rare to the point where nearly half of all marriages end in divorce. Even among professing Christians, divorces are distressingly common. As a result we have seen the rapid growth of single-parent families, frequently resulting in impoverished homes and psychologically scarred children.

Given the attitudes current in our society, there is no easy solution to this problem. As Christians, however, we must not surrender to the values of our society. We must teach our children the biblical standards for marriage both by word and by example. We need to start when they are young and keep repeating these teachings at every opportunity.

The church must also provide help for those whose marriages are in trouble. It isn't enough just to preach and condemn. Fortunately, there are many Christian marriage counselors available who can help people whose marriages are struggling. Even those of us who are not professional counselors can often give helpful advice to such couples. Above all we can pray for them.

Discovery Learning

This page contains an alternate lesson plan emphasizing learning activities. Classes desiring such student involvement will find these suggestions helpful. The next page is a reproducible activity page to further enhance discovery learning.

LEARNING GOALS

After this lesson students should be able to:

1. Recite the standards Paul set for both married and single persons in our text.

2. Tell how today's society illustrates the folly of abandoning God's guidelines for marriage.

3. Take steps to promote and model these guidelines in the family, the church, and the community.

INTO THE LESSON

As your students arrive, give them copies of the following agree/disagree exercise, or direct their attention to the student book, where it is reprinted. Allow two minutes to complete the exercise and five more to discuss their answers.

1. Under no circumstances should Christians divorce. Agree or disagree?

2. Every preacher should have a family to relate better to his congregation. Agree or disagree?

3. Single Christians are better situated than married ones to deal with this sinful world. Agree or disagree?

4. Christians are commanded by God (Genesis 1) to marry and have children. Agree or disagree?

After the discussion, tell your students that today's lesson addresses each statement.

Option: Have three students perform the skit "The Couples Class" (use the script on the next page). Afterward, ask the students what they think about Bob and Karen's advice. Do not comment on their responses, but encourage all to find God's answer in today's text.

INTO THE WORD

Many of the topics in 1 Corinthians were occasioned by a letter addressed to Paul. The seventh chapter contains the first such topic. Ask your students to work in pairs to read each passage indicated below and compose the question they think Paul was answering. Possible questions are indicated in parentheses. As the pairs report, use the additional questions cited after each one to further your class discussion of these issues.

7:1-6 (With all the sexual immorality in Corinth, should we abstain from sex entirely?)

According to Paul, what is the proper view of marital intimacy? What potential problems face married couples if they avoid intimacy? When is it permissible for couples temporarily to cease sexual relations?

7:7-9 (Should unmarried believers be discouraged from marrying?)

Why did Paul wish all were unmarried, as he was? What advantages might a single Christian have over a married one? When might it be better for a Christian to marry than to remain single?

7:10-16 (To protect his faith, should a believer divorce his unbelieving spouse?)

What is the Lord's view of divorce between believers? When is divorce allowed? If believers divorce for any other reason, what can they do? What can they not do? What is Paul's teaching on mixed marriages between believers and unbelievers? How is an unbeliever sanctified by a believing spouse? What does Paul mean about their children being either "unclean" or "holy"? What breaks the marriage bonds between a believer and an unbeliever? Is the believer then free to remarry? Compare verse 15 with verse 39, where Paul uses similar language of widows.

INTO LIFE

Ask each pair of students who completed the previous exercise to write a brief response to one of the situations below. Assign every situation to at least one pair of students to make sure that all are covered. Each situation is based on an agree/disagree statement from the opening activity.

1. Bruce and his wife Beth, both Christians, have been having marital problems over money and in-laws for several years. Bruce has decided to file for divorce. What would you tell him?

2. You serve on the pulpit committee of your congregation. A great prospect for the minister's position has applied, but he is single and some of the committee members think that his marital status would hinder his work. What would you say to the committee?

3. Tom, a forty-something bachelor, would love to settle down to be a family man, but he has yet to meet the right woman. He is deeply depressed because he feels he is past his prime and his chances for happiness are gone. What would you write to reassure him?

4. Luke believes that now is the right time to have children, but his wife is afraid to raise a child in today's violent, pagan society. What would you tell them?

Close the class session with prayer, asking specifically for God to bless each of the marriages represented in the class.

The Couples Class

For this skit you will need three chairs, arranged in a row at the front of the class, facing the back of the classroom. The scene opens with Bob and Karen sitting together in Sunday morning Sunday school class, sipping coffee and munching donuts. George enters, carrying a cup of coffee and his Bible.

Karen: Hi, George! Come join us over here.

George: Thanks, don't mind if I do.

Bob: How's the insurance business these days, George?

George: Couldn't be better. This building boom is great for the company.

Karen: Is Michelle going to join you for the class potluck today after church?

George: No, she had a business trip this weekend.

Bob: Does she travel every weekend? It seems that we never see her anymore.

George: I don't see much of her either, these days. She's usually gone two weekends a month.

Karen: It sure would be great if she could be here for Bible school and worship with you.

George: I know, but her career is number one with her right now. She wants to be a vice president before she turns forty.

Karen: It's a shame she doesn't share your beliefs. Every Christian needs a soul mate, if you know what I mean, George.

Bob: George, I don't mean to pry, but have you ever thought of breaking out of that unequal yoke?

George: What do you mean?

Bob: Well, I believe the Bible says it's ok to divorce a non-Christian spouse.

George: It does?

Karen: Yes, George, remember that verse that says, "Don't cast your pearls before swine"? That's what it's talking about.

George: Really? This is all a little confusing. I thought the Christian thing was to be a faithful husband and witness to Michelle and try to win her to the Lord.

Bob: No, no, George. Jesus told the Canaanite woman his food is for his children, not for the dogs. It's not right to waste good food, George. (Bob crams his donut into his mouth.)

George: No, I suppose it isn't.

Karen: Well, I see that class is about to begin. Anyway, George, give it some thought, and remember, we're always here for you when you need us. That's what Christians are for, right?

Helping a Church Confront Crisis

Unit 2: Unity in Human Relationships
(Lessons 5-9)

LOVE AND KNOWLEDGE

WHY TEACH THIS LESSON?

Much of the discussion about what may be called "disputable matters" centers around what Christians may do even though some people think they ought not to do so. Siding with the "strong," these people are convinced they can drink this or watch that without any harm to their spiritual lives. They will refrain only in the presence of a "weaker brother" who might have a problem with their behavior.

That is the right position to take toward the weaker brother, but there is more to this issue. Today's lesson text should also challenge your students to examine such behaviors in the light of what possible good they can do.

The issue is the superiority of love over knowledge. What greater act of love than to pursue only the best—those behaviors that strengthen their faith and that of any who may observe them—so that their example is worth following even when they are not aware that another is watching!

INTRODUCTION

A. HAYMOW THEOLOGY

Some teenage boys often played in the neighbor's barn. From the top of the barn they had suspended a long rope. On it they would swing from the haymow on one side of the barn across the open area in the middle to the haymow on the other side, landing safely on the loose hay.

This game, which seemed safe enough for the older boys, went on for several weeks. Then one day a younger brother, seeing the older boys swinging on the rope, decided to try it. Before the older boys could stop him, he grabbed the rope and jumped. But he lost his grip, fell to the floor below, and was seriously injured.

The next day the older boys, without any urging from their parents, took down the rope. They realized that what was safe for them posed serious dangers for one not so strong or experienced. This illustrates what Paul was talking about when he stated that he was willing to give up any activities that might cause a weaker brother to stumble and fall into sin.

B. LESSON BACKGROUND

Today's lesson, which includes all of 1 Corinthians 8, continues Paul's discussion of practical problems facing the church at Corinth. Apparently one of the issues that had been raised in the Corinthians' letter to Paul was whether or not a Christian could eat meat that had been sacrificed to idols. There were primarily two ways to handle this matter, and they are found within today's lesson title: "Love and Knowledge." According to Paul, knowledge may make some people puffed up and arrogant. Those who see debatable issues, such as eating meat offered to idols, from the perspective of knowledge alone often insist on their freedom of behavior, even though the exercise of that freedom might be harmful to some of their fellow Christians. Love, on the other hand, seeks to help and encourage other Christians, especially those who are weaker in the faith.

DEVOTIONAL READING:
1 CORINTHIANS 10:23—11:1
BACKGROUND SCRIPTURE:
1 CORINTHIANS 8
PRINTED TEXT:
1 CORINTHIANS 8

LESSON AIMS

After this lesson students should be able to:

1. Summarize Paul's teaching about love and knowledge as it applies to the issue of eating meat sacrificed to idols.

2. Compare the issue Paul addressed with disputable matters that concern Christians today.

3. Determine to make choices based on love for Christ and his church more than on personal freedom.

○ Apr 9

KEY VERSE

The man who thinks he knows something does not yet know as he ought to know. But the man who loves God is known by God. —1 Corinthians 8:2, 3

I. LIVING BY KNOWLEDGE (1 CORINTHIANS 8:1-8)

A. THE DANGER OF KNOWLEDGE (vv. 1-3)

1. Now about food sacrificed to idols: We know that we all possess knowledge. Knowledge puffs up, but love builds up.

The phrase *now about* indicates that Paul was addressing a question that the Corinthians had raised in their letter to Paul (see the similar language in 7:1). While the specific subject involved is not an issue in our society today, the principle that Paul lays down to deal with the matter certainly applies to many issues that modern Christians face.

Some of the Corinthians were troubled about whether it was right to eat meat that had been *sacrificed to idols*. Part of such a sacrifice was consumed on the altar, some was eaten by the priests, and what was left over was commonly sold in the meat market (1 Corinthians 10:25). Persons only recently converted from paganism understandably had some reservations about eating such meat.

Apparently some of the more mature Christians, recognizing that the pagan idols were nothing, had no qualms about eating this meat. Paul, however, pointed out that this knowledge can sometimes be dangerous. *Knowledge puffs up;* that is, it can cause a person to become arrogant and domineering over others and to believe that everyone should think as he does. On the other hand, *love builds up* others in the faith. It seeks to work with people and help them, regardless of their level of knowledge.

It is important to note that Paul was not commending ignorance. His quarrel was with the exercise of the kind of knowledge that is self-centered. Love, by contrast, is always concerned about others first. Love is the attitude that will help us to use our knowledge in a way pleasing to God. It would be better if we all possess love than if *we all possess knowledge*.

2. The man who thinks he knows something does not yet know as he ought to know.

One can be knowledgeable about many things; but if this knowledge leads a person to become vain and conceited, then that individual *does not yet know* about the things *he ought to know*—the things that really matter.

3. But the man who loves God is known by God.

Rather than desiring knowledge, we should seek to be *known by God*. This happens when we love him, thereby fulfilling "the first and greatest commandment" (Matthew 22:37, 38). As Paul will state in verse 4, some of the Corinthians were correct in their knowledge that the idols were nothing and that the meat sacrificed to them was in no way contaminated. However, it is not enough for one to hold correct views about certain matters. One who truly knows God and loves him will express his love to God by caring for the weaker believers around him. Most of us have known people who were sound in the faith but expressed their faith in an arrogant and unloving fashion. Others were driven away from Christ, not drawn to him.

B. THE TRUTH ABOUT IDOLS (vv. 4-6)

4. So then, about eating food sacrificed to idols: We know that an idol is nothing at all in the world and that there is no God but one.

Paul agreed with those who knew that the *idols* were *nothing*. Though many of them had come from polytheistic backgrounds (worshiping many gods), they had come to the mature understanding that *there is no God but one*.

5, 6. For even if there are so-called gods, whether in heaven or on earth (as indeed there are many "gods" and many "lords"), yet for us there is but one God, the Father, from whom all things came and for whom we live; and there is but one Lord, Jesus Christ, through whom all things came and through whom we live.

WHAT DO YOU THINK?

As 1 Corinthians 8:2 reminds us, we do not know as much as we should know. How can we overcome tendencies toward excessive pride regarding our biblical and religious knowledge?

WHAT DO YOU THINK?

Not many people have a problem with meat sacrificed to idols today. Suggest a contemporary issue in which "strong" and "weak" Christians may take differing views. How should the "strong" and the "weak" relate to one another?

In contrast to the many supposed entities that are *so-called gods* and that are worshiped and treated as though they were gods, *there is but one God*. In addition, he is *the Father,* indicating his warm personal relationship with those who serve him. He is the Creator of *all things* and the source of all that is necessary for man's livelihood. In contrast to the many lords of the pagans, *there is but one Lord, Jesus Christ*. Through him has come God's plan for human redemption.

Corinth: *Temples and Temptations*

Use this visual to remind students of the prevalence of paganism in Corinth and how that would have been the occasion for temptations in every area of life.

"THE KING IS DEAD; LONG LIVE THE KING"

We've probably all glanced at the tabloid headlines while waiting in line at the grocery store. With amazing regularity they announce another sighting of Elvis Presley—"the king of rock and roll." Elvis died in August of 1977, but some of his fans simply cannot acknowledge that an out-of-control lifestyle led him to an early grave. As if to keep the delusion alive nearly a quarter of a century after his death, there are still competitions to see which Elvis impersonator looks most like his idol.

Ted Harrison, author of *Elvis People—The Cult of the King,* says, "The worship, adoration and the perpetuation of the memory of Elvis today closely resembles a religious cult." He cites the thousands of fans who go to Presley's Graceland mansion in Memphis every year on the anniversary of his death, as well as the talk of being loved by Elvis and having a personal relationship with him! Harrison's verdict is that the "Elvis cult" could eventually become a "full-fledged religion."

How little human nature has changed in twenty centuries! It is tragic that spiritually needy people still create their own gods just as they did in Paul's day. Whether the god is an idol of stone or the memory of a musician who destroyed himself with alcohol and drugs, it makes no difference. The truth is as Paul states it: "There is but one God." Let us worship him—the King of kings!   —C. R. B.

C. A WEAK CHRISTIAN'S CONSCIENCE (vv. 7, 8)

7. But not everyone knows this. Some people are still so accustomed to idols that when they eat such food they think of it as having been sacrificed to an idol, and since their conscience is weak, it is defiled.

We noted in last week's lesson how the pagan environment out of which the Corinthian Christians came may have influenced their views on marriage and sex. The same was probably true with attitudes concerning idols. Some Christians saw great harm in eating meat offered to an *idol* because it had been used for pagan purposes. To them, eating such meat was tantamount to worshiping the idol.

Instead of scolding the *weak* Christians who were not secure in the knowledge described in verse 6, Paul encouraged the stronger Christians to be careful lest they cause the weaker ones to stumble. The strong Christian had no problem with meat sacrificed to idols, but the weak Christian, following the example of the strong, might be tempted to eat the meat even though it violated his *conscience*. As a result his conscience would become *defiled;* he would be more susceptible to engage in acts that were clearly sinful, without remorse.

8. But food does not bring us near to God; we are no worse if we do not eat, and no better if we do.

The act of eating *meat* is in itself neither morally good nor bad. It *does not bring us near to God;* that is, in the eyes of God eating does not gain any merit for the Christian, nor is anyone the *worse* for abstaining from eating meat.

II. LIVING BY LOVE (1 CORINTHIANS 8:9-13)

A. NOT MISLEADING OTHERS (vv. 9, 10)

9. Be careful, however, that the exercise of your freedom does not become a stumbling block to the weak.

WHAT DO YOU THINK?

The poet R. L. Sharpe has written:

Each is given a bag of tools,
A shapeless mass, a book of rules;
And each must make, ere life is flown,
A stumbling-block or a stepping stone.

How might keeping this in mind help us as we make decisions about what we do?

Paul acknowledged that the stronger Christians have the *freedom* to eat meat sacrificed to idols. Had they been in a different situation where there were no Christians with sensitive consciences, Paul's discussion might have ended at this point. They would have been free to eat the meat without hesitation. But freedom in Christ does not mean complete lack of restraints on a Christian's behavior. When the stronger Christian uses his freedom without carefully considering the impact his actions may have on *weak* Christians, then he is abusing his freedom. He may become a *stumbling block* to others.

Whenever our freedom to participate in certain actions threatens the spiritual well-being of another person, then our love for that person must transcend our personal freedom, or our "rights," as we often say. Paul encouraged the Galatians to use their freedom in Christ to "serve one another in love" (Galatians 5:13).

10. For if anyone with a weak conscience sees you who have this knowledge eating in an idol's temple, won't he be emboldened to eat what has been sacrificed to idols?

Were some Christians actually sitting in an *idol's temple* and *eating* what was *sacrificed to idols*? Not necessarily. The expression may be a hyperbole, describing the effect on the weaker brother. To him, eating the meat that had been sacrificed to an idol was equivalent to participating in the ceremony at the temple.

Another suggestion has also been offered. Paul may refer to attending a banquet of a civic or social nature that was held in pagan temples. These temples provided convenient meeting places for such gatherings, and Christians might occasionally attend these kinds of banquets. (Perhaps it is just such an occasion Paul refers to in 1 Corinthians 10:27.) Upon seeing other Christians present at one of these occasions, a weaker Christian who did not know better might suppose that they were participating in a pagan ceremony. Or the weaker brother might believe that any activity performed in the temple had religious significance—even social or civic functions. In either case, the weaker brother would be *emboldened* to participate also, violating his *conscience* in the matter.

B. CONSIDERING CHRIST (vv. 11, 12)

11. So this weak brother, for whom Christ died, is destroyed by your knowledge.

By having his conscience thus violated, the *weak brother* might have been led into further actions that were clearly sinful (a result similar to his conscience being "defiled" in verse 7). This could lead to his being lost eternally—and all because the stronger brother, perhaps not realizing the impact of his deeds, had acted by his *knowledge* rather than his love for a fellow Christian.

The same may happen today. Suppose a Christian attends an "R" rated movie that he has carefully selected according to what he considers strict standards. Another believer, knowing the former is a strong Christian, may conclude that attending any "R" rated movie is okay—with tragic results!

We must always consider how our actions may influence others. This may seem a heavy burden to carry, limiting our freedom. But *Christ died* for the weaker brother—as well as the stronger one. Thus, we really have no choice but to shoulder this burden, relying on the Lord to give us the strength to carry it graciously.

12. When you sin against your brothers in this way and wound their weak conscience, you sin against Christ.

We do not live the Christian life in a vacuum. We do have a clear responsibility to our *brothers* and sisters. If we neglect this responsibility and *wound their weak conscience*, increasing the likelihood that they will fall deeper into sin, we *sin against* them. But that does not conclude the matter. We also *sin against Christ*. We harm someone for whom Jesus died, and we do damage to a part of his body. A part of that body cannot be hurt without the Head's feeling the pain.

WHAT DO YOU THINK?

First Corinthians 8:11 speaks of the danger of causing a weak brother, "for whom Christ died," to be destroyed. How can we cultivate better concern for our Christian brothers and sisters to see that this does not happen? What difference would it make in our lives if we did?

HOW TO SAY IT

Corinth. KOR-inth.
Corinthians. Kor-IN-thee-unz.
polytheism. PAHL-uh-thee-iz-um.

C. WILLING TO ADAPT (v. 13)

13. Therefore, if what I eat causes my brother to fall into sin, I will never eat meat again, so that I will not cause him to fall.

Paul concluded his discussion with a statement of his own convictions and of how much he was willing to sacrifice his freedom in Christ for the sake of a weaker Christian. *Meat* in this context refers to meat sacrificed to idols. It was not Paul's intent to argue that Christians should give up all meat and become vegetarians. He is setting forth a fundamental rule governing the behavior of Christians. The standards of Christian behavior are not to be set by knowledge or law, but by love—love for Christ and love for one's Christian brothers and sisters. What a difference it would make if Christians everywhere understood this principle and applied it in their daily living!

HOW MUCH IS A PERSON WORTH?

Suppose you were asked, "What would be the perfect job?" Most people have a fantasy about a "dream job" in which the responsibilities, working conditions, co-workers, and salary all combine to approach perfection.

Many people (especially children!) might say that John Harrison of Oakland, California, has such a job. He is the official taste tester for Dreyer's Ice Cream—one of the premium brands on the U.S. West Coast. Harrison's trained taste buds are so important to him (and to the company) that they are insured for one million dollars! To make sure that he stays in top form for his job, Harrison avoids spicy foods, alcoholic beverages, tobacco, and caffeine. All of these substances either "clog the taste buds," deaden them, or distort the flavor of the ice cream.

So, what are taste buds *really* worth? One million dollars? Five million? Ten million? Another question: what is the spiritual welfare of another person worth? There is no way to put a monetary value on it, but Paul suggests that there is a way to show how much we value it: whether we are willing to limit (or even sacrifice) our freedom in order to protect a Christian brother or sister from stumbling.

How highly do we value fellow Christians? As highly as Christ valued us?

—C. R. B.

CONCLUSION

A. I-STRAIN

"Do your own thing!" How many times have we heard that expression in recent years! Someone has observed that our culture suffers from a severe case of "I-strain." On every hand we see examples of the insistence on one's "rights" to the neglect or even injury of others. It is this selfish attitude that Paul rejects.

As we labor to set forth the Christian ideal that the individual must be willing to subordinate his own wishes and desires for the good of others, we must recognize that we are going against the flow of our times. For every individual who gives his or her life in selfless service to others, there are millions who think only of themselves. As we examine our own lives, we are forced to admit that we have on many occasions fallen short of the ideal Paul sets forth. If we desire to change our own lives to measure up to this ideal, we need to recognize that it will not be an easy task. People are likely to misunderstand us, question our motives, and laugh at us.

B. OUR BROTHERS' KEEPERS

"Am I my brother's keeper?" Cain's hypocritical answer, which he gave in an effort to cover up the murder of his brother Abel, has echoed down through the centuries. For the Christian the answer is *yes* and *no*. The answer is *yes* in the sense that we do have a responsibility first to God and then second to every part

DAILY BIBLE READINGS

Monday, Apr. 3—*Knowledge Puffs Up; Love Builds Up (1 Corinthians 8:1-6)*

Tuesday, Apr. 4—*Don't Cause Another to Stumble (1 Corinthians 8:7-13)*

Wednesday, Apr. 5—*Love Has Priority Over "Rights" (1 Corinthians 9:1-12)*

Thursday, Apr. 6—*Preaching the Gospel Is Reward Enough (1 Corinthians 9:13-18)*

Friday, Apr. 7—*Do Whatever It Takes (1 Corinthians 9:19-27)*

Saturday, Apr. 8—*Learn From Lessons of the Past (1 Corinthians 10:1-13)*

Sunday, Apr. 9—*Flee From the Worship of Idols (1 Corinthians 10:14-22)*

PRAYER

Dear God, help us to be sensitive to the spiritual needs of those about us. Show us how to live in such a way that we will never be a hindrance or a stumbling block to others. Help us to have knowledge, but above all help us to love you and your children. In Christ's name we pray. Amen.

THOUGHT TO REMEMBER

"If what I eat causes my brother to fall into sin, I will never eat meat again" (1 Corinthians 8:13).

WHAT DO YOU THINK?

At times we must stand up for our rights, for certain unscrupulous people will prey upon us if we do not. But we must beware of insisting on our rights even when other people will be hurt, or when we can be of more help to another by yielding. How can we balance our "rights" with our responsibility to serve others? What are some examples of circumstances in which we must achieve such a balance?

of God's creation. This especially applies to the crowning gem of God's creation—the human race, made in his own image.

Obviously we cannot extend our concern to all of creation in the way that God can, but he does expect us to act appropriately within the limits of our wisdom and strength. For example, not so very long ago many Christians took a strong stand against any use of alcoholic beverages. In our more morally relaxed times, some Christians have taken the position that such a viewpoint denies them their freedom. How would Paul react to this thinking? In view of the high cost that alcohol imposes on our society—broken homes, crime, and shattered lives—there is little doubt that he would say, "If drinking alcohol (even only a beer now and then) causes my brother to offend, then I will drink no alcohol so long as the world stands." He would take the same position against many other activities in our current society, including many of the movies and television programs we see and the literature we read.

On the other hand, we must also answer *no* to Cain's question. First of all, we must recognize that we cannot control all the actions of all the people around us. We can teach and we can set good examples, but each person ultimately must make his or her own decisions about moral matters.

Repeated efforts have been made to control people's behavior by laws. Recall how the Pharisees in Jesus' day, for example, attempted to control people's actions by laws that spelled out right and wrong behavior in great detail. In real life it didn't work. In addition, it produced a spiritual pride and arrogance on the part of the Pharisees that led them to oppose Jesus and eventually nail him to the cross.

Paul's solution is not to ignore our brothers or attempt to legislate their behavior, but to try to live our lives in such a way that we are sensitive and loving examples for others.

C. THE WEAKER BROTHER

Many years ago when the game of Monopoly was first introduced, my brother, my cousin, and several neighborhood youngsters would spend hours on rainy days playing the game. But a problem soon arose when we played at our house. To determine moves we had to roll dice. In the eyes of my grandmother, this was sinful because dice were used in gambling. We finally solved the problem by devising a spinner that determined our moves. The irony of all this is that no one questioned the object of the game, which was to bankrupt your opponent by lucky moves or clever trading. Perhaps the game was relatively harmless, yet its subtle emphasis was on greed.

We may smile at this childhood experience, but it does point to a problem that we must face as we try to live in such a way that we do not cause others to stumble. By concentrating on minor details, we may neglect the larger, more important issues of Christian living.

In Romans 14 Paul discusses in detail the principle of concern for the weaker brother. There he points out that we cannot make the conscience of the weaker brother the only standard for our actions. If we do, the weaker brother may become a moral dictator, controlling everyone's behavior by his delicate conscience.

In the Romans passage Paul warns the strong not to despise the weak and the weak not to judge the strong (Romans 14:1-3). Interestingly enough, Paul makes no mention, either in the Romans passage or in today's lesson text, that the weak should become strong. In many matters we may not know which position the inspired apostle would label "weak" and which he would call "strong." All we know is that we disagree. No matter. Act according to your own conscience and accept the brother who disagrees without judging—whether weak or strong.

Discovery Learning

This page contains an alternate lesson plan emphasizing learning activities. Classes desiring such student involvement will find these suggestions helpful. The next page is a reproducible activity page to further enhance discovery learning.

LEARNING GOALS

After this lesson your students should be able to:

1. Summarize Paul's teaching about love and knowledge as it applies to the issue of eating meat sacrificed to idols.

2. Compare the issue Paul addressed with disputable matters that concern Christians today.

3. Determine to make choices based on love for Christ and his church more than on personal freedom.

INTO THE LESSON

Distribute copies of the following scenario and ask your students to pretend they are members of the same church as "James." Ask them what they might say to him in response to this incident.

James is a professional athlete who claims to be a "born-again Christian." After his arrest for drunk driving, he told reporters, "It's a free country and what I do with my life, as long as I don't hurt anyone, is my business. I've never told anyone else to pattern his life after mine, and I don't need anyone to tell me how to live my life."

Discuss their responses briefly for now; then move on to the next exercise.

INTO THE WORD

Introduce the issue of eating meat offered to idols as background information. (Use the material in the comments on 1 Corinthians 8:1.) Then divide your class into groups of three or four each. Distribute copies of Exercise 1 to half the groups and copies of Exercise 2 to the other half (or refer them to the student books). Ask each group to complete its exercise (correct answers are in parentheses). Allow five to ten minutes for the group activities; then bring the class together to review their conclusions.

EXERCISE 1

Read 1 Corinthians 8:1-3, 10-13, and complete the chart below, contrasting knowledge and love. Then discuss the questions that follow.

Verse	Knowledge	Love
1	Puffs up	(Builds up)
2, 3	(Lacks full knowledge)	Is known by God
10-13	Can destroy a weak brother	(Won't cause a weak brother to stumble)

1. What kind of knowledge was Paul talking about in verse 1?

2. What does it mean that a person who thinks he knows something knows nothing (v. 2)?

3. How are love and knowledge related (v. 3)?

4. How could one Christian's knowledge cause another to stumble (vv. 10-13)?

5. How could wounding a weak conscience be a sin against Christ (v. 12)?

6. Should a Christian avoid doing something that is not sinful simply because someone might be offended by it? Why or why not?

EXERCISE 2

From 1 Corinthians 8:4-10, identify the statements below as true or false; then discuss the questions that follow:

1. Paul said that idols are not real beings. (True, v. 4.)

2. According to Paul, there really are many gods. (False, vv. 5, 6.)

3. Some consciences are defiled by eating meat offered to idols. (True, v. 7.)

4. We are better, in God's eyes, for not eating some foods. (False, v. 8.)

5. Our freedom can cause others to stumble into sin. (True, vv. 9, 10.)

1. What did Paul mean when he said an idol is "nothing at all in the world" (v. 4)?

2. Did Paul really believe that there are many "gods" (vv. 5, 6)?

3. How would eating meat offered to an idol defile another's weak conscience (v. 7)?

4. What does verse 8 mean, "But food does not bring us near to God"?

5. How can a Christian's freedom become a stumbling block to a weak brother (vv. 9, 10)?

Option: Distribute copies of Exercise A from the next page to guide the class, as a whole or in small groups, in a study of today's text.

INTO LIFE

Return to the "Into the Lesson" exercise. In light of Paul's teaching, would your students make any changes or additions to their first efforts?

Distribute copies of Exercise B from the next page. Divide the class into three groups, and assign each situation to one of the groups.

Exercise A

As you read the text for today's lesson, 1 Corinthians 8:1-13, fill in the blanks below:

1. Now about food _____ to idols: We know that we all possess _____.

2. But the man who _____ God is known by God.

3. So then, about _____ food _____ to idols: We know that an idol is _____ at all in the world and that there is no God but one.

4. For even if there are so-called gods, whether in _____ or on _____ (as indeed there are many "gods" and many "_____"), yet for us there is but one God, the _____, from whom all things came and for whom we ____; and there is but one ____, Jesus Christ, through whom all things came and through whom ___ ____.

5. Some people are still so _____ to idols that when they eat such food they think of it as having been _____ to an idol, and since their _____ is weak, it is defiled.

6. Be careful, however, that the exercise of your _____ does not become a _____ _____ to the weak.

7. For if anyone with a weak conscience sees you who have this knowledge eating in an idol's _____, won't he be _____ to eat what has been sacrificed to idols?

8. So this weak brother, for whom _____ ____, is destroyed by your knowledge.

9. When you sin against your _____ in this way and wound their weak _____, you sin against _____.

Exercise B

Read each of the following situations below and, using Paul's "stumbling block" principle in 1 Corinthians 8:9-13, decide what response would be appropriate. To what other, similar situations, could you apply Paul's principle?

1. Dave, a deacon in a local congregation, regularly buys tickets in the state lottery. Recently, he celebrated a $1000 win by purchasing a new TV/VCR for the church. Mary, whose husband is a member of Gamblers' Anonymous, has complained to the elders that Dave's gambling is threatening her husband's recovery. What should the elders do?

2. Bill and Pam, avid golfers, are members of the local country club. Their Bible school teachers, Mark and Cheryl, recently criticized the country club in class, because of the social drinking that goes on there. Now Bill and Pam are unsure about whether or not to continue their membership. What should they do?

3. Eleven-year-old Jessica is having a sleep-over birthday party. One of the guests, Alicia, has shown up with an R-rated video that several of the girls are anxious to see. Jessica's parents do not want her to view the video, and they are concerned that some of the other parents would be upset with them if their daughters viewed it. What should they say to Alicia and her parents?

SPIRITUAL GIFTS

LESSON 7

WHY TEACH THIS LESSON?

Michael Jordan, who retired from professional basketball last year, is probably the greatest player ever to play in the NBA. The records he set and the honors he won speak for themselves. But Michael Jordan never won an NBA championship. The Chicago Bulls won six while he played for them, and it's fair to say that Jordan led the team to those titles. But Michael Jordan alone never won a championship.

Basketball is a team sport. It blends the gifts and talents of several players. Some shoot well and some rebound; some handle the ball well and others are fierce on defense. Occasionally a standout comes along who can do everything well—but even he cannot do it all by himself. He still needs the team.

Spiritual gifts are like that. We need the combined efforts of all whom God has gifted. If your students are not "spiritual Michael Jordans," that's okay. God will take the talents and gifts of each of them and build the church just the same.

INTRODUCTION

A. NAILED TOGETHER

One day the parts of a sailing vessel got into a terrible argument about which was the most important. "I am the most important," said the sail, "for I enable the ship to move."

"But," responded the mast, "without me you would be nothing but a piece of canvas."

Then the deck got into the argument: "Without me there would be no place for the sailors who man the ship to stand."

"Yes," replied the rudder, "but without me no one could steer the ship."

Thus the argument went back and forth. Finally, in the midst of all the debate, a tiny voice was heard: "Without me none of you would be part of a boat at all." Looking around, the various parts discovered that the tiny voice came from the nails that were absolutely necessary to hold the boat together.

Thus it is with the church. Every member of the church is important, but without the power of the Holy Spirit to hold the parts together there could be no church. That is the point Paul makes in today's lesson.

B. LESSON BACKGROUND

The previous lessons in this quarter have dealt with some of the problems and controversies plaguing the church at Corinth. Today's lesson deals with another controversial matter—the place of spiritual gifts in the church. This issue was not settled once and for all in the first century. In fact, within the past three or four decades it has become a subject of debate in hundreds of congregations and most major denominations.

God has poured out many wonderful gifts upon mankind, including the "indescribable gift" of his only Son (2 Corinthians 9:15). Today's lesson, however, deals with the special gifts that he granted to his church, which are often called "spiritual gifts" or "charismatic gifts." Several of these gifts are mentioned in the New Testament (Romans 12:6-8; 1 Corinthians 12:4-11, 28-30; Ephesians 4:7-12).

DEVOTIONAL READING:
ROMANS 12:1-8

BACKGROUND SCRIPTURE:
1 CORINTHIANS 12:1-30

PRINTED TEXT:
1 CORINTHIANS 12:4-20, 24b-26

LESSON AIMS

After this lesson each student will be able to:

1. Tell how the various spiritual gifts in a church body function together for the health and unity of the body.

2. Tell what Paul says about the variety of gifts and why that variety is so important in the church.

3. Identify at least one spiritual gift he or she possesses and describe how it can be used to edify others in the body.

Apr
16

KEY VERSE

There are different kinds of gifts, but the same Spirit. . . . There are different kinds of working, but the same God works all of them in all men.

—1 Corinthians 12:4, 6

LESSON 7 NOTES

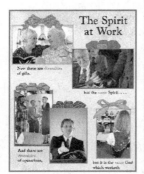

Today's visual illustrates our Key Verse. Discuss how unity is seen in diversity in the church today as well as in the first century.

WHAT DO YOU THINK?

First Corinthians 12:7 tells us that every spiritual gift is given "for the common good." Every believer should be excited to realize that he or she has something to contribute to the good of the church. We often hear the lament, "I don't feel like a part of the church!" But when we ponder how a certain talent we possess is important to the congregation's evangelistic outreach or worship or teaching programs, we will be assured that we are an important part. How does thinking of our gifts or talents as existing "for the common good" help you to appreciate the value of your gifts and the gifts of others?

The term *charismatic* is derived from the Greek word *charisma*, meaning "gift." This word is used in the New Testament to describe much more than just the gifts mentioned in today's text. Eternal life is called a *charisma* in Romans 6:23. The lifestyle of being single or married is called a *charisma* in 1 Corinthians 7:7.

Spiritual gifts have afforded great blessings to the church, but they have also been a source of problems, as illustrated by the situation in Corinth. There spiritual gifts became a source of unholy pride. Some believers were jealous of the possession of certain gifts, especially the ability to speak in tongues (1 Corinthians 14:1-25). Thus the gifts became a divisive force, threatening the unity of the church.

Paul begins 1 Corinthians 12 with these words: "Now about spiritual gifts, brothers, I do not want you to be ignorant." Similar wording has been seen before (see 7:1; 8:1). It is generally agreed that this refers to another matter raised in the letter from the Corinthians to Paul. One reason this question may have been raised was that certain activities associated with pagan worship resembled some of the spiritual gifts. It is obvious from Paul's emphasis on *one body* throughout chapter 12 that the exercise of these gifts had become more important than the pursuit of unity in Christ.

I. DIVERSITY OF GIFTS (1 CORINTHIANS 12:4-11)

A. SOURCE OF GIFTS (vv. 4-6)
4. There are different kinds of gifts, but the same Spirit.

In verses 1-3 of 1 Corinthians 12 Paul reminds his readers that they had come from pagan backgrounds and from the worship of "mute idols" (v. 2). In the pagan temples and religious services, they had likely witnessed a variety of phenomena that they had believed were evidence of the pagan gods' activities. The point Paul makes is that the real test of any "gift" is whether or not it leads people to acclaim Jesus as Lord.

The members of the Corinthian church had displayed a variety of *gifts*. Since in the pagan world different gods were associated with different gifts, Paul wanted to assure the Corinthians that the *different kinds of gifts* within the church all had a common source—*the same Spirit.*

5. There are different kinds of service, but the same Lord.

While Paul speaks of *different kinds of service*, the intent is the same as "different kinds of gifts" in verse 4. The source of these is described as *the same Lord.*

6. There are different kinds of working, but the same God works all of them in all men.

Another similar phrase, *different kinds of working*, is seen in this verse. All spiritual gifts come from the Godhead, whose triune nature is expressed in verses 4-6 as the Spirit, the Lord (Jesus), and *God*. Such harmony of purpose ought to be demonstrated by God's people.

B. VARIETY OF GIFTS (vv. 7-11)
7. Now to each one the manifestation of the Spirit is given for the common good.

The *manifestation of the Spirit* is a particular gift of God given through the Holy Spirit. Paul affirms here that some such gift has been given to *each one*. Every Christian has received one or more spiritual gifts. In the verses that follow Paul specifically mentions some of these, but it does not appear that he intends to make this list exhaustive (other lists include gifts that Paul does not mention here, and he includes some here that are not mentioned elsewhere). The purpose of these gifts must not be overlooked: they are *given for the common good*—that is, to provide for the mutual encouragement and edification of everyone in the church.

FOR THE GOOD OF EVERYONE

Can you remember when making a telephone call involved picking up the earpiece, cranking the handle on the box on the wall, and shouting into the mouthpiece so the operator could hear you? Then she would connect you with the person to whom you wished to talk.

Then came dial phones, and soon we had prefixes to the numbers, such as "Gladstone" or "Jackson." Next came all-number dialing, and an ever-increasing number of digits in the phone numbers. Now we have push-button phones and a growing number of area codes; sometimes area codes even overlap within the same area.

This might seem unnecessarily complicated, but those hundreds of millions of phone lines are essential if we are to benefit from the fax machines and computers in our homes and offices, not to mention conduct ordinary conversation. The multiplicity of numbers lets our technology work for the greater good of everyone.

The gifts that the Spirit gives are a lot like those phone numbers. The multiplicity of gifts lets the various members of a congregation work for the "common good" of everyone (1 Corinthians 12:7). Those who fail to discover and use the gift or gifts that the Spirit has given them deprive themselves and their church of numerous blessings. When the church isn't blessed by the use of our gifts, the fault is with *us*—not the Spirit!   —C. R. B.

8. To one there is given through the Spirit the message of wisdom, to another the message of knowledge by means of the same Spirit.

One of the difficulties we have in understanding spiritual gifts lies in the fact that Paul does not explain what each of these gifts enabled someone to do. In some cases, the best we can do is to use the names themselves and try to determine what the exercise of the gifts may have included.

One may gain certain types of *wisdom* through experience and study. The wisdom Paul lists here as a gift must be something beyond such "ordinary" wisdom. The same is true of *knowledge*. It would seem that both of these had something to do with God's revelation of truth to an individual. This was especially important during the early years of the church, before the written New Testament was completed.

9. . . . to another faith by the same Spirit, to another gifts of healing by that one Spirit.

The word *faith* carries several different meanings in the New Testament. Here it may describe an extraordinary level of faith, such as the "mountain-moving" faith described in 1 Corinthians 13:2, where faith is listed among several other gifts that clearly are miraculous.

The phrase *gifts of healing* refers to healings that are miraculous, instantaneous, and complete. (The plural *gifts* may be used because of the many kinds of sickness that were healed.) The healings produced by this gift should not be confused with the healings that came in answer to prayer. These latter healings would have differed from miraculous healings primarily in two ways. First, healings that came in answer to prayer did not usually occur instantaneously. Furthermore, all Christians could have prayed for healing, not just a few persons who had the gift of miraculous healing.

10. . . . to another miraculous powers, to another prophecy, to another distinguishing between spirits, to another speaking in different kinds of tongues, and to still another the interpretation of tongues.

A more literal translation of *miraculous powers* is "workings of powers." This expression would include miracles other than those of healing. Some suggest that it may refer to such acts as raising people from the dead or drinking poison without any ill effects (Mark 16:18).

HOW TO SAY IT

Agabus. AG-uh-bus.
charisma (Greek). kah-RISS-ma.
charismatic. care-iz-MAT-ik.
Corinth. KOR-inth.
Corinthians. Kor-IN-thee-unz.

WHAT DO YOU THINK?

Compare the role of the "prophet" with that of the "preacher" in today's church. How are they alike? How are they different?

Literature of the Greco-Roman period contains numerous references to so-called prophecies, often known as oracles. The *prophecy* mentioned here differs from these accounts in that it came from the Holy Spirit, insuring its accuracy. The role of the prophet was not merely to predict the future (recall Agabus's warning to Paul—in Acts 21:10, 11—that if he went to Jerusalem, he would be bound and delivered to the Gentiles), but more importantly to teach spiritual truth. It is this aspect of prophecy that Paul especially commended to the church at Corinth (as in 1 Corinthians 14:1-5). The *distinguishing between spirits* appropriately follows that of prophecy, for this gift would allow its possessor to distinguish false prophets from true prophets.

On the Day of Pentecost, the apostles began to speak with "other tongues" (Acts 2:4). This was the result of a unique outpouring of the Holy Spirit, and the listeners heard the message in their own languages (Acts 2:8). The *different kinds of tongues* here refers to languages as well. The *interpretation of tongues* was the ability to translate instantaneously something spoken in an unknown language—especially if it was spoken as an expression of the gift of tongues. Paul later called tongues a "sign" to unbelievers (1 Corinthians 14:22). He taught that Christians should not speak in tongues in public worship unless an interpreter was present (1 Corinthians 14:27, 28). These gifts would have been quite useful in a busy commercial city such as Corinth, where people from many nations were found.

It is important to note that all of these miraculous gifts served a vital purpose in the early church. In the case of gifts such as wisdom and knowledge, the purpose was to provide divine guidance until the time when the writings of the New Testament were completed. The working of miracles and the speaking in tongues served to confirm the gospel message when it was first delivered (Mark 16:17-20).

Note that these miraculous gifts (prophecies, tongues, knowledge) are described as those that will "cease," "be stilled," and "pass away" when "perfection comes" (1 Corinthians 13:8-10). Some believe that this "perfection" describes the New Testament Scriptures. Once these were completed, there was no need for additional revelation or for the gifts of confirmation to continue; for the record of the confirmation could be found in the Scriptures.

11. All these are the work of one and the same Spirit, and he gives them to each one, just as he determines.

Paul emphasizes that all gifts come from *the same Spirit*. No one has any reason to boast about the gift or gifts that he has received.

II. ANALOGY OF THE BODY (1 CORINTHIANS 12:12-20)

A. ONE BODY, MANY MEMBERS (v. 12)

12. The body is a unit, though it is made up of many parts; and though all its parts are many, they form one body. So it is with Christ.

Even though the human *body* has *many parts*, it still functions as a *unit*. *So it is with Christ*. In the verses that follow, Paul compares the diversity of gifts in the body of Christ with the various parts of the human body that work together to make the body complete.

B. UNITY BY ONE SPIRIT (v. 13)

13. For we were all baptized by one Spirit into one body—whether Jews or Greeks, slave or free—and we were all given the one Spirit to drink.

Through being *baptized*, believers become a part of the *one body* of Christ. The *Spirit* is closely involved in this process. On the Day of Pentecost Peter proclaimed that penitent believers would receive the "gift of the Holy Spirit" when they were baptized (Acts 2:38).

In the body of Christ the various categories into which people are often placed lose their significance. *Jews, Greeks, slave,* and *free* are equal before God because they *were all given the one Spirit to drink*—that is, all have received the Holy Spirit, who, like God the Father, does not show favoritism (Acts 10:34).

C. Unity in Diversity (vv. 14-20)

14. Now the body is not made up of one part but of many.

This verse states what is obvious to anyone who has given the matter a passing thought. It sets the stage for the examples that Paul uses in the verses that follow.

15. If the foot should say, "Because I am not a hand, I do not belong to the body," it would not for that reason cease to be part of the body.

We do not think much about a *foot* unless it is hurt or crippled. Otherwise, our feet do not receive much attention or respect. Paul may have deliberately used the feet as an example for that very reason. Perhaps they represented members of the Corinthian church who were snubbed because their gifts did not seem important. But that did not give them an excuse to secede from the rest of the *body.* To suggest that something like that could happen to the human body is absurd.

16. And if the ear should say, "Because I am not an eye, I do not belong to the body," it would not for that reason cease to be part of the body.

After considering two extremities, the feet and the hands, Paul turns to two sensory organs, the *ear* and the *eye.* While these organs perform very different functions, both are necessary if *the body* is to operate at its greatest efficiency.

17. If the whole body were an eye, where would the sense of hearing be? If the whole body were an ear, where would the sense of smell be?

No one organ or other member of the body can exist apart from the other members. Each part performs a unique function that is necessary for the well-being of *the whole body.* This fact is perfectly obvious when dealing with the human body, and is just as true of Christ's body.

18. But in fact God has arranged the parts in the body, every one of them, just as he wanted them to be.

While the human body's diversity in function is quite evident to nearly everyone, that same diversity in the church is often not as appreciated as it should be. Paul reminds the fragmented Corinthians that the source of that diversity is *God.*

19, 20. If they were all one part, where would the body be? As it is, there are many parts, but one body.

Paul clinches his argument with a rhetorical question. What kind of a *body* would one have if every *part* were exactly like every other part? The church would be totally helpless if every member were exactly alike, coming from the same mold. The immediate application of this principle was to the variety and use of gifts within the Corinthian church, but it is equally applicable to other aspects of church life today.

III. GOD'S CONCERN FOR THE BODY (1 CORINTHIANS 12:24b-26)

A. God Honors All Parts (v. 24b)

24b. But God has combined the members of the body and has given greater honor to the parts that lacked it.

Paul now makes the application from what he has said. God designed the physical *body* so that every member performs a function essential to the well-being of the whole. Some of the smallest or most obscure organs or *members* of the body may actually be among the most important. Thus has God *given greater honor* to the *parts* that seem to lack it. Every part of the body should be respected for its contribution to the good of the body. This is true in the body of Christ as well.

What Do You Think?

What are some gifts or ministries that we may be inclined to regard as less important in the church? Why do we do that? How can we correct the situation?

What Do You Think?

What are some church programs in which the blending of the members' various talents and gifts can be easily demonstrated?

B. SO SHOULD HIS PEOPLE (vv. 25, 26)

25. . . . so that there should be no division in the body, but that its parts should have equal concern for each other.

Paul insists that there not be any *division* within the *body* of Christ. The church at Corinth seems to have been more blessed with spiritual gifts than other congregations in New Testament times, yet it was characterized by a more divisive spirit than that found in other congregations.

Paul's words indicate that this divisiveness stemmed from the Corinthians' lack of *equal concern for each other.* Were Paul to visit many congregations today, he would, unfortunately, find this same condition. If the situation in Corinth mirrors the situation in the church where we serve, then we ought to repent in humility and act to restore the unity that God wants in his church and for which Jesus prayed (John 17:20, 21).

AN ACT OF UNUSUAL CONCERN

Too often the focus of the news media seems to be only on crime, violence, and natural disasters. It is refreshing, then, when good news is reported, even if it comes as the result of something bad that has happened.

Such was the case a couple of years ago. An eighty-year-old woman with a puppy was put off a commercial bus at a deserted Florida truck stop at 3:00 A.M. She did not know that animals were not allowed on the bus. Her plight was made more serious by the fact that her hearing and eyesight were failing and that she used a crutch.

The good news is that a security guard called the area sheriff, who enlisted the help of deputies in five neighboring counties. They gave the woman food and carried her in their patrol cars, one after the other, to her home. The last deputy helped her walk right to her front door.

The fact that this woman was elderly may have helped her obtain some extra care from the deputies, but isn't it refreshing to see the institutions of society working together to accomplish good? However, in society at large—*and* in the church—we should not have to rely on "officials" to do good. The biblical principle is that we *all* should demonstrate "equal concern for each other" (1 Corinthians 12:25).

Can the world count on us who are Christians to live this way? Is this the way you and I are known for living *our* lives?   —C. R. B.

26. If one part suffers, every part suffers with it; if one part is honored, every part rejoices with it.

All of us recognize how true this is of our own bodies. If we have a severe headache, the whole body suffers; if we catch a cold, the whole body is uncomfortable. The reverse is just as true. When the members of our body are well, we feel good all over and we are also mentally and emotionally healthy. The application to the church is obvious. (See Paul's admonition in Romans 12:15: "Rejoice with those who rejoice; mourn with those who mourn.")

CONCLUSION

Today we have studied Paul's use of the human body to illustrate that unity and diversity can (and must) exist alongside one another in the body of Christ. The world of music provides other helpful examples. Certainly an orchestra includes many different instruments of various shapes and sounds. However, this diversity does not stand in the way of unity. A skilled conductor knows just how to bring harmony out of the diversity, resulting in a pleasant listening experience for an audience.

Let us resolve that our church's diversity in gifts and abilities will be united under the direction of our "Conductor"—Jesus Christ.

Discovery Learning

This page contains an alternate lesson plan emphasizing learning activities. Classes desiring such student involvement will find these suggestions helpful. The next page is a reproducible activity page to further enhance discovery learning.

LEARNING GOALS

After this lesson each student will be able to:

1. Tell how the various spiritual gifts in a church body function together for the health and unity of the body.

2. Tell what Paul says about the variety of gifts and why that variety is so important in the church.

3. Identify at least one spiritual gift he or she possesses and describe how it can be used to edify others in the body.

INTO THE LESSON

Display three small pieces of wood: one of natural wood, one of plywood, and one of particleboard. Tell the class members to assume that all three pieces are from the same type of tree, such as a pine. Then ask them to rate the three pieces in terms of strength, from weakest to strongest. (Particleboard is weakest because it is simply made of wood particles held together by glue. The board is only as strong as the glue that binds the pieces together. Natural wood is much stronger than particleboard, but it can crack and split along the grain. Plywood is strongest because it is made of thin layers of wood glued and pressed together with the grain of each layer running in a different direction to prevent splitting. Thus, each layer reinforces the others around it, making the whole piece strong.)

Discuss your class's ratings, then explain to them that today's lesson from 1 Corinthians 12 will show how God unites individual Christians with their particular gifts to make a strong church.

INTO THE WORD

Distribute copies of the following exercise (without the material in parentheses) or the corresponding activity in the student book. Ask each student to read 1 Corinthians 12:4-20, 24-26 and then to fill in the blanks for each statement below. (Correct answers and the verses where they are found are supplied in parentheses for the teacher's convenience.)

1. There are different kinds of gifts, but the same _____. There are different kinds of _____, but the same Lord. (*Spirit, service, vv. 4, 5*)

2. There are different kinds of _____, but the same God. (*working, v. 6*)

3. To each one the _____ of the Spirit is given for the common good. (*manifestation, v. 7*)

4. To one there is given through the Spirit the message of _____, to another the message of _____. (*wisdom, knowledge, v. 8*)

5. To another _____ by the same Spirit, to another gifts of _____ by that one Spirit, to another _____ _____, to another _____, to another _____ between spirits, to another speaking in _____ kinds of _____, and to still another the _____ of tongues. (*faith, healing, miraculous powers, prophecy, distinguishing, different, tongues, interpretation, vv. 9, 10*)

6. For we were all _____ by one _____ into one body. (*baptized, Spirit v. 13*)

7. If the _____ should say, "Because I am not a _____, I do not belong to the body," it would not for that reason cease to be part of the body. (*foot, hand, v. 15*)

8. And if the _____ should say, "Because I am not an _____, I do not belong to the _____," it would not for that reason cease to be part of the body. (*ear, eye, body, v. 16*)

9. If the whole body were an eye, where would the sense of _____ be? If the whole body were an ear, where would the sense of _____ be? (*hearing, smell, v. 17*)

10. But God has combined the members of the body and has given greater _____ to the parts that lacked it. (*honor, v. 24*)

11. The parts of the body should have _____ concern for each other. (*equal, v. 25*)

12. If one part _____, every part suffers with it; if one part is honored, every part rejoices with it. (*suffers, v. 26*)

Using the students' answers and the lesson commentary, discuss Paul's teaching on the variety of spiritual gifts in the church.

INTO LIFE

There is a saying, "Our strength is our diversity." Ask the class in what way that slogan is true of the church. Ask for examples.

Divide the class into pairs. Ask each student to list the spiritual gifts he or she has and to make another list of the gifts of his or her partner. Have the partners compare their lists and to discuss any gifts that appear on both lists but are not currently being used. Have them discuss ways to put those gifts to work for the church's good and to pray together for opportunities to do that.

Option: Use the reproducible activity on the next page to make application of today's lesson.

Hand-Eye Coordination

Look at the picture below. Number the parts of the body shown from one to ten, with one being the most important to you. Which part of the body could you get along without most easily? Why? In what situations would some parts become more necessary than others? What body parts need others to function properly?

What Part of the Body Are You?

From the picture above, first circle the body part that best represents your current role in the church—the body of Christ. In the space to the left or right of the figure, briefly explain how you function as that organ or limb. Next, circle the body part that best represents the way you would like to be serving. It could be the same part you've already circled or another one. Write below an explanation for your choice.

CHRIST'S RESURRECTION AND OURS

LESSON 8

WHY TEACH THIS LESSON?

In Jerusalem, Paul asserted that he was on trial because of his "hope in the resurrection of the dead" (Acts 23:6). In Rome he met with Jewish leaders and told them, "It is because of the hope of Israel that I am bound with this chain" (Acts 28:20). The "hope of Israel" was, indeed, the "hope in the resurrection of the dead." It is today the hope of Christians. Therefore, it is something we need to understand as clearly as possible. We may not be bound with chains or stand trial because of our hope, but we will be tested. (See Romans 5:3-5.) This lesson provides an opportunity to provide a sure anchor for your students' hope.

INTRODUCTION

A. RECYCLED RAGS

In the process of producing textiles, there are always scraps of material that cannot be used. These are sometimes sent to a paper mill. From other sources, old and worn-out clothes are gathered and sent to the same mill. All of these are then processed and added to wood pulp. The end product is a beautiful, high-grade bond paper on which especially important documents are printed.

If a paper maker can take useless scraps and ragged old clothes and make a valuable product from them, why should we doubt that God, the "people maker," can take our feeble, worn-out bodies and make glorious new bodies from them?

B. LESSON BACKGROUND

Apparently there were some in the Corinthian church who were denying the resurrection of the dead (1 Corinthians 15:12). The exact details of this false belief are not clear, but Paul leaves no doubt about its consequences if carried to its logical conclusion. "If there is no resurrection of the dead, then not even Christ has been raised" (v. 13). This in turn meant that the Corinthians' (and all Christians') faith was in vain and that they were still in their sins.

The disheartening conclusion of Paul's argument is stated in verse 19: "If only for this life we have hope in Christ, we are to be pitied more than all men." Our printed text begins with the next verse, where Paul begins to examine some of the key issues surrounding the resurrection.

I. CHRIST'S RESURRECTION (1 CORINTHIANS 15:20-23)

A. ITS CERTAINTY (v. 20)

20. But Christ has indeed been raised from the dead, the firstfruits of those who have fallen asleep.

The origin of this skepticism is not certain. Some believe it stemmed from certain Greek philosophers who believed the soul was immortal but that the body was not resurrected. Others see its source in an early form of the what later came to be known as Gnosticism, which insisted that the material world was evil.

DEVOTIONAL READING:
1 CORINTHIANS 15:12-19, 50-58
BACKGROUND SCRIPTURE:
1 CORINTHIANS 15
PRINTED TEXT:
1 CORINTHIANS 15:20-27, 35-44

LESSON AIMS

After completing this lesson, each student should be able to:

1. Tell what Paul says about the certainty of Christ's resurrection and his role as the "firstfruits," guaranteeing believers' resurrection.

2. Contrast the Christian perspective on the future with that of the unbeliever.

3. Give thanks to God that the resurrection of Christ remains the sure foundation of Christian faith and hope.

Apr
23

KEY VERSE

But Christ has indeed been raised from the dead, the firstfruits of those who have fallen asleep. . . . For as in Adam all die, so in Christ all will be made alive. –1 Corinthians 15:20, 22

LESSON 8 NOTES

WHAT DO YOU THINK?

Skeptics deny that Jesus actually rose from the dead. How would you answer if an unbeliever challenged your faith in the resurrection of Jesus?

In the face of this doubt, Paul thundered forth an absolute certainty: *But Christ has indeed been raised from the dead.* The resurrection of Christ marks the *firstfruits* of those who have died. This term had rich overtones for those who understood the Old Testament. In dedicating the firstfruits of a crop, a farmer was demonstrating his assurance that God would provide the entire harvest. The portion offered was a pledge, signifying that the rest of the harvest would one day be gathered. Thus Christ's resurrection stands as the assurance that all others who have died will also be raised. Since this is true, it was appropriate for Paul to speak of them as *those who have fallen asleep.* Death is not final; we shall "awaken" from it.

B. ADAM AND CHRIST CONTRASTED (vv. 21-23)

21, 22. For since death came through a man, the resurrection of the dead comes also through a man. For as in Adam all die, so in Christ all will be made alive.

Because of the sin of *Adam, death* came as a punishment, not to Adam alone but to the entire human race. As a result, man's eternal status remained hopeless until *Christ* came. His *resurrection* has given new hope to humanity. In him *all will be made alive.* All who have died will be raised when he returns, as the next verse states. This does not mean that all will be saved. Assuredly all will be raised, but some to eternal life and some to eternal punishment (John 5:28, 29; Acts 24:15).

23. But each in his own turn: Christ, the firstfruits; then, when he comes, those who belong to him.

The Greek word translated *turn* described an army unit properly organized to move in a strategic manner. Thus, declared Paul, the resurrection will proceed according to a plan—obviously a divine plan. Christ will be the head of the procession, for he has already risen; then *when he comes, those who belong to him* will follow. First Thessalonians 4:13-18 tells us that at Jesus' return "the dead in Christ will rise first," then those "who are still alive and are left will be caught up . . . to meet the Lord in the air."

RENEWED, NOT REBURIED

Czar Nicholas II went into exile in 1917 as the Russian Revolution was beginning. He and his family were assassinated by a Bolshevik firing squad the following year. Their bodies were burned in a pit and then buried.

More than sixty years later the bones were discovered. After several more years went by, and following the collapse of the Communist empire, the royal remains were transferred to a morgue. Finally, on July 17, 1998, eighty years to the day after their murders, the members of the royal family were given a belated Russian state funeral and reburied in a ceremony of "repentance and atonement," as one report of the event described it.

Such an act reminds us of man's limitations concerning death. People can conduct a reburial, even adding touches of dignity and decor, but they cannot bring about a resurrection.

Because of Jesus' resurrection, however, man's limitations are overshadowed by God's power. When the dead in Christ are raised at his return, not only will our decayed physical bodies be changed into a new and glorious form, they shall be inhabited again by our spirits, never to die again. That is far better than any state funeral, no matter how belated or how richly deserved. —C. R. B.

The glorious resurrection of Christ is the theme of today's visual. You may want to display it on other occasions besides today's class session.

II. CHRIST'S ULTIMATE VICTORY (1 CORINTHIANS 15:24-27)

A. AUTHORITY ASSERTED (v. 24)

24. Then the end will come, when he hands over the kingdom to God the Father after he has destroyed all dominion, authority and power.

The end refers to the end of this present age. While men have attempted to discern when this will occur, we really know for certain only this: Jesus will return! The book of Revelation speaks of the occasion in these words: "The kingdom of the world has become the kingdom of our Lord and of his Christ, and he will reign for ever and ever" (Revelation 11:15).

Obviously that time has not yet come. While, in a sense, Christ does rule even now, the kingdoms of this world are anything but in subjection to him. In fact, many of the kingdoms of our day stand in defiant rejection of his authority.

When Jesus returns, he will destroy *all dominion, authority and power.* He will not wait until we have everything in order before he comes to take charge. He will come at the time designated by his *Father,* and he will come with full and absolute authority. As Paul tells us in Philippians 2:10 and 11, every knee will then bow at the name of Jesus and every tongue will confess him as Lord. Thus it is urgent that we so live that we will be ready whenever that triumphant day arrives.

B. ALL ENEMIES CONQUERED (vv. 25-27)
25. For he must reign until he has put all his enemies under his feet.

Paul told the Ephesian church that God has set Jesus "at his right hand . . . far above all rule and authority, power and dominion, and every title that can be given." From this lofty throne he reigns "not only in the present age but also in the one to come." God has "placed all things under his feet and appointed him to be head over everything for the church" (Ephesians 1:20-22).

This passage in Ephesians helps us to understand what Paul means here. Jesus will continue to *reign* as Head of the church until "the end" (verse 24), when he will have *put all his enemies under his feet*—an expression that conveys the idea of total victory over an enemy and the enemy's complete subjection. This language has its roots in the Old Testament, specifically the messianic prophecy of Psalm 110:1: "The Lord says to my Lord: 'Sit at my right hand until I make your enemies a footstool for your feet.'"

26. The last enemy to be destroyed is death.

Death is the ultimate *enemy* of the human race. Every person born into this world must, unless the Lord returns first, exit through the gate of death. The Bible records the resurrection of several persons, but each of these persons eventually had to drink the cup of mortality. Medical science has made many advances in the past generation and has extended the life expectancy of human beings. All that these breakthroughs have done, however, is to postpone the inevitable.

With the coming of Christ, man's outlook on death changed dramatically. That death has already been dealt a fatal blow because of Jesus is clear from Hebrews 2:14, 15: "so that by his death he might destroy him who holds the power of death—that is, the devil—and free those who all their lives were held in slavery by their fear of death." Thus those who are born into the new life in Christ have already begun to experience some of the blessings that come by knowing that death is no longer able to cast a dark shadow over their lives. Jesus has given us the promise that those who believe on God and who know God have eternal life already (John 5:24; 17:3). When Jesus returns and has finally put all of his other enemies under his feet, then death itself will be *destroyed*—for eternity (Revelation 20:14).

27. For he "has put everything under his feet." Now when it says that "everything" has been put under him, it is clear that this does not include God himself, who put everything under Christ.

Here Paul adds a further comment on his previous statements, making use of a passage from Psalm 8:6. That *everything* is *under* Jesus' *feet* does not literally

WHAT DO YOU THINK?

What excites you about the idea that Jesus will at last reign? Why? Do you feel any other emotions about it? If so, what? Why?

WHAT DO YOU THINK?

Not only do we anticipate Christ's future reign, but Paul tells us that we can enjoy Christ's present reign as Head of the church. What excites you about the idea that Jesus is even now reigning? Why?

HOW TO SAY IT

Bolshevik. BOWL-sheh-vick.
Corinth. KOR-inth.
Corinthians. Kor-IN-thee-unz.
Ephesian. Ee-FEE-zhun.
Gnosticism. NAHSS-tih-sizz-um.
messianic. mess-ee-AN-ick.

DAILY BIBLE READINGS

Monday, Apr. 17—*The Resurrection of Christ the Lord (1 Corinthians 15:1-11)*

Tuesday, Apr. 18—*How Can You Deny the Resurrection? (1 Corinthians 15:12-19)*

Wednesday, Apr. 19— *The Resurrected Christ Destroys Death (1 Corinthians 15:20-28)*

Thursday, Apr. 20—*The Dead Are Raised: Believe It! (1 Corinthians 15:29-34)*

Friday, Apr. 21—*How Are the Dead Raised? (1 Corinthians 15:35-41)*

Saturday, Apr. 22—*Raised a Spiritual Body (1 Corinthians 15:42-49)*

Sunday, Apr. 23—*We Have Victory Through Jesus Christ! (1 Corinthians 15:50-58)*

mean *everything*. The exception is God, the One *who put everything under Christ*. Though Christ will eventually subject all things to his authority, he himself will still be subordinate to the Father. Verse 28 completes Paul's thought in regard to this matter. When Christ returns and has put all other things in subjection to himself, then he in turn will "will be made subject" to God.

III. OUR RESURRECTION (1 CORINTHIANS 15:35-44)

A. KEY QUESTIONS (v. 35)

35. But someone may ask, "How are the dead raised? With what kind of body will they come?"

In the first part of today's printed text, Paul has firmly established the fact of the resurrection; but he realizes that this has not completely satisfied the skeptics. Two of their questions are stated in this verse. The first is, *How are the dead raised?* Paul does not specifically address this question, for God has not revealed to any of us the process of how he will accomplish this. However, he does respond to the second question (*With what kind of body will they come?*) by drawing on illustrations from nature.

B. EARTHLY BODIES (vv. 36-39)

36. How foolish! What you sow does not come to life unless it dies.

Paul used rather strong language (*foolish*) to express his criticism of someone who raised questions about the resurrection. He certainly would have been more gentle toward one whom he considered an honest seeker after truth. Apparently Paul knew his readers better than we do and addressed his reply to those who stubbornly persisted in their doubts. Perhaps he had in mind the kind of person described in Psalm 14:1: "The fool says in his heart, 'There is no God.'"

Paul then proceeded to discuss the nature of the resurrection. In this verse he emphasized the fact that death must precede a resurrection. That is quite obvious with the sowing of seeds. The original seed is decomposed and is absorbed into the new life that later emerges from the ground.

37. When you sow, you do not plant the body that will be, but just a seed, perhaps of wheat or of something else.

When *wheat* or some other *seed* is planted, it sprouts and grows. The green plant does not at all resemble the brown grain of wheat. What is sown is not what *will be*. It was planted as one kind of a *body* and is raised a different kind of a body.

Undoubtedly the Corinthians had witnessed this process many times and had accepted it as part of life. Paul's implied question was, "Why, then, do you have trouble accepting the resurrection of the human body in a new and different form?"

38. But God gives it a body as he has determined, and to each kind of seed he gives its own body.

Seeds come in all kinds of sizes and shapes, from a tiny mustard seed to a coconut. The plants they produce vary just as widely. All of these differences are planned by God in his infinite wisdom. Grain is planted as one kind of *body*, and it is raised a different kind of body. If God can accomplish this in the physical realm, why should he not be able to do the same in the spiritual realm?

39. All flesh is not the same: Men have one kind of flesh, animals have another, birds another and fish another.

To reinforce his point, Paul then turned to the animal kingdom. *All flesh is not the same*. This is obvious to anyone who is at all observant of nature. *Men, animals, birds*, and *fish* all have different types of flesh and different bodies. If God could make such a variety of physical bodies to populate his earth, why should the Corinthians have any problem believing that he could also create the spiritual body to be different from the physical body?

C. Heavenly Bodies (vv. 40, 41)

40. *There are also heavenly bodies and there are earthly bodies; but the splendor of the heavenly bodies is one kind, and the splendor of the earthly bodies is another.*

Paul then drew an illustration from some of the inanimate objects of creation. In this verse he contrasts *heavenly bodies* (sun, moon, and stars, note v. 41) with *earthly bodies*. We do not know exactly what earthly bodies Paul had in mind (some believe the great mountains, canyons, and seas), but that information is not essential to understanding the point he is making. Each of the bodies possesses certain characteristics that give it a distinct *splendor*. The heavenly bodies are entirely different in their composition from the earthly bodies. God is able to take similar physical material and design it to accomplish his purposes, whether in the heavens or on the earth.

41. *The sun has one kind of splendor, the moon another and the stars another; and star differs from star in splendor.*

In the previous verse, Paul highlighted the distinction between two very different categories of objects—earthly bodies and heavenly bodies. Now, in this verse, he focuses on the differences between the bodies in the celestial class. Everyone would readily acknowledge the difference between the *splendor* of the *sun* and that of the *moon*. Even if one did not understand that the brightness of the sun is caused by a vast and continuous nuclear reaction while the moon simply reflects the light of the sun, the difference in their brightness would still be obvious. No one has to be an astronomer to understand the point Paul is making here.

D. Our Resurrected Bodies (vv. 42-44)

42. *So will it be with the resurrection of the dead. The body that is sown is perishable, it is raised imperishable.*

Paul now applied the comparisons he had made to the issue at hand—*the resurrection of the dead*. It (referring to the physical body) *is perishable* Just as the seed must decay when it is planted, so the physical body, composed of mortal flesh, must also decompose when it is *sown* (planted or buried) at death.

But that is not the end of the story. Just as the decaying seed is transformed into new life as a plant springs forth, the body *is raised imperishable*. The new body sheds its mortality and takes on immortality, no longer subject to the limitations of the flesh.

43. *. . . it is sown in dishonor, it is raised in glory; it is sown in weakness, it is raised in power.*

Paul continued a series of contrasts in order to drive home his point. The body *is sown in dishonor*. No matter how great a person may be in the eyes of the world, he or she must face death. But, praise God, because of Jesus' resurrection that dishonor is replaced by *glory* and that mortal *weakness* is exchanged for eternal *power*.

44. *. . . it is sown a natural body, it is raised a spiritual body.*

If there is a natural body, there is also a spiritual body.

Just as there are many differences between one form of animal and another, Paul says, so there is a difference between one form of human *body* (the *natural*) and the other (*spiritual*). And just as there are differences between one celestial body and another, so there are differences between these two forms of human body. But there is a body in that spiritual realm—*there is also a spiritual body.*

Thought to Remember
"*Christ has indeed been raised from the dead*" (1 Corinthians 15:20).

Prayer
Troubled as we are by so many things in the world about us, dear Father, we offer up thanks to you for the assurance that beyond the resurrection there awaits a glorious life for all those who accept your Son as Lord and Savior. In his name we offer this prayer. Amen.

Some of the Corinthians may have believed that the physical or *natural body* was weak, even evil, and that the ideal situation was attained when one could free himself from it and become a disembodied spirit. Paul completely rejected this notion. A Christian will be *raised a spiritual body.* We cannot begin to understand what this resurrected body will be like, but we can be absolutely sure of this: it will be different from (and far superior to) the natural body with all of its limitations and frailties.

CONCLUSION

A. SKEPTICS OF THE RESURRECTION

The doctrine of the resurrection is at the very heart of the gospel. Without it there really is no gospel—no good news. Today those who believe in the resurrection are under attack from at least two directions. Leading one attack are the materialists, who believe that the only real world is the physical world. In their view, anything that cannot be seen, touched, or weighed simply does not exist. They reject the account of Jesus' resurrection and the belief in a resurrected life after this life as myths that educated people no longer believe. Unfortunately, some who claim to be Christians (even some who hold prominent positions within the church) have accepted this materialistic view of Christianity. Such a view makes observing Easter (or going to church at all, for that matter) an empty charade.

A second challenge to the Christian view of the resurrection comes from strange religious beliefs that have recently become prominent in the Western world. Some of these, such as Hinduism and Buddhism, are ancient religions imported from the East. Reports indicate that both of these religions are gaining followers because they claim to fill a spiritual need that many feel. What an indictment against Christians! Why have we not found ways to fill this void with the truth of the gospel?

Christians are also challenged by many new cults, often built around a person with unusual personal charisma. Claiming special knowledge or some unique revelation about topics such as life after death, these cults have been able to lead many astray.

Just as Paul countered the doubts toward and rejections of the resurrection with a vigorous affirmation of this doctrine, so must we today. Jesus' resurrection allows us to say, with enthusiasm, "Thanks be to God! He gives us the victory through our Lord Jesus Christ" (1 Corinthians 15:57).

B. WHAT KIND OF BODY?

When we come to believe in the resurrection, we are tempted to speculate about what kind of a body we will have in the world to come. Today's lesson affirms certain important facts about the resurrection, but it leaves many questions unanswered. What will we look like in the future life? Will we be able to recognize one another? Will there be work for us to do in the next world?

On one occasion Paul was "caught up to the third heaven." There he heard words "that man is not permitted to tell" (2 Corinthians 12:2-4), meaning, presumably, that he could not find words to describe what he witnessed during that experience. We would be wise to follow Paul's example here and avoid undue speculation about all that the resurrected life will involve. The Scripture in today's lesson indicates that the next world will be different from this world. Other passages of Scripture (for example, Revelation 21 and 22) indicate that it will be far better than anything we can imagine. This ought to provide us with the confidence that we need to face each day joyfully and triumphantly!

WHAT DO YOU THINK?

Many unbelievers declare, "When you're dead, you're dead!" Others hold to a vague kind of hope regarding life after death. How do we respond to them?

WHAT DO YOU THINK?

Even Christians have many questions about the exact nature of the life we will live in our new bodies. How would you answer a new Christian who says he just can't figure out what life after death will be like?

Discovery Learning

This page contains an alternate lesson plan emphasizing learning activities. Classes desiring such student involvement will find these suggestions helpful. The next page is a reproducible activity page to further enhance discovery learning.

LEARNING GOALS

After this lesson your students should be able to:

1. Tell what Paul says about the certainty of Christ's resurrection and his role as the "firstfruits," guaranteeing believers' resurrection.

2. Contrast the Christian perspective on the future with that of the unbeliever.

3. Give thanks to God that the resurrection of Christ remains the sure foundation of Christian faith and hope.

INTO THE LESSON

Distribute copies of Henry Wadsworth Longfellow's "A Psalm of Life" (or refer your students to the poem in their student books).

> Life is real! Life is earnest!
> And the grave is not its goal;
> Dust thou art, to dust returnest
> Was not spoken of the soul.

Ask your students whether they agree or disagree with Longfellow. Have each one write his or her evaluation of the verse. Then have several volunteers share their evaluations and briefly discuss their views. Tell your students that in the first century, as today, many people rejected the possibility of life after death (see Acts 17:32). Today's lesson deals with Paul's arguments against such skepticism.

INTO THE WORD

Divide your class into pairs and have each pair choose an "A" reader and a "B" reader. Give everyone a copy of the reproducible page that follows, and read the text (1 Corinthians 15:17-27, 35-44) antiphonally. Then give each pair a copy of the following arguments against the possibility of our resurrection. Using today's text, each pair of students should write a response to each argument. (Relevant verses are cited in parentheses.)

1. Even if Jesus rose from the dead, there is no guarantee that we will. (vv. 20-23)

2. If Jesus were going to return, he would have done so already, so we have no hope of a future resurrection. (vv. 24-27)

3. Resurrection is impossible because there is nothing left to raise; the body is decayed, gone. (vv. 35-39)

4. Even if God did raise our bodies from the dead, we would simply grow old and die again. (vv. 40-44)

After your students finish their responses, ask several to share their work, one argument at a time. Then discuss the questions below:

1. What are "firstfruits"? (See Leviticus 23:9-14.) How is Jesus, by virtue of his resurrection, the firstfruits of our resurrection?

2. What contrast does Paul make between Adam and Christ?

3. How was Jesus' resurrection different from those before his, such as that of Lazarus?

4. What order of resurrection is indicated in this section? Compare verse 23 with Daniel 12:2 and 1 Thessalonians 4:16.

5. How long must Christ reign before the end of the world?

6. What must happen before Christ can deliver up the kingdom to God? What does it mean to "put all his enemies under his feet"? Who is exempted from that subjection?

7. How is death an enemy? See Hebrews 2:14, 15. How will it be destroyed?

8. How is the resurrection likened to a seed that has been planted?

9. Why must something die to come to life?

10. How, from his reference to animals, birds, and fish, does Paul demonstrate that the resurrected body is different from the natural body?

11. How is Paul's argument in verses 40, 41 parallel to the one in verse 39?

12. What argument does Paul offer to prove that resurrected people will not die again?

13. In what sense is the natural body sown in dishonor and weakness? What gives the resurrected body its glory and power?

INTO LIFE

Return to the discussion of Longfellow's poem from the opening activity. How accurately did the poet capture Paul's teaching in today's text? Distribute paper and pencils as needed, and ask your students to write their own poems, based on 1 Corinthians 15, praising God for the promise of the resurrection. To conclude the lesson, ask for volunteers to share their poetry.

Option: Use the antiphonal reading of the text on the next page to close the session instead of, or in addition to, reading it earlier.

The Resurrection of the Dead

Use the printed text below as the basis for an antiphonal reading of today's lesson text. One individual or group should read the lines marked "A" and another individual or group replies with the lines marked "B."

A: If Christ has not been raised,
B: your faith is futile; you are still in your sins.

A: Then those also who have fallen asleep in Christ are lost.
B: If only for this life we have hope in Christ,

A: we are to be pitied more than all men.
B: But Christ has indeed been raised from the dead,

A: the firstfruits of those who have fallen asleep.
B: For since death came through a man,

A: the resurrection of the dead comes also through a man.
B: For as in Adam all die,

A: so in Christ all will be made alive.
B: But each in his own turn: Christ the firstfruits;

A: then, when he comes, those who belong to him.
B: Then the end will come,

A: when he hands over the kingdom to God the Father
B: after he has destroyed all dominion, authority and power.

A: For he must reign until he has put all his enemies under his feet.
B: The last enemy to be destroyed is death.

A: For he "has put everything under his feet."
B: Now when it says that "everything" has been put under him,

A: it is clear that this does not include God himself,
B: who put everything under Christ.

A: But someone may ask, "How are the dead raised?
B: With what kind of body will they come?"

A: How foolish! What you sow does not come to life unless it dies.
B: When you sow, you do not plant the body that will be,

A: but just a seed, perhaps of wheat or of something else.
B: But God gives it a body as he has determined,

A: and to each kind of seed he gives its own body.
B: All flesh is not the same:

A: Men have one kind of flesh,
B: animals have another,

A: birds another and fish another.
B: There are also heavenly bodies and there are earthly bodies;

A: but the splendor of the heavenly bodies is one kind,
B: and the splendor of the earthly bodies is another.

A: The sun has one kind of splendor,
B: the moon another and the stars another;

A: and star differs from star in splendor.
B: So it will be with the resurrection of the dead.

A: The body that is sown is perishable,
B: it is raised imperishable;

A: it is sown in dishonor,
B: it is raised in glory;

A: it is sown in weakness,
B: it is raised in power;

A: it is sown a natural body,
B: it is raised a spiritual body.

A: If there is a natural body,
B: there is also a spiritual body.

LOVE'S BETTER WAY

LESSON 9

WHY TEACH THIS LESSON?

"All we need is love!" It's been more than thirty years since the Beatles sang those words. The philosophy is too simplistic, and we wonder whether they really knew what love was, but they were not far from the truth.

While love may not be "all" we need, it is clear that nothing else we do or have makes much sense without it. Obviously you will want your students to be able to recite the grand and noble things Paul says are meaningless without love—miraculous faith, heroic benevolence, even martyrdom.

Something that is not so obvious is the value of simple loving actions. Routine acts done *with* love are extremely valuable, just as grand acts done *without* love are worthless. Challenge your students to evaluate their behavior. Are they putting on a show, attempting to look good by what they do? The solution is not necessarily to give up the behavior, but to change the motive! The same thing that was meant to "put on a show" can be directed instead toward showing genuine love and concern for another.

INTRODUCTION

A. LOVE "IS NOT SELF-SEEKING"

Early in the nineteenth century a missionary worked alone among the slaves in the British West Indies. The planters sneered at him or ignored him, but the slaves came to love him. Eventually the missionary, exhausted by his hard labors, fell dangerously ill. With no one to attend him, it seemed certain that he would never recover. Then one day one of the slaves who had become a faithful Christian through the missionary's efforts appeared at the door with the simple announcement: "I am yours now. Just tell me what to do."

Inquiry disclosed that the slave converts had become worried about the missionary's health, but were not certain what they could do to help. Finally they arrived at a solution. By combining their meager savings, earned through years of extra work, they were able to purchase one of their own number from his master and present him to the missionary. In so doing each had postponed indefinitely his or her individual hope of freedom in order to comfort the one who had taught them the meaning of brotherly love.

B. LESSON BACKGROUND

In the lesson two weeks ago we saw that a problem had developed within the Corinthian church regarding spiritual gifts. The church was blessed with a variety of spiritual gifts, but pride and selfishness had led some of the members to abuse these gifts so that they had become a source of division rather than the harmony that God intended.

Today's lesson text is actually a continuation of the theme Paul began in 1 Corinthians 12. At the conclusion of that chapter, Paul pointed the Corinthians to "the most excellent way"—the way of *agape* love. The chapter that follows is one of the most cherished portions of Scripture in the entire Bible. In it Paul gives us a description of what Christian love is and challenges us to live by its standards.

DEVOTIONAL READING:
1 JOHN 4:7-21
BACKGROUND SCRIPTURE:
1 CORINTHIANS 12:31—13:13
PRINTED TEXT:
1 CORINTHIANS 12:31—13:13

LESSON AIMS

After this lesson each student will be able to:

1. Summarize what Paul says about love and what makes it the "most excellent way."

2. Suggest some actions love might prompt a person to take.

3. Commit himself or herself to act with genuine love toward a specific person.

Apr
30

KEY VERSE

And now these three remain: faith, hope and love. But the greatest of these is love.
—*1 Corinthians 13:13*

I. PRIORITY OF LOVE (1 CORINTHIANS 12:31—13:3)

A. Eloquence Without Love (12:31—13:1)

31. But eagerly desire the greater gifts.

And now I will show you the most excellent way.

But eagerly desire the greater gifts. As Paul's statement reads, it is a command; however, the Greek construction of this statement can also be understood as a description of what the people were actually doing ("you are earnestly desiring"). *The greater gifts* were those gifts that the Corinthians had thought most important—perhaps the gifts that Paul cited in 1 Corinthians 13:1 and 2. There Paul wanted to emphasize the supremacy of love over the gifts: love is the *most excellent way.* Love is not a spiritual gift; it is a fruit of the Spirit (Galatians 5:22) that must govern how gifts are used. If the Corinthians are to desire anything, it should be to love one another. This leads to Paul's timeless description of love.

1. If I speak in the tongues of men and of angels, but have not love, I am only a resounding gong or a clanging cymbal.

Since Paul uses the personal pronoun in verses 1-3, some commentators think that these verses are autobiographical, with Paul describing some of his own gifts. However, it seems more likely that he was presenting hypothetical situations and making himself the subject of them out of consideration for the feelings of the Corinthians.

Since the gift of *tongues* was particularly controversial in Corinth, it was appropriate for Paul to mention it here in order to draw attention to the importance of *love.* The phrase *a resounding gong or a clanging cymbal* suggests discordant notes that are little more than noise. That, says Paul, is what speaking in tongues amounts to unless it is done with a discerning love for the members of the congregation.

B. Gifts Without Love (v. 2)

2. If I have the gift of prophecy and can fathom all mysteries and all knowledge, and if I have a faith that can move mountains, but have not love, I am nothing.

Paul now calls attention to three of the spiritual gifts that he had mentioned in the previous chapter. While he esteemed the gift of *prophecy* quite highly (as 1 Corinthians 14:1 indicates), if it was practiced without *love* it was *nothing.* The gift of *knowledge* apparently gave one the power to understand some of the *mysteries* of God's dealings with man—an understanding that not everyone possessed.

The power to *move mountains* may have included the ability to work miracles in the realm of nature. Jesus mentioned moving mountains on occasion (Matthew 17:20; 21:21; Mark 11:23), although he may have used this expression as a hyperbole (an extreme exaggeration for emphasis). In any case, the point of Paul's proposition is obvious. One might perform the most astounding miracle imaginable, but if it is done without love, it is *nothing.*

C. Giving Without Love (v. 3)

3. If I give all I possess to the poor and surrender my body to the flames, but have not love, I gain nothing.

People have been known to give part of what they *possess* to benefit others, but it is often for the wrong motives. Jesus criticized those who gave to *the poor* when they did so in order to receive the plaudits of men (Matthew 6:1-4). Paul's hypothetical example goes far beyond giving just a part of one's goods; here, the donor gives *all* he possesses *to the poor.*

Then Paul goes a step further, supposing that the person gives not merely all his possessions but himself—his *body to the flames* in an act of martyrdom. Such

What Do You Think?

Some people speak of love as merely a feeling, something one "falls" into—and just as easily falls out of. But in speaking of love as a requirement, Paul makes it clear that we have the ability to control whether or not we demonstrate love. What can we do to be sure we are acting with love?

What Do You Think?

Paul pointed out that acts of charity and sacrifice toward others do us little good if they are not done in love. Why not?

extreme examples of giving highlight the importance of *love*; as impressive as they may seem, they are totally meaningless if one does not do them out of love.

MIXED MESSAGE

A twenty-six-year-old woman in Tustin, California, provided an interesting example of the "road rage" phenomenon. This term describes an aggressive driving style that some people adopt in which they take out their frustrations on other drivers. This young woman became angry at the driver of the truck in front of her because she thought he wasn't driving fast enough. So she took a baseball bat that she had in her car and attempted to hit the side of the truck several times as she pulled alongside it.

The policeman who arrested her noted that her license plate read "PEACE 95." When he questioned her about it, she told the officer that she got the personalized plate because she thought there was too much violence in our society!

Psychologists would probably call this a case of "cognitive dissonance." It's what happens when a person's behavior doesn't match his stated beliefs—and yet the person himself sees no contradiction. This was the situation in the Corinthian church that Paul was addressing. When we pride ourselves on the gifts or talents that make us seem very spiritual, and yet do not exercise them in a spirit of love, something is seriously wrong with our Christianity.   —C. R. B.

II. PRACTICE OF LOVE (1 CORINTHIANS 13:4-7)

A. LOVE IS HUMBLE (v. 4)

4. Love is patient, love is kind. It does not envy, it does not boast, it is not proud.

Having identified several actions that are meaningless without love, Paul turns to love's positive side. Some of these attributes were conspicuously absent from the Corinthian congregation.

A very important part of love is humility. *Love is patient;* that is, love leads one to work patiently with others, even those who may be considered "difficult." The loving person is willing to labor in the shadow of others, allowing them to receive credit for what he may have done. Love is also *kind.* It is not merely passive in its longsuffering; it actively pursues what is in the best interests of another.

It does not envy. It is clear that some in the Corinthian church had become envious of the gifts that others had received. Envy, however, is not a mark of true love. *It does not boast, it is not proud.* One who lives a life controlled by love is not proud or arrogant. Yet how subtly Satan tempts us in this respect. We want to be "number one," or to "keep up with the Joneses." Such pride blinds us to the source of our possessions and our talents. They all come from God.

B. LOVE IS UNSELFISH (v. 5)

5. It is not rude, it is not self-seeking, it is not easily angered, it keeps no record of wrongs.

Love *is not rude.* Unseemly behavior is any conduct that brings reproach to Christ or his church. Many of us are shocked by the growing rudeness we see in the society around us. Often this stems from ignorance; children have not been taught simple politeness such as saying "please" and "thank you." But in other cases rudeness is the product of the selfish spirit that seems to be the trademark of our times.

Love *is not easily angered.* Some people are like prickly cactuses. It is painful to approach them from any direction. Nearly every office and every church probably has at least one person who is irritable and hard to get along with. Whatever reasons one may have for this attitude, the underlying problem is that such a person lacks love and consideration for others.

HOW TO SAY IT

agape (Greek). uh-GAH-pay.
Clairvaux. Clair-VOH.
Corinth. KOR-inth.
Corinthians. Kor-IN-thee-unz.

WHAT DO YOU THINK?

What are some forms of self-ish behavior in the church that love can overcome?

Love *keeps no record of wrongs*; it does not dwell on wrongs done, trying to devise ways of "getting even." Love forgives and forgets.

C. LOVE REJOICES IN THE TRUTH (v. 6)
6. Love does not delight in evil but rejoices with the truth.

Today we are immersed in a sea of *evil*. Radio, movies, television, and now various electronic media intrude into our homes with offensive words and images. We have to be alert every minute to keep our minds pure. Living by God's *truth* can help us attain that purity because it helps us determine right from wrong.

D. LOVE IS PATIENT (v. 7)
7. It always protects, always trusts, always hopes, always perseveres.

The Greek word translated *protects* comes from the word for "roof." Thus love protects others (from threatening situations or negative talk), as a roof protects what is inside a building.

Love *always trusts*. This certainly does not mean that we are to be naive, believing everything that we are told or chasing after every strange idea that appears on the horizon. The point here is that love gives us a positive attitude toward others that is eager to believe the best, not the worst, about people. Love continues to believe that God has ways of reaching out and saving wayward souls. It gives us an optimistic, patient perspective toward life.

Love also *always hopes* and *always perseveres*. Love looks toward the future positively. It refuses to fold in the face of difficult people or circumstances. It is thoroughly loyal—to God and to others.

III. PERMANENCE OF LOVE (1 CORINTHIANS 13:8-13)
A. GIFTS WILL CEASE (v. 8)
8. Love never fails. But where there are prophecies, they will cease; where there are tongues, they will be stilled; where there is knowledge, it will pass away.

In verses 1-3 Paul declared that even the most coveted spiritual gifts and the most commendable actions, if exercised without love, are empty and meaningless. In verses 4-7 he listed the qualities of love that make it the "most excellent way." Now in the closing verses of this chapter he shows that love is superior to the spiritual gifts because love is permanent, while the gifts are temporary.

B. THE PARTIAL AND THE PERFECT (vv. 9-12)
9. For we know in part and we prophesy in part.

Knowledge and prophecy refer back to two of the spiritual gifts that were mentioned in 1 Corinthians 12:8 and 10. Although Paul, as an apostle, had received by revelation a special knowledge of God's purposes in Christ (Galatians 1:11, 12), he readily recognized that his understanding was only partial. There were at least two reasons for this. First of all, God in his infinite wisdom had not chosen to reveal all of his mysteries at that time. Second, if he had, man in his human weakness would not have been able to comprehend it. In the same way, the ability to *prophesy* resulted in only partial understanding.

10. . . . but when perfection comes, the imperfect disappears.

This verse has been the source of considerable discussion. Some understand *perfection* to refer to the revelation of the New Covenant embodied in the New Testament Scriptures. The special spiritual gifts were necessary in the first century and shortly thereafter to authenticate this new and final revelation of God's will to man. (See the reference to how the Lord "confirmed his word" in Mark 16:20.) According to this view, the gifts ceased once the New Testament was completed.

WHAT DO YOU THINK?

It is a very human tendency to want to imagine ourselves superior to others. In order to fulfill this tendency, we focus on what we perceive as the faults or inadequacies of others. Through love Christians can learn to believe the best about one another. How important do you think this quality is? Why?

Another view is that *perfection* looks to the second coming of Christ. When he who is the perfect revelation of God returns, then special gifts will no longer be needed.

Still others believe that *perfection* means "maturity," as it does in various passages (Colossians 1:28; James 3:2). As such, it may refer to a mature individual or a mature church. When a person or congregation has attained "unity in the faith and in the knowledge of the Son of God" and "the whole measure of the fullness of Christ" (Ephesians 4:13), there will no longer be a need for the gifts of knowledge and prophecy. Or when the church as a whole becomes "mature," it no longer needs the foundational gifts of the apostles and prophets (Ephesians 2:20).

11. When I was a child, I talked like a child, I thought like a child, I reasoned like a child. When I became a man, I put childish ways behind me.

Paul elaborates on the point he made in the previous verse. The *child* represents the time in which Paul was writing (first century) while the *man* points to maturity at some time future to Paul. As noted under verse 10, the time represented by this analogy varies according to one's view of what the "perfection" is. Under the first view—and probably the third—we are in that time now. But if one takes the perfection to be the return of Christ, then that time is, obviously, still future to us today.

12. Now we see but a poor reflection as in a mirror; then we shall see face to face. Now I know in part; then I shall know fully, even as I am fully known.

A *mirror* in Paul's day was not made of glass but of polished metal. With such a mirror one's *reflection* would be dim and distorted. But at some future time *we shall see face to face.* To use a contemporary illustration, we might compare a person's photograph to the person himself. A photograph may show certain aspects of a person accurately, but it in no way adequately shows the real person. When "perfection comes" (v. 10), we will have more complete knowledge about those matters that we now *know in part.*

Again, one's understanding of when this happens depends on his interpretation of what "perfection" means. Those who believe it refers to the return of Jesus would say that at that time we will see him face to face. Those who say that "perfection" designates the completion of the New Testament or the attainment of maturity may take a more symbolic understanding of *face to face.* Some will combine both views, seeing the arrival of "perfection" as beginning a process that makes the foundational gifts unnecessary before Christ returns, but not necessarily granting full knowledge *even as I am fully known* until his return.

C. "THE GREATEST OF THESE" (v. 13)

13. And now these three remain: faith, hope and love. But the greatest of these is love.

The closing verse of this chapter brings Paul's discussion to a fitting conclusion. The spiritual gifts that had created so much controversy in the Corinthian church were not permanent. What really matters are the qualities of *faith, hope,* and *love.* This triad sums up quite succinctly the crucial elements that lie at the heart of Christian living.

In one sense, faith will not be needed in the next world, for then we shall "walk by sight." But in another sense it will exist there as fulfilled faith. The same is true of hope. Hope is a wonderful source of encouragement in this life, but in Heaven we will no longer need that kind of hope. However, it will exist as hope that has been realized and rewarded.

The greatest of these is love. Love is greater than faith and hope, because in Heaven it will be most necessary. Faith and hope are not divine attributes, but

WHAT DO YOU THINK?

Whatever view one takes of when "perfection" arrives, Paul's point about adults' "put[ting] childish ways behind" them is applicable to us today. How does the mature Christian demonstrate love in ways a non-Christian might not? What are some goals we might set for ourselves in order to grow in love?

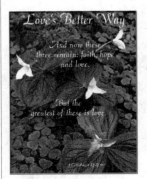

The beautiful visual that goes with today's lesson reminds us of the importance and power of love. Display it as you begin to discuss verse 13.

PRAYER

Loving Father, we raise our voices in a prayer for forgiveness—forgiveness for not loving you as we should, forgiveness for not accepting your love, and forgiveness for not sharing that love with others. Melt our hearts now, and give us the strength and wisdom to become the kind of people you want us to be. In Jesus' name. Amen.

THOUGHT TO REMEMBER

"The true measure of loving God is to love him without measure."   —*Bernard of Clairvaux*

DAILY BIBLE READINGS

Monday, Apr. 24—The Gift of Love (1 Corinthians 13:1-7)

Tuesday, Apr. 25—Love Is the Greatest Gift (1 Corinthians 13:8-13)

Wednesday, Apr. 26—Love: An Old New Commandment (1 John 2:7-17)

Thursday, Apr. 27—Show Your Love for One Another (1 John 3:11-17)

Friday, Apr. 28—Believe in Jesus and Love One Another (1 John 3:18-24)

Saturday, Apr. 29—Let Us Love as God Loves (1 John 4:7-12)

Sunday, Apr. 30—We Abide in God If We Love (1 John 4:13-21)

human ones. After all, God does not need faith and hope; we do. But "God is love" (1 John 4:8), and if we are to relate to him throughout all eternity, then we must possess love above all else.

SYMBOL OF LASTING LOVE

Yvonne Saunders runs an unusual business in West Vancouver, British Columbia: she preserves wedding bouquets. She sends an airtight shipping box to the bride who wants her bouquet preserved. When the flowers arrive at Saunders' studio, they are photographed, disassembled, and dried, flower by flower, in chemicals that will preserve even the colors of the petals, leaves, and stems. Then the bouquet is reassembled, placed on a background of velvet (or a piece of the fabric from which the bride's gown was made), and sealed in a frame. The cost of this service ranges from under $100 to over $600.

The carefully preserved flowers are intended to symbolize the eternal nature of the love that the happy couple have pledged to each other. (One might observe that this could be a symbolic first lesson to the newlyweds of how much love can cost!)

Paul describes the eternal nature of love in 1 Corinthians 13, noting that it "never fails" (v. 8). While the words of this chapter are often read as part of a wedding ceremony, they can truly be understood only by looking to the God who is this kind of love. His love is a love that lasts a lifetime and beyond.   —C. R. B.

CONCLUSION

Love is not just a term that theologians discuss or about which scholars write books. It is at the heart of everything that Christianity stands for. Love must be active and involved in the real, everyday world. Consider the extent and variety of circumstances in today's world where love can make a genuine difference.

For example, love transcends race and nationality. Paul wrote in Ephesians 2:14 that the sacrificial love of Christ "has destroyed the barrier, the dividing wall of hostility" between Jews and Gentiles. Laws may sometimes help dissipate the racism that so plagues our world; but until our hearts have surrendered to the power of *agape* love, racism will never be eliminated.

We are distressed by the ethical behavior of men and women in places of prominence in our land. Codes of ethics and laws may be helpful, but without love our society will never solve this problem.

In our major cities are thousands of homeless individuals without adequate food or shelter. Unless the power of *agape* love compels us to leave our comfortable suburbs and go down into the inner city to minister to them, the problem will remain.

All of us are distressed by the growing number of broken marriages and single-parent families and the countless problems they cause. Yet without love, all of the efforts to meet these problems are like adhesive bandage strips plastered over a gnawing cancer.

Our society has surrendered its soul to materialism. Many are blessed beyond their dreams by God's gifts, and yet in the midst of their plenty they never seem to be satisfied; they always want more and better things. They pursue these items with the love and zeal that rightly should be directed toward God and his creation. Until they are willing to make God and others the objects of their love, they are doomed to drown in their own discontent.

Deep down, we usually come to realize that we all need to embrace *agape* love; but *agape* love exacts a price. We must be willing to surrender to Christ, accept his love, and then share his love with others.

Discovery Learning

This page contains an alternate lesson plan emphasizing learning activities. Classes desiring such student involvement will find these suggestions helpful. The next page is a reproducible activity page to further enhance discovery learning.

LEARNING GOALS

After this lesson each student will be able to:

1. Summarize what Paul says about love and what makes it the "most excellent way."

2. Suggest some actions love might prompt a person to take.

3. Commit himself or herself to act with genuine love toward a specific person.

INTO THE LESSON

Over the years, many writers, poets, and lyricists have tried to capture the essence of love. Ask your students to read the following statements and decide which ones accurately reflect the meaning of love and how they do so.

"Love means never having to say you're sorry."

"Love is always sweeter the second time around."

"All you need is love."

"Love can touch us one time and last for a lifetime."

"Love was when God became a man."

Discuss these ideas briefly; then tell your class that today we will see what the Holy Spirit inspired Paul to write about the nature of love.

Option: Use the crossword puzzle on the next page to introduce today's lesson.

INTO THE WORD

For this exercise, divide your class into three sections. Each student in section 1 will write a paraphrase of 1 Corinthians 12:31—13:3; students in section 2 will paraphrase 13:4-7, and those in section three will paraphrase 13:8-13. Encourage students to express the meaning of the passage, not simply to rewrite it in slightly different words. After a few minutes ask for volunteers to share their paraphrases with the class. Then discuss the meaning of the chapter, using the questions below.

1. What are the "greater gifts" to which Paul refers?

2. Is it wrong to desire God's gifts? Why?

3. What does Paul mean by his reference to "a resounding gong" and "a clanging cymbal"?

4. What is the relationship of love to the gifts and deeds mentioned in verses 2 and 3?

5. What does Paul mean, "Love is patient"?

6. What do the positive characteristics of love in verse 4 have in common?

7. How are the negative characteristics of love in verse 5 the opposite of those in verse 4?

8. What does it mean to "delight in evil"? How does verse 6 contradict the idea that lying is a good way to spare someone's feelings?

9. Is it naive to be someone who "always trusts," as Paul says love does? In what kinds of situations will love protect and persevere?

10. Why will love outlast the various spiritual gifts, including prophecy, tongues, and knowledge?

11. To whom does Paul refer in verse 9? What does he mean to "prophesy in part"?

12. What is "perfection" in verse 10? Why will its coming signify the end of the partial gifts?

13. What is the point of Paul's illustration about his childhood in verse 11?

14. What is the "mirror" Paul refers to in verse 12? What does this allusion say about love?

15. Why is love greater than faith or hope (13:13)?

INTO LIFE

Distribute copies of the chart below, omitting the material in parentheses. Have each class member look up the following passages; then write a brief description of what God expects a Christian to do to express love. Ask students to add to the list other loving deeds that are not mentioned in these passages.

After his list is complete, each student should then go back and evaluate it. If a student believes he is now expressing love in this way to the best of his ability, he should put a plus (+) next to the verse. If he believes he could do better, he should put a minus (–). From the deeds marked with the minus signs, each student should select at least one loving deed that he will determine to do this week and put an asterisk (*) beside it. Emphasize that he will *not* be asked to share his evaluation with the class.

VERSE	LOVING DEED	EVALUATION (+, –, *)
1 John 3:17	(Help the needy)	
1 John 5:2, 3	(Keep commands)	
James 2:1-9	(Be impartial)	
3 John 5-8	(Show hospitality)	
Romans 14	(Respect a brother's conscience)	

Discuss the meaning of the passages as well as other ways to express love. Close with prayer for your students, that they may follow through in their plans to demonstrate love this week.

Puzzled About Love?

Read 1 Corinthians 13, then complete the puzzle below, using the numbered clues.

DOWN

1. Now we see this, as in a mirror.

3. These three remain: _____, hope, and love.

5. When I was a child, I _____ like a child.

6. If I have all this, and a faith that can move mountains, but lack love, I am nothing.

7. Love keeps no _____ of wrongs.

9. Along with faith, it is one of the lesser things that remain.

11. The ability to fathom all of these is inferior to love.

13. If I _____ my body to the flames, but have not love, I gain nothing.

14. Love is the _____ of these.

17. Not the whole.

19. The opposite of rich.

ACROSS

2. When this comes, the imperfect disappears.

4. Love is _____, love is kind.

8. This will be done to tongues.

10. When I became a man, I put these things behind me.

12. What will happen to the imperfect.

15. Love always hopes, always _____.

16. A gift closely related to knowledge and faith.

20. Love does this with the truth.

"And now these three remain: faith, hope and love. But the greatest of these is love."

Helping a Church Confront Crisis

Unit 3: Unity Expressed in Ministry
(Lessons 10-13)

CHRISTIAN MARCH OF TRIUMPH

LESSON 10

WHY TEACH THIS LESSON?

Some people see the apostle Paul as a stern, even unforgiving, character. His refusal to allow John Mark to accompany him on the second missionary journey (Acts 15:36-38) is cited as an example. These people fail to consider "the rest of the story." Paul later asked for John Mark, and he said the younger man was helpful to him in his ministry (2 Timothy 4:11).

Today's lesson gives us another "rest of the story." In 1 Corinthians 5 we saw Paul's stern judgment against the incestuous brother. The sin was blatant, and few would argue that harsh measures were warranted. But even so, Paul was not vindictive, and in our lesson today we will see his recommendation that the erring one be forgiven and restored. Let the lesson be a challenge to each of your students to be ready to forgive and restore any who have sinned against them.

INTRODUCTION

A. FROM A BLOT TO A BLESSING

A friend once showed John Ruskin, a nineteenth-century British writer, a very expensive silk handkerchief that had been ruined by an ink blot. All efforts to remove the stain had failed, so the man decided to throw the handkerchief away. Ruskin, however, offered to find a way to save it. A few days later he returned the handkerchief to the man. He had not removed the stain, but, using the stain as a starting point, he had used a pen and some India ink to create an intricate and attractive design. From a ruined handkerchief, Ruskin created a valuable work of art.

This somewhat resembles the situation Paul dealt with in Corinth. In 1 Corinthians 5 he urged that a man involved in a serious sin be disciplined. It is apparent in today's lesson that the man had repented, so Paul encouraged the church to welcome him back in love. In this way the Corinthians were able to help in turning an individual badly stained by sin into a spiritual "work of art."

B. LESSON BACKGROUND

The remaining four lessons in this quarter will be based on texts taken from the book of 2 Corinthians. Before considering the background for today's printed text, let us examine the background of the letter itself. After Paul's successful ministry in Corinth, which lasted about a year and a half (Acts 18:11), he had traveled to Jerusalem and then returned to Antioch, thus completing his second missionary journey (Acts 18:22).

Not long afterward, Paul began his third missionary journey, which took him through Galatia and Phrygia to Ephesus (Acts 18:23; 19:1). Here he had another very successful ministry, which lasted about three years (20:31). Its success, however, brought him into conflict with the craftsmen of Ephesus, whose lucrative business had been impinged by the message of the gospel (19:23-27). While in Ephesus, Paul had written 1 Corinthians. In this letter (as we have

DEVOTIONAL READING:
2 CORINTHIANS 1:3-11
BACKGROUND SCRIPTURE:
2 CORINTHIANS 1, 2
PRINTED TEXT:
2 CORINTHIANS 2:4-17

LESSON AIMS

After this lesson students will be able to:

1. Tell the reasons for Paul's sense of triumph concerning the Corinthians.

2. Suggest some situations over which God's love and grace can triumph today.

3. Pinpoint a current situation in the church or in their personal relationships where Christian love needs to triumph.

May 7

KEY VERSE

But thanks be to God, who always leads us in triumphal procession in Christ and through us spreads everywhere the fragrance of the knowledge of him.

—2 *Corinthians 2:14*

LESSON 10 NOTES

noted in previous studies this quarter), he addressed some of the situations in the church that had threatened its unity and had undermined its witness to the pagans.

At this point, a question arises concerning Paul's visits to the Corinthians. It appears that some time after the writing of 1 Corinthians, Paul made a brief stop in Corinth to try to address personally the problems there. We know that a second visit occurred because 2 Corinthians 12:14 and 13:1, 2 mention *two* prior visits. In addition, 2 Corinthians 2:1 indicates that one of the two earlier visits was "painful." This does not seem to be a good description of Paul's first visit to Corinth, recorded in Acts 18:1-18, so it must refer to another. In 2 Corinthians 1:15-23 Paul mentions his plans for a third visit to Corinth; in fact, he was on his way when he wrote 2 Corinthians. He had left Ephesus, passed through Troas, and had gone as far as Macedonia when he met Titus, returning from Corinth, and penned the epistle (2 Corinthians 2:12, 13; 7:5-7).

Though some believe that the man mentioned in today's lesson text is someone who had attacked Paul by challenging his apostolic credentials (someone whom he had met during his second visit to Corinth), it has generally been held that he is the man mentioned in 1 Corinthians 5, who was involved in an incestuous relationship with his father's wife. Today's lesson gives us a good example of how Paul, a man with a servant's heart, dealt with sin in the body of Christ—firmly and yet with mercy and forgiveness.

I. CHRISTIAN LOVE UNITES (2 CORINTHIANS 2:4-11)

A. IN SYMPATHY (v. 4)

4. For I wrote you out of great distress and anguish of heart and with many tears, not to grieve you but to let you know the depth of my love for you.

The phrase *out of great distress and anguish of heart* describes the emotions that Paul experienced when he felt compelled to write to the Corinthian church in rather firm tones. Some believe that the words *I wrote* refer to a letter Paul had written to the Corinthians after the letter that we today call 1 Corinthians. According to this view, this "lost epistle" or "severe letter" contained very harsh language, which is the reason Paul felt so anguished about it. Others maintain that 1 Corinthians is this letter, and that the situations it describes would certainly have been disturbing enough to move an earnest man like Paul to *many tears.*

Paul took no pleasure in admonishing the Corinthians, just as a parent takes no joy in punishing a child. But his *love* for them required him to take such action. Paul wanted to assure the Corinthians of *the depth* of that love.

"BIG BOYS DON'T CRY"

There may be a scientific reason behind the old adage that "big boys don't cry." Ramsey Clinic in St. Paul, Minnesota, has a Dry Eye and Tear Research Center. Researchers at the Center have found that, up to approximately age twelve, boys and girls cry about the same amount; but by the time they are adults, women cry much more frequently than men. Women in the study experienced crying on an average of 5.3 times per month; men cried only 1.4 times a month. Seventy-one percent of men said that they had only watery eyes when they cried, but forty-seven percent of women reported that tears flowed when they cried. Forty-five percent of men versus six percent of women said they did not cry at all.

Of course, part of the differences may be attributed to the different ways in which women and men are conditioned by cultural factors to respond in a certain manner. But the researchers think that some of these differences have to do with biochemistry. Tears that are triggered by our emotions contain the hormone prolactin, and women have sixty percent more of it in their blood than men do.

WHAT DO YOU THINK?

The Corinthians had caused Paul "great distress and anguish of heart." Still, he loved them and worked hard to help them. How do you think a leader develops the kind of love that keeps on in spite of "great distress and anguish"?

Nevertheless, it is significant when a man such as Paul acknowledges that his love and concern for the Corinthian church had caused him anguish of heart and had brought "many tears." Perhaps Paul is telling us, by word and example, that in our modern sophistication we may not be moved to tears as often as we should be at the sin we find in the world—and sometimes even in the church.   —C. R. B.

B. In Punishment (vv. 5, 6)

5, 6. *If anyone has caused grief, he has not so much grieved me as he has grieved all of you, to some extent—not to put it too severely. The punishment inflicted on him by the majority is sufficient for him.*

As noted in the Lesson Background, the individual mentioned here is likely the man guilty of incest, whom Paul had told the Corinthians to discipline (1 Corinthians 5). Paul noted that the *grief* the man had *caused* was not confined to Paul but had affected the entire congregation. As Christians we need to realize that when we sin, or even engage in questionable activities, our actions reflect negatively on the congregation where we serve.

The Corinthians were told to "hand this man over to Satan" (1 Corinthians 5:5). (See the comments on this verse in lesson 4.) This *punishment*, which had been *inflicted on him by the majority* and thus represented the entire congregation, had achieved the desired results. Paul considered it *sufficient* for the man.

C. In Forgiveness (vv. 7-11)

7, 8. *Now instead, you ought to forgive and comfort him, so that he will not be overwhelmed by excessive sorrow. I urge you, therefore, to reaffirm your love for him.*

In Paul's opinion the man had suffered enough. Two steps were now necessary. First, the Corinthians were to *forgive . . . him,* perhaps in a public meeting of the congregation. The restoration process then required another step. The man needed to sense the *comfort,* or support, of the congregation, lest he *be overwhelmed by excessive sorrow.* In some situations an offender may be so burdened with remorse that he needs continued help and support from other Christians. If he does not sense that they have forgiven him, he may find it difficult, if not impossible, to forgive himself.

When the offense against others has been quite painful, this is not an easy step to take. In such a situation the most effective tool that one can use is the kind of love Paul describes in 1 Corinthians 13.

9. *The reason I wrote you was to see if you would stand the test and be obedient in everything.*

Paul had written the Corinthians primarily out of a concern that the man living in sin be disciplined, but he had another motive. He was testing whether the Corinthians had the maturity to deal with this problem effectively. No doubt Paul was pleased that they had accepted his authority, which some in the congregation had challenged. Paul's response to their criticism is found in 2 Corinthians 10:1—11:33.

10. *If you forgive anyone, I also forgive him. And what I have forgiven—if there was anything to forgive—I have forgiven in the sight of Christ for your sake.*

Forgive is the key word in this verse. Since the man in question had shown repentance and had been punished by being excommunicated from the congregation, it was time for healing to begin. The congregation had already started the process, and Paul now gave his approval to their actions. When the problem first arose, Paul had to prod the Corinthians to take action; but in extending forgiveness, they had taken the initiative. Paul commended them by expressing his agreement with their action.

WHAT DO YOU THINK?

It has been said that a church leader is to "comfort the afflicted and afflict the comfortable." How would you apply this maxim to the problem of dealing with a member's sin?

HOW TO SAY IT

Antioch. AN-tee-ock.
Corinth. KOR-inth.
Ephesus. EFF-uh-sus.
Galatia. Guh-LAY-shuh.
Macedonia. Mass-eh-DOE-
    nee-uh.
Phrygia. FRIJ-ee-uh.
Troas. TRO-az.

I have forgiven in the sight of Christ. By forgiving the man Paul was acting in the spirit of Christ—the spirit that he wanted the Corinthians to demonstrate. It is difficult for people to know that Christ forgives them if those who claim to follow Christ do not forgive them.

SAVING A SINKING CHURCH

Construction of Mexico City's Metropolitan Cathedral began in 1563. Builders were warned that the ground was unstable, and, proving the skeptics right, the building started to sink soon after construction was started.

During the growth of the city to its present population of more than eighteen million, aquifers beneath the city have been its water supply. So much ground water has been pumped that in the last hundred years, the ground has subsided more than twenty-five feet. As a result, the great cathedral has also been sinking. Because it sank unevenly, a point was reached a few years ago where one end was eight feet lower than the other. Engineers proposed a radical, counterintuitive scheme to solve the problem: remove the earth that supports the high end of the building in order to level it. It is working, and the church has been stabilized.

The Corinthian church was "sinking" also—not the building, but the body of Christ in Corinth. Paul's solution to at least one of their problems was bold and perhaps counterintuitive to some. Rather than gloating over the sin of their stumbling member and their success in having forced him to repent, they were to forgive him—especially once the desired end of their discipline had been realized. The sinking moral tone of the church had been stopped. Forgiving love would put the situation in Corinth back "on the level."   —C. R. B.

WHAT DO YOU THINK?

What are some devices Satan employs to wreak havoc in a typical church?

[CAUTION: Teacher, if there is an issue causing more than the usual differences of opinion in your church, be very careful that this discussion does not erupt into a "blame game." Keep the discussion focused on issues, not people.]

11. . . . *in order that Satan might not outwit us. For we are not unaware of his schemes.*

Had the church or some of its leaders remained at odds with Paul or defiant of his advice, *Satan* would have taken advantage of the opportunity to create havoc among the believers. Satan has many *schemes,* many weapons in his arsenal. Immorality is a weapon he often uses to ensnare Christians. But he also uses disagreements to create a spirit of division among believers, and in many situations this weapon can be just as devastating.

II. CHRISTIAN LOVE REACHES OUT (2 CORINTHIANS 2:12-17)
A. IN EVANGELISM (vv. 12, 13)

12. *Now when I went to Troas to preach the gospel of Christ and found that the Lord had opened a door for me.*

Earlier Paul had expressed his intention to visit the Corinthians on his way from Ephesus to Macedonia, then to stop by Corinth again on his way to Judea (1:15, 16). However, he had changed his mind about the visit, no doubt out of a concern that the time was not right: "it was in order to spare you that I did not return to Corinth" (v. 23).

Instead he sent Titus to check on things in Corinth and to bring him word, intending to meet Titus in Troas (verse 13). Apparently Paul left Ephesus because of the riot recorded in Acts 19 (see Acts 20:1). He *went to Troas* (Acts 20:6) where he found that *the Lord had opened a door* for him *to preach the gospel of Christ.* (Compare Paul's language with that in 1 Corinthians 16:9, where "a great door for effective work" was "opened" to Paul in Ephesus.) Paul preached enough in Troas to determine that the door was open, but, as the next verse tells us, he was not able to continue long in that city.

13. *. . . I still had no peace of mind, because I did not find my brother Titus there. So I said good-by to them and went on to Macedonia.*

Because of the circumstances under which Paul left Ephesus, we may assume he left somewhat sooner than he had intended when he sent *Titus* to Corinth with plans to meet him in Troas. Thus Titus was not in Troas when Paul was, and Paul was not able to learn of the conditions in Corinth. This left him restless—he *had no peace of mind.* So in spite of the "open door" in Troas, Paul felt compelled to go *on to Macedonia* and to continue his search for Titus.

B. IN TRIUMPH (vv. 14-16)

14. But thanks be to God, who always leads us in triumphal procession in Christ and through us spreads everywhere the fragrance of the knowledge of him.

Apparently somewhere in Macedonia, Paul finally met with Titus and was relieved to learn that the Corinthians had received his letter in a positive spirit and were addressing the matters about which he had written (2 Corinthians 7:4-9, 13-16). This led Paul, as he often did in his writings, to offer a tribute of praise to God.

To emphasize his gratitude, Paul used a striking metaphor. The phrase *leads us in triumphal procession in Christ* pictures a conquering Roman general at the head of a victory parade in his honor. Behind him marched his victorious troops; then came the prisoners and the spoils of war that had been seized. Christians are likely represented by the triumphant soldiers, for they march victoriously behind the leadership of Christ (though some believe that Christians are portrayed by the prisoners, for they have given themselves as willing "captives" of Christ).

The phrase *fragrance of the knowledge of him* alludes to another practice that accompanied victory processions. Incense was offered as part of the sacrifices that were made to give thanks to the Roman gods. The victory was also celebrated with the release of perfumes along the parade route. Paul equates these fragrances with the spread of the knowledge of Christ wherever his gospel is preached.

15, 16. For we are to God the aroma of Christ among those who are being saved and those who are perishing. To the one we are the smell of death; to the other, the fragrance of life. And who is equal to such a task?

In the previous verse Paul used "fragrance" to describe the knowledge of Christ as it is spread through the efforts of Christians. Here *aroma* is used of Christians themselves. Certainly this is a sweet aroma *among those who are being saved.* In contrast, those who refuse to accept the message that Christians proclaim are described as *perishing.* So it was with the aroma of incense and perfume at the Roman victory procession; it was the *smell of death* to the conquered peoples, for they would be executed at the conclusion of the celebration. Paul expressed a similar contrast in 1 Corinthians 1:18: "For the message of the cross is foolishness to those who are perishing, but to us who are being saved it is the power of God."

Who is equal to such a task? With this rhetorical question Paul raises the issue of the awesome responsibility of those who convey the gospel message. In a sense no human is worthy or competent to deliver this message. Yet this is the means that God has chosen to convey his saving truths—through fallible humans. Thus we must always enter into the ministry of the Word with humility and trembling.

Later Paul gives an answer to this question, asserting that his "competence comes from God" (2 Corinthians 3:5). It behooves us to be imitators of Paul in this respect, looking to God for direction and strength as we carry out the ministry he has given us. As Jesus emphasized in his teaching on the vine and the branches, "Apart from me you can do nothing" (John 15:5).

C. IN SINCERITY (v. 17)

17. Unlike so many, we do not peddle the word of God for profit. One the contrary, in Christ we speak before God with sincerity, like men sent from God.

WHAT DO YOU THINK?

Paul seems to have left an open door in Troas unentered because of his great concern for the Corinthians. When do you think it is okay to ignore a door "that the Lord [has] opened," and when would you feel compelled to enter in spite of other circumstances?

The "procession" in today's visual is composed of young people from missionary families displaying the flags of the many nations where they serve.

WHAT DO YOU THINK?

In what kind of efforts or ministries are you most likely to say with Paul, "Who is equal to such a task?" Name some situations when you have most appreciated that "our competence comes from God."

PRAYER

We thank you, O Father, for the inspired words of Paul and the other biblical writers that give us practical guidance for the problems that we face as we serve in your church. Give us the grace and wisdom to accept and apply these lessons in a manner pleasing to you. In Jesus' name. Amen.

THOUGHT TO REMEMBER

Lord, teach us how to forgive—and to forget.

DAILY BIBLE READINGS

Monday, May 1—God Consoles Us in Our Afflictions (2 Corinthians 1:1-11)

Tuesday, May 2—Sealed by God's Spirit (2 Corinthians 1:12-22)

Wednesday, May 3—Love Prevails Over Pain and Conflict (2 Corinthians 1:23—2:4)

Thursday, May 4—Christian Forgiveness for the Offender (2 Corinthians 2:5-11)

Friday, May 5—The Gospel: the Fragrance of Life (2 Corinthians 2:12-17)

Saturday, May 6—Good News Written on Human Hearts (2 Corinthians 3:1-11)

Sunday, May 7—Freed and Transformed by the Spirit (2 Corinthians 3:12-18)

Paul established himself as an authentic spokesman for God in contrast to *so many* who *peddle the word of God for profit*. The *many* does not necessarily indicate that there were a great number of false teachers, only that the number was large in comparison with the teachers of truth. This certainly would have included false teachers in other churches as well as in Corinth. The word *peddle* calls attention to the real motives of these individuals: they were interested primarily in making a profit from their teaching. God's truth was nothing more than a commodity for them to "sell."

CONCLUSION

A. APOSTOLIC TRIUMPHS

In today's lesson text Paul expresses his thanks for the triumph he had experienced in Christ. There were several blessings for which he could be thankful. First of all, he was thankful that the man who had been overtaken by sin had repented. Paul found great joy in the man's change of heart.

Second, the Corinthians' actions in disciplining the man brought joy to Paul's heart. They could have resented Paul's criticism of their slowness to act in this case. Many today react negatively to any criticism, even when it is appropriate and given sincerely and gently. The Corinthians accepted Paul's counsel and acted to correct the problem.

Third, Paul found joy in the Corinthians' willingness to forgive the man who had created the problem. All too often when conflict occurs within a congregation, people are slow to forgive and even slower to forget. Some find it much easier to blame everyone else for their problems, and they hold grudges that cripple a church for years. But the Corinthians forgave the man and encouraged him, lest he be "overwhelmed by excessive sorrow" (2 Corinthians 2:7). Serious wounds that result from conflicts within a congregation are sometimes slow to heal. The soothing balm of love must be applied frequently and over a long period of time to effect complete healing.

Finally, Paul could rejoice that he had been given the opportunity to preach in Troas. While he could not take full advantage of the open door there, he was never happier than when he was sharing the good news with those who had never heard it. He was ready to preach in any circumstance—in jail, to angry mobs, to legalistic Jews, to scholars. No situation could curb his desire to preach.

B. SATAN'S DEVICES

Satan never seems to lack ways to attack Christians. Sometimes he is a "roaring lion" that "prowls around . . . looking for someone to devour" (1 Peter 5:8). At other times he is subtle, appearing as an "angel of light" (2 Corinthians 11:14). He often attacks us through our enemies, using them to lead us into temptation. But he may also get to us through our friends or members of our own families.

Paul could say that "we are not unaware of [Satan's] schemes" (2 Corinthians 2:11); however, he did not mean by that that we can take him for granted. Just the opposite! We know he will attempt to catch us at our weakest moment—that is one of his favorite "schemes"! Thus, we need all the help we can get to protect us from Satan's wiles. Since "our struggle is not against flesh and blood, but against the rulers, against the authorities, against the powers of this dark world and against the spiritual forces of evil in the heavenly realms," we need to "put on the full armor of God" (Ephesians 6:11, 12). Among other items, this includes a better understanding of the Scriptures—something that this present study is designed to give.

Discovery Learning

This page contains an alternate lesson plan emphasizing learning activities. Classes desiring such student involvement will find these suggestions helpful. The next page is a reproducible activity page to further enhance discovery learning.

LEARNING GOALS

After this lesson students will be able to:

1. Tell the reasons for Paul's sense of triumph concerning the Corinthians.

2. Suggest some situations over which God's love and grace can triumph today.

3. Pinpoint a current situation in the church or in their personal relationships where Christian love needs to triumph.

INTO THE LESSON

Prior to students' arriving, write the word "conflict" on the chalkboard. Begin the lesson by directing their attention to the board and asking them to "identify the various types of conflict there are in the world today." Write their suggested answers (racial, marital, interpersonal, religious, employer/employee, ideological, political, international) on the board.

After looking at these various types of conflict, ask the class to "describe how conflict affects people's attitudes and behavior—the way people relate to each other while in conflict." Possible responses include the following: separation of people, avoidance of people, refusal to make eye contact, lack of communication, angry criticism.

Next, ask the class to describe what often happens between people who are in conflict—i.e., how conflict is "acted out" (fighting, lawsuits, verbal and/or physical abuse). In today's study, we find that a conflict that could have separated people was not acted out but was resolved by love. God, who is love, "leads us in triumphal procession in Christ" (v. 14)—by restoring not only broken relationships between people, but broken relationships with God.

INTO THE WORD

Read 2 Corinthians 2:4-11 aloud. Write on the chalkboard "Steps to Unite Broken Relationships." Ask the class to identify the ways that the Corinthians' faith united their congregation and resolved their conflict. Write their answers on the board. From the text, possible answers include forgive the erring brother, comfort him, reaffirm your love. Ask: "Why should the Corinthians forgive the erring brother?" Paul gives three possible answers: 1. punishment was sufficient to bring repentance (v. 6); 2. failure to forgive would overwhelm the man with sorrow (v. 7); and 3. failure to forgive would give Satan an advantage (v. 11).

Point out that love triumphs in restoring a broken relationship with God. Have a volunteer read 2 Corinthians 2:12-17. Ask the students to work with a neighbor in answering the following questions:

1. What is meant by the "opened" door (v. 12)?

2. Describe how you believe Paul felt when he said, "I still had no peace of mind" (v. 13).

3. What is meant by the word "aroma" (v. 15)?

4. Why does the aroma result in two different responses (v. 16)?

Allow four or five minutes to complete this activity. Then go over the questions, having the students respond with their answers.

INTO LIFE

Distribute copies of the reproducible page that follows. Have the students work individually or in groups of three to five to complete the chart, "Satan's Schemes/ Savior's Solutions." Under the first heading students should list as many possible ways that Satan deceives, separates, and causes conflict among people as they can think of. *(Possible answers include immorality, worry, false teaching, disagreements, divisiveness, worldliness, and arguments.)* Students should then identify possible solutions to avoid those schemes and list them under the second heading, Savior's Solutions. *(Suggested answers: knowledge of God's Word; obedience to God; personal confrontation of sin; genuine concern for the person; active involvement in sharing the message of Christ; indwelling presence of the Holy Spirit; personal forgiveness, love, and comfort.)*

Answers will come from the text as well as from inference and personal experience. Allow time for the students to work; then ask for reports. Use the students' responses to compile a master list.

Next, ask each student to look at the bottom of the handout. With assurances that the students will not be asked to reveal what they write, have each one write the four "schemes" that most often give them trouble in their personal relationships and evaluate how often he or she is employing the "Savior's solution" the class identified as appropriate to address each of them. Challenge students to work to raise the frequency in each case. Close with prayer.

Satan's Schemes/Savior's Solutions

In the left column list some ways that Satan deceives, separates, and causes conflict among people. To the right of each "scheme" cite one or two ways the Savior helps us to avoid or defeat the devil's work.

SATAN'S SCHEMES	SAVIOR'S SOLUTIONS

Choose four of these schemes that give you the most trouble. Evaluate how often you are practicing the Savior's solutions to that scheme. What do the results suggest you need to do in your battles with Satan?

Scheme: _____

Solution: _____
Rarely
Practiced   1.........2.........3.........4.........5.........6.........7.........8.........9 10   Usually Practiced

Scheme: _____

Solution: _____
Rarely
Practiced   1.........2.........3.........4.........5.........6.........7.........8.........9 10   Usually Practiced

Scheme: _____

Solution: _____
Rarely
Practiced   1.........2.........3.........4.........5.........6.........7.........8.........9 10   Usually Practiced

Scheme: _____

Solution: _____
Rarely
Practiced   1.........2.........3.........4.........5.........6.........7.........8.........9 10   Usually Practiced

TRIALS AND TRIUMPHS OF CHRISTIAN MINISTRY

LESSON 11

WHY TEACH THIS LESSON?

Don't let your students assume from the word "Christian Ministry" in the title to today's lesson that this is just for and about preachers. Perhaps the first thing you can accomplish in this lesson is to challenge your students to be involved in some kind of ministry for the Lord.

From there you will want to demonstrate the balance that exists between trial and triumph. Too many people are won to the Lord with shallow promises of bliss and rest; they are ill-equipped for the trials and even persecutions they will face in their new way of life. We have planted the seed in shallow, rocky soil—to borrow Jesus' picture from the parable of the sower. Let this lesson be a reality check for your students. They need to know that trials will come. But you can also assure them of the promise of triumph—full and final and eternal triumph! Trials can be endured when hope for victory is in sight!

INTRODUCTION

A. A GREATER HONOR

During the American Civil War, General William T. Sherman created a special corps to carry out his campaign against the Confederates in Georgia. He passed over the man who had expected to command this corps, giving this duty instead to General O. O. Howard, a man of strong Christian faith who had a distinguished combat record. When the war was over, the Union army prepared for a victory parade in Washington, D.C. The night before the grand parade, General Sherman called Howard to his quarters.

"General Howard," said Sherman, "I have a problem. The man that you were chosen ahead of to direct the special corps has some powerful friends in Washington, and they are demanding that he lead the corps in the parade."

"But, General Sherman," Howard protested, "I earned the right to lead that corps."

"I know that, Howard," Sherman replied. "But I also know that you are a Christian and that you know how to handle disappointment."

"Since you put it that way," Howard replied, "I'll accept your decision."

"Thank you, Howard. Report to me at nine in the morning." When General Howard reported the next morning, General Sherman brought him to the head of the parade and ordered him to ride by his side.

This is similar to the experience of Paul, who endured much suffering and many disappointments in his service for Christ. But he never complained, for he knew that he would one day be part of the heavenly parade, enjoying the eternal glory that "far outweighs" any "light and momentary troubles."

B. LESSON BACKGROUND

Despite Paul's best efforts to help the Corinthian church and address its problems, some in the church had become critical of Paul and his ministry. He begins

DEVOTIONAL READING:
2 CORINTHIANS 6:1-10

BACKGROUND SCRIPTURE:
2 CORINTHIANS 4

PRINTED TEXT:
2 CORINTHIANS 4:5-18

LESSON AIMS

After completing this lesson, students should be able to:

1. Recite the trials and the blessings Paul said accompanied his service for the Lord.

2. Explain how we, like Paul, can persevere through the trials of Christian ministry.

3. Focus on the eternal in order to bear the trials and appreciate the blessings that come with serving Christ.

May 14

KEY VERSE

We are hard pressed on every side, but not crushed; perplexed, but not in despair; persecuted, but not abandoned; struck down, but not destroyed.
—2 Corinthians 4:8, 9

his response to these critics in the third chapter of 2 Corinthians. In today's lesson text (taken from chapter 4), Paul continues the defense of his ministry by affirming his complete trust in Christ and his desire to make Christ the heart of his ministry. The trials and personal conflicts he experienced had not shaken that trust. Because Paul's vision was focused on that which is eternal, he could deal with any trials with an attitude of triumph.

Every Christian at one time or another has experienced trials or setbacks while serving Christ, some of them quite severe. Paul's testimony is one from which we can draw strength and encouragement for these occasions. The Source of Paul's triumph can be ours as well!

I. MINISTRY'S FOCUS (2 CORINTHIANS 4:5-7)

A. THE MESSAGE (vv. 5, 6)

5. For we do not preach ourselves, but Jesus Christ as Lord, and ourselves as your servants for Jesus' sake.

In the previous verses of this chapter, Paul referred to those who were accusing him of preaching the gospel for his own personal gain and glory. He asserted that he had "renounced secret and shameful ways" and had refused to "distort the word of God." *We do not preach ourselves,* he declares (apparently including those who had accompanied him on his journeys); instead, we preach *Jesus Christ as Lord.* Paul had stated in his first letter: "I resolved to know nothing while I was with you except Jesus Christ and him crucified" (1 Corinthians 2:2).

Paul was also clear about his and his companions' duty, speaking of them as *your servants for Jesus' sake.* The word translated *servants* is more accurately rendered "bondservants" or "slaves." Paul's emphasis is one that every follower of Christ ought to emulate.

6. For God, who said, "Let light shine out of darkness," made his light shine in our hearts to give us the light of the knowledge of the glory of God in the face of Christ.

Here Paul states the reason that he had become a slave of Christ. In mentioning the *light* that shone *out of darkness,* he describes the experience of all who come to know Christ as "the light of the world" (John 8:12). They are thereby delivered from spiritual "darkness" (Colossians 1:12, 13) "into his wonderful light" (1 Peter 2:9). Their lifestyle is described as walking in the light (1 John 1:7).

This verse calls to mind God's words at the beginning of creation: "Let there be light" (Genesis 1:3). Through Jesus God has initiated a spiritual re-creation, declaring to those in the darkness of sin, "Let there be light!" The reference to seeing *the glory of God in the face of Christ* recalls Paul's contrast of Moses' veiled face under the Old Covenant with Christ's unveiled face under the New (3:12-18).

B. THE MESSENGERS (v. 7)

7. But we have this treasure in jars of clay to show that this all-surpassing power is from God and not from us.

God in his infinite wisdom has chosen to reveal his message of salvation through human beings. This message is the *treasure* of which Paul speaks. We who carry the message are the *jars of clay!* In using this expression, Paul probably had in mind the practice of rulers of that day who kept their captured wealth of gold and silver in clay pots. The cheap clay vessels, contrasting sharply with the vast wealth they contained, did not attract the attention of potential robbers.

In the same way, the use of weak human vessels to convey God's message is contrasted with the *all-surpassing power* of that message. That power is not *from us;* it is *from God.* We are merely the clay pots; the treasure is that which is in us—the power of the indwelling Spirit of God. Later Paul would note how what he describes as a "thorn in my flesh" was used of God to demonstrate the sufficiency of his grace and the power of Christ (12:7-10).

Worthless Treasure

In 1857 the S.S. *Central America* sank off the coast of South Carolina during a hurricane. It was carrying passengers from the California gold fields and a cargo of gold bullion worth about twenty-one million dollars in today's value.

For 130 years the wreckage lay lost on the ocean floor. Then in 1987 a group of investors funded an expedition that found the ruined ship. In the process of recovering the cargo, the salvagers spent some thirty million dollars. To add insult to injury, a court awarded ten percent of the twenty-one million dollars to the company that originally insured the cargo. The judge commented that he wished the cargo had been worth a billion dollars so that it would have been worth the salvage effort.

Compare that vessel and its cargo with the "jars of clay" and their contents of which Paul wrote. The containers in each case are mere physical "stuff," but how much the contents differ! The things of this world often are not worth the trouble or the cost required to obtain them. The gospel, however, is a priceless treasure of which Jesus said a person ought to give all he has to possess (Matthew 13:44).

It is a prize that life's storms cannot harm or destroy. Instead of being salvaged, this treasure has the unique power to salvage the one who seeks it!   —C. R. B.

II. MINISTRY'S TRIALS (2 CORINTHIANS 4:8-12)

A. Severe but Bearable (vv. 8, 9)

8, 9. We are hard pressed on every side, but not crushed; perplexed, but not in despair; persecuted, but not abandoned; struck down, but not destroyed.

At this point (approximately A.D. 56) there was very little persecution of Christians by the Roman Empire. That would not become severe until the next decade under Emperor Nero. The Jewish leaders, however, exerted whatever pressure they could in an effort to stop the spread of Christianity. For Paul and his companions, the problems and sufferings they had endured for Christ's sake had often been intense. Later in this same letter Paul gave a more detailed and graphic description of some of his own trials (11:23-28). In spite of the severity of these circumstances, Paul acknowledged that he was *not crushed, not in despair, not abandoned,* and *not destroyed.* Whenever the Corinthians faced persecution, they could look to Paul's example and take courage. The key to his perseverance was not his own strength but his trust in God to sustain him through each crisis.

B. Serving a Purpose (vv. 10-12)

10. We always carry around in our body the death of Jesus, so that the life of Jesus may also be revealed in our body.

According to 2 Corinthians 11:24 and 25, five times Paul received thirty-nine lashes with a whip, three times he was beaten with rods, and once he was stoned. Not all of these incidents are mentioned in the New Testament; the record of his stoning at Lystra during his first missionary journey is found in Acts 14:19.

Paul did not believe he could suffer in the way that Jesus did on the cross. The phrase *carry around in our body the death of Jesus* is explained in the next verse.

11. For we who are alive are always being given over to death for Jesus' sake, so that his life may be revealed in our mortal body.

For Paul to bear in his body "the death of Jesus" means *always being given over to death for Jesus' sake.* Paul constantly faced hazardous, life-threatening situations for the cause of Christ. This theme is found in other writings of Paul. In Romans 8:36 he quotes Psalm 44:22: "For your sake we face death all day long." In 1 Corinthians 15:31 he writes, "I die every day."

What Do You Think?

In spite of all the trouble Paul faced, he never felt defeated. What resources do we Christians have so that, as we face disappointments, frustrations, and trials, we can have confidence of victory?

While there's nothing funny about persecution, the humorous illustration on today's visual reminds us that God is with us in these tough times as well as in good times.

The *we* in this verse may include Paul and his companions, or it may be more extensive, including the apostles and others who had been martyred for Christ. Paul and others were willing to suffer in order that Christ's *life may be revealed in our mortal body.* This is similar in meaning to the "clay pot" language of verse 7: God uses human frailty to demonstrate his power.

12. So then, death is at work in us, but life is at work in you.

Death was *at work* in Paul and others who brought the gospel, in the sense that they frequently suffered potentially lethal persecution. Those who courageously faced such circumstances did so in order that their example might call attention to the message of eternal *life.* Paul was not saying that suffering and death in themselves have intrinsic value. Their value lies in the fact that the manner in which the Christian faces suffering and death provides a compelling testimony to others of the reality of his faith.

TARGET PRACTICE

William Tell was a legendary Swiss patriot. No doubt the most familiar story told about him is reputed to have taken place in the year 1307. Tell was forced to shoot an arrow into an apple placed on his son's head, because he refused to acknowledge Austrian authority over his land. Tell's aim was true, and his son was spared any injury. Tell was still imprisoned, however, because he later commented that if he had injured his son, he would have put his second arrow through the Austrian governor's heart.

Perhaps inspired by this tale, a Portland, Oregon, man tried to shoot a one-gallon fuel can off the head of his friend, Anthony Roberts. The incident took place as part of an initiation into an adventurers' group called Mountain Men Anonymous. As you might have guessed, both men were reported to have been drinking at the time. Roberts lost an eye, but suffered no brain damage. He later said, "I feel really stupid."

Roberts suffered a serious injury and came very close to being killed, and for no legitimate purpose whatsoever! Paul, however, was willing to be a target of the devil's "arrows" for the noblest purpose of all—spreading the gospel of Christ. The injuries he suffered he willingly endured for the sake of bringing others to know Christ, whose power had made such a dramatic change in his own life. —C. R. B.

III. MINISTRY'S HOPE (2 CORINTHIANS 4:13-18)

A. FIRMLY FOUNDED (vv. 13, 14)

13, 14. It is written: "I believed; therefore I have spoken." With that same spirit of faith we also believe and therefore speak, because we know that the one who raised the Lord Jesus from the dead will also raise us with Jesus and present us with you in his presence.

The word *spirit* in this verse probably does not refer to the Holy Spirit, but to the attitude or perspective *of faith,* since faith is the subject of the Old Testament text Paul cites. The quotation from Psalm 116:10 is appropriate, for the psalmist seems to have been experiencing some of the same difficulties as Paul. In Psalm 116:3 he writes: "The cords of death entangled me, the anguish of the grave came upon me; I was overcome by trouble and sorrow." Paul could readily identify with this situation. No doubt he also found consolation in the later verses of the Psalm (vv. 12-19) in which the writer testifies how he found deliverance in the Lord.

Paul's hope for deliverance from his present troubles was grounded in his faith in the resurrection of Jesus. He knew that as God *raised the Lord Jesus,* he *will also raise us with Jesus and present us with you in his presence.* On the day Jesus returns, God will raise those "who have fallen asleep in Christ" (1 Corinthians 15:18) and present the faithful before his throne in glory and honor. Paul's faith in the

HOW TO SAY IT

Corinth. KOR-inth.
Corinthians. Kor-IN-thee-unz.
Damascus. Duh-MASS-kus.
Lystra. LISS-truh.

resurrection and in the return of Christ sustained him through all kinds of difficulties. He encouraged his readers in Corinth to live by that same faith.

B. RENEWED DAILY (vv. 15, 16)

15. All this is for your benefit, so that the grace that is reaching more and more people may cause thanksgiving to overflow to the glory of God.

All this refers to the afflictions and humiliations that Paul had suffered. Paul never suggests that there is any virtue in suffering as such. Rather, his suffering had been *for* the Corinthians' *benefit*. Paul had committed his life to winning as many *people* to Christ as he could. Whatever pain he may have experienced in the past was for the purpose of bringing others like the Corinthians into a saving relationship with Jesus Christ. In so doing he was making available God's abundant *grace*. God is glorified when people accept his grace, so the greater the number who accept it, the greater the number who offer their thanks *to the glory of God*.

This principle is still valid. Jesus' Great Commission to carry the gospel into all the world has never been repealed. Unfortunately, many Christians today have never understood the Great Commission or have little concern for it. With perhaps as many as four billion people in the world who have never come to God through Jesus Christ, we have vast opportunities to labor for God's glory.

16. Therefore we do not lose heart. Though outwardly we are wasting away, yet inwardly we are being renewed day by day.

The Greek term for *lose heart*, which appears also in verse 1 of this chapter, may refer either to physical weakness or to spiritual weariness. The latter appears to be Paul's primary emphasis. Paul often must have become physically exhausted, but he never became disheartened so that he wanted to quit the Lord's work.

God never intended our physical bodies to be immortal. *Outwardly* we cannot escape the limitations imposed by time and disease. Paul had no problem accepting these limitations, for he was able to rejoice that *inwardly we are being renewed day by day*. That renewal comes through daily communion with God through prayer and the study of his Word.

C. FIXED ON ETERNITY (vv. 17, 18)

17. For our light and momentary troubles are achieving for us an eternal glory that far outweighs them all.

Most of us would not look upon all that Paul suffered as *light and momentary troubles*! For most of us these experiences would represent crushing burdens. But Paul knew that his afflictions were *momentary*. Many today live just for the moment, or view life and set priorities by temporal standards. Paul, on the other hand, saw life through an eternal telescope, which allowed him to see *an eternal glory* that made his present afflictions seem light in comparison.

18. So we fix our eyes not on what is seen, but on what is unseen. For what is seen is temporary, but what is unseen is eternal.

Many today are obsessed with *what is seen*. To them, if something cannot be experienced through one or more of the five senses, then it does not really exist, or at least it cannot be important. Paul turns this view on its head, asserting that just the opposite is true. What we see is only *temporary* and is relatively insignificant in view of the *unseen*, but lasting, realities of what is *eternal*.

CONCLUSION

A. "WE DO NOT LOSE HEART"

On every hand the forces of secularism, demonstrated by a ceaseless quest for pleasure and possessions, seem to be winning. Pollsters tell us that many people

WHAT DO YOU THINK?

How can we make sure that we, like Paul, are "inwardly . . . renewed day by day"?

[Perhaps your students can tell some of the methods or materials they have used for effective quiet times with the Word.]

WHAT DO YOU THINK?

When we face afflictions, it is hard to think of them as "light." But that is exactly how Paul described them. How can we keep our troubles in perspective? How can we keep the promised "eternal glory" in focus while facing our "light and momentary troubles"?

PRAYER

O God, give us the eyes to see beyond the temporary trials we all must face and to catch a glimpse of the grand triumph you have in store for us. At the same time, give us the zeal to share that vision with others about us who are lost in the darkness. In Jesus' name. Amen.

THOUGHT TO REMEMBER

Keep your eyes on "what is unseen."

DAILY BIBLE READINGS

Monday, May 8—God's Light Shines in Our Hearts (2 Corinthians 4:1-7)

Tuesday, May 9—God Raised Jesus and Will Raise Us (2 Corinthians 4:8-15)

Wednesday, May 10—We Walk and Live by Faith (2 Corinthians 4:16—5:10)

Thursday, May 11— Reconciled to Be Reconcilers (2 Corinthians 5:11-21)

Friday, May 12—Open Wide Your Hearts (2 Corinthians 6:1-11)

Saturday, May 13—We Are Temples of the Living God (2 Corinthians 6:14—7:1)

Sunday, May 14—Paul's Joy at the Corinthians' Repentance (2 Corinthians 7:2-16)

---

still believe in God, but we know very well that such an expression of faith is at best shallow and uninformed. People in some parts of the world are facing severe persecution such as Paul suffered, while the worst that many of us may suffer for Christ's sake is a polite rebuff or a condescending sneer when we present the claims of the gospel to others. Yet even such "light and momentary troubles" as these may cause us to become fainthearted and discouraged.

Paul's response to the trials he faced was a ringing "we do not lose heart." His words were not based on youthful bravado or blissful ignorance. Nor were they the response of an emotionally unstable man who did not know what he was talking about. At the time that Paul (then known as Saul) journeyed to Damascus for the purpose of persecuting Christians (about two decades prior to writing this letter to the Corinthians), he had gained a reputation among his Jewish countrymen as a scholar and a zealot for the Jewish faith.

Paul knew that once he became a disciple of Jesus, all that would change. He knew that his conversion to Christianity would cost him most of his friends and the honors that he had gained among his own people. He knew that his actions could lead to his imprisonment and even his death. Yet Paul did not hesitate in making the decision to follow Christ. Years later he looked back with this observation: "I consider everything a loss compared to the surpassing greatness of knowing Christ Jesus my Lord, for whose sake I have lost all things. I consider them rubbish, that I may gain Christ" (Philippians 3:8).

B. THIS WORLD IS NOT MY HOME

There was a reason that Paul could endure trials and persecutions: he realized that this world is in no way the real or final home of Christians; we are just passing through. Like Abraham, we are strangers and sojourners "longing for a better country—that is, a heavenly one" (Hebrews 11:16). Of necessity we must live under a worldly government, and that citizenship requires us to behave in a certain way. We ought to obey the laws of the land unless they require us to engage in an activity that violates God's laws. However, our true citizenship is in Heaven; and that citizenship also carries certain obligations. Concerning this issue, Peter wrote, "I urge you, as aliens and strangers in the world, to abstain from sinful desires, which war against your soul" (1 Peter 2:11).

Paul understood the principle of dual citizenship, and he knew where his priorities lay. "Outwardly" his physical body may waste away; but that did not greatly concern him, for "inwardly" his spirit was "renewed day by day." Through the eyes of faith he could focus on "what is unseen," knowing that he would share in the glory that is promised to all who faithfully serve Jesus.

C. CHRISTIANS CAN!

Christians can handle disappointments because they are not self-centered. We often suffer disappointments because we want the wrong things for selfish purposes. But if we put Christ and others first, these lesser goals are seen for what they are—short-sighted and inadequate.

Christians can handle disappointments because they help bear one another's burdens. Every church ought to be a caring support group for its members in times of trouble. Whether these times involve illness, financial difficulties, or moral issues, the church should always be there to offer guidance and assistance.

Christians can handle disappointments because they understand that any present "light and momentary troubles" are but for a moment. They can look beyond such temporary inconveniences, knowing that God has in store for them "an eternal glory that far outweighs them all!"

Discovery Learning

This page contains an alternate lesson plan emphasizing learning activities. Classes desiring such student involvement will find these suggestions helpful. The next page is a reproducible activity page to further enhance discovery learning.

LEARNING GOALS

After this lesson each student will be able to:

1. Recite the trials and the blessings Paul said accompanied his service for the Lord.

2. Explain how we, like Paul, can persevere through the trials of Christian ministry.

3. Focus on the eternal in order to bear the trials and appreciate the blessings that come with serving Christ.

INTO THE LESSON

Write the words "Trials" and "Blessings" on the chalkboard or an overhead projector transparency. Ask the class to suggest blessings they have experienced since coming to know the Lord, and list these under the word *Blessings*. Do the same with *Trials*. Continue until you have more than just a few. Ask, "Which ones—from either column—have come to us specifically because we are Christians? Which have also come to many non-Christians? How did we Christians react differently to these blessings and trials from the way non-Christians reacted?" Lead into the Bible text by stating: "In today's lesson, the apostle Paul tells us how he persisted in his faith in spite of many trials. Through it all he remained joyful because God helped him—just as he can help us triumph over the trials we face."

Option: Use the "Trials . . ." part of the reproducible activity on page 324 to introduce today's lesson. (Use the ". . . and Triumph" section to conclude the lesson.)

INTO THE WORD

Divide the class into at least three smaller groups. Assign one of the following sections to each group. Have them write their answers and then report to the class.

1. **Proclaim the Message.** Read 2 Corinthians 4:1-7, 13. Paul had received a ministry (v. 1) and as a result had "renounced secret and shameful ways" (v. 2). Answer the following questions to better understand that ministry: 1. What specific characteristics describe this renouncing of secret and shameful ways (v. 2)? (*not using deception; not distorting the word of God; setting forth the truth plainly*) 2. What is the "treasure in jars of clay" (v. 7)? (*gospel message that Jesus Christ is Lord*) 3. With whom does Paul say he has the "same spirit of faith" (v. 13)? (*the psalmist who wrote Psalm 116:10*) 4. What is the point of this comparison? (*making an audible expression of faith regardless—even when facing death.*)

2. **Persist Under God's Power.** Read 2 Corinthians 4:1, 7-12, 16. In this section Paul affirms his unyielding loyalty to the lordship of Christ. The phrase that is translated "do not lose heart" in verses 1 and 16 is used four more times in the New Testament (Luke 18:1; Galatians 6:9; Ephesians 3:13; 2 Thessalonians 3:13). 1. What are some other words or expressions that mean the same as "lose heart"? (*quit; give up; throw in the towel; drop out; become discouraged or brokenhearted*) 2. Paul contrasts the eternal, incorruptible, glorious gospel with the temporal, corruptible, non-glorious human vessel that proclaims it. How does Paul identify the frailty of the clay jar (vv. 8, 9)? (*hard pressed, perplexed, persecuted, struck down*) 3. What is the point of this description of weakness? (*God manifests his power in his servant's weakness so that we never have to give up*) 4. What does Paul mean by the phrase "carry around in our body the death of Jesus" (v. 10)? (*servanthood involves self-sacrifice, a willingness to suffer physically, mentally, socially, etc.*)

3. **Point to Eternal Glory.** Read 2 Corinthians 4:13-18. Paul was able to remain loyal to the lordship of Jesus in spite of severe trials because of his continuous focus. 1. What guarantee does Paul give for our own resurrection (v. 14)? (*Christ's resurrection*) 2. To what does the "all this" refer in v. 15? (*whatever is suffered or endured for Christ*) 3. What terms in this chapter refer to the "outward" part of a person (v. 16)? (*clay jar, v. 7; body, v. 10; mortal body, v. 11*) 4. Why does Paul's focus help him to persist? (*trials are seen in the light of the eternal perspective*)

INTO LIFE

Paul would not give up when he faced trials or difficulties. Yet, many Christians give up on God when they face problems. Discuss why this happens and how a focus on eternity affects one's personal attitude about the difficulties of life.

Ask the class to brainstorm the following question: "What trials or difficulties do you believe most Christians struggle under today?" Write their ideas on the chalkboard. Then ask: What trials or difficulties do you personally face today? Based upon this study, how should our attitudes be adjusted when we encounter trials?

State: "Let's put on our eternal goggles and see life as only a brief moment in time, and rejoice that God gives us the power to triumph in Christ."

Trials . . .

Use each of the letters of the word *trials* to form another word synonymous with, or related to, the trials you face as a Christian. The letters may start, end, or merely appear in the new words.

T

R

I

A

L

S

. . . and Triumph

Use the space below to write a brief note about how God is working, or will work, each situation represented in your words on the *trials* acrostic to bring "triumph." For example, perhaps your "T" word above was *tears*. You might write below, "God will wipe away every tear from their eyes" (Revelation 7:17).

COLLECTION FOR
JERUSALEM CHRISTIANS

LESSON 12

WHY TEACH THIS LESSON?

Perhaps there is no more controversial subject in all the Bible than "giving." Many preachers will not announce in advance that they will be preaching on the topic because they know attendance will be down when the appointed day arrives. Churches that have annual stewardship emphases often note that attendance is generally lower during those weeks than their average for the year.

If the church membership reacts negatively to the subject, one can imagine how unbelievers react. "All they want down there at that church is my money!" is the stereotype against which churches have to battle. As a result, many churches have quit talking about giving, at least in their worship services. Others will mention it, but they are quite apologetic when they do.

But if we believe that *all* Scripture is given by inspiration of God, and that it is all "useful for teaching, rebuking, correcting and training in righteousness" (see 2 Timothy 3:16), then giving is a subject that we simply cannot avoid.

Teach the lesson today without apology! Those students who take in the Word with an open heart will be blessed if you do.

INTRODUCTION

A. KNOTTY GENEROSITY

John Eliot, a seventeenth-century missionary to the Indians of New England, was noted for his unbounded generosity. His yearly salary of fifty pounds was often given almost entirely to charity. On one occasion the secretary of the missionary society that supported Eliot tried to protect him from his own generosity. To keep him from giving away his entire quarterly stipend before he reached home, the secretary took Eliot's pay and tied a portion of it in each of the four corners of a handkerchief. Then he pulled the knots and tightened them as much as he could before handing the handkerchief to the missionary.

On his way home Eliot met a woman whose appearance indicated dire poverty. He stopped to speak to her, and his heart was so touched that he reached into his pocket to get a coin for her. For some time he pulled and pulled at the knots in his handkerchief, trying to loosen one of them. But he could not do so. Finally he rolled the handkerchief up into a ball and handed it to the astonished woman with these words: "My dear woman, I think the Lord meant for you to have it all."

Eliot had learned what many Christians need to learn: "God loves a cheerful giver."

B. LESSON BACKGROUND

Being a follower of Jesus Christ in first-century Jerusalem was not always easy. Poverty was a problem for some right from the beginning, but it seems that other believers had the resources to deal with the situation (Acts 4:32-37; 6:1). Intimidation and persecution were growing problems (Acts 4:1-18; 5:17, 18, 26-40;

DEVOTIONAL READING:
2 CORINTHIANS 8:1-15

BACKGROUND SCRIPTURE:
2 CORINTHIANS 9

PRINTED TEXT:
2 CORINTHIANS 9:1-13

LESSON AIMS

After this lesson students will be able to:

1. Recite Paul's instructions about the Corinthians' participation in the collection for the Jerusalem Christians.

2. Summarize the principles of Christian giving found in today's text.

3. Apply the principles in today's text to their personal financial giving to the Lord's work.

KEY VERSE

Each man should give what he has decided in his heart to give, not reluctantly or under compulsion, for God loves a cheerful giver.
—2 Corinthians 9:7

May
21

6:9-12), increasing after the stoning of Stephen (Acts 7:54-60) to the point that most of the Christians fled. "On that day," says Acts 8:1, "a great persecution broke out against the church at Jerusalem."

Persecution and poverty continued. It may be that some of the believers had property confiscated at this time (see Hebrews 10:34). In addition, a great famine (Acts 11:27, 28) added to their poverty. In response—or, rather, in prophetic anticipation—the church at Antioch of Syria sent a contribution to the elders of the Jerusalem church (Acts 11:29, 30).

Later, at the Jerusalem conference reported in Acts 15, the issue of poverty was apparently discussed. Luke does not mention this in Acts, but Paul says in Galatians 2:9 and 10 that the apostles and elders (he mentions "James, Peter and John") encouraged him to "remember the poor," something Paul was "eager to do."

Paul began his second missionary journey "some time later" after that conference (Acts 15:36-41). During this journey, Paul demonstrated his eagerness to "remember the poor" by arranging to gather contributions from the churches he visited and to have them sent to the church at Jerusalem. Apparently Paul began this effort among the Galatian churches and then urged the Corinthians to follow their example (1 Corinthians 16:1). In the eighth chapter of 2 Corinthians, Paul mentioned the need once again, citing the generosity of the churches in Macedonia in order to challenge the Corinthians in their giving (vv. 1-6). In the ninth chapter, from which today's text is taken, Paul provided further and more detailed instructions about giving.

I. CHALLENGED TO GIVE (2 CORINTHIANS 9:1-5)
A. PAUL'S COMMENDATION (vv. 1, 2)
1, 2. *There is no need for me to write to you about this service to the saints. For I know your eagerness to help, and I have been boasting about it to the Macedonians, telling them that since last year you in Achaia were ready to give; and your enthusiasm has stirred most of them to action.*

In the previous chapter Paul mentioned that he was sending Titus and two other brothers to Corinth to oversee the collection for the *service to the saints*—that is, to help the Jerusalem Christians (vv. 18-22). Since Paul had come under attack by some in the Corinthian church, he wisely limited his involvement in this activity, lest his enemies would have an occasion to bring further charges against him.

It is unfortunate that some in the ministry have handled money in such a way as to arouse suspicions about their honesty. By sending these well-known and respected men, Paul removed the likelihood that any could challenge his integrity. We today would be wise to follow his example to "do what is right, not only in the eyes of the Lord but also in the eyes of men" (2 Corinthians 8:21).

There is no need for me to write to you. In this way Paul complimented the Corinthians on their *eagerness* to fulfill their ministry to the Jerusalem Christians. In fact, he had been *boasting* about the generosity of the churches in *Achaia* (the province in which Corinth was located) to the churches in Macedonia (the province in northern Greece where cities such as Philippi and Thessalonica were located). Paul noted that his words had had an impact on these other churches: *your enthusiasm has stirred most of them to action.*

B. THE CHURCH'S PREPARATION (vv. 3, 4)
3. *But I am sending the brothers in order that our boasting about you in this matter should not prove hollow, but that you may be ready, as I said you would be.*

Titus and the two other *brothers* had been sent on ahead to make the necessary preparations for receiving the collection. After Paul had commended the generosity of the Corinthians, he did not want his words to *prove hollow*. We do not know how this collection was organized, but in 1 Corinthians 16:2, Paul wrote, "On the first day of every week, each one of you should set aside a sum of money in keeping with his income, saving it up, so that when I come no collections will have to be made." Evidently the collections were taken weekly when the congregation assembled for worship.

4. For if any Macedonians come with me and find you unprepared, we—not to say anything about you—would be ashamed of having been so confident.

Paul said that some of the *Macedonians* might accompany him when he returned to Corinth. (Whether they did or not we do not know.) Should that happen, Paul said, then not only those in Corinth but also he and his companions would have been embarrassed because of how *confident* Paul had been concerning the Corinthians.

C. PAUL'S CONCERN (v. 5)

5. So I thought it necessary to urge the brothers to visit you in advance and finish the arrangements for the generous gift you had promised. Then it will be ready as a generous gift, not as one grudgingly given.

Paul wanted the Corinthians' collection to be *ready* before he arrived so that he would not have to press the issue of giving with them. If he should have to coerce them or plead with them to give, it would appear as though he were trying to obtain the money for himself. (In that day it was not uncommon for itinerant teachers to extort money from their students.) Paul wanted to avoid any controversy about his motives, for this would only further antagonize those in Corinth who were already critical of him.

ENCOURAGEMENT TO GIVE

How do you finance a college education? These days it is not at all uncommon for a year's tuition, room and board, and incidentals to total ten thousand dollars or more. Of course, if "incidentals" include the three "C"s—computer, car, and cash for extracurricular activities—the cost can go *much* higher!

A few years ago Mike Hayes of Rochelle, Illinois, wrote to Bob Greene, a columnist for the *Chicago Tribune*. Mike asked each of Greene's readers to send him a penny to help finance his college education.

The response was amazing: Mike received eighty-eight thousand letters, and the contributions totaled more than fourteen thousand dollars! In addition to pennies, he received dollar bills and checks for one hundred dollars. (With this kind of entrepreneurial spirit, we'll assume Mike decided to become a business major!) However, just to make sure Mike would be the right kind of student, one donor wrote, "Here's a penny. If you use it to buy drugs I hope a bolt of lightning strikes you dead."

While Mike Hayes may be commended for his creativity, Paul is a more noble example for us. Paul encouraged the Corinthians to give, not for his own profit, but for the benefit of impoverished Christians in the Jerusalem church. Most of us don't need any encouragement to be selfish! We need encouragement to give willingly and even sacrificially for the good of others—as Jesus did.   —C. R. B.

II. PRINCIPLES OF GIVING (2 CORINTHIANS 9:6-13)

A. SOWING BOUNTIFULLY (v. 6)

6. Remember this: Whoever sows sparingly will also reap sparingly, and whoever sows generously will also reap generously.

Paul's words sound like a proverb; however, nothing resembling this saying can be found in the book of Proverbs. His observation is quite apparent: a farmer

Use today's visual to illustrate verse 7. Discuss what it means to give "grudgingly, or of necessity," and what it means to be a "cheerful giver."

Every man according as he purposeth in his heart, so let him give; not grudgingly, or of necessity: for God loveth a cheerful giver.
2 Corinthians 9:7

WHAT DO YOU THINK?

Human emotions are prone to going up and down. If we give only when we "feel like it," our giving will be inconsistent. On the other hand, giving must not be only a cold, calculated act—just another item in our budgets. As our lesson writer says, "Good Christian stewardship requires that we give intelligently as well as emotionally." How can we achieve a proper balance in this?

who plants a small plot is not as likely to enjoy as large a harvest as the farmer who plants a large plot. Likewise, if one skimps on seeds in order to save money, he is not likely to enjoy the abundant harvest of one who plants the necessary amount of seeds.

We should not understand Paul to mean that one should give much in order to get much in return. More important than the amount one gives is his motive in giving (a point that Paul will touch on shortly). Jesus commended the poor widow, who gave only two small coins ("all she had to live on"), rather than the rich, who "gave their gifts out of their wealth" (Luke 21:1-4).

B. GIVING CHEERFULLY (v. 7)
7. Each man should give what he has decided in his heart to give, not reluctantly or under compulsion, for God loves a cheerful giver.

When one is cajoled or pressured into giving, his gift is likely to be given *reluctantly.* No doubt Paul would have serious reservations about some of the fund-raising tactics used today by churches and Christian organizations. One who gives *what he has decided in his heart to give* is more likely to give generously and certainly more cheerfully than one who has been pressured or manipulated into giving.

Giving from the heart, however, does not mean that giving should be based entirely on emotions. Good Christian stewardship requires that we give intelligently as well as emotionally. In fact, long-lasting joy is more likely to result from intelligent giving than from giving that is the product of spur-of-the-moment emotions.

C. TRUSTING GOD'S PROMISES (vv. 8-11)
8. And God is able to make all grace abound to you, so that in all things at all times, having all that you need, you will abound in every good work.

Some argue that if we give generously, God will reward us generously. This may seem to be true in some cases. When we are seriously committed to Christ and give generously to his church, we are likely to be better off financially, in part because we no longer need or want many of the expensive "toys" that have become status symbols in our culture. But that is not Paul's point here. God provides *all things at all times* in order that we may *abound in every good work.* In other words, he blesses us that we may use those blessings to help others, not to better ourselves.

9. As it is written: "He has scattered abroad his gifts to the poor; his righteousness endures forever."

Paul reinforced his point with a quotation from Psalm 112:9. *He has scattered abroad.* In the context of the Psalm, this statement is describing a righteous man. One mark of such a man is his generosity. Because of his deep concern for others, as reflected in the fact that he has given unselfishly *to the poor, his righteousness endures forever.* This *righteousness* refers to good deeds that often have positive consequences long after the initial gift has been given. For example, a child may give money to support a missionary who carries the gospel to some who had never heard it. These converts pass their faith on to their children, who do the same with their children, and so forth, resulting in many generations' becoming Christians. Only eternity will measure the worth and the impact of the child's gift.

10. Now he who supplies seed to the sower and bread for food will also supply and increase your store of seed and will enlarge the harvest of your righteousness.

This verse seems to reflect in part Isaiah 55:10. Here the word *he* refers to God, rather than to a righteous man. Such a man who is also generous does not really create the wealth that he shares with others. Both the *seed* and the *bread* come from God. Paul is reminding us that as we have freely received from God, so we should freely share with others our blessings. God will *enlarge* the impact of our giving beyond anything we can imagine.

11. You will be made rich in every way so that you can be generous on every occasion, and through us your generosity will result in thanksgiving to God.

The contributions that the Corinthians and others were sending to the saints in Jerusalem would provide relief for some of their physical needs. But it would also benefit the givers, providing them the joy that comes from helping others. Furthermore, this gift would lead the recipients to render *thanksgiving to God.* No doubt the Jerusalem Christians had prayed for help in their time of need. The fact that their prayers had been answered through the *generosity* of the Gentile churches would strengthen their faith in God and help dispel any reservations they may have had toward Gentile Christians.

D. MEETING NEEDS (v. 12)
12. This service that you perform is not only supplying the needs of God's people but is also overflowing in many expressions of thanks to God.

In this verse Paul reiterated two important blessings that resulted from the Gentile churches' generosity (and should accompany ours as well). First, they were *supplying the needs of God's people;* that is, they supplied what the Jerusalem Christians needed or lacked. Second, their giving was the source of *many expressions of thanks to God*—a point that Paul elaborates on in verse 13.

AN ANONYMOUS DONOR
The severe winter of 1996-97 combined with a very wet spring to bring disastrous flooding to the upper Midwest of the United States. Thousands of square miles of farmland were inundated by the Red River, which flows between Minnesota and North Dakota. Ninety percent of the twin cities of Grand Forks, North Dakota, and East Grand Forks, Minnesota, were destroyed. Many buildings in those cities were first flooded, then they burned to the waterline when the fire department could not get to them to fight the fires that came in the flood's wake.

But spirits of the flood victims were raised when someone gave fifteen million dollars to be distributed, two thousand dollars to each family. The donor requested that her identity not be revealed. The news media could not resist researching such a story, however, and finally traced the gift to Joan Kroc, the widow of Ray Kroc, who made the McDonald's restaurant chain a success. Mrs. Kroc said that the press's attention should be given to the victims and not to her. She didn't want to "take away from their story."

Paul gets to the "heart" of the matter concerning giving when he challenges us to look at our motives. We should seek to supply the "needs of God's people" and we should desire that God be glorified through what we do (2 Corinthians 9:12). We ought to be more interested in doing good *for* others to God's glory than in receiving acclaim *from* others to our own glory.

Each of us would do well to ask himself, "What are *my* aims in giving?"

—C. R. B.

E. GLORIFYING GOD (v. 13)
13. Because of the service by which you have proved yourselves, men will praise God for the obedience that accompanies your confession of the gospel of Christ, and for your generosity in sharing with them and with everyone else.

The Jerusalem Christians would *praise God*, being convinced of the Corinthians' *obedience* as demonstrated by their *generosity in sharing* their resources. One's faith can be measured by how well his life measures up to the standards set by Jesus. Our Lord's life was a living example of generosity. The Corinthians

---

WHAT DO YOU THINK?

When we give to people in need, we generate occasions of praise and thanksgiving to God. How important do you think this is? Why?

WHAT DO YOU THINK?

There was no "welfare" or other government relief in the first century, but we today have a variety of sources of secular help for the poor. How, if at all, does the presence of this aid affect our responsibility to minister to the poor today? What is unique about the relief that comes from the church and from Christian people as compared with that which comes from a secular source?

THOUGHT TO REMEMBER

"It is more blessed to give than to receive" (Acts 20:35).

would demonstrate that they understood this if they gave generously. In other words, they could put some "walk in their talk" or "put their money where their mouth is" by their giving.

The phrase *with everyone else* reminds us that while Christians have a special responsibility to those of the "family of believers," their benevolence must not be limited to fellow Christians (Galatians 6:10).

CONCLUSION

A. RULES FOR GIVING

The Old Testament set some specific standards, both by example and by law, for giving. Abram, returning from a victory over a coalition of invading kings, gave Melchizedek, a "priest of God Most High," a tithe (a tenth) of the goods he had recovered (Genesis 14:17-20). After his dream at Luz (Bethel), Jacob promised to return to God a tenth of all that God gave him (Genesis 28:19-22).

According to the law of Moses, each Israelite was required to give a tenth of his crops, herds, and flocks to the Lord (Leviticus 27:30-32). This tithe went to support the Levites who cared for the tabernacle and helped conduct worship services (Numbers 18:24). The Levites, in turn, gave a tenth of what they received to support the priests (Numbers 18:25-32). In addition, other tithes were required under the law.

However, under the New Covenant no such specific requirements are set. Our motives for giving are to be guided, not by law, but by grace. We are not our own; we have been "bought at a price" (1 Corinthians 6:20)—the death of God's Son on the cross. Thus we are slaves, and our lives, our talents, and *all* our possessions belong to God. We are required to be good stewards of *all* that God has entrusted to us, using everything carefully and wisely for his glory. One who gives only a tithe of his income and feels generous does not understand the New Testament concept of stewardship.

B. PURPOSES FOR GIVING

Christians must give, but they also must give intelligently. It is important that we know *why* we are giving. Jesus left his heavenly home, humbled himself by taking on the form of a human being, and died on the cross for our sins. What have we done for Christ?

Not only do we give because of what Christ has given us, but we also give because there are real needs in the world. Many of us reside in comfortable suburban areas where our lives are rarely touched by many of these needs. We have been content to allow the government to address them. However, Christians can and should make a real difference in reaching the lives of those in need. Jesus set the standard for what God expects of us in Matthew 25:40: "Whatever you did for one of the least of these brothers of mine, you did for me."

We give also as a witness to the lost. If we are selfish toward others and stingy in our giving, we are not likely to convince many in the unbelieving world that we serve a loving and generous God. Someone who serves Christ selflessly in the squalor of an inner city slum is likely to have a far greater impact on the world than all the pronouncements we make in our solemn assemblies.

One other important reason for giving is that it will bring happiness and personal satisfaction to us. To feed a hungry person, to clothe and house an orphan, to visit one who is sick or lonely, to counsel one who is in the depths of despair—these are actions that Jesus equated with caring for him (Matthew 25:34-40). And as he said in another context, "Now that you know these things, you will be blessed if you do them" (John 13:17).

Discovery Learning

*This page contains an alternate lesson plan emphasizing learning activities. Classes
desiring such student involvement will find these suggestions helpful. The next page
is a reproducible activity page to further enhance discovery learning.*

LEARNING GOALS

After this lesson students will be able to:

1. Recite Paul's instructions about the Corinthians' participation in the collection for the Jerusalem Christians.

2. Summarize the principles of Christian giving found in today's text.

3. Apply the principles in today's text to their personal financial giving to the Lord's work.

INTO THE LESSON

Prepare one set of index cards for every three students (i.e., a class of fifteen will need five sets of cards). Each set will contain five cards with one of the following scrambled words written on each: DGO VEOLS A FECLURHE VGEIR. Place each set of cards in an envelope.

At the beginning of class, move the students into groups of three (if you have one or two students left over, then make one or two groups of four). Give an envelope to each group and explain that it contains five index cards with scrambled words on them. The group's task is to unscramble the words on each card and then rearrange the cards in the proper order. The correct answer is: "God loves a cheerful giver" (2 Corinthians 9:7). The group that completes the task first should receive a small reward (i.e., a doughnut hole, small muffin, etc.) for each person in the group.

State: "Just as these letters and words were scrambled, sometimes our thinking is scrambled too—especially on today's subject of giving. Some people think that they just can't afford to give. But the lesson today teaches us that we can't afford *not* to give."

INTO THE WORD

Ask for a volunteer to read 2 Corinthians 9:1-13 aloud. Divide the class into two groups and assign each group one of the following sections. Give the students several minutes to work with someone sitting nearby; then review the questions, having the students give the answers.

Option: Use the "Giving Explained" questions to lead a general class discussion. Then distribute copies of the reproducible activity page and have the students complete the "Benefits of Giving Generously" activity.

Giving Explained (2 Corinthians 9:1-5)

1. Who are the "brothers" of v. 3? (*See 2 Corinthians 8:16-24 to find Titus and two others.*)

2. What was Paul's twofold purpose in sending the brothers to Corinth? (*His boasting would not prove hollow, v. 3; their bounty would be prepared prior to his coming, v. 5.*)

3. Whose honor was at stake if the Corinthians failed to fulfill their promised commitment to give? (*Paul's, v. 3, and the Corinthians', v. 4.*)

Giving Encouraged (2 Corinthians 9:6-13)

1. Read 2 Corinthians 9:6; Proverbs 11:24, 25; Luke 6:38. Describe how these verses teach that giving is a demonstration of faith. (*Giving generously beyond what you can spare is a statement of faith and trust in God's ability to supply what you need; reaping is dependent upon the sowing.*)

2. How should the act of giving be done? (*Intentional, "what he has decided in his heart to give," v. 7; cheerfully, v. 7; faithfully, v. 8.*)

3. How should the act of giving *not* be done? (*Sparingly, v. 6; reluctantly, v. 7; under compulsion, v. 7.*)

After a brief discussion, ask for some volunteers to form three teams of at least two people. Each team will write and perform a brief skit to demonstrate giving in one of the three ways listed in question 3 above. Allow a couple of minutes to prepare. These skits will be easy for the students to prepare, and they will probably be quite humorous.

After the presentations, state: "Though we laughed about these improper ways to give, perhaps we need to look a little more closely at our own giving in light of today's biblical teaching."

INTO LIFE

Begin this section by stating, "Sometimes we need to feel the emotions that rise up within a person as a result of generous giving." Ask the class to write a thank-you note on behalf of a young widow in Jerusalem with three children who was helped by a generous gift from the Corinthian Christians. They should try to describe how this person felt. Provide both paper and pens for this exercise. After several minutes, have several volunteers read their thank-you notes.

Next, use the reproducible activity page to have the class evaluate their own giving to various needs. After sufficient time has been given, ask the students to select one of the four areas cited and make a commitment to increase their giving. Close with a prayer of commitment.

Benefits of Giving Generously

Using the following Scripture references, list some specific benefits of giving generously.

PERSONAL BENEFIT, 2 Corinthians 9:8-11

PRACTICAL BENEFIT, 2 Corinthians 9:12a

PRAISE BENEFIT, 2 Corinthians 9:11b, 12b

PROOF BENEFIT, 2 Corinthians 9:13

(See shaded box below for answers.)

Personal Giving Analysis

Using the following scale, evaluate your personal giving habits as they relate to four areas of giving.

	RELUCTANTLY	SPARINGLY	COMPULSION	CHEERFULLY	GENEROUSLY
A. Giving to the Local Church	❏	❏	❏	❏	❏
B. Giving to Missions	❏	❏	❏	❏	❏
C. Giving to Religious Non-Profit Organizations	❏	❏	❏	❏	❏
D. Giving in Emergency Situations	❏	❏	❏	❏	❏

PERSONAL= your needs will be provided for; PRACTICAL = needs of the recipients will be met; PRAISE = thanksgiving to God on behalf of the giver; PROOF = a test of the sincerity of faith.

LIVING IN THE FAITH

LESSON 13

WHY TEACH THIS LESSON?

In school we often concluded a term of study with a "final examination." Preparing for that exam was a stressful experience because passing the test was so important. That is something like our lesson today—only you won't have to grade any tests! This lesson contains Paul's exhortation to the Corinthians to give themselves an examination—and passing the test was extremely important. Passing meant that Christ Jesus was in the Corinthians. Failing the test—well, that was unthinkable!

Challenge your own students to examine themselves today. Are they in Christ? Do they accept the Word of God as their unerring guide for faith and practice? Do they submit to God-ordained authority? Do they pass the test?

INTRODUCTION

A. AUTHORITY UNDER ATTACK

A young lieutenant was assigned the command of a company of soldiers that had a reputation for being sullen and unruly. Not only was the lieutenant green and inexperienced, he was also short of stature, making him a ready target for the men's remarks.

The young officer was overwhelmed by this lack of respect, and finally blurted out in desperation, "Tomorrow at zero seven hundred you will assemble here with full field equipment. I will lead you on a twenty-five-mile hike." His words were met with sneers and defiance.

Just then, a tough old veteran officer stepped out from behind the barracks where he had been observing the episode. "You heard Lieutenant Jones," he shouted. "You will do exactly as he commanded. You will assemble here in the morning with full field equipment to take a twenty-five-mile hike. And Lieutenant Jones will lead you—riding my horse!"

The situation facing the young lieutenant was somewhat similar to the one that confronted Paul in dealing with some of the people in the Corinthian church. They had made derogatory comments about him and had questioned his authority as an apostle. According to today's printed text, Paul told them that he planned to return to Corinth to address the situation, promising that he would be as "harsh" (v. 10) as necessary in order to bring about the Corinthians' obedience.

B. LESSON BACKGROUND

In 2 Corinthians 10–12 Paul went to some length to defend himself against his detractors in Corinth. They accused him of being a coward because he wrote strong letters but was weak in his personal appearance (10:10). They apparently accused him of preaching only for money. Paul defended himself by pointing out that he was "free of charge" while he labored in Corinth and that any support he needed had been received from the Macedonian churches (11:7-9). Some of Paul's critics may have been Jews, which led Paul to present his impeccable Jewish credentials (11:22).

DEVOTIONAL READING:
ACTS 4:32-37
BACKGROUND SCRIPTURE:
2 CORINTHIANS 13
PRINTED TEXT:
2 CORINTHIANS 13

LESSON AIMS

After this lesson each student should be able to:

1. Summarize Paul's challenge to the Corinthians as he prepared for his third visit to them.

2. Tell why the discipline of examining one's self is so important for the Christian.

3. Set up a plan (perhaps involving another Christian) by which regular self-examination can take place.

KEY VERSE

Examine yourselves to see whether you are in the faith; test yourselves. Do you not realize that Christ Jesus is in you—unless, of course, you fail the test?
—2 Corinthians 13:5

May
28

Paul deeply regretted that he was forced to boast about his accomplishments and his sufferings for Christ (12:1, 11). He related an experience of having been "caught up to the third heaven," as further proof of authority from God for his ministry (12:2-6). Immediately following this account, he told of how a messenger of Satan ("a thorn in my flesh") had been allowed to torment him. Paul prayed three times for its removal, but God did not grant his request. Instead he promised, "My grace is sufficient for you" (vv. 7-10).

Although the situation in Corinth made Paul's disclosure of this information necessary, he was not at all happy about having to spend his time and energy in such an effort. He concluded the letter with a final appeal for the Corinthians to set their house in order lest he be forced to be more aggressive with them when he returned.

I. FINAL APPEALS (2 CORINTHIANS 13:1-10)

A. PAUL'S WARNINGS (vv. 1-4)

1. This will be my third visit to you. "Every matter must be established by the testimony of two or three witnesses."

The phrase *my third visit* raises the issue of Paul's visits to Corinth and when these occurred. The book of Acts mentions only one previous visit to Corinth (Acts 18:1). We do not know exactly where to fit a second visit into a chronology of Paul's life. (See the discussion of this matter in the Lesson Background for lesson 10.) Probably it occurred sometime during Paul's three-year ministry in Ephesus (Acts 20:31).

Paul had already stated his plan to make a third visit to the Corinthians in 12:14. By repeating his intentions, perhaps he hoped that his warnings to them would be taken seriously.

By the testimony of two or three witnesses refers to a judicial procedure under the Mosaic law (Deuteronomy 19:15). It is not clear just what Paul meant by using this quotation. Some understand him to mean that each of his visits to the Corinthians counted as a witness to his integrity and apostolic authority; thus his third visit would provide the three witnesses that the law deemed sufficient to consider a matter *established*, or adequately proven.

Others hold that this was Paul's way of affirming that he would institute disciplinary proceedings against his detractors when he returned to Corinth (similar to those actions taken against the man mentioned in 1 Corinthians 5). The *three witnesses* would then be three of Paul's supporters in the Corinthian church.

2. I already gave you a warning when I was with you the second time. I now repeat it while absent: On my return I will not spare those who sinned earlier or any of the others.

Apparently on his *second* visit to Corinth Paul had confronted his critics, but his efforts to correct them had been ignored. Since we have no specific information about this confrontation, we are led to conclude that it was a somewhat mild one. This may have been the reason that Paul's opponents accused him of weakness (2 Corinthians 10:10) and ignored his efforts to correct them.

I will not spare. It will be different the next time, Paul assured the Corinthians. He wanted to make sure that they understood his resolve to settle this matter decisively. The most severe step he could take was to excommunicate those who had *sinned* (1 Corinthians 5:1-5).

3. . . . since you are demanding proof that Christ is speaking through me. He is not weak in dealing with you, but is powerful among you.

Paul's critics had been *demanding proof* that Paul really spoke for *Christ*. While we do not know what specific miracles Paul performed in Corinth, he mentions

WHAT DO YOU THINK?

"I will not spare those who sinned," Paul wrote. Wow! When, if ever, should church leaders today take so firm a stand against a church member or group of church members? Why?

that everyone there had had an opportunity to witness this manifestation of God's power: "the things that mark an apostle—signs, wonders, and miracles—were done among you with great perseverance" (2 Corinthians 12:12). Paul assured the Corinthians that if they wanted further proof of his authority, the severity with which he would deal with the rebels among them would show that the Christ he represented was *not weak . . . but . . . powerful.*

4. For to be sure, he was crucified in weakness, yet he lives by God's power. Likewise, we are weak in him, yet by God's power we will live with him to serve you.

Though Christ had unlimited power, he meekly submitted to his persecutors, surrendering himself to be *crucified.* His enemies saw this as *weakness,* but that weakness was transformed into the victory of the resurrection *by God's power.* In similar fashion Paul had seemed *weak* in Christ to the Corinthians (10:1, 10), but he now assured them that he would *by God's power . . . live with him to serve you.* Most likely this is not referring to the future resurrection when Jesus returns. Paul was reiterating that his next visit to the Corinthians would demonstrate the power that some thought was lacking in his ministry.

B. PAUL'S CONCERNS (vv. 5-9)

5. Examine yourselves to see whether you are in the faith; test yourselves. Do you not realize that Christ Jesus is in you—unless, of course, you fail the test?

Paul's critics had been demanding proof of his apostleship and authority. Now he turned the challenge back on them: *Examine yourselves.* The test was *whether you are in the faith.* The Corinthians' questioning of Paul's authority and their defiant attitude had raised serious doubts about whether they really understood the nature of the Christian faith. The issue was not just whether *Christ Jesus* was present in Paul (v. 3), but whether he lived in the Corinthians. One of the themes of Paul's ministry was, "Christ in you, the hope of glory" (Colossians 1:27).

A SPIRITUAL BEAUTY CONTEST

We are all familiar with beauty pageants, in which hopeful young women compete for college scholarships and a few minutes of fame. A less well-known form of beauty pageant is the "Pride & Polish Truck Beauty Contest." As many as twenty such contests are held each year across North America. We are not talking about pickups here; these are "eighteen-wheelers," dump trucks, and other heavy-duty industrial vehicles. They are judged for their extra equipment, perfection of paint and bodywork, and "spit-and-polish" cleanliness—even of their chassis and engine compartments.

It is common for such vehicles to cost over a hundred thousand dollars, in part because of their special equipment. Contestants have been known to spend as much as forty thousand dollars on the interior of the cab, complete with a kitchen equipped with microwave oven, refrigerator, and freezer (not to mention the on-board shower)!

Our Scripture today urges us to "examine" ourselves to see that we are approved by God. In other words, we are to do our best to appear beautiful before him, with lives that match the standards by which he shall judge us and award our eternal prize.   —C. R. B.

6. And I trust that you will discover that we have not failed the test.

If the Corinthians really had Christ in them, they would have had no trouble understanding that while Paul was among them, he possessed all the credentials that demonstrated his apostolic authority.

7. Now we pray to God that you will not do anything wrong. Not that people will see that we have stood the test but that you will do what is right even though we may seem to have failed.

WHAT DO YOU THINK?

Self-examination can be a healthy thing, or it can become a kind of brooding, unhealthy self-consciousness. How can we develop the healthy kind and avoid that which is unhealthy?

Today's visual illustrates the need to "examine yourselves," to see whether your own pattern of behavior reflects biblical standards.

Paul had already made it clear that as an apostle he had the authority to discipline the erring brothers in Corinth who were demeaning him and challenging his apostleship. However, he preferred that they cease doing what was *wrong* and do what was honest and *right*. If they chose to change their behavior and end their defiant spirit, then Paul would not need to exert his apostolic authority.

Of course, if Paul did not use his authority, then some might conclude that he was bluffing and really did not have the power he claimed. Paul was willing to accept such a judgment, even if it made him and his companions look like they had *failed* (which he claimed they had not in verse 6). Paul was more concerned with the Corinthians' spiritual well-being than with his own reputation.

8, 9. *For we cannot do anything against the truth, but only for the truth. We are glad whenever we are weak but you are strong; and our prayer is for your perfection.*

Paul elaborates on the point he made in verse 7. If the Corinthians have been acting according to *the truth*, then he has no need to reprimand them. When he does not exercise his authority as an apostle, he may seem *weak*; but he is willing to accept that if it makes the Corinthians appear *strong*.

Paul's fervent desire was that the Corinthians continue to grow in the faith even to *perfection*. This word does not imply sinlessness. In New Testament times the Greek word was used to describe the act of a physician in setting a broken bone; it may be translated "restoration."

In these verses Paul reveals his servant's heart. Even though he had the authority of an apostle of Christ, he chose not to use that power in an authoritarian way. He chose instead to defer to the best interests of the Corinthians. Christian leaders can learn much from Paul's example, whose primary concern was always his people, not his ego.

C. Paul's Purpose (v. 10)

10. *This is why I write these things when I am absent, that when I come I may not have to be harsh in my use of authority—the authority the Lord gave me for building you up, not for tearing you down.*

This verse concludes the section of 2 Corinthians that began with chapter 10. In these previous chapters Paul had dealt with the claims of his detractors that he wrote strong, bold letters but was weak and powerless in person. Here Paul explained his actions. He wrote forceful letters so that when he did come in person, he would *not have to be harsh* in his dealings with the Corinthians. He assured them once again that *the Lord* had given him *authority* to deal forcefully should the situation require it. However, his goal was to work for their *building . . .up*, not their *tearing . . . down*. The choice of whether Paul would have to take harsher measures with the Corinthians was really up to them, as he had written previously: "What do you prefer? Shall I come to you with a whip, or in love and with a gentle spirit?" (1 Corinthians 4:21).

To Build or to Destroy?

Attitudes of American citizens toward the Internal Revenue Service range from "it's a necessary evil" to "it's an unconstitutional means the government uses to destroy its citizens." The latter attitude owes much to the well-publicized troubles of citizens such as Thomas Treadway, a Pennsylvania businessman.

Agents from the IRS audited one of Treadway's tax returns and erroneously assessed him $247,000. In fighting the claim, Treadway lost his business and everything he owned. Finally, an appeals officer revoked the assessment, but IRS agents threatened "to do the whole thing all over again." Even a former IRS official has acknowledged that the agency "is intent on driving taxpayers to the wall."

What Do You Think?

The lesson writer says, "Paul was more concerned with the Corinthians' spiritual well-being than with his own reputation." How important do you think such an attitude is for Christian leaders today? What difference does it make?

What Do You Think?

Paul said his authority was given to him to build people up, not to tear them down. We all probably know leaders who were quicker to tear down whatever did not suit them than they were to build people up. Without mentioning the names of any contemporary leaders, contrast the two styles.

The severity of Paul's dealings with the Corinthians was not intended to destroy them, regardless of what some in Corinth might have thought. Paul used his apostolic authority to build them up—an example of how *all* authority ought to be used.

We who are in positions of authority over others must continually be watchful of how we exercise that authority.   —C. R. B.

II. FINAL COUNSEL (2 CORINTHIANS 13:11-14)

A. CHALLENGES (v. 11)

11. Finally, brothers, good-by. Aim for perfection, listen to my appeal, be of one mind, live in peace. And the God of love and peace will be with you.

Paul closed this letter on a warm note with a series of general admonitions, as he did certain other letters (1 Corinthians 16:13, 14; 1 Thessalonians 5:16-22, 25, 26). The Greek word translated *good-by* literally means "rejoice." The command to *aim for perfection* reflects Paul's concern for the Corinthians' "perfection" in verse 9. As noted in the comments on that verse, this Greek word signifies a restoration of strength and wholeness. Paul was urging the Corinthians to restore their relationships with one another and with God.

The words *listen to my appeal* express Paul's gentle urging that the Corinthians accept those teachings in the earlier part of the letter that might have seemed harsh. With the command *be of one mind*, Paul was not suggesting that they agree on everything, but on "the faith"—those doctrines that are central to Christianity.

Paul's final challenge was to *live in peace*, especially concerning the matters that were dividing the congregation. If the Corinthians followed Paul's admonitions, they could be assured that *the God of love and peace* would be *with* them.

B. GREETINGS (vv. 12, 13)

12, 13. Greet one another with a holy kiss. All the saints send their greetings.

The *kiss* was a typical greeting in the first century (see Luke 7:44, 45; 22:47, 48), even as it is in some cultures today. (In other Western cultures the handshake is what the kiss was then.) Among Christians it was considered *holy* because it symbolized a common commitment to Christ and would be a mark of peace and reconciliation among the members of the Corinthian church.

All the saints included not only Paul and his companions, but the members of the Macedonian churches to whom Paul had referred previously (8:1; 9:1-4; 11:9). While most of them were not personally acquainted with the saints in Corinth, their joint concern for the cause of Christ united them in spite of the miles that separated them.

C. BENEDICTION (v. 14)

14. May the grace of the Lord Jesus Christ, and the love of God, and the fellowship of the Holy Spirit be with you all.

Paul includes a reference to *grace* at the conclusion of each of his letters. Here he specifies *the grace of the Lord Jesus Christ* and adds *the love of God, and the fellowship of the Holy Spirit* as a reminder that the Father, the Son, and the Holy Spirit will be involved in every aspect of the Corinthians' daily lives. The Corinthians should seek to be one in the same way that the members of the Trinity are one (John 17:21).

CONCLUSION

A. GOOD LEADERS

Observers who evaluate our society today all acknowledge that one of the biggest problems we face is the lack of adequate leadership. This complaint is

HOW TO SAY IT

Corinth. KOR-inth.
Corinthians. Kor-IN-thee-unz.
Ephesus. EFF-uh-sus.
Macedonian. Mass-eh-DOE-nee-un.
Mosaic. Mo-ZAY-ik.
Silas. SIGH-luss.

WHAT DO YOU THINK?

In spite of all the strong words he had to write, Paul concluded 2 Corinthians in a very gracious, winsome manner. What does that say about the way we handle difficult situations?

THOUGHT TO REMEMBER

Rarely can one become a good leader until he has learned to be a good follower.

heard from business, industry, education, government, and, sadly, even from the church. Leadership comes in many styles. One who is a leader in education might make a very poor military leader. In turn, a great military leader would not likely make a good leader in the field of medicine.

What attributes are required in a good leader? Some qualities are obvious: intelligence, appearance, good education, speaking ability, people skills, patience, stamina, good health, willingness to delegate responsibilities, high moral standards, commitment to an important cause, and courage. The list could go on for several paragraphs.

How would the apostle Paul measure up to some of these standards? Intelligence he certainly had, but appearance? Some traditions indicate that he was not at all attractive. He had a good education and apparently was a powerful preacher. He had the stamina to travel great distances without all the conveniences of modern travel, but he apparently had some physical disability ("a thorn in my flesh") that plagued him. Paul had inexhaustible courage and a commitment to the greatest of all causes—carrying the gospel to dying sinners.

While Paul lacked some of the qualities that we may deem important in a leader, still he provides an excellent model for leadership in our congregations. His handling of the difficult situation in the Corinthian church gives us insight into his leadership during a time of crisis. The challenge to his authority, which came from certain elements in the church, was one he could not ignore. To do so would have allowed control of the church to fall into the hands of arrogant and self-serving men.

In his counsel to the Corinthians, Paul encouraged them to solve problems on their own without his intervention. However, he left no doubt that he would act firmly to address these problems if he had to. In other situations, Paul knew how to be gentle and forgiving. Most important, he never allowed his ego to get in the way of his ministry. As we have seen in today's lesson, he was quite willing to become "weak" if it allowed the Corinthians to become strong.

How can we develop good leaders for our churches? One method Paul used was to serve as a mentor for younger, less experienced men, such as Timothy, Titus, Silas, and others who accompanied him on his missionary ventures. Older, experienced leaders in the congregation can render a great service by following Paul's example.

B. GOOD FOLLOWERS

Good leadership is necessary if the church is to grow and prosper in our times. But good leaders are almost powerless unless they are supported by good followers. And in case anyone hasn't noticed, good followers are about as hard to come by as are good leaders.

Many of the same qualities that we look for in our leaders are also necessary traits for good followers. In addition, good followers need a sense of humility that allows them to work in the background and out of the limelight. In the New Testament we see Andrew bringing Peter to Christ and then quietly moving to the background as Peter assumed leadership among the disciples. We watch John the Baptist, who was content to take a secondary role when Jesus arrived on the scene: "He must become greater; I must become less" (John 3:30).

Followers may have skills that qualify them as experts, and yet if they refuse to follow their leaders, chaos can result. Imagine how a choir would sound if the members refused to follow the direction of the leader. That is how the church "sounds" to the world when we fail to support our leaders and when we all fail to follow the leadership of Jesus.

Discovery Learning

*This page contains an alternate lesson plan emphasizing learning activities. Classes
desiring such student involvement will find these suggestions helpful. The next page
is a reproducible activity page to further enhance discovery learning.*

LEARNING GOALS

After this lesson each student will be able to:

1. Summarize Paul's challenge to the Corinthians as he prepared for his third visit to them.

2. Tell why the discipline of examining one's self is so important for the Christian.

3. Set up a plan (perhaps involving another Christian) by which regular self-examination can take place.

INTO THE LESSON

Prior to the lesson prepare two graffiti statements: "A Leader likes . . ." and "A Leader dislikes. . . ." Write them on two sheets of blank newsprint or butcher paper. Tape them near the door and hang a couple of markers there so students coming to class can jot down items to complete the sentences.

After the class arrives, move the filled-in newsprint to the front of the classroom. Briefly review the items written under each statement. Ask, "What would happen to a leader who did only those responsibilities he liked to do?" (*He would not fulfill his own leadership responsibilities and would probably be fired.*) State: "Effective leaders fulfill both kinds of responsibilities. In our lesson today, the apostle Paul reveals those responsibilities he does not like to fulfill but will if the Corinthians fail to follow his leadership. Let's read our lesson text, 2 Corinthians 13, and find out what those are."

INTO THE WORD

Ask each student to select a partner with whom to answer the following questions. (They are listed in the student book.) Each group of two should be assigned two questions from the following:

1. What is the meaning of the "two or three witnesses" in v. 1? (*See Deuteronomy 19:15. Possible views are: each of his visits represents a witness; when he arrives, he will verify all charges against some of the Corinthians with witnesses.*)

2. What do you think Paul meant by the phrase, "I will not spare" (v. 2)? (*See 1 Corinthians 5:1-5; 2 Corinthians 1:23. Possible views: public humiliation and censure; excommunication.*)

3. Why did the Corinthians seek proof that Paul really spoke for Christ? (*See 2 Corinthians 10:1; 13:2, 3, 10. Paul was accused of being bold and authoritative in his letters but meek and too lenient in person.*)

4. What did Paul mean when he said, "By God's power we will live with [Christ] to serve you" (v. 4)? (*See the comments on page 335.*)

5. What was Paul's primary desire for the Corinthians (vv. 7, 9)? (*Repent and do what is right, to become perfect in Christ.*)

6. What was Paul's primary desire for himself (vv. 7, 10)? (*He did not want to use his authority and inflict punishment even though he would appear to be weak.*)

7. Why did Paul give the command to "examine yourselves" in verse 5? (*The Corinthians' questioning of Paul's authority raised doubts about their own faith.*)

8. What is the predominant idea of the word "perfection" in v. 9? (*See page 336.*)

Allow time to review the questions; then ask for the students' answers. State: "Church leaders today experience similar kinds of problems."

INTO LIFE

Ask the students to recall their experiences of being in the church and brainstorm the various types of problems or difficulties that church leadership has faced or faces today. (*Possible answers: incorrect doctrine of teachers; immorality among the leadership or church members; strife and dissension; undermining efforts for growth.*)

Churches are sometimes held back by unruly members who stymie the leaders' vision for growth. Ask, "How do you think Paul felt about the situation in Corinth?" (*See 2 Corinthians 2:4, 13.*) Leaders today find no pleasure in confronting individuals in the church. Yet, such confrontation and admonition are necessary if they are going to lead with integrity and be true to Scripture.

Distribute copies of the reproducible page that follows. Allow a few minutes for the students to work, encouraging them to be specific; then ask, "What are some ways that followers in the church could be better at following?" (*See Hebrews 13:17—"obey your leaders," "submit" to leaders; 2 Corinthians 13—do not do anything wrong; be honest; be of one mind; live in peace; be perfect or complete.*) Write all ideas on the chalkboard. Then ask each to select one way that he or she can become a better follower. Ask each student to make a commitment to God, asking for his strength, so that the leaders' "work will be a joy, not a burden" (Hebrews 13:17). Encourage the students to sign the commitment pledges at the bottom of their reproducible pages.

Followers Who Follow

What are some ways that followers in the church could be better at "following"?

"Helping Leaders Serve With Joy"
Pledge of Commitment

"Obey your leaders and submit to their authority. They keep watch over you as men who must give an account. Obey them so that their work will be a joy, not a burden, for that would be of no advantage to you" (Hebrews 13:17).

As a pledge of respect and appreciation for the care my church leadership gives for my soul, I commit myself to live in such a way that their work will be a joy and not a burden.

One specific way that I can make their work more joyful is . . .

Signed: _____

Summer Quarter, 2000

New Life in Christ

(Ephesians, Philippians, Colossians, Philemon)

Special Features

Lessons

Unit 1: Living in Christ

Unit 2: Called by Christ

Unit 3: Christ Above All

About These Lessons

The lessons for the present quarter give us a special look at the heart of the apostle Paul as well as timeless words of wisdom to live by. Paul wrote these letters while a prisoner in Rome, yet they show no bitterness, no anger, no resentment. May Paul's example be as instructive as his words as you study these texts.

Jun 4

Jun 11

Jun 18

Jun 25

Jul 2

Jul 9

Jul 16

Jul 23

Jul 30

Aug 6

Aug 13

Aug 20

Aug 27

Christ Is the Center

by J. Michael Shannon

The studies for this summer quarter of lessons are focused on Jesus Christ. Drawn from Paul's Prison Epistles, the lessons are divided into three units: "Living in Christ," "Called by Christ," and "Christ Above All." Each lesson challenges us to make Jesus the center of every area of life.

UNIT 1: LIVING IN CHRIST

JUNE

The first unit of lessons, entitled, "Living in Christ," consists of four lessons from Philippians. **Lesson 1**, "Living Is Christ," comes from Philippians 1:12-26. This text communicates how Christians can face difficult circumstances with a firm and unshakable hope. This lesson will encourage us to glorify Christ, "whether by life or by death" (Philippians 1:20). **Lesson 2**, "Having the Mind of Christ," is taken from Philippians 2:1-13. In this lesson the class will learn the importance of a humble, Christlike attitude. **Lesson 3** is entitled, "Pressing On in Christ." Through a study of Philippians 3:7-21, class members will learn something of what it takes to remain faithful to Christ when they feel like giving up. Using images from the athletic world, Paul encourages Christians to "press on" (Philippians 3:14). **Lesson 4**, "Rejoicing in Christ," is taken from Philippians 4:4-19. It will challenge followers of Jesus to "rejoice in the Lord always." Regardless of our situation, Christ is unchanging and always faithful.

UNIT 2: CALLED BY CHRIST

JULY

The five lessons in Unit 2 are taken from the book of Ephesians. **Lesson 5**, from Ephesians 1:1-14, is entitled, "Called to Spiritual Blessings in Christ." It describes the wondrous "riches" that we possess in Jesus. **Lesson 6**, based on Ephesians 2:8-22, centers on unity. Jesus unites us to the Father, and he unites us to others who are united to the Father! Too often the discussion of spiritual gifts tends to center on controversial gifts. **Lesson 7** (from Ephesians 4:1-16) will provide a helpful perspective by emphasizing that every Christian has at least one gift that should be used to edify the church. **Lesson 8**, taken from Ephesians 5 and 6, will deal with the Christian's responsibility to live a life consistent with his calling. This lesson will deal particularly with our responsibilities to honor Christ in our homes. In **lesson 9**, from Ephesians 6:10-24, Paul borrows military imagery to assure Christians that God has provided the resources necessary for victory.

UNIT 3: CHRIST ABOVE ALL

AUGUST

The third unit includes three lessons from Colossians and one from Philemon. **Lesson 10**, "The Supremacy of Christ," is taken from Colossians 1:15-29. This study will provide a panoramic view of the glory of Jesus as Lord of creation and Lord of the church. **Lesson 11**, "Complete Life in Christ," warns against the seduction of false philosophies. **Lesson 12**, from Colossians 3:1-17, presents specific character qualities that should accompany the new life in Christ. **Lesson 13** comes from Paul's brief letter to Philemon—probably his most personal correspondence. Still, the letter can be applied to a variety of contemporary settings that involve individuals of different backgrounds, races, etc.

This quarter will teach us many great doctrines and instruct us about many great virtues. But above all, this quarter is about *Jesus Christ.* May you prepare and teach these lessons "for the praise of his glory" (Ephesians 1:12)!

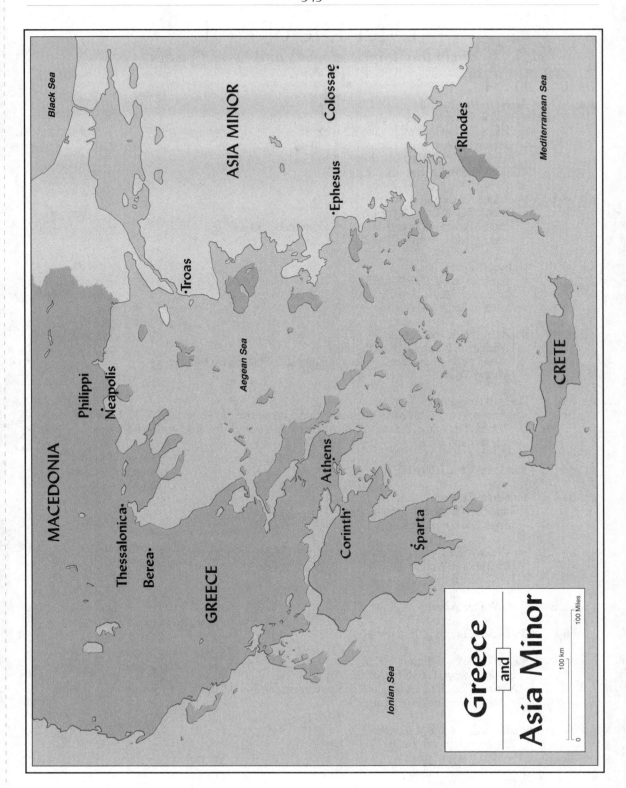

Greece and Asia Minor

Black Sea

ASIA MINOR

Colossae

Rhodes

Mediterranean Sea

Ephesus

Troas

Aegean Sea

CRETE

Philippi

Neapolis

MACEDONIA

Athens

Thessalonica

Berea

Corinth

Sparta

GREECE

Ionian Sea

Greece
and
Asia Minor

100 km

100 Miles

0

Later Life of Paul
Including Imprisonments and Later Epistles

DATE	EVENT
A.D. 58	Arrest in Jerusalem (Acts 21:17, 27-36)
	Held in Tower of Antonia (Acts 21:37; 22:24; 23:10)
	Defense Before the People (Acts 22:1-23)
	Defense Before the Sanhedrin (Acts 22:30—23:10)
	Plot Against Paul's Life Discovered (Acts 23:11-22)
	Transferred to Caesarea (Acts 23:23-33)
A.D. 58–60	Imprisoned in Caesarea (Acts 23:35; 24:27)
	Defense Before Felix (Acts 24:1-27)
	Defense Before Festus and Appeal to Caesar (Acts 25:1-12)
	Defense Before Agrippa (Acts 25:13—26:32)
A.D. 60, 61	Journey to Rome
	Shipwrecked (Acts 27:9—28:1)
	Ministry on Melita (Acts 28:2-10)
	Arrival in Rome (Acts 28:16)
A.D. 61–63	Imprisoned in Rome (Acts 28:16, 30)
	Preaching in Prison (Acts 28:17-31)
	Prison Epistles (Colossians, Philemon, Ephesians, Philippians) Written
	Hebrews Written?
A.D. 63	Released From Prison
	(Acts closes with Paul "two whole years" under house arrest in Rome [28:30]. Probably Paul was released at that time, but the evidence for what he did after that is scant. The following is one possible scenario.)
A.D. 63	Traveled to Crete (Titus 1:5)
A.D. 64	Traveled to Ephesus (1 Timothy 1:3)
	Joined by Timothy (1 Timothy 1:3)
	Trip to Colosse and Return to Ephesus (Philemon 22)
A.D. 65	Traveled to Macedonia (1 Timothy 1:3), including Philippi (Philippians 2:24)
	First Timothy Written
	Titus Written
A.D. 65, 66	Spent Winter in Nicopolis (Titus 3:12)
A.D. 66	Traveled to Corinth (2 Timothy 4:20)
A.D. 67	Traveled to Troas (2 Timothy 4:13)
	Possibly Stopped at Miletus on the Way (2 Timothy 4:20)
	Arrested (That Paul left his cloak and parchments in Troas [2 Timothy 4:13] suggests to many a hasty departure, as in an arrest.)
A.D. 67, 68	Imprisoned in Rome (2 Timothy 2:9)
	First Trial (2 Timothy 4:16, 17)
	Second Timothy Written
	Second Trial (2 Timothy 4:6)
	Executed in Rome

LIVING IS CHRIST

LESSON 1

WHY TEACH THIS LESSON?

"Now this is living!" Those words have been uttered in response to a variety of experiences, but most of them pale in comparison with the subject of today's lesson. A connoisseur might react to an elegant meal with such an exclamation. One who has never been able to own or drive a luxury automobile might respond this way to a ride in a limousine. Still another, perhaps a middle- or lower-class wage earner, might so react to a night in a penthouse suite at a fine hotel. Inherent to every such declaration is a longing to make the experience a regular part of one's life.

But "what good is it for a man to gain the whole world [with its richest foods, shiniest limousines, and most plush penthouses], yet forfeit his soul?" (Mark 8:36). There is more to consider than the baubles that make our temporary residence on this physical planet more convenient. Real life extends beyond, into eternity, which is to be spent with Christ Jesus. Use today's lesson to encourage your students to see that living is greater than all the accoutrements that may be added to our temporal existence on this earth—"living is Christ!"

INTRODUCTION

A. LIVING SPACE

A television series called "America's Castles" described the magnificent dwellings built by immensely wealthy men for themselves, their families, and their guests. (Perhaps some space was needed also to house symbols of their pride and vanity.) The rooms in one of "America's Castles" would number in the scores, many of them with towering ceilings and with magnificent hand-carved woodwork imported from great distances. Furniture and decor were brought from all over the world at the whim of the buyer. A dining room, splendidly furnished, would seat as many as fifty guests.

Some of the owners lived for many years in the luxury of their mansions, some died shortly after moving in, and some did not even live to see their projects finished. One is reminded of Oliver Wendell Holmes's poem about a sea creature, the chambered nautilus, that develops a shell of ever-increasing proportions until at last the creature dies and leaves an empty shell. One portion of the poem says,

Build thee more stately mansions, O my soul,
    As the swift seasons roll!
    Leave thy low-vaulted past!
Let each new temple, nobler than the last,
Shut thee from heaven with a dome more vast,
    Till thou at length art free,
Leaving thine outgrown shell by life's unresting sea!

Proud words are those about a proud effort. But the person who lives in Christ has a "stately mansion" of God's making rather than his own. He sees freedom, not in being "shut . . . from heaven," but in living with the sure hope of going there someday. That is the assurance described for us in today's text.

DEVOTIONAL READING:
1 PETER 1:3-9

BACKGROUND SCRIPTURE:
PHILIPPIANS 1:12-30

PRINTED TEXT:
PHILIPPIANS 1:12-26

LESSON AIMS

After this lesson the student will be able to:

1. Tell how Paul used his Roman imprisonment and his concern for the Philippian Christians to illustrate that Christ must come first.

2. Explain how Paul's conviction that "to live is Christ" expresses what a Christian's priorities should be.

3. Determine to face each circumstance of the coming week with the goal that "Christ will be exalted."

KEY VERSE

For to me, to live is Christ and to die is gain.
                    —Philippians 1:21

The visual for today is a map that locates each of the cities to which Paul addressed the prison epistles. It will be useful throughout the quarter.

B. LESSON BACKGROUND

The church in the city of Philippi, located in the province of Macedonia, was the first established by Paul in what we know as Europe. This took place during his second missionary journey. Acts 16 tells of Paul's vision of a man of Macedonia who pleaded with Paul to come there (v. 9). In Philippi the apostle's efforts resulted in the conversion of Lydia and her household, Paul and Silas's imprisonment after they cast a fortune-telling demon out of a servant girl, and finally the conversion of the prison keeper and his household. Thus began what became a strong and generous congregation. The church at Philippi sent gifts to help Paul when he moved on to Thessalonica (Philippians 4:16) and later when his journeys took him to Corinth (2 Corinthians 11:9).

That spirit of generosity was still present approximately ten years later, when, while Paul was a prisoner at Rome, the Philippian church sent Epaphroditus, one of their leaders, with a substantial gift. Epaphroditus stayed for a time as a helper to Paul, but he became seriously ill while he was there. When Epaphroditus was able to travel, Paul sent him home with the letter of thanks and encouragement that we have come to call the Epistle to the Philippians (Philippians 2:25-30). Among Paul's writings, this one is especially notable for its warm and affectionate tone and for its persistent expression of rejoicing in Christ. It will provide our texts for study in the next four lessons.

The first chapter opens with Paul's typical greeting (vv. 1, 2), then expresses affectionate thanks for the Philippians' constant fellowship in the gospel. It displays confidence in their ongoing maturity in the Lord (vv. 3-8). Verses 9-11 include a prayer for continued growth in love, knowledge, and judgment; in appreciation for what is best; in lifelong sincerity and purity; and in fruitfulness springing from the righteousness that comes through Christ Jesus.

The following verses (12-26), from which our text for today is taken, testify that Paul himself possessed the same qualities that he urged his friends in Philippi to demonstrate.

I. PROGRESS OF THE CAUSE (PHILIPPIANS 1:12-18)

A. THE GOSPEL ADVANCES (vv. 12, 13)

12. Now I want you to know, brothers, that what has happened to me has really served to advance the gospel.

Paul's ministry had been somewhat limited since he was seized by the Jews in the temple area of Jerusalem (Acts 21:27-33). His enemies thought that this would initiate a series of events that would destroy him and his influence—in fact, they had hoped to murder him (Acts 23:12-15). However, these men succeeded only in broadening and making more permanent the apostle's accomplishments. Letters such as this one, written from Rome during Paul's incarceration, provide examples of the apostle's ongoing ministry.

Acts 28:30, 31 notes a period of two years during which Paul lived "in his own rented house" in Rome and received visitors whom he taught and counseled, "without hindrance"—though he was always accompanied by a soldier of the palace guard (Acts 28:16). Most likely those persons whom he taught were in a position to teach others. And, of course, the letters known as Paul's "prison epistles" (Ephesians, Philippians, Colossians, and Philemon) continue to teach and encourage Christians everywhere.

Persecution has often served to make the church more firm in its faith and in its eagerness to spread the gospel. The persecutors fail to realize that, while they can hinder the movements of the messengers, they cannot suppress the power of the message!

13. As a result, it has become clear throughout the whole palace guard and to everyone else that I am in chains for Christ.

To all the *palace guard*, beginning with and spreading from the soldiers who were with Paul most directly, it was evident that his imprisonment came not from any real crime, but from his commitment to preaching the gospel. Like Daniel, Paul could not be charged with any offense except for his unusual commitment to an unpopular form of religion (Daniel 6:4, 5). In both instances God's man won respect both for himself and for the Lord whom he served.

B. OTHERS ARE ENCOURAGED (v. 14)

14. Because of my chains, most of the brothers in the Lord have been encouraged to speak the word of God more courageously and fearlessly.

Christians in Rome knew that Paul was physically restrained by being imprisoned. Rather than being intimidated by the fact, however, *most* of them had become *encouraged* by Paul's example *to speak the word of God more courageously and fearlessly* and to accept the consequences. No doubt some also responded to the need for faithful persons to pick up the work where Paul had been forced to lay it down.

Paul was providing evidence of the blessings one receives in the service of Christ, even under less than ideal conditions. He was also giving a powerful demonstration that the claims he had made in other letters about God's presence during difficulties (as in Romans 8:28 and 2 Corinthians 12:9, 10) were more than mere words.

A DANGEROUS PRISONER

Wherever he was, the apostle Paul was engaged in evangelism. The Christians at Philippi understood this. No doubt most of them knew of his imprisonment during his first visit to their city and how he had led the local jailer and his family to Christ. Now, with Paul in prison in Rome, they were not surprised that he continued to be concerned about the souls of others—even of those who kept him confined.

When the Communists were in control of the former Soviet Union and of eastern Europe, they encountered numerous examples of this kind of evangelistic fervor. They put Christians in prison for preaching, and the Christians continued to preach, leading fellow prisoners and even some of their captors to faith. They were as dangerous to the Communist cause inside the prison as they had been outside. In some cases they were actually released early because their evangelistic success in prison embarrassed the government!

When John Bunyan, the seventeenth-century preacher and author, was put in prison in England, the authorities offered to release him if he would agree never to preach again. He replied, "If you release me today I will preach tomorrow." Such determination ought to shame us, who have the freedom to witness of our faith but often remain silent. Sometimes we claim we have no opportunities to win anyone to Jesus. The problem is that we have many such occasions but fail to take advantage of them.

Many may have figured that an imprisoned Paul had few or no opportunities to witness for Christ. An imprisoned *and* determined Paul *made* opportunities.

—R. C. S.

C. MINOR SETBACKS (vv. 15-17)

15. It is true that some preach Christ out of envy and rivalry, but others out of goodwill.

Most likely there were already leaders among the Christians in Rome before Paul arrived (Acts 28:13-15). Some of them apparently were envious of his

WHAT DO YOU THINK?

Seeing Paul in prison had made the Philippians more bold and less fearful. Do you think having one of our Christian leaders unjustly arrested and imprisoned would make us speak more or less boldly for Christ? Why?

WHAT DO YOU THINK?

*When good is done—such as preaching Christ—in what sense does motive not matter? In what sense **does** motive matter?*

influence and his success in winning people to Christ. They were tempted to show that whatever Paul could do, they could do better.

On the other hand, many Christians in Rome knew that Paul's highest priority was the advancement of the kingdom; and their eager efforts to cooperate in that enterprise would have pleased him greatly. He could rejoice in the demonstration of such *goodwill*.

16, 17. *The latter do so in love, knowing that I am put here for the defense of the gospel. The former preach Christ out of selfish ambition, not sincerely, supposing that they can stir up trouble for me while I am in chains.*

Love is a source of encouragement to any preacher—both love for the Lord and love for his messenger. Any church is doubly blessed when the highest priority—love for the Lord—is enforced by a warm regard for the proclaimer of his truth. It is less well served when love for the preacher (or lack of it) takes precedence over love for the Lord.

The insincere proclaimers, governed at least partly by a desire to embarrass Paul while he was imprisoned, were sufficiently rebuked by the revelation of their motives. Paul refused to go any farther in judging or suggesting any kind of discipline. Since the competitors had not succeeded in embarrassing him or hindering his ministry, why should he dwell anymore on the subject? The mention of their tainted motivation is a rare negative element in an otherwise positive and joyous letter.

D. Yet Christ Is Preached (v. 18)

18. *But what does it matter? The important thing is that in every way, whether from false motives or true, Christ is preached. And because of this I rejoice.*
   Yes, and I will continue to rejoice.

The negotiable element here was the motive and spirit of the proclaimer, not the message being proclaimed. The truth in *Christ* was never to be compromised: "Even if we or an angel from heaven should preach a gospel other than the one we preached to you, let him be eternally condemned!" (Galatians 1:8). The basis of Paul's rejoicing was the spreading of the gospel and the welfare of the church. His own welfare was a minor concern.

II. PERSONAL TESTIMONY (PHILIPPIANS 1:19-26)

At this point the apostle turned to matters more personal—his own relationship with Christ during the present times of difficulty and the strength that this relationship supplied for what lay ahead.

A. I Want to Exalt Christ (vv. 19, 20)

19. *. . . for I know that through your prayers and the help given by the Spirit of Jesus Christ, what has happened to me will turn out for my deliverance.*

Through the *prayers* of his friends and the *help given by the Spirit of Jesus Christ*, Paul's present plight would lead to better things ahead, specifically to his *deliverance*. In this context *deliverance* could describe the apostle's release from prison or his ultimate deliverance into the glorious presence of Christ. As Paul states the matter in verse 20, he desires to be Christ's man in either circumstance.

20. *I eagerly expect and hope that I will in no way be ashamed, but will have sufficient courage so that now as always Christ will be exalted in my body, whether by life or by death.*

I eagerly expect translates a Greek expression that speaks literally of "stretching out the head." As one craning his neck to see who or what is coming, Paul anticipated that he would remain firm in his courageous representation of Christ. He

What Do You Think?

How much confidence do we have that the prayers of our friends and the "help given by the Spirit" will turn our hard situation into something better? How do we gain such confidence?

would refuse to be ashamed of the gospel that could have appeared at times to have let him down (Romans 1:16). He would also avoid being disappointed or embarrassed by any apparent failure of God's promises. He could, and would, continue to rejoice in the gospel of Christ.

Paul desired that *Christ . . . be exalted* through the *body* in which he lived. Certainly the apostle had his physical limitations (2 Corinthians 10:10; 12:7-10), and they did not disappear with the passing of time. Yet his physical body—heart, hands, feet, eyes, voice, and mind—was his only available tool with which to serve his beloved Lord. His chief desire was that every thought, word, and act reflect the lordship of Jesus. Each day he wanted to be able to say, "I have been crucified with Christ and I no longer live, but Christ lives in me" (Galatians 2:20).

The possibility of an early *death* for Paul was very real. His enemies had plotted and tried in every conceivable way to destroy him. They had testified against him in every available court, and might do so again before Caesar. But as Paul had lived for Christ, he was ready also to die for him. That *Christ will be exalted*: this was Paul's ultimate motive. May it be ours as well.

B. SHOULD I HURRY TO HEAVEN? (vv. 21-24)

21. For to me, to live is Christ and to die is gain.

To live is Christ. Paul's daily being was an expression of Christ. To be without Christ would mean spiritual and eternal death.

To die is gain. Paul expressed this more fully in 2 Corinthians 5:6-8: "Therefore we are always confident and know that as long as we are at home in the body we are away from the Lord. We live by faith, not by sight. We are confident, I say, and would prefer to be away from the body and at home with the Lord." To the Christian, physical death opens the way to the eternal fulfillment of his purpose for living. Until one can say with conviction, "To live is Christ," he cannot say with confidence, "To die is gain."

GAIN AND LOSS

We have some interesting ways to avoid using the word *death*. We use expressions such as, "He went away," "God took her," or "I lost him." But *lost* is a most inaccurate word to describe the death of a Christian.

Nowadays everyone talks about the "bottom line." For a Christian the bottom line concerning death is that it is a gain and never a loss. We all can accept this in our heads, but sometimes it is hard for us to accept it in our hearts. The apostle Paul, however, was firmly convinced that he would never *lose* his life. He might *give* his life for the cause of Christ (and we can be fairly certain that he did), but he never would have wanted anyone to speak of it as a loss. For Paul death was more like the return on an investment. He had invested his life in the service of the Lord Jesus Christ, and after death he would receive the "full benefits" from that investment.

No doubt we will always speak of death as a "loss," and that is all right as long as we remember that the loss is on our side. We grieve, and we have every right to grieve. We have lost the companionship of one we love. But if that person was a Christian, he or she has gained the eternal companionship of God the Father and Christ the Savior. For a Christian it is always true that "to die is gain."   —R. C. S.

22. If I am to go on living in the body, this will mean fruitful labor for me. Yet what shall I choose? I do not know!

While "to die is gain," Paul realized that, if he should *go on living in* his earthly *body*, it would provide a means of *fruitful labor* among the people around him. This presented quite a quandary: if he had to *choose* immediately between living

---

HOW TO SAY IT

Caesar. SEE-zer.
Colossians. Kuh-LOSH-unz.
Corinth. KOR-inth.
Corinthians. Kor-IN-thee-unz (th as in thin).
Epaphroditus. Ee-PAF-ro-DYE-tus.
Ephesians. Ee-FEE-zhunz.
Lydia. LID-ee-uh.
Macedonia. Mass-eh-DOE-nee-uh.
Philemon. Fih-LEE-mun or Fye-LEE-mun.
Philippi. Fih-LIP-pie or FIL-ih-pie.
Philippians. Fih-LIP-ee-unz.
Silas. SIGH-luss.
Thessalonians. THESS-uh-LO-nee-unz (th as in thin).
Thessalonica. THESS-uh-lo-NYE-kuh (th as in thin).

WHAT DO YOU THINK?

Life presents daily choices between serving self or serving others, even when to do either is a good thing. Paul's dilemma (vv. 23, 24) is a large example of that which comes to us in small "bits" each day: to do what makes us happier or what blesses another. Paul made the better choice.

When is the last time you had to choose between your own welfare and that of another? How did you choose? Why?

PRAYER

O Lord, our God, you have provided living space for us, temporarily in this world of your creation and eternally in Jesus Christ, your Son and our Lord. Help us to live in him now, with all our being and all our belongings, that we may be prepared to live with him eternally. In his name we ask. Amen.

THOUGHT TO REMEMBER

"I have been crucified with Christ and I no longer live, but Christ lives in me. The life I live in the body, I live by faith in the Son of God, who loved me and gave himself for me" (Galatians 2:20).

and dying, he wouldn't *know* which way to cast his ballot. Both possibilities were good; which was better? Paul was in a "win-win" situation.

Thankfully there are some issues in which we do not have to choose one way or the other. Let us join with Paul in doing God's will as we are able, and pray that he will be glorified in the result. Beyond that, it was not the prerogative of even the great apostle to know the time of his death.

23, 24. I am torn between the two: I desire to depart and be with Christ, which is better by far; but it is more necessary for you that I remain in the body.

Paul felt himself *torn between . . . two* alternatives, both of which were favorable. An early death, with escape from present difficulties into the everlasting presence of his beloved Lord (2 Corinthians 5:8), would be greatly to his own advantage. On the other hand, if he were true to his own admonition in Philippians 2:3 and 1 Corinthians 10:24 (to consider others' interests ahead of one's own), he would continue making himself helpfully available to his brethren for as long as possible.

C. I EXPECT TO STAY (vv. 25, 26)

25, 26. Convinced of this, I know that I will remain, and I will continue with all of you for your progress and joy in the faith, so that through my being with you again your joy in Christ Jesus will overflow on account of me.

Paul's conclusion brought him back to the theme of *joy* that characterizes this epistle. It was the joy that would come to the Philippian Christians as they were blessed by his further ministry, especially through his *being with* them *again*.

It may seem that Paul was rather presumptuous in assuming that his friends would rejoice in his continued ministry, and particularly at the prospect of seeing and hearing him again. Is it presumptuous, though, for the member of a family or the partner in a long and close friendship to expect a joy-filled welcome home? Wouldn't a relationship seem hollow if it did not exhibit that kind of expectation? And the natural warmth of Christian love is not hollow!

First Timothy 1:3 speaks of a visit by Paul to Macedonia, which evidently took place after his first imprisonment in Rome. The joyous reunion with the Philippian Christians that most likely took place during this journey surely must have fulfilled Paul's expectation that the Philippians' joy in Christ would be increased by his presence. In turn his joy would be enhanced by being able to witness how the Philippians had grown in dedication to Christ. Apart from Jesus such joy, even in the midst of severe hardship, is not possible.

CONCLUSION

In many of the telephone conversations that involve family members, the final words are, "We'll be in touch." Times, methods, and circumstances are not spelled out, but there is a firm commitment to ongoing communication. It was so, too, in Paul's relationship with the Philippians. He had said that he expected to see them in Philippi, but he was not sure exactly when. He had affirmed his commitment and his confidence with regard to living in Christ for time and eternity. Of that he was very sure!

So, regardless of when Paul saw the Philippians again, he would stay in touch, expecting to hear that they had joined him in putting Christ above all else, in being steadfast in that commitment, and in suffering with and for Christ without wavering (Philippians 1:27-30). Should not we, who also have received the message Paul wrote to the Philippians, accept the same responsibility? We'll be in touch—with one another and especially with God's Word and God's Son. In him we live!

Discovery Learning

This page contains an alternate lesson plan emphasizing learning activities. Classes desiring such student involvement will find these suggestions helpful. The next page is a reproducible activity page to further enhance discovery learning.

LEARNING GOALS

After participating in this lesson, each student will be able to:

1. Tell how Paul used his Roman imprisonment and his concern for the Philippian Christians to illustrate that Christ must come first.

2. Explain how Paul's conviction that "to live is Christ" expresses what a Christian's priorities should be.

3. Determine to face each circumstance of the coming week with the goal that "Christ will be exalted."

INTO THE LESSON

Prepare a handout with a list of activities (see below) down the left side. To the right of the list make two columns with a large plus sign (+) at the top of the left column and a large minus sign (–) over the right. Students are to consider each activity and determine whether it would likely serve to advance the gospel (+) or hinder it (–). List the following (and perhaps some additional) activities:

Learning the language of the people
Economic recession or depression
Serious illness or physical handicap
The arrest of a popular preacher
Publishing Christian literature
Preaching an unpopular message

Give the students a few minutes to respond; then discuss their findings. There probably will not be complete agreement on every item; discuss how some of these may be positive or negative, depending on other factors. Tell the class that Paul made a positive out of just about all of these factors—even his arrest and imprisonment in Rome, he said, had served to advance the gospel.

Option: Use the similar activity "In Chains for Christ" on the next page to introduce today's lesson.

INTO THE WORD

On the chalkboard or on a large poster write, "To live is Christ." Ask the class what they think that means. After a very brief discussion, tell the class we are beginning a series of lessons from the book of Philippians that remind us of the joys and responsibilities of living in Christ's church. Remind the class of Paul's adventures in establishing the Philippian church (see Acts 16:11-40 and the "Lesson Background"). Then have a volunteer read Philippians 1:12-26.

After the text is read, recall the phrase, "To live is Christ." Ask, "How does Paul's experience in Rome illustrate this principle? How do his priorities demonstrate the truth of this statement?" Here are some possible points to note in this discussion:

Verses 12-14. Paul's imprisonment had served to advance the gospel.

Verses 15-18. Paul was not jealous of the success of others or bitter about those who tried to make him look bad. The spread of the gospel was his first concern.

Verse 19. He expressed confidence that God would answer the Philippians' prayers for his "deliverance."

Verses 20-23. Paul lived with hope in Christ and could die in that hope, confident of eternal life with Christ.

Verses 24-26. Paul was eager to serve the Lord, especially to minister to the Philippians, so he was confident that God's will included his release so he could do that.

To help understand Paul's statement in verse 21, use this brainstorm activity. Write two headings on the chalkboard or marker board: "Advantages of Going to Heaven" and "Advantages in Staying Here." Then ask students to brainstorm ideas for each column as you write them on the chalkboard.

INTO LIFE

Tell the students that the phrase "To live is Christ" is the theme of this text. The phrase is both inspirational and challenging to readers today. We live in the body of Christ. Refer to the poster completed in the introductory activity, reminding students of the joy, satisfaction, and peace that come from living in Christ's body.

Note Paul's confidence that Christ would be "exalted" in his life or in his death (verse 20). Ask, "How has Christ been exalted in your life recently?" Be prepared to give a personal example to get people thinking of tangible ways they exalt the Lord. For example, any act of kindness rendered to a person in need or taking a stand for morality in a PTA meeting or some other public forum exalts the Lord. (Use the activity "Living . . . for the Gospel" on the next page to supplement this discussion.)

Note that some people occasionally exalt the Lord while others, like Paul, seem to do it automatically. Observe that it takes a mind set on Christ to have a life that continually exalts him. Close with prayer that each student will develop a determination to exalt the Lord in every circumstance of life.

In Chains for Christ

The apostle Paul, when writing to the Philippians, was a prisoner in Rome. Yet he wrote that his difficult and trying circumstances had really served to spread the gospel. How could the following trying circumstances serve to advance the gospel through your life?

Financial Hardship

Losing Your Eyesight

Death of a Spouse

Job Transfer to Korea

Living . . .   for the Gospel

Paul wrote, "To live is Christ and to die is gain" (Philippians 1:21). He knew that his continued life on earth meant "fruitful labor" for him (v. 22). Specifically, that labor meant "I will continue with all of you for your progress and joy in the faith" (v. 25).

Complete your own personal version of Paul's words with a statement of the "fruitful labor" that God can achieve through you.

If I am to go on living in the body, this will mean fruitful labor for me. . . . I know that I will remain, and I will . . .

Like Paul, while we are on this earth, we desire to share the gospel of Jesus Christ. What do you think you might do to strengthen your witness in the following environments:

To your family?

To your next-door neighbors?

To your co-workers?

HAVING THE
MIND OF CHRIST

LESSON 2

WHY TEACH THIS LESSON?

"W W J D?" You have probably seen those letters on a bracelet, a T-shirt, a cap, or some other article of clothing. The letters remind us to ask, "What would Jesus do?" Inspired by Charles Sheldon's *In His Steps,* asking that question is a good practice for those who would follow the Savior.

A young girl reported that she had engaged in some not-so-kind behavior toward a classmate at school. Taking advantage of the opportunity, her father asked if she thought Jesus would have been pleased with her actions. "Oh, it's okay, Daddy," she said. "I wasn't wearing my W W J D bracelet!"

Today's lesson will challenge your students to go beyond outward shows of discipleship to have the attitude of Christ Jesus himself, the attitude of a servant bringing honor to his Lord.

INTRODUCTION

A. OF DOGS AND DISCIPLES

The dog is recognized as "man's best friend"—and with good reason. A dog tends to remain ardently loyal to a considerate master. Stories have been told about brave dogs that served courageously in war or risked their lives to save those in danger. The St. Bernard is particularly famous for its ability to travel through deep snow and rescue lost or trapped travelers.

Unfortunately, such "dogged" determination is often lacking among those who claim Jesus as Master. We are too easily influenced by the apathetic attitude of our time rather than by an unwavering devotion to duty. Today's study will offer this challenge to each of us: "Your attitude should be the same as that of Christ Jesus" (Philippians 2:5). Jesus' sole purpose was to do the will of the Father who sent him (John 6:38). Luke 9:51 says, "As the time approached for him to be taken up to heaven, Jesus resolutely set out for Jerusalem." Knowing the cross was before him, he boldly undertook the task he had come to perform.

Have we "resolutely set out" to accomplish the task we have been given?

B. LESSON BACKGROUND

Always in view throughout the Philippian letter is the theme of rejoicing in Christ. In last week's study, we observed how chapter 1 of Philippians deals with the manner of life—regarding matters here and hereafter—that expresses our faith in Christ and thus promotes joy and peace in the body of believers. The final four verses of chapter 1 urge steadfastness in the face of difficulties such as Paul and his Philippian friends were enduring. Their faithfulness would provide a powerful testimony to unbelievers. What, though, should be said of relationships *within* the church? That is the emphasis of chapter 2.

Philippians 2 begins by urging the readers to act in such a way as to promote peace and unity in the body. It continues by calling attention to three persons—

DEVOTIONAL READING:
2 PETER 3:8-18
BACKGROUND SCRIPTURE:
PHILIPPIANS 2:1-18
PRINTED TEXT:
PHILIPPIANS 2:1-13

LESSON AIMS

As a result of studying this lesson, students will be able to:

1. Tell how Paul used Jesus as an example to challenge Christians to selfless service.

2. Explain why Jesus' example is critical to church life and to the church's witness to the world.

3. Identify specific situations in their church, home, or work where demonstrating the attitude of Jesus could make a positive difference.

KEY VERSE

Your attitude should be the same as that of Christ Jesus.
—*Philippians 2:5*

LESSON 2 NOTES

all known to the Philippians—who demonstrated the qualities recommended by Paul. The second and third were Timothy and Epaphroditus (Philippians 2:19-30). First and most important was Jesus himself.

I. BE OF ONE MIND (PHILIPPIANS 2:1-4)

A. LOOKING TO JESUS (vv. 1, 2)

1, 2. If you have any encouragement from being united with Christ, if any comfort from his love, if any fellowship with the Spirit, if any tenderness and compassion, then make my joy complete by being like-minded, having the same love, being one in spirit and purpose.

At the first reading of verse 1, the repeated *if* might suggest that Paul doubted whether the Philippians had received *any encouragement* from being *united with Christ, any comfort from his love, any* meaningful *fellowship* with the Holy *Spirit*, or *any tenderness and compassion*. With Christ all of these blessings are surely to be found without limit and enjoyed beyond measure. Any uncertainty about possessing these treasures is to be traced to the saints' limited receptiveness of them.

The *if* in this sentence introduces a construction known as a "particular condition." It means that on the condition stated in the first clause, a particular response is warranted. It does not question the fact of the condition, but simply states "if this, then that"—or even, "*since* this, then that." For this reason, we may rightly understand Paul to be saying, "Since all of the virtues listed are to be expected in persons who are in Christ, let those God-given forces be put to work where they are not present in order to achieve the healing of whatever problems exist!"

Paul exhorted the Philippians to *make* his *joy complete.* He had already expressed his joy in their Christian maturity (Philippians 1:3-5). There was still room for spiritual growth, however, and Paul's joy would increase as they achieved it.

Being like-minded, having the same love, . . . being one in spirit and purpose. Paul did not expect total uniformity in the Philippians' preferences and opinions; but he did expect their mind-set, attitude, and commitment to be centered on Christ. When their love for him was complete, differences in other matters would be insignificant. When their dominating purpose was to glorify him, other loyalties would fade into the background. And when they loved him more than all else, then they would love other persons who also belonged to him. Those who are close to Jesus will be close to one another.

B. NOT SELF-CENTERED (v.3)

3. Do nothing out of selfish ambition or vain conceit, but in humility consider others better than yourselves.

Selfish ambition describes a combative spirit that puts others down to advance oneself. *Vain conceit* refers to the empty honor frequently associated with wealth, position, or power. Romans 12:3 offers the corrective: "I say to every one of you: Do not think of yourself more highly then you ought, but rather think of yourself with sober judgment, in accordance with the measure of faith God has given you."

Humility has been described as the position of one who has stooped down to lift another up. Paul put it this way when writing to the Roman Christians: "Be devoted to one another in brotherly love. Honor one another above yourselves" (Romans 12:10). "It is more blessed to give than to receive" tributes, credit, and words of encouragement as well as money and material goods!

Paul's command to *consider* others as *better than* ourselves contrasts sharply with the me-centered philosophy of our age. But if we are honest, we can easily recognize that others are better than we at something. Let us freely acknowledge the fact, especially if doing so will encourage them in their service to the Lord.

WHAT DO YOU THINK?

The lesson writer notes that the if *in verse 1 does not question the fact of the presence of "any encouragement from . . . Christ, . . . comfort from his love . . . fellowship with the Spirit . . . [and] tenderness and compassion." Tell how you have experienced some of these in significant ways or at special times.*

WHAT DO YOU THINK?

How can we spot the "others-oriented" person? How can we be "others oriented"?

C. CONSIDERING OTHERS (v 4)

4. Each of you should look not only to your own interests, but also to the interests of others.

We are to *look . . . to the interests of others,* not with a covetous heart, but with a concerned one. Thoughtful consideration of the wishes and needs of others is the order of the Christian's day. That is the reason one associate minister would whistle a tune as he walked through the empty halls of the large church building on weekdays. It assured the lone secretary that the footsteps echoing in the otherwise silent corridors were friendly ones.

The same thoughtfulness persuades a friend to listen patiently to another's long story of minor adventures when his own experience could produce vastly more interesting narratives. He doesn't need to talk; he is more than happy to let the other person do so.

This is not to say that one must neglect his own daily needs and responsibilities while caring for those of others. The words *not only . . . also* tell us that others are to be considered in addition to, not instead of, one's own legitimate needs.

II. CHRIST SHOWS THE WAY (PHILIPPIANS 2:5-8)

Some Bible students believe that verses 6-11 of this chapter comprised an early Christian hymn that Paul included in his letter at this point. However, Paul was quite capable of writing in a poetic style (as illustrated by 1 Corinthians 13), and may well have written these lines himself. (They could have become part of a hymn at a later time.) Whatever their origin, this passage is a magnificent statement concerning Jesus and illustrates the principle of serving others.

A. HIS EXAMPLE (v. 5)

5. Your attitude should be the same as that of Christ Jesus.

A person's dominant *attitude* will be reflected in all he thinks about, says, and does. The verse before us presents *Christ Jesus* as the One who should be the determining influence in the believer's mind-set. That happens in two ways. First, Christ is the example to be followed. His attitude should be reproduced in the minds of his followers. Second, Christ himself is the power who enables the Christian to live by that example: "Christ in you, the hope of glory" (Colossians 1:27).

B. HIS SURRENDER (vv. 6, 7)

6. Who, being in very nature God, did not consider equality with God something to be grasped.

Jesus was in his *very nature God*—eternally. When he did what verse 7 describes ("made himself nothing"), he was not surrendering a glory that he had unfairly taken; he was determining not to hold on to Heaven's glory as his possession. This is the meaning of the phrase *did not consider equality with God something to be grasped.* Jesus surrendered his advantages willingly for the sake of rescuing lost humanity.

7. . . . but made himself nothing, taking the very nature of a servant, being made in human likeness.

The eternal Word, who was with God and was God, emptied himself of heavenly glory and, through his birth in Bethlehem, accepted the limitations and difficulties that accompany *being made in human likeness.* Isaiah 53 describes him as the suffering *servant* who was "pierced for our transgressions" and "crushed for our iniquities" (v. 5). The difference between Jesus and other men was not in his physical appearance, but in his thoughts, words, and deeds. These were all governed by the fact that the Lord of Heaven came to earth, not to be served, but to

Today's visual illustrates the truth of verse 5. Discuss what it means to have the "attitude" of Christ.

WHAT DO YOU THINK?

In Paul's "hymn to Christ," vv. 6-11, he includes this important truth to be believed: "Christ Jesus . . . did not consider equality with God something to be grasped, . . . made in human likeness" (vv. 5-7). The truth of the incarnation is critical for our evangelistic message! What factors make declaring that truth challenging in our culture? What specific errors does this truth confront?

HOW TO SAY IT

Epaphroditus. Ee-PAF-ro-DYE-tus.

Isaiah. Eye-ZAY-uh.

Philippi. Fih-LIP-pie or FIL-ih-pie.

Philippians. Fih-LIP-ee-unz.

Zoroastrianism. Zor-o-AS-tree-uh-niz-um.

DAILY BIBLE READINGS

Monday, June 5—Imitate Christ's Humility in Your Lives (Philippians 2:1-11)

Tuesday, June 6—Rejoice in One Another's Faithfulness (Philippians 2:12-18)

Wednesday, June 7—Timothy, a Faithful Servant of Christ (Philippians 2:19-24)

Thursday, June 8—Welcome Epaphroditus in Christ (Philippians 2:25-30)

Friday, June 9—Repay Evil With a Blessing (1 Peter 3:8-12)

Saturday, June 10—Suffering for Doing Right (1 Peter 3:13-22)

Sunday, June 11—You Are Participants in God's Nature (2 Peter 1:1-11)

serve others (Matthew 20:28). He taught and gave directions—even issued commandments—but never for his own self-promotion.

THE VERY NATURE OF A SERVANT

In the historical district of Charleston, South Carolina, a little after seven o'clock in the morning, one can see a seventy-five-year-old man carrying a plastic grocery bag. Those who follow him for his two-mile walk will see him picking up the trash with which people have littered the streets the night before. Many will find it hard to believe that this volunteer trash collector is James J. Kilpatrick—one of the most widely read columnists in America. His column is in scores of newspapers, and he is considered an authority on the English language. He is financially secure. Yet he does not think it beneath his dignity to help clean up the streets of his beloved city.

How often people will refuse to do work that needs to be done in a community, a school, or even the church! No doubt the people who dropped the trash in the streets were far less gifted than Kilpatrick. No doubt he cleans up after people who make a lot less money than he does, and who will never know the fame he enjoys.

Of course, this kind of humble service is very minor compared with what Jesus did when he "made himself nothing" and took "the very nature of a servant." Certainly our imitation of Christ will always pale beside his example. Still, we can and should learn much from that example. Jesus stooped to wash his disciples' feet. He stooped to cook their breakfast beside the sea.

Someone has wisely observed, "Only the strong can stoop." What have we done lately to "stoop" and help another in need?   —R. C. S.

C. HIS SACRIFICE (v. 8)

8. And being found in appearance as a man, he humbled himself and became obedient to death—even death on a cross!

Jesus accepted human limitations without complaint. He knew weariness, hunger and thirst, and temptation (Matthew 4:1, 2; John 4:6, 7). He was tested just as other human beings are (Hebrews 4:15). He demonstrated the servant role most memorably when he washed his disciples' feet during the observance of the Passover meal (John 13:1-5).

Jesus became the servant of men because he was first and foremost the *obedient* servant/Son of God. His *death on a cross* was the supreme test of that obedience. Designed as the ultimate punishment of the most despised and vicious criminals, crucifixion was the epitome of suffering and shame. For Jesus the cross demonstrates the extreme to which he was willing to go in loving, serving, and saving us.

III. GOD HONORS HIS SON (PHILIPPIANS 2:9-11)

A. THE HIGHEST NAME (v. 9)

9. Therefore God exalted him to the highest place and gave him the name that is above every name.

In spoken words as well as by constant empowerment, God expressed his pleasure in what Jesus did on earth (Matthew 3:17; 17:5; John 12:28-30; Acts 10:38). In response to Jesus' fulfillment of God's purpose, the Father's pleasure was expressed in this manner: God "raised him from the dead and seated him at his right hand in the heavenly realms, far above all rule and authority, power and dominion, and every title that can be given, not only in the present age but also in the one to come. And God placed all things under his feet and appointed him to be head over everything for the church, which is his body, the fullness of him who fills everything in every way" (Ephesians 1:20-23).

What is the superior *name* given by God? At birth his Son was to be called Jesus; following Jesus' resurrection, the titles of "Lord and Christ" took on special meaning (Acts 2:33-36). Isaiah 9:6 speaks of him as "Wonderful Counselor, Mighty God, Everlasting Father, Prince of Peace." The term *name*, however, may signify position or office (as in the Ephesians passage cited above). The risen Lord himself declared, "All authority in heaven and on earth has been given to me" (Matthew 28:18).

God's recognition of his servant/Son is a compelling illustration of what Jesus told his followers: "Whoever exalts himself will be humbled, and whoever humbles himself will be exalted" (Matthew 23:12). Jesus knows and shows what he is talking about!

B. THE HIGHEST ADORATION (vv. 10, 11)

10. . . . *that at the name of Jesus every knee should bow, in heaven and on earth and under the earth.*

The purpose of Jesus' exaltation is that *every knee should bow* to his *name* and every tongue confess that he is Lord (v. 11). No realm is excluded from this expression of adoration; those *in heaven* and *earth* and those *under the earth* (likely referring to the hosts of Satan) will pay homage to Jesus' lordship.

Jesus' claim to all authority in Matthew 28:18 was followed by his command that all nations are to be made his disciples and directed to follow his commands (vv. 19, 20). The recognition of Jesus' authority will occur, either willingly by faith (leading to salvation) or forcefully at the judgment (resulting in condemnation).

A FAMOUS NAME

A suburban homeowner got to thinking one day about all the people who served him who were not really known to him. He didn't know the name of the policeman, the fireman, the man who delivered his newspaper, or the man who picked up his trash. He decided to remedy that; so one day he stopped the garbage man and introduced himself. The garbage man said, "My name is Albert Einstein."

The man responded, "That's a very famous name."

And the trash collector replied, "Well, it should be. I've been collecting the trash on this street for ten years!"

No name is more widely known than the name of Jesus. No name is more honored than the name of Jesus. Even many who do not believe his claims pay a certain amount of homage to his name and his character. It always surprises us to visit a country like Mexico and see people whose first name is Jesus (pronounced Haysoose). But in Jesus' day the name *Jesus* was as common as John or Joe is to us today. Jesus took an ordinary name and gave it extraordinary significance.

Is this not what Jesus has done for us? He has taken our ordinary, commonplace lives and given them extraordinary meaning. He loved us when we were dead in our sins and suffered "even death on a cross" for us. His name deserves to be remembered, honored, and praised—by our words and by our lives.   —R. C. S.

11. . . . *and every tongue confess that Jesus Christ is Lord, to the glory of God the Father.*

Submission to Jesus will be expressed, not only by the gesture of bending the knee, but in words. To *confess* is to say the truth plainly and boldly: *Jesus Christ is Lord*. His authority deserves to be listened to with respect and obeyed implicitly. He takes no pleasure in those who call him Lord and do not follow his direction (Luke 6:46-49).

To the glory of God the Father. God is most highly honored when individuals agree with him in recognizing, acknowledging, and honoring his Son. From our viewpoint that means following Jesus' example and direction in loving and serving, rather than in loving to be served.

WHAT DO YOU THINK?

Paul reveals that "at the name of Jesus every knee should bow" (v. 10). Few Christians kneel in contemporary worship. Why is that? Is kneeling necessary? Desirable? Why or why not?

IV. GOD WORKS IN HIS PEOPLE (PHILIPPIANS 2:12, 13)

Paul returns now to the exhortation with which the chapter began. He had urged the kind of unselfish care for one another that allows the church to grow and be one body. He had called attention to Jesus as the perfect example of an unselfish attitude. Now he challenges his readers to put his words into practice.

12. Therefore, my dear friends, as you have always obeyed—not only in my presence, but now much more in my absence—continue to work out your salvation with fear and trembling.

The saints at Philippi had a good "track record" on which to build their ongoing Christian experience. They and Paul loved one another genuinely (Philippians 1:3-8; 4:1, 10, 14-16). The Philippians' eager response to Paul's teaching had reflected something of Jesus' wholehearted obedience to the will of God. They were obedient *not only* when Paul was in their city, but, more important, they continued to be so in his *absence.* They respected God's message for them, even when its messenger was far away.

Now Paul urged his readers to *continue* their consistent obedience and to *work out* their *salvation.* Paul is not saying that salvation is based on works; the work he commands is the expression of the Philippians' commitment to Christ (Philippians 1:6). They must follow to its fulfillment the salvation course on which they had embarked. The attitude of *fear and trembling,* which acknowledges the holiness of God and the danger posed by sin, would mark their commitment. This is not a matter to be taken lightly. We are to "worship God acceptably with reverence and awe" (Hebrews 12:28).

13. For it is God who works in you to will and to act according to his good purpose.

Our salvation is God's accomplishment, not our own. He desires that none should perish, but that all should come to repentance and salvation (1 Timothy 2:4; 2 Peter 3:9); and he *works* continually toward that purpose. His Holy Spirit also works to accomplish that goal—through the Scriptures and *in* individuals who are committed to carrying out God's *good purpose* in a sinful world.

"Do not put out the Spirit's fire" (1 Thessalonians 5:19); that is, don't clog the channels of his working in us. As Christians we wear Christ's name, and God will not hold that one guiltless who wears his Son's name irreverently. Let's give God his way in us!

CONCLUSION

A Christian minister counsels a young couple in preparation for their June wedding, to be conducted in a place dedicated to Christian worship. Much that they discuss is common to most marriage counseling: finances, personal relationships, shared responsibilities, communication, to name just a few matters. What, though, will set this wedding and this marriage apart from other June bridal arrangements?

It is not simply that the wedding will take place in a house of worship and will include prayers for God's blessing. Most important, it will focus on Jesus as both the example and the divine presence that can enable this couple to fulfill the promises they will make before God and man. It is not their personal skills that will produce success, but their recognition that the strength of their marriage depends on God working in and through them. Standing and kneeling shoulder to shoulder, they must pray as Jesus prayed, "Your will be done."

This same principle applies if we desire a Christian home, a Christian business, or anything else that bears the name Christian. Just calling something Christian does not make it so. Calling on Christ for his power and presence will make the difference.

Discovery Learning

This page contains an alternate lesson plan emphasizing learning activities. Classes desiring such student involvement will find these suggestions helpful. The next page is a reproducible activity page to further enhance discovery learning.

LEARNING GOALS

After this lesson each student will be able to:

1. Tell how Paul used Jesus as an example to challenge Christians to selfless service.

2. Explain why Jesus' example is critical to church life and to the church's witness to the world.

3. Identify a specific situation in his or her church, home, or work where demonstrating the attitude of Jesus can make a positive difference.

INTO THE LESSON

The introduction to the theme of this lesson will focus on the attitude of submission to Christ. The attitude of believers should be of joyful submission because we wish to please our Master.

To introduce this concept, talk about dog-obedience training. Point out that the dog's ultimate motivation for submission and obedience is that he wants to please his master. To do this, you may choose to bring a dog-obedience trainer to class. He could demonstrate dog obedience with his dog. Or, if you do not wish to have an animal present, he could talk about the key concept . . . *the dog wishes to please his master*. Or you could show a segment of a video (from your public library or a pet shop) on training dogs. Look for a segment that emphasizes the dog's pleasure in pleasing his master.

Make your transition from this activity by telling the class that the dog develops a strong attachment to its master and takes genuine delight in pleasing the one he loves. Just as Jesus found delight and purpose in doing the will of his Father who sent him (John 6:38), we also should find joy in submitting to our Master.

Option: If your students enjoy word-search puzzles, give them copies of the reproducible page that follows to introduce the lesson.

INTO THE WORD

Form at least three discussion groups of three to six people each. Give the groups written instructions, and provide a poster board and marking pens for each group.

Group 1: Read Philippians 2:5-8; list the illustrations of Christ's submission to the Father. Be ready to explain each of these.

Group 2: Read Philippians 2:9-11, and list the honors given Christ because he submitted to the Father. Be ready to explain each of these.

Group 3: Read Philippians 2:2-5, 12, 13. Remembering that we are to have the mind of Christ in joyful surrender to God's will, list on poster board the words and phrases in these verses that suggest practical demonstrations of Christlike obedience. Be ready to clarify or explain these concepts to the class.

Encourage the groups to do their research and prepare for reports quickly. Ask each group to put its poster on the wall after completing the assigned task.

Before the groups report, use your lesson commentary to give a brief explanation of verses 1 and 2. Explain that Paul is not calling for total uniformity by using the word *like-minded*. He is simply asking that his readers' loyalty be to Christ. Their love for him will be the source of joyful and willful submission to his will.

A spokesperson for each group should recite the group's findings. After each group reports, you should be ready to explain or clarify concepts.

To make the transition from group 2's report to group 3, put up a poster you have prepared with these words from verse 5, "Your attitude should be the same as that of Christ Jesus." (Or use visual 2 from the visuals pack; see page 355.) Explain that Jesus was cited by Paul in this passage as an illustration of how we are to live. Group 3 will share some of Paul's principles.

To wrap up this portion of the study, summarize group reports. Remind the students that group 1 discovered that Jesus' obedience was a willful act, something he chose to do. He was not trapped nor forced into leaving Heaven or dying on the cross. Group 2 found that Jesus' submission was pleasing to God and that God exalted Jesus. Group 3 listed practical principles for submitting to and pleasing the Master.

INTO LIFE

Ask class members to hear these questions and answer them to themselves. Question 1: "What are two things you believe you need to do to demonstrate submission to God's authority and to please your Master?" (Give them time to think about these.) Question 2: "Which of those tasks or challenges would you like to start right now?"

Conclude by having the class sing (or recite) "In My Life, Lord, Be Glorified" or "Take My Life and Let It Be." (Be sure to provide songbooks for those who do not know the words.)

Searching for a Christlike Heart

Paul tells us, "Your attitude should be the same as that of Christ Jesus." In the heart below find eighteen qualities or actions typical of a Christlike heart. Each word can be found in Philippians 2:1-13. You may use the blank lines and verses below to find clues for words to seek.

_____ v. 1	_____ v. 2	_____ v. 10
_____ v. 1	_____ v. 3	_____ v. 11
_____ v. 1	_____ v. 3	_____ v. 12
_____ v. 2	_____ v. 5	_____ v. 12
_____ v. 2	_____ v. 7	_____ v. 12
_____ v. 2	_____ v. 8	_____ v. 12

v. 1: tenderness, compassion, united; v. 2: joy, love, purpose, spirit; v. 3: humility, consider others; v. 5: attitude; v. 7: servant; v. 8: obedient; v. 10: bow; v. 11: confess; v. 12: obeyed, salvation, fear, work

PRESSING ON IN CHRIST

LESSON 3

DEVOTIONAL READING:
HEBREWS 10:19-25, 32-36
BACKGROUND SCRIPTURE:
PHILIPPIANS 3
PRINTED TEXT:
PHILIPPIANS 3:7-21

Jun
18

WHY TEACH THIS LESSON?

"Selective forgetfulness." If you are a parent, you have probably encountered it. You tell the kids, "Take out the trash after dinner," and they are likely to forget. Tell them, "Maybe we'll get ice cream a little later," and they will make sure you don't forget! Somehow they seem to forget what they want to forget.

Today's lesson recommends—no, commands—a certain selective forgetfulness. "Forgetting what is behind," Paul says, "I press on." But just two verses later he says, "Let us live up to what we have already attained." How can we "live up to what we have already attained" if we have forgotten "what is behind"? Selective forgetfulness! Today's lesson will clear up the mystery.

INTRODUCTION

A. THE PEACE OF PROGRESS

Traffic moved smoothly that afternoon along the interstate, and we fully expected to reach home on schedule. Then suddenly, on the highway before us, there appeared a slowing, crowding, and finally a complete stoppage of vehicles in every lane of the wide highway. Eventually our progress was also brought to a standstill. What had happened? How long would it be until we could move again? We waited with an increasingly tense frustration.

After what seemed like a very long hour there was movement, irregular at first, and then more steady as the mass of traffic filtered, one car at a time, past the distant roadblock. Even the first slow movement, however, brought what an acquaintance of mine used to call "the peace of progress"—relief and relaxation in the assurance that we were moving toward home.

As Christians we are on the way toward the home prepared for us by the Lord who has gone before. But are we really moving in the right direction? Or have we stalled in our progress? Is it possible that some difficulty has even caused us to move away from, rather than toward, the Lord who waits to welcome us home? Today's text from Philippians 3:7-21 points us to the way of progress and peace, guaranteed to get us home safely under the direction of Jesus.

B. LESSON BACKGROUND

Philippians is a Christ-centered letter! Chapter 1 presents Jesus as the focus and goal of Paul's life: "For to me, to live is Christ" (1:21). Chapter 2 presents Christ as the perfect example of the self-sacrificing spirit that will build the church in peace and unity. Chapter 3 opens with an exhortation to "rejoice in the Lord"—a theme that rings throughout the letter. Paul then warns the Philippians of certain "dogs," or false teachers, who are encouraging people to put their "confidence in the flesh" (outward conformity to Jewish law) rather than in Christ. He proceeds to list some of the items in his own background that gave him more than enough reason to have such confidence (v. 4). He does so to emphasize that such dependence on the flesh can never make a person right with God. Only by following the course that is urged in the succeeding verses, which comprise our printed text, can we be made right with God.

LESSON AIMS

After this lesson each student will be able to:

1. Describe the attitude, actions, and goal that, according to Paul, are part of "pressing on in Christ."

2. List some personal possessions or activities that he or she considers expendable in his or her own discipleship.

3. Evaluate his or her life to determine whether there is any part that needs to be "considered as loss" for the sake of knowing Christ better.

KEY VERSE

I press on toward the goal to win the prize for which God has called me heavenward in Christ Jesus.   —Philippians 3:14

I. THE GOAL IS CHRIST (PHILIPPIANS 3:7-11)

In verses 5 and 6 the apostle has noted that his "bragging rights" in relation to the Jewish law were far better than those of others who depended on the law for their acceptance with God. All of that, however, constituted a *program* to be carried out. For Paul that program had been replaced with a *Person* to be loved, honored, and served for time and eternity.

A. COUNTING EVERYTHING LOSS (vv. 7, 8)

7. But whatever was to my profit I now consider loss for the sake of Christ.

Paul recognized that any part of his background or reputation that encouraged reliance on anything but *Christ* for his salvation was a handicap to him. The more desirable these items had been, the greater would be their potential to become a hindrance. They must now be moved from the *profit* side of his personal and spiritual ledger to the *loss* side *for the sake of* his relationship with Christ. A Christian must ask himself occasionally which of his "assets" have become liabilities because they compete with Christ for top priority in his time and attention.

8. What is more, I consider everything a loss compared to the surpassing greatness of knowing Christ Jesus my Lord, for whose sake I have lost all things. I consider them rubbish, that I may gain Christ.

To know and serve and be with Christ is a blessing so great as to be sought at any and all costs. It begins with considering the information about Jesus found in the Gospels; it moves to an acceptance of Jesus as Savior and Lord; it then grows into the kind of intimacy described by Paul as *the surpassing greatness of knowing Christ Jesus my Lord*. Thus does one become prepared for the further intimacy of an eternity with Jesus.

Note that Paul was not promising some price that he would pay; he was giving a sober account of what he had *already paid*. His position in the Jewish community; his family and friends; his home with all its comforts and security—these and other assets had been tossed aside that he might *gain Christ*.

Did the apostle miss these items and mourn their loss? To the contrary, he rejoiced in his glorious exchange, regarding the losses as *rubbish*, or material for the garbage can. Needless to say, that kind of evaluation by Paul did not sit well with the Jewish community whose heritage he appeared to dismiss so lightly. And the world in which we live is not inclined to look favorably on our absolute preference for Jesus Christ above any and all of the benefits or "perks" it offers. The downgrading of what the world holds dear may be taken as an insult to be resented and resisted. Can we avoid the offense? Probably not if we express our preference as clearly as Paul did.

B. HAVING HIS RIGHTEOUSNESS (v. 9)

9. . . . and be found in him, not having a righteousness of my own that comes from the law, but that which is through faith in Christ—the righteousness that comes from God and is by faith.

Paul says it again: a person's *righteousness*, or becoming right with God, comes not through outward conformity to *the law* of Moses but through belief in and commitment to God through his Son Jesus. The phrase *in him* describes a vital and intimate relationship with *Christ* that begins in time and continues throughout eternity.

If one could become acceptable with God through obedience to the law, then his salvation would be by means of his good behavior and thus an earned reward. But that is impossible, because no one—except for Jesus—has yet fully kept the law. Paul recognized the hopelessness of his position under the law (in spite of his

WHAT DO YOU THINK?

What "assets" do we have that may well be "liabilities" because they compete with Christ for top priority in our lives? How can we "consider them as loss for Christ"?

WHAT DO YOU THINK?

The Christian who minimizes the importance of the things most people value runs the risk of being resented and resisted by others. That threat may tempt us to compromise our value system. How can we resist that temptation?

own "faultless" standing before the law; see v. 6), and recognized that his salvation must come not from himself but *from God* through Christ. It must be received *by faith*—the belief that expresses itself through complete trust and obedience.

C. KNOWING HIM (vv. 10, 11)

10. I want to know Christ and the power of his resurrection and the fellowship of sharing in his sufferings, becoming like him in his death.

To *know Christ* was Paul's constant passion and purpose. In order to attain such an intimate acquaintance, the apostle was willing to share to the greatest possible degree the experiences of his Lord and Savior. If he was to experience the *power* that raised Christ from the dead, he would need to follow Jesus through the giving of his life daily in service to God (note his statement, "I die every day," in 1 Corinthians 15:31), and also through a willingness even to die in the service of Jesus (Revelation 2:10). This was no halfhearted effort!

A UNIQUE FELLOWSHIP

Many Christians enjoy singing the hymn, "Leaning on the Everlasting Arms." Whenever we sing, "What a fellowship, what a joy divine!" we usually think of person-to-person fellowship, though this verse is actually describing the relationship we have with Jesus. And often the occasions when we are singing the hymn are happy times spent with fellow believers.

Paul, however, recognized that there is another side to fellowship. It may surprise us to hear him speak of the fellowship of sharing in Christ's sufferings. Yet when Christians suffer for Christ's sake, they share a unique partnership with him. They come to know Christ in a way that those of us who live in more comfortable surroundings will never experience.

At the same time, the blessing of this fellowship can encourage those who suffer in more "ordinary" ways. A minister once told of visiting a member in the hospital, who spoke of her intense pain. She said to him, "You don't know what I am suffering." He agreed that indeed he did not. Then he told her, "But Christ does. He suffered intense pain on the cross, and he knows what you are going through." The minister noted that immediately he saw a look of comfort come over the woman's face. It made a difference to her to realize that Christ knows what it is to suffer, and that when we suffer there is a unique bond between us and him.

"What a fellowship"—the precious fellowship of suffering!   —R. C. S.

11. . . . and so, somehow, to attain to the resurrection from the dead.

The Scriptures teach that a *resurrection from the dead* will be shared by both saint and sinner—the one to life eternal and the other to condemnation (John 5:28, 29; Acts 24:15). Resurrection to life with Christ is a goal worth more than whatever can be invested in striving toward it.

Attain here signifies the arrival at a chosen destination. Paul had his eye on the goal and was on his way to reaching it. This does not mean, however, that eternal life is achieved on the basis of one's personal effort. It is a gift from God to be accepted and received. Its value increases as the recipient grows in his familiarity with the Provider.

II. THE APPROACH IS COMMITMENT (PHILIPPIANS 3:12-16)

A. PRESSING ON (v. 12)

12. Not that I have already obtained all this, or have already been made perfect, but I press on to take hold of that for which Christ Jesus took hold of me.

Paul described himself as *not . . . made perfect.* He was not yet a finished product of God's workmanship. That, however, did not keep him from pursuing his

---

HOW TO SAY IT

Epaphroditus. Ee-PAF-ro-DYE-tus.

Macedonia. Mass-eh-DOE-nee-uh.

Philippi. Fih-LIP-pie or FIL-ih-pie.

Philippians. Fih-LIP-ee-unz.

WHAT DO YOU THINK?

It is a universally accepted truism that "no one's perfect." How might that truth be misused to justify bad behavior? Why is it dangerous to do so?

goal patiently to the end. *I press on:* as a patient hunter tracks his game, so Paul resolved to stay the course with dogged persistence.

Here was Paul's fervent desire: that *I take hold of that for which Christ Jesus took hold of me.* The action is comparable to a drowning person's being seized by his rescuer and brought to grasp the rope he hadn't known was there. The lifesaving is accomplished by the rescuer, but it requires the cooperation of the rescued one. The Lord has laid hold on all of us through the gospel; through the same gospel we lay hold on him and are saved.

Today's visual illustrates Paul's metaphor of "pressing on." Discuss the similarities between an athlete's perseverance and a Christian's.

B. FORGETTING AND EXPECTING (vv. 13, 14)

13, 14. Brothers, I do not consider myself yet to have taken hold of it. But one thing I do: Forgetting what is behind and straining toward what is ahead, I press on toward the goal to win the prize for which God has called me heavenward in Christ Jesus.

Brothers. Paul regarded his readers as equals with him in the family of God. He and they had shared in the opportunities and responsibilities of the gospel. We share in them, too!

Paul had not yet reached his *goal:* he did not claim *to have taken hold of* his reward. He had not yet crossed the finish line in the Christian race, but he was committed to going all out in order to reach it.

One thing I do! The Greek text does not include the words *I do,* and is really more powerful without it. This is it! Nothing else matters!

Forgetting what is behind—this could include much of the "rubbish" from Paul's past: his Jewish heritage and cultural advantages; his sins and failures; his impressive array of accomplishments. None of these must be allowed to divert his attention from the opportunities before him.

Straining toward. As a runner leaning forward and extending himself to the limit, Paul was exerting the utmost effort to reach his objective.

I press on toward the goal. Paul was not following a general compass direction of "living a good life." His eyes were fixed on a specific goal.

The verse concludes with Paul's description of his goal: *the prize for which God has called me heavenward in Christ Jesus.* On reaching that goal Paul would receive the everlasting, never-fading "crown of righteousness" (1 Corinthians 9:25; 2 Timothy 4:8) given to those who are "faithful, even to the point of death" (Revelation 2:10). If there is anything more wonderful than being "in Christ," it will be the joy of being "with Christ!"

FACING FORWARD

During a discussion on changes and improvements in airplane design, someone suggested that airplane seats be turned around so that all the passengers are facing backward. Industry analysts claim that the public will never accept this. Why? Because people want to see where they are going, not where they have been. Everyone wants to face forward—at least physically.

In a more symbolic sense, there is always the temptation to face backward—that is, to live in the past. Sometimes this desire can be attributed to a nostalgia for supposedly better days. Sometimes it is caused by guilt over things that one did or failed to do.

In Savannah, Georgia, there is a statue in Madison Square honoring Sergeant William Jasper, who died during the siege of Savannah in 1779. The cool shaded square offers a striking contrast to the dust and heat that must have characterized the battlefield that day. But one thing is the same: Sergeant Jasper is pictured as he died—running *forward.*

Facing forward offers many advantages. One's eye is focused on future opportunities, not on past failures. One concentrates on building up character for days to come, not on reliving sins of the past. Satchel Paige, one of the greatest pitchers in the history of baseball, offered some sound advice when he said, "Don't look back. Something might be gaining on you."

Given the "prize" that awaits faithful Christians, there is no need for us to look back—ever.   —R. C. S.

C. PRESERVING THE GAINS (vv. 15, 16)

15. All of us who are mature should take such a view of things. And if on some point you think differently, that too God will make clear to you.

Having presented clearly his own position and perspective, the apostle recommended the same course to the *mature* Christians among his readers. Any who considered themselves to be complete in their spiritual development were exhorted to *take such a view of things.* However, if some differences of viewpoint still remained, Paul would leave the matter to *God,* trusting that he would *make clear* what the less mature needed to know. Such individuals required further teaching, perhaps by experience, perhaps by a more complete understanding of Christ and his Word, or perhaps by the example of mature Christians. Agreement would not be compelled, even by an apostle.

16. Only let us live up to what we have already attained.

Even those who have not yet *attained* the level of maturity that others have should not stand around doing nothing while God is bringing them "up to speed." Let them *live* by the truth they have already learned. Thus they will not lose the ground they have gained, but will be in a position to advance—learning more, doing more, and growing more toward the likeness of Christ.

III. THE COMPANY IS CHOSEN (PHILIPPIANS 3:17-21)

Neither the apostle Paul nor his friends in Philippi walked alone in the way to which they were committed. No one travels the road of life alone, but each must choose carefully his fellow travelers.

A. FOLLOW GOOD EXAMPLES (v. 17)

17. Join with others in following my example, brothers, and take note of those who live according to the pattern we gave you.

Again, Paul refers to his readers as *brothers*—as equals in God's family. *Join with others in following my example.* Whatever flaws might be found in Paul, he had still reached a level of commitment and maturity that merited respect and imitation. The most important aspect of his example was his steadfast imitation of Christ (1 Corinthians 11:1).

Take note of faithful folk around you—Timothy and Epaphroditus, for examples (Philippians 2:19-30)—whose way of life is worthy of being observed, appreciated, encouraged, and followed. Then when others say, concerning some wickedness, "Everyone is doing it!" you can reply, "Not everyone, and I can point to some who are not!"

B. SHUN BAD EXAMPLES (vv. 18, 19)

18, 19. For, as I have often told you before and now say again even with tears, many live as enemies of the cross of Christ. Their destiny is destruction, their god is their stomach, and their glory is in their shame. Their mind is on earthly things.

The intensity of expression here leads one to suppose that the *enemies of the cross* included some who had claimed salvation in Christ but had forsaken the Christian way. Those who had never known the Savior would not be likely to

WHAT DO YOU THINK?

Characterize the persons whose "god is their stomach." What do we see of ourselves in such a characterization?

Prayer

Thank you, our Father, for Jesus—"the way and the truth and the life." May we never lose sight of him as the goal worthy of all our striving. When we falter or fail, lift us, please, toward a better and more successful effort for his sake. In his name, amen.

Thought to Remember

"Run in such a way as to get the prize" (1 Corinthians 9:24).

exert much influence on the saints in Philippi, but the falling away of those once in Christ would bring the tearful agony here expressed.

In describing the guilty ones, Paul mentions the final *destiny* of their wickedness—*destruction*. Paul also describes the lifestyle that leads these individuals to ruin. They give priority to physical appetites, disregarding exhortations to self-discipline. Thus *their god is their stomach*. Their sense of values becomes distorted: *their glory is in their shame*. They brag about actions of which they ought to be ashamed. The Christian belongs to a better company and has a better influence to cultivate!

C. Live in Hope (vv. 20, 21)

20. But our citizenship is in heaven. And we eagerly await a Savior from there, the Lord Jesus Christ.

In contrast with the earthbound enemies of the cross, *our* (the construction is emphatic) vital ties are elsewhere—*in heaven*. The issue of *citizenship* would have been very important to the Philippians, whose city was recognized as a Roman colony and whose people were citizens of Rome. They lived in the province of Macedonia, but their loyalty and their security were closely tied to a city that was some distance away.

In the same way, Christians live *in* the world and are involved *with* it; yet they are not *of* it. Their real home is far away. They must guard against becoming naturalized worldlings, giving this temporary residence top priority.

21. . . . who, by the power that enables him to bring everything under his control, will transform our lowly bodies so that they will be like his glorious body.

Most of the miracles worked by our Lord during his earthly ministry dealt with the diseased, disabled, and even dead bodies of persons whom he restored to health and activity. All who saw his healings were amazed at his *power*. The results, however, were limited. The healed ones grew old, or became ill, and died in due time.

Immeasurably greater power will be seen when Jesus comes in glory and changes the *bodies* of all the saints to be *like his* own *glorious* spiritual *body* (1 Corinthians 15:42-53; 1 John 3:2). The physical body is called *lowly* not in the sense of being unimportant or worthless, but in contrast with the glory of Christ's body.

The miracle of conversion is seen in the spiritual change that occurs when a person is transformed from sinner to saint (Romans 6:1-11). The miracle of resurrection will be seen when the saint's physical body is transformed into one that is, like the Lord's, imperishable and immortal (1 Corinthians 15:51-54). It is a goal worthy of our utmost attention!

CONCLUSION

Where, we may ask, is a race in which one participant may enjoy the "thrill of victory" without causing others to experience "the agony of defeat"? The answer is easy. The win-win outcome is most natural among those in Christ who are determined to "press on toward the goal" as Paul did.

This is especially clear in Paul's final letter to Timothy. He had fought the good fight against the powers of darkness. He had finished the race. He was ready to receive the winner's crown, which the righteous Judge will bestow, "not only to me, but also to all who have longed for his appearing" (2 Timothy 4:7, 8). We sense that Paul's victory would be enhanced by the presence of every one whom he had helped over the finish line. There is room in the "winners' circle" for all we can bring with us!

Discovery Learning

This page contains an alternate lesson plan emphasizing learning activities. Classes desiring such student involvement will find these suggestions helpful. The next page is a reproducible activity page to further enhance discovery learning.

LEARNING GOALS

After this lesson each student will be able to:

1. Describe the attitude, actions, and goal that, according to Paul, are part of "pressing on in Christ."

2. List some personal possessions or activities that he or she considers expendable in his or her own discipleship.

3. Evaluate his or her life to determine whether there is any part that needs to be "considered as loss" for the sake of knowing Christ better.

INTO THE LESSON

Ask each class member to identify one or two goals he or she is working toward at the present time. Students may suggest short-range or long-range goals. The goals may involve learning new skills, perfecting some they already know, correcting disorders—any goals they may be trying to accomplish. Ask for volunteers to relate their goal(s) to the rest of the class.

Conclude this sharing time by telling the class that goal-setting is an everyday part of life. Sometimes goals are accomplished quickly. Some goals take much longer. It is important that every person determine the ultimate goal or purpose of his or her life. However, sometimes that is very difficult to do. Today's study will help you determine life's goal and how to accomplish that goal.

INTO THE WORD

Distribute copies of the reproducible page that follows. Give the students about five minutes to examine the text and to fill in the blanks on the page. Then follow the directions given below labeled "Review."

Option: Prepare a study guide to be distributed to each class member. The study guide should have the following information: A heading should read "Determining and Accomplishing Life's Ultimate Goal." Print the Scripture reference (Philippians 3:7-21) under the heading. Print these three sub-headings and references evenly spaced down the left-hand side of the page: *The Goal Is Christ* (Philippians 3:7-11), *Pressing Toward the Goal* (Philippians 3:12-16), and *Choosing Friends and Examples* (Philippians 3:17-21). At the bottom of the page, print the words, "My life's goal is. . . ."

Ask the class to work in groups of three persons. Each group should read the entire text together. Then ask the groups to go back and re-read each passage listed down the left-hand side of the page. Their first task is to summarize the primary thought of each section in one sentence and write it in the space provided. After they have accomplished that task, ask several of the groups to read their summary sentences.

Review: Whether you used the reproducible page or made the alternate handout, follow the directions below to review the passage.

Discuss these questions:

1. What were some of the things Paul considered as "loss" for Christ? (vv. 7, 8).

2. Paul's goal was to know Christ (v. 10). What did he mean when he said he wanted to become "like him in his death"? Then, using the lesson commentary and Romans 3:21-26, emphasize that it is impossible to become acceptable with God through the law. Righteousness comes from God through Jesus Christ.

Display the words of verse 12 on a poster or a projected transparency. Using your lesson commentary, prepare a brief lecture about the colorful language and significance of verses 12-16.

Use these questions to stimulate discussion on the conclusion of the passage:

1. Why do you think it is so important to identify good examples in determining our life's goal?

2. Would you consider Heaven our goal or our reward for knowing Christ (v. 20)? Why?

INTO LIFE

Ask each class member to complete this sentence: "My life's goal is. . . ." (If you used the alternate handout, note this activity at the bottom.)

The next two activities can be facilitated with the reproducible activity "Gaining Christ" on page 368. Remind the students that Paul had decided his credentials were nothing but rubbish compared with knowing Christ. Ask the students to list a few of their credentials that they would consider rubbish compared with knowing Christ. Cite examples: lots of money, Christian parents, position in the community, etc.

Finally, call the class's attention to the words "take note" in verse 17. Ask them to list one or two persons they know who would serve as good models for their lives in following Christ.

Ask the groups to pray for each other's progress in pursuing life's ultimate goal.

Looking Toward Heavenly _ _ _ _ z _ _ _ _ _ _!

Read Philippians 3:7-21. Find words in this passage to fill in the blanks of each of these statements or phrases.

The surpassing greatness of knowing _ _ _ _ _ _. (v. 8)

I have lost all _ _ _ _ _ _. (v. 8)

The _ _ _ _ _ _ _ _ _ _ _ _ _ that comes from God. (v. 9)

Our lowly bodies . . . will be like his _ _ _ _ _ _ _ _ body. (v. 21)

Join with others in following my _ _ _ _ _ _ _ _. (v. 17)

The fellowship of sharing in his _ _ _ _ _ _ _ _ _ _ _. (v. 10)

Whatever was to my profit I now consider _ _ _ _. (v. 8)

Righteousness . . . is by _ _ _ _ _. (v. 9)

Forgetting what is _ _ _ _ _ _. (v. 13)

Live according to the _ _ _ _ _ _ _ _. (v. 17)

Use the ten underlined letters in your responses to complete the heading for this page.

Gaining Christ

Paul reviews his credentials in Philippians 3:4-6. He says, however, that he considers them "a loss compared to . . . knowing Christ Jesus" (v. 8). What are some of your "credentials" you would consider a loss compared to knowing Jesus?

Paul encourages readers to "take note of those who live according to the pattern we gave you" (v. 17). Name some of your acquaintances you would consider a good example in following Jesus.

REJOICING IN CHRIST

LESSON 4

WHY TEACH THIS LESSON?

Henry Ford reportedly said a customer could buy any color "Model T" that he wanted—as long as he wanted black! Paul implies a similar promise in today's text. We can have everything we need to make us content, as long as we're content with what we need! Too often we confuse wants and needs. We think we "need" something that we do not have, and that we would be content if we had it. It is only when we learn to trust God so completely that we believe his promise to supply all our needs that we will find true contentment. This lesson should be a start to finding that kind of trust.

INTRODUCTION

A. SHAKESPEARE'S RECOVERY SONG

One of William Shakespeare's more familiar sonnets tells of the poet's notable recovery from a spell of the "blues." It begins on a low, low note:

When, in disgrace with fortune and men's eyes,
I all alone beweep my outcast state
And trouble deaf heaven with my bootless cries
And look upon myself and curse my fate. . . .

You may have been there, and you probably came out of it. How? Shakespeare thought of a good and generous friend:

Yet in these thoughts myself almost despising
Haply I think on thee, and then my state,
Like to the lark at break of day arising
From sullen earth, sings hymns at heaven's gate;
For thy sweet love remember'd such wealth brings
That then I scorn to change my state with kings.

The pits of a Shakespeare-like depression could be avoided entirely if, like the apostle Paul, one would spend the dark hours with Christ, the best of all friends, and so discover that the "break of day" he provides is the best of all times for pure rejoicing. That discovery is the focus of today's study.

B. LESSON BACKGROUND

From beginning to end, both Paul's experience in the city of Philippi and his Philippian letter are characterized by a theme of rejoicing in the face of difficulties. Among the highlights of the apostle's ministry in Philippi is the occasion when he and Silas sang praises to God at midnight in a prison—and afterward baptized the jailer and his household as believers in Jesus (Acts 16:25-34).

Approximately ten years later we find Paul again in prison, this time at Rome, and writing to the Philippians to encourage them in their own difficulties. Each chapter in Philippians begins with an encouragement to joy and rejoicing. Paul prayed with *joy* for the Philippian saints and their faithful "partnership in the

DEVOTIONAL READING:
1 THESSALONIANS 1:2-10
BACKGROUND SCRIPTURE:
PHILIPPIANS 4:4-20
PRINTED TEXT:
PHILIPPIANS 4:4-19

Jun
25

LESSON AIMS

As a result of studying this lesson, each student will be able to:

1. Describe the joy and contentment that Paul both urged and modeled for the Philippians.

2. Tell what makes Christian joy different from the surface happiness that the world promises and promotes.

3. Express appreciation to one who has helped him or her or has been an encouragement through example.

KEY VERSE

Rejoice in the Lord always. I will say it again: Rejoice!
—Philippians 4:4

LESSON 4 NOTES

gospel" (1:3-5). He pleaded for their unity so that his *joy* might be complete (2:2). He confessed to being repetitious in exhorting them to *"rejoice* in the Lord" (3:1). He insisted that they do so always (4:4).

There were, however, occasional interruptions to the joyous mood. Some brethren were preaching the gospel with motives that were less than ideal (1:15-18). Warnings not to engage in "complaining or arguing" were necessary (2:14). Self-seeking "enemies of the cross" persisted in their opposition (3:18, 19). And Euodias and Syntyche still needed help to overcome their differences (4:2, 3). None of these difficulties, however, must be allowed to stifle the saints' rejoicing in the Lord—always!

I. CONSTANT REJOICING (PHILIPPIANS 4:4-7)

A. GOD'S PRESENCE (vv. 4, 5)

4. Rejoice in the Lord always. I will say it again: Rejoice!

Rejoice is used to translate five different Greek words in the New Testament. The word found here appears in some form in approximately fifty passages, all of which are related to Christ or to the Christian's life in Christ.

Rejoice in the Lord always. Continual rejoicing requires a constant, steadfast basis. We find that constancy only in God, of whom we sing, "Thou changest not, Thy compassions, they fail not; As Thou hast been Thou forever wilt be."

That basis for rejoicing is most evident when circumstances seem to undermine any reason to rejoice. Recall Jesus' words: "Blessed are you when people insult you, persecute you and falsely say all kinds of evil against you because of me. Rejoice and be glad, because great is your reward in heaven" (Matthew 5:11, 12). The Christian's joy in Jesus is always "in season," whatever national, international, or personal conditions may be.

I will say it again: Rejoice! Paul has said it before (3:1), and, like any effective teacher, he will say it again and again!

5. Let your gentleness be evident to all. The Lord is near.

Gentleness reflects the divine nature described in Psalm 103:8: "The Lord is compassionate and gracious, slow to anger, abounding in love." He who constantly rejoices in the Lord will not respond angrily in word or deed to small vexations. He can answer a scowl with a smile and an insult with a favor, because he knows that the Lord is constantly present to provide patience and to dispense in his own time whatever judgment is appropriate.

B. PRAYER AND PEACE (vv. 6, 7)

6. Do not be anxious about anything, but in everything, by prayer and petition, with thanksgiving, present your requests to God.

"The Lord is near" (v. 5) to prevent the killjoy attitudes of worry, anxiety, or perplexity that haunt persons who do not acknowledge his presence. The phrase *do not be anxious about anything* simply means, "Don't worry." It echoes the themes of part of Jesus' Sermon on the Mount (Matthew 6:25-34). Many medical caregivers testify that prayer helps in the treatment of their patients; but prayer loses something of its value if it is used for anything other than communication between a child of God and the loving heavenly Father.

Our text provides a well-balanced menu for *prayer.* Along with general communication it includes *petition* and *thanksgiving.* A petition recognizes dependence on God for all we really need—in both the material and spiritual realms. Thanksgiving brings a smile of remembrance in recalling countless blessings already received in answer to requests made (and sometimes without any requests made!). It discovers joy and covers disappointment. It is an exercise in continual rejoicing!

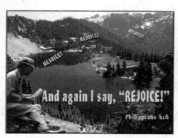

Today's visual suggests that our rejoicing should continually "echo" throughout our lives. Post it before you begin the lesson.

WHAT DO YOU THINK?

Worry and anxiety are characteristic of the modern culture. Why is that true? Why is such a mind-set antithetical to Christian living?

7. And the peace of God, which transcends all understanding, will guard your hearts and your minds in Christ Jesus.

Peace suggests a wholeness and serenity of spirit very different from the pulled-apart feeling of anxiety. Anything laid before the Lord in honest prayer is on the way to a solution. Because the Lord is "able to do immeasurably more than all we ask or imagine" (Ephesians 3:20), the resultant tranquillity indeed *transcends all understanding.* Its source, however, is clear; it comes through *Christ Jesus.* This is a peace, "not . . . as the world gives" (John 14:27). It is Christ's answer to the trouble and fear that one encounters in the world (John 16:33).

The Greek word translated *guard* refers to the protection of a security guard standing at a door. The mind thus protected will scarcely be invaded by such intruders as bitterness, depression, or anxiety. Like the joy highlighted earlier, Heaven's peace abides within the Christian regardless of his surroundings.

II. CLEAR THINKING (PHILIPPIANS 4:8, 9)

To be kept from invasion by negative forces, the mind needs nourishment from positive sources.

A. UPBEAT THOUGHTS (v. 8)

8. Finally, brothers, whatever is true, whatever is noble, whatever is right, whatever is pure, whatever is lovely, whatever is admirable—if anything is excellent or praiseworthy—think about such things.

Finally: Paul offers one more series of exhortations before expressing his gratitude for the recent gift sent to him by the Philippians. He has written about Christians' attitudes; he turns now to the mental diet that feeds those attitudes. What are Christians to look at, listen to, think about, or discuss? Even in a wicked world filled with "junk food" for the mind, some constructive subject matter is available.

Paul names eight qualities of a good mental diet, and all of them are associated with God. The list falls naturally into four pairs: *true* and *noble, right* and *pure, lovely* and *admirable,* and *excellent* and *praiseworthy.* The first two describe what is upright and dependable, despising deceitfulness in all its forms. The second pair describes what is incorruptible and undefiled; it is not tainted by a sinful world. The third pair describes what is seen and known to be above reproach; it is both pleasant and wholesome. The fourth pair describes what is most respectable and respected—of highest quality and known to be so.

One adjective describes all these subjects recommended for consideration: *Christlike!* "Turn your eyes [and your mind] upon Jesus." Fix and hold your attention on *such things,* and you will never lack for reasons to smile! Neither will you lack for material to occupy conversations and to form plans, imaginations, and actions that will please the God who has blessed you with a mind.

B. UPLIFTING EXAMPLE (v. 9)

9. Whatever you have learned or received or heard from me, or seen in me—put into practice. And the God of peace will be with you.

Paul did not ask his friends to act simply on the basis of abstract principles. He provided a "visual aid" to offer guidance where needed and to show that these principles really work. And that visual aid was Paul himself!

Christian truth is not something only for intellectual stimulation; one must *put into practice* what he has *learned.* Just as Paul's teaching would have been ineffective without the confirmation provided by his actions, so the Philippians' learning would have been empty without expression of the truth in their daily

WHAT DO YOU THINK?

Paul says we are to fill our minds with good and wholesome things (v. 8). How can we evaluate ourselves in this regard?

WHAT DO YOU THINK?

What are some of the things we have learned, received, heard, and seen that we have yet to put into practice?

How to Say It

Caesarea. Sess-uh-REE-uh.
Corinth. KOR-inth.
Corinthians. Kor-IN-thee-unz (th as in thin).
Epaphroditus. Ee-PAF-ro-DYE-tus.
Euodias. You-O-dee-us.
Macedonia. Mass-eh-DOE-nee-uh.
Philippi. Fih-LIP-pie or FIL-ih-pie.
Philippians. Fih-LIP-ee-unz.
Syntyche. SIN-tih-key.
Thessalonica. THESS-uh-lo-NYE-kuh (th as in thin).

behavior. With that combination of knowing and doing firmly in place, they could be sure that *the God of peace* would shelter them with his presence.

III. CONTENTMENT (PHILIPPIANS 4:10-13)

A. Renewed Care (v. 10)

10. I rejoice greatly in the Lord that at last you have renewed your concern for me. Indeed, you have been concerned, but you had no opportunity to show it.

Paul's own "rejoicing in the Lord always" had been encouraged by Epaphroditus's arrival from Philippi with gifts from the church. We may wonder why Paul waited until the conclusion of his letter to mention this. Perhaps he had sent a grateful acknowledgment earlier, possibly with the news of Epaphroditus's illness (Philippians 2:26).

Paul's rejoicing was not so much for the gift, however, as for the loving *concern* that prompted the giving. Some time had passed since the Philippians' last communication with Paul. He recognized this delay, not as a sign of their indifference, but as a reflection of circumstances. His imprisonment had placed certain restrictions on his ability to correspond with others and be contacted by them (thus one of the reasons for writing this letter). Recall that his Roman imprisonment was preceded by at least two years of imprisonment in Caesarea (Acts 24:27).

B. Satisfied Regardless (vv. 11, 12)

11. I am not saying this because I am in need, for I have learned to be content whatever the circumstances.

Paul wanted to make it clear that he was not expressing a *need* for more gifts. He had *learned* through a considerable amount of practice (read of his sufferings for Christ in 2 Corinthians 11:23-28) how to get along with much or with little. Thus he was indifferent to what most people consider important or necessary. He would have been embarrassed to have anyone think otherwise. Paul was always concerned that others' reception of the gospel would not be affected negatively by what might be interpreted as greed on his part (1 Thessalonians 2:5, 9).

The key word in this verse is *content*. It translates a Greek word that means "self-sufficient," in the sense that Paul needed no outward props to sustain his faith. In Christ he possessed an inner strength that erased any dependence on external help. His sense of self-worth and well-being did not depend on the state of his outward *circumstances*. He could deal with companionship or solitude, popularity or rejection, comfort or pain, good health or illness. Have we *learned* to live in that same contentment?

To Be Content

Many people have been caught up in the craze known as "lottery fever" and have spent huge (and unnecessary) amounts of money in trying to find a cure. However, a Kentucky newspaper reporter found some people who were not at all swept up in the enthusiasm. The reporter interviewed one lady who claimed that all that money could be more trouble than it's really worth. "Look at all the wealthy people who are still unhappy." Later the reporter talked with a man who said, "Frankly, what am I supposed to do with all those millions of dollars? I can't think of anything else I really need. I'm content."

Obviously this reporter had talked to two very astute people. It simply doesn't matter how much you have if you are discontented. And it doesn't matter how little you have if you are contented. Note that Paul said that he had *learned* to be content. It was not something that came naturally to him. More than likely it does not come naturally to any of us. But we can learn contentment, and we can do so in the same way Paul learned it—by enrollment in the school of Christian living. Here one learns not only contentment, but a host of other virtues that make one "educated" in the subjects that matter most.   —R. C. S.

12. I know what it is to be in need, and I know what it is to have plenty. I have learned the secret of being content in any and every situation, whether well fed or hungry, whether living in plenty or in want.

To live one's life each day under conditions that seldom vary does not pose a formidable challenge to faith. However, to be able to adjust gracefully, as Paul did, to the roller-coaster experiences of poverty and *plenty*, hunger and feasting, and to do so in many locations and surroundings, requires a sense of true contentment.

This does not mean that Paul passively accepted the circumstances he faced. He prayed for relief from the "thorn in my flesh." But when he did not receive that for which he prayed, he thanked God for the grace to bear testimony to Christ's power in him (2 Corinthians 12:7-10). His contentment came from a source greater than his surroundings, as the next verse indicates.

C. CHRIST, THE SOURCE (v. 13)

13. I can do everything through him who gives me strength.

Paul's contentment, or self-sufficiency, was really Christ-sufficiency. While the word *Christ* does not appear in the Greek text of this verse, it is surely implied. Jesus supplied the *strength* that Paul needed to run the Christian race to its completion and receive the "crown of righteousness" (2 Timothy 4:8). At this point the strength he needed was the endurance to serve joyously in the circumstances he was now enduring. What a comfort to the apostle to know that his imprisonment could not shut out the companionship of Christ!

IV. CARING CHRISTIANS (PHILIPPIANS 4:14-19)

A. THE PHILIPPIANS' GIVING (vv. 14-16)

14. Yet it was good of you to share in my troubles.

Paul's comparative indifference to material things might make him seem ungrateful for his friends' generosity. That was not the case at all. The Philippians were aware of his *troubles*, living as a prisoner and probably on limited resources. Their gift made them participants in his ministry, and he sincerely appreciated such partnership.

15. Moreover, as you Philippians know, in the early days of your acquaintance with the gospel, when I set out from Macedonia, not one church shared with me in the matter of giving and receiving, except you only.

The close bond between Paul and the *Philippians* began when the apostle first entered what we know as the European continent. Philippi was the first city in that region to receive the *gospel*, and it was eager to join in Paul's ministry of taking the gospel to others. Paul cites the Philippians' "partnership in the gospel from the first day until now" (Philippians 1:5). They did not wait to receive letters of appeal from Paul or to see what other churches would do; on their own initiative they acted to participate in what Paul was doing. Theirs was the true joy of *giving*. It was a joy in which others could not share because they waited to be asked.

16. For even when I was in Thessalonica, you sent me aid again and again when I was in need.

Here Paul recalls the Philippians' assistance during his rather stormy experience at *Thessalonica*, which was also in Macedonia (Acts 17:1-9). It appears that they also provided similar assistance to Paul at Corinth; for later he wrote to the Corinthians, "When I was with you and needed something, I was not a burden

WHAT DO YOU THINK?

Some people think, "If I just had this, then I would be content." Probably not! What is keeping us from reaching Paul's state of contentment?

DAILY BIBLE READINGS

Monday, June 19—Rejoice and Be Gentle With One Another (Philippians 4:2-7)

Tuesday, June 20—Keep On Keeping On in Christ (Philippians 4:8-14)

Wednesday, June 21—Paul's Thanks for the Philippian Church (Philippians 4:15-23)

Thursday, June 22—Life Among the Early Believers (Acts 2:42-47)

Friday, June 23—Paul's Thanks for the Thessalonian Church (1 Thessalonians 1:1-10)

Saturday, June 24—Lives Pleasing to God (1 Thessalonians 4:1-12)

Sunday, June 25—Faithfulness Brings Great Joy (3 John 1-8)

PRAYER

Some of childhood's joys are no longer with me, Lord; so give me grace to appreciate the richer gifts of a growing faith. And when I no longer have some strengths I now enjoy, give me grace to enjoy the riper pleasures and greater expectations I then shall have in Christ my Lord. Amen.

to anyone, for the brothers who came from Macedonia supplied what I needed" (2 Corinthians 11:9).

B. PAUL'S PRIORITIES (vv. 17, 18)

17. Not that I am looking for a gift, but I am looking for what may be credited to your account.

Paul was bold in urging liberality toward others who were in need (2 Corinthians 8, 9), but would never request, or even suggest, that any kind of *gift* be given to him. "What I want is not your possessions but you," he insisted (2 Corinthians 12:14).

Paul did, however, rejoice in the blessing that came to his friends from their faithful giving. Here he uses an interesting commercial term in expressing his pleasure at seeing "credits" added to the Philippians' *account.* They were laying up treasures in Heaven, which would never be lost nor depleted (Matthew 6:19-21). In that Paul openly rejoiced.

18. I have received full payment and even more; I am amply supplied, now that I have received from Epaphroditus the gifts you sent. They are a fragrant offering, an acceptable sacrifice, pleasing to God.

Paul had been "paid in *full*" and had all that he needed. *Epaphroditus* apparently brought *gifts* of more than one kind (perhaps money and warm clothing). Here Paul referred to them in terms like those used to describe Old Testament sacrifices: *a fragrant offering, an acceptable sacrifice, pleasing to God* (cf. Exodus 29:18; Leviticus 1:9, 13, 17; 2:2). Sheer generosity creates its own pleasant aroma.

C. GOD'S PROVISION (v. 19)

19. And my God will meet all your needs according to his glorious riches in Christ Jesus.

God had provided through Paul a dramatic demonstration of Jesus' promise concerning life's necessities: "Seek first his kingdom and his righteousness, and all these things will be given to you as well" (Matthew 6:33). The apostle was convinced that the saints in Philippi had set these same priorities and could claim the same provision.

God's provision in Christ, however, goes far beyond material *needs*. It includes all the glories of living daily *in Christ Jesus* and the indescribable glories of his presence in eternity. Such *riches* come in their own unique and dependable "currency." They are not subject to the woes that befall worldly wealth, for they are the riches of Heaven!

CONCLUSION

You may have heard of Pollyanna, the young minister's daughter who could find, or make, something to be glad about in whatever happened. Pollyanna's optimism was more respected in 1913, when her story was published, than it has been in more recent (and more cynical) times. Her perspective has been dubbed "vapid sentimentality" or "head-in-the-sand idealism" by those who prefer to look on the darker side of things.

The "glad" approach did not begin with Pollyanna, though, nor with Eleanor Hodgman Porter, who wrote her story. It is at least as old as the apostle Paul and the Christ-centered optimism that led him to say, "I have learned to be content whatever the circumstances," and to advise, "Rejoice in the Lord always."

It takes considerable courage in this present world to promote this "Paulyanna" brand of optimism. Such courage, as well as the joy that accompanies it, comes with a stubborn faith in the Son of God.

WHAT DO YOU THINK?

The world constantly urges us to provide for ourselves all that money can buy—even if on credit. If we can't afford it, we can finance it. If the bank won't lend us the money, there are places that are more "creative" with their financing. How well do most Christians demonstrate that they believe the truth Paul states: "My God will meet all your needs according to his glorious riches in Christ Jesus"? How can we live with greater confidence in this truth?

THOUGHT TO REMEMBER

Our grounds for rejoicing are as constant as the love of God.

Discovery Learning

This page contains an alternate lesson plan emphasizing learning activities. Classes desiring such student involvement will find these suggestions helpful. The next page is a reproducible activity page to further enhance discovery learning.

LEARNING GOALS

As a result of studying this lesson, each student will be able to:

1. Describe the joy and contentment that Paul both urged and modeled for the Philippians.

2. Tell what makes Christian joy different from the surface happiness that the world promises and promotes.

3. Express appreciation to one who has helped him or her or has been an encouragement through example.

INTO THE LESSON

Before class prepare and post a banner with the words, "Rejoice in the Lord always."

Begin this study by asking the class to sing the chorus, "Rejoice in the Lord Always." (A larger class can sing the song as a round.) Tell the class the words on the banner are the words in the key verse to today's study.

Ask two class members to be the scribes at chalkboards or posters. Ask class members to call out names of other choruses and hymns that indicate Christian joy and happiness. The hymnbooks and chorus books are filled with songs of joy, such as "The Joy of the Lord," "This Is the Day," "Let There Be Praise," "He Keeps Me Singing," "Sunshine in My Soul," and "O Happy Day."

After the exercise, ask the class what this long list of songs tells them about Christianity. The answer you are looking for is that one of the products of our faith is a deep sense of joy.

Option: Instead of having the members call out song or hymn titles, have them look for expressions of joy in the Psalms. Use the reproducible page that follows to facilitate the activity.

INTO THE WORD

This portion of the lesson will be done in two parts. For the first part of the Bible study, prepare handouts to be given each student and an identical large poster (or an overhead transparency) to use in this portion of the study. The heading to the posters and handouts should read "Tips for Peace and Joyful Living." Under the heading should be three columns. The smaller heading for column 1 should be "Do." The heading for column 2 should be "Do Not." Column 3's heading should read "Rewards." Ask a student to read Philippians 4:4-19. Then ask the class to scan the text looking for answers to write in the columns. As the students discover answers, write their responses on the large poster (transparency).

Do: rejoice in the Lord, v. 4; be gentle, v. 5; present your requests to God, v. 6; think on good things, v. 8; rejoice at benevolent care, v. 10; be content, v. 11; acknowledge blessings and gifts, vv. 14-17.

Do not: worry, v. 6.

Rewards: the peace of God, vv. 7, 9; I can do everything through him, v. 13; God will meet all your needs, v. 19.

Summarize this part of the study by observing that Paul has given us very helpful tips for joyful living. Tell the class that we will look more closely at this passage in two sections. The first section (vv. 4-9) will give us some tips for finding true joy and peace. The second section (vv. 10-19) will focus on Paul's example in learning contentment.

After re-reading vv. 4-9, use the following questions to lead a discussion:

• Why would Paul say, "I will say it *again*: Rejoice" (v. 4)?

• What makes Christian joy different from and deeper than other kinds of joy?

• What kind of peace is Paul talking about?

• What is the opposite of this kind of peace (v. 7)?

Prepare a short lecture on Paul's example and tips for finding contentment (vv. 10-19), using the lesson commentary. Remember, the lecture should be brief.

INTO LIFE

As you distribute envelopes to the students, point out that Paul says he has found joy in persons who have encouraged him. This Philippian letter expresses his gratitude for such acts. He thanks his friends for their financial help during times of trouble. Tell the class of someone who, down through the years, has been a Christian encouragement to you and brought joy to your life.

Ask each student to identify someone who has done that for him or her. Have the students write those names on their envelopes and then take the envelopes home and write letters to the ones they identified, expressing gratitude and joy for sharing in their lives.

Give the students copies of Philippians 4:4-7 and ask them to memorize this text. Make the arrangements to have a "Scripture choir" in a worship service in the near future. The Scripture recitation can become the core of a song service built around Christian joy.

Joyful Songs From the Psalmist's Heart

We are so fortunate to have God as our source of joy. Many of the Psalms are songs of joy—often intended to be used in worship. Read the references from the Psalms listed below and make a brief note about the significance of joy in each reference.

Psalm 21:6 _____

Psalm 66:1 _____

Psalm 30:11 _____

Psalm 96:12 _____

Psalm 43:4 _____

Psalm 107:22 _____

Psalm 51:12 _____

Psalm 119:111 _____

A Joyful Song From My Heart

This is your chance to be a songwriter. We need some new stanzas to the popular song, "Jesus Loves Me." Using the ideas from today's text, write one or two stanzas that express your joy and faith in Christ. The first words of the song should be "Jesus Loves Me. . . ."

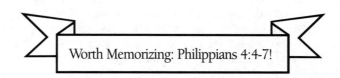

Worth Memorizing: Philippians 4:4-7!

CALLED TO SPIRITUAL BLESSINGS IN CHRIST

LESSON 5

WHY TEACH THIS LESSON?

"Gobbledygook." My freshman English students couldn't believe I was asking them to learn how to spell it. They couldn't imagine ever needing to use it. I think some of them did not even believe it was a real word! But it was there in their vocabulary book, and it is in the dictionary: "wordy and generally unintelligible jargon."

That is just what many unbelievers think about "church talk." There are certain words that Christians like to use but that unbelievers find to be "unintelligible jargon"—gobbledygook! Among these are sanctification, justification, predestination, redemption, reconciliation. And—truth be told—many Christians are not entirely sure about the meaning of some of them!

Ephesians seems to have a lot of these words. In today's lesson, and in the lessons you will study throughout this month, you will be able to clear up some of the gobbledygook that has been mucking up your students' faith. With an improved understanding, it is hoped, they will be able to live it and articulate it more clearly.

INTRODUCTION

A. THREE CHEERS FOR GOD!

Have you ever become so excited about something that you started talking and couldn't stop—you just talked and talked without "coming up for air"? It takes an extraordinary event to generate that degree of excitement.

The first few verses of Paul's letter to the Ephesians comprise just such an outburst. Language scholars have criticized the style, but no one can criticize the sentiment. What is it that gets Paul so excited? It is his realization of the many wonderful blessings that God has given all Christians.

If we do get as excited as Paul, it is rarely over spiritual blessings; yet these are the very topics that ought to thrill us most. The blessings and benefits we receive from God are exhilarating. That is the reason Paul begins his letter to the Ephesians by saying, in effect, "Three Cheers for God!"

B. LESSON BACKGROUND

The book of Ephesians is thought by many Bible students to have been a circular letter—that is, that it was addressed to a group of churches rather than to one specific congregation. Two reasons are often cited for this conclusion. The first is the lack of personal information and references included in the letter. Paul was closely associated with the Ephesian church—he spent three years in Ephesus (Acts 20:31)—yet this letter does not contain the kind of warm, personal language that one would expect to see.

The second piece of evidence for believing that Ephesians was a circular letter is that the earliest copies of the book do not have the words "in Ephesus" in the

DEVOTIONAL READING:
ROMANS 1:8-17
BACKGROUND SCRIPTURE:
EPHESIANS 1
PRINTED TEXT:
EPHESIANS 1:1-14

Jul
2

LESSON AIMS

After this lesson each student will be able to:

1. Summarize the "spiritual blessings" that Christians possess.

2. Tell how a knowledge of these blessings will affect their walk with Christ and witness to the world.

3. Write or say a prayer of thanksgiving for the spiritual blessings he or she has received in Christ.

KEY VERSE

Praise be to the God and Father of our Lord Jesus Christ, who has blessed us in the heavenly realms with every spiritual blessing in Christ.
—*Ephesians 1:3*

LESSON 5 NOTES

opening verse. Why, then, did the letter come to be called the book of Ephesians? The church in Ephesus may have been the largest one or most prominent among the group of churches to which the letter was sent. Perhaps it was the church that took custody of the letter.

On the other hand, the letter is not completely without personal language. Paul mentions his prayers for the recipients (1:15-23; 3:14-19) and asks for theirs (6:18-20). He also notes that Tychicus would bring them personal information about him (6:21, 22). And, of course, we do not have the original copy of the letter, so we do not know whether the words "in Ephesus" were part of the original or not. Nor were the words necessary since the letter was probably carried directly to its destination(s) by Tychicus, one of Paul's friends (Ephesians 6:21). It did not have to be "addressed" like a modern letter sent by the post office.

The idea of a circular letter is not foreign to the New Testament. Paul told the Colossians, "After this letter has been read to you, see that it is also read in the church of the Laodiceans and that you in turn read the letter from Laodicea" (Colossians 4:16). Note, however, that both Colossians and "the letter from Laodicea" seem to have been intended for a particular church first and for circulation second. If Ephesians was a circular letter, it was probably delivered to the Ephesians first and then circulated as much as was feasible. (In fact, there are some scholars who believe the letter to the Ephesians was "the letter from Laodicea" that Paul mentioned in Colossians 4:16.)

Ephesus was a thriving and fairly modern city when Paul was there. (Its ruins are still being studied by archaeologists.) Paul's first recorded visit occurred at the conclusion of his second missionary journey, but the visit was brief (Acts 18:19-21). It was not until the third missionary journey that Paul spent any significant time in the city.

One of the most outstanding features in Ephesus was the temple dedicated to the Greek goddess Artemis (also known by her Roman name Diana), considered one of the seven wonders of the ancient world. Silversmiths established a lucrative business in making and selling silver images of Artemis. Paul's success in converting people to Christianity became the source of great concern to these silversmiths, who sparked a riot in the city by stirring up the Ephesians' pride in their temple and the goddess who was worshiped there (Acts 19:23-41).

Ephesians, Philippians, Colossians, and Philemon are usually called Paul's prison epistles. What is perhaps most striking about these four letters is Paul's positive attitude in all of them. (We have already noted the theme of joy that characterizes Philippians.) It is surely an insight into the apostle's relationship with Christ that he could maintain such a vibrant faith while in prison. Paul himself may have been in bonds, but his spirit was always free—with the freedom that only Jesus can give.

I. GOD'S GRACIOUS CHOICE (EPHESIANS 1:1-6)

While words like *chosen*, *election*, and *predestination* have fueled many a theological debate, we cannot ignore them. As difficult as these issues may be to grasp, we must give attention to them and seek to examine them from a biblical perspective.

A. CHOSEN FOR A PURPOSE (vv. 1-4)

1, 2. Paul, an apostle of Christ Jesus by the will of God,
    To the saints in Ephesus, the faithful in Christ Jesus:
    Grace and peace to you from God our Father and the Lord Jesus Christ.

HOW TO SAY IT

Abraham. AY-bruh-ham.
Antioch. AN-tee-ock.
Artemis. AR-teh-miss.
Colossians. Kuh-LOSH-unz.
Ephesians. Ee-FEE-zhunz.
Ephesus. EF-uh-sus.
Ezekiel. Ee-ZEEK-yul or
    Ee-ZEEK-ee-ul.
Laodicea. Lay-ODD-uh-SEE-uh.
Laodiceans. Lay-ODD-uh-SEE-unz.
Philemon. Fih-LEE-mun or Fye-
    LEE-mun.
Philippians. Fih-LIP-ee-unz.
predestination. pree-DESS-tin-
    AY-shun.
Tychicus. TICK-ih-cuss.

As with most letters in the Greco-Roman world, this one begins with the writer's identifying himself. *Paul describes himself* (as he often does in his letters) as *an apostle of Christ Jesus.* He addresses his letter *to the saints.* The world generally considers *saints* to be special people who belong to an elite class of super-spirituality. But the word *saints* simply means "holy ones" or "separated ones," which is a characteristic of all Christians.

Paul also uses his typical greeting of *grace and peace.* Since *grace* was the typical Greek greeting and *peace* was the typical Jewish greeting, the use of both terms together was particularly significant in this letter, which emphasizes the oneness of Jew and Gentile in Christ (Ephesians 2:11-22).

3. Praise be to the God and Father of our Lord Jesus Christ, who has blessed us in the heavenly realms with every spiritual blessing in Christ.

Paul describes the blessings Christians have received as being *in the heavenly realms,* or, literally, "in the heavenlies." This is a phrase unique to Ephesians, appearing four other times in this book besides here (1:20; 2:6; 3:10; 6:12). It is instructive to note the use of the term in these passages. According to 1:20, 21, Christ is now at God's right hand *"in the heavenly realms,* far above all rule and authority, power and dominion." Ephesians 2:6 says that Christians are privileged to be "seated . . . *in the heavenly realms* in Christ Jesus." The reference in 6:12 says that the "struggle" of Christians is "against the spiritual forces of evil *in the heavenly realms.*"

These passages emphasize that the victory gained by Jesus through his resurrection is one that he shares with his followers. We are reminded that our true home is in Heaven (Philippians 3:20) and that we have a taste of that now by being "in the heavenlies" with Jesus.

4. For he chose us in him before the creation of the world to be holy and blameless in his sight. In love . . .

This verse takes us into controversial territory. Theologians have long debated the issues of predestination and free will. Is this verse saying that God chooses who will be saved? If so, how does this fit with Scriptures indicating that God desires that all be saved (1 Timothy 2:4) and that man has the freedom to choose whether or not to accept God's salvation (John 3:16; Revelation 22:17)? How do we reconcile the sovereignty of God with man's free will?

Some believe that *chose* means that God has chosen (or elected) certain individuals to believe in Jesus Christ and be saved, while the rest of mankind (everyone not chosen) is condemned and lost forever. Many people, however, wonder how this position can be held in light of those Scriptures that call individuals to choose to obey God (Deuteronomy 30:19; Revelation 22:17) and that indicate that God does not want any individual to perish (Ezekiel 18:32; 2 Peter 3:9).

One way of understanding the doctrine of election is to see the choice as corporate; that is, it describes God's dealings with a group rather than with individuals. Thus, when Paul says, *"He chose us in him before the creation of the world,"* he may be talking about the church. Just as Israel had been God's chosen people under the Old Covenant, so the church has become God's chosen people under the New Covenant.

At the same time, some Scriptures indicate that election has an individual nature as well as corporate. Peter writes to Christians whom he calls "chosen according to the foreknowledge of God the Father" (1 Peter 1:2). This passage tells us that election occurs according to God's foreknowledge. This means that God chooses or elects certain individuals to be saved and to enjoy the blessings of salvation on the basis of his advance knowledge of the choice they will make concerning Jesus Christ. Thus, God does not cause some to be saved and some to be

WHAT DO YOU THINK?

God's having "blessed us in the heavenly realms with every spiritual blessing in Christ" certainly includes the blessing of salvation. What are some other blessings included in "every spiritual blessing in Christ"?

The large letters on today's visual spell the word Blessings. Ask the class what blessings Paul describes in our text; then compare the small background words to see which ones match the class's list.

THOUGHT TO REMEMBER

Don't be afraid to raise a phrase of praise.

lost, but rather he knows in advance who will accept his gracious offer of salvation. And "those God foreknew he also predestined to be conformed to the likeness of his Son. . . . And those he predestined, he also called" (Romans 8:29, 30).

Note also the purpose of this election: *to be holy and blameless in his sight*—or, as Paul told the Romans, "to be conformed to the likeness of his Son." As God's people *in Christ,* we are to be holy (or, be "saints," see v. 1) and blameless, just as Christ was while he walked on this earth. And someday, we will be just as he is in glory (1 John 3:2).

B. ADDED TO A FAMILY (vv. 5, 6)

5, 6. . . . he predestined us to be adopted as his sons through Jesus Christ, in accordance with his pleasure and will—to the praise of his glorious grace, which he has freely given us in the One he loves.

Part of God's eternal plan is that we who accept his *grace* become his *sons.* Paul is the only New Testament writer to use the metaphor of being *adopted,* though the concept is consistent with other New Testament images (see, for example, John 1:12).

All of this is pleasing to God and is *to the praise of his glorious grace* (words similar to these are also found in verses 12 and 14). The salvation of lost individuals delights God and causes people to give him glory.

II. GOD'S GRACIOUS SACRIFICE (EPHESIANS 1:7, 8)

A. PROVIDING FORGIVENESS (v. 7)

7. In him we have redemption through his blood, the forgiveness of sins, in accordance with the riches of God's grace.

Sin exacts a terrible price; thus the plan to save mankind from it was not without a staggering cost. The word *redemption* is a word that signifies the freeing of a slave by payment of a price. The picture is clear: God saw us on the auction block, as it were, and as slaves to sin. He was willing to pay the redemption price—the *blood* of his only Son—to set us free.

God's blessings are granted *in accordance with the riches of God's grace.* Too many see God as someone who enjoys dispensing his justice but is stingy with his grace. That is not at all the picture the Bible gives us. In Ephesians, Paul refers six times to the richness of what God has done for us (here; 1:18; 2:4, 7; 3:8, 16).

THE ALTAR OF FORGIVENESS

If you ever visit the renowned cathedral in downtown Mexico City, you will see a magnificent altar known as the Altar of Forgiveness. An interesting story lies behind its construction. A young artist was accused of a capital crime and sentenced to a year in prison, after which he was to be executed. While in prison he painted such a touching and inspiring picture that he was pardoned and set free. Eventually this painting became the central feature of a majestic golden altar that was placed in the cathedral in Mexico City.

Some years ago fire destroyed much of the inside of the cathedral. When officials surveyed the ruins to determine the cause of the fire, they discovered a short circuit in the electrical system. That short circuit was in, of all places, the Altar of Forgiveness!

We need not worry that the true Altar of Forgiveness will ever experience a short circuit—for that Altar is the cross of Jesus Christ. On the cross Jesus died and offered himself as the sacrifice that made forgiveness of sins possible for us all. He is the only person who can provide this forgiveness, and his cross is the only place

DAILY BIBLE READINGS

Monday, June 26—God Has Blessed Us in Christ (Ephesians 1:1-6)

Tuesday, June 27—God's Grace Lavished on Us in Christ (Ephesians 1:7-14)

Wednesday, June 28—Paul's Prayer for the Ephesian Christians (Ephesians 1:15-23)

Thursday, June 29—Called to Belong to Jesus Christ (Romans 1:1-7)

Friday, June 30—The Gospel: God's Power for Salvation (Romans 1:8-17)

Saturday, July 1—Bear the Fruit of the Spirit (Galatians 5:16-26)

Sunday, July 2—Bear One Another's Burdens (Galatians 6:1-10)

where it can be found. There will never be a short circuit in this altar. The "riches of God's grace" found there will never be depleted.   —R. C. S.

B. PROVIDING IN ABUNDANCE (v. 8)

8. . . . that he lavished on us with all wisdom and understanding.

Among God's other blessings, we also receive both *wisdom and understanding.* There is only a shade of difference in the meaning of these two words. We might interpret them as telling us that God has blessed us with the ability to see situations as they are and the ability to know what to do about them.

III. GOD'S GRACIOUS MESSAGE (EPHESIANS 1:9, 10)

A. ONCE HIDDEN (v. 9)

9. And he made known to us the mystery of his will according to his good pleasure, which he purposed in Christ.

Paul says that God has *made known to us* what was once a *mystery.* We think of a mystery as something that we need to figure out, such as the identity of the guilty party in a mystery novel. With Paul, however, the word describes something once unknown that has now been revealed by God. Since his *good pleasure* and purposes are involved, the mystery encompasses something that it was not possible for us to reason out for ourselves. God had to reveal the answer.

B. NOW REVEALED (v. 10)

10. . . . to be put into effect when the times will have reached their fulfillment— to bring all things in heaven and on earth together under one head, even Christ.

As part of God's "good pleasure," Paul says that in the end (*when the times will have reached their fulfillment*) God will *bring all things in heaven and on earth together under one head, even Christ.* The Greek word translated *bring . . . together under one* is a mathematical term and describes the way that numbers were totaled in New Testament times. Whenever a column of figures was added, the total was placed at the top (not at the bottom as most of us are accustomed to doing). Paul is saying that at the end, everything will "add up" to Christ.

This is not to be taken as a form of syrupy universalism that says everyone will go to Heaven. (This would contradict other passages in Ephesians as well as countless other Scriptures.) It simply means that all of history is pointing to the second coming of Jesus and will be consummated when he returns (1 Corinthians 15:24-28). What an encouragement to know that we will reign with him!

IV. GOD'S GRACIOUS PROMISE (EPHESIANS 1:11-14)

A. OUR INHERITANCE (vv. 11, 12)

11. In him we were also chosen, having been predestined according to the plan of him who works out everything in conformity with the purpose of his will.

Under the Old Covenant, Israel was God's *chosen* people. Now, however, under the New Covenant Gentiles are included—a theme to be developed later by Paul (Ephesians 2:11-22). Christians are now God's "chosen people" (1 Peter 2:9).

Notice once more the use of *predestined.* From the beginning of time God has had a particular "destiny" in mind for his people, those who by faith are children of Abraham. The church was not an afterthought in God's *plan,* but was part of his *purpose* all along.

12. . . . in order that we, who were the first to hope in Christ, might be for the praise of his glory.

WHAT DO YOU THINK?

If God has "lavished on us . . . all wisdom and understanding," why do you think we continue to do so many foolish things? Even the best of us occasionally revert to our old ways. Peter, who clearly saw that God had accepted the Gentiles (Acts 10, 11), reverted to his old way of behaving in Antioch (Galatians 2:11-14). What can we do to demonstrate more of God's wisdom?

WHAT DO YOU THINK?

God has always had a plan culminating in Christ. He worked his plan to the letter. All history is "his story." Do we have a plan? How are we doing in working it out?

WHAT DO YOU THINK?

How can we "be for the praise of [God's] glory"?

[Your discussion should focus not only on verse 12 of the text, from which the quotation comes, but also on the similar language in verses 6 and 14, and the immediate context for each verse. Note the similarities: predestination (vv. 5 and 11), redemption (vv. 7 and 14); God's will (vv. 5 and 9).]

WHAT DO YOU THINK?

Gentiles as well as Jews had trusted in Christ and found salvation in him. This represented the removal of a major barrier between peoples. What barriers need to be removed in our world today? In our church?

Does your church exhibit the same demographics as your community? If not, why not? Are there barriers that need to come down? Brainstorm some ways to remove the barriers and open your church to all peoples.

PRAYER

Lord, thank you for the songs you place in our hearts and the smiles you place on our faces. When language fails, we will still try to praise your holy name. Words may be inadequate, but accept the sentiment of our hearts. We are grateful for your grace, your gifts, and your glory. Through Christ, who is above all, amen.

The ultimate purpose of what God has done is that those who are blessed by his work should bring *praise* to him. But to whom is Paul referring when he speaks of those *who were the first to hope in Christ*? Most likely he is describing the Jews (of whom Paul was one); since in the next verse his use of *you also* would seem to include Gentile Christians, which would characterize most of those reading Paul's letter.

B. OUR DOWN PAYMENT (vv. 13, 14)

13, 14. And you also were included in Christ when you heard the word of truth, the gospel of your salvation. Having believed, you were marked in him with a seal, the promised Holy Spirit, who is a deposit guaranteeing our inheritance until the redemption of those who are God's possession—to the praise of his glory.

Gentile Christians (*you also*) are now described as full participants in the blessings of the *gospel* of *salvation*. They are also described as *marked in [Christ] with a seal*. Just as a letter was sealed by an owner in order to guarantee its authenticity, or an item was sealed to insure its safety while being transported to another location, Christians have been *marked* as God's property by the *Holy Spirit*.

In addition, the Spirit is described as *a deposit guaranteeing our inheritance*. The word *deposit* was taken from the business world and described what we would call a "down payment" (as when we put a "deposit" on an item that we wish to purchase). The final *redemption* (that is, the time when we receive "in full" what God has promised) will take place when we get to Heaven. Until then, we have the Holy Spirit to assist us in living the Christian life as well as to give us a touch of Heaven.

THE NOTARY'S SEAL

Most everyone is familiar with the notary's seal. It takes the place of that more ancient seal in which a bit of hot wax was placed on a document and then an image was pressed into it. Today we use a metal stamp that embosses the image signifying the author directly into the paper itself. While a photocopy machine may duplicate such a document, the presence of the seal assures you that what you have is not a copy but the real document.

In one respect, our modern notary's seal may actually serve as a better illustration of our being "marked" with the "seal" of the Holy Spirit than the ancient seal. Just as the notary seal is embossed into the paper itself, so the Holy Spirit comes *into* the believer to become a part of his life. Sometimes we call this the indwelling of the Spirit. In another passage, Paul wrote that a Christian "is a temple of the Holy Spirit, who is in you" (1 Corinthians 6:19).

God does not want us to have any uncertainty about our forgiveness. The presence of the Holy Spirit gives us a blessed assurance that we truly belong to him. We can know that our forgiveness is real and that we are members of the family of God. We ought to rejoice in the seal of the Spirit—God's assurance of his presence now and of greater blessings yet to come!   —R. C. S.

CONCLUSION

One dear saint (but a very reserved one) was pondering the many blessings of the Lord. She told a friend, "The Lord's been so good to me, I can hardly keep from smiling." It should be hard not to feel some measure of gratitude when we consider all that God has done for us in Christ. It's all right to get a bit emotional about his great blessings. Emotionalism may be dangerous, but emotion based on and appropriate to the facts is always healthy.

If you put your mind to it, couldn't you, like Paul in today's text, find abundant reason to break forth into praise?

Discovery Learning

This page contains an alternate lesson plan emphasizing learning activities. Classes desiring such student involvement will find these suggestions helpful. The next page is a reproducible activity page to further enhance discovery learning.

LEARNING GOALS

After this lesson each student will be able to:

1. Summarize the "spiritual blessings" that Christians possess.

2. Tell how a knowledge of these blessings will affect their walk with Christ and witness to the world.

3. Write or say a prayer of thanksgiving for the spiritual blessings he or she has received in Christ.

INTO THE LESSON

Distribute copies of the handout described below. (This exercise is also included in the student book.) On the handout, print "CURSE OR BLESSINGS?" Under this heading print the following instructions: "Paul tells us that Christ has redeemed us from the curse of the law (Galatians 3:13). One of the final promises of the Bible is *'No longer will there be any curse'* (Revelation 22:3). Remove the letters of that promise—in order—from the list of letters below. The remaining letters will reveal a wonderful message that is the key to our study today. Write the solution below." Under these instructions print the letters "P R A N I S E O B E L O T O N G T E H E R G O D W W I H O L L H A T S H E B L R E E S S B E E D U S W I A T H N E V Y E R C Y S P I R U I T R U S A L B L E E S S I N G."

Give the students a couple of minutes to solve the puzzle; then ask for the solution, which is "Praise be to the God . . . who has blessed us . . . with every spiritual blessing" (Ephesians 1:3). Tell the class that today's study will provide us with a wonderful list of spiritual blessings.

INTO THE WORD

Use your lesson commentary to outline and deliver a brief lecture about the background of the book of Ephesians. Conclude with remarks about Paul's greeting in verses 1 and 2.

Ask a student to serve as scribe to write blessings on the chalkboard. Ask the other members of the class to read Ephesians 1:1-14 and look for the blessings Paul mentions. As they discover a blessing, they are to tell it to the scribe so that he or she can add it to the list. The list will include the following: spiritual blessings in the heavenly realms (v. 3), God chose us (v. 4), holiness (v. 4), blamelessness (v. 4), adoption (v. 5), God's grace (v. 6), redemption (v. 7), forgiveness of sins (v. 7), the riches of God's grace (v. 7), wisdom (v. 8), understanding (v. 8), knowledge of God's will (v. 9), marked with the seal of the Holy Spirit (v. 13), and the deposit guaranteeing our inheritance (v. 14). Is it any wonder that Christians celebrate when we realize the many wonderful and powerful gifts God has given us?

Next, review and clarify the following issues:

1. The issue of predestination, vv. 4, 5. During the week before class ask a class member to prepare a brief report on this issue. Let the student study the lesson commentary and other sources you can make available. Have the student report to the class at this time.

2. Give each student a copy of the reproducible activity "Definitions and Explanations" for the next page. Give them a few minutes to define the terms listed there; then ask for reports. Use the lesson commentary to complement the class's answers.

3. Explore the concept of adoption by asking, "What are the benefits of being adopted? Why is this such a precious concept to Christians?"

4. Ask the class, "What is a 'deposit' (when we are talking about money), and how does understanding that help us understand verse 14?"

Summarize the study by reminding the class that Paul's wonderful list of blessings was written from prison. But his positive attitude, optimism, and enthusiasm tell us that his spirit remained free.

INTO LIFE

Point to the list of blessings created earlier and remind the class that these blessings are theirs! Distribute copies of the reproducible activity "Adopted Into the Family of God" from the next page. Ask the students to work as pairs to complete this activity, listing a number of blessings associated with being a child of God. Ask volunteers to tell what blessings mean the most to them.

Then ask the students to turn the handout over and use the blank side to express gratitude or praise by writing a prayer using the word "Bless" or "Praise" for an acrostic. (This activity is also in the student book.) Display this sample on a large red heart:

You have **B**lessed me, Lord!
I will **L**ive with the joy
of b**E**ing your child,
redeemed by your **S**on and
bathing in the riche**S** of your grace.

Definitions and Explanations

Define or explain the words or phrases listed below that are used in today's text. Resources for this project might include other translations of the Bible, a Bible dictionary or Bible encyclopedia, or a commentary on Ephesians.

Saints (v. 1) _____

Predestined (v. 5) _____

Adopted (v. 5) _____

Redemption (v. 7) _____

Mystery (v. 9) _____

Deposit (v. 14) _____

Adopted Into the Family of God

Verse 5 of our text reminds us we have been adopted into the family of God. Read the Scriptures below and write the privileges or blessings implied for God's children. In the third column, write the emotion or reaction you experience from this blessing.

Scripture	Privileges or Blessings	My Reaction/Emotion
Romans 8:17		
Romans 8:23		
Galatians 3:26, 27		
Galatians 3:28		
Galatians 3:29		
Galatians 4:4, 5		
Galatians 4:6		
Galatians 4:7		
Hebrews 12:7		

CALLED TO ONENESS IN CHRIST

WHY TEACH THIS LESSON?

I think they called it the "identity axiom" in math class. "If A=B and B=C, then A=C." Sounds basic enough in academia, but how about in the "real world"? Is it still as easy? If Nate is a Christian and Steve is a Christian, then Nate and Steve are equals. That doesn't seem so hard.

It did in the early church, however. If Nathaniel (a Jewish name) is a Christian and Stephanas (a Greek name) is a Christian, are Nathaniel and Stephanas equals? Can Jews and Greeks be equal? Can blacks and whites? Can North Americans and Latinos? Can Irish and British? Can Serbs and Croatians?

This lesson is intended to remind your students that unity in Christ is possible across all racial and geographic boundaries. If I have been joined with Christ, then I am one with anyone and everyone else who has been joined with Christ!

INTRODUCTION

A. BEFORE AND AFTER

People who sell diet programs or muscle-building devices often show before-and-after pictures to dramatize the difference that their products allegedly have made in the lives of people who have used the products. They hope that others will be impressed enough by this difference to buy those same products.

Paul, in our text for today, provides some before-and-after pictures comparing our lives before Christ came with what he has made of them. In particular, he calls attention to what the Gentiles were like before and after Christ came. The difference is striking!

Often the advertisers of the aforementioned products have to admit that their before-and-after pictures are not necessarily typical and that results may vary from user to user. Paul, however, could promise results without any disclaimers. Everyone who comes to Christ can experience the changes he describes. These changes make it hard to imagine that anyone could consider them and then not want his "product."

B. LESSON BACKGROUND

This lesson covers a text that contains some of the most significant doctrinal themes found in this letter to the Ephesians. In certain respects our text reminds us of the themes found in Paul's letter to the Romans, though they are considered here in a much more concise manner.

Paul was commissioned by Jesus to be an apostle to the Gentiles (Acts 26:17; cf. Romans 11:13). However, Paul was a Jew, with an especially impressive Jewish heritage and upbringing (Philippians 3:4-6). This placed him in the thick of occasional controversies, such as that which led to the convening of the Jerusalem Conference (Acts 15:1, 2) and that which resulted in Paul's confronting Peter in Antioch (Galatians 2:11-14).

DEVOTIONAL READING:
JOHN 17:1-11, 20-23
BACKGROUND SCRIPTURE:
EPHESIANS 2
PRINTED TEXT:
EPHESIANS 2:8-22

Jul
9

LESSON AIMS

As a result of studying this lesson, each student will be able to:

1. Tell how the grace that provides salvation also eliminates barriers that had previously separated those who are now saved.

2. Suggest some modern walls or barriers that need to be eliminated by the gospel.

3. Tell one specific way he or she can work for unity within the body.

KEY VERSE

Consequently, you are no longer foreigners and aliens, but fellow citizens with God's people, and members of God's household, built on the foundation of the apostles and prophets, with Christ Jesus himself as the chief cornerstone.

—Ephesians 2:19, 20

Lesson 6 Notes

What Do You Think?

Why do some of us have difficulty accepting the fact that salvation comes by God's grace and not by our works?

Solution to puzzle on page 392.

In today's text Paul emphasizes that Christ died for both Jew and Gentile—to bring an end to the separation between the two. He encourages us to remember that we are all sinners who have been reconciled to God by Jesus' death on the cross. If we have been thus accepted by God, then we must accept each other—something that is often easier said than done.

Today's text highlights what we once were because of our sins and what we now are because of what Jesus did for us.

I. SAVED! (EPHESIANS 2:8-10)
A. By Grace Through Faith (vv. 8, 9)

8. For it is by grace you have been saved, through faith—and this not from yourselves, it is the gift of God.

In spite of the questions this verse raises, we marvel at how concisely Paul explains the substance of the gospel, drawing attention to salvation, grace, and faith in one verse. Certainly the verse offers much comfort in the assurance that *by grace you have been saved.* This frees us from trying to earn or deserve Heaven, which we can never do in the first place.

A certain amount of controversy has arisen over the words *this not from yourselves, it is the gift of God.* What is it that is not of ourselves? What exactly is the gift of God? Some believe that faith itself is the gift of God. They maintain that those who respond to God were first given the gift of faith by the Holy Spirit so that they would believe; thus it is impossible for them not to believe. This position, however, diminishes the factor of man's free will, which is emphasized in "whoever" passages such as John 3:16 and Revelation 22:17.

There is also a linguistic problem with this position. In the Greek text the pronoun *this* (in *this not from yourselves*) is a neuter pronoun. It cannot, then, refer to *faith* because *faith* is feminine in gender. *This* refers not to any actual word in the text but to the concept expressed, that is, to the entire process of salvation. Our salvation is a gift from God. That this understanding is the better way to view this verse becomes more clear when the next verse is considered—"not by works." The idea of earning one's salvation is as ancient as it is wrong, but it still persists and shows up in some of the most surprising places. Longtime believers can be caught up in a process of trying to "do enough" to merit salvation rather than accept the fact that we are saved by God's grace. Good works are important, but not as the source of our salvation. Paul addresses the role of works in verse 10.

9. . . . not by works, so that no one can boast.

One of the consequences of understanding that we are saved by grace should be a sense of genuine humility. The plan of salvation is the work of God, *so that no one can boast.* No one can ever say that he is going to Heaven on the basis of his own *works.* While we should always seek to be obedient and to live in a manner pleasing to God, that is not what gets us to Heaven.

Let us keep in mind a phrase that appeared in last week's text from Ephesians 1: "for [or to] the praise of his glory" (vv. 12, 14). This is one of the consequences of salvation: that God is praised by those who have received it. Obviously if we could win salvation through our own merits, we would have something about which to boast. As it is, we should boast about God: "Let him who boasts boast in the Lord" (1 Corinthians 1:31).

In Our Nothingness

Our house guests had sent their two small children upstairs to get ready for bed. Soon the older sister came down to complain about her younger brother. "He won't go to bed," she said, "and he's running around up there in his nothingness."

That's a fitting description of what we have to offer when we come to God for forgiveness: our nothingness. For him to make something out of our nothingness is a testimony to the power of his "amazing grace." We sing of that in the beloved hymn *Rock of Ages*:

Nothing in my hand I bring,
Simply to Thy cross I cling;
Naked, come to Thee for dress;
Helpless, look to Thee for grace.

Can we name one good reason that God should forgive us? Absolutely not. The only reason is that this is the kind of God he is. Forgiveness can never be based on *our* goodness—only on *his* goodness. All our accomplishments, all our possessions, and all our abilities put together amount to nothing before God. We could not trade them all for pardon for a single sin.

We cannot earn forgiveness. We cannot buy forgiveness. We cannot barter for forgiveness. We can only accept the forgiveness lovingly offered by the God of grace. That is the reason there is no room for boasting. But there is more than enough room for gratitude and praise. A God who does so much for us who deserve so little is worthy of all the gratitude, praise, and love that we can offer.

—R. C. S.

B. FOR GOOD WORKS (v. 10)

10. For we are God's workmanship, created in Christ Jesus to do good works, which God prepared in advance for us to do.

While salvation is "not by works," we must never think that works are meaningless. However, they must be understood in proper relationship to our faith. In order to emphasize the significance of *good works*, Paul points out that *God prepared in advance* that we should *do* them. It is God's will for us as Christians that in this life we should display good works and thus let our light shine (Matthew 5:16). Thus works do not justify us, but they do identify us. As F. F. Bruce says, Paul "repudiated good works as a ground of salvation. [Still] no one more wholeheartedly insisted on works as the fruit of salvation."

While we cannot hope to earn Heaven by our works, knowing what Jesus did for us should move us to fill our lives with works that honor him. The result of salvation is not just eternal life in Heaven, but a better, more fulfilling life on earth.

This verse also describes Christians as *God's workmanship*. The Greek word used here carries the connotation of a "work of art." (It is the source of our word "poem.") Perhaps we could translate it as "God's masterpiece."

II. RECONCILED! (EPHESIANS 2:11-18)

Next, Paul describes Christians as enemies of God who have been reconciled to him. Many non-Christians are uncomfortable with any suggestion that they are God's enemies. But they are dead in sin and, in fact, at enmity with God.

In this section of our text, Paul deals with what we might call our "double alienation": we are separated from God and from each other.

A. A GREAT CHASM (vv. 11, 12)

11. Therefore, remember that formerly you who are Gentiles by birth and called "uncircumcised" by those who call themselves "the circumcision" (that done in the body by the hands of men).

Paul reminded his Gentile readers what their condition was like before they knew Christ. They were *called "uncircumcised"* as a derisive way of noting that they lacked the covenant sign of Israelite males.

WHAT DO YOU THINK?

Religious and ethnic differences often are the grounds for derogatory name-calling. When the Jews called Gentiles the "uncircumcised," they were simply doing what others had done and others still do. What are the usual bases for such name-calling? Why is such a practice foolish?

Circumcision was first commanded of Abraham (Genesis 17:10-14). Eventually the practice became to the Jews a symbol of their presumed superiority to the *Gentiles.* Peter, for example, was accused of going to uncircumcised men and eating with them following his visit to the house of Cornelius (Acts 11:1-3).

Paul, however, explained that Christ has provided a new kind of circumcision. In Colossians 2:11 Paul wrote that Christians are "circumcised . . . not with a circumcision done by the hands of men." To the Philippians, he wrote, "For it is we who are the circumcision, we who worship by the Spirit of God, who glory in Christ Jesus, and who put no confidence in the flesh" (Philippians 3:3).

12. . . . remember that at that time you were separate from Christ, excluded from citizenship in Israel and foreigners to the covenants of the promise, without hope and without God in the world.

At that time (before they became Christians), the Gentiles were *separate from Christ.* They were *excluded from citizenship in Israel.* They were not part of God's chosen people and did not share in *the covenants of the promise* made with individuals such as Abraham, Moses, and David, and given to the nation of Israel. Gentiles were both hopeless and Godless. It is hard to imagine a more desperate situation.

B. A GREATER BRIDGE (vv. 13-18)

13. But now in Christ Jesus you who once were far away have been brought near through the blood of Christ.

Verse 13 introduces a much brighter picture, thanks to the phrase *but now.* (Other significant uses of this phrase are found in Romans 6:22; 7:6; Colossians 3:8.) The Gentiles, who for so long had been *far away* have now been *brought near* to God *in Christ Jesus.* Those who have been "on the outside looking in" have seen the barriers come down. No separation exists between God and the Gentiles; therefore no separation exists between Jew and Gentile. How did this happen? It happened through the cross, where Jesus shed his *blood.*

Today there is considerable concern about the divisions—racial, social, economic, and others—that exist in our society. We need to keep in mind the degree of hostility that was present between Jew and Gentile in Paul's day. Read the book of Acts to see how challenging it was for the church, which began among the Jews, to understand that God wanted to save Gentiles as well. A gathering of the leadership (recorded in Acts 15) was required to settle the issue, and even that did not put the issue to rest. No less a figure than the apostle Peter had trouble living out the new understanding of God's love for Gentiles as well as Jews. (See Galatians 2:11-14.) Yet it is one of the impressive accomplishments of the gospel of Christ that it could and did transcend such formidable barriers. Can anything but the gospel heal the divisions present in our fragmented world?

14. For he himself is our peace, who has made the two one and has destroyed the barrier, the dividing wall of hostility.

Paul does not say merely that Jesus brought peace, but that *he himself is our peace.* There are two ways Paul describes the difference Jesus has made. First, he *has made the two one.* Any differences between Jew and Gentile mean nothing now. Paul told the Galatians, "There is neither Jew nor Greek [Gentile], . . . for you are all one in Christ Jesus" (Galatians 3:28).

Second, Paul says that Christ *destroyed the barrier, the dividing wall of hostility.* The Greek word rendered *barrier* is a general term that can refer to any kind of wall or fence, including a wall that was used to protect a vineyard (Mark 12:1). Perhaps Paul was thinking of the "wall" that existed in the Jerusalem temple, where gates leading into the inner courts displayed warning signs barring Gentiles from going any farther. Violation of this warning was punishable by death.

WHAT DO YOU THINK?

Why is it that Christians sometimes act as if they do not believe that those who are "separate from Christ" and "foreigners to the covenants of the promise" are indeed "without hope and without God in the world"?

THOUGHT TO REMEMBER

What you were is not what you are, and what you are is not what you will be.

Recall the uproar that resulted when Paul was accused of bringing Gentiles into a forbidden area of the temple (Acts 21:27-36).

15. . . . by abolishing in his flesh the law with its commandments and regulations. His purpose was to create in himself one new man out of the two, thus making peace.

Jesus is described as *abolishing in his flesh the law with its commandments and regulations*. Some see this statement as contradictory to Jesus' declaration that he did not come "to abolish the Law or the Prophets; . . . but to fulfill them" (Matthew 5:17). These two verses simply offer two different perspectives on what Jesus did concerning the law. Jesus fulfilled the law by living according to its standards of righteousness and by emphasizing its underlying principles (as seen throughout the Sermon on the Mount). Through his coming the law's purpose was fulfilled in that it is meant to "lead us to Christ" (Galatians 3:24).

In this passage from Ephesians, Paul seems to place special emphasis on the ceremonial aspects of the law—*commandments and regulations*. These are the portions of the law (including such matters as feast days, food regulations, and rituals) that drove a wedge between Jew and Gentile. Colossians 2:14 says that Jesus "canceled the written code, with its regulations, that was against us and that stood opposed to us; he took it away, nailing it to the cross."

Under the New Covenant, the portions of the law concerning moral issues (for example, the Ten Commandments) can still provide guidance as a standard of conduct, but not a means of salvation. Only Jesus' death supplies that. His sacrifice has allowed those who have broken the law to be forgiven.

The impact of Jesus' death is described as making *one new man out of the two*. Some believe that this is to be taken in a corporate sense, picturing the church as God's new humanity that includes both Jews and Gentiles. Others see the phrase as descriptive of the new individual or "new creation" in Christ (2 Corinthians 5:17). This person is neither Jew nor Gentile; he is a Christian!

16. . . . and in this one body to reconcile both of them to God through the cross, by which he put to death their hostility.

Since the cross has done away with what once separated Jews and Gentiles, and has reconciled them *to God*, they can now be reconciled to each other.

17. He came and preached peace to you who were far away and peace to those who were near.

This verse tells us that Jesus *came and preached peace* to those *far away* (Gentiles) and *to those who were near* (Jews). But Jesus' earthly ministry was primarily for the sake of "the lost sheep of Israel" (Matthew 15:24). When did he preach peace to Gentiles? Probably Paul is describing the impact of Jesus' ministry, particularly his death and resurrection, on all peoples, to whom his followers are told to go and preach (Mark 16:15). Thus Peter could speak to the Gentiles in the house of Cornelius of "the message God sent to the people of Israel, telling the good news of peace through Jesus Christ" (Acts 10:36). He then concluded, "Everyone who believes in him receives remission of sins through his name" (Acts 10:43).

18. For through him we both have access to the Father by one Spirit.

Through Jesus all peoples, Jews and Gentiles alike, have *access* to God as their *Father*. The Greek word rendered *access* is related to a word that describes the official who would usher someone into a king's presence. Now *both* Jews and Gentiles can walk in daily fellowship with the King of Heaven.

III. INCLUDED! (EPHESIANS 2:19-22)

In this portion of our text, Paul uses what our high school English teacher would have called a mixed metaphor. He combines the figures of a nation, a

---

How to Say It

Colossians. Kuh-LOSH-unz.
Cornelius. Kor-NEEL-yus.
Ephesians. Ee-FEE-zhunz.
Ephesus. EF-uh-sus.
Philippians. Fih-LIP-ee-unz.
Pyrenees. PEER-uh-neez.

Daily Bible Readings

Monday, July 3—Saved and Made Alive by Grace (Ephesians 2:1-10)

Tuesday, July 4—One Body in Jesus Christ (Ephesians 2:11-16)

Wednesday, July 5—God Dwells in You (Ephesians 2:17-22)

Thursday, July 6—Jesus Commits Disciples to God's Care (John 17:1-6)

Friday, July 7—Jesus Prays for the Disciples' Protection (John 17:7-13)

Saturday, July 8—Jesus Prays for the Disciples' Unity (John 17:14-21)

Sunday, July 9—May God's Love Be in Christ's Disciples (John 17:22-26)

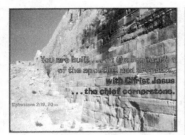

Today's visual illustrates our Key Verse for the day, Ephesians 2:19, 20. Display it as you begin to discuss that passage.

WHAT DO YOU THINK?

What are the responsibilities of being a citizen of a nation? What are the responsibilities of being "fellow citizens with God's people"?

WHAT DO YOU THINK?

What are some of the human "building blocks" necessary to a church that is truly "a holy temple . . . in which God lives by his Spirit"?

PRAYER

Thank you, gracious Father, for saving me, bringing me to yourself, and including me in your wonderful enterprise. I freely admit that I do not deserve such treatment. While I know I am unworthy of your grace, I will treasure it and seek to live a life that honors you. Through Jesus, who paid the price and built the bridge between us, amen.

family, and a building to illustrate that Christians (both Jews and Gentiles) belong together because they belong to God.

A. IN GOD'S FAMILY (v. 19)

19. Consequently, you are no longer foreigners and aliens, but fellow citizens with God's people and members of God's household.

Paul offers a before-and-after picture of what we were before Christ's coming and what we are now, thanks to him. We were *foreigners and aliens*; we had no place among *God's people*. But that is *no longer* true; now we have been designated *fellow citizens*. We enjoy the full privileges of being citizens of the kingdom of Heaven and *members of God's household* (family).

B. IN GOD'S TEMPLE (vv. 20-22)

20. . . . built on the foundation of the apostles and prophets, with Christ Jesus himself as the chief cornerstone.

Paul now pictures Christians as building blocks in a great temple that God is constructing. He describes the *apostles and prophets* as the *foundation* of this building. This makes sense, since the apostles and prophets were instrumental in delivering the first inspired messages to the early church.

Then Paul designates *Christ Jesus himself as the chief cornerstone*. Today cornerstones are largely symbolic. In the first century, however, the cornerstone was a vital part of the construction of a building. Great care was taken to be sure the cornerstone was perfectly square and level. It then stood as a standard of reference for all the measurements relating to the construction of the rest of the building.

21. In him the whole building is joined together and rises to become a holy temple in the Lord.

Each Christian might be called a "brick" in God's *building*. Paul pictures this building as in the process of constant growth. Anyone who becomes a Christian is added to the structure. Every part belongs; every part has purpose. *Together* the parts constitute *a holy temple in the Lord*—his dwelling place (1 Corinthians 3:16).

22. And in him you too are being built together to become a dwelling in which God lives by his Spirit.

Now Paul goes a step farther. Not only is this great building—this holy temple—being *built* by God, but he himself dwells in it *by* the presence of *his Spirit*. Of course, Paul is not talking about a literal building. Just as God has created "one new man" including both Jews and Gentiles (v. 15), so he has constructed one new building—his church, composed of the people (both Jews and Gentiles) in whom he *lives* through his Spirit.

CONCLUSION

When the same royal family ruled both Spain and France during the seventeenth century, someone declared, "There are no more Pyrenees." For centuries those mountains had divided the two nations, serving as both a military and a psychological barrier. When the two royal families united, it was seen as an opportunity for two nations that had been geographically and politically separated to be at least politically united. However, the mountains remained in place and so did the mistrust. The union did not last; the hopes went unfulfilled.

With Jesus the barriers that divide nations, groups, families, and individuals are meant to come down for good. When we see how much God dislikes walls of separation and the effort he put forth at the cross to tear them down, we should be motivated to do all we can to bring them down in the name of Jesus—and to refuse to allow any new walls to take their place.

Discovery Learning

*This page contains an alternate lesson plan emphasizing learning activities. Classes
desiring such student involvement will find these suggestions helpful. The next page
is a reproducible activity page to further enhance discovery learning.*

LEARNING GOALS

As a result of participating in this lesson, each student will be able to:

1. Tell how the grace that provides salvation also eliminates barriers that had previously separated those who are now saved.

2. Suggest some modern walls or barriers that need to be eliminated by the gospel.

3. Tell one specific way he or she can work for unity within the body.

INTO THE LESSON

Give every person a copy of a handout with the heading, *My Immediate Family!* Under the heading should appear these instructions: *Name each person in your immediate family. Then write something about each person named that makes him or her unique or different from other family members.* Ask the class members to take a few moments to complete the exercise and share their answers in groups of two or three persons.

Tell the class that today's Scripture identifies us as "members of God's household." Just as members of your family are unique and different from each other, so are members of God's family. Yet, like your family, we are to enjoy a "oneness" in God's family. The questions that face us today include, "In what ways are we to be one?" And, "What can I do to promote unity in God's family?"

Option: Use the crossword puzzle on the next page to introduce the text.

INTO THE WORD

Ask the students to turn their handouts over and divide the back page into two columns. Ask them to write, "Images of the Church That Indicate Unity (Ephesians 2:19-22)" at the top of column 1. About halfway down the page they should write, "Foundations for Christian Unity (Ephesians 2:8-10)." At the very bottom of column 1 have them write, "Issues Concerning Unity in Ephesus (Ephesians 2:11-18)."

Tell the class, "Read Ephesians 2:19-22, looking for names or images that indicate unity in Christ's church. Write these under the first heading." (Answers may include *fellow citizens with God's people, members of God's household, a building, a holy temple, a dwelling in which God lives.*) Prepare a poster identical to the handout and write comments on it as they are given.

Next, have the class read verses 8-10 and look for clues to the basis for Christian unity. (Answers will focus on the means of our salvation. Salvation is *by grace . . . through faith.* Salvation does not come *from yourselves.* Salvation is *not by works.* Instead, we are saved *to do good works.*) Tell the class that we will explore the wonderful truths and implications of this text later in the lesson.

Read verses 11-18. Using your lesson commentary, give a brief lecture about the issues raised in this passage. Include information about the identity and issues of the "*uncircumcised*" and "*the circumcision.*" While this text teaches that Gentiles are no longer separated from God, it also emphasizes the unity of Jews and Gentiles.

INTO LIFE

Tell the class that the issue of unity in the local church is as important to our church as it was for the Ephesian Christians. Ask class members to write "Implications for My Church" at the top of column 2 on the handout. Ask them, "As you read through the list of descriptions and names for the church in column 1, what principles for unity do you see implied for our church?" Again, write their comments on the poster you have prepared.

Ask the class to review their notes about the "Foundations for Christian Unity." Ask and discuss: "How can understanding the means of salvation help to break down the barriers to unity in the church? How does understanding grace and salvation draw people together?"

Tell the class, "The issue of the relationship of Jews and Gentiles is not an issue in our church. However, there may be other walls or barriers to fellowship we are experiencing." Ask the students to identify differences that may separate people in your congregation. The answers may focus on music, worship styles, leadership struggles, economic strata, ethnic issues, quarrels, etc.

Ask, "What have we learned today that will help to destroy these walls or barriers to fellowship in our church family?"

To make this lesson personal, ask the students to turn back to page 1 of the handout. At the bottom of the page ask them to write these words: "I am concerned about this barrier to complete fellowship and unity in our congregation," and "I will do this one thing to strengthen the fellowship in my church." Ask each student to write a response to each of those; then close with small groups praying for the concerns on their lists.

Living in Unity

One of Paul's themes in Ephesians is that Christians should live together in unity. Find key words, phrases, or tools for living together in the family of God from these verses in Ephesians to complete the crossword puzzle.

ACROSS

1. "For he _____ is our peace" (v. 14).
6. Gentiles were said to be "foreigners to the _____ of the promise" (v. 12).
7. Jesus created "in himself one new man . . . thus making _____" (v. 15).
8. Jesus has removed "the _____ wall of hostility" (v. 14).
10. "It is by grace you have been saved, through _____" (v. 8).
12. "Built on the _____ of the apostles and prophets" (v. 20).
14. The Jews called Gentiles "_____" (v. 11).
18. Our salvation is a _____ from God (v. 8).
19. Salvation is not a matter of works, so no one can _____ (v. 9).
20. We are "God's _____," his masterpiece (v. 10).

DOWN

1. Without Jesus, we are "without _____ and without God in the world" (v. 12).
2. Gentiles were "_____ from citizenship in Israel" (v. 12).
3. We are "saved by _____" (v. 8).
4. "In him the whole building is _____ together" (v. 21).
5. Jesus "came and _____ peace" to those far away and near (v. 17).
9. Jesus abolished "in his flesh the law with its _____ and regulations" (v. 15).
11. "Built on the foundation of the _____ and prophets, with Christ Jesus himself as the chief cornerstone" (v. 20).
13. Jesus "has destroyed the barrier, the dividing wall of _____" (v. 14).
15. "You who once were far away have been brought near through the blood of _____" (v. 13).
16. "We are God's workmanship, _____ in Christ Jesus to do good works" (v. 10).
17. Jesus "has _____ the barrier" between Jew and Gentile (v. 14).

(The solution to the puzzle can be found on page 386 of *The NIV® Standard Lesson Commentary*, 1999-2000.)

CALLED TO USE SPIRITUAL GIFTS

LESSON 7

WHY TEACH THIS LESSON?

"Use tools right," the farmer admonished his son. "Never pound with a big wrench when a little one will do!" We smile at the twist on what should have been good advice. Each tool is made for a certain function, and it works best when it is used for that function and not another. Similarly, even a difficult job is made much easier when a person has the right tools at his or her disposal.

Spiritual gifts are like tools. The Lord has supplied the church with a variety of them to engage in a variety of tasks or ministries. Just as a wrench is not jealous of a hammer, so one gifted member should not be jealous of another. Nor would a hammer look down on a screw driver. Use this lesson to encourage each member of the class to discern what his or her particular gift or gifts are, and to use them to the glory of God.

INTRODUCTION

A. GET ORGANIZED

In an old *Peanuts* comic strip, Lucy tries to get Linus to let her watch what she wants to see on television. Linus says, "Give me one good reason I should let you."

Holding up her hand, Lucy responds, "I'll give you five." She then pulls each of her fingers one by one into a ball, makes a fist, and shakes it at Linus.

In the last frame of the comic strip, Linus looks at his hand and says, "Why can't you guys get organized like that?"

Sometimes we feel like asking the church that same question. We wonder how much more powerful and effective the church could be if its members would work together and "get organized." In today's text, Paul challenges us to "keep the unity of the Spirit through the bond of peace" for the sake of the cause of Christ.

B. LESSON BACKGROUND

The first two lessons in this unit from Ephesians were taken from the doctrinal portion of the letter (chapters 1-3). Chapter 4 begins what might be considered the more practical portion of the letter, where Paul addresses concerns relevant to Christian living. (Most of Paul's letters could be outlined in this manner.)

At the same time, what Paul considers as chapter 4 begins is closely tied to the preceding material. (Note the word "then" in verse 1.) The doxology at the close of chapter 3 (vv. 20, 21) includes the phrase "to him [God] be glory in the church and in Christ Jesus." In chapter 4 Paul proceeds to address how the church can bring glory to God. His initial topic of concern is unity in Christ—a matter that the church must make a top priority.

I. RECOGNIZING UNITY (EPHESIANS 4:1-6)

Christian unity is rarely, if ever, achieved by accident. Essential to its attainment is the cultivation of Christlike attitudes in those who claim to be his followers.

DEVOTIONAL READING:
EPHESIANS 3:14-21
BACKGROUND SCRIPTURE:
EPHESIANS 4:1-16
PRINTED TEXT:
EPHESIANS 4:1-16

LESSON AIMS

This lesson should enable students to:

1. Summarize Paul's discussion of unity in terms of its source, expression, and result.

2. Tell how a variety of differing gifts can contribute to unity.

3. Identify a specific ministry gift that he or she has and suggest how the use of that gift can contribute to unity within the body.

Jul
16

KEY VERSE

But to each one of us grace has been given as Christ apportioned it. —Ephesians 4:7

A. ESSENTIAL ATTITUDES (vv. 1-3)

1. As a prisoner for the Lord, then, I urge you to live a life worthy of the calling you have received.

Paul's use of the word *urge* indicates the critical nature of his discussion of unity. He begins his plea by expressing his desire that his readers *live a life worthy*—"practice what they preach," or "walk the talk." He wants that walk to reflect *the calling you have received.* All Christians are called to cultivate the attitudes that follow.

2. Be completely humble and gentle; be patient, bearing with one another in love.

Here Paul begins to describe what it means to "live a life worthy." He wants followers of Jesus to *be patient, bearing with one another in love.* Working together with others requires patience; and if we are going to have that kind of patience, then we must possess the related qualities of being *humble and gentle.* People will inevitably disappoint us and will tax our patience at times. What we must never forget is how much we need people to be patient with us.

WHAT DO YOU THINK?

As Paul discusses unity, he begins with individual godly behavior as the basis for that unity. How does the absence of the qualities cited in verses 1 and 2 create disunity?

UNNECESSARY GENTLENESS

One of Bud Blake's *Tiger* comic strips shows a group of children playing football. One little boy stands and watches as a girl carries the football right past him. When he is asked why he didn't tackle her, he replies, "I was afraid I would hurt her." Later, on his way home, he is complaining about what happened to him. He says, "I got thrown out for unnecessary gentleness." In certain sports a player is sometimes thrown out for unnecessary roughness, but never for unnecessary gentleness!

In the life and work of the church, we must learn to be gentle. We must follow Paul's admonition to "be completely humble and gentle; be patient, bearing with one another in love" (Ephesians 4:2). Roughness is always unnecessary in the church.

Love is to be the trademark that identifies followers of Jesus (John 13:35). Love demands courtesy and kindness. Love demands that we learn how to disagree without being disagreeable. Love desires to handle both the sinning believer (Galatians 6:1) and the one who requires further instruction (2 Timothy 2:24, 25) *gently.* If we exercise gentleness, we can keep the unity of the church intact. If we fail to be gentle—if we use "unnecessary roughness" with others—we risk dividing the body of Christ.

Even the soldiers who crucified Jesus would not divide the *robe* of Christ. Let us not be guilty of dividing the *body* of Christ.   —R. C. S.

3. Make every effort to keep the unity of the Spirit through the bond of peace.

Notice that *unity* and *peace* are linked in this verse. In a sense, peace is the by-product of unity; peace, in turn, serves to keep unity alive and well. This unity is said to be *of the Spirit.* Elsewhere Paul tells us, "We were all baptized by one Spirit into one body . . . and we were all given the one Spirit to drink" (1 Corinthians 12:13). The Spirit is also the source of the gifts (1 Corinthians 12:4, 7, 11) that are to be used to achieve "unity in the faith" (Ephesians 4:13).

B. ESSENTIAL PRINCIPLES (vv. 4-6)

What follows is a seven-part statement of Christian unity. It seems more than coincidental that Paul lists seven items, since seven is a frequent symbol in the Scriptures for completeness.

4. There is one body and one Spirit—just as you were called to one hope when you were called.

The *one body,* of course, is the church. Today the various denominations that exist make it difficult for many to see the church as one body. This was not the

Today's visual is a graphic reminder that the church is called to oneness. Display it as you discuss verses 4-6 in the text.

case in Paul's day, and this is not the case in God's eyes. In spite of the divisions created by man, to him there is still only one body.

The *one Spirit* is the Holy Spirit. Every Christian has the gift of the Holy Spirit (Acts 2:38; 5:32). Sadly, the purpose for which the Spirit has been given (to glorify Jesus, according to John 16:14) has been lost amid numerous questions and controversies concerning the Spirit's work.

The *one hope* to which we are *called* is no doubt the hope of eternal life. This hope is firmly grounded in the resurrection of Jesus, who declared, "Because I live, you also will live" (John 14:19).

5. . . . one Lord, one faith, one baptism.

It is obvious that the *one Lord* is Jesus himself. What does Paul mean by *one faith*? It may refer to the fact that Christians "have been saved, through faith" (Ephesians 2:8). However, it could also describe the substance of what we believe. A similar usage is found in the phrase "the faith that was once for all entrusted to the saints" (Jude 3).

Paul also mentions *one baptism.* Many might respond to Paul's claim by saying, "Wait a minute; there are many baptisms mentioned in the Bible: John the Baptist's baptism, baptism in the Holy Spirit, and water baptism." However, since Jesus included water baptism as part of what should be preached to all the world (Matthew 28:19, 20; Mark 16:16) and since Paul describes it as the act by which one is brought "into Christ" (Romans 6:3, 4; Galatians 3:27), it seems clear that the one baptism is water baptism.

This, however, does not end the discussion. A question might be raised concerning the mode of baptism—that is, how it is done. Some use sprinkling, others believe in pouring, and still others advocate immersion. Which is the *one baptism*? When we consider the meaning of the word *baptism* (the verb form means "to dip or plunge") and the evidence provided in the book of Acts (Acts 8:38, 39, for example, where Philip and the eunuch "went down into the water" and "came up out of the water"), it is clear that originally baptism was done by immersion.

6. . . . one God and Father of all, who is over all and through all and in all.

Last in Paul's description of the basics of Christian unity (though first in prominence and authority) is *God* himself. He is described as the *Father of all,* and his authority is affirmed in the phrase *who is over all and through all and in all.*

Notice in these verses the mention of the three persons of the Trinity: one Spirit, one Lord (Jesus), and one God.

II. RESPECTING DIVERSITY (EPHESIANS 4:7-12)

A. SOURCE OF OUR GIFTS (vv. 7-10)

7. But to each one of us grace has been given as Christ apportioned it.

Paul now moves from stating the principles of unity to considering the expression of unity in church life. He reminds his readers that *each one of us . . . has been given* some kind of spiritual gift that can be exercised in some ministry of the church. Here Paul describes these gifts as given by *Christ,* but these are also gifts of the Holy Spirit, as noted in 1 Corinthians 12:7-11.

8. This is why it says: "When he ascended on high, he led captives in his train and gave gifts to men."

Here Paul cites a passage from the Old Testament (Psalm 68:18). The text pictures a conquering hero rising up a mountain and then giving of the spoils of his victory as *gifts* to his people. Paul's main point is to affirm that the church has been given gifts by our Conqueror, Christ Jesus, who has *ascended* into Heaven. Each person has been given a gift, and all gifts are to be exercised for the good of the church.

WHAT DO YOU THINK?

Paul says that we who are called in Christ have one hope— the hope of eternal life. What value does that hope have in focusing, simplifying, and easing our lives?

WHAT DO YOU THINK?

People gifted by God have God's purpose to accomplish. In what ways do we see that "gift-and-purpose" strategy at work in our church?

HOW TO SAY IT

Agabus. AG-uh-bus.
Barak. BAIR-uk.
Ephesians. Ee-FEE-zhunz.
eunuch. YOU-nick.
Hades. HAY-deez.

What is meant by the phrase *he led captives in his train*? Some believe that the captives are those who march in triumph behind the victorious Christ and are the recipients of his gifts. (A similar idea is expressed in 2 Corinthians 2:14.) More likely, however, the phrase here describes Jesus' victory over his spiritual enemies. Colossians 2:15 supports this view by noting that at the cross Jesus, "having disarmed the powers and authorities, . . . made a public spectacle of them, triumphing over them by the cross." Judges 5:12 tells how Barak was commanded to "take captive your captives" and then describes in the succeeding verses Israel's victory over its oppressors. Thus the idea of conquest over one's enemies seems to be what the phrase implies.

Of special note in considering Paul's quotation from Psalm 68:18 is that it varies from the text found there, which reads, "You *received* [not *gave*] gifts from [the Hebrew more accurately reads "on behalf of"] men." Perhaps Paul recognized that the gifts Christ gives to his church have been given to him by God; however, in this verse he chooses to emphasize what Christ has given, since he has alluded to what Christ has "apportioned" in verse 7.

However we understand what Paul is saying, we can trust that, under the inspiration of the Holy Spirit, he is providing the correct understanding and application of the verse from Psalms.

9. (What does "he ascended" mean except that he also descended to the lower, earthly regions?

Since the passage Paul cited spoke of Christ's having *ascended,* then he must *also* have *descended.* To where did Christ descend? Paul says he *descended to the lower, earthly regions,* but that phrase is also confusing. What does Paul mean?

Some believe that this refers to the earth itself and is speaking of what happened in the incarnation: Jesus left the glories of Heaven, "became flesh and made his dwelling among us" (John 1:14), and then later ascended back to Heaven. Others claim that *the lower, earthly regions* refers to the grave or to Hades, the abode of the dead. Those who hold this view often cite 1 Peter 3:18-20 for support.

10. He who descended is the very one who ascended higher than all the heavens, in order to fill the whole universe.)

When he had accomplished his Father's task ("after he had provided purification for sins," Hebrews 1:3), Jesus *ascended higher than all the heavens* to "the right hand of the throne of God" (Hebrews 12:2). He is in this position of authority and prominence *in order to fill the whole universe*—perhaps a reference to his giving of the Spirit (Acts 2:33) and the gifts that accompany the Spirit's presence. Paul now proceeds to describe some of these gifts and their purpose.

B. VARIETY OF OUR GIFTS (v. 11)

11. It was he who gave some to be apostles, some to be prophets, some to be evangelists, and some to be pastors and teachers.

This verse describes some of the people whom God has gifted in order to help the church fulfill its mission. It is not surprising that this list begins with the office of the *apostles.* They were the men commissioned by Jesus to lead in the proclamation of the gospel and the establishment of the church.

Next, Paul mentions the *prophets.* Prophets were inspired by God to utter special proclamations of divine truth. A good example is Agabus, mentioned in Acts 11:28 and 21:10-12. Both apostles and prophets make up what Paul calls the "foundation" of the church (Ephesians 2:20).

Following the prophets is the office of *evangelists.* This word comes from a Greek verb meaning "to bring good news." An evangelist proclaims the good news found in the gospel. It would seem that the main focus of the evangelist's work is to reach lost people with the gospel. (Perhaps evangelists could be considered the equivalent of today's church planters.)

Only one person in the Bible is given the title of *evangelist*, and that is Philip (Acts 21:8). Timothy is told to do the work of an evangelist (2 Timothy 4:5), so many conclude that the title properly belongs to him as well. Their conclusion is probably correct.

Paul also mentions *pastors and teachers*. Frequently in modern usage, the word *pastor* is used to refer to the preaching minister of a congregation. While the preaching minister may perform a variety of pastoral duties, such duties are usually associated in the New Testament with the office of elder (also called "overseer"). The word for *pastor* literally means "shepherd," and it is the elders who are exhorted to "be shepherds of the church of God" (Acts 20:17, 28; 1 Peter 5:1, 2).

In the Greek text each of these offices has a definite article except *teachers*. Most students believe this indicates that the last two terms describe one office ("pastor-teachers" or "teaching elders"), not two. This office may well describe the "elders . . . whose work is preaching and teaching" (1 Timothy 5:17).

All of the leadership gifts mentioned in this verse are given for a special purpose, which Paul goes on to explain.

C. Purpose of Our Gifts (v. 12)

12. . . . *to prepare God's people for works of service, so that the body of Christ may be built up.*

What are these gifted leaders supposed to accomplish? They are *to prepare God's people for works of service*. The Greek word translated *prepare* was used in New Testament times to describe the setting of a broken bone. It is used in the New Testament itself to describe the mending of nets (Matthew 4:21). The expression here conveys the idea of "equipping" the saints.

Thus it is clear that one of the most important tasks of the leaders in any church is to encourage those in the congregation to exercise their gifts, carry out their ministries effectively, and thus bless the church. This, of course, does not mean that the church will ever outgrow the need for a vocational ministry. There is far too much work to do in the church for anyone in that position to work himself out of a job. It is true, however, that all Christians are ministers in the sense of being "servants." And as all exercise their gifts and fulfill their ministries, they will fulfill the purpose for which Christ has given these gifts: *so that the body of Christ may be built up.*

III. REACHING MATURITY (EPHESIANS 4:13-16)

A. The Process (vv. 13, 14)

13. . . . *until we all reach unity in the faith and in the knowledge of the Son of God and become mature, attaining to the whole measure of the fullness of Christ.*

The church achieves *unity* in Christ and becomes *mature* when each Christian is willing to use his or her gift or gifts to help others grow toward *the whole measure of the fullness of Christ*. To be like Jesus—this is the true measure of our progress.

14. *Then we will no longer be infants, tossed back and forth by the waves, and blown here and there by every wind of teaching and by the cunning and craftiness of men in their deceitful scheming.*

To be childlike in humility is commended by Jesus (Matthew 18:1-4), but here the immaturity of *infants* is something to be avoided. Paul wants Christians to be

What Do You Think?

How are some Christians being "blown here and there by every wind of teaching" in our culture?

knowledgeable enough not to be unstable. The word Paul uses for *tossed back and forth* describes a dizzying kind of spinning motion.

Christians should beware of both questionable doctrines and the men who use *cunning and craftiness* to deceive others. The mature must not be taken in by spiritual con artists and their clever words. They should know the Word well enough to be able to recognize the "counterfeit" message of the dishonest teacher or preacher.

B. The Product (vv. 15, 16)

15. Instead, speaking the truth in love, we will in all things grow up into him who is the Head, that is, Christ.

Truth without *love* can come across as harsh and vindictive. Love without truth can come across as sloppy and undisciplined sentimentality. The combination of both is necessary in order to enhance the process of growth toward the likeness of *Christ*.

16. From him the whole body, joined and held together by every supporting ligament, grows and builds itself up in love, as each part does its work.

Paul uses various medical terms in this verse to describe a *body* that is healthy and fully functioning. *Each part* is important to the whole. *Love* enables the parts to work together so that the body *grows and builds itself up*.

Of course, it is *from* Christ the Head (v. 15) that the health of the body comes. When all parts of the body respect his headship, the body will demonstrate the unity that will lead others to believe in Jesus (John 17:21).

A Healthy Body

David Feldman has written a book with an interesting title: *"How Does Aspirin Find a Headache?"* Perhaps we've wondered just how medicine is able to "find" the area that it is supposed to help. Or we've gone to the doctor for treatment on one part of the body, and are surprised when he or she starts examining some other part.

These peculiarities remind us that the body is a unit, and that each part is connected to the whole. While modern medicine has become very specialized, many physicians are seeing the value of what is called holistic medicine—looking at the individual as a whole person and considering more than just one's physical problems. Some now acknowledge the need to give spiritual matters a higher priority than they once did.

This interconnectedness is the reason that the body is one of the most frequently used metaphors for the church. Each part of the church is meant to function for the spiritual health of the entire church. No part functions alone or lives in isolation from the rest.

What part of the body should you be? God has already decided that through the gifts he has given you. You need only to identify those gifts and determine that you will use them as effectively as possible—not for your own benefit, but for the good of the body.
—R. C. S.

CONCLUSION

Every tool in the toolbox is important. Each one has a unique role to play. A toolbox made up of all hammers or all saws is useless to the handyman. However, when it is stocked with various types of tools, it can serve the handyman well and keep him prepared for any situation he might face. No tool is unnecessary, and none is more important than another.

The same is true in the church. We should not look down on our own gift(s) or disparage the gift(s) of a brother or sister. We must all lovingly offer our gifts to be used for the common goal of building the body of Christ.

What Do You Think?

The phrase "speaking the truth in love" implies it is possible to speak the truth without love. How can truth be loveless? Can love be truthless? Why or why not?

Prayer

Father, help me to discern the gifts you have given me. Grant me the courage to use those gifts. Help me to do my part to make my church the dynamic body of Christ that it needs to be. Through your Son, the greatest gift of all. Amen.

Thought to Remember

God has given you many gifts. Your gift to him is to use the gifts he has given you.

Discovery Learning

This page contains an alternate lesson plan emphasizing learning activities. Classes desiring such student involvement will find these suggestions helpful. The next page is a reproducible activity page to further enhance discovery learning.

LEARNING GOALS

After this lesson each student will be able to:

1. Summarize Paul's discussion of unity in terms of its source, expression, and result.

2. Tell how a variety of differing gifts can contribute to unity.

3. Identify a specific ministry gift that he or she has and suggest how the use of that gift can contribute to unity within the body.

INTO THE LESSON

Ask class members to name their favorite books (other than the Bible). Ask them to categorize the books (historical, fiction, western, biography, or some other). Write on a large poster the categories they name.

After the exercise, point out the diverse reading interests of the class. Then ask, "How is the church like a library of books?" (*There is a variety of interests and skills; each person is different and makes a unique contribution. Yet we are bound together into one body.*) Today, the apostle Paul will help us understand how important each of us is to the church and how the unity of believers blesses the church and each member of it.

INTO THE WORD

As you read Ephesians 4:1-16, ask students to watch for clues to the problems Paul was concerned about at Ephesus (*unity & maturity*). After reading the text and discovering the problems, tell the class that Paul has several tips for living together in God's family. Write these tips on a poster as you complete the following activities.

Option: Use the reproducible page that follows to supplement the following activities.

Tip #1: Qualities of a Good Family Member (vv. 2, 3). Assign each of the terms *humility, gentleness, patience, bearing with one another, love, unity,* and *peace* to a different person or group. Have each one define the assigned term and tell how it contributes to a healthy church.

Tip #2: Things That Bind Us Together (vv. 4-6). Ask the class to name the seven "Ones." Discuss, "In which of these areas is Christendom united? Where are the differences? What is the impact of division on the effectiveness of Christianity around the world?"

Tip #3: Remember That Our Various Gifts Come From God (vv. 7-10). Prepare a brief lecture on, or explanation of, these verses.

Tip #4: Appreciate the Diversity of Gifts (v. 11). Draw a sketch of books on a shelf. Ask the class to name and explain these gifts as you write their names on the spines of the books. (Explain that this is not a complete list. Other teachings about gifts can be found in other New Testament passages.)

Tip #5: Reach for the Goals (vv. 12-16). Ask the class members to scan verses 12-16 and list the various goals for the church (*preparing Christians for service, building up the body of Christ, unity, knowledge of the Son of God, maturity, doctrinal stability, etc.*). Write the class's answers on your visual poster. Then comment on Paul's imagery of a healthy body in verse 16. Point out Paul's emphasis on "each part does its work."

On the chalkboard write, "Unity in Christ's Church." Under this heading list *Source, Expression, Results.* Ask and discuss the following:

"What is the source of Christian unity?"

"How is unity expressed in the church?"

"What are the results of unity in the church?"

INTO LIFE

Tell the class that God teaches in 1 Peter 4:10 and 11 that each Christian has a gift to contribute to the church. Discuss, "How do we discover our gifts?" Then give each student a handout with the following questions listed under the heading "How to Unwrap Your Gifts."

1. What do you WANT or LIKE to do?

2. What are you willing to TRY?

3. What spiritual abilities do OTHERS SEE in you and what are you ASKED to do?

4. What are you NEVER asked to do?

5. What kind of service can you render BEST to Christ's body?

Discuss how these questions can help, giving brief illustrations.

Tell the class that we have a "library" of gifted people in our class—and we are a part of the church. Ask groups of four to take a few moments to work together and list what they see are "gifts" of each person in the group. After the group discussion, ask groups to shout out some of the gifts that were in their groups.

Tell the class, "This brief exercise answered questions 3 and 4 on the handout. Now focus on question 5 and pray a silent prayer committing yourself to use your gift(s) for God to bless and strengthen his church."

Searching for Unity in the Body of Christ

In Ephesians 4:1-16 Paul pleads for unity in the body of Christ. He commands his readers to display five qualities for living in harmony and then cites five kinds of gifts that God gave the church to foster unity. He also lists seven "ones" that demonstrate the unity of the church. Find the information needed in the Scriptures and locate them in the puzzle grid.

Five Qualities for Living in Harmony (verse 2): "Be completely _____ and _____; be _____, _____ with one another in _____."

Five Gifts Christ Gave the Church (v. 11)

_____

_____

_____

_____

The Seven "Ones" That Demonstrate the Unity of the Church (vv. 4-6)

_____

_____

_____

_____

_____

_____

_____

```
A P O S T L E S B B N T
I R L H O O O C K A L I
U O O G E V Q R R P K P
T P A T I E N T D T V P
E H S Q A S P I R I T A
A E V A N G E L I S T S
C T M H S Q E H J M M T
H S O D E L B M U H F O
E T A B T Q C O H V S R
R M I N R D J G D K F S
S B E A R I N G Y Y J I
T G O D F Q R T L S Z E
```

Appreciating Gifted Christian Friends

Name one or two Christian friends who have effectively used their spiritual gift(s) for the Lord's church. Write their name(s) and the gifts they use for Christ in this space.

Send these special persons a gift expressing your appreciation for their contribution to the lives of God's people. Gift ideas: a home-made card, a t-shirt with an appropriate logo, an offer of service such as baby-sitting for a night out. Be creative and expressive as you encourage these gifted people. Note the kind and design of your gift in this space.

Answers for the puzzle grid: Humble, gentle, patient, bearing, love; apostles, prophets, evangelists, pastors, teachers; body, Spirit, hope, Lord, faith, baptism, God.

New Life in Christ
Unit 2: *Called by Christ*
(Lessons 5-9)

CALLED TO RESPONSIBLE LIVING

LESSON 8

WHY TEACH THIS LESSON?

Why do so many people wander from the church until they become parents? What is it about parenthood that draws so many of them back to the church? It's called *responsibility*—that sense that the welfare of another depends on oneself. A person may treat his or her own life with reckless abandon, but when a child is added to the home, many times the person will "wake up" and act with more responsibility.

Perhaps you have some in your class who have returned to the church after a time of irresponsibility. Surely there are some who have been faithful since their youth. Others may be just discovering the church, from a variety of backgrounds. Whatever route has brought them to your classroom, you have an opportunity today to help them become more responsible. Paul gives extremely practical tips that are as helpful today as they were when he wrote them.

INTRODUCTION

A. WASH UP

A little boy was having trouble with his pronunciation. On one occasion he meant to say, "We go to church to worship." Instead it came out, "We go to church to wash up." Paul, however, may well have agreed with this young man. We go to church both to worship God and to learn how to "wash up" our lives so that they become pleasing to God. Sunday worship and daily living are tightly bound together. Some like to try to separate these, but the Bible will not let us get away with that. Sincere Christians want to do right between Sundays as well as on them.

Worship is not for those who are perfect. No one should stay away from church because he has sinned. Going to church is probably just what such a person needs to give him what he needs to "wash up" (stop sinning) and to live in a manner pleasing to God.

B. LESSON BACKGROUND

Last week's lesson brought us to the portion of Ephesians where Paul considers issues that involve practical Christian living. Beginning with 4:17, he calls followers of Jesus to "put off" the way of living associated with their pre-Christian lifestyles (v. 22) and to "put on the new self, created to be like God in true righteousness and holiness" (v. 24). Paul then gives a series of exhortations concerning a Christian's conduct (vv. 25-32).

The text for our lesson today, taken from portions of chapters 5 and 6, continues these exhortations, with a special emphasis on responsible conduct in the world, the church, and the home. In each of these areas of life, we have a duty to live by the highest standards of behavior—the standards of Christ himself.

Despite the two thousand years that separate us from Paul's time, the need for his words is just as great today as it was then. His words speak to a society

DEVOTIONAL READING:
EPHESIANS 5:6-21
BACKGROUND SCRIPTURE:
EPHESIANS 5:1—6:9
PRINTED TEXT:
EPHESIANS 5:1-5, 18-29; 6:1-4

LESSON AIMS

After this lesson the student will be able to:

1. Relate Paul's description of proper Christian conduct in the community, the church, and the home.

2. Contrast Christ's call to responsible living with the thinking that governs much of modern society.

3. Pinpoint an area of personal, home, or church life where a more responsible commitment to Christ is needed, and devise a plan to address that need.

Jul
23

KEY VERSE

Submit to one another out of reverence for Christ.
—Ephesians 5:21

Today's visual is a delightful illustration of a child's fondness for imitating his or her parents. Discuss: "Are we as fond of imitating God?"

WHAT DO YOU THINK?

What was it about your childhood heroes that made you want to be like them? What about God makes you want to be like him?

WHAT DO YOU THINK?

What sins do we especially need to be on guard against so that there will "not be even a hint of" them among us? How can we do that?

that is becoming increasingly uncivil and immoral. They speak to a society in which churches battle each other rather than the real enemy. They speak to a society that seems helpless as marriages continue to collapse at an alarming rate.

I. RESPONSIBLE IN THE WORLD (EPHESIANS 5:1-5)

A. IMITATE THE FATHER (v. 1)

1. Be imitators of God, therefore, as dearly loved children.

Young people will always choose someone to imitate, and their primary model is their parents. Since we are *children* of God, we should want to be like our Father.

The Greek word translated *imitators* comes from a word that gives us our English term *mimic*. Parents consider it a great compliment when their children want to be like them. Surely it pleases our Father when we want to be like him.

B. WALK IN LOVE (v. 2)

2. And live a life of love, just as Christ loved us and gave himself up for us as a fragrant offering and sacrifice to God.

If we are true imitators of God, one of our first priorities will be to *live a life of love*. Paul defines the standard of this love: *just as Christ loved us.* Our Father's love for us is illustrated by his willingness to give his Son to die for us.

The impact of Jesus' death is described using terminology taken from the Old Testament sacrificial system. The word *offering* is the term normally used for a grain, or cereal, offering. The word *sacrifice* normally indicates an offering during which an animal was slain. Both kinds of offerings would have been quite familiar to people who were acquainted with Judaism.

The presence of a *fragrant offering* was frequently associated with the Old Testament sacrificial system (note the phrase "a pleasing aroma" or "an aroma pleasing to the Lord" in Exodus 29:18; Leviticus 1:9, 13, 17; 2:2). The usage of the term here indicates that God accepted Jesus' sacrifice as an atonement for the sins of the world. Paul used similar language in expressing his appreciation for a gift from the Philippians (Philippians 4:18).

C. AVOID IMMORALITY (v. 3)

3. But among you there must not be even a hint of sexual immorality, or of any kind of impurity, or of greed, because these are improper for God's holy people.

As Paul continues his description of behavior that is consistent with Christian commitment, he issues a warning against *sexual immorality*. This was an area where those who had come to Christ out of paganism (and out of the sexual perversion associated with it) needed special guidance.

The phrase *sexual immorality* translates the Greek word *porneia*, which is the source of our English word "pornography." *Porneia* is a general term for sexual misconduct. The word *impurity* is a literal translation of the Greek term and can describe any kind of immoral behavior.

We often interpret *greed* to mean an inordinate desire for money or possessions. The same Greek word is translated "lust" in Ephesians 4:19, where it is again linked with "impurity." Carelessness in these matters is incompatible with the *holy* lifestyle that is to characterize followers of Jesus. Paul's counsel concerning each of these sins is firm: *there must not be even a hint* that any of them is present.

D. AVOID IMPURE SPEECH (v. 4)

4. Nor should there be obscenity, foolish talk or coarse joking, which are out of place, but rather thanksgiving.

In discussing one's personal speech, Paul uses three terms that are used nowhere else in the New Testament. *Obscenity* describes any kind of shameful or crude speech. *Foolish talk* is literally "the speech of morons." These two terms are combined with *coarse joking*, which could well include the double entendre and other kinds of "off-color" humor that are so prevalent in our world. These forms of speech are *out of place*—inappropriate or unbecoming. Sadly, however, much of this kind of talk is common in our churches today. Instead of improper speech, Paul admonishes Christians to let the trademark of their talk be *thanksgiving*.

E. REMEMBER THIS (v. 5)

5. For of this you can be sure: No immoral, impure or greedy person—such a man is an idolater—has any inheritance in the kingdom of Christ and of God.

The persons described here are essentially those who have committed the sins mentioned in verse 3. The word *immoral* translates another form of the word *porneia* ("sexual immorality"). The *greedy person* is further described as an *idolater* (Paul also links these two sins in Colossians 3:5). The connection is not hard to grasp: one who covets anything is in grave danger of allowing that item to have a more important place in his life than God does. The item, in effect, becomes that individual's idol.

One dare not treat the sins Paul has listed here as trivial, for too much is at stake. The person whose life is controlled by one of these evils has no *inheritance in the kingdom of Christ and of God*. The follower of Christ must be determined not to compromise in any way his standards of speech and behavior.

II. RESPONSIBLE IN THE CHURCH (EPHESIANS 5:18-21)

A. OUR INNER POWER (v. 18)

18. Do not get drunk on wine, which leads to debauchery. Instead, be filled with the Spirit.

This prohibition against drunkenness shows that alcohol abuse was a problem in the first century. Drunkenness not only harms the body of the person who consumes the *wine*, but it often causes behavior that harms others. Here its ill effects are described with the word *debauchery*. The Greek term behind this word implies waste. The staggering number of lives ruined and wasted by alcohol abuse is one of the saddest statistics of our time.

Instead of merely telling people not to drink, Paul provides a positive alternative: *be filled with the Spirit*. The Holy Spirit can bring about far better and more productive results than the artificial and temporary "high" of alcoholic "spirits." It should be noted that the verb form in the phrase *be filled with the Spirit* does not indicate a one-time filling, but a constant condition ("go on being filled"). This was not something that Paul's readers had never experienced before. It was something they were already experiencing, in which Paul wanted them to continue.

B. OUR CORPORATE WORSHIP (vv. 19, 20)

19. Speak to one another with psalms, hymns and spiritual songs. Sing and make music in your heart to the Lord.

A church made up of people filled with the Spirit expresses itself in meaningful corporate worship. Christians are to *speak to one another with psalms, hymns and spiritual songs. Psalms* almost certainly refers to the book of Psalms in the Old Testament. No doubt the early church integrated certain Psalms into their times of worship. Some believe that the word *hymns* describes Christian compositions, examples of which may be recorded in some of Paul's letters. (See Philippians 2:6-8 and 1 Timothy 3:16.) The term *spiritual songs* may describe songs that were sung

WHAT DO YOU THINK?

Paul suggests an alternative to drunkenness: being Spirit-filled. How is true conversion the solution to such soul-killing behavior?

WHAT DO YOU THINK?

Paul describes a worship service where people "sing and make music . . . to the Lord" and are "always giving thanks to God the Father for everything." What is the key to having such beneficial worship times?

spontaneously in the worship assemblies. Whatever these words mean specifically, they indicate that there was a variety of music used in first-century worship.

The phrase *make music* translates a word that describes playing a stringed instrument; thus some see in the two terms used here a reference to both vocal and instrumental music. Others think that form is not at issue since this music is to be performed in the *heart*. They believe the point is one of personal sincerity and purpose in worship.

20. . . . always giving thanks to God the Father for everything, in the name of our Lord Jesus Christ.

The personality of a local congregation should always be marked by an attitude of gratitude. Most definitely our thanksgiving should never be limited to one "official" Thanksgiving Day each year!

C. A VITAL PRINCIPLE (v. 21)

21. Submit to one another out of reverence for Christ.

Paul now moves from the subject of worship to interpersonal relationships. His command to *submit* has received much attention, mostly because of its use in verse 22. At this point notice that, in the church, everyone is to *submit to one another*. Such mutual submission is based on our common *reverence for Christ*—that is, our respect for his authority.

III. RESPONSIBLE IN THE HOME (EPHESIANS 5:22-29; 6:1-4)

A. WORDS FOR WIVES (vv. 22-24)

22. Wives, submit to your husbands as to the Lord.

Here Paul applies the principle of submission, introduced in verse 21, to *wives*. When Paul admonishes wives to *submit to your husbands, as to the Lord,* he does not mean that a wife should treat her husband as if he were Jesus. Paul is saying that a wife's submission to her husband is a service that she does unto the Lord, or for the Lord's glory. A similar phrase is used in encouraging servants to obey their masters "just as you would obey Christ" (Ephesians 6:5-7).

23. For the husband is the head of the wife as Christ is the head of the church, his body, of which he is the Savior.

The authority given to the *husband* is certainly not absolute. That he is *the head of the wife* does not give him license to coerce his wife into submission. The standard against which his headship must be measured is clear: *as Christ is the head of the church.* This indicates that marriage is truly "holy matrimony." It is meant to give both husband and wife a deeper appreciation of their relationship to Christ.

Notice the close ties between home and church: the order in the home is to reflect how Christ and the church are related. Whether a man really knows Christ and follows his example will be evident from the state of his household. Thus one qualification of the would-be elder is that he "manage his own family well" (1 Timothy 3:4). The next verse then asks, "If anyone does not know how to manage his own family, how can he take care of God's church?"

24. Now as the church submits to Christ, so also wives should submit to their husbands in everything.

Paul's teaching that *wives should submit to their husbands in everything* is not meant to demean women. (It is important to remember that Christianity brought to women a sense of dignity that the pagan world of the first century had not provided.) His teaching establishes a sense of order in the home. It does not mean that men are smarter or more valuable than women. In any football team, the quarterback may not be the smartest player; however, order in the huddle requires someone to take the role of leader. In an army the general may not be more intelligent than the private, yet the necessity of discipline and order in a military unit requires that someone be in charge. Paul is establishing a similar arrangement of authority in the Christian home, modeled on the arrangement that every Christian understands: the submission of the church to Jesus.

B. WORDS FOR HUSBANDS (vv. 25-29)

25. Husbands, love your wives, just as Christ loved the church and gave himself up for her.

While *submit* is the primary command to *wives*, the priority for *husbands* is *love*. Paul's command is followed with an extraordinary standard for husbands to follow. Husbands are to love their wives *just as Christ loved the church*. How did he love the church? He *gave himself up for her*. That is the kind of sacrificial love with which husbands are to treat their wives.

26. . . . to make her holy, cleansing her by the washing with water through the word.

Paul then comments briefly on the degree with which Jesus loves the church and desires what is best for it. He says that Jesus gave himself in order *to make her holy* and provided for her *cleansing . . . by the washing with water through the word*. Most likely this cleansing with water is a reference to Christian baptism (cf. Acts 22:16). *The word* is the word of God (the gospel), which Peter describes as the "imperishable" seed that produces the new birth (1 Peter 1:23-25).

27. . . . and to present her to himself as a radiant church, without stain or wrinkle or any other blemish, but holy and blameless.

Jesus also wants his *church* (his bride) to be *a radiant church, without stain or wrinkle or any other blemish*. As the loving husband, Jesus took it upon himself to do what was necessary to make his bride beautiful. He took care of all the spots, wrinkles, and blemishes caused by sin through his sacrifice on the cross.

28, 29. In this same way, husbands ought to love their wives as their own bodies. He who loves his wife loves himself. After all, no one ever hated his own body, but he feeds and cares for it, just as Christ does the church.

Paul applies Christ's love for the *church* to the *love* of *husbands* for their *wives*. He says that husbands *ought to love their wives as* they do *their own bodies*.

Many men have bought into the self-centered spirit of our time and have abandoned their responsibilities at home. Believing that these duties stood in the way of their personal happiness, they have selfishly pursued interests outside the home and family. Here Paul declares that a man's love of self and of his wife are interconnected: *he who loves his wife loves himself*. For the husband to love his wife *just as Christ does the church* is in his own best interests and brings him the greatest sense of fulfillment as a man.

Some may ask whether (or to what degree) Paul's teaching is applicable in situations where the husband or the wife is not a Christian. Guidance for proper conduct in these situations is provided in such Scriptures as 1 Corinthians 7: 12-16 and 1 Peter 3:1-6. Certainly Paul's teaching should encourage us to take seriously his words about not being "yoked together with unbelievers" (2 Corinthians 6:14-18). Our youth need to receive special instruction in these matters to avoid substantial heartache in the future.

HIS MOST IMPORTANT TITLES

The man had already enjoyed an outstanding career of public service when he was elected a United States Congressman. After serving there, he was made head of the Central Intelligence Agency. When the United States reopened diplomatic relations with China, he was appointed Chief Liaison Officer in China. Then he was

DAILY BIBLE READINGS

Monday, July 17—Turn Your Backs on Pagan Ways (Ephesians 5:1-5)

Tuesday, July 18—Live as Children of the Light (Ephesians 5:6-14)

Wednesday, July 19—Serve and Worship With Thanks (Ephesians 5:15-20)

Thursday, July 20—Words for Christians in Families (Ephesians 5:21-27)

Friday, July 21—Love as Christ Loved the Church (Ephesians 5:28-33)

Saturday, July 22—Treat Everyone With Love and Respect (Ephesians 6:1-9)

Sunday, July 23—Hear God's Word and Obey (Luke 6:43-49)

made chairman of the Republican National Committee. After that he was elected vice president of the United States. And last, but certainly not least, he was elected President of the United States. When his distinguished public life had ended, George Bush claimed that he still held his three most important titles: husband, father, and grandfather!

What an example this is for us all! It is noble to carry the title of husband. No one should ever take it lightly. It is equally noble to have the title of wife. To be a father or a mother is one of the greatest privileges one can ever enjoy. And every grandparent knows that to be a grandfather or a grandmother is such a wonderful blessing that it fully deserves the description of *grand*.

In an age and in a society that takes such wonders as these so very lightly, it is refreshing to hear a former President of the United States express his personal satisfaction in the simple titles of husband, father, and grandfather. Whatever our other achievements in life, the roles we fulfill in our families are of true and eternal significance.   —R. C. S.

C. WORDS FOR CHILDREN (6:1-4)

1-3. Children, obey your parents in the Lord, for this is right. "Honor your father and mother"—which is the first commandment with a promise—"that it may go well with you and that you may enjoy long life on the earth."

Children are admonished to *obey* their *parents*. They are to do so *in the Lord*, or as part of their duty to the Lord. Similar language occurs in connection with the wife's submission to her husband (Ephesians 5:22) and with slaves' obedience of their masters (6:5-7).

Paul strengthens his words with a *promise* from the Ten Commandments (Exodus 20:12): *that it may go well with you and that you may enjoy long life on the earth.* This is not a guarantee of long life to all obedient children, but it does call attention to the fact that obedient, God-fearing children are far less likely to engage in the kind of behavior that shortens so many lives.

4. Fathers, do not exasperate your children; instead, bring them up in the training and instruction of the Lord.

Fathers held a position of great authority in the ancient world. In some cases they possessed an almost dictatorial power over their *children*. Paul tells Christian fathers that in the exercise of their leadership they must not *exasperate* their children. All children will get angry at times, and no parent can avoid that. Paul is encouraging fathers not to be the source of such anger by their hasty words or thoughtless actions. Remember, fathers, that our children's perception of the heavenly Father will depend in large part on the kind of fathers we are!

CONCLUSION

Why do we have to be concerned about the public aspects of our faith? "Isn't Christianity a private matter?" some wonder. It is true that certain areas of the Christian life are private (one's prayer life, for example), but a Christian's testimony is meant to have public consequences. This is the implication of Jesus' challenge to us: we are to be "the salt of the earth" and "the light of the world" (Matthew 5:13, 14). We are not to be hermits. We must live our lives where people can see the difference Jesus has made.

Each of us has a sphere of influence for Christ that no one else possesses. There are people we contact each day whom no one else has the opportunity to reach with the gospel. We need to accept the challenge to leave our "comfort zones" and make an impact on a world that is dying. After all, the purpose of Christianity is not just to make us comfortable. It is to make us righteous. And sometimes we have to be made uncomfortable in order to learn righteousness.

Discovery Learning

*This page contains an alternate lesson plan emphasizing learning activities. Classes
desiring such student involvement will find these suggestions helpful. The next page
is a reproducible activity page to further enhance discovery learning.*

LEARNING GOALS

After participating in this lesson, each student will be able to:

1. Relate Paul's description of proper Christian conduct in the community, in the church, and in the home.

2. Contrast Christ's call to responsible living with the thinking that governs much of modern society.

3. Pinpoint an area of personal, home, or church life where a more responsible commitment to Christ is needed, and devise a plan to address that need.

INTO THE LESSON

Before class, write each of the letters of the word *imitate* on a different sheet of construction paper. Begin the class time by giving the seven sheets of paper to seven class members, one to each person. Ask them to arrange themselves so that they spell a word. When they have formed the word *imitate,* thank them and ask them to mount the letters on a wall or bulletin board.

Then ask the class members to share with a partner the name of one person they like to imitate and why. After a moment of sharing, ask, "What are some of the qualities of character or skills that you find you like to imitate?" Write their answers on a chalkboard. Tell the class, "Sometimes it is difficult to imitate people because their lives are so much better than ours. The standards are so high. Yet Paul tells us to imitate God. What a lofty goal!"

INTO THE WORD

Prepare a large visual poster for the class. At the top of the poster write, "Imitators of God." Below the heading make two columns headed "*Dos*" and "*Don'ts*."

As you begin the activity, call attention to the first four words of Ephesians 5:1: *Be imitators of God.* God gives us a very practical and easily understood list of things to do or not do as we imitate him. Then read Ephesians 5:1-5, 18—6:4, pausing after each verse to ask, "What are we to do or not do as imitators of God?" Have a class member write the answers on the poster.

When you begin reading and listing *dos* and *don'ts* from verses 21 and following, explain that this is God's will for the Christian home. Then proceed with the activity through the end of the Scripture text. Be sure to keep this activity moving. Do not let it drag.

INTO LIFE

Ask the class to review the list of *dos* and *don'ts,* looking for teachings that are contrary to the teachings or practices of our culture. There will be many! Circle each one they mention with a colored marker, asking *why* or *how* this is different from what our culture accepts.

Then discuss the following questions:

1. Why does God ask us to do or not do the things that are listed? What are the practical outcomes of the behavior he is requesting from us? (You will need to take time to allow students to review each of the items on the list, but keep the discussion moving.)

2. Why do you think our culture reacts negatively to the teaching about wives' submitting to husbands in verse 22? Be sure to read the lesson commentary for help in applying this verse. Also ask, "Does the context of this passage imply selfish power or selfless service by the husband? Why?" Another question that could be used in this context is, "How could Paul's teaching about submission be misused or misapplied?"

3. What, according to our text, are our motivations or reasons for imitating God? (See 5:1, 2, 5.)

To make the lesson personal, give each person a letter-size sheet of paper with the heading, "My Commitment to Be an Imitator of God." Below that print, "I have been an 'Imitator of God' by obeying these teachings." (Students will write commands from the *dos* and *don'ts* list that they believe they have obeyed fairly well.)

Almost midway down the page print, "My failure to obey these commands shows that I have not always been an 'Imitator of God,' and I need to improve." (Students will write commands from the *dos* and *don'ts* list that they believe they have not obeyed well.)

Near the bottom of the page print, "My plan or steps to bring honor to God by changing the above-mentioned behavior is to do this." (Here the students will suggest specific actions they can take to improve their obedience to the Master.)

Option: To make application of the lesson, distribute copies of the reproducible page that follows. Have the students "gauge" themselves on doing what Paul commands here. (Keep the students' responses private.)

Play a tape recording of an appropriate song, such as "I Surrender All" or "More Like the Master," while the students complete the handout described above or the reproducible page. Close with a prayer.

God's Desire and Our Response

In today's lesson God calls us to imitate him. Below are summations of several of the behaviors God asks of his people in today's Scripture text. "Gauge" your response to God's will by drawing an arrow that indicates how well you believe you are fulfilling God's desire for you.

Poor Very Well	Poor Very Well	Poor Very Well
Example	Sexually Pure	Not Greedy
Poor Very Well	Poor Very Well	Poor Very Well
Pure Speech	No Drunkenness	Sing and Make Music in Your Heart to the Lord
Poor Very Well	Poor Very Well	Poor Very Well
Submissive to My Husband/ Love and Sacrifice for My Wife	Obedient to My Parents	Bringing Up My Children to Know the Lord

A Commitment to One I Love

Read Ephesians 5:22—6:4. If you are married, engaged, or a parent, write a brief letter of commitment to your spouse or children based on these verses. If you are a single adult, write a brief prayer, based on the principles in this text, for a married couple or parent you know and love.

CALLED TO STAND FIRM

LESSON 9

WHY TEACH THIS LESSON?

Sitting in an office in Ohio, an editor has a hard time imagining all the places a lesson will be used. Certainly the vast majority will be used in the United States and Canada, where Christianity is relatively easy. Very few believers in North America run any risk of physical injury or death. To them, the idea of Christian "armor" may sound quite strange.

Other users, however, may wish they could have a literal armor. Christians in areas dominated by militant adherents to other religions do actually find their lives in jeopardy. More Christians have been martyred in the twentieth century than in any century before. If the Lord tarries, the twenty-first will probably see even more!

But the battle about which Paul writes is not a physical battle. Encourage your students to see the real danger—those spiritual forces of darkness. Whether your students sit comfortably in a magnificent edifice or huddle in an inconspicuous location to avoid detection, their enemy is one and the same. And the ones in the comfortable chairs may be more at risk than the others!

INTRODUCTION

A. IS LIFE A BATTLE?

Some years ago, a controversy developed within a group of churches over the use of hymns that included military terminology. The leadership convened to study the issue and made the decision to have the questionable hymns removed from church hymnals. Protests, however, immediately arose from the "rank and file" within the church.

While some likely protested because of the nostalgia associated with these hymns, others objected because they found personal strength and encouragement in these songs. Their personal experience testified that life is sometimes very much like a battle.

As we study today's text, we will see how Paul used military metaphors (particularly the parts of a soldier's armor) to emphasize the seriousness of the Christian life. For those who have experienced the battles of life, these words will offer real hope. They will reassure us that God has given us all the resources we need to wage war victoriously and to overcome our enemy.

B. LESSON BACKGROUND

The passage before us today is well known to many. Young people who grew up attending church, Sunday school, and church camp may well have been asked to memorize the portion of this lesson that outlines the armor of God.

We have seen how Paul has touched on many important theological issues in his letter to the Ephesians. In the first chapter he brought us to the "heavenly realms" (v. 3), where he gave us insights into God's marvelous plan for the universe. In today's text we will see how the apostle brings us "back to earth" and to the harsh realities of living a Christlike life in a hostile world. At the same time, he calls our attention to the fact that the real conflict of which we are a part is not on earth, but in the "heavenly realms" (Ephesians 6:12).

DEVOTIONAL READING:
JOHN 14:15-27

BACKGROUND SCRIPTURE:
EPHESIANS 6:10-24

PRINTED TEXT:
EPHESIANS 6:10-24

LESSON AIMS

After this lesson each student will be able to:

1. List the items included in "the whole armor of God."

2. Tell why military metaphors are appropriate for explaining the nature of the Christian life.

3. Suggest a specific way to "put on" a particular piece of the armor of God.

Jul
30

KEY VERSE

Finally, be strong in the Lord and in his mighty power.
—*Ephesians 6:10*

Our real enemy is not of this world; he is a spiritual being. We cannot overcome him in our own strength. Today's text will reveal the source of divine power by which we can defeat him!

I. OUR CONFLICT (EPHESIANS 6:10-12)

A. The Challenge (v. 10)

10. Finally, be strong in the Lord and in his mighty power.

Paul reminds us that the Christian life is a conflict so intense that whatever strength we can muster of ourselves is not enough to survive. We must *be strong in the Lord and in his mighty power*. Paul has already noted that this *mighty power* is that "which he [God] exerted in Christ when he raised him from the dead and seated him at his right hand in the heavenly realms" (1:19, 20).

WE DON'T KNOW OUR OWN STRENGTH

When a person shakes our hand and squeezes too hard, or hugs us and embraces too tightly, we sometimes say, "He doesn't know his own strength!" In some cases there is more truth to that statement than meets the eye. We read of individuals coming to the aid of a loved one who is pinned under the wreckage of an automobile accident. Suddenly they find themselves able to lift something they could not ordinarily lift. The crisis gave them a "rush" of adrenaline that provided a strength far beyond their ordinary ability.

Something similar to this may be said with regard to our spiritual strength. Because that strength comes from God and not from us, it is far greater than we realize. Many people have found themselves able to endure a period of suffering that they would never have thought they could endure. Many have found victory over temptations that they had thought too strong for them. Martin Luther said it well in his great hymn, "A Mighty Fortress Is Our God": "Did we in our own strength confide, Our striving would be losing."

Regardless of the situation we face, even if we have never faced it before, God's strength will never prove inadequate. For every Christian it can truly be said, "He doesn't know his own strength"—for the Christian's strength is God's. —R. C. S.

B. The Adversary (vv. 11, 12)

11. Put on the full armor of God so that you can take your stand against the devil's schemes.

Paul was quite familiar with the *armor* used by Roman soldiers. Paul was writing this epistle as a prisoner in Rome, where, according to Acts 28:16, he "was allowed to live by himself, with a soldier to guard him." Perhaps Paul was reflecting on this soldier's attire when writing these words in our text. (Of course, he had been in the presence of Roman soldiers on other occasions.) It is also possible that Paul's words were based on an Old Testament passage in Isaiah 59:17, where God himself is portrayed as wearing certain pieces of armor. If so, Paul would have truly been describing the "armor of God."

The purpose of equipping ourselves with this *armor* is so that we will be able to *take [our] stand against the devil's schemes*. The word Paul uses for *stand* is the common military term for holding one's ground. Paul reminds us that however difficult our struggle, at the end of the battle we will stand—victorious—in the strength of the Lord.

12. For our struggle is not against flesh and blood, but against the rulers, against the authorities, against the powers of this dark world and against the spiritual forces of evil in the heavenly realms.

Our battle is first and foremost a *spiritual* battle. It is not against people (the unsaved are not our enemy). Our struggle is *not against flesh and blood, but* against the rulers, against the authorities, against the powers of this dark world. Clearly these are references to Satan and his forces; Satan is called "the prince of this world" (John 12:31; 14:30; 16:11) and "the ruler of the kingdom of the air" (Ephesians 2:2). In Acts 26:18 darkness is associated with the power of Satan.

The phrase *in the heavenly realms* (literally, "in the heavenlies") calls attention to the same territory where both Christ (Ephesians 1:20) and his followers (2:6) are said to dwell. Thus to be "in the heavenlies" is to be part of the spiritual battlefield, where God's forces and the forces of the devil continue to wage war.

II. OUR EQUIPMENT (EPHESIANS 6:13-17)

A. ITS IMPORTANCE (v. 13)

13. Therefore put on the full armor of God, so that when the day of evil comes, you may be able to stand your ground, and after you have done everything, to stand.

The forces of God will *be able to stand* against the attacks of the opponents described in verse 12. The book of Revelation shows that Christ and his church will reign forever. However, in the here and now the church must be prepared for an intense battle. Every piece of *the full armor of God* has its purpose in this battle.

The day of evil does not likely refer to some great outpouring of evil. It probably refers to any period of time during which the Christian finds himself under severe attack from the enemy. (The *New English Bible* translates it, "when things are at their worst.") Obviously Satan can mount an assault at any time, yet most of us can testify to instances when his opposition seemed especially fierce. On those occasions, the armor of God will never let us down or prove to be inferior.

B. THE BELT (v. 14a)

14a. Stand firm then, with the belt of truth buckled around your waist.

The first piece of armor mentioned is the *belt*. The belt was a basic and practical piece of equipment. First, it helped to keep the breastplate in place. It also included a place for the soldier to keep his sword where it could be drawn at a moment's notice. Besides that, the soldier could pull his tunic up and tuck it under his belt, which would allow him to run without hindrance.

Paul states that the Christian's *belt* is *truth*. Our enemy Satan is the father of lies (John 8:44), so truth is, like the belt, a basic and practical piece of our equipment. The believer knows, not only that "the truth . . . is in Jesus" (Ephesians 4:21), but that Jesus himself is the truth (John 14:6). Such knowledge gives the Christian the ability to detect falsehood whenever it surfaces.

C. THE BREASTPLATE (v. 14b)

14b. . . . with the breastplate of righteousness in place.

The second item mentioned is *the breastplate of righteousness*. The main purpose of the breastplate was to protect the vital organs, particularly the heart and lungs, where a wound would almost certainly be fatal. Some have maintained that, since breastplates would not have covered one's back, Paul's words are to be understood as exhorting Christians to face the enemy and never retreat. That is good advice; however, breastplates in the first century commonly covered the back as well as the front of the soldier.

What is meant by the word *righteousness*? Frequently in his writings Paul uses this word to describe the righteousness that we receive through Jesus (Romans 3:21, 22; 2 Corinthians 5:21; Philippians 3:9), for we can never be righteous enough on our own to deserve Heaven. At other times he uses the term to refer to the Christian's righteous lifestyle (Romans 6:19; Ephesians 5:8, 9). Righteousness in either form is a powerful and effective defense against evil.

The humorous illustration in today's visual reminds us that we have a strength not our own as we face the schemes and the assaults of the devil.

How to Say It

Colosse. Ko-LAHSS-ee.
Ephesians. Ee-FEE-zhunz.
Ephesus. EF-uh-sus.
Isaiah. Eye-ZAY-uh.
Philippians. Fih-LIP-ee-unz.
Tychicus. TICK-ih-cuss.

The importance of the heart in Scripture makes significant the fact that the breastplate covered the heart. The heart is the center of one's moral discernment. That is the reason Jesus blessed those who are "pure in heart" (Matthew 5:8). Satan would like nothing more than to see that purity soiled and ruined.

D. THE SHOES (v. 15)

15. . . . *and with your feet fitted with the readiness that comes from the gospel of peace.*

Since an army marches on its *feet*, its footwear is very important. Often soldiers would wear shoes with spikes in the soles to give additional stability on rugged terrain. The Christian's footwear is *the readiness that comes from the gospel of peace*. While we are at war with the devil, we are to communicate to the world a message of *peace*—peace between God and man and peace between individuals who were formerly hostile toward one another (cf. Ephesians 2:14-17).

This verse brings to mind a portion of Paul's declaration of the priority of preaching: "How beautiful are the feet of those who bring good news!" (Romans 10:15, from Isaiah 52:7).

E. THE SHIELD (v. 16)

16. *In addition to all this, take up the shield of faith, with which you can extinguish all the flaming arrows of the evil one.*

The *shield* in New Testament times protected its bearer from spears or arrows. Here the Christian is described as having to ward off *the flaming arrows of the evil one.* Such a reference emphasizes the intensely personal nature of the Christian's battle. We do not fight some vague impersonal "force," but a real person: Satan. His attacks are intense and his weapons are life-threatening, but our *shield of faith* has the ability not just to deflect the arrows but to *extinguish all* of them. "This is the victory that has overcome the world, even our faith" (1 John 5:4).

F. THE HELMET (v. 17a)

17a. *Take the helmet of salvation.*

Next to the heart, the head was the most vulnerable area of the soldier. To protect it, the first-century soldier wore a *helmet* of bronze and leather. Today we recognize how important protecting the head is—not just to soldiers, but to football and baseball players, bike riders, skateboarders, race car drivers, and many others.

It is fitting to think of our *salvation* as protecting our minds. The battle for our souls is also a battle for our minds. It is in the mind where evil takes hold, and it is the mind that God wants to transform (Romans 12:2; Ephesians 4:23).

G. THE SWORD (v. 17b)

17b. . . . *and the sword of the Spirit, which is the word of God.*

The final item mentioned is *the sword of the Spirit, which is the word of God.* This verse reminds us how Jesus countered the devil's temptations in the wilderness by quoting Scripture. The Word of God is infinitely more powerful than the devil. Realizing this should impress upon us how vital it is to make the diligent study and memorization of Scripture a priority in our lives.

It has been noted by some that this is the only offensive weapon that Paul mentions. Our battle with Satan is not only a matter of defending ourselves. We need also to launch an offensive against evil. Jesus' picture of the gates of Hades' not prevailing against the church (Matthew 16:18) is a picture of the church attacking and breaking down the gates, not merely holding off an offensive launched from them.

Daily Bible Readings

Monday, July 24—*Be Strong in the Lord* (Ephesians 6:10-15)

Tuesday, July 25—*Pray Always in the Spirit* (Ephesians 6:16-20)

Wednesday, July 26—*Grace, Peace, and Love From God* (Ephesians 6:21-24)

Thursday, July 27—*God's Spirit Will Strengthen You* (John 14:15-27)

Friday, July 28—*Abide in Christ and Bear Fruit* (John 15:1-11)

Saturday July 29—*Chosen by Christ* (John 15:12-27)

Sunday, July 30—*Your Pain Will Turn to Rejoicing* (John 16:16-24)

UNUSED ARMOR

In the city of Graz, Austria, there is a fascinating museum called the Provincial Arsenal. This museum dates from the seventeenth century and contains one of the largest collections of medieval weapons and armor in the world—enough, in fact, to equip twenty-eight thousand soldiers! Despite such an impressive display of swords, spears, helmets, and shields, this armor and weaponry will never be used. It is meant only to be seen and admired.

The Christian's armor is not simply for decorative purposes. We do not wear it so that people will admire our virtues. We wear it to use it in battle. Perhaps someday the armor in Graz *may* be brought out for some reenactment of an historical event. But our spiritual battle is not a mock battle; it is real spiritual warfare, and we all desperately need "the full armor of God" if we are to triumph.

Are you wearing the belt of truth? Is your breastplate of righteousness in place? Are your feet fitted with the preparation of the gospel of peace? Do you have the shield of faith always at hand? Are you protected by the helmet of salvation? Do you know how to wield "the sword of the Spirit"? Christians are not mannequins in a museum to be viewed, admired, and later forgotten. The battle is real. War has been declared.

We must be prepared. —R. C. S.

III. OUR CONCERNS (EPHESIANS 6:18-24)

A. FOR ALL SAINTS (v. 18)

18. And pray in the Spirit on all occasions with all kinds of prayers and requests. With this in mind, be alert and always keep on praying for all the saints.

Paul now moves to the subject of prayer. While prayer is not described using a specific piece of armor, it is without question part of our battle against "the spiritual forces of evil in the heavenly realms" (v. 12). Paul recommends that Christians *pray . . . on all occasions*. No circumstance that we face ever provides an inappropriate time to pray.

What does it mean to pray *in the Spirit*? Perhaps it means that when we pray, we are in communication with the Holy Spirit. Possibly it means that when we pray, the power of the Holy Spirit is applied to answering our prayer. Or, Paul may be saying that our prayer is aided in some sense by the Holy Spirit. This latter position is supported by Paul's teaching in Romans 8:26, where he notes that "the Spirit himself intercedes for us with groans that words cannot express."

Notice that not only are we to pray at all times, but we are to pray *for all the saints*. Such prayer acknowledges that all Christians have been targeted by the enemy and must therefore be undergirded with prayer. Just as Satan is unrelenting in his efforts toward Christians, so Christians must *always keep on praying*.

B. FOR GOD'S MESSENGER (vv. 19, 20)

19. Pray also for me, that whenever I open my mouth, words may be given me so that I will fearlessly make known the mystery of the gospel.

Paul was not afraid or ashamed to ask for prayer on his own behalf. Here he has a specific request in mind. He wants his readers to *pray that words may be given* him in his preaching and teaching. He wants to be able to express *fearlessly . . . the mystery of the gospel*. Earlier he had explained that mystery in these words: "that through the gospel the Gentiles are heirs together with Israel, members together of one body, and sharers together in the promise in Christ Jesus" (Ephesians 3:6).

20. . . . for which I am an ambassador in chains. Pray that I may declare it fearlessly, as I should.

In this verse Paul uses a strange image that seems to some to be a contradiction in terms. He describes himself as *an ambassador in chains*. An ambassador's

WHAT DO YOU THINK?

Who are some of the saints for whom you "keep on praying"? For whom should you be praying?

[If your church has a prayer list suggesting people for whom the saints should pray, look the list over. How many of the requests relate to physical issues (health, needing a job, etc.), and how many relate to spiritual warfare? Perhaps your class could take the names of all your church members, divide them into seven groups, and then pray for one group every day.]

performance of his duties would appear to require that he not be restricted in any way. He must have free access so that he may represent his nation to the officials of a foreign government. However, it is characteristic of Paul's optimistic spirit that even though he was imprisoned, he still saw himself as an *ambassador* for Christ. Paul had the knack for turning every event in his life into an evangelistic opportunity. He refused to be silenced or intimidated by his surroundings.

C. FOR DEAR FRIENDS (vv. 21-24)

21. Tychicus, the dear brother and faithful servant in the Lord, will tell you everything, so that you also may know how I am and what I am doing.

Paul also wanted to communicate to his friends how his ministry was progressing, so he promised that *Tychicus* would *tell* them *everything* they needed to know. Tychicus is also described as fulfilling the same role (in much the same language) for the Christians in Colosse (Colossians 4:7-9). We do not know much more about Tychicus, but the other times he is mentioned indicate that Paul must have considered him a very dependable servant of the Lord (Acts 20:4; 2 Timothy 4:12; Titus 3:12). Tychicus may have been from the region around Ephesus. It is even possible that he took the dictation for this letter.

22. I am sending him to you for this very purpose, that you may know how we are, and that he may encourage you.

Part of Tychicus's *purpose* was to *encourage* those who were concerned about Paul. Paul did not want his friends to be discouraged because of what had happened to him. He wanted them to know that the work of the Lord was progressing and that the gospel was being preached even during his imprisonment (Philippians 1:12-14).

23. Peace to the brothers, and love with faith from God the Father and the Lord Jesus Christ.

This is a fairly typical benediction, with some slight variations from the closing words in Paul's other epistles. Here he mentions the blessings of *peace, love,* and *faith*. We recall other places where the apostle makes a triad out of faith, hope, and love (the most notable in 1 Corinthians 13:13). In this letter *peace* replaces hope. That is appropriate, however, because peace, love, and faith have been important themes in this letter. The reference to *peace* may reflect Paul's burden that Jews and Gentiles understand and express their oneness in Christ (Ephesians 2:13-18).

24. Grace to all who love our Lord Jesus Christ with an undying love.

Thus this powerful epistle begins (1:2) and ends with the blessing of *grace*.

CONCLUSION

The Roman orator Cato is said to have ended every speech he made in the Roman senate with the words, "Carthage must be destroyed." He saw the threat of this north African city as so ominous that he constantly reminded his audience of what he thought needed to be done. His persistent warnings were a factor in Carthage's ultimate defeat.

In the back of our minds there should always be the words, "Sin must be destroyed." When we fight against sin, it is not because we are prudish; it is not because we want to oppress people. We are against sin because it is so terribly harmful to society as a whole and to the individual in particular. The defeat of sin is the defeat of what dehumanizes us and makes us far less than what God created us to be.

Yes, sin must be destroyed. Praise God that he has given us all the resources we need to do so!

WHAT DO YOU THINK?

The letters of Paul were designed to let his loved ones know his condition and to bring comfort and encouragement to the readers. What do we do that is similar?

PRAYER

Father, we will face many challenges in life. Those challenges will often fill us with fear. Relieve us, not by removing the challenges, but by helping us to be ready for them. In the name of Christ our Conqueror we pray. Amen.

THOUGHT TO REMEMBER

The battle belongs to the Lord, but you must fight it.

Discovery Learning

This page contains an alternate lesson plan emphasizing learning activities. Classes desiring such student involvement will find these suggestions helpful. The next page is a reproducible activity page to further enhance discovery learning.

LEARNING GOALS

After this lesson each student will be able to:

1. List the items included in "the whole armor of God."

2. Tell why military metaphors are appropriate for explaining the nature of the Christian life.

3. Suggest a specific way to "put on" a particular piece of the armor of God.

INTO THE LESSON

To introduce the lesson, ask class members to name songs and choruses that picture the Christian life as a battle or use military terms to describe the Christian life. Many are listed under headings like "Victory" or "Christian Warfare" in songbooks. You can stimulate thought by naming a song or two, such as "A Mighty Fortress Is Our God," "Lead On, O King Eternal," "Stand Up, Stand Up for Jesus," "The Battle Belongs to the Lord," etc. As the students suggest a song or chorus, ask, "What is some of the imagery and its significance in the lines of that song?" For example, from "A Mighty Fortress" we learn that God is our protector from evil. (You may wish to have a songbook ready for reference.)

Make the transition to Bible study by telling the class that the writers of Christian music with militaristic themes have a scriptural model. Today's text includes imagery from the Roman soldier to teach us how to be firm in our faith.

INTO THE WORD

Prepare and distribute a handout with today's Scripture text printed on the left side and room on the right half for the students to write notes. Print the heading "Our Conflict" over verses 10-12 of the text, "Our Equipment" over verses 13-17, and "Our Concerns" over verses 18-24.

Assign the following tasks to discussion groups of three to six persons each. Larger classes may need more than one group to do the same task. Give each group a piece of poster board with one of the following assignments printed at the top.

Group 1: Read Ephesians 6:10-12. Notice the words "the devil's schemes." List on this poster some of the strategies Satan uses to attack Christians in today's world.

Group 2: Read Ephesians 6:13-17. List the six pieces of armor mentioned and write the purpose or significance of each piece for contemporary Christians.

Group 3: Read Ephesians 6:18-24. Prayer is an important part of our preparation for the battle with Satan. Please list and answer the following questions: 1. Pray How? 2. Pray for Whom? 3. Pray When? 4. How does prayer fit into the battle with Satan?

Ask a reporter from each group to put its poster on the wall and report the group's conclusions. After group 1 reports, ask, "What is at stake if we are *not* prepared for the battle against Satan?" After group 2 reports, highlight the significance of the battle for our hearts and minds. (See the lesson commentary on verses 14 and 17.) Distribute the reproducible activity page that follows. Have the class complete the "G.I. Christian" section. Compare the modern soldier's equipment with the resources a Christian has for spiritual battle. After group 3 reports, mention the significance of prayer for *all* the saints. We are part of a team that fights and stands together.

INTO LIFE

Distribute a handout on which you have written, "Evaluate Your Spiritual Armor." Below this heading list the six pieces of armor in the left column: "My Belt of Truth," "My Breastplate of Righteousness," "My Shoes of the Gospel of Peace," "My Shield of Faith," "My Helmet of Salvation," "My Sword of the Spirit." To the right of each piece of armor print the words, "Good Shape"; "Moldy and Rusty"; "Non-existent." Ask the class members to evaluate each piece of their own spiritual armor and circle the word that best describes its condition and effectiveness.

Refer to the lower part of the reproducible page, "Spiritual Battle." When students have had a moment to write some ideas, discuss the various fronts in the battle with Satan's forces.

Ask, "Where is Satan attacking you the hardest?" Encourage class members to think about their fiercest struggles with Satan. (Do not ask anyone to answer this aloud, but everyone should give it serious consideration.)

Then ask, "What do you need to do to be better prepared for spiritual battle with Satan?" Ask each student to decide what piece of armor he or she needs to put on to deal with Satan's attacks. In small groups have each student tell what piece of armor he or she needs.

Conclude by reminding the class that Paul calls us to pray for the saints. Ask each class member to pray for the person to his or her left in the small group, mentioning the specific need that person expressed.

G.I. Christian!

Paul illustrates the importance of being ready for spiritual warfare by using an illustration from the clothing and weapons of the Roman soldier. If you were to rewrite this passage using the clothing and equipment of a contemporary soldier, what principle or concept would you attach to the following?

Camouflage clothing _____

_____

Binoculars _____

_____

Field Radio _____

_____

Helmet _____

_____

Firearm _____

_____

Spiritual Battle

Paul tells us we are involved in a spiritual battle. What evidences do you see of the battle on each of the following fronts?

Your Community

Your Nation

The World

The Church

Paul asks us to pray for all the saints (v. 18). Prayer is a wonderful weapon in spiritual warfare. Select one of the four areas of battle named above to make as a focus of your prayer this week.

THE SUPREMACY OF CHRIST

LESSON 10

WHY TEACH THIS LESSON?

"Who do people say the Son of Man is?" Jesus asked his disciples (Matthew 16:13). And then—"Who do you say I am?" (v. 15). It is a question every disciple must answer. If he or she cannot state clearly who Jesus is, then that person's faith is on a tenuous foundation, for our faith is in Jesus.

Peter's answer is good: Jesus is "the Christ, the Son of the living God" (Matthew 16:16). Without Peter's Jewish background, however, we may not fully comprehend the significance of this good answer. We need a fuller explanation, a more complete description, and in today's lesson we get it.

One of the lesson aims today is that the students will suggest a specific way to honor Christ as Lord. If the truth of the lesson, the supremacy of Christ, really gets through to them, they cannot help but to honor him thus!

INTRODUCTION

A. "WHAT DO YOU THINK ABOUT THE CHRIST?"

Most people who read about Jesus are attracted to him and even admire him. The real challenge comes when we ask someone, "Do you believe that Jesus is who he said he was?"

Today's text from Paul's letter to the Colossians highlights what makes Jesus unique. It will not allow us to get away with saying that Jesus was just a good man, a prophet, or a great teacher. Paul declares that Jesus is nothing less than "the image of the invisible God" (Colossians 1:15). People find it much more convenient to believe in a God who is indefinable, impersonal, and can be described as "way out there" because they do not believe themselves to be accountable to such a distant God. But Jesus shows us God in the flesh—"the glory of the One and Only, who came from the Father" (John 1:14).

Today's lesson will focus on some of the most important truths about Jesus. These are truths that we who are his followers must believe and proclaim—without compromise.

B. LESSON BACKGROUND

Our study today covers the second half of the first chapter of Paul's letter to the Colossians. This letter, like Ephesians, Philippians, and Philemon, is one of Paul's "prison epistles" and, like the rest, was probably written from Rome around A.D. 63. Like Ephesians, it was sent by the hand of Tychicus (Colossians 4:7-9).

The city of Colosse was located some one hundred miles east of Ephesus, in what is modern-day Turkey. We do not know when the church there was formed, for Colosse is never mentioned in the book of Acts. Probably it was established during Paul's ministry at Ephesus. Luke tells us that Paul used the school of Tyrannus as his headquarters in Ephesus for two years, and that as a result "all the Jews and Greeks who lived in the province of Asia heard the word of the Lord" (Acts 19:9, 10). Otherwise, all we know of the Colossian church is what we can learn from this letter and from Paul's letter to Philemon (which was carried by Onesimus, who most likely lived in Colosse).

DEVOTIONAL READING:
JOHN 3:25-36
BACKGROUND SCRIPTURE:
COLOSSIANS 1
PRINTED TEXT:
COLOSSIANS 1:15-29

LESSON AIMS

As a result of studying this lesson, each student will be able to:

1. Summarize how Paul described the supremacy of Christ and its impact on his ministry.

2. Tell why the supremacy of Christ must continue to remain at the heart of the church's ministry and message.

3. Suggest a way to honor Christ as Lord through some specific ministry undertaken in his behalf.

Aug
6

KEY VERSE

For God was pleased to have all his fullness dwell in him, and through him to reconcile to himself all things . . . by making peace through his blood, shed on the cross. —Colossians 1:19, 20

LESSON 10 NOTES

DAILY BIBLE READINGS

Monday, July 31—Paul Gives Thanks for the Colossians (Colossians 1:1-8)

Tuesday, Aug. 1—Paul Prays for the Colossians (Colossians 1:9-14)

Wednesday, Aug. 2—The Fullness of God Dwells in Christ (Colossians 1:15-20)

Thursday, Aug. 3—God's Mystery Revealed to the Saints (Colossians 1:21-29)

Friday, Aug. 4—Jesus Christ: God's Word and Light (John 1:1-9)

Saturday, Aug. 5—God's Word Lived Among Us (John 1:10-18)

Sunday, Aug. 6—Christ Is Superior Even to Angels (Hebrews 1:1-14)

HOW TO SAY IT

Colosse. Ko-LAHSS-ee.

Colossians. Kuh-LOSH-unz.

Epaphras. EP-uh-frass.

Ephesians. Ee-FEE-zhunz.

Ephesus. EF-uh-sus.

Gnosticism. NAHSS-tih-sizz-um.

Gnostics. NAHSS-tiks.

Immanuel. Ih-MAN-you-el.

Onesimus. Oh-NESS-ih-muss.

Philemon. Fih-LEE-mun or Fye-LEE-mun.

Philippians. Fih-LIP-ee-unz.

reconciliation. REC-un-sill-ee-AY-shun.

Tychicus. TICK-ih-cuss.

Tyrannus. Ty-RAN-us.

It is important to note the similarities between Colossians and Ephesians. They cover the same basic topics and exhibit a similar structure. In some instances the wording is very similar (compare, for example, Colossians 4:7-9 and Ephesians 6:21, 22). Probably they were both written at the same time, with Tychicus delivering Ephesians first and then continuing on to Colosse to deliver Colossians.

Despite the similarities between Ephesians and Colossians, there are important differences, many of which can be attributed to the reason Paul wrote this letter. Apparently Paul had received some disturbing news from Epaphras (mentioned in Colossians 1:7 and 4:12) that certain false doctrines were being propagated in the Colossian church, including an early form of what would later be known as Gnosticism.

It is difficult to explain Gnosticism briefly, but we must make a few observations about it before our study of Colossians begins. The name *Gnosticism* comes from a Greek word meaning "knowledge." Gnostics believed that they possessed a secret knowledge of spiritual truth that the average or "unenlightened" person could not possess. That is the reason Paul, in writing to the Colossians, emphasizes that in Christ alone are "all the treasures of wisdom and knowledge" (Colossians 2:3; cf. 1:9, 10). Only in Christ (not in the Gnostics' doctrine) is God's true "mystery" revealed (1:26, 27; 2:2).

Gnostics also believed that material things, including the physical world itself, were evil, created by an evil god. There was also a good god, they believed, who was spirit only, for only the spirit was good. They believed in a spiritual world full of divine beings (one of whom was Jesus) who came forth from this good god. Apparently some of these emanations became confused with angels, resulting in the actual worship of angels among some in the Colossian church. Paul warns against this practice in Colossians 2:18.

The Gnostic teaching that all flesh was evil had a devastating impact on Christian doctrine; for if flesh is evil, then Jesus would never have come as a human being. Gnostics thus saw Jesus as a kind of phantom who only appeared to be human. We will notice, as our study in Colossians proceeds, how Paul countered this error by insisting that Jesus had a body (Colossians 1:22; 2:9).

Since Gnostics considered the body to be evil, many of them advocated treating it harshly, denying it any pleasures. This resulted in a strict set of rules governing one's conduct. Paul alludes to these rules in Colossians 2:16, 17, 20-23. Others, however, went to the opposite extreme. They claimed that since the body was evil anyway, one's behavior did not matter. Thus they engaged in blatant immorality, against which Paul writes in Colossians 3:5.

As he does with his letter to the Ephesians, Paul begins his epistle to the Colossians with a tribute of praise to the Lord Jesus Christ. In our text the apostle presents three word pictures of Christ: he is Creator, he is Reconciler, and he is Commander.

I. CHRIST, OUR CREATOR (COLOSSIANS 1:15-18)

A. HIS IDENTITY (v. 15)

15. He is the image of the invisible God, the firstborn over all creation.

Jesus is described as *the image of the invisible God*. The Greek word translated *image* is a word that gives us our English word "icon." It could describe an image on a coin or a person's reflection in a mirror. Thus does Paul counter the false teaching that Jesus was simply one of many beings who came from God. Jesus was Immanuel—"God with us." Later Paul will affirm that in Christ "all the fullness of the Deity lives in bodily form" (Colossians 2:9). The nature of God is perfectly represented in Jesus.

Jesus is also *the firstborn over all creation*. Although this phrase may seem to portray Jesus as a created being, we should understand the term *firstborn* to highlight the role of Christ, not his origin. It was common in the first century to bestow on the firstborn special rights and obligations. Paul thus sets the stage for his declaration in the next two verses that Jesus Christ is Lord over all of the created world.

B. HIS ACTIVITY (y. 16)

16. For by him all things were created: things in heaven and on earth, visible and invisible, whether thrones or powers or rulers or authorities; all things were created by him and for him.

As one with the Father, Jesus was involved in the creation of this world. (See John 1:1-3.) This verse counters the Gnostic notion of the world's creation by an evil god.

Notice also that Paul places Christ above all *thrones or powers or rulers or authorities*. These include the authorities *in heaven and on earth*. The reference to heavenly powers may reflect Paul's concern about the worship of angels within the Colossian church.

C. HIS SUPREMACY (vv. 17, 18)

17. He is before all things, and in him all things hold together.

Christ is not only superior in that he existed *before* the created world, but it is through him that the entire created world is sustained. Jesus is the "glue" of this universe. If not for Jesus, there would be chaos.

18. And he is the head of the body, the church; he is the beginning and the firstborn from among the dead, so that in everything he might have the supremacy.

Not only is Christ the head of the created world, but he is specifically *the head of the body, the church*. The idea of the church as a body with Jesus as the head is one of Paul's favorite images of the church. It has been wisely said that the church is not just an organization; it is an organism.

Whereas Jesus was described as "the firstborn over all creation" in verse 15 (indicating his supremacy as Creator of all things), here he is called *the firstborn from among the dead*. This is obviously referring to his resurrection. Jesus raised certain individuals from the dead; however, they were brought back in their physical bodies and eventually died again. Jesus was the first to rise from the dead, never to die again.

Because he is "the firstfruits of those who have fallen asleep" (1 Corinthians 15:20), it is the "blessed hope" (Titus 2:13) of all followers of Jesus to be resurrected and to be "clothed with . . . immortality" when he returns (Romans 8:11; 1 Corinthians 15:51-54).

The resurrection is the primary reason that Jesus has been given *supremacy*. Paul says that Jesus was "declared with power to be the Son of God by his resurrection from the dead" (Romans 1:4).

LIBERTY, EQUALITY, FRATERNITY

The slogan of the French Revolution in the late eighteenth century consisted of three words: *Liberty, Equality, Fraternity*. In some sense each of these three words applies to the church, yet each must be properly understood. We are certainly free in Christ. Paul's letters make that very plain. But they also warn us that our liberty is not license; we cannot do as we please. The word *fraternity* fits the concept of the church as the family of God. We are brothers and sisters in Christ. But we must keep in mind that Jesus is the Elder Brother (Hebrews 2:11, 12).

WHAT DO YOU THINK?

Equality with God, participation in creation, supremacy, superiority to all things, headship of the church, incarnation, sacrificial and redemptive death, and being the basis of our hope of eternal life—all these critical doctrines of Christ are capsulized in Colossians 1. However, many today make false statements about the nature of Christ. What is there in today's text that we can use to make his claims known to those who oppose or just don't understand the real claims of the gospel?

Today's visual recalls the supreme price paid for our reconciliation. Post it as you begin to discuss verse 19.

The word *equality* reminds us that we are all equal before God. We are all equal in our need for a Savior. Distinctions that often separate people in society are eliminated in Christ. However, one Person in the church is above us all, and that is Jesus. He is "the head of the body, the church" (Colossians 1:18). He has supremacy. No matter how long we have been Christians, our primary purpose as part of the body of Christ is always to lift up the Head.

Maturity is usually viewed as being able to get along independently of others, without having to resort to their help in making decisions or handling problems when they arise. But in the Christian life, maturity is shown by our increasing dependence on Jesus. We cannot exist and function apart from the Head. —R. C. S.

II. CHRIST, OUR RECONCILER (COLOSSIANS 1:19-23a)

A. MEANS OF RECONCILIATION (vv. 19, 20)

19, 20. For God was pleased to have all his fullness dwell in him, and through him to reconcile to himself all things, whether things on earth or things in heaven, by making peace through his blood, shed on the cross.

The phrase *to have all his [God's] fullness dwell in him [Jesus]* refers to the incarnation of Christ. The Word through whom all things were created (John 1:1-3) "became flesh and made his dwelling among us. We have seen his glory, the glory of the One and Only, who came from the Father" (v. 14). This is another point at which Paul refutes the Gnostics' belief that Jesus was one of many spirit beings who came from God (cf. v. 15). *All* the fullness of God is found in Jesus—and in no one else!

This verse also calls attention to the purpose for which Jesus "became flesh": *to reconcile to himself all things.* The means of this reconciliation was *his blood, shed on the cross* (note the similarity to Ephesians 2:16). It is through Jesus' death and our acceptance that what happened there happened for us that we are able to be at peace with God.

Why does Paul mention both *things on earth* and *things in heaven* being reconciled? Probably he is indicating how far-reaching is the impact of Jesus' death. Just as "by him all things were created: things in heaven and on earth" (v. 16), now all things are reconciled to God by him. That "the whole creation" is affected by the work of Christ is clear from Romans 8:19-22. Again, Paul's words are similar to his teaching in Ephesians: that God will one day "bring all things in heaven and on earth together under one head, even Christ" (1:10).

B. EFFECT OF RECONCILIATION (vv. 21-23a)

21. Once you were alienated from God and were enemies in your minds because of your evil behavior.

Paul now moves from considering the universal impact of the work of Christ to a more personal perspective. Our position of being *alienated from God* affects our *minds.* Man's mind is a wonderful creation; however, if unredeemed it is capable of producing increasingly *evil behavior.*

22. But now he has reconciled you by Christ's physical body through death to present you holy in his sight, without blemish and free from accusation.

Notice Paul's emphasis that God has reconciled us *by Christ's physical body.* As noted earlier, Gnostics rejected the idea that Jesus was really God in the flesh, for they viewed all flesh as evil. They taught that Jesus had only the appearance of humanity. Paul affirms that it was *by Christ's physical body through death* that Jesus accomplished the work of reconciliation.

The purpose of Christ's redeeming work is to *present* those who once were alienated as *holy in his sight, without blemish and free from accusation.* The word

WHAT DO YOU THINK?

Paul says Jesus can make us "holy in his sight, without blemish and free from accusation." God has taken that which was unholy, blemished, and worthy of accusation in our lives, and—by the covering blood of Christ—made them all the opposite. How does that affect our behavior?

holy means "set apart." Holy objects are set apart for God in service or worship. Holiness is not some attribute for the "super spiritual"; it is expected of all Christians.

A person *without blemish* is not sinless, but his character is consistently Christ-like. Others are drawn toward Christ, not driven away from him, by his behavior.

Finally, we are described as *free from accusation*. This term describes a person whose conduct provides no basis for a charge of wrongdoing.

23a. . . . if you continue in your faith, established and firm, not moved from the hope held out in the gospel. This is the gospel that you heard and that has been proclaimed to every creature under heaven.

Here Paul encourages his readers to remain true to *the hope held out in the gospel*. The word *faith* can describe either the content of doctrinal truth or our own personal belief in those truths. We who have accepted the gospel must resolve not to be *moved from* its truth.

Paul's description of the gospel as having been *proclaimed to every creature under heaven* is a bit of hyperbole—an intentional exaggeration to make a point. Certainly the gospel had not been preached at that point to every individual on earth. It had, however, been proclaimed in virtually all the great urban centers of the Roman world. Keep in mind also that on the Day of Pentecost people "from every nation under heaven" (Acts 2:5) were present to hear Peter's message.

III. CHRIST, OUR COMMANDER (COLOSSIANS 1:23b-29)

A. CALLED TO SUFFER (vv. 23b, 24)

23b, 24. . . . and of which I, Paul, have become a servant. Now I rejoice in what was suffered for you, and I fill up in my flesh what is still lacking in regard to Christ's afflictions, for the sake of his body, which is the church.

Paul was able to *rejoice in what was suffered* because he saw his sufferings as coming for the benefit of the Colossians. In addition, his sufferings linked him with *Christ's afflictions* and with *the church* as a whole. But how could Paul have expected to *fill up in* his *flesh what is still lacking in regard to Christ's afflictions*? Did Paul see something insufficient in Jesus' sufferings?

It may be better to look at Paul's words, not as a statement that something was lacking in Christ's death, but that something was lacking in Paul himself. As Christ's *servant*, Paul had suffered even as Jesus promised he would (Acts 9:16). Now, in prison, he was continuing to suffer in accordance with that promise; and he would do so until this part of his service to Christ was fulfilled.

REJOICING IN SUFFERING

It would seem strange indeed to many in our self-centered, comfortable age to hear Paul speak of rejoicing in his sufferings (Colossians 1:24). Yet to Christians in other parts of the world, this does not sound strange at all. If anything, suffering is part of their routine.

For decades the Soviet Union and the Communist countries of eastern Europe persecuted Christians. Those believers' view of such suffering was surprising. They said, "Christians in the West see prosperity as a sign of God's favor. We see suffering as a sign of God's favor. It shows that God thinks that we are strong enough to endure it."

Recently the church's attention has been drawn to the intensifying persecution of believers in certain parts of the world. Their hardships reinforce the truth that the cost of following Jesus is sometimes very high—a fact that Christians who live in more comfortable surroundings can easily forget.

These sufferers, however, are our brothers and sisters. We must not forget them.

—R. C. S.

WHAT DO YOU THINK?

In Paul's day the gospel had been preached in all the major urban centers of the world. Since that time, however, the gospel has been shut out from much of the world. Literally billions of people have no prospect of hearing the gospel preached in their lifetimes! What is our congregation doing to see that the gospel is once again available to all peoples? What more can we do?

[Try to mention by name each mission work supported by your church. Perhaps your class could adopt a missionary family and send assistance and greetings on a regular basis.]

WHAT DO YOU THINK?

Paul humbly speaks of the things he does and what he suffers for the sake of Christ's body, the church. Every Christian needs to ask himself or herself, "What am I doing, what am I suffering, for the sake of Christ's body, the church?" How would you answer the question?

B. CALLED TO SPEAK (vv. 25-28)

25. I have become its servant by the commission God gave me to present to you the word of God in its fullness.

Again Paul describes himself as a *servant* of Christ *by the commission God gave me*. The word *commission* can be translated "management plan" or "strategy" (cf. Ephesians 1:10). Paul recognized that God's plan for him was that he *present . . . the word of God in its fullness*. He explains that message and his response to it in the remaining verses of our text.

26. . . . the mystery that has been kept hidden for ages and generations, but is now disclosed to the saints.

The word *mystery*, as we noted in our study of Ephesians 1:9; 6:19, refers to a truth once hidden from mankind that God has *disclosed*. Paul's use of this word ran counter to the Gnostics' claim to possess secret knowledge. The *saints* are blessed with insight into the plan of God!

27. To them God has chosen to make known among the Gentiles the glorious riches of this mystery, which is Christ in you, the hope of glory.

The *mystery* involves the sharing of the *riches* of the gospel with the *Gentiles*—a theme that is prominent in Ephesians (Ephesians 2:11-19; 3:1-6). But it also involves something deeper and more personal. The *mystery* is more than just God's acceptance of a class of people; it is *Christ* actually dwelling *in* a person, regardless of his or her ethnic background. That personal indwelling comes through the Holy Spirit, who is described as "a deposit guaranteeing our inheritance" in Ephesians 1:14. This produces *the hope of glory* within us, allowing us to look forward to the ultimate fulfillment of God's plan in eternity.

28. We proclaim him, admonishing and teaching everyone with all wisdom, so that we may present everyone perfect in Christ.

Christian work has both a negative and a positive side. Sometimes people need *admonishing* (given words of warning), so Paul warned the Colossians about false teachings being spread among them. He also engaged in faithful *teaching* of the truth so that people would be able to recognize falsehood when it appeared.

The purpose of these efforts is to *present everyone perfect in Christ*. Remember that *perfect* in this context does not mean flawless or faultless; it is better rendered as "complete," "mature," or "fully formed."

C. CALLED TO STRIVE (v. 29)

29. To this end I labor, struggling with all his energy, which so powerfully works in me.

The word Paul uses here for *labor* describes hard, demanding work—the kind that takes every ounce of one's effort. The Greek word translated *struggling* is the source of our English word *agony*. But Paul does not view these rigorous labors as dependent on his own stamina. He understands that God *works* through him and does so *powerfully*. Paul's use of so many similar words for work and power create a dramatic cumulative effect. Clearly, there is no power shortage here!

CONCLUSION

Paul has given us a marvelous picture of who Jesus is, what he has done, and what he wants to do for us. Think of it: Jesus is the One in whom all the fullness of God dwells, and we as Christians have that fullness dwelling in us!

What are we to do with this fullness? Consider what one preacher said when a lady remarked to him, "Preacher, my cup is filled to overflowing."

He responded, "Then go out there and slosh on somebody!"

We have been filled with Jesus. Is there someone we can "slosh on"?

Discovery Learning

This page contains an alternate lesson plan emphasizing learning activities. Classes desiring such student involvement will find these suggestions helpful. The next page is a reproducible activity page to further enhance discovery learning.

LEARNING GOALS

After this lesson each student will be able to:

1. Summarize how Paul described the supremacy of Christ and its impact on his ministry.

2. Tell why the supremacy of Christ must continue to remain at the heart of the church's ministry and message.

3. Suggest a way to honor Christ as Lord through some specific ministry undertaken in his behalf.

INTO THE LESSON

Prepare a handout for each student with Colossians 1:15-29 printed on it. Ask the students to scan verses 15-22 and select words or phrases that describe Jesus. Have a student write them on a poster under the heading "Jesus." Then do a similar exercise with verses 22-29, this time looking for words or phrases that describe the Christian life. Put these words on the poster under the heading "And Me."

After the exercise, tell the class this text is one of the most complete, yet concise, descriptions of Jesus in the Bible. Our faith is centered on Jesus, so we must clearly understand who he is. Some of the Christians at Colosse were confused about Jesus, and this letter was written to make Jesus' nature and authority clear to them and us.

Early in the week, ask a student to prepare a brief report on Gnosticism in the early church. Ask the student to deliver that report at this time. Summarize his or her report by saying that the beliefs of the Gnostics caused the early church great trouble, and the seeds of this destructive belief system are seen in the issues Paul addressed in Colossians. While Gnosticism is not a problem today, many people remain confused about the nature of Jesus. This text gives us tools to address the confusion in our own world even as it helped to solve ancient problems.

INTO THE WORD

If you are a skilled lecturer, the visual list made earlier of names and qualities of Jesus and Christians provides a wonderful visual and outline for your lecture. Use the lesson commentary to clarify the significance of these descriptions.

However, to encourage active participation in studying this passage, you may want to study it in small groups. Give each group the instructions printed for that group, paper and pencils, and (if possible) a hymnbook.

Group 1: Read Colossians 1:15-18. Explain the significance of the titles and descriptive words assigned to Jesus in this text. Also, make a list of worship hymns or choruses that recall some of these qualities.

Group 2: Read Colossians 1:19-23a. Paraphrase these verses, making the major concepts in this passage as clear as possible. Also, make a list of hymns or choruses that celebrate the thoughts of this passage.

Group 3: Read Colossians 1:23b-29. Explain the significance of the words in our opening activity under the heading "And Me." Also, make a list of hymns or choruses that call these principles to mind.

Ask each group to report on its findings. Supplement the reports with information from the commentary as needed. After group 1 reports, discuss these questions:

1. What are some other views of Jesus in today's world? (For example, who would the Muslim say Jesus is? the Jew? the atheist?)

2. Why is it important that Jesus' supremacy remain at the heart of the church's ministry and message?

Option: Instead of, or in addition to, the above activity, distribute copies of the reproducible page that follows. Have the students work individually or in small groups to fill in the "thought bubbles." Use the section at the bottom of the page at the conclusion of the session to make application.

INTO LIFE

Call attention to the list of words under "Jesus" on the poster made earlier. Ask each person to select one of those words or phrases and share why that description of our Lord is richer or more significant to him because of today's study. (This activity may be done in the small groups formed earlier.)

Next, observe that Paul tells us he works hard for Christ's kingdom. Ask the students to think of works they have seen other persons doing for the Lord this past year and list those on a visual. You might list these in categories such as physical labor, proclamation, spiritual encouragement, and other appropriate headings. Then draw a scale (1–10) on the chalkboard. Tell the class, "Paul was able to say he works hard for Christ. Think about where on this scale you would make a mark to measure your work for Christ." Then ask them to consider "stepping up the pace" in service and mentally circle the areas of service they would like to explore and try.

Thought-Full Bubbles

Read Colossians 1:15-29. Write your thoughts or reactions to it in the "thought bubbles" provided. Your thoughts may be a profound discovery to you, a surprising impact on your mind, a question, or something you wish to do.

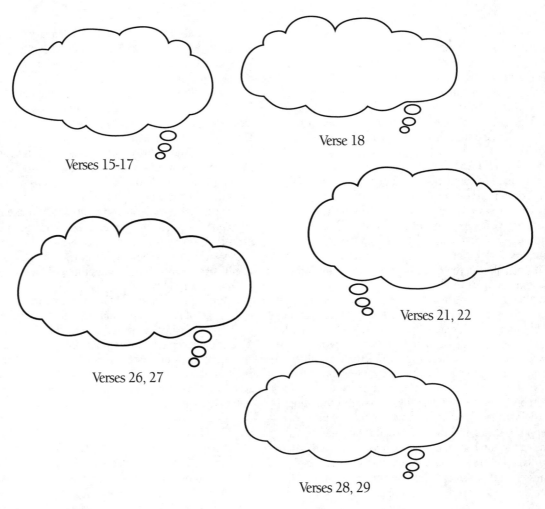

Verses 15-17

Verse 18

Verses 26, 27

Verses 21, 22

Verses 28, 29

The key thought in this passage is that Christ is Supreme (v. 18). What does Christ's supremacy imply or mean to:

The Church? _____

_____

Theology? _____

_____

My Life? _____

_____

COMPLETE LIFE IN CHRIST

LESSON 11

WHY TEACH THIS LESSON?

In our convenience-seeking society, the word *complete* is a powerful marketing tool. We want the kit to be *complete* so we don't have to run to the hardware store for screws to put the unit together. We want the box dinner to be *complete* so we don't have to add anything from the cupboard. We want things to be complete because we want them to be quick and easy.

Unfortunately, this kind of thinking sometimes affects our discipleship. We want it to be quick and easy, too, but often it is not. Most spiritual graces take a long time to develop. That does not mean our lives are not complete—it just means they are not completed!

Use this lesson to assure your students that, in Christ, they have all they need for the abundant life. Their lives are truly complete if they are in Christ. But they still have a long way to go to become all that God wants them to be. The "complete" life still has room for growth. It is only when their lives are "completed" (finished) that they will join the assembly of "righteous men made perfect"—that is to say, "made *complete*" (Hebrews 12:23).

INTRODUCTION

A. BARGAINS?

An auto mechanic once put up this sign in his shop: "Beware of bargains in life rafts, brain surgery, parachutes, and auto repairs." We have all, no doubt, had the experience of getting a bargain that turned out to be no bargain! Yet some people apply a "bargain mentality" to religious faith. They want what promises the most and requires the least. They don't want to do the hard work of maturing in the faith.

Christian maturity doesn't happen overnight any more than physical maturity does. Yes, there are numerous blessings to being a Christian; we have considered many of them during this quarter's study, and we will examine more in today's lesson. But these blessings are not automatic. They come as a result of our committing ourselves to the never-ending process of Christian growth.

Christianity is a bargain in the sense that we can never earn, or deserve, the blessings God gives us. It is a bargain in the sense that we will receive far more than we ever contribute. Still, we must recognize that while one can become a Christian in just a few moments, it takes a lifetime to learn the Christian life. (In a similar way, we may get married in a ceremony of only minutes, but it takes a lifetime to make a marriage.) Today's lesson will describe what it means to grow in Christ. It will both encourage us to remain faithful and warn us to beware of obstacles to our growth.

B. LESSON BACKGROUND

In last week's lesson we touched on how what appears to be the seeds of a false teaching called Gnosticism had infiltrated the Colossian church. (See the Lesson Background to last week's study.) In today's text we see Paul issuing more direct warnings concerning some of these pre-Gnostic doctrines.

DEVOTIONAL READING:
ROMANS 8:31-39

BACKGROUND SCRIPTURE:
COLOSSIANS 2:6-19

PRINTED TEXT:
COLOSSIANS 2:6-19

LESSON AIMS

After this lesson each student will be able to:

1. Explain how Paul describes the Christian's completeness in Christ, and the ways in which the Colossians were being led astray from their completeness.

2. Give some modern examples of teachings and philosophies that constitute a threat to our completeness in Christ.

3. Express an exclusive faith in Jesus, rejecting all other systems of belief.

Aug
13

KEY VERSE

So then, just as you received Christ Jesus as Lord, continue to live in him, rooted and built up in him, strengthened in the faith as you were taught, and overflowing with thankfulness.

—Colossians 2:6, 7

LESSON 11 NOTES

The visual for today's lesson is a striking representation of the Christian's need to be "rooted" in Christ. Display it as you discuss verses 6 and 7.

WHAT DO YOU THINK?

Biologists tell us that a root's primary function is to give the plant stability. Roots are also the plant's connection to its sources of nourishment. In what ways can our church help to ensure that its members are "rooted" in Christ?

The heretical teachings in Colosse included elements from different sources. Some teachings appeared to be derived from pagan philosophy, but they used certain Christian terminology to heighten their appeal. Other teachings seemed to advocate a rigid adherence to the Old Testament ceremonial regulations. Much of the language that the false teachers used appeared to correspond to what Paul was teaching. It is easy to see how newer Christians especially could be led astray.

If these false teachers had one characteristic in common, it was probably their attempt to add to the gospel, thus saying, in effect, that the work and ministry of Jesus was insufficient. Such a position was something that Paul could not tolerate. Chapter 2 of Colossians begins with his expression of concern for the Colossians' spiritual welfare (and for others besides them). He notes that in Christ "are hidden all the treasures of wisdom and knowledge" (v. 3), thereby countering the Gnostics' claim to a special secret knowledge of spiritual matters. He wants the Colossians to possess an "orderly" and "firm" faith in Christ (v. 5). Paul is doing more than just exposing false information; he is acting to preserve the eternal destiny of brothers and sisters in Christ!

I. THE STEADY CHRISTIAN (COLOSSIANS 2:6, 7)

A. WALKING IN CHRIST (v. 6)

6. So then, just as you received Christ Jesus as Lord, continue to live in him.

To Paul, the logical conclusion of having *received Christ Jesus as Lord* is that we *continue to live* as he would have us to live. Every aspect of our lives and our conduct should be influenced by our relationship with Jesus Christ.

B. ROOTED IN CHRIST (v. 7)

7. . . . rooted and built up in him, strengthened in the faith as you were taught, and overflowing with thankfulness.

Paul, by describing us as being *rooted*, illustrates the stability that should characterize all Christians. The verb *rooted* is in the perfect tense, which indicates a past event. By our acceptance of Jesus as Savior and Lord, we became planted in him.

Not only are we rooted in Christ, but Paul also says that we are *built up in him*. Here the verb is present tense, which indicates an ongoing process. Growing in the Lord is just that. Consider the growth of a plant: the better rooted it is, the better chance it has to grow strong and the better it will be able to withstand storms and other threats to its existence.

Furthermore, we are *strengthened in the faith*. In this verse, the word *faith* probably refers to the entire system of doctrinal truth that Christians believe, since faith is described as something that the Colossians have been *taught*.

Paul also describes the prevailing attitude of our life in Christ—that we should be *overflowing with thankfulness*. Christians should be constantly thanking God for his blessings and for his work in their lives.

NO FORWARDING ADDRESS

Some years ago the television program *Real People* told a story about a package that had been mailed to an inmate of a penitentiary. The package was returned to the sender marked: "ESCAPED: LEFT NO FORWARDING ADDRESS." You can be certain that an escaped prisoner left no forwarding address!

By God's grace we have escaped from sin—and we must not leave a forwarding address! In today's lesson Paul emphasizes the fact that we who have found forgiveness in Jesus must now walk in him and remain rooted in him. Our break with sin must be complete and final. Our new allegiance to Christ must be complete and final.

It is said that Augustine, one of the outstanding theologians of early church history, once met a woman whom he had known before his conversion. She called to him, "Augustine! It is I!" He replied, "But it is not I!" He was a new person! His break with sin was such that he could not go back to the old ways.

Unfortunately, some who claim allegiance to Christ make only a tentative break with sin. They escape, but they leave a forwarding address so that the devil will know where to find them. A gospel song we often sing at Christian camps reminds us of the commitment we have made: "I have decided to follow Jesus. . . . No turning back. No turning back."

            —R. C. S.

II. THE DISCERNING CHRISTIAN (COLOSSIANS 2:8-10)

A. CAUTIOUS OF ERROR (v. 8)

8. See to it that no one takes you captive through hollow and deceptive philosophy, which depends on human tradition and the basic principles of this world rather than on Christ.

Is Paul condemning the study of *philosophy* in this verse? Not exactly. What he is condemning is false philosophy, or philosophy that refuses to acknowledge God. Since *philosophy* literally means "love of wisdom," and since "all the treasures of wisdom and knowledge" are in Christ (Colossians 2:3), then genuine philosophy must pay homage to Christ. Obviously the philosophy being promoted by the false teachers in Colosse included ideas contrary to Christian truth.

Paul describes some as having been taken *captive* by these philosophies—in much the same way that items or individuals are taken captive during battle. Those who are thus captured are robbed of all they have been given in Christ.

This false philosophy is *hollow and deceptive*, for it *depends on human tradition*. Paul could be referring to either Jewish or pagan traditions, either of which were to be avoided if they led their followers away from Christ. These traditions were as dangerous as those of which Jesus warned the Pharisees and scribes (Mark 7:5-13). All such teachings must give way to the authoritative word of Jesus.

Paul also describes the false teaching as being dependent on *the basic principles of this world*. The Greek word rendered *basic principles* was often used to describe the components of something. Here it could refer to either the fundamental principles of the false teachers' philosophy or to the beings who were part of the spirit world and whose worship was promoted by the false teachers (Colossians 2:18). In either case, Paul was exposing the error in something that was clearly not focused *on Christ*.

B. COMPLETE IN CHRIST (vv. 9, 10)

9. For in Christ all the fullness of the Deity lives in bodily form.

This is a very important verse when considering the nature of Christ. It stresses Jesus' human and divine nature. Jesus was divine (*all the fullness of the Deity*), even though that divinity was housed in humanity (*in bodily form*). This is the significance of the term *incarnation*, which literally means being in flesh. Paul's statement refuted the Gnostic contention that Jesus was just one of many manifestations of God.

10. . . . and you have been given fullness in Christ, who is the head over every power and authority.

Christians have found their *fullness* in the One who is the fullness of God. How could any false teacher improve on this—then or now? Why seek after any other claims of authority when Jesus is *the head over every power and authority*?

WHAT DO YOU THINK?

What are some examples of "hollow and deceptive philosophy" in the contemporary world that threaten to subvert Christian faith?

DAILY BIBLE READINGS

Monday, Aug. 7—Paul Commends the Colossian Christians (Colossians 2:1-5)

Tuesday, Aug. 8—God Dwells Fully in Jesus Christ (Colossians 2:6-10)

Wednesday, Aug. 9—Dead to the Flesh, Alive in Christ (Colossians 2:11-15)

Thursday, Aug. 10—Hold Fast to Christ, Our Head (Colossians 2:16-23)

Friday, Aug. 11—Jesus: Mediator of a New Covenant (Hebrews 8:1-7)

Saturday, Aug. 12—The Blood of Christ Purifies Us (Hebrews 9:11-15)

Sunday, Aug. 13—Christ Perfects Those Who Are Sanctified (Hebrews 10:11-18)

THE COMPLETE PACKAGE

The June 1969 issue of *National Geographic* reported the discovery of relics from a Spanish ship that had sunk in 1588. A man named Robert Senuit located the wreckage of the ship off the coast of Ireland. Among the objects he found was a man's engagement ring. Although some 380 years had passed since the tragic death of the person who wore it, one could still see engraved on the ring an outstretched hand and a phrase written in Spanish meaning, "I have nothing more to give."

The Lord Jesus could have spoken those very words at Calvary. When he gave his life on the cross, he had nothing more to give. Indeed nothing more *needed* to be given. His work of atonement was complete.

The same words can also describe our response to Jesus' sacrifice at Calvary. When we give our lives to him, we have nothing more to give. It may seem that giving our lives to him is not really much of a gift. Sin has ruined our lives, making them distorted, dirty, and ugly. But they are the very gifts Jesus wants. He died so that ruined lives could be made new.

Is this not part of what Paul means when he writes that we "have been given fullness in Christ" (Colossians 2:10)? His gift of life for us was full and complete. The gift of our lives to him must also be full and complete. Then we can sing, "Jesus Paid It *All*" and "*All* to Jesus I Surrender."   —R. C. S.

III. THE FORGIVEN CHRISTIAN (COLOSSIANS 2:11-13)

A. DEAD TO SIN (v. 11)

11. In him you were also circumcised, in the putting off of the sinful nature, not with a circumcision done by the hands of men but with the circumcision done by Christ.

Circumcision was the covenant sign instituted by God with Abraham (Genesis 17:10-14) and performed on all Israelite males. Here Paul describes a spiritual *circumcision*. It cannot be *done by the hands of men*, for it involves a procedure that only *Christ* can perform. Instead of cutting away part of human flesh (as physical circumcision does), the spiritual circumcision cuts away from one's life *the sinful nature*. (The Greek term is the word meaning *flesh*, which describes the kind of perspective that defies God's authority and seeks to gratify one's own desires.) Gentiles were not required to undergo physical circumcision, but all believers in Jesus from whatever background must receive the spiritual circumcision, which Paul proceeds to explain.

B. ALIVE IN CHRIST (vv. 12, 13)

12. . . . having been buried with him in baptism and raised with him through your faith in the power of God, who raised him from the dead.

The book of Hebrews tells of many Old Testament practices and institutions that were given a deeper and fuller meaning with the coming of Christ. Here Paul points out that circumcision's fuller meaning is found in the act of Christian *baptism*. It would be wrong to say that circumcision and baptism are exactly parallel to one another, for circumcision was performed on male Israelite infants when they were eight days old. The spiritual circumcision of baptism follows repentance from sins (Acts 2:38) and provides a washing away of sins (Acts 22:16).

Paul also describes baptism as a burial. This alludes to the normal mode of baptism in the New Testament, which was by immersion in water. (The word *baptism* comes from a verb meaning to immerse.) Because baptism follows a dying to sin, the candidate for baptism is symbolically *buried* (lowered into the water) and raised up from it, symbolizing his resurrection to new life (Romans 6:3-6). Paul then links baptism with faith when he says that we are *raised with him* [Christ] *through your faith in the power of God*. Baptism without faith is of no

HOW TO SAY IT

Colosse. Ko-LAHSS-ee.

Colossians. Kuh-LOSH-unz.

Ephesians. Ee-FEE-zhunz.

Gnosticism. NAHSS-tih-sizz-um.

Gnostics. NAHSS-tiks.

Philippians. Fih-LIP-ee-unz.

use and has no real meaning. Faith in Jesus expressed by the obedience of baptism receives the full blessing of God.

13. When you were dead in your sins and in the uncircumcision of your sinful nature, God made you alive with Christ. He forgave us all our sins.

This describes what happens in the process of experiencing the spiritual circumcision. We who were once uncircumcised (in a spiritual sense, indicating our separation from God and from his people) and who were *dead in* our *sins* are *made . . . alive with Christ*. Note that we are made alive after we have died *to* sins, and we are made alive by being brought out of the state of being dead *in* sins. We are forgiven of *all our sins;* they cannot be held against us anymore.

IV. THE LIBERATED CHRISTIAN (COLOSSIANS 2:14-19)

A. FREE FROM THE LAW (vv. 14, 15)

14. . . . having canceled the written code, with its regulations, that was against us and that stood opposed to us; he took it away, nailing it to the cross.

What does this *written code* mean? The Greek word rendered *written code* is taken from the business world and describes a certificate of indebtedness signed by the debtor acknowledging his obligation. Some believe that this phrase is describing a list of our sins. However, the emphasis of the verse is on *regulations*, which most likely refers to the law of Moses and the many commandments found within it. While the Colossian church was largely made up of Gentiles, part of the false teaching there seems to have been a legalistic insistence on keeping the Mosaic law. This code *was against us* and *stood opposed to us* because it was impossible for us to keep its requirements. But because Jesus kept the law perfectly and then took the penalty that was due lawbreakers, the debt has been canceled. Jesus *took it away* at the *cross*.

15. And having disarmed the powers and authorities, he made a public spectacle of them, triumphing over them by the cross.

Roman generals celebrated their victories on the battlefield by marching in an impressive parade. All prisoners of war were forced to march in this parade, and all the spoils of battle that the army had captured were displayed.

Here Paul uses the description of such a celebration to highlight the triumph of Jesus at the *cross*. At the cross Jesus *disarmed the powers and authorities*. Most likely this phrase refers to those "powers of this dark world" that hold individuals captive to sin and against whom Christians still "struggle" (Ephesians 6:12). Jesus broke the stranglehold of these powers so that their captives could be set free.

B. FREE FROM LEGALISM (vv. 16, 17)

16. Therefore do not let anyone judge you by what you eat or drink, or with regard to a religious festival, a New Moon celebration or a Sabbath day.

Here Paul specifically addresses the false teachers in the Colossian church who were promoting a rigid legalism. The Colossians need not concern themselves with those who *judge* them on the basis of how they handle certain religious rituals—in this case, keeping various Old Testament regulations and festivals. This is indicated from the references to the *New Moon celebration* and to the *Sabbath day*, which were part of the Jewish calendar. The references to what individuals *eat* and *drink* likely called attention to the dietary regulations of the law of Moses. It is also possible that the false teachers in Colosse had developed their own dietary restrictions.

It was not wrong for Jewish Christians to observe the customs outlined in the law of Moses. Paul himself observed some of them (Acts 16:3; 18:20, 21; 21:26). The key issue in the early church was whether Christians—especially Gentile

WHAT DO YOU THINK?

Jesus taught us to pray, "Forgive us our debts" (Matthew 6:12). Paul says God "forgave us all our sins." Why do we need to pray for forgiveness if we're already forgiven?

WHAT DO YOU THINK?

It seems that people in every era and every generation fall prey to the trap of legalism. In the Old Testament, God's prophet Micah had to ask, "What does the Lord require of you? To act justly and to love mercy and to walk humbly with your God" (Micah 6:8). Even in that prescribed system of law, God was concerned about the heart and the mind. Yet some today still judge their fellow Christians according to rules not taught in the New Testament. Why is legalism so appealing? How can we avoid it in our own lives?

converts—should be *required* to observe them. While Paul voluntarily circumcised Timothy (Acts 16:3), in another circumstance he refused to have Titus circumcised because others (certain false teachers) were trying to force the issue (Galatians 2:3-5).

Brothers and sisters in Christ should not judge each other on the basis of whether they keep or do not keep certain customs. The false teachers in Colosse were only promoting division when they encouraged such activity. Read Paul's additional teaching on this matter in Romans 14:1-12.

17. *These are a shadow of the things that were to come; the reality, however, is found in Christ.*

Paul maintains that the Old Testament regulations and holy days were just *a shadow* of the *reality* that would come later *in Christ*. This is the reason they should not become tests of faith and fellowship. We should not grasp at shadows when we can embrace the reality and the fullness found in Jesus.

C. FREE FROM DECEPTION (vv. 18, 19)

18. *Do not let anyone who delights in false humility and the worship of angels disqualify you for the prize. Such a person goes into great detail about what he has seen, and his unspiritual mind puffs him up with idle notions.*

Paul describes the high price of being led astray by the false teachers. Some of the Christians in Colosse were in danger of forfeiting their *prize* (cf. Philippians 3:14) by following after those who had lost contact with Christ the Head (v. 19).

Later Paul will encourage the Colossians to "clothe yourselves with . . . humility" (Colossians 3:12). Here, however, he speaks of a *false humility* (although the word he uses is the same word found in 3:12). This seems to be tied in some way to the *worship of angels*. Perhaps the false teachers were claiming to be humble by worshiping angels rather than the sovereign God. We have noted that the erroneous teaching in Colosse was characterized by a belief in a series of spirit beings who were thought to have come from God.

In addition, the false teachers seemed to take great pride in informing their hearers about what they had *seen*. In other words, they were claiming to have received special visions of some kind. These were not, however, visions from God, but simply *idle notions* produced by an *unspiritual mind*.

19. *He has lost connection with the Head, from whom the whole body, supported and held together by its ligaments and sinews, grows as God causes it to grow.*

Here is the real cause of the false teachers' problems: they have *lost connection with the Head*—that is, with Christ, the Head of the church. For any part of the *body* of Christ to stay spiritually healthy, it must remain connected to the Head. Paul's description of how the body grows is similar to his words in Ephesians 4:16.

CONCLUSION

In many cities, when spring melts the heavy snows of winter and cars splash the resulting "slush" on everything nearby, road crews must come along and scrub all the street signs. They become obscured to the point that people cannot read what they say.

In a sense, that is what Paul is doing in our lesson today. He is trying to wash off the spiritual warning signs (which have been obscured by the "slush" of the false teachers) so that the Christians in Colosse can know where to go and what to do. These signs have not been posted to limit our freedom; they are there to give us the freedom to travel the right road and avoid danger. Thus we can reach our destination safely.

WHAT DO YOU THINK?

From television to collectibles, angels are very popular today! How, if at all, is the modern fascination with angels similar to the Colossian heresy of worshiping angels?

PRAYER

Forgive me, Father, when I have been content with what is partial and "shadowy." Help me to be dissatisfied with stunted spiritual growth. Keep me aware of all the riches that I have in Christ, and help me to find my completeness in him. Through him I pray. Amen.

THOUGHT TO REMEMBER

To be a complete Christian, I need to be completely Christ's.

Discovery Learning

This page contains an alternate lesson plan emphasizing learning activities. Classes desiring such student involvement will find these suggestions helpful. The next page is a reproducible activity page to further enhance discovery learning.

LEARNING GOALS

After this lesson each student will be able to:

1. Explain how Paul describes the Christian's completeness in Christ, and the ways in which the Colossians were being led astray from their completeness.

2. Give some modern examples of teachings and philosophies that constitute a threat to our completeness in Christ.

3. Express an exclusive faith in Jesus, rejecting all other systems of belief.

INTO THE LESSON

Be sure there is a supply of paper and pencils available, and begin this lesson by playing a "word association" game. This is a light, fast-moving activity that will involve all students in a non-threatening way. You will say a word, and the students will quickly write down the first word or thought that comes to mind. Use the following words: *Faith, Jesus, Baptism, Circumcision,* and *Complete.*

Review the list, asking a few volunteers to tell what they wrote for each word. Keep this activity brief.

Then say, "We might ask, 'What do these five words have in common?' While some words have an obvious commonality, some just don't seem to fit the list. For example, what do *circumcision* and *baptism* have in common? All five are key words in today's text. And all five words are clues to living a full and mature Christian life."

INTO THE WORD

Do a brief lecture, reviewing the setting for this text, from the Lesson Background in the commentary. Distribute copies of the reproducible page that follows. Observe that verse 10 tells us we "have been given fullness in Christ" and that today's text is filled with clues to what it means to be full or complete or mature in Christ. Have the students work individually or in small groups to search the verses cited on the activity page, looking for marks of a Christian who is full, complete, or mature. When they have listed the items for each verse, they can unscramble the letters in the shaded area to spell *complete.*

6: Living in Christ.

7: Rooted and built up in him, strengthened in the faith, and overflowing with thankfulness.

8: Refusing to be robbed or taken captive by human philosophies.

11: Putting off, or dead to, sin.

12: Buried and raised with Christ in baptism.

13: Dead in one's sins, made alive with Christ, forgiven.

16, 17: Free from traditions or legalism.

18, 19: Committed to Christ's headship, free from falsehood.

Allow eight to ten minutes for this activity. Then review the students' findings, using the lesson commentary to explain passages that seem difficult to understand.

Read and review the text in the four sections listed in your commentary (vv. 6, 7; 8-10; 11-13; 14-19). After reading and discussing each section, write on a poster the words "The complete Christian is _____." Beneath that write each of the following headings (taken from the commentary) as you summarize your discussion: *steady* (vv. 6, 7); *discerning* (vv. 8-10); *forgiven* (vv. 11-13); *liberated* (vv. 14-19).

As you review these verses, be sure to include a discussion of these three issues:

1. Explain Paul's warning about "philosophy" and "tradition" (v. 8). Ask, "What does this warning mean to us today? What philosophies or traditions might be 'of this world rather than . . . Christ'? Why is the Christian perspective superior to these teachings?"

2. Explain the human and divine nature of Christ (v. 9).

3. Review Christ's work on our behalf (vv. 14, 15).

INTO LIFE

Display this incomplete statement: "Living as a complete or mature Christian is like living as a _____." Have persons fill in the blank with their own vocations (e.g., carpenter, salesperson, retiree, housewife). Then have them think why this statement is an appropriate analogy. Example: An investment counselor might say his life is vested in Christ and growing beyond his imagination. Or a farmer might say that completeness in Christ is like being a laborer in God's harvest. Members of the class can share their analogies in small groups, with those sitting next to them, or with the entire class.

Remind the class that we may be tested in our maturity or completeness in Christ as the Colossians were tested. Christ, however, is the only true way to know and worship God.

Complete in Christ

Read Colossians 2:6-19. Use the following clues to find a word that describes living in Christ. Write that word in the corresponding blanks. Then unscramble the highlighted letters to spell an important concept from this part of Paul's writing. (The words may come directly from, or be a paraphrase of, the text.)

Colossians 2:6: _____ in Christ
Colossians 2:7: _____ and built up in him.
Colossians 2:8: Refusing to be taken _____
Colossians 2:11: _____ off sin

Colossians 2:12: _____ and raised with Christ
Colossians 2:13: Made _____ in Christ.
Colossians 2:16, 17: Free from _____
Colossians 2:18, 19: _____ to Christ's headship

v. 6

v. 7

v. 8

v. 11

v. 12

v. 13

vv. 16, 17

vv. 18, 19

Scrambled Word: _____

Paul cautions believers to beware of deceptive philosophy which depends on human tradition rather than on Christ (Colossians 2:8). Below are listed a few of the religious sayings frequently heard in today's world. Consider why they are wrong and not built on Scriptural doctrine. Then write a more Scriptural view and at least one supporting Scripture.

Sayings	A More Scriptural Doctrine	A Supporting Text
"It doesn't matter what you believe as long as you are sincere."		
"We are all going to the same place."		
"Baptism isn't important. It's how you live that counts."		

New Life in Christ
Unit 3: Christ Above All
(Lessons 10-13)

THE WAY TO RIGHTEOUSNESS

LESSON 12

WHY TEACH THIS LESSON?

Dressing up for church seems out of vogue these days. It used to be that people dressed in their finest for worship. Thus, we called certain clothes our "Sunday best" or our "Sunday-go-to-meetin' clothes." It was assumed that if God deserves our best efforts, then we ought also to give him our best in how we dress.

It was a good tradition—though we don't want to get legalistic about it or suggest that those who dress casually are less spiritual. But it would help us understand today's text, where Paul uses a clothing metaphor to describe the Christian life. Use this lesson to encourage your students to dress in their "Sunday best"—not on the outside, but on the inside. And not just on Sunday, but every day.

INTRODUCTION

A. THE MIRROR

In one of Hans Christian Andersen's stories, he tells of a mirror that made every good and pretty thing look bad. Many people have just such a distorted view of life. Paul once made this observation: "To the pure, all things are pure, but to those who are corrupted and do not believe, nothing is pure. In fact, both their minds and consciences are corrupted" (Titus 1:15). Often those who use such a "mirror" find that it also makes bad things look good.

Today's study from Colossians reminds us that only when we find new life in Christ and begin to look at people and situations through the mirror of God's Word (James 1:23-25) can we enjoy a clear view of them. The best way to see the world is from Heaven's perspective!

B. LESSON BACKGROUND

Our two previous studies from Colossians were taken from the portions of the letter that focus particularly on doctrinal issues: the supremacy of Christ (chapter 1) and false teachings being spread among the Colossians (chapter 2). Both lessons highlighted the fullness of the Father that dwelt in Jesus (Colossians 1:19; 2:9) and the fact that Christians have received "fullness" through the presence of Christ in us (1:27; 2:10).

Today's study moves on to the more practical part of Colossians, challenging us who have been "raised with Christ" (3:1) to express that new life in our attitudes, words, and deeds.

I. TRUTHS TO CELEBRATE (COLOSSIANS 3:1-4)

A. RISEN WITH CHRIST (vv. 1, 2)

1. Since, then, you have been raised with Christ, set your hearts on things above, where Christ is seated at the right hand of God.

Paul urges Christians to *set their hearts on* the highest possible ideals—*things above*, or, the things of Heaven. The phrase *set your hearts on* is literally "seek" in

DEVOTIONAL READING:
MARK 12:28-34

BACKGROUND SCRIPTURE:
COLOSSIANS 3:1-17

PRINTED TEXT:
COLOSSIANS 3:1-17

LESSON AIMS

After this lesson students will be able to:

1. List several things Paul says a Christian must "put off" and things he says a Christian must "put on" in order to grow in the way of righteousness.

2. Tell why the process of "putting off" and "putting on" is a continual challenge for the Christian.

3. Suggest a specific way to "put on" one of the virtues Paul commends.

KEY VERSE

Aug
20

Whatever you do, whether in word or deed, do it all in the name of the Lord Jesus, giving thanks to God the Father through him.
—*Colossians 3:17*

LESSON 12 NOTES

DAILY BIBLE READINGS

Monday, Aug. 14—*Revealed With Christ in Glory (Colossians 3:1-6)*

Tuesday, Aug. 15—*Put on the New Self (Colossians 3:7-11)*

Wednesday, Aug. 16—*Live Faithfully, Joyfully, and Thankfully (Colossians 3:12-17)*

Thursday, Aug. 17—*Love and Honor All People (Colossians 3:18—4:1)*

Friday, Aug. 18—*Live and Speak in Christian Love (Colossians 4:2-6)*

Saturday, Aug. 19—*Paul's Faithful Supporters (Colossians 4:7-11)*

Sunday, Aug. 20—*Paul's Final Words to the Colossians (Colossians 4:12-18)*

WHAT DO YOU THINK?

Earthly things pound persistently on our mind's door, demanding to be let in. Basic human needs and desires must be met, but we must not let them dominate and control our thinking. How do we "set [our] minds on things above, not on earthly things"?

the Greek text, and has the sense of "keep on seeking." This emphasizes that the seeking must become a priority in our lives. To accept Christ as Savior is, in one sense, the end of our searching—we have found the one and only source of salvation! In another sense, however, it is just the beginning. The Christian life is a continual adventure of seeking to know Christ better.

The expression *raised with Christ* recalls Paul's words in the previous chapter. Colossians 2:12 says: "Buried with [Christ] in baptism and raised with him through your faith in the power of God, who raised him from the dead." Baptism marks a rebirth—a beginning of a new life (Romans 6:4). The one so raised must continually walk with the Lord, seeking those things that are above.

Here Jesus is described as *seated at the right hand of God*. To be at the right hand of a sovereign or king is to be stationed at the place of highest privilege. Even today a person may refer to a close friend or associate as his right-hand man.

THE MAN WHO CAME BACK FROM THE DEAD

When a guest minister came to a certain church one Sunday to preach, the people asked him, "Would you like to meet a man who came back from the dead?" They then introduced him to an older man in the congregation. They explained that some time ago the man had become very ill and was taken to the hospital, where he was declared dead. Then someone noticed a slight movement. Quickly doctors resuscitated the man, who soon became known as "the man who came back from the dead." Of course, these people understood that their friend was not really dead, though he was certainly near death. Only Jesus is honored as the One who really came back from the dead.

In a spiritual sense, however, all Christians have come back from the dead. We died to sin. Our old person was buried with Christ in baptism (Colossians 2:12), and a new person was raised up. We are now declared "raised with Christ" (Colossians 3:1). As he came back from physical death we have come back from spiritual death—and the same power is responsible for both events! Now that resurrection power lives in us, enabling us to live as Christ lived.

We need to remind ourselves from time to time of the difference Christ has made in our lives. We are indeed people who have come back from the dead. —R. C. S.

2. Set your minds on things above, not on earthly things.

Perhaps we have known someone whom we would describe as having a mind that was "in the gutter." Here Paul admonishes us to have the opposite. We are to *set* our *minds on things above*. True, not all *earthly things* are evil, but they are inferior to what is heavenly.

B. HIDDEN WITH CHRIST (v. 3)
3. For you died, and your life is now hidden with Christ in God.

What does Paul mean by telling us that we *died*? He means that our old sinful life is dead with Christ (Romans 6:8-11). Our *life is now hidden with Christ in God*. We dwell "in the heavenly realms" (Ephesians 2:6) with Christ (Ephesians 1:20). *Hidden* calls attention to the fact that the world does not understand our new life; it is too preoccupied with "earthly things." The word may also carry with it the idea of being protected.

C. GLORIFIED WITH CHRIST (v. 4)
4. When Christ, who is your life, appears, then you also will appear with him in glory.

This describes what will happen at the second coming of *Christ*. This "blessed hope" (Titus 2:13) provides us a strong motivation to continue thinking about heavenly things and thus to keep ourselves pure (1 John 3:3). We will be part of the great victory that Christ achieves when he returns. The life once "hidden" from the world (v. 3) will be gloriously revealed, for Christ himself is our *life*.

II. VICES TO ELIMINATE (COLOSSIANS 3:5-11)

A. IMMORAL BEHAVIOR (vv. 5-7)

5. Put to death, therefore, whatever belongs to your earthly nature: sexual immorality, impurity, lust, evil desires and greed, which is idolatry.

While we have died to sin (Romans 6:2) so that sin is no longer controlling our lives as it once did, we still have to deal with individual temptations. To do this, says Paul, we must *put to death . . . whatever belongs to* our *earthly nature. Earthly nature* translates a Greek word meaning "members," which refers to the parts of the body and here represents the entire body and its desires. Paul is obviously not asking for a literal killing of the body; he is telling us to avoid the sins he proceeds to list, which involve the use of the body. (Read his similar exhortation in Romans 6:19.)

The Greek word for *sexual immorality* is the source of our English word *pornography*. Paul's counsel is deemed irrelevant by many in our society today, where sexual standards have been greatly relaxed. However, regardless of what society says, Christians are still obligated to live lives of purity before a holy God.

Impurity is similar to, but covers a much wider area of behavior than, *sexual immorality*. Then comes *lust*. This is actually the Greek word *pathos,* which is the root of such words as empathy and sympathy. While the Greeks used *pathos* of either a good or bad feeling or desire, in the New Testament it always refers to inappropriate feelings or uncontrolled desires.

The Greek term translated *evil desires* describes intense desire, particularly sexual desire—though the word is not limited to the sexual context. Of itself it can be good or evil. It is the same word used to describe how Jesus "eagerly desired" to eat the Last Supper with his apostles (Luke 22:15). Paul makes clear that it is the *evil* desires that must be put to death, not just intense desires of any kind. Indeed, a Christian should have an ardent desire for good causes.

The last sin Paul cites is *greed.* This means more than just the desire for money; it is a warning against a selfish desire for anything or anyone. Note how Paul equates greed with *idolatry*: if we put our desires and wants above what God wants for us, then we have indeed made idols and worshiped them.

6. Because of these, the wrath of God is coming.

While God is loving and forgiving, we dare not think that he is casual about sin. Paul reminds us that these sins provoke *the wrath of God.*

7. You used to walk in these ways, in the life you once lived.

Paul reminds the Colossians that at one time they committed these sins. Their lives prior to being "raised with Christ" were characterized by all kinds of evil.

B. HOSTILE ATTITUDES (v. 8a)

8a. But now you must rid yourselves of all such things as these: anger, rage, malice.

Paul continues with another list of evils that the Christian is to *rid* himself of like soiled clothing. These sins deal more with our attitudes and our speech toward others. The first three words are all related: *anger, rage,* and *malice*. James tells us simply, "Man's anger does not bring about the righteous life that God desires" (James 1:20).

C. IMPROPER SPEECH (vv. 8b, 9a)

8b, 9a. . . . slander, and filthy language from your lips. Do not lie to each other.

WHAT DO YOU THINK?

If we are preoccupied with the demands and pleasures of everyday living, anything future can easily be ignored. Thus, the second coming of Christ gets very little thought time and talk time with most of us. What can we do to give it more attention, more space in our lives?

WHAT DO YOU THINK?

We, too, "used to walk" in evil practices and a wrong lifestyle. How much thought do you think a Christian should give to his or her former life? How can an awareness of the past help the believer to be faithful in the present and into the future?

Slander describes the kind of insulting talk that can be directed toward God or toward other people. *Filthy language* translates a Greek word that suggests communication that is abusive or obscene. This is another term that seems especially relevant in our day. Nearly every movie and television program contains what might be described as *filthy language*. The language is used either to shock or to provide a twisted form of humor, neither of which is an acceptable use of God's precious gift of speech.

Verse 9 continues the admonitions concerning our speech by reminding us that Christians are to be honest people. Anyone who claims to be a follower of the One who is the truth (John 14:6) should find lying intolerable. It is actually the speech of the devil (John 8:44). A Christian's speech, Paul will later say, should be "always full of grace, seasoned with salt" (Colossians 4:6).

D. REMEMBER WHO YOU ARE (vv. 9b-11)

9b, 10. . . . since you have taken off your old self with its practices and have put on the new self, which is being renewed in knowledge in the image of its Creator.

The use of the terms *taken off* and *put on* highlights the difference that being "raised with Christ" ought to make in the resurrected person's life. The *new self*, or new person, in Christ *is being renewed in knowledge.* This is probably a reference to the knowledge of God, since the knowledge mentioned here causes the individual to become more and more like God. Such a person grows *in the image of* his *Creator,* thus becoming what God created him to be.

11. Here there is no Greek or Jew, circumcised or uncircumcised, barbarian, Scythian, slave or free, but Christ is all, and is in all.

This verse emphasizes the unity found in Christ. Paul says that in him those barriers that divide and frustrate people are brought down. *There is no Greek or Jew.* Since the time of Alexander the Great, Greek culture had been spread over the entire world. But since it was a pagan culture, it was resisted by the Jews. The love of Christ was able to penetrate such barriers of culture and nationalism.

A religious barrier divided the *circumcised* and the *uncircumcised.* The *circumcised* referred to the Jews, for whom this act was the covenant sign required of all males. To the Jews, all non-Jews were labeled *uncircumcised.* But the sign of the Old Covenant is meaningless in the New, so this barrier was also removed in Christ.

The term *barbarian* referred to anyone who did not speak Greek. The Greek word used here imitated how foreigners sounded to Greek ears—as if they were saying, "baa, baa, baa, baa." Thus we get the term *barbarian.* Perhaps this suggests that the language barrier is removed in Christ.

A *Scythian* was part of a particularly hated group of barbarians in Paul's day. They originated from what is today southern Russia. The term probably suggests that no one is beyond the reach of God's grace in Christ.

Finally, Paul declares that in Christ no one is considered *slave or free.* Slavery was a fact of life in the biblical world. Few probably even considered the possibility of its nonexistence. Here Paul does not speak directly to the issue of slavery; he simply affirms that in Christ the slave and the free person are one.

That the distinctions Paul mentions in this verse could be eliminated in Christ is a testimony to the power of the gospel. It also challenges us as Christians today to apply that same power to the divisions around us.

III. VIRTUES TO CULTIVATE (COLOSSIANS 3:12-17)

A. A MERCIFUL SPIRIT (v. 12)

12. Therefore, as God's chosen people, holy and dearly loved, clothe yourselves with compassion, kindness, humility, gentleness and patience.

WHAT DO YOU THINK?

Many of our divisions are the same as those in Paul's day. Reaching across the dividing lines may pull us out of our comfort zones, but we must make the effort. The cross was outside Jesus' comfort zone, too! What can we do about eliminating the divisions that separate people in our world? [Consider cultural, ethnic, and national differences as well as those caused by history and tradition, language barriers, economic differences, and any other divisions you and your class can name.]

Earlier Paul described what we should "take off." Now he tells us how we must *clothe* ourselves. He describes us as *God's chosen people*. This term, along with *holy and dearly loved*, calls attention to our standing as the people of God. Note that being *chosen* does not do away with human responsibility. We are to take to heart all the commands that Paul proceeds to give.

Paul follows this reminder of who we are with a list of qualities that we need to cultivate. First, he says that we should clothe ourselves with *compassion*. The Greek text literally reads, "bowels of compassion." This reflects the belief of Paul's day that emotions originated, not in the heart (as we usually describe them), but in the intestinal area. It is still true that people often feel strong emotion in their stomachs. (Thus we occasionally speak of a "gut feeling.")

The word for *kindness* is the common word for this virtue. In the original language it sounds very much like the name *Christ. Humility* and *gentleness* are attitudes that will produce acts of kindness toward others.

Finally, Paul admonishes us to clothe ourselves with *patience*, which we will also demonstrate if we have cultivated humility and gentleness. Patience is a virtue both in handling the trials and struggles of life and in dealing with people and all of their complexities.

B. A FORGIVING SPIRIT (v. 13)

13. Bear with each other and forgive whatever grievances you may have against one another. Forgive as the Lord forgave you.

To *bear with each other* describes a willingness to remain even-tempered with others whose actions or words irritate us. It is demonstrated by what we do not do. On the other hand, *forgive* is a more active virtue in that we determine not to hold someone's offensive act or deed against him anymore. This admonition is made stronger by the challenge to forgive *as the Lord forgave* us. All of us have been the recipients of an "amazing grace," and it behooves us to exhibit it toward others. This is the point of Jesus' parable of the unforgiving servant (Matthew 18:21-35).

C. A LOVING SPIRIT (v. 14)

14. And over all these virtues put on love, which binds them all together in perfect unity.

Paul completes his list of virtues with the "crown jewel" of *love*. The word for *love* is the Greek word *agape*. Paul says that love *binds . . . together in perfect unity*, or is the gluing power behind, *all* the other virtues he has listed. This is consistent with his teaching in 1 Corinthians 13 about the priority and excellence of love.

D. A PEACEFUL SPIRIT (v. 15)

15. Let the peace of Christ rule in your hearts, since as members of one body you were called to peace. And be thankful.

The word for *rule* is taken from the sports world of Paul's day. The word described the action of a judge, or umpire, in deciding the outcome of a competition. Thus Paul is saying that God's *peace* is to act as an arbiter governing all of our relationships in the church. He even goes so far as to say that we are *called to peace*. We are not to treat peace as optional; Paul tells the Romans, "If it is possible, as far as it depends on you, live at peace with everyone" (Romans 12:18). If Christians would give peace this kind of priority, we would go a long way toward becoming *one body*.

Then Paul adds *and be thankful*. Certainly the refreshing change in our lives that results from removing the vices and embracing the virtues should make us grateful people indeed.

WHAT DO YOU THINK?

Why are bearing with each other and forgiving each other often forgotten among Christian friends? How can we cultivate an ability to practice these more faithfully?

HOW TO SAY IT

agape (Greek). uh-GAH-pay.
Barbarian. Bar-BARE-ee-un.
Colossians. Kuh-LOSH-unz.
Ephesians. Ee-FEE-zhunz.
pathos. PAY-thahss.
Scythian. SITH-ee-un.

This visual illustrates the principle of verse 17. Discuss how a believer can do everything ("whatever you do") in the name of Christ.

CELEBRATE THANKSGIVING DAYS

On the island of St. Croix (*kroy*) in the Virgin Islands, two Thanksgiving days are celebrated. In addition to the one celebrated by all Americans, the residents observe a Hurricane Thanksgiving Day on October 25. It is linked to the observance of Supplication Day, which is on July 25, the beginning of hurricane season. On Supplication Day all the citizens of St. Croix are urged to pray that their tiny island will be spared the ravages of a hurricane. They have then appointed a day at the end of hurricane season, October 25, to thank God for answering their prayers.

Most of us probably have many supplication days, but far too few thanksgiving days. Over and over we receive that for which we prayed, yet we seldom thank God for his answers. Of course, we don't need something as dramatic as a hurricane to make us thankful. One little boy made a list of blessings for Thanksgiving Day and showed it to his family. One item on the list was quite puzzling: the boy said that he was thankful for his eyeglasses. Since most little boys don't want to wear glasses, the family wondered why he would list that. He explained that he was thankful for his glasses for two reasons: "They keep the boys from hitting me, and they keep the girls from kissing me."

All of us have unnoticed blessings for which we need to be thankful. And we need to remember that it is just as important to thank God for the little things as it is to thank him for the big things. —R. C. S.

E. A GRATEFUL SPIRIT (vv. 16, 17)

16. Let the word of Christ dwell in you richly as you teach and admonish one another with all wisdom, and as you sing psalms, hymns and spiritual songs with gratitude in your hearts to God.

What does it mean to *let the word of Christ dwell* in us? The *word of Christ* probably refers to the message of the gospel. The gospel is not just truth to be grasped intellectually; it should find a home in our minds and our hearts, affecting all our relationships. Its presence allows us to share a rich fellowship with others in the church, who also know that indwelling.

Paul says that we are to express this fellowship *as we teach and admonish one another* in our worship. The terms *psalms, hymns,* and *spiritual songs* were discussed in lesson 8 under the study of Ephesians 5:19 (pages 403, 404).

17. And whatever you do, whether in word or deed, do it all in the name of the Lord Jesus, giving thanks to God the Father through him.

This is an appropriate summary of Paul's exhortations in this passage. He tells us that every *word* that we speak and every *deed* that we perform ought to be done *in the name of the Lord Jesus.* Every aspect of our lives should be lived in recognition of his lordship, *giving thanks to* our heavenly *Father* for his goodness, with the Lord Jesus as our intercessor.

CONCLUSION

Have you ever watched a crowd of people watching a tennis match? No doubt you have noticed how their heads move back and forth in perfect unison as they follow the flight of the ball from one side of the court to the other and back again.

Many people try to live the Christian life in just that manner. They want to give their allegiance to *both* God and the world in an effort to gain "the best of both worlds." Paul tells us, "Set your minds on things above, not on earthly things" (Colossians 3:2). What works for watching a tennis match spells disaster in the spiritual realm. Let's stay focused, for this is a "match" with eternity at stake!

Discovery Learning

This page contains an alternate lesson plan emphasizing learning activities. Classes desiring such student involvement will find these suggestions helpful. The next page is a reproducible activity page to further enhance discovery learning.

LEARNING GOALS

As a result of studying this lesson, each student will be able to:

1. List several things Paul says a Christian must "put off" and things he says a Christian must "put on" in order to grow in the way of righteousness.

2. Tell why the process of "putting off" and "putting on" is a continual challenge for the Christian.

3. Suggest a specific way to "put on" one of the virtues Paul commends.

INTO THE LESSON

On the chalkboard or on a large poster list the following events: the inauguration of a president (or other government leader), a football game, a wedding, a polar expedition, an engine overhaul. Divide the class into small groups and assign one event to each group, or have the entire class consider each item on the list. Ask, "How would you dress to attend or participate in this event?" (or, ". . . in each of these events?")

Obviously the way one dresses to attend an inauguration will be much different from the way he dresses to overhaul an engine! A polar expedition requires one to "put on" some very special clothing. Observe that today's lesson will tell us how to dress for the Christian life—what to take off and what to put on.

INTO THE WORD

Divide the class into small groups, and give each group two pieces of paper. The heading for one should read "Behaviors of My Old Self." The heading for the other paper should read "Qualities or Behaviors of My New Self." Ask each group to read Colossians 3:1-17 and then list all the old and new qualities or behaviors mentioned in the text, citing the verse reference for each. ("Old Self" behaviors will be found in verses 5, 8, and 9. "New Self" behaviors may be found in verses 1, 2, 3, 5, 10, 11, 12, 13, 14, 15, and 16.)

Option: Use the reproducible page that follows to supplement this activity, or in place of it. The first activity and questions 1 and 2 of the second will facilitate a discussion of "old self" issues; question 3 will help you discuss "new self" matters. Review as suggested below.

After the exercise is completed, it may be necessary to elaborate on some of the behaviors or qualities listed. Begin by reviewing the "Old Self" qualities. Ask

for definitions or examples of each. Write these definitions on a poster. Use the material in the commentary as needed to clarify explanations. After completing the first list, remind the class that these are behaviors that God expects his children to abandon or avoid.

To review the "New Self" behaviors and qualities, ask these questions:

1. Paul tells us to "set [our] hearts" (and our minds) "on things above" in verses 1 and 2. Why? Does he assume that all things on earth are evil?

2. What does Paul mean when he says that we "died" (v. 3)?

3. What does it mean to "put to death . . . whatever belongs to your earthly nature" (v. 5)?

4. What are the differences in the three types of music mentioned in verse 16? How can they be used to "teach and admonish one another"?

Use the commentary section to help answer questions and clarify other issues as needed.

INTO LIFE

Tell the class, "This list appears to be a 'before and after' list." Then discuss these questions:

1. Do you think this transformation is likely to be completed at the moment of conversion? Or do you think this transformation is a continuing process? Why?

2. What can make this transition to the "new self" difficult for believers? What can we as a church do to encourage this transformation in our members?

Read verse 17. Note that this verse is a great summary statement of Paul's teaching and of living as a Christian.

Make the lesson personal by distributing lists of the characteristics of the old and new self. (Prepare these lists before class.) They may not be identical to the lists prepared earlier, but will be very similar. Ask class members to take a moment to look at the first list. Ask them to circle one of the behaviors of the "Old Self" that they may be having trouble letting go. Have a time for silent, personal prayer, asking God's help to abandon this dishonoring behavior.

Then ask each person to look at the second list and place a check mark by each virtue he or she would like to develop or improve to bring honor to Christ. Ask each to share one of those items with a person sitting next to him or her. Ask the students to pray for each other's goals; then close with a prayer for all your students.

Discovering Life

Paul tells believers to "put to death . . . whatever belongs to your earthly nature." Remove the letters of that statement (in order) from the list of letters below. The remaining letters will reveal an encouragement for living the Christian life.

L P U E T T T O T H E D E A W T H O W H R A D T E V E R O B F E L C O N H G S R T I O S Y O T
U R D W E E A R T L H L L Y I N N A T U Y R E O U

Write the solution in the box below. What verse in our text is the source for this wonderful teaching?

Discovering Change

Colossians 3:1-17 is packed with tips for changing our lives as followers of Christ. Paul tells us to take off our old self and put on a new self (vv. 9, 10). Read this very practical Scripture and answer these questions about Christian living.

1. Killer Christians! What are Christians to put to death? (v. 5)

2. Cleaning House. What are Christians to get rid of? (v. 8)

3. All Dressed Up! What clothing are we to wear as believers . . . and what is the belt that binds it all together? (vv. 12-14)

Now, circle the qualities or behaviors in question 3 that you feel are often present in your life. Thank God that you honor him with these characteristics.

Then, underline qualities or behaviors in questions 1, 2 and 3 you frequently struggle with. Select at least one of these that you will immediately begin to work on "in the name of the Lord Jesus." (v. 17)

Answer to "Discovering Life": Let the word of Christ dwell in you (v. 16).

WELCOMING OTHERS IN CHRIST

LESSON 13

WHY TEACH THIS LESSON?

We were a small church and proud of our friendly spirit. Everyone knew everyone, and we genuinely enjoyed being with one another. A sister congregation and the local evangelism association had offered to assist us so that we could hire a full-time preaching minister. We were interviewing the man who would become our minister when someone mentioned the friendly spirit of our small church.

"Yes," the minister replied, "small churches are the friendliest churches. And they are the hardest to get into!" He went on to explain to the suddenly sobered leaders gathered there that small churches take on an almost family-like relationship. Your family may welcome many guests, but it would be rare indeed to adopt your guests into your family. A similar dynamic prevents newcomers from being accepted into the small church "family."

Larger churches have their own problems, but all churches, whether large or small, have to make an effort to welcome their guests and make them want to belong. Let Paul's efforts on behalf of Onesimus be a model for your students of the degree to which they need to go to welcome others into your fellowship.

INTRODUCTION

A. PEOPLE LIKE US

It is generally true that we like people who are most like ourselves. And, in contrast, we tend not to build friendships as quickly with people who are not like us. Sometimes, if we are not careful, prejudices can develop toward those who are not like us.

Today's lesson from Philemon encourages us to take a closer look at how we view people and to see them as Jesus sees them. This letter is not a theological treatise; it is a very personal letter permeated with genuine emotion. It does not deal with issues in the abstract; it deals with them in the context of a very real set of circumstances being addressed by very real people.

Obviously Philemon was one of the individuals involved in the situation behind Paul's writing of this letter, for it is addressed to him. The other was an escaped slave named Onesimus. They were asked to become models of the reconciliation made possible through Jesus. This was no easy task for either of them. In the world of the first century they were miles apart on the socio-economic scale: Philemon was an apparently well-to-do businessman; Onesimus, a humble slave. How they responded to Paul's appeal had the potential to provide an impressive testimony to the uniting power of the gospel.

There is an important lesson here for all of us. It is quite possible for us to believe that the gospel should go to everyone, even people who are not like us, but at the same time refuse to accept such people into our own fellowship. Paul appealed to Philemon to display a willingness to break down social barriers in the name of Jesus. His appeal is addressed to us, too.

DEVOTIONAL READING:
JAMES 2:1-13

BACKGROUND SCRIPTURE:
PHILEMON

PRINTED TEXT:
PHILEMON 4-21

LESSON AIMS

After completing this lesson, each student should be able to:

1. Identify Philemon and Onesimus and tell what Paul hoped to accomplish on their behalf with his letter to Philemon.

2. Tell what made Paul's actions regarding Onesimus such a bold testimony to Christ's love.

3. Take steps to break down barriers and develop a friendship for Christ's sake with someone who needs a Christian's testimony.

KEY VERSE

I pray that you may be active in sharing your faith, so that you will have a full understanding of every good thing we have in Christ.   —Philemon 6

Aug
27

LESSON 13 NOTES

HOW TO SAY IT

Apphia. AF-ee-uh or AP-fee-uh.
Archippus. Ar-KIP-us.
Colosse. Ko-LAHSS-ee.
Colossians. Kuh-LOSH-unz.
Ephesians. Ee-FEE-zhunz.
Ephesus. EF-uh-sus.
Onesimus. Oh-NESS-ih-muss.
Philemon. Fih-LEE-mun or Fye-
    LEE-mun.
Philippians. Fih-LIP-ee-unz.
Tychicus. TICK-ih-cuss.

Paul prayed that Philemon would be active in sharing his faith. Today's visual illustrates a modern believer sharing his faith.

However, we will see in this study that there is more than just social change at stake; the importance of forgiveness is also a pivotal issue. This, too, is difficult. According to the standards of the day, Philemon would have been under no obligation to be kind to or forgive his slave. But Paul knew of Philemon's Christian commitment and appealed to him to "go the second mile" with a person whom society would have said did not deserve such treatment. This appeal also is addressed to us.

B. LESSON BACKGROUND

Some believe that Philemon is the most personal book in the Bible. Certainly there is no other book quite like it. It deals with a very sensitive set of circumstances. The problem was a runaway slave named Onesimus. He had fled from his master, Philemon (and may even have stolen something before he left). When Onesimus reached Rome, he met Paul and his companions. As a result, he became a Christian.

Now what was Paul to do? Should he tell Onesimus to go back to his master (where he might be punished), or should he tell him to stay in Rome and thus remain a fugitive? Paul chose a third course of action—one that illustrates the gospel's ability to heal the divisions that characterize a sinful world. He would send Onesimus back, but plead for Philemon to treat him as a brother rather than a slave—in other words, to allow their relationship in Christ to overrule their relationship in society.

Some Bible students wish that Paul (and the New Testament in general) had more to say about the evils of slavery. Actually it comments very little on the subject (perhaps the closest to a criticism of slavery comes in Paul's reference to "slave traders" in 1 Timothy 1:10). Slavery was simply a part of first-century culture. No one would have given serious consideration to abandoning it, for they could not have conceived of an alternative. But Paul put into effect the transformation of the master-slave relationship by urging Philemon to treat Onesimus as a brother in Christ rather than as a slave. It seems that Paul did not try to change society as such, but to change individuals and to encourage them to apply Christian principles to every situation. In that way, society would be changed.

Not only does Paul address Philemon in this letter, but he also mentions Apphia and Archippus (v. 2). Some Bible students believe Apphia to be Philemon's wife and Archippus his son, but there is no proof of this.

Philemon is one of the prison epistles, most likely written around the same time as Ephesians, Philippians, and Colossians. Since Paul sent Onesimus with Tychicus to Colosse (see Colossians 4:7-9), it seems likely that Philemon lived in or near that town. Onesimus probably delivered Paul's letter to Philemon. This, of course, would have added an extra touch of tenderness to Paul's appeal.

I. PAUL'S OLD FRIEND (PHILEMON 4-7)

A. HIS LOVE AND FAITH (vv. 4, 5)

4. I always thank my God as I remember you in my prayers.

Paul begins the body of this letter in much the same fashion as he does his other letters. He expresses thanksgiving to God and reminds the recipient, Philemon, of his *prayers* for him. So much of our prayer lives is devoted to our wants. It appears that much of Paul's prayer life was devoted to others rather than to his own wants or needs.

Paul does not identify himself as an "apostle" in this letter, though that is common in his other letters (Romans 1:1; 1 Corinthians 1:1; 2 Corinthians 1:1; Galatians 1:1; Ephesians 1:1; Colossians 1:1; 1 Timothy 1:1; 2 Timothy 1:1;

Titus 1:1). This attests to the personal nature of this letter. Titles are not as important when corresponding with a friend.

Paul was particularly grateful for the household of Philemon and for the church that met in his home (v. 2). This indicates that Philemon was a man of hospitality and of some means, and that he was probably a leader in that church. And if he was a leader, then his response in the matter involving Onesimus would set a compelling example for others in the church.

5. . . . because I hear about your faith in the Lord Jesus and your love for all the saints.

Interestingly, the name *Philemon* means "loving." Philemon's Christian commitment was expressed in his *faith in the Lord Jesus* and his *love for all the saints.* (Of course, Paul was about to ask Philemon to do a very loving thing for Onesimus.)

This twofold dimension of love should call to mind Jesus' statement of the two greatest commandments: love God with all your heart, soul, mind, and strength; and love your neighbor as yourself. It is not possible to separate these two aspects of Christianity. Our relationship with God will always affect the relationships we have with others. It has often been noted that Christianity has both a vertical dimension (toward God) and a horizontal dimension (toward others). These two dimensions are also seen in the Ten Commandments; the first four of them emphasize our reverence for God, and the last six stress our responsibility to others.

B. His Evangelistic Success (v. 6)

6. I pray that you may be active in sharing your faith, so that you will have a full understanding of every good thing we have in Christ.

As Philemon participates in the *sharing* of his *faith* in Christ, that faith will become more effective because he will understand more fully the goodness of God. It is certainly true that the more we give our faith away, the more it grows.

C. His Support (v. 7)

7. Your love has given me great joy and encouragement, because you, brother, have refreshed the hearts of the saints.

Philemon's *love* has been a source of *great joy and encouragement* to Paul and to others. The Greek word for *encouragement* literally means a calling alongside (for the purpose of rendering some kind of assistance). Paul commended Philemon because other Christians had been encouraged and *refreshed* through his efforts.

It is obvious at this point that Paul is preparing Philemon for the favor he will ask. He is depending on Philemon's compassion to govern how he will treat his runaway slave.

II. PAUL'S NEW SON (PHILEMON 8-16)

A. No Longer Useless (vv. 8-11)

8. Therefore, although in Christ I could be bold and order you to do what you ought to do.

Paul now begins his appeal to Philemon. He first suggests to Philemon that there is abundant reason for him to *order* Philemon to do what he desires, but he will not do so. Paul prefers to appeal to Philemon's own conscience that he will do what he *ought to do* simply because it is the right thing to do.

9. Yet I appeal to you on the basis of love. I then, as Paul—an old man and now also a prisoner of Christ Jesus.

Although Paul appeals to Philemon to grant his request *on the basis of love*, he is not unwilling to tug at Philemon's emotions. His description of himself as *an old man* is a bit of hyperbole. While Paul was a mature man at this point, he probably

WHAT DO YOU THINK?

Paul has some very nice—even flattering—things to say about Philemon before asking of him a huge favor. Do you think it's okay, then, to "butter up" a person before asking a favor? Why or why not?

WHAT DO YOU THINK?

Sometimes even when we are in a position to insist on another's doing our bidding, it is better to make a request than an order. What circumstances tell us the right times to do this? What makes this the better approach?

was not what we would consider *old*. Perhaps Paul used the term in a spiritual sense, describing himself as someone older in the faith, which would have given some degree of authority to his request. Along with his reference to being *also a prisoner of Christ Jesus*, it would have appealed to Philemon's sympathy.

10. I appeal to you for my son Onesimus, who became my son while I was in chains.

Paul finally mentions the name of the person for whom he is interceding: *Onesimus*, a slave. Philemon must have been surprised to see the words *my son* attached to the name of Onesimus. It was clear he would have to begin to see his slave in a new light!

As far as we know, Paul had no children (none is mentioned in the New Testament). But he had many "sons in the faith," including Titus (Titus 1:4), Timothy (1 Timothy 1:2), and others whom he led to Christ (1 Corinthians 4:14, 15).

Onesimus was someone Paul had begotten *while . . . in chains*. Even while in prison Paul had many opportunities to present the gospel (Philippians 1:12, 13). Onesimus had responded positively and had become a son to Paul. The issue now was whether Philemon would treat him as a brother.

Something should be said about the faith of Onesimus. He was doing something quite courageous by returning to Philemon—something that demonstrated the sincerity of his commitment to Christ. Onesimus could have remained a fugitive, but he chose to return instead. Paul said he was sending Onesimus (v. 12), but Paul was in no position to force him to return. While Paul may have urged him, we have to see this as a voluntary act on the part of Onesimus.

OPEN MY EYES

Anyone who puts on glasses for the very first time is amazed at the difference they make in his vision. A person doesn't realize what he has been missing! Only after wearing and using his glasses does he realize how blurred different objects and people have looked.

Today's study of Philemon and Onesimus challenges us to see people as God sees them and as they can be in Christ. Sometimes it is hard to see the potential in others. Their past obscures the possibilities for their future. Yet every one of us probably knows someone who, by the grace of God, has made a dramatic change in his or her life and achieved a level of spirituality we never dreamed the person could reach. (In fact, we would probably be surprised at how many people think that about us!)

In today's lesson we have two examples of being able to see others better because of the improved vision that God provides. Paul saw the potential in Onesimus. He knew that the runaway slave could become a trusted servant. He also saw the potential in Philemon. He knew that this master could become a brother to the man who was his slave.

Many today have given up on humanity, and they see no hope. (Suppose God had felt that way!) As Christians we are relieved of this pessimism when we see by faith the potential that God sees in the human race. May it be said of us, "So from now on we regard no one from a worldly point of view" (2 Corinthians 5:16).

—R. C. S.

11. Formerly he was useless to you, but now he has become useful both to you and to me.

This verse includes an interesting play on words. The name Onesimus means *useful*, but he had been to Philemon quite *useless*—especially since he had run away. Paul claims that Onesimus will no longer be useful in name only, but in reality. Paul then proceeds to explain how this is so.

DAILY BIBLE READINGS

Monday, Aug. 21—Paul Gives Thanks for Philemon (Philemon 1-7)

Tuesday, Aug. 22—Paul Expresses His Love for Onesimus (Philemon 8-12)

Wednesday, Aug. 23—Paul Intercedes for Onesimus (Philemon 13-18)

Thursday, Aug. 24—Paul's Challenge to Philemon (Philemon 19-25)

Friday, Aug. 25—Don't Let Fine Clothes Deceive You! (James 2:1-7)

Saturday, Aug. 26—Show Mercy and Love All People (James 2:8-13)

Sunday, Aug. 27—Have True Faith; Do Good Works (James 2:14-26)

B. NO LONGER A SLAVE (vv. 12-16)

12. I am sending him—who is my very heart—back to you.

Paul continues his emotional appeal. By describing Onesimus as *my very heart*, he indicates that this slave is not just another convert. He is precious to Paul.

13. I would have liked to keep him with me so that he could take your place in helping me while I am in chains for the gospel.

Paul admits that he considered keeping Onesimus with him so that he could have assisted Paul during his imprisonment in the proclamation of the *gospel*. If he had done so, Onesimus would have been serving Paul in Philemon's *place*. To do this, however, would have violated the law and jeopardized the friendship of Paul and Philemon. However helpful this new brother might be to Paul, the apostle chose a different course of action.

14. But I did not want to do anything without your consent, so that any favor you do will be spontaneous and not forced.

Paul does not mention the legal issue involved in keeping Onesimus with him but goes right to the matter of his friendship with Philemon. He does not want to take advantage of his friend by acting *without* Philemon's *consent* or to force Philemon to accept Onesimus, but for Philemon to act willingly. A gift given out of necessity is no gift at all, but "God loves a cheerful giver" (2 Corinthians 9:7).

15, 16. Perhaps the reason he was separated from you for a little while was that you might have him back for good—no longer as a slave, but better than a slave, as a dear brother. He is very dear to me but even dearer to you, both as a man and as a brother in the Lord.

Paul believed that God had been at work in this situation. He suggests there may have been a purpose behind Onesimus's running away and meeting Paul. Though Onesimus had been temporarily *separated from* his master, now, in Christ, Philemon would have Onesimus *back for good . . . as a dear brother*.

There is some speculation that Paul was also hinting that Philemon should free Onesimus and send him back to Paul. This, however, involves speculation and a reading between the lines. There is no evidence that this was either Paul's intention or the eventual result of his letter to Philemon.

III. PHILEMON'S NEW BROTHER (PHILEMON 17-21)

A. COUNT HIM A FRIEND (v. 17)

17. So if you consider me a partner, welcome him as you would welcome me.

As if Paul had not already appealed to Philemon enough, he now says that Philemon should *welcome* Onesimus as if he were Paul himself. Can you imagine the respect and honor that Philemon would have given Paul if he were his house guest? Can he show that kind of hospitality to Onesimus? Paul depends on Philemon's fellowship as a *partner* in Christ as a basis for his request.

B. FORGIVE HIS PAST OFFENSES (vv. 18-21)

18. If he has done you any wrong or owes you anything, charge it to me.

This verse suggests that Onesimus may have taken some money or something else of value from Philemon. Paul says that if this is the case, then *charge it to me*. Such a gesture showed that Paul was willing to do more than just request favors of Philemon; he, too, was offering to make some sacrifices on behalf of Onesimus.

19. I, Paul, am writing this with my own hand. I will pay it back—not to mention that you owe me your very self.

Why does Paul emphasize that he is *writing this with* his *own hand*? We know that Paul dictated his epistle to the Romans to an individual (Romans 16:22). In another letter he mentions writing the closing salutation with his own hand,

WHAT DO YOU THINK?

Paul suggests that perhaps Onesimus's running away was within the providence and plan of God. Onesimus had found faith in meeting Paul. Now things could be better than they ever had been before.

What can we generalize about God's providence on the basis of fortuitous happenings?

WHAT DO YOU THINK?

It takes a special kind of love to agree to be accountable for another's debts. Paul showed such love for Onesimus when he wrote, "If he has done you any wrong or owes you anything, charge it to me." For whom could you say that? Why?

WHAT DO YOU THINK?

How do we plead with others to "refresh [our hearts] in Christ"?

"which is the distinguishing mark in all my letters" (2 Thessalonians 3:17). Here Paul was probably trying to demonstrate the earnestness of his appeal to Philemon by taking the pen in his own hand and concluding his letter.

In addition, Paul reminds Philemon that he owes his very life to Paul. This may refer to the part Paul played in leading Philemon to Christ.

20. I do wish, brother, that I may have some benefit from you in the Lord; refresh my heart in Christ.

Philemon could become the source of true joy to Paul by doing exactly as he requested in his treatment of Onesimus. Philemon had a reputation as a man of great compassion. Paul calls upon him to manifest that compassion in the midst of a very delicate situation.

21. Confident of your obedience, I write to you, knowing that you will do even more than I ask.

Paul is *confident* that Philemon will *do* as he has asked. He then goes a step farther and expresses his conviction that Philemon *will do even more*. Again, this calls attention to Philemon's reputation as a deeply committed and compassionate servant of Christ.

According to tradition, early in the second century one of the leaders of the church in the city of Ephesus was a man named Onesimus. Is this the same man as the Onesimus in today's study? There is no way to know, but isn't it fascinating to think of this runaway slave becoming a leader in the church?

PRAYER

Give me the grace, dear Lord, to treat people the way you would have me treat them. Help me to realize that you do not take note of social status. Forgive me when I have done so. Help me not to think so highly of myself that I demean other people. Help me to forgive those who have wronged me. Through Jesus, in whom there is true unity. Amen.

BROTHER LOVE

Gil Contreras is a Mexican preacher who works among the Otomi Indians in his native land. During his efforts to communicate the gospel to them, he discovered that they had no word for love. They could only say, "I hate you" or "I don't hate you." Contreras lived among those Indians, ate their meager food, and slept on their rough benches. Through such acts they began to comprehend the idea of love. As a result they borrowed a word from the Spanish language, and now they call Contreras "Brother Love."

We do not know how the situation involving Philemon and Onesimus turned out. Given Philemon's reputation as a loving and compassionate Christian, we trust that the master/slave relationship became one between brothers in Christ. Think of the impact this must have had on those who became aware of what had happened!

This is the kind of love that Christians are called to demonstrate as their trademark (John 13:35). Our culture has so overworked the word *love* that merely talking about it will not suffice. We must support our talk with actions so that others will be drawn to the true love—God's love.

If others are to know that the Father loves them, they must see that love in the lives of his children.

—R. C. S.

CONCLUSION

The day that the Iron Curtain fell will be remembered as one of the twentieth century's most remarkable events. The collapse of the wall that once divided the city of Berlin spoke of a new hope for freedom and for reconciliation between cultures and political systems that once seemed forever alienated from one another.

Paul's letter to Philemon tells of the apostle's efforts to tear down one of the most intimidating social walls of his day: the wall between a master and a runaway slave. The usual response to such an occurrence included severe punishment. But the presence of Christ in the parties involved meant that this was not to be handled in the usual way. Whether the century is the first or the twenty-first, any man-made barriers that separate groups or individuals can be torn down—through the love of Jesus Christ.

THOUGHT TO REMEMBER

All are family who have God as Father and Christ as Elder Brother.

Discovery Learning

This page contains an alternate lesson plan emphasizing learning activities. Classes desiring such student involvement will find these suggestions helpful. The next page is a reproducible activity page to further enhance discovery learning.

LEARNING GOALS

After completing this lesson, each student should be able to:

1. Identify Philemon and Onesimus and tell what Paul hoped to accomplish on their behalf with his letter to Philemon.

2. Tell what made Paul's actions regarding Onesimus such a bold testimony to Christ's love.

3. Take steps to break down barriers and develop a friendship for Christ's sake with someone who needs a Christian's testimony.

INTO THE LESSON

Begin this lesson with a "brainstorming" activity. Ask the class to "brainstorm," or list quickly, a few kinds or illustrations of human prejudices in today's world. Write their answers on a visual under the heading "Human Prejudice." (Their list might include religious prejudice, racial prejudice, prejudice against handicapped persons, political prejudice, economic prejudice, and others.) Then make the transition to Bible study by saying, "It seems that we tend to like people who are like us and not to like people who are different from us. Today's text forces us to address and deal with our differences and the impact they have on our attitudes toward each other."

INTO THE WORD

First, use the Lesson Background to prepare and deliver a lecture, telling how Onesimus ran away from Philemon and was converted by Paul. Mention Paul's dilemma about wanting to keep Onesimus with him but knowing the need to send him back to Philemon.

Have a volunteer read Philemon 4-21 aloud. Then distribute copies of the following page. Have the students answer the questions there about Philemon, Onesimus, and Paul.

While the students are writing their answers, write the italicized headings listed below on the chalkboard. Review the information from the text by discussing the questions listed below each name.

Philemon

1. What does this text imply or say about Philemon's stature in the community?

2. What does it imply about his faith?

3. For what does Paul thank Philemon?

Onesimus

1. What was his occupation?

2. At the writing of the letter, what was his relationship with the Lord?

3. Why would Paul say Onesimus was once useless but now is useful? (Tell the class that Onesimus's name means useful.)

Paul's Plea

1. What was Paul asking of Philemon?

2. Paul said he would like to keep Onesimus, but was sending him back to Philemon. Why? What was the ethical issue at stake?

3. What was the basis of Paul's plea to Philemon (v. 9)?

4. Why would Paul mention his age as he makes this request of Philemon?

5. What point of leverage is Paul making in verse 12? Verse 17? Verse 19?

6. What did Paul mean by his remark in verse 15?

INTO LIFE

Point out that there were great differences between Philemon and Onesimus. One was a slave, the other a slave owner. One was well-to-do, the other was a debtor. One had social status, the other had none. Yet Paul urges Philemon to accept Onesimus as a Christian brother and forgive him.

Then remind the class of the introductory activity. Differences and prejudices often have the potential to divide believers. However, our differences can also be a blessing. Ask how the following differences can be a blessing to the church: Religious Backgrounds, Racial Differences, Economic Differences, Physical Handicaps.

Tell the class you are confident Paul would encourage acceptance and fellowship with everyone we've talked about. Ask, "What are the attitudes or values that are necessary to bring fellowship, harmony, and a sense of purpose among Christians who come from different backgrounds?" Write their answers on the chalkboard. Then ask, "What can we do to foster these attitudes or values in our church and community?"

Ask each class member to identify a Christian who comes from a different background from himself or herself. Ask the students to evaluate their acceptance of and fellowship with the individuals they identified. Ask each student to determine to become better acquainted with that person and to work together for God's glory.

Who's Who?

Read Philemon 4-21. Then answer the following questions to complete the "files" on Philemon, Onesimus, and Paul.

Philemon

1. What were some of the spiritual characteristics of this Christian?

2. Why did Philemon's love give Paul joy and encouragement?

3. What did Paul want Philemon to do for Onesimus?

Onesimus

1. Who was Onesimus? What was his occupation?

2. What was Onesimus's crime? How serious do you think would be his punishment?

3. Why did Paul call Onesimus "my son"?

Paul

1. Paul was concerned about Onesimus and would have liked to keep him as an assistant. Yet he chose to return Onesimus to Philemon. Why?

2. What was the basis of Paul's request of Philemon?

3. What did Paul mean by his remark in verse 15?